Anna Karenina

Anna Karenina

Leo Tolstoy

Translated by Constance Garnett

BARNES & NOBLE

NEW YORK

Barnes & Noble, Inc.
122 Fifth Avenue
New York, NY 10011

ISBN: 978-1-4351-3962-6

Printed and bound in China

3 5 7 9 10 8 6 4

PART ONE

CHAPTER I

HAPPY FAMILIES ARE ALL ALIKE; EVERY UNHAPPY FAMILY IS UNHAPPY IN ITS own way.

Everything was in confusion in the Oblonskys' house. The wife had discovered that the husband was carrying on an intrigue with a French girl, who had been a governess in their family, and she had announced to her husband that she could not go on living in the same house with him. This position of affairs had now lasted three days, and not only the husband and wife themselves, but all the members of their family and household, were painfully conscious of it. Every person in the house felt that there was no sense in their living together, and that the stray people brought together by chance in any inn had more in common with one another than they, the members of the family and household of the Oblonskys. The wife did not leave her own room, the husband had not been at home for three days. The children ran wild all over the house; the English governess quarreled with the housekeeper, and wrote to a friend asking her to look out for a new situation for her; the man-cook had walked off the day before just at dinner-time; the kitchen-maid and the coachman had given warning.

Three days after the quarrel, Prince Stepan Arkadyevitch Oblonsky— Stiva, as he was called in the fashionable world—woke up at his usual hour, that is, at eight o'clock in the morning, not in his wife's bedroom, but on the leather-covered sofa in his study. He turned over his stout, well-cared-for person on the springy sofa, as though he would sink into a long sleep again; he vigorously embraced the pillow on the other side and buried his face in it; but all at once he jumped up, sat up on the sofa, and opened his eyes.

"Yes, yes, how was it now?" he thought, going over his dream. "Now, how was it? To be sure! Alabin was giving a dinner at Darmstadt; no, not Darmstadt, but something American. Yes, but then, Darmstadt was in America. Yes, Alabin was giving a dinner on glass tables, and the tables sang, *Il mio tesoro*—not *Il mio tesoro* though, but something better, and there were some sort of little decanters on the table, and they were women, too," he remembered.

Stepan Arkadyevitch's eyes twinkled gaily, and he pondered with a smile. "Yes, it was nice, very nice. There was a great deal more that was delightful, only there's no putting it into words, or even expressing it in one's thoughts awake." And noticing a gleam of light peeping in beside one of the serge curtains, he cheerfully dropped his feet over the edge of the sofa, and felt about with them for his slippers, a present on his last birthday, worked for him by his wife on gold-colored morocco. And, as he had done every day for the last nine years, he stretched out his hand, without getting up, towards the place where his dressing-gown always hung in his bedroom. And thereupon he suddenly remembered that he was not sleeping in his wife's room, but in his study, and why: the smile vanished from his face, he knitted his brows.

"Ah, ah, ah! Oo!..." he muttered, recalling everything that had happened. And again every detail of his quarrel with his wife was present to his imagination, all the hopelessness of his position, and worst of all, his own fault.

"Yes, she won't forgive me, and she can't forgive me. And the most awful thing about it is that it's all my fault—all my fault, though I'm not to blame. That's the point of the whole situation," he reflected. "Oh, oh, oh!" he kept repeating in despair, as he remembered the acutely painful sensations caused him by this quarrel.

Most unpleasant of all was the first minute when, on coming, happy and good-humored, from the theater, with a huge pear in his hand for his wife, he had not found his wife in the drawing-room, to his surprise had not found her in the study either, and saw her at last in her bedroom with the unlucky letter that revealed everything in her hand.

She, his Dolly, forever fussing and worrying over household details, and limited in her ideas, as he considered, was sitting perfectly still with the letter in her hand, looking at him with an expression of horror, despair, and indignation.

"What's this? this?" she asked, pointing to the letter.

And at this recollection, Stepan Arkadyevitch, as is so often the case, was not so much annoyed at the fact itself as at the way in which he had met his wife's words.

There happened to him at that instant what does happen to people when they are unexpectedly caught in something very disgraceful. He did not succeed in adapting his face to the position in which he was placed towards his wife by the discovery of his fault. Instead of being hurt, denying, defending himself, begging forgiveness, instead of remaining indifferent even—anything would have been better than what he did do—his face utterly involuntarily (reflex spinal action, reflected Stepan Arkadyevitch, who was fond of physiology)—utterly involuntarily assumed its habitual, good-humored, and therefore idiotic smile.

This idiotic smile he could not forgive himself. Catching sight of that smile, Dolly shuddered as though at physical pain, broke out with her characteristic heat into a flood of cruel words, and rushed out of the room. Since then she had refused to see her husband.

"It's that idiotic smile that's to blame for it all," thought Stepan Arkadyevitch.

"But what's to be done? What's to be done?" he said to himself in despair, and found no answer.

CHAPTER II

S TEPAN ARKADYEVITCH WAS A TRUTHFUL MAN IN HIS RELATIONS WITH himself. He was incapable of deceiving himself and persuading himself that he repented of his conduct. He could not at this date repent of the fact that he, a handsome, susceptible man of thirty-four, was not in love with his wife, the mother of five living and two dead children, and only a year younger than himself. All he repented of was that he had not succeeded better in hiding it from his wife. But he felt all the difficulty of his position and was sorry for his wife, his children, and himself. Possibly he might have managed to conceal his sins better from his wife if he had anticipated that the knowledge of them would have had such an effect on her. He had never clearly thought out the subject, but he had vaguely conceived that his wife must long ago have suspected him of being unfaithful to her, and shut her eyes to the fact. He had even supposed that she, a worn-out woman no longer young or good-looking, and in no way remarkable or interesting, merely a good mother, ought from a sense of fairness to take an indulgent view. It had turned out quite the other way.

"Oh, it's awful! oh dear, oh dear! awful!" Stepan Arkadyevitch kept repeating to himself, and he could think of nothing to be done. "And how well things were going up till now! how well we got on! She was contented and happy in her children; I never interfered with her in anything; I let her manage the children and the house just as she liked. It's true it's bad *her* having been a governess in our house. That's bad! There's something common, vulgar, in flirting with one's governess. But what a governess!" (He vividly recalled the roguish black eyes of Mlle. Roland and her smile.) "But after all, while she was in the house, I kept myself in hand. And the worst of it all is that she's already…it seems as if ill-luck would have it so! Oh, oh! But what, what is to be done?"

There was no solution, but that universal solution which life gives to all questions, even the most complex and insoluble. That answer is: one must live in the needs of the day—that is, forget oneself. To forget himself in sleep was impossible now, at least till night-time; he could not go back now to the music sung by the decanter-women; so he must forget himself in the dream of daily life.

"Then we shall see," Stepan Arkadyevitch said to himself, and getting up he put on a gray dressing-gown lined with blue silk, tied the tassels in a knot, and, drawing a deep breath of air into his broad, bare chest, he walked to the window with his usual confident step, turning out his feet that carried his full frame so easily. He pulled up the blind and rang the bell loudly. It was at once answered by the appearance of an old friend, his valet, Matvey, carrying his clothes, his boots, and a telegram. Matvey was followed by the barber with all the necessaries for shaving.

"Are there any papers from the office?" asked Stepan Arkadyevitch, taking the telegram and seating himself at the looking-glass.

"On the table," replied Matvey, glancing with inquiring sympathy at his master; and, after a short pause, he added with a sly smile, "They've sent from the carriage-jobbers."

Stepan Arkadyevitch made no reply, he merely glanced at Matvey in the looking-glass. In the glance, in which their eyes met in the looking-glass, it was clear that they understood one another. Stepan Arkadyevitch's eyes asked: "Why do you tell me that? don't you know?"

Matvey put his hands in his jacket pockets, thrust out one leg, and gazed silently, good-humoredly, with a faint smile, at his master.

"I told them to come on Sunday, and till then not to trouble you or themselves for nothing," he said. He had obviously prepared the sentence beforehand.

Stepan Arkadyevitch saw Matvey wanted to make a joke and attract attention to himself. Tearing open the telegram, he read it through, guessing at the words, misspelt as they always are in telegrams, and his face brightened.

"Matvey, my sister Anna Arkadyevna will be here to-morrow," he said, checking for a minute the sleek, plump hand of the barber, cutting a pink path through his long, curly whiskers.

"Thank God!" said Matvey, showing by this response that he, like his master, realized the significance of this arrival—that is, that Anna Arkadyevna, the sister he was so fond of, might bring about a reconciliation between husband and wife.

"Alone, or with her husband?" inquired Matvey.

Stepan Arkadyevitch could not answer, as the barber was at work on his upper lip, and he raised one finger. Matvey nodded at the looking-glass.

"Alone. Is the room to be got ready up-stairs?"

"Inform Darya Alexandrovna: where she orders."

"Darya Alexandrovna?" Matvey repeated, as though in doubt.

"Yes, inform her. Here, take the telegram; give it to her, and then do what she tells you."

"You want to try it on," Matvey understood, but he only said, "Yes sir."

Stepan Arkadyevitch was already washed and combed and ready to be dressed, when Matvey, stepping deliberately in his creaky boots, came back into the room with the telegram in his hand. The barber had gone.

"Darya Alexandrovna told me to inform you that she is going away. Let him do—that is you—do as he likes," he said, laughing only with his eyes, and putting his hands in his pockets, he watched his master with his head on one side. Stepan Arkadyevitch was silent a minute. Then a good-humored and rather pitiful smile showed itself on his handsome face.

"Eh, Matvey?" he said, shaking his head.

"It's all right, sir; she will come round," said Matvey.

"Come round?"

"Yes, sir."

"Do you think so? Who's there?" asked Stepan Arkadyevitch, hearing the rustle of a woman's dress at the door.

"It's I," said a firm, pleasant, woman's voice, and the stern, pockmarked face of Matrona Philimonovna, the nurse, was thrust in at the doorway.

"Well, what is it, Matrona?" queried Stepan Arkadyevitch, going up to her at the door.

Although Stepan Arkadyevitch was completely in the wrong as regards his wife, and was conscious of this himself, almost every one in the house (even the nurse, Darya Alexandrovna's chief ally) was on his side.

"Well, what now?" he asked disconsolately.

"Go to her, sir; own your fault again. Maybe God will aid you. She is suffering so, it's sad to see her; and besides, everything in the house is topsy-turvy. You must have pity, sir, on the children. Beg her forgiveness, sir. There's no help for it! One must take the consequences..."

"But she won't see me."

"You do your part. God is merciful; pray to God, sir, pray to God."

"Come, that'll do, you can go," said Stepan Arkadyevitch, blushing suddenly. "Well now, do dress me." He turned to Matvey and threw off his dressing-gown decisively.

Matvey was already holding up the shirt like a horse's collar, and, blowing off some invisible speck, he slipped it with obvious pleasure over the well-groomed body of his master.

CHAPTER III

WHEN HE WAS DRESSED, STEPAN ARKADYEVITCH SPRINKLED SOME scent on himself, pulled down his shirt-cuffs, distributed into his pockets his cigarettes, pocketbook, matches, and watch with its double chain and seals, and shaking out his handkerchief, feeling himself clean, fragrant, healthy, and physically at ease, in spite of his unhappiness, he walked with a slight swing on each leg into the dining-room, where coffee was already waiting for him, and beside the coffee, letters and papers from the office.

He read the letters. One was very unpleasant, from a merchant who was buying a forest on his wife's property. To sell this forest was absolutely essential; but at present, until he was reconciled with his wife, the subject could not be discussed. The most unpleasant thing of all was that his pecuniary interests should in this way enter into the question of his reconciliation with his wife. And the idea that he might be led on by his interests, that he might seek a reconciliation with his wife on account of the sale of the forest—that idea hurt him.

When he had finished his letters, Stepan Arkadyevitch moved the office-papers close to him, rapidly looked through two pieces of business, made a few notes with a big pencil, and pushing away the papers, turned to his coffee. As he sipped his coffee, he opened a still damp morning paper, and began reading it.

Stepan Arkadyevitch took in and read a liberal paper, not an extreme one, but one advocating the views held by the majority. And in spite of the fact that science, art, and politics had no special interest for him, he firmly held those views on all these subjects which were held by the majority and by his paper, and he only changed them when the majority changed them—or, more strictly speaking, he did not change them, but they imperceptibly changed of themselves within him.

Stepan Arkadyevitch had not chosen his political opinions or his views; these political opinions and views had come to him of themselves, just as he did not choose the shapes of his hat and coat, but simply took those that were being worn. And for him, living in a certain society—owing to the need, ordinarily developed at years of discretion, for some degree of mental activity—to have views was just as indispensable as to have a hat. If there was a reason for his preferring liberal to conservative views, which were held also by many of his circle, it arose not from his considering liberalism more rational, but from its being in closer accordance with his manner of life. The liberal party said that in Russia everything is wrong, and certainly Stepan Arkadyevitch had many debts and was decidedly short of money. The liberal party said that marriage is an institution quite out of date, and that it needs reconstruction; and family life certainly afforded Stepan Arkadyevitch little gratification, and forced him into lying and hypocrisy, which was so repulsive to his nature. The liberal party said, or rather allowed it to be understood, that religion is only a curb to keep in check the barbarous classes of the people; and Stepan Arkadyevitch could not get through even a short service without his legs aching from standing up, and could never make out what was the object of all the terrible and high-flown language about another world when life might be so very amusing in this world. And with all this, Stepan Arkadyevitch, who liked a joke, was fond of puzzling a plain man by saying that if he prided himself on his origin, he ought not to stop at Rurik and disown the first founder of his family—the monkey. And so liberalism had become a habit of Stepan Arkadyevitch's, and he liked his newspaper, as he did his cigar after dinner, for the slight fog it diffused in his brain. He read the leading article, in which it was maintained that it was quite senseless in our day to raise an outcry that radicalism was threatening to swallow up all conservative elements, and that the government ought to take measures to crush the revolutionary hydra; that, on the contrary, "in our opinion the danger lies not in that fantastic revolutionary hydra, but in the obstinacy of traditionalism clogging progress," etc., etc. He read another article, too, a financial one, which alluded to Bentham and Mill, and dropped some innuendoes reflecting on the ministry. With his characteristic quick-wittedness he caught the drift of each innuendo, divined whence it came, at whom and on what ground it was aimed, and that afforded him, as it always did, a certain satisfaction. But to-day that satisfaction was embittered by Matrona Philimonovna's advice and the unsatisfactory state of the household. He read, too, that Count Beist was rumored to have left for Wiesbaden, and that one need have no more gray hair, and of the sale of a light carriage, and of a young person seeking a situation; but these items of information did not give him, as usual, a quiet, ironical gratification. Having finished the paper, a second cup of coffee and a roll and butter, he got up, shaking the crumbs of the roll off his waistcoat; and, squaring his broad chest, he smiled joyously: not because there was anything particularly agreeable in his mind—the joyous smile was evoked by a good digestion.

But this joyous smile at once recalled everything to him, and he grew thoughtful.

Two childish voices (Stepan Arkadyevitch recognized the voices of Grisha, his youngest boy, and Tanya, his eldest girl) were heard outside the door. They were carrying something, and dropped it.

"I told you not to sit passengers on the roof," said the little girl in English; "there, pick them up!"

"Everything's in confusion," thought Stepan Arkadyevitch; "there are the children running about by themselves." And going to the door, he called them. They threw down the box, that represented a train, and came in to their father.

The little girl, her father's favorite, ran up boldly, embraced him, and hung laughingly on his neck, enjoying as she always did the smell of scent that came from his whiskers. At last the little girl kissed his face, which was flushed from his stooping posture and beaming with tenderness, loosed her hands, and was about to run away again; but her father held her back.

"How is mamma?" he asked, passing his hand over his daughter's smooth, soft little neck. "Good-morning," he said, smiling to the boy, who had come up to greet him. He was conscious that he loved the boy less, and always tried to be fair; but the boy felt it, and did not respond with a smile to his father's chilly smile.

"Mamma? She is up," answered the girl.

Stepan Arkadyevitch sighed. "That means that she's not slept again all night," he thought.

"Well, is she cheerful?"

The little girl knew that there was a quarrel between her father and mother, and that her mother could not be cheerful, and that her father must be aware of this, and that he was pretending when he asked about it so lightly. And she blushed for her father. He at once perceived it, and blushed too.

"I don't know," she said. "She did not say we must do our lessons, but she said we were to go for a walk with Miss Hoole to grandmamma's."

"Well, go, Tanya, my darling. Oh, wait a minute, though," he said, still holding her and stroking her soft little hand.

He took off the mantelpiece, where he had put it yesterday, a little box of sweets, and gave her two, picking out her favorites, a chocolate and a fondant.

"For Grisha?" said the little girl, pointing to the chocolate.

"Yes, yes." And still stroking her little shoulder, he kissed her on the roots of her hair and neck, and let her go.

"The carriage is ready," said Matvey; "but there's some one to see you with a petition."

"Been here long?" asked Stepan Arkadyevitch.

"Half an hour."

"How many times have I told you to tell me at once?"

"One must let you drink your coffee in peace, at least," said Matvey, in the affectionately gruff tone with which it was impossible to be angry.

"Well, show the person up at once," said Oblonsky, frowning with vexation.

The petitioner, the widow of a staff captain Kalinin, came with a request impossible and unreasonable; but Stepan Arkadyevitch, as he generally did, made her sit down, heard her to the end attentively without interrupting her, and gave her detailed advice as to how and to whom to apply, and even wrote her, in his large, sprawling, good and legible hand, a confident and fluent little note to a personage who might be of use to her. Having got rid of the staff captain's widow, Stepan Arkadyevitch took his hat and stopped to recollect whether he had forgotten anything. It appeared that he had forgotten nothing except what he wanted to forget—his wife.

"Ah, yes!" He bowed his head, and his handsome face assumed a harassed expression. "To go, or not to go!" he said to himself; and an inner voice told him he must not go, that nothing could come of it but falsity; that to amend, to set right their relations was impossible, because it was impossible to make her attractive again and able to inspire love, or to make him an old man, not susceptible to love. Except deceit and lying nothing could come of it now; and deceit and lying were opposed to his nature.

"It must be some time, though: it can't go on like this," he said, trying to give himself courage. He squared his chest, took out a cigarette, took two whiffs at it, flung it into a mother-of-pearl ash-tray, and with rapid steps walked through the drawing room, and opened the other door into his wife's bedroom.

CHAPTER IV

D ARYA ALEXANDROVNA, IN A DRESSING JACKET, AND WITH HER NOW scanty, once luxuriant and beautiful hair fastened up with hairpins on the nape of her neck, with a sunken, thin face and large, startled eyes, which looked prominent from the thinness of her face, was standing among a litter of all sorts of things scattered all over the room, before an open bureau, from which she was taking something. Hearing her husband's steps, she stopped, looking towards the door, and trying assiduously to give her features a severe and contemptuous expression. She felt she was afraid of him, and afraid of the coming interview. She was just attempting to do what she had attempted to do ten times already in these last three days—to sort out the children's things and her own, so as to take them to her mother's—and again she could not bring herself to do this; but now again, as each time before, she kept saying to herself, "that things cannot go on like this, that she must take some step" to punish him, put him to shame, avenge on him some little part at least of the suffering he had caused her. She still continued to tell herself that she should leave him, but she was conscious that this was impossible; it was impossible because she could not get out of the habit of regarding him as her husband and loving him. Besides this, she realized that if even here in her own house she could hardly manage to look after her five children properly, they would be still worse off where she was going with them all. As it was, even in the course of these three days, the youngest was unwell from being given unwholesome soup, and the others had almost gone without their dinner the day before. She was conscious that it was impossible to go away; but, cheating herself, she went on all the same sorting out her things and pretending she was going.

Seeing her husband, she dropped her hands into the drawer of the bureau as though looking for something, and only looked round at him when he had come quite up to her. But her face, to which she tried to give a severe and resolute expression, betrayed bewilderment and suffering.

"Dolly!" he said in a subdued and timid voice. He bent his head towards his shoulder and tried to look pitiful and humble, but for all that he was radiant with freshness and health. In a rapid glance she scanned his figure that beamed with health and freshness. "Yes, he is happy and content!" she thought; "while I... And that disgusting good nature, which every one likes him for and praises—I hate that good nature of his," she thought. Her mouth stiffened, the muscles of the cheek contracted on the right side of her pale, nervous face.

"What do you want?" she said in a rapid, deep, unnatural voice.

"Dolly!" he repeated, with a quiver in his voice. "Anna is coming to-day."

"Well, what is that to me? I can't see her!" she cried.

"But you must, really, Dolly...."

"Go away, go away, go away!" she shrieked, not looking at him, as though this shriek were called up by physical pain.

Stepan Arkadyevitch could be calm when he thought of his wife, he could hope that she would *come round*, as Matvey expressed it, and could quietly go on reading his paper and drinking his coffee; but when he saw her tortured, suffering face, heard the tone of her voice, submissive to fate and full of despair, there was a catch in his breath and a lump in his throat, and his eyes began to shine with tears.

"My God! what have I done? Dolly! For God's sake!... You know..." He could not go on; there was a sob in his throat.

She shut the bureau with a slam, and glanced at him.

"Dolly, what can I say?... One thing: forgive...Remember, cannot nine years of my life atone for an instant..."

She dropped her eyes and listened, expecting what he would say, as it were beseeching him in some way or other to make her believe differently.

"—instant of passion?"... he said, and would have gone on, but at that word, as at a pang of physical pain, her lips stiffened again, and again the muscles of her right cheek worked.

"Go away, go out of the room!" she shrieked still more shrilly, "and don't talk to me of your passion and your loathsomeness."

She tried to go out, but tottered, and clung to the back of a chair to support herself. His face relaxed, his lips swelled, his eyes were swimming with tears.

"Dolly!" he said, sobbing now; "for mercy's sake, think of the children; they are not to blame! I am to blame, and punish me, make me expiate my fault. Anything I can do, I am ready to do anything! I am to blame, no words can express how much I am to blame! But, Dolly, forgive me!"

She sat down. He listened to her hard, heavy breathing, and he was unutterably sorry for her. She tried several times to begin to speak, but could not. He waited.

"You remember the children, Stiva, to play with them; but I remember them, and know that this means their ruin," she said—obviously one of the phrases she had more than once repeated to herself in the course of the last few days.

She had called him "Stiva," and he glanced at her with gratitude, and moved to take her hand, but she drew back from him with aversion.

"I think of the children, and for that reason I would do anything in the world to save them, but I don't myself know how to save them. By taking them away from their father, or by leaving them with a vicious father—yes, a vicious father.... Tell me, after what...has happened, can we live together? Is that possible? Tell me, eh, is it possible?" she repeated, raising her voice, "after my husband, the father of my children, enters into a love-affair with his own children's governess?"

"But what could I do? what could I do?" he kept saying in a pitiful voice, not knowing what he was saying, as his head sank lower and lower.

"You are loathsome to me, repulsive!" she shrieked, getting more and more heated. "Your tears mean nothing! You have never loved me; you have neither heart nor honorable feeling! You are hateful to me, disgusting, a stranger—yes, a complete stranger!" With pain and wrath she uttered the word so terrible to herself—*stranger*.

He looked at her, and the fury expressed in her face alarmed and amazed him. He did not understand how his pity for her exasperated her. She saw in him sympathy for her, but not love. "No, she hates me. She will not forgive me," he thought.

"It is awful! awful!" he said.

At that moment in the next room a child began to cry; probably it had fallen down. Darya Alexandrovna listened, and her face suddenly softened.

She seemed to be pulling herself together for a few seconds, as though she did not know where she was, and what she was doing, and getting up rapidly, she moved towards the door.

"Well, she loves my child," he thought, noticing the change of her face at the child's cry, "my child: how can she hate me?"

"Dolly, one word more," he said, following her.

"If you come near me, I will call in the servants, the children! They may all know you are a scoundrel! I am going away at once, and you may live here with your mistress!"

And she went out, slamming the door.

Stepan Arkadyevitch sighed, wiped his face, and with a subdued tread walked out of the room. "Matvey says she will come round; but how? I don't see the least chance of it. Ah, oh, how horrible it is! And how vulgarly she shouted," he said to himself, remembering her shriek and the words— "scoundrel" and "mistress." "And very likely the maids were listening!

Horribly vulgar! horrible!" Stepan Arkadyevitch stood a few seconds alone, wiped his face, squared his chest, and walked out of the room.

It was Friday, and in the dining-room the German watchmaker was winding up the clock. Stepan Arkadyevitch remembered his joke about this punctual, bald watchmaker, "that the German was wound up for a whole lifetime himself, to wind up watches," and he smiled. Stepan Arkadyevitch was fond of a joke: "And maybe she will come round! That's a good expression, 'come round,'" he thought. "I must repeat that."

"Matvey!" he shouted. "Arrange everything with Darya in the sitting-room for Anna Arkadyevna," he said to Matvey when he came in.

"Yes, sir."

Stepan Arkadyevitch put on his fur coat and went out onto the steps.

"You won't dine at home?" said Matvey, seeing him off.

"That's as it happens. But here's for the housekeeping," he said, taking ten roubles from his pocketbook. "That'll be enough."

"Enough or not enough, we must make it do," said Matvey, slamming the carriage door and stepping back onto the steps.

Darya Alexandrovna meanwhile having pacified the child, and knowing from the sound of the carriage that he had gone off, went back again to her bedroom. It was her solitary refuge from the household cares which crowded upon her directly she went out from it. Even now, in the short time she had been in the nursery, the English governess and Matrona Philimonovna had succeeded in putting several questions to her, which did not admit of delay, and which only she could answer: "What were the children to put on for their walk? Should they have any milk? Should not a new cook be sent for?"

"Ah, let me alone, let me alone!" she said, and going back to her bedroom she sat down in the same place as she had sat when talking to her husband, clasping tightly her thin hands with the rings that slipped down on her bony fingers, and fell to going over in her memory all the conversation. "He has gone! But has he broken it off with her?" she thought. "Can it be he sees her? Why didn't I ask him! No, no, reconciliation is impossible. Even if we remain in the same house, we are strangers—strangers forever!" She repeated again with special significance the word so dreadful to her. "And how I loved him! my God, how I loved him!... How I loved him! And now don't I love him? Don't I love him more than before? The most horrible thing is," she began, but did not finish her thought, because Matrona Philimonovna put her head in at the door.

"Let us send for my brother," she said; "he can get a dinner anyway, or we shall have the children getting nothing to eat till six again, like yesterday."

"Very well, I will come directly and see about it. But did you send for some new milk?"

And Darya Alexandrovna plunged into the duties of the day, and drowned her grief in them for a time.

CHAPTER V

STEPAN ARKADYEVITCH HAD LEARNED EASILY AT SCHOOL, THANKS TO HIS excellent abilities, but he had been idle and mischievous, and therefore was one of the lowest in his class. But in spite of his habitually dissipated mode of life, his inferior grade in the service, and his comparative youth, he occupied the honorable and lucrative position of president of one of the government boards at Moscow. This post he had received through his sister Anna's husband, Alexey Alexandrovitch Karenin, who held one of the most important positions in the ministry to whose department the Moscow office belonged. But if Karenin had not got his brother-in-law this berth, then through a hundred other personages—brothers, sisters, cousins, uncles, and aunts—Stiva Oblonsky would have received this post, or some other similar one, together with the salary of six thousand absolutely needful for him, as his affairs, in spite of his wife's considerable property, were in an embarrassed condition.

Half Moscow and Petersburg were friends and relations of Stepan Arkadyevitch. He was born in the midst of those who had been and are the powerful ones of this world. One-third of the men in the government, the older men, had been friends of his father's, and had known him in petticoats; another third were his intimate chums, and the remainder were friendly acquaintances. Consequently the distributors of earthly blessings in the shape of places, rents, shares, and such, were all his friends, and could not overlook one of their own set; and Oblonsky had no need to make any special exertion to get a lucrative post. He had only not to refuse things, not to show jealousy, not to be quarrelsome or take offense, all of which from his characteristic good nature he never did. It would have struck him as absurd if he had been told that he would not get a position with the salary he required, especially as he expected nothing out of the way; he only wanted what the men of his own age and standing did get, and he was no worse qualified for performing duties of the kind than any other man.

Stepan Arkadyevitch was not merely liked by all who knew him for his good-humor, but for his bright disposition, and his unquestionable honesty. In him, in his handsome, radiant figure, his sparkling eyes, black hair and eyebrows, and the white and red of his face, there was something which produced a physical effect of kindliness and good-humor on the people who met him. "Aha! Stiva! Oblonsky! Here he is!" was almost always said with a smile of delight on meeting him. Even though it happened at times that after a conversation with him it seemed that nothing particularly delightful had happened, the next day, and the next, every one was just as delighted at meeting him again.

After filling for three years the post of president of one of the government boards at Moscow, Stepan Arkadyevitch had won the respect, as well as the liking, of his fellow-officials, subordinates, and superiors, and all who had had business with him. The principal qualities in Stepan Arkadyevitch which had gained him this universal respect in the service consisted, in the first place, of his extreme indulgence for others, founded on a consciousness of his own shortcomings; secondly, of his perfect liberalism—not the liberalism he read of in the papers, but the liberalism that was in his blood, in virtue of which he treated all men perfectly equally and exactly the same, whatever their fortune or calling might be; and thirdly—the most important point—his complete indifference to the business in which he was engaged, in consequence of which he was never carried away, and never made mistakes.

On reaching the offices of the board, Stepan Arkadyevitch, escorted by a deferential porter with a portfolio, went into his little private room, put on his uniform, and went into the boardroom. The clerks and copyists all rose, greeting him with good-humored deference. Stepan Arkadyevitch moved quickly, as ever, to his place, shook hands with his colleagues, and sat down. He made a joke or two, and talked just as much as was consistent with due decorum, and began work. No one knew better than Stepan Arkadyevitch how to hit on the exact line between freedom, simplicity, and official stiffness necessary for the agreeable conduct of business. A secretary, with the good-humored deference common to every one in Stepan Arkadyevitch's office, came up with papers, and began to speak in the familiar and easy tone which had been introduced by Stepan Arkadyevitch.

"We have succeeded in getting the information from the government department of Penza. Here, would you care?..."

"You've got them at last?" said Stepan Arkadyevitch, laying his finger on the paper. "Now, gentlemen..."

And the sitting of the board began.

"If they knew," he thought, bending his head with a significant air as he listened to the report, "what a guilty little boy their president was half an hour ago." And his eyes were laughing during the reading of the report. Till two o'clock the sitting would go on without a break, and at two o'clock there would be an interval and luncheon.

It was not yet two, when the large glass doors of the board-room suddenly opened and some one came in.

All the officials sitting on the further side under the portrait of the Tsar and the eagle, delighted at any distraction, looked round at the door; but the doorkeeper standing at the door at once drove out the intruder, and closed the glass door after him.

When the case had been read through, Stepan Arkadyevitch got up and stretched, and by way of tribute to the liberalism of the times took out a cigarette in the board-room and went into his private room. Two of the members of the board, the old veteran in the service, Nikitin, and the *Kammerjunker* Grinevitch, went in with him.

"We shall have time to finish after lunch," said Stepan Arkadyevitch.

"To be sure we shall!" said Nikitin.

"A pretty sharp fellow this Fomin must be," said Grinevitch of one of the persons taking part in the case they were examining.

Stepan Arkadyevitch frowned at Grinevitch's words, giving him thereby to understand that it was improper to pass judgment prematurely, and made him no reply.

"Who was that came in?" he asked the doorkeeper.

"Some one, your excellency, crept in without permission directly my back was turned. He was asking for you. I told him: when the members come out, then ... "

"Where is he?"

"Maybe he's gone into the passage, but here he comes anyway. That is he," said the doorkeeper, pointing to a strongly built, broad-shouldered man with a curly beard, who, without taking off his sheepskin cap, was running lightly and rapidly up the worn steps of the stone staircase. One of the members going down—a lean official with a portfolio—stood out of his way and looked disapprovingly at the legs of the stranger, then glanced inquiringly at Oblonsky.

Stepan Arkadyevitch was standing at the top of the stairs. His good-naturedly beaming face above the embroidered collar of his uniform beamed more than ever when he recognized the man coming up.

"Why, it's actually you, Levin, at last!" he said with a friendly mocking smile, scanning Levin as he approached. "How is it you have deigned to look me up in this den?" said Stepan Arkadyevitch, and not content with shaking hands, he kissed his friend. "Have you been here long?"

"I have just come, and very much wanted to see you," said Levin, looking shyly and at the same time angrily and uneasily around.

"Well, let's go into my room," said Stepan Arkadyevitch, who knew his friend's sensitive and irritable shyness, and, taking his arm, he drew him along, as though guiding him through dangers.

Stepan Arkadyevitch was on familiar terms with almost all his acquaintances, and called almost all of them by their Christian names: old men of sixty, boys of twenty, actors, ministers, merchants, and adjutant-generals, so that many of his intimate chums were to be found at the extreme ends of the social ladder, and would have been very much surprised to learn that they had, through the medium of Oblonsky, something in common. He was the familiar friend of every one with whom he took a glass of champagne, and he took a glass of champagne with every one, and when in consequence he met any of his *disreputable* chums, as he used in joke to call many of his friends, in the presence of his subordinates, he well knew how, with his characteristic tact, to diminish the disagreeable impression made on them. Levin was not a disreputable chum, but Oblonsky, with his ready tact, felt that Levin fancied he might not care to show his intimacy with him before his subordinates, and so he made haste to take him off into his room.

Levin was almost of the same age as Oblonsky; their intimacy did not rest merely on champagne. Levin had been the friend and companion of his early youth. They were fond of one another in spite of the difference of their characters and tastes, as friends are fond of one another who have been together in early youth. But in spite of this, each of them—as is often the way with men who have selected careers of different kinds—though in discussion he would even justify the other's career, in his heart despised it. It seemed to each of them that the life he led himself was the only real life, and the life led by his friend was a mere phantasm. Oblonsky could not restrain a slight mocking smile at the sight of Levin. How often he had seen him come up to Moscow from the country where he was doing something, but what precisely Stepan Arkadyevitch could never quite make out, and indeed he took no interest in the matter. Levin arrived in Moscow always excited and in a hurry, rather ill at ease and irritated by his own want of ease, and for the most part with a perfectly new, unexpected view of things. Stepan Arkadyevitch laughed at this, and liked it. In the same way Levin in his heart despised the town mode of life of his friend, and his official duties, which he laughed at, and regarded as trifling. But the difference was that Oblonsky, as he was doing the same as every one did, laughed complacently and good-humoredly, while Levin laughed without complacency and sometimes angrily.

"We have long been expecting you," said Stepan Arkadyevitch, going into his room and letting Levin's hand go as though to show that here all danger was over. "I am very, very glad to see you," he went on. "Well, how are you? Eh? When did you come?"

Levin was silent, looking at the unknown faces of Oblonsky's two companions, and especially at the hand of the elegant Grinevitch, which had such long white fingers, such long yellow filbert-shaped nails, and such huge shining studs on the shirt-cuff, that apparently they absorbed all his attention, and allowed him no freedom of thought. Oblonsky noticed this at once, and smiled.

"Ah, to be sure, let me introduce you," he said. "My colleagues: Philip Ivanitch Nikitin, Mihail Stanislavitch Grinevitch"—and turning to Levin—"a district councilor, a modern district council man, a gymnast who lifts thirteen stone with one hand, a cattle-breeder and sportsman, and my friend, Konstantin Dmitrievitch Levin, the brother of Sergey Ivanovitch Koznishev."

"Delighted," said the veteran.

"I have the honor of knowing your brother, Sergey Ivanovitch," said Grinevitch, holding out his slender hand with its long nails.

Levin frowned, shook hands coldly, and at once turned to Oblonsky. Though he had a great respect for his half-brother, an author well known to all Russia, he could not endure it when people treated him not as Konstantin Levin, but as the brother of the celebrated Koznishev.

"No, I am no longer a district councilor. I have quarreled with them all, and don't go to the meetings any more," he said, turning to Oblonsky.

"You've been quick about it!" said Oblonsky with a smile. "But how? why?"

"It's a long story. I will tell you some time," said Levin, but he began telling him at once. "Well, to put it shortly, I was convinced that nothing was really done by the district councils, or ever could be," he began, as though some one had just insulted him. "On one side it's a plaything; they play at being a parliament, and I'm neither young enough nor old enough to find amusement in playthings; and on the other side" (he stammered) "it's a means for the coterie of the district to make money. Formerly they had wardships, courts of justice, now they have the district council—not in the form of bribes, but in the form of unearned salary," he said, as hotly as though some one of those present had opposed his opinion.

"Aha! You're in a new phase again, I see—a conservative," said Stepan Arkadyevitch. "However, we can go into that later."

"Yes, later. But I wanted to see you," said Levin, looking with hatred at Grinevitch's hand.

Stepan Arkadyevitch gave a scarcely perceptible smile.

"How was it you used to say you would never wear European dress again?" he said, scanning his new suit, obviously cut by a French tailor. "Ah! I see: a new phase."

Levin suddenly blushed, not as grown men blush, slightly, without being themselves aware of it, but as boys blush, feeling that they are ridiculous through their shyness, and consequently ashamed of it and blushing still more, almost to the point of tears. And it was so strange to see this sensible, manly face in such a childish plight, that Oblonsky left off looking at him.

"Oh, where shall we meet? You know I want very much to talk to you," said Levin.

Oblonsky seemed to ponder.

"I'll tell you what: let's go to Gurin's to lunch, and there we can talk. I am free till three."

"No," answered Levin, after an instant's thought, "I have got to go on somewhere else."

"All right, then, let's dine together."

"Dine together? But I have nothing very particular, only a few words to say, and a question I want to ask you, and we can have a talk afterwards."

"Well, say the few words, then, at once, and we'll gossip after dinner."

"Well, it's this," said Levin; "but it's of no importance, though."

His face all at once took an expression of anger from the effort he was making to surmount his shyness.

"What are the Shtcherbatskys doing? Everything as it used to be?" he said.

Stepan Arkadyevitch, who had long known that Levin was in love with his sister-in-law, Kitty, gave a hardly perceptible smile, and his eyes sparkled merrily.

"You said a few words, but I can't answer in a few words, because...Excuse me a minute...."

A secretary came in, with respectful familiarity and the modest consciousness, characteristic of every secretary, of superiority to his chief in the knowledge of their business; he went up to Oblonsky with some papers, and began, under pretense of asking a question, to explain some objection.

Stepan Arkadyevitch, without hearing him out, laid his hand genially on the secretary's sleeve.

"No, you do as I told you," he said, softening his words with a smile, and with a brief explanation of his view of the matter he turned away from the papers, and said: "So do it that way, if you please, Zahar Nikititch."

The secretary retired in confusion. During the consultation with the secretary Levin had completely recovered from his embarrassment. He was standing with his elbows on the back of a chair, and on his face was a look of ironical attention.

"I don't understand it, I don't understand it," he said.

"What don't you understand?" said Oblonsky, smiling as brightly as ever, and picking up a cigarette. He expected some queer outburst from Levin.

"I don't understand what you are doing," said Levin, shrugging his shoulders. "How can you do it seriously?"

"Why not?"

"Why, because there's nothing in it."

"You think so, but we're overwhelmed with work."

"On paper. But, there, you've a gift for it," added Levin.

"That's to say, you think there's a lack of something in me?"

"Perhaps so," said Levin. "But all the same I admire your grandeur, and am proud that I've a friend in such a great person. You've not answered my question, though," he went on, with a desperate effort looking Oblonsky straight in the face.

"Oh, that's all very well. You wait a bit, and you'll come to this yourself. It's very nice for you to have over six thousand acres in the Karazinsky district, and such muscles, and the freshness of a girl of twelve; still you'll be one of us one day. Yes, as to your question, there is no change, but it's a pity you've been away so long."

"Oh, why so?" Levin queried, panic-stricken.

"Oh, nothing," responded Oblonsky. "We'll talk it over. But what's brought you up to town?"

"Oh, we'll talk about that, too, later on," said Levin, reddening again up to his ears.

"All right. I see," said Stepan Arkadyevitch. "I should ask you to come to us, you know, but my wife's not quite the thing. But I tell you what; if you want to see them, they're sure now to be at the Zoological Gardens from four to five. Kitty skates. You drive along there, and I'll come and fetch you, and we'll go and dine somewhere together."

"Capital. So good-bye till then."

"Now mind, you'll forget, I know you, or rush off home to the country!" Stepan Arkadyevitch called out laughing.

"No, truly!"

And Levin went out of the room, only when he was in the doorway remembering that he had forgotten to take leave of Oblonsky's colleagues.

"That gentleman must be a man of great energy," said Grinevitch, when Levin had gone away.

"Yes, my dear boy," said Stepan Arkadyevitch, nodding his head, "he's a lucky fellow! Over six thousand acres in the Karazinsky district; everything before him; and what youth and vigor! Not like some of us."

"You have a great deal to complain of, haven't you, Stepan Arkadyevitch?"

"Ah, yes, I'm in a poor way, a bad way," said Stepan Arkadyevitch with a heavy sigh.

CHAPTER VI

WHEN OBLONSKY ASKED LEVIN WHAT HAD BROUGHT HIM TO TOWN, Levin blushed, and was furious with himself for blushing, because he could not answer, "I have come to make your sister-in-law an offer," though that was precisely what he had come for.

The families of the Levins and the Shtcherbatskys were old, noble Moscow families, and had always been on intimate and friendly terms. This intimacy had grown still closer during Levin's student-days. He had both prepared for the university with the young Prince Shtcherbatsky, the brother of Kitty and Dolly, and had entered at the same time with him. In those days Levin used often to be in the Shtcherbatskys' house, and he was in love with the Shtcherbatsky household. Strange as it may appear, it was with the household, the family, that Konstantin Levin was in love, especially with the feminine half of the household. Levin did not remember his own mother, and his only sister was older than he was, so that it was in the Shtcherbatskys' house that he saw for the first time that inner life of an old, noble, cultivated, and honorable family of which he had been deprived by the death of his father and mother. All the members of that family, especially the feminine half, were pictured by him, as it were, wrapped about with a mysterious poetical veil, and he not only perceived no defects whatever in them, but under the poetical veil that shrouded them he assumed the existence of the loftiest sentiments and every possible perfection. Why it was the three young ladies had one day to speak French, and the next English; why it was that at certain hours they played by turns on the piano, the sounds of which were audible in their brother's room above, where the students used to work; why they were visited by those professors of French literature, of music, of drawing, of dancing; why at certain hours all the three young ladies, with Mademoiselle Linon, drove in the coach to the Tversky boulevard, dressed in their satin cloaks, Dolly in a long one, Natalia in a half-long one, and Kitty in one so short that her shapely legs in tightly-drawn red stockings were visible to all beholders; why it was they had to walk about the Tversky boulevard escorted by a footman with a gold cockade in his hat— all this and much more that was done in their mysterious world he did not understand, but he was sure that everything that was done there was very good, and he was in love precisely with the mystery of the proceedings.

In his student-days he had all but been in love with the eldest, Dolly, but she was soon married to Oblonsky. Then he began being in love with the second. He felt, as it were, that he had to be in love with one of the sisters, only he could not quite make out which. But Natalia, too, had hardly made her appearance in the world when she married the diplomat Lvov. Kitty was still a child when Levin left the university. Young Shtcherbatsky went into the navy, was drowned in the Baltic, and Levin's relations with the Shtcherbatskys, in spite of his friendship with Oblonsky, became less intimate. But when early in the winter of this year Levin came to Moscow, after a year in the country, and saw the Shtcherbatskys, he realized which of the three sisters he was indeed destined to love.

One would have thought that nothing could be simpler than for him, a man of good family, rather rich than poor, and thirty-two years old, to make the young Princess Shtcherbatskaya an offer of marriage; in all likelihood he would at once have been looked upon as a good match. But Levin was in love, and so it seemed to him that Kitty was so perfect in every respect that she was a creature far above everything earthly; and that he was a creature so low and so earthly that it could not even be conceived that other people and she herself could regard him as worthy of her.

After spending two months in Moscow in a state of enchantment, seeing Kitty almost every day in society, into which he went so as to meet her, he abruptly decided that it could not be, and went back to the country.

Levin's conviction that it could not be was founded on the idea that in the eyes of her family he was a disadvantageous and worthless match for the charming Kitty, and that Kitty herself could not love him. In her family's eyes he had no ordinary, definite career and position in society, while his contemporaries by this time, when he was thirty-two, were already, one a colonel, and another a professor, another director of a bank and railways, or president of a board like Oblonsky. But he (he knew very well how he must appear to others) was a country gentleman, occupied in breeding cattle, shooting game, and building barns; in other words, a fellow of no ability, who had not turned out well, and who was doing just what, according to the ideas of the world, is done by people fit for nothing else.

The mysterious, enchanting Kitty herself could not love such an ugly person as he conceived himself to be, and, above all, such an ordinary, in no way striking person. Moreover, his attitude to Kitty in the past—the attitude of a grown-up person to a child, arising from his friendship with her brother—seemed to him yet another obstacle to love. An ugly, good-natured man, as he considered himself, might, he supposed, be liked as a friend; but to be loved with such a love as that with which he loved Kitty, one would need to be a handsome and, still more, a distinguished man.

He had heard that women often did care for ugly and ordinary men, but he did not believe it, for he judged by himself, and he could not himself have loved any but beautiful, mysterious, and exceptional women.

But after spending two months alone in the country, he was convinced that this was not one of those passions of which he had had experience in his early youth; that this feeling gave him not an instant's rest; that he could not live without deciding the question, would she or would she not be his wife, and that his despair had arisen only from his own imaginings, that he had no sort of proof that he would be rejected. And he had now come to Moscow with a firm determination to make an offer, and get married if he were accepted. Or...he could not conceive what would become of him if he were rejected.

CHAPTER VII

ON ARRIVING IN MOSCOW BY A MORNING TRAIN, LEVIN HAD PUT UP AT THE house of his elder half-brother, Koznishev. After changing his clothes he went down to his brother's study, intending to talk to him at once about the object of his visit, and to ask his advice; but his brother was not alone.

With him there was a well-known professor of philosophy, who had come from Harkov expressly to clear up a difference that had arisen between them on a very important philosophical question. The professor was carrying on a hot crusade against materialists. Sergey Koznishev had been following this crusade with interest, and after reading the professor's last article, he had written him a letter stating his objections. He accused the professor of making too great concessions to the materialists. And the professor had promptly appeared to argue the matter out. The point in discussion was the question then in vogue: Is there a line to be drawn between psychological and physiological phenomena in man? and if so, where?

Sergey Ivanovitch met his brother with the smile of chilly friendliness he always had for every one, and introducing him to the professor, went on with the conversation.

A little man in spectacles, with a narrow forehead, tore himself from the discussion for an instant to greet Levin, and then went on talking without paying any further attention to him. Levin sat down to wait till the professor should go, but he soon began to get interested in the subject under discussion.

Levin had come across the magazine articles about which they were disputing, and had read them, interested in them as a development of the first principles of science, familiar to him as a natural science student at the university. But he had never connected these scientific deductions as to the origin of man as an animal, as to reflex action, biology, and sociology, with those questions as to the meaning of life and death to himself, which had of late been more and more often in his mind.

As he listened to his brother's argument with the professor, he noticed that they connected these scientific questions with those spiritual problems, that at times they almost touched on the latter; but every time they were close upon what seemed to him the chief point, they promptly beat a hasty retreat, and plunged again into a sea of subtle distinctions, reservations, quotations, allusions, and appeals to authorities, and it was with difficulty that he understood what they were talking about.

"I cannot admit it," said Sergey Ivanovitch, with his habitual clearness, precision of expression, and elegance of phrase. "I cannot in any case agree with Keiss that my whole conception of the external world has been derived from perceptions. The most fundamental idea, the idea of existence, has not been received by me through sensation; indeed, there is no special sense-organ for the transmission of such an idea."

"Yes, but they—Wurt, and Knaust, and Pripasov—would answer that your consciousness of existence is derived from the conjunction of all your sensations, that that consciousness of existence is the result of your sensations. Wurt, indeed, says plainly that, assuming there are no sensations, it follows that there is no idea of existence."

"I maintain the contrary," began Sergey Ivanovitch.

But here it seemed to Levin that just as they were close upon the real point of the matter, they were again retreating, and he made up his mind to put a question to the professor.

"According to that, if my senses are annihilated, if my body is dead, I can have no existence of any sort?" he queried.

The professor, in annoyance, and, as it were, mental suffering at the interruption, looked round at the strange inquirer, more like a bargeman than a philosopher, and turned his eyes upon Sergey Ivanovitch, as though to ask: What's one to say to him? But Sergey Ivanovitch, who had been talking with far less heat and one-sidedness than the professor, and who had sufficient breadth of mind to answer the professor, and at the same time to comprehend the simple and natural point of view from which the question was put, smiled and said:

"That question we have no right to answer as yet."

"We have not the requisite data," chimed in the professor, and he went back to his argument. "No," he said; "I would point out the fact that if, as Pripasov directly asserts, perception is based on sensation, then we are bound to distinguish sharply between these two conceptions."

Levin listened no more, and simply waited for the professor to go.

CHAPTER VIII

WHEN THE PROFESSOR HAD GONE, SERGEY IVANOVITCH TURNED TO HIS brother.

"Delighted that you've come. For some time, is it? How's your farming getting on?"

Levin knew that his elder brother took little interest in farming, and only put the question in deference to him, and so he only told him about the sale of his wheat and money matters.

Levin had meant to tell his brother of his determination to get married, and to ask his advice; he had indeed firmly resolved to do so. But after seeing his brother, listening to his conversation with the professor, hearing afterwards the unconsciously patronizing tone in which his brother questioned him about agricultural matters (their mother's property had not been divided, and Levin took charge of both their shares), Levin felt that he could not for some reason begin to talk to him of his intention of marrying. He felt that his brother would not look at it as he would have wished him to.

"Well, how is your district council doing?" asked Sergey Ivanovitch, who was greatly interested in these local boards and attached great importance to them.

"I really don't know."

"What! Why, surely you're a member of the board?"

"No, I'm not a member now; I've resigned," answered Levin, "and I no longer attend the meetings."

"What a pity!" commented Sergey Ivanovitch, frowning.

Levin in self-defense began to describe what took place in the meetings in his district.

"That's how it always is!" Sergey Ivanovitch interrupted him. "We Russians are always like that. Perhaps it's our strong point, really, the faculty of seeing our own shortcomings; but we overdo it, we comfort ourselves with irony which we always have on the tip of our tongues. All I say is, give such rights as our local self-government to any other European people—why, the Germans or the English would have worked their way to freedom from them, while we simply turn them into ridicule."

"But how can it be helped?" said Levin penitently. "It was my last effort. And I did try with all my soul. I can't. I'm no good at it."

"It's not that you're no good at it," said Sergey Ivanovitch; "it is that you don't look at it as you should."

"Perhaps not," Levin answered dejectedly.

"Oh! do you know brother Nikolay's turned up again?"

This brother Nikolay was the elder brother of Konstantin Levin, and half-brother of Sergey Ivanovitch; a man utterly ruined, who had dissipated the greater part of his fortune, was living in the strangest and lowest company, and had quarreled with his brothers.

"What did you say?" Levin cried with horror. "How do you know?"

"Prokofy saw him in the street."

"Here in Moscow? Where is he? Do you know?" Levin got up from his chair, as though on the point of starting off at once.

"I am sorry I told you," said Sergey Ivanovitch, shaking his head at his younger brother's excitement. "I sent to find out where he is living, and sent him his I O U to Trubin, which I paid. This is the answer he sent me."

And Sergey Ivanovitch took a note from under a paperweight and handed it to his brother.

Levin read in the queer, familiar handwriting: "I humbly beg you to leave me in peace. That's the only favor I ask of my gracious brothers.—NIKOLAY LEVIN."

Levin read it, and without raising his head stood with the note in his hands opposite Sergey Ivanovitch.

There was a struggle in his heart between the desire to forget his unhappy brother for the time, and the consciousness that it would be base to do so.

"He obviously wants to offend me," pursued Sergey Ivanovitch; "but he cannot offend me, and I should have wished with all my heart to assist him, but I know it's impossible to do that."

"Yes, yes," repeated Levin. "I understand and appreciate your attitude to him; but I shall go and see him."

"If you want to, do; but I shouldn't advise it," said Sergey Ivanovitch. "As regards myself, I have no fear of your doing so; he will not make you quarrel with me; but for your own sake, I should say you would do better not to go. You can't do him any good; still, do as you please."

"Very likely I can't do any good, but I feel—especially at such a moment— but that's another thing—I feel I could not be at peace."

"Well, that I don't understand," said Sergey Ivanovitch. "One thing I do understand," he added; "it's a lesson in humility. I have come to look very differently and more charitably on what is called infamous since brother Nikolay has become what he is … you know what he did...."

"Oh, it's awful, awful!" repeated Levin.

After obtaining his brother's address from Sergey Ivanovitch's footman, Levin was on the point of setting off at once to see him, but on second thought he decided to put off his visit till the evening. The first thing to do to set his heart at rest was to accomplish what he had come to Moscow for. From his brother's Levin went to Oblonsky's office, and on getting news of the Shtcherbatskys from him, he drove to the place where he had been told he might find Kitty.

CHAPTER IX

A T FOUR O'CLOCK, CONSCIOUS OF HIS THROBBING HEART, LEVIN STEPPED
out of a hired sledge at the Zoological Gardens, and turned along the
path to the frozen mounds and the skating-ground, knowing that he
would certainly find her there, as he had seen the Shtcherbatskys' carriage at
the entrance.

It was a bright, frosty day. Rows of carriages, sledges, drivers, and policemen were standing in the approach. Crowds of well-dressed people, with hats
bright in the sun, swarmed about the entrance and along the well-swept little
paths between the little houses adorned with carving in the Russian style. The
old curly birches of the gardens, all their twigs laden with snow, looked as
though freshly decked in sacred vestments.

He walked along the path towards the skating-ground, and kept saying
to himself—"You mustn't be excited, you must be calm. What's the matter
with you? What do you want? Be quiet, stupid," he conjured his heart. And
the more he tried to compose himself, the more breathless he found himself.
An acquaintance met him and called him by his name, but Levin did not even
recognize him. He went towards the mounds, whence came the clank of the
chains of sledges as they slipped down or were dragged up, the rumble of the
sliding sledges, and the sounds of merry voices. He walked on a few steps,
and the skating-ground lay open before his eyes, and at once, amidst all the
skaters, he knew her.

He knew she was there by the rapture and the terror that seized on his heart.
She was standing talking to a lady at the opposite end of the ground. There was
apparently nothing striking either in her dress or her attitude. But for Levin she
was as easy to find in that crowd as a rose among nettles. Everything was made
bright by her. She was the smile that shed light on all round her. "Is it possible
I can go over there on the ice, go up to her?" he thought. The place where she
stood seemed to him a holy shrine, unapproachable, and there was one moment
when he was almost retreating, so overwhelmed was he with terror. He had to
make an effort to master himself, and to remind himself that people of all sorts
were moving about her, and that he too might come there to skate. He walked
down, for a long while avoiding looking at her as at the sun, but seeing her, as
one does the sun, without looking.

On that day of the week and at that time of day people of one set, all acquainted with one another, used to meet on the ice. There were crack skaters

there, showing off their skill, and learners clinging to chairs with timid, awkward movements, boys, and elderly people skating with hygienic motives. They seemed to Levin an elect band of blissful beings because they were here, near her. All the skaters, it seemed, with perfect self-possession, skated towards her, skated by her, even spoke to her, and were happy, quite apart from her, enjoying the capital ice and the fine weather.

Nikolay Shtcherbatsky, Kitty's cousin, in a short jacket and tight trousers, was sitting on a garden seat with his skates on. Seeing Levin, he shouted to him:

"Ah, the first skater in Russia! Been here long? First-rate ice—do put your skates on."

"I haven't got my skates," Levin answered, marveling at this boldness and ease in her presence, and not for one second losing sight of her, though he did not look at her. He felt as though the sun were coming near him. She was in a corner, and turning out her slender feet in their high boots with obvious timidity, she skated towards him. A boy in Russian dress, desperately waving his arms and bowed down to the ground, overtook her. She skated a little uncertainly; taking her hands out of the little muff that hung on a cord, she held them ready for emergency, and looking towards Levin, whom she had recognized, she smiled at him, and at her own fears. When she had got round the turn, she gave herself a push off with one foot, and skated straight up to Shtcherbatsky. Clutching at his arm, she nodded smiling to Levin. She was more splendid than he had imagined her.

When he thought of her, he could call up a vivid picture of her to himself, especially the charm of that little fair head, so freely set on the shapely girlish shoulders, and so full of childish brightness and good-humor. The childishness of her expression, together with the delicate beauty of her figure, made up her special charm, and that he fully realized. But what always struck him in her as something unlooked for, was the expression of her eyes, soft, serene, and truthful, and above all, her smile, which always transported Levin to an enchanted world, where he felt himself softened and tender, as he remembered himself in some days of his early childhood.

"Have you been here long?" she said, giving him her hand. "Thank you," she added, as he picked up the handkerchief that had fallen out of her muff.

"I? I've not long ... yesterday ... I mean to-day ... I arrived," answered Levin, in his emotion not at once understanding her question. "I was meaning to come and see you," he said; and then, recollecting with what intention he was trying to see her, he was promptly overcome with confusion and blushed.

"I didn't know you could skate, and skate so well."

She looked at him earnestly, as though wishing to make out the cause of his confusion.

"Your praise is worth having. The tradition is kept up here that you are the best of skaters," she said, with her little black-gloved hand brushing a grain of hoarfrost off her muff.

"Yes, I used once to skate with passion; I wanted to reach perfection."

"You do everything with passion, I think," she said smiling. "I should so like to see how you skate. Put on skates, and let us skate together."

"Skate together! Can that be possible?" thought Levin, gazing at her.

"I'll put them on directly," he said.

And he went off to get skates.

"It's a long while since we've seen you here, sir," said the attendant, supporting his foot, and screwing on the heel of the skate. "Except you, there's none of the gentlemen first-rate skaters. Will that be all right?" said he, tightening the strap.

"Oh, yes, yes; make haste, please," answered Levin, with difficulty restraining the smile of rapture which would overspread his face. "Yes," he thought, "this now is life, this is happiness! *Together,* she said; *let us skate together!* Speak to her now? But that's just why I'm afraid to speak—because I'm happy now, happy in hope, anyway.... And then?.... But I must! I must! I must! Away with weakness!"

Levin rose to his feet, took off his overcoat, and scurrying over the rough ice round the hut, came out on the smooth ice and skated without effort, as it were, by simple exercise of will, increasing and slackening speed and turning his course. He approached with timidity, but again her smile reassured him.

She gave him her hand, and they set off side by side, going faster and faster, and the more rapidly they moved the more tightly she grasped his hand.

"With you I should soon learn; I somehow feel confidence in you," she said to him.

"And I have confidence in myself when you are leaning on me," he said, but was at once panic-stricken at what he had said, and blushed. And indeed, no sooner had he uttered these words, when all at once, like the sun going behind a cloud, her face lost all its friendliness, and Levin detected the familiar change in her expression that denoted the working of thought; a crease showed on her smooth brow.

"Is there anything troubling you?—though I've no right to ask such a question," he added hurriedly.

"Oh, why so?... No, I have nothing to trouble me," she responded coldly; and she added immediately: "You haven't seen Mlle. Linon, have you?"

"Not yet."

"Go and speak to her, she likes you so much."

"What's wrong? I have offended her. Lord help me!" thought Levin, and he flew towards the old Frenchwoman with the gray ringlets, who was sitting on a bench. Smiling and showing her false teeth, she greeted him as an old friend.

"Yes, you see we're growing up," she said to him, glancing towards Kitty, "and growing old. *Tiny bear* has grown big now!" pursued the Frenchwoman, laughing, and she reminded him of his joke about the three young ladies whom he had compared to the three bears in the English nursery tale. "Do you remember that's what you used to call them?"

He remembered absolutely nothing, but she had been laughing at the joke for ten years now, and was fond of it.

"Now, go and skate, go and skate. Our Kitty has learned to skate nicely, hasn't she?"

When Levin darted up to Kitty her face was no longer stern; her eyes looked at him with the same sincerity and friendliness, but Levin fancied that in her friendliness there was a certain note of deliberate composure. And he felt depressed. After talking a little of her old governess and her peculiarities, she questioned him about his life.

"Surely you must be dull in the country in the winter, aren't you?" she said.

"No, I'm not dull, I am very busy," he said, feeling that she was holding him in check by her composed tone, which he would not have the force to break through, just as it had been at the beginning of the winter.

"Are you going to stay in town long?" Kitty questioned him.

"I don't know," he answered, not thinking of what he was saying. The thought that if he were held in check by her tone of quiet friendliness he would end by going back again without deciding anything came into his mind, and he resolved to make a struggle against it.

"How is it you don't know?"

"I don't know. It depends upon you," he said, and was immediately horror-stricken at his own words.

Whether it was that she had heard his words, or that she did not want to hear them, she made a sort of stumble, twice struck out, and hurriedly skated away from him. She skated up to Mlle. Linon, said something to her, and went towards the pavilion where the ladies took off their skates.

"My God! what have I done! Merciful God! help me, guide me," said Levin, praying inwardly, and at the same time, feeling a need of violent exercise, he skated about describing inner and outer circles.

At that moment one of the young men, the best of the skaters of the day, came out of the coffee-house in his skates, with a cigarette in his mouth. Taking a run, he dashed down the steps in his skates, crashing and bounding up and down. He flew down, and without even changing the position of his hands, skated away over the ice.

"Ah, that's a new trick!" said Levin, and he promptly ran up to the top to do this new trick.

"Don't break your neck! it needs practice!" Nikolay Shtcherbatsky shouted after him.

Levin went to the steps, took a run from above as best he could, and dashed down, preserving his balance in this unwonted movement with his hands. On the last step he stumbled, but barely touching the ice with his hand, with a violent effort recovered himself, and skated off, laughing.

"How splendid, how nice he is!" Kitty was thinking at that time, as she came out of the pavilion with Mlle. Linon, and looked towards him with a smile of quiet affection, as though he were a favorite brother. "And can it be my fault, can I have done anything wrong? They talk of flirtation. I know it's not he that I love; but still I am happy with him, and he's so jolly. Only, why did he say that? ..." she mused.

Catching sight of Kitty going away, and her mother meeting her at the steps, Levin, flushed from his rapid exercise, stood still and pondered a minute. He took off his skates, and overtook the mother and daughter at the entrance of the gardens.

"Delighted to see you," said Princess Shtcherbatskaya. "On Thursdays we are home, as always."

"To-day, then?"

"We shall be pleased to see you," the princess said stiffly.

This stiffness hurt Kitty, and she could not resist the desire to smooth over her mother's coldness. She turned her head, and with a smile said:

"Good-bye till this evening."

At that moment Stepan Arkadyevitch, his hat cocked on one side, with beaming face and eyes, strode into the garden like a conquering hero. But as he approached his mother-in-law, he responded in a mournful and crestfallen tone to her inquiries about Dolly's health. After a little subdued and dejected conversation with his mother-in-law, he threw out his chest again, and put his arm in Levin's.

"Well, shall we set off?" he asked. "I've been thinking about you all this time, and I'm very, very glad you've come," he said, looking him in the face with a significant air.

"Yes, come along," answered Levin in ecstasy, hearing unceasingly the sound of that voice saying, "Good-bye till this evening," and seeing the smile with which it was said.

"To the England or the Hermitage?"

"I don't mind which."

"All right, then, the England," said Stepan Arkadyevitch, selecting that restaurant because he owed more there than at the Hermitage, and consequently considered it mean to avoid it. "Have you got a sledge? That's first-rate, for I sent my carriage home."

The friends hardly spoke all the way. Levin was wondering what that change in Kitty's expression had meant, and alternately assuring himself that there was hope, and falling into despair, seeing clearly that his hopes were insane, and yet all the while he felt himself quite another man, utterly unlike what he had been before her smile and those words, "Good-bye till this evening."

Stepan Arkadyevitch was absorbed during the drive in composing the menu of the dinner.

"You like turbot, don't you?" he said to Levin as they were arriving.

"Eh?" responded Levin. "Turbot? Yes, I'm *awfully* fond of turbot."

CHAPTER X

WHEN LEVIN WENT INTO THE RESTAURANT WITH OBLONSKY, HE COULD not help noticing a certain peculiarity of expression, as it were, a restrained radiance, about the face and whole figure of Stepan Arkadyevitch. Oblonsky took off his overcoat, and with his hat over one ear walked into the dining-room, giving directions to the Tatar waiters, who were clustered about him in evening coats, bearing napkins. Bowing to right and left to the people he met, and here as everywhere joyously greeting acquaintances, he went up to the sideboard for a preliminary appetizer of fish and vodka, and said to the painted Frenchwoman decked in ribbons, lace, and ringlets, behind the counter, something so amusing that even that Frenchwoman was moved to genuine laughter. Levin for his part refrained from taking any vodka simply because he felt such a loathing of that Frenchwoman, all made up, it seemed, of false hair, *poudre de riz*, and *vinaigre de toilette*. He made haste to move away from her, as from a dirty place. His whole soul was filled with memories of Kitty, and there was a smile of triumph and happiness shining in his eyes.

"This way, your excellency, please. Your excellency won't be disturbed here," said a particularly pertinacious, white-headed old Tatar with immense hips and coat-tails gaping widely behind. "Walk in, your excellency," he said to Levin; by way of showing his respect to Stepan Arkadyevitch, being attentive to his guest as well.

Instantly flinging a fresh cloth over the round table under the bronze chandelier, though it already had a table-cloth on it, he pushed up velvet chairs, and came to a standstill before Stepan Arkadyevitch with a napkin and a bill of fare in his hands, awaiting his commands.

"If you prefer it, your excellency, a private room will be free directly; Prince Golistin with a lady. Fresh oysters have come in."

"Ah! oysters."

Stepan Arkadyevitch became thoughtful.

"How if we were to change our program, Levin?" he said, keeping his finger on the bill of fare. And his face expressed serious hesitation. "Are the oysters good? Mind now."

"They're Flensburg, your excellency. We've no Ostend."

"Flensburg will do, but are they fresh?"

"Only arrived yesterday."

"Well, then, how if we were to begin with oysters, and so change the whole program? Eh?"

"It's all the same to me. I should like cabbage soup and porridge better than anything; but of course there's nothing like that here."

"*Porridge à la Russe*, your honor would like?" said the Tatar, bending down to Levin, like a nurse speaking to a child.

"No, joking apart, whatever you choose is sure to be good. I've been skating, and I'm hungry. And don't imagine," he added, detecting a look of dissatisfaction on Oblonsky's face, "that I shan't appreciate your choice. I am fond of good things."

"I should hope so! After all, it's one of the pleasures of life," said Stepan Arkadyevitch. "Well, then, my friend, you give us two—or better say three—dozen oysters, clear soup with vegetables...."

"*Printanière*," prompted the Tatar. But Stepan Arkadyevitch apparently did not care to allow him the satisfaction of giving the French names of the dishes.

"With vegetables in it, you know. Then turbot with thick sauce, then ... roast beef; and mind it's good. Yes, and capons, perhaps, and then sweets."

The Tatar, recollecting that it was Stepan Arkadyevitch's way not to call the dishes by the names in the French bill of fare, did not repeat them after him, but could not resist rehearsing the whole menu to himself according to the bill:—"*Soupe printanière, turbot, sauce Beaumarchais, poulard à l'estragon, macédoine de fruits* ... etc.," and then instantly, as though worked by springs, laying down one bound bill of fare, he took up another, the list of wines, and submitted it to Stepan Arkadyevitch.

"What shall we drink?"

"What you like, only not too much. Champagne," said Levin.

"What! to start with? You're right though, I dare say. Do you like the white seal?"

"*Cachet blanc,*" prompted the Tatar.

"Very well, then, give us that brand with the oysters, and then we'll see."

"Yes, sir. And what table wine?"

"You can give us Nuits. Oh, no, better the classic Chablis."

"Yes, sir. And *your* cheese, your excellency?"

"Oh, yes, Parmesan. Or would you like another?"

"No, it's all the same to me," said Levin, unable to suppress a smile.

And the Tatar ran off with flying coat-tails, and in five minutes darted in with a dish of opened oysters on mother-of-pearl shells, and a bottle between his fingers.

Stepan Arkadyevitch crushed the starchy napkin, tucked it into his waist-coat, and settling his arms comfortably, started on the oysters.

"Not bad," he said, stripping the oysters from the pearly shell with a silver fork, and swallowing them one after another. "Not bad," he repeated, turning his dewy, brilliant eyes from Levin to the Tatar.

Levin ate the oysters indeed, though white bread and cheese would have pleased him better. But he was admiring Oblonsky. Even the Tatar, uncorking the bottle and pouring the sparkling wine into the delicate glasses, glanced at Stepan Arkadyevitch, and settled his white cravat with a perceptible smile of satisfaction.

"You don't care much for oysters, do you?" said Stepan Arkadyevitch, emptying his wine-glass, "or you're worried about something. Eh?"

He wanted Levin to be in good spirits. But it was not that Levin was not in good spirits; he was ill at ease. With what he had in his soul, he felt sore and uncomfortable in the restaurant, in the midst of private rooms where men were dining with ladies, in all this fuss and bustle; the surroundings of bronzes, looking-glasses, gas, and waiters—all of it was offensive to him. He was afraid of sullying what his soul was brimful of.

"I? Yes, I am; but besides, all this bothers me," he said. "You can't conceive how queer it all seems to a country person like me, as queer as that gentleman's nails I saw at your place...."

"Yes, I saw how much interested you were in poor Grinevitch's nails," said Stepan Arkadyevitch, laughing.

"It's too much for me," responded Levin. "Do try, now, and put yourself in my place, take the point of view of a country person. We in the country try to bring our hands into such a state as will be most convenient for working with. So we cut our nails; sometimes we turn up our sleeves. And here people purposely let their nails grow as long as they will, and link on small saucers by way of studs, so that they can do nothing with their hands."

Stepan Arkadyevitch smiled gaily.

"Oh, yes, that's just a sign that he has no need to do coarse work. His work is with the mind...."

"Maybe. But still it's queer to me, just as at this moment it seems queer to me that we country folks try to get our meals over as soon as we can, so as to be ready for our work, while here are we trying to drag out our meal as long as possible, and with that object eating oysters...."

"Why, of course," objected Stepan Arkadyevitch. "But that's just the aim of civilization—to make everything a source of enjoyment."

"Well, if that's its aim, I'd rather be a savage."

"And so you are a savage. All you Levins are savages."

Levin sighed. He remembered his brother Nikolay, and felt ashamed and sore, and he scowled; but Oblonsky began speaking of a subject which at once drew his attention.

"Oh, I say, are you going to-night to our people, the Shtcherbatskys', I mean?" he said, his eyes sparkling significantly as he pushed away the empty rough shells, and drew the cheese towards him.

"Yes, I shall certainly go," replied Levin; "though I fancied the princess was not very warm in her invitation."

"What nonsense! That's her manner.... Come, boy, the soup! ... That's her manner—*grande dame*," said Stepan Arkadyevitch. "I'm coming, too, but I have to go to the Countess Bonina's rehearsal. Come, isn't it true that you're a savage? How do you explain the sudden way in which you vanished from Moscow? The Shtcherbatskys were continually asking me about you, as though I ought to know. The only thing I know is that you always do what no one else does."

"Yes," said Levin, slowly and with emotion, "you're right. I am a savage. Only, my savageness is not in having gone away, but in coming now. Now I have come …"

"Oh, what a lucky fellow you are!" broke in Stepan Arkadyevitch, looking into Levin's eyes.

"Why?"

"I know a gallant steed by tokens sure,
And by his eyes I know a youth in love,"

declaimed Stepan Arkadyevitch. "Everything is before you."

"Why, is it over for you already?"

"No; not over exactly, but the future is yours, and the present is mine, and the present—well, it's not all that it might be."

"How so?"

"Oh, things go wrong. But I don't want to talk of myself, and besides I can't explain it all," said Stepan Arkadyevitch. "Well, why have you come to Moscow, then? … Hi! take away!" he called to the Tatar.

"You guess?" responded Levin, his eyes like deep wells of light fixed on Stepan Arkadyevitch.

"I guess, but I can't be the first to talk about it. You can see by that whether I guess right or wrong," said Stepan Arkadyevitch, gazing at Levin with a subtle smile.

"Well, and what have you to say to me?" said Levin in a quivering voice, feeling that all the muscles of his face were quivering too. "How do you look at the question?"

Stepan Arkadyevitch slowly emptied his glass of Chablis, never taking his eyes off Levin.

"I?" said Stepan Arkadyevitch, "there's nothing I desire so much as that—nothing! It would be the best thing that could be."

"But you're not making a mistake? You know what we're speaking of?" said Levin, piercing him with his eyes. "You think it's possible?"

"I think it's possible. Why not possible?"

"No! do you really think it's possible? No, tell me all you think! Oh, but if … if refusal's in store for me! … Indeed I feel sure …"

"Why should you think that?" said Stepan Arkadyevitch, smiling at his excitement.

"It seems so to me sometimes. That will be awful for me, and for her too."

"Oh, well, anyway there's nothing awful in it for a girl. Every girl's proud of an offer."

"Yes, every girl, but not she."

Stepan Arkadyevitch smiled. He so well knew that feeling of Levin's, that for him all the girls in the world were divided into two classes: one class—all the girls in the world except her, and those girls with all sorts of human weaknesses, and very ordinary girls: the other class—she alone, having no weaknesses of any sort and higher than all humanity.

"Stay, take some sauce," he said, holding back Levin's hand as it pushed away the sauce.

Levin obediently helped himself to sauce, but would not let Stepan Arkadyevitch go on with his dinner.

"No, stop a minute, stop a minute," he said. "You must understand that it's a question of life and death for me. I have never spoken to any one of this. And there's no one I could speak of it to, except you. You know we're utterly unlike each other, different tastes and views and everything; but I know you're fond of me and understand me, and that's why I like you awfully. But for God's sake, be quite straight-forward with me."

"I tell you what I think," said Stepan Arkadyevitch, smiling. "But I'll say more: my wife is a wonderful woman ..." Stepan Arkadyevitch sighed, remembering his position with his wife, and, after a moment's silence, resumed—"She has a gift of foreseeing things. She sees right through people; but that's not all; she knows what will come to pass, especially in the way of marriages. She foretold, for instance, that Princess Shahovskaya would marry Brenteln. No one would believe it, but it came to pass. And she's on your side."

"How do you mean?"

"It's not only that she likes you—she says that Kitty is certain to be your wife."

At these words Levin's face suddenly lighted up with a smile, a smile not far from tears of emotion.

"She says that!" cried Levin. "I always said she was exquisite, your wife. There, that's enough, enough said about it," he said, getting up from his seat.

"All right, but do sit down."

But Levin could not sit down. He walked with his firm tread twice up and down the little cage of a room, blinked his eyelids that his tears might not fall, and only then sat down to the table.

"You must understand," said he, "it's not love. I've been in love, but it's not that. It's not my feeling, but a sort of force outside me has taken possession of me. I went away, you see, because I made up my mind that it could never be, you understand, as a happiness that does not come on earth; but I've struggled with myself, I see there's no living without it. And it must be settled."

"What did you go away for?"

"Ah, stop a minute! Ah, the thoughts that come crowding on one! The questions one must ask oneself! Listen. You can't imagine what you've done for me by what you said. I'm so happy that I've become positively hateful; I've forgotten everything. I heard to-day that my brother Nikolay ... you know, he's here ... I had even forgotten him. It seems to me that he's happy too. It's a sort of madness. But one thing's awful.... Here, you've been married, you know the feeling ... it's awful that we—old—with a past ... not of love, but of sins ... are brought all at once so near to a creature pure and innocent; it's loathsome, and that's why one can't help feeling oneself unworthy."

"Oh, well, you've not many sins on your conscience."

"Alas! all the same," said Levin, "when with loathing I go over my life, I shudder and curse and bitterly regret it.... Yes."

"What would you have? The world's made so," said Stepan Arkadyevitch.

"The one comfort is like that prayer, which I always liked: 'Forgive me not according to my unworthiness, but according to Thy loving-kindness.' That's the only way she can forgive me."

CHAPTER XI

LEVIN EMPTIED HIS GLASS, AND THEY WERE SILENT FOR A WHILE.
"There's one other thing I ought to tell you. Do you know Vronsky?" Stepan Arkadyevitch asked Levin.

"No, I don't. Why do you ask?"

"Give us another bottle," Stepan Arkadyevitch directed the Tatar, who was filling up their glasses and fidgeting round them just when he was not wanted.

"Why you ought to know Vronsky is that he's one of your rivals."

"Who's Vronsky?" said Levin, and his face was suddenly transformed from the look of childlike ecstasy which Oblonsky had just been admiring to an angry and unpleasant expression.

"Vronsky is one of the sons of Count Kirill Ivanovitch Vronsky, and one of the finest specimens of the gilded youth of Petersburg. I made his acquaintance in Tver when I was there on official business, and he came there for the levy of recruits. Fearfully rich, handsome, great connections, an aide-de-camp, and with all that a very nice, good-natured fellow. But he's more than simply a good-natured fellow, as I've found out here—he's a cultivated man, too, and very intelligent; he's a man who'll make his mark."

Levin scowled and was dumb.

"Well, he turned up here soon after you'd gone, and as I can see, he's over head and ears in love with Kitty, and you know that her mother…"

"Excuse me, but I know nothing," said Levin, frowning gloomily. And immediately he recollected his brother Nikolay and how hateful he was to have been able to forget him.

"You wait a bit, wait a bit," said Stepan Arkadyevitch, smiling and touching his hand. "I've told you what I know, and I repeat that in this delicate and tender matter, as far as one can conjecture, I believe the chances are in your favor."

Levin dropped back in his chair; his face was pale.

"But I would advise you to settle the thing as soon as may be," pursued Oblonsky, filling up his glass.

"No, thanks, I can't drink any more," said Levin, pushing away his glass. "I shall be drunk…. Come, tell me how are you getting on?" he went on, obviously anxious to change the conversation.

"One word more: in any case I advise you to settle the question soon. To-night I don't advise you to speak," said Stepan Arkadyevitch. "Go round to-morrow morning, make an offer in due form, and God bless you…."

"Oh, do you still think of coming to me for some shooting? Come next spring, do," said Levin.

Now his whole soul was full of remorse that he had begun this conversation with Stepan Arkadyevitch. A feeling such as his was profaned by talk of the rivalry of some Petersburg officer, of the suppositions and the counsels of Stepan Arkadyevitch.

Stepan Arkadyevitch smiled. He knew what was passing in Levin's soul.

"I'll come some day," he said. "But women, my boy, they're the pivot everything turns upon. Things are in a bad way with me, very bad. And it's all through women. Tell me frankly now," he pursued, picking up a cigar and keeping one hand on his glass; "give me your advice."

"Why, what is it?"

"I'll tell you. Suppose you're married, you love your wife, but you're fascinated by another woman...."

"Excuse me, but I'm absolutely unable to comprehend how... just as I can't comprehend how I could now, after my dinner, go straight to a baker's shop and steal a roll."

Stepan Arkadyevitch's eyes sparkled more than usual. "Why not? A roll will sometimes smell so good one can't resist it.

> "Himmlisch ist's, wenn ich bezwungen
>   Meine irdische Begier;
>   Aber doch wenn's nich gelungen
>   Hatt' ich auch recht huebsch Plaisir!"

As he said this, Stepan Arkadyevitch smiled subtly. Levin, too, could not help smiling.

"Yes, but joking apart," resumed Stepan Arkadyevitch, "you must understand that the woman is a sweet, gentle, loving creature, poor and lonely, and has sacrificed everything. Now, when the thing's done, don't you see, can one possibly cast her off? Even supposing one parts from her, so as not to break up one's family life, still, can one help feeling for her, setting her on her feet, softening her lot?"

"Well, you must excuse me there. You know to me all women are divided into two classes ... at least no ... truer to say: there are women and there are ... I've never seen exquisite fallen beings, and I never shall see them, but such creatures as that painted Frenchwoman at the counter with the ringlets are vermin to my mind, and all fallen women are the same."

"But the Magdalen?"

"Ah, drop that! Christ would never have said those words if He had known how they would be abused. Of all the Gospel those words are the only ones remembered. However, I'm not saying so much what I think, as what I feel. I have a loathing for fallen women. You're afraid of spiders, and I of these vermin. Most likely you've not made a study of spiders and don't know their character; and so it is with me."

"It's very well for you to talk like that; it's very much like that gentleman in Dickens who used to fling all difficult questions over his right shoulder. But to deny the facts is no answer. What's to be done—you tell me that, what's to be done? Your wife gets older, while you're full of life. Before you've time to look round, you feel that you can't love your wife with love, however much you may esteem her. And then all at once love turns up, and you're done for, done for," Stepan Arkadyevitch said with weary despair.

Levin half smiled.

"Yes, you're done for," resumed Oblonsky. "But what's to be done?"

"Don't steal rolls."

Stepan Arkadyevitch laughed outright.

"Oh, moralist! But you must understand, there are two women; one insists only on her rights, and those rights are your love, which you can't give her; and the other sacrifices everything for you and asks for nothing. What are you to do? How are you to act? There's a fearful tragedy in it."

"If you care for my profession of faith as regards that, I'll tell you that I don't believe there was any tragedy about it. And this is why. To my mind, love … both the sorts of love, which you remember Plato defines in his Banquet, served as the test of men. Some men only understand one sort, and some only the other. And those who only know the non-platonic love have no need to talk of tragedy. In such love there can be no sort of tragedy. 'I'm much obliged for the gratification, my humble respects'—that's all the tragedy. And in platonic love there can be no tragedy, because in that love all is clear and pure, because …"

At that instant Levin recollected his own sins and the inner conflict he had lived through. And he added unexpectedly:

"But perhaps you are right. Very likely…. I don't know, I don't know."

"It's this, don't you see," said Stepan Arkadyevitch, "you're very much all of a piece. That's your strong point and your failing. You have a character that's all of a piece, and you want the whole of life to be of a piece too—but that's not how it is. You despise public official work because you want the reality to be invariably corresponding all the while with the aim—and that's not how it is. You want a man's work, too, always to have a defined aim, and love and family life always to be undivided—and that's not how it is. All the variety, all the charm, all the beauty of life is made up of light and shadow."

Levin sighed and made no reply. He was thinking of his own affairs, and did not hear Oblonsky.

And suddenly both of them felt that though they were friends, though they had been dining and drinking together, which should have drawn them closer, yet each was thinking only of his own affairs, and they had nothing to do with one another. Oblonsky had more than once experienced this extreme sense of aloofness, instead of intimacy, coming on after dinner, and he knew what to do in such cases.

"Bill!" he called, and he went into the next room where he promptly came across an aide-de-camp of his acquaintance and dropped into conversation with him about an actress and her protector. And at once in the conversation with the aide-de-camp Oblonsky had a sense of relaxation and relief after the conversation with Levin, which always put him to too great a mental and spiritual strain.

When the Tatar appeared with a bill for twenty-six roubles and odd kopecks, besides a tip for himself, Levin, who would another time have been horrified, like any one from the country, at his share of fourteen roubles, did not notice it, paid, and set off homewards to dress and go to the Shtcherbatskys' there to decide his fate.

CHAPTER XII

THE YOUNG PRINCESS KITTY SHTCHERBATSKAYA WAS EIGHTEEN. IT WAS THE first winter that she had been out in the world. Her success in society had been greater than that of either of her elder sisters, and greater even than her mother had anticipated. To say nothing of the young men who danced at the Moscow balls being almost all in love with Kitty, two serious suitors had already this first winter made their appearance: Levin, and immediately after his departure, Count Vronsky.

Levin's appearance at the beginning of the winter, his frequent visits, and evident love for Kitty, had led to the first serious conversations between Kitty's parents as to her future, and to disputes between them. The prince was on Levin's side; he said he wished for nothing better for Kitty. The princess for her part, going round the question in the manner peculiar to women, maintained that Kitty was too young, that Levin had done nothing to prove that he had serious intentions, that Kitty felt no great attraction to him, and other side issues; but she did not state the principal point, which was that she looked for a better match for her daughter, and that Levin was not to her liking, and she did not understand him. When Levin had abruptly departed, the princess was delighted, and said to her husband triumphantly: "You see I was right." When Vronsky appeared on the scene, she was still more delighted, confirmed in her opinion that Kitty was to make not simply a good, but a brilliant match.

In the mother's eyes there could be no comparison between Vronsky and Levin. She disliked in Levin his strange and uncompromising opinions and his shyness in society, founded, as she supposed, on his pride and his queer sort of life, as she considered it, absorbed in cattle and peasants. She did not very much like it that he, who was in love with her daughter, had kept coming to the house for six weeks, as though he were waiting for something, inspecting, as though he were afraid he might be doing them too great an honor by making an offer, and did not realize that a man, who continually visits at a house where there is a young unmarried girl, is bound to make his intentions clear. And suddenly, without doing so, he disappeared. "It's as well he's not attractive enough for Kitty to have fallen in love with him," thought the mother.

Vronsky satisfied all the mother's desires. Very wealthy, clever, of aristocratic family, on the highroad to a brilliant career in the army and at court, and a fascinating man. Nothing better could be wished for.

Vronsky openly flirted with Kitty at balls, danced with her, and came continually to the house, consequently there could be no doubt of the seriousness of his intentions. But, in spite of that, the mother had spent the whole of that winter in a state of terrible anxiety and agitation.

Princess Shtcherbatskaya had herself been married thirty years ago, her aunt arranging the match. Her husband, about whom everything was well known beforehand, had come, looked at his future bride, and been looked at. The matchmaking aunt had ascertained and communicated their mutual impression. That impression had been favorable. Afterwards, on a day fixed beforehand, the expected offer was made to her parents, and accepted. All had passed very simply and easily. So it seemed, at least, to the princess. But over her own daughters she had felt how far from simple and easy is the business, apparently so commonplace, of marrying off one's daughters. The panics that had been lived through, the thoughts that had been brooded over, the money that had been wasted, and the disputes with her husband over marrying the two elder girls, Darya and Natalia! Now, since the youngest had come out, she was going through the same terrors, the same doubts, and still more violent quarrels with her husband than she had over the elder girls. The old prince, like all fathers indeed, was exceedingly punctilious on the score of the honor and reputation of his daughters. He was irrationally jealous over his daughters, especially over Kitty, who was his favorite. At every turn he had scenes with the princess for compromising her daughter. The princess had grown accustomed to this already with her other daughters, but now she felt that there was more ground for the prince's touchiness. She saw that of late years much was changed in the manners of society, that a mother's duties had become still more difficult. She saw that girls of Kitty's age formed some sort of clubs, went to some sort of lectures, mixed freely in men's society; drove about the streets alone, many of them did not curtsey, and, what was the most important thing, all the girls were firmly convinced that to choose their husbands was their own affair, and not their parents'. "Marriages aren't made nowadays as they used to be," was thought and said by all these young girls, and even by their elders. But how marriages were made now, the princess could not learn from any one. The French fashion—of the parents arranging their children's future—was not accepted; it was condemned. The English fashion of the complete independence of girls was also not accepted, and not possible in Russian society. The Russian fashion of matchmaking by the offices of intermediate persons was for some reason considered unseemly; it was ridiculed by every one, and by the princess herself. But how girls were to be married, and how parents were to marry them, no one knew. Every one with whom the princess had chanced to discuss the matter said the same thing: "Mercy on us, it's high time in our day to cast off all that old-fashioned business. It's the young people have to marry; and not their parents; and so we ought to leave the young people to arrange it as they choose." It was very easy for any one to say that who had no daughters, but the princess realized that in the process of getting to know each other, her daughter might fall in love, and fall in love with some one who did not care to marry her or who was quite unfit to be her husband. And, however much it was instilled into the princess that in our times young people ought to arrange their lives for themselves, she was unable to believe it, just as she would have been unable to believe that, at any time whatever, the most suitable playthings for children five years old ought to be loaded pistols. And so the princess was more uneasy over Kitty than she had been over her elder sisters.

Now she was afraid that Vronsky might confine himself to simply flirting with her daughter. She saw that her daughter was in love with him, but tried to comfort herself with the thought that he was an honorable man, and would not do this. But at the same time she knew how easy it is, with the freedom of manners of to-day, to turn a girl's head, and how lightly men generally regard such a crime. The week before, Kitty had told her mother of a conversation she had with Vronsky during a mazurka. This conversation had partly reassured the princess; but perfectly at ease she could not be. Vronsky had told Kitty that both he and his brother were so used to obeying their mother that they never made up their minds to any important undertaking without consulting her. "And just now, I am impatiently awaiting my mother's arrival from Petersburg, as peculiarly fortunate," he told her.

Kitty had repeated this without attaching any significance to the words. But her mother saw them in a different light. She knew that the old lady was expected from day to day, that she would be pleased at her son's choice, and she felt it strange that he should not make his offer through fear of vexing his mother. However, she was so anxious for the marriage itself, and still more for relief from her fears, that she believed it was so. Bitter as it was for the princess to see the unhappiness of her eldest daughter, Dolly, on the point of leaving her husband, her anxiety over the decision of her youngest daughter's fate engrossed all her feelings. To-day, with Levin's reappearance, a fresh source of anxiety arose. She was afraid that her daughter, who had at one time, as she fancied, a feeling for Levin, might, from extreme sense of honor, refuse Vronsky, and that Levin's arrival might generally complicate and delay the affair so near being concluded.

"Why, has he been here long?" the princess asked about Levin, as they returned home.

"He came to-day, mamma."

"There's one thing I want to say …" began the princess, and from her serious and alert face, Kitty guessed what it would be.

"Mamma," she said, flushing hotly and turning quickly to her, "please, please don't say anything about that. I know, I know all about it."

She wished for what her mother wished for, but the motives of her mother's wishes wounded her.

"I only want to say that to raise hopes …"

"Mamma, darling, for goodness' sake, don't talk about it. It's so horrible to talk about it."

"I won't," said her mother, seeing the tears in her daughter's eyes; "but one thing, my love; you promised me you would have no secrets from me. You won't?"

"Never, mamma, none," answered Kitty, flushing a little, and looking her mother straight in the face, "but there's no use in my telling you anything, and I … I … if I wanted to, I don't know what to say or how … I don't know…."

"No, she could not tell an untruth with those eyes," thought the mother, smiling at her agitation and happiness. The princess smiled that what was taking place just now in her soul seemed to the poor child so immense and so important.

CHAPTER XIII

AFTER DINNER, AND TILL THE BEGINNING OF THE EVENING, KITTY WAS feeling a sensation akin to the sensation of a young man before a battle. Her heart throbbed violently, and her thoughts would not rest on anything.

She felt that this evening, when they would both meet for the first time, would be a turning-point in her life. And she was continually picturing them to herself, at one moment each separately, and then both together. When she mused on the past, she dwelt with pleasure, with tenderness, on the memories of her relations with Levin. The memories of childhood and of Levin's friendship with her dead brother gave a special poetic charm to her relations with him. His love for her, of which she felt certain, was flattering and delightful to her; and it was pleasant for her to think of Levin. In her memories of Vronsky there always entered a certain element of awkwardness, though he was in the highest degree well-bred and at ease, as though there were some false note—not in Vronsky, he was very simple and nice, but in herself, while with Levin she felt perfectly simple and clear. But, on the other hand, directly she thought of the future with Vronsky, there arose before her a perspective of brilliant happiness; with Levin the future seemed misty.

When she went up-stairs to dress, and looked into the looking-glass, she noticed with joy that it was one of her good days, and that she was in complete possession of all her forces,—she needed this so for what lay before her: she was conscious of external composure and free grace in her movements.

At half-past seven she had only just gone down into the drawing-room, when the footman announced, "Konstantin Dmitrievitch Levin." The princess was still in her room, and the prince had not come in. "So it is to be," thought Kitty, and all the blood seemed to rush to her heart. She was horrified at her paleness, as she glanced into the looking-glass. At that moment she knew beyond doubt that he had come early on purpose to find her alone and to make her an offer. And only then for the first time the whole thing presented itself in a new, different aspect; only then she realized that the question did not affect her only—with whom she would be happy, and whom she loved—but that she would have that moment to wound a man whom she liked. And to wound him cruelly. What for? Because he, dear fellow, loved her, was in love with her. But there was no help for it, so it must be, so it would have to be.

"My God! shall I myself really have to say it to him?" she thought. "Can I tell him I don't love him? That will be a lie. What am I to say to him? That I love someone else? No, that's impossible. I'm going away, I'm going away."

She had reached the door, when she heard his step. "No! it's not honest. What have I to be afraid of? I have done nothing wrong. What is to be, will be! I'll tell the truth. And with him one can't be ill at ease. Here he is," she said to herself, seeing his powerful, shy figure, with his shining eyes fixed on her. She looked straight into his face, as though imploring him to spare her, and gave her hand.

"It's not time yet; I think I'm too early," he said glancing round the empty drawing-room. When he saw that his expectations were realized, that there was nothing to prevent him from speaking, his face became gloomy.

"Oh, no," said Kitty, and sat down at the table.

"But this was just what I wanted, to find you alone," he began, not sitting down, and not looking at her, so as not to lose courage.

"Mamma will be down directly. She was very much tired....Yesterday ..."

She talked on, not knowing what her lips were uttering, and not taking her supplicating and caressing eyes off him.

He glanced at her; she blushed, and ceased speaking.

"I told you I did not know whether I should be here long ... that it depended on you...."

She dropped her head lower and lower, not knowing herself what answer she should make to what was coming.

"That it depended on you," he repeated. "I meant to say ... I meant to say ... I came for this ... to be my wife!" he brought out, not knowing what he was saying; but feeling that the most terrible thing was said, he stopped short and looked at her....

She was breathing heavily, not looking at him. She was feeling ecstasy. Her soul was flooded with happiness. She had never anticipated that the utterance of love would produce such a powerful effect on her. But it lasted only an instant. She remembered Vronsky. She lifted her clear, truthful eyes, and seeing his desperate face, she answered hastily:

"That cannot be ... forgive me."

A moment ago, and how close she had been to him, of what importance in his life! And how aloof and remote from him she had become now!

"It was bound to be so," he said, not looking at her.

He bowed, and was meaning to retreat.

CHAPTER XIV

BUT AT THAT VERY MOMENT THE PRINCESS CAME IN. THERE WAS A LOOK OF horror on her face when she saw them alone, and their disturbed faces. Levin bowed to her, and said nothing. Kitty did not speak nor lift her eyes. "Thank God, she has refused him," thought the mother, and her face lighted up with the habitual smile with which she greeted her guests on Thursdays. She sat down and began questioning Levin about his life in the country. He sat down again, waiting for other visitors to arrive, in order to retreat unnoticed.

Five minutes later there came in a friend of Kitty's, married the preceding winter, Countess Nordston.

She was a thin, sallow, sickly, and nervous woman, with brilliant black eyes. She was fond of Kitty, and her affection for her showed itself, as the affection of married women for girls always does, in the desire to make a match for Kitty after her own ideal of married happiness; she wanted her to marry Vronsky. Levin she had often met at the Shtcherbatskys' early in the winter, and she had always disliked him. Her invariable and favorite pursuit, when they met, consisted in making fun of him.

"I do like it when he looks down at me from the height of his grandeur, or breaks off his learned conversation with me because I'm a fool, or is condescending to me. I like that so; to see him condescending! I am so glad he can't bear me," she used to say of him.

She was right, for Levin actually could not bear her, and despised her for what she was proud of and regarded as a fine characteristic—her nervousness, her delicate contempt and indifference for everything coarse and earthly.

The Countess Nordston and Levin had got into that relation with one another not seldom seen in society, when two persons, who remain externally on friendly terms, despise each other to such a degree that they cannot even take each other seriously, and cannot even be offended by each other.

The Countess Nordston pounced upon Levin at once.

"Ah, Konstantin Dmitrievitch! So you've come back to our corrupt Babylon," she said, giving him her tiny, yellow hand, and recalling what he had chanced to say early in the winter, that Moscow was a Babylon. "Come, is Babylon reformed, or have you degenerated?" she added, glancing with a simper at Kitty.

"It's very flattering for me, countess, that you remember my words so well," responded Levin, who had succeeded in recovering his composure, and at once from habit dropped into his tone of joking hostility to the Countess Nordston. "They must certainly make a great impression on you."

"Oh, I should think so! I always note them all down. Well, Kitty, have you been skating again?..."

And she began talking to Kitty. Awkward as it was for Levin to withdraw now, it would still have been easier for him to perpetrate this awkwardness than to remain all the evening and see Kitty, who glanced at him now and then and avoided his eyes. He was on the point of getting up, when the princess, noticing that he was silent, addressed him.

"Shall you be long in Moscow? You're busy with the district council, though, aren't you, and can't be away for long?"

"No, princess, I'm no longer a member of the council," he said. "I have come up for a few days."

"There's something the matter with him," thought Countess Nordston, glancing at his stern, serious face. "He isn't in his old argumentative mood. But I'll draw him out. I do love making a fool of him before Kitty, and I'll do it."

"Konstantin Dmitrievitch," she said to him, "do explain to me, please, what's the meaning of it. You know all about such things. At home in our village of Kaluga all the peasants and all the women have drunk up all they possessed, and now they can't pay us any rent. What's the meaning of that? You always praise the peasants so."

At that instant another lady came into the room, and Levin got up.

"Excuse me, countess, but I really know nothing about it, and can't tell you anything," he said, and looked round at the officer who came in behind the lady.

"That must be Vronsky," thought Levin, and, to be sure of it, glanced at Kitty. She had already had time to look at Vronsky, and looked round at Levin. And simply from the look in her eyes, that grew unconsciously brighter, Levin knew that she loved that man, knew it as surely as if she had told him so in words. But what sort of a man was he? Now, whether for good or for ill, Levin could not choose but remain; he must find out what the man was like whom she loved.

There are people who, on meeting a successful rival, no matter in what, are at once disposed to turn their backs on everything good in him, and to see only what is bad. There are people, on the other hand, who desire above all to find in that lucky rival the qualities by which he has outstripped them, and seek with a throbbing ache at heart only what is good. Levin belonged to the second class. But he had no difficulty in finding what was good and attractive in Vronsky. It was apparent at the first glance. Vronsky was a squarely built, dark man, not very tall, with a good-humored, handsome, and exceedingly calm and resolute face. Everything about his face and figure, from his short-cropped black hair and freshly shaven chin down to his loosely fitting, brand-new uniform, was simple and at the same time elegant. Making way for the lady who had come in, Vronsky went up to the princess and then to Kitty.

As he approached her, his beautiful eyes shone with a specially tender light, and with a faint, happy, and modestly triumphant smile (so it seemed to Levin), bowing carefully and respectfully over her, he held out his small broad hand to her.

Greeting and saying a few words to everyone, he sat down without once glancing at Levin, who had never taken his eyes off him.

"Let me introduce you," said the princess, indicating Levin. "Konstantin Dmitrievitch Levin, Count Alexey Kirillovitch Vronsky."

Vronsky got up and, looking cordially at Levin, shook hands with him.

"I believe I was to have dined with you this winter," he said, smiling his simple and open smile; "but you had unexpectedly left for the country."

"Konstantin Dmitrievitch despises and hates town and us townspeople," said Countess Nordston.

"My words must make a deep impression on you, since you remember them so well," said Levin, and, suddenly conscious that he had said just the same thing before, he reddened.

Vronsky looked at Levin and Countess Nordston, and smiled.

"Are you always in the country?" he inquired. "I should think it must be dull in the winter."

"It's not dull if one has work to do; besides, one's not dull by oneself," Levin replied abruptly.

"I am fond of the country," said Vronsky, noticing, and affecting not to notice, Levin's tone.

"But I hope, count, you would not consent to live in the country always," said Countess Nordston.

"I don't know; I have never tried for long. I experienced a queer feeling once," he went on. "I never longed so for the country, Russian country, with bast shoes and peasants, as when I was spending a winter with my mother in Nice. Nice itself is dull enough, you know. And indeed, Naples and Sorrento are only pleasant for a short time. And it's just there that Russia comes back to me most vividly, and especially the country. It's as though …"

He talked on, addressing both Kitty and Levin, turning his serene, friendly eyes from one to the other, and saying obviously just what came into his head.

Noticing that Countess Nordston wanted to say something, he stopped short without finishing what he had begun, and listened attentively to her.

The conversation did not flag for an instant, so that the princess, who always kept in reserve, in case a subject should be lacking, two heavy guns—the relative advantages of classical and of modern education, and universal military service—had not to move out either of them, while Countess Nordston had not a chance of chaffing Levin.

Levin wanted to, and could not, take part in the general conversation; saying to himself every instant, "Now go," he still did not go, as though waiting for something.

The conversation fell upon table-turning and spirits, and Countess Nordston, who believed in spiritualism, began to describe the marvels she had seen.

"Ah, countess, you really must take me, for pity's sake do take me to see them! I have never seen anything extraordinary, though I am always on the lookout for it everywhere," said Vronsky, smiling.

"Very well, next Saturday," answered Countess Nordston. "But you, Konstantin Dmitrievitch, do you believe in it?" she asked Levin.

"Why do you ask me? You know what I shall say."

"But I want to hear your opinion."

"My opinion," answered Levin, "is only that this table-turning simply proves that educated society—so called—is no higher than the peasants. They believe in the evil eye, and in witchcraft and omens, while we …"

"Oh, then you don't believe in it?"

"I can't believe in it, countess."

"But if I've seen it myself?"

"The peasant women too tell us they have seen goblins."

"Then you think I tell a lie?"

And she laughed a mirthless laugh.

"Oh, no, Masha, Konstantin Dmitrievitch said he could not believe in it," said Kitty, blushing for Levin, and Levin saw this, and, still more exasperated, would have answered, but Vronsky with his bright frank smile rushed to the support of the conversation, which was threatening to become disagreeable.

"You do not admit the conceivability at all?" he queried. "But why not? We admit the existence of electricity, of which we know nothing. Why should there not be some new force, still unknown to us, which …"

"When electricity was discovered," Levin interrupted hurriedly, "it was only the phenomenon that was discovered, and it was unknown from what it proceeded and what were its effects, and ages passed before its applications were conceived. But the spiritualists have begun with tables writing for them, and spirits appearing to them, and have only later started saying that it is an unknown force."

Vronsky listened attentively to Levin, as he always did listen, obviously interested in his words.

"Yes, but the spiritualists say we don't know at present what this force is, but there is a force, and these are the conditions in which it acts. Let the scientific men find out what the force consists in. No, I don't see why there should not be a new force, if it …"

"Why, because with electricity," Levin interrupted again, "every time you rub tar against wool, a recognized phenomenon is manifested, but in this case it does not happen every time, and so it follows it is not a natural phenomenon."

Feeling probably that the conversation was taking a tone too serious for a drawing-room, Vronsky made no rejoinder, but by way of trying to change the conversation, he smiled brightly, and turned to the ladies.

"Do let us try at once, countess," he said; but Levin would finish saying what he thought.

"I think," he went on, "that this attempt of the spiritualists to explain their marvels as some sort of new natural force is most futile. They boldly talk of spiritual force, and then try to subject it to material experiment."

Every one was waiting for him to finish, and he felt it.

"And I think you would be a first-rate medium," said Countess Nordston; "there's something enthusiastic in you."

Levin opened his mouth, was about to say something, reddened, and said nothing.

"Do let us try table-turning at once, please," said Vronsky. "Princess, will you allow it?"

And Vronsky stood up, looking about for a little table.

Kitty got up to fetch a table, and as she passed, her eyes met Levin's. She felt for him with her whole heart, the more because she was pitying him for suffering of which she was herself the cause. "If you can forgive me, forgive me," said her eyes, "I am so happy."

"I hate them all, and you, and myself," his eyes responded, and he took up his hat. But he was not destined to escape. Just as they were arranging themselves round the table, and Levin was on the point of retiring, the old prince came in, and after greeting the ladies, addressed Levin.

"Ah!" he began joyously. "Been here long, my boy? I didn't even know you were in town. Very glad to see you." The old prince embraced Levin, and talking to him did not observe Vronsky, who had risen, and was serenely waiting till the prince should turn to him.

Kitty felt how distasteful her father's warmth was to Levin after what had happened. She saw, too, how coldly her father responded at last to Vronsky's bow, and how Vronsky looked with amiable perplexity at her father, as though trying and failing to understand how and why anyone could be hostilely disposed towards him, and she flushed.

"Prince, let us have Konstantin Dmitrievitch," said Countess Nordston; "we want to try an experiment."

"What experiment? Table-turning? Well, you must excuse me, ladies and gentlemen, but to my mind it is better fun to play the ring game," said the old prince, looking at Vronsky, and guessing that it had been his suggestion. "There's some sense in that, anyway."

Vronsky looked wonderingly at the prince with his resolute eyes, and, with a faint smile, began immediately talking to Countess Nordston of the great ball that was to come off next week.

"I hope you will be there?" he said to Kitty. As soon as the old prince turned away from him, Levin went out unnoticed, and the last impression he carried away with him of that evening was the smiling, happy face of Kitty answering Vronsky's inquiry about the ball.

CHAPTER XV

AT THE END OF THE EVENING KITTY TOLD HER MOTHER OF HER conversation with Levin, and in spite of all the pity she felt for Levin, she was glad at the thought that she had received an *offer*. She had no doubt that she had acted rightly. But after she had gone to bed, for a long while she could not sleep. One impression pursued her relentlessly. It was Levin's face, with his scowling brows, and his kind eyes looking out in dark dejection below them, as he stood listening to her father, and glancing at her and at Vronsky. And she felt so sorry for him that tears came into her eyes. But immediately she thought of the man for whom she had given him up. She vividly recalled his manly, resolute face, his noble self-possession, and the good-nature conspicuous in everything towards every one. She remembered the love for her of the man she loved, and once more all was gladness in her soul, and she lay on the pillow, smiling with happiness. "I'm sorry, I'm sorry; but what could I do? It's not my fault," she said to herself; but an inner voice told her something else. Whether she felt remorse at having won Levin's love, or at having refused him, she did not know. But her happiness was poisoned by doubts. "Lord, have pity on us; Lord, have pity on us; Lord, have pity on us!" she repeated to herself, till she fell asleep.

Meanwhile there took place below, in the prince's little library, one of the scenes so often repeated between the parents on account of their favorite daughter.

"What? I'll tell you what!" shouted the prince, waving his arms, and at once wrapping his squirrel-lined dressing-gown round him again. "That you've no pride, no dignity; that you're disgracing, ruining your daughter by this vulgar, stupid matchmaking!"

"But, really, for mercy's sake, prince, what have I done?" said the princess, almost crying.

She, pleased and happy after her conversation with her daughter, had gone to the prince to say good-night as usual, and though she had no intention of telling him of Levin's offer and Kitty's refusal, still she hinted to her husband that she fancied things were practically settled with Vronsky, and that he would declare himself so soon as his mother arrived. And thereupon, at those words, the prince had all at once flown into a passion, and began to use unseemly language.

"What have you done? I'll tell you what. First of all, you're trying to catch an eligible gentleman, and all Moscow will be talking of it, and with good reason. If you have evening parties, invite everyone, don't pick out the possible suitors. Invite all the young bucks. Engage a piano-player, and let them dance, and not as you do things nowadays, hunting up good matches. It makes me sick, sick to see it, and you've gone on till you've turned the poor wench's head. Levin's a thousand times the better man. As for this little Petersburg swell, they're turned out by machinery, all on one pattern, and all precious rubbish. But if he were a prince of the blood, my daughter need not run after anyone."

"But what have I done?"

"Why, you've ..." The prince was crying wrathfully.

"I know if one were to listen to you," interrupted the princess, "we should never marry our daughter. If it's to be so, we'd better go into the country."

"Well, and we had better."

"But do wait a minute. Do I try and catch them? I don't try to catch them in the least. A young man, and a very nice one, has fallen in love with her, and she, I fancy ..."

"Oh, yes, you fancy! And how if she really is in love, and he's no more thinking of marriage than I am! ... Oh, that I should live to see it! ... Ah! spiritualism! Ah! Nice! Ah! the ball!" And the prince, imagining that he was mimicking his wife, made a mincing curtsey at each word. "And this is how we're preparing wretchedness for Kitty; and she's really got the notion into her head ..."

"But what makes you suppose so?"

"I don't suppose; I know. We have eyes for such things, though womenfolk haven't. I see a man who has serious intentions, that's Levin: and I see a peacock, like this feather-head, who's only amusing himself."

"Oh, well, when once you get an idea into your head! ..."

"Well, you'll remember my words, but too late, just as with Dolly."

"Well, well, we won't talk of it," the princess stopped him, recollecting her unlucky Dolly.

"By all means, and good-night!"

And signing each other with the cross, the husband and wife parted with a kiss, feeling that they each remained of their own opinion.

The princess had at first been quite certain that that evening had settled Kitty's future, and that there could be no doubt of Vronsky's intentions, but her husband's words had disturbed her. And returning to her own room, in terror before the unknown future, she, too, like Kitty, repeated several times in her heart, "Lord, have pity; Lord, have pity; Lord, have pity."

CHAPTER XVI

VRONSKY HAD NEVER HAD A REAL HOME-LIFE. HIS MOTHER HAD BEEN IN HER youth a brilliant society woman, who had had during her married life, and still more afterwards, many love-affairs notorious in the whole fashionable world. His father he scarcely remembered, and he had been educated in the Corps of Pages.

Leaving the school very young as a brilliant officer, he had at once got into the circle of wealthy Petersburg army men. Although he did go more or less into Petersburg society, his love affairs had always hitherto been outside it.

In Moscow he had for the first time felt, after his luxurious and coarse life at Petersburg, all the charm of intimacy with a sweet and innocent girl of his own rank, who cared for him. It never even entered his head that there could be any harm in his relations with Kitty. At balls he danced principally with her. He was a constant visitor at their house. He talked to her as people commonly do talk in society—all sorts of nonsense, but nonsense to which he could not help attaching a special meaning in her case. Although he said nothing to her that he could not have said before everybody, he felt that she was becoming more and more dependent upon him, and the more he felt this, the better he liked it, and the tenderer was his feeling for her. He did not know that this mode of behavior in relation to Kitty had a definite character, that it is courting young girls with no intention of marriage, and that such courting is one of the evil actions common among brilliant young men such as he was. It seemed to him that he was the first who had discovered this pleasure, and he was enjoying his discovery.

If he could have heard what her parents were saying that evening, if he could have put himself at the point of view of the family and have heard that Kitty would be unhappy if he did not marry her, he would have been greatly astonished, and would not have believed it. He could not believe that what gave such great and delicate pleasure to him, and above all to her, could be wrong. Still less could he have believed that he ought to marry.

Marriage had never presented itself to him as a possibility. He not only disliked family life, but a family, and especially a husband was, in accordance with the views general in the bachelor world in which he lived, conceived as something alien, repellent, and, above all, ridiculous.

But though Vronsky had not the least suspicion what the parents were saying, he felt on coming away from the Shtcherbatskys' that the secret spiritual bond which existed between him and Kitty had grown so much stronger that evening that some step must be taken. But what step could and ought to be taken he could not imagine.

"What is so exquisite," he thought, as he returned from the Shtcherbatskys', carrying away with him, as he always did, a delicious feeling of purity and freshness, arising partly from the fact that he had not been smoking for a whole evening, and with it a new feeling of tenderness at her love for him—"what is so exquisite is that not a word has been said by me or by her, but we understand each other so well in this unseen language of looks and tones, that this evening more clearly than ever she told me she loves me. And how secretly, simply, and most of all, how trustfully! I feel myself better, purer. I feel that I have a heart, and that there is a great deal of good in me. Those sweet, loving eyes! When she said: 'Indeed I do....'

"Well, what then? Oh, nothing. It's good for me, and good for her." And he began wondering where to finish the evening.

He passed in review of the places he might go to. "Club? a game of bezique, champagne with Ignatov? No, I'm not going. Château des Fleurs; there I shall find Oblonsky, songs, the cancan. No, I'm sick of it. That's why I like the Shtcherbatskys', that I'm growing better. I'll go home." He went straight to his room at Dussot's Hotel, ordered supper, and then undressed, and as soon as his head touched the pillow, fell into a sound sleep.

CHAPTER XVII

NEXT DAY AT ELEVEN O'CLOCK IN THE MORNING VRONSKY DROVE TO THE station of the Petersburg railway to meet his mother, and the first person he came across on the great flight of steps was Oblonsky, who was expecting his sister by the same train.

"Ah! your excellency!" cried Oblonsky, "whom are you meeting?"

"My mother," Vronsky responded, smiling, as every one did who met Oblonsky. He shook hands with him, and together they ascended the steps. "She is to be here from Petersburg to-day."

"I was looking out for you till two o'clock last night. Where did you go after the Shtcherbatskys'?"

"Home," answered Vronsky. "I must own I felt so well content yesterday after the Shtcherbatskys' that I didn't care to go anywhere."

"I know a gallant steed by tokens sure,
And by his eyes I know a youth in love,"

declaimed Stepan Arkadyevitch, just as he had done before to Levin.

Vronsky smiled with a look that seemed to say that he did not deny it, but he promptly changed the subject.

"And whom are you meeting?" he asked.

"I? I've come to meet a pretty woman," said Oblonsky.

"You don't say so!"

"*Honi soit qui mal y pense!* My sister Anna."

"Ah! that's Madame Karenina," said Vronsky.

"You know her, no doubt?"

"I think I do. Or perhaps not ... I really am not sure," Vronsky answered heedlessly, with a vague recollection of something stiff and tedious evoked by the name Karenina.

"But Alexey Alexandrovitch, my celebrated brother-in-law, you surely must know. All the world knows him."

"I know him by reputation and by sight. I know that he's clever, learned, religious somewhat.... But you know that's not ... *not in my line,*" said Vronsky in English.

"Yes, he's a very remarkable man; rather a conservative, but a splendid man," observed Stepan Arkadyevitch, "a splendid man."

"Oh, well, so much the better for him," said Vronsky, smiling. "Oh, you've come," he said, addressing a tall old footman of his mother's, standing at the door; "come here."

Besides the charm Oblonsky had in general for every one, Vronsky had felt of late specially drawn to him by the fact that in his imagination he was associated with Kitty.

"Well, what do you say? Shall we give a supper on Sunday for the *diva?*" he said to him with a smile, taking his arm.

"Of course. I'm collecting subscriptions. Oh, did you make the acquaintance of my friend Levin?" asked Stepan Arkadyevitch.

"Yes; but he left rather early."

"He's a capital fellow," pursued Oblonsky. "Isn't he?"

"I don't know why it is," responded Vronsky, "in all Moscow people—present company of course excepted," he put in jestingly, "there's something uncompromising. They are all on the defensive, lose their tempers, as though they all want to make one feel something...."

"Yes, that's true, it is so," said Stepan Arkadyevitch, laughing good-humoredly.

"Will the train soon be in?" Vronsky asked a railway official.

"The train's signaled," answered the man.

The approach of the train was more and more evident by the preparatory bustle in the station, the rush of porters, the movement of policemen and attendants, and people meeting the train. Through the frosty vapor could be seen workmen in short sheepskins and soft felt boots crossing the rails of the curving line. The hiss of the boiler could be heard on the distant rails, and the rumble of something heavy.

"No," said Stepan Arkadyevitch, who felt a great inclination to tell Vronsky of Levin's intentions in regard to Kitty. "No, you've not got a true impression of Levin. He's a very nervous man, and is sometimes out of humor, it's true, but then he is often very nice. He's such a true, honest nature, and a heart of gold. But yesterday there were special reasons," pursued Stepan Arkadyevitch, with a meaning smile, totally oblivious of the genuine sympathy he had felt the day before for his friend, and feeling the same sympathy now, only for Vronsky. "Yes, there were reasons why he could not help being either particularly happy or particularly unhappy."

Vronsky stood still and asked directly: "How so? Do you mean he made your *belle-sœur* an offer yesterday?"

"Maybe," said Stepan Arkadyevitch. "I fancied something of the sort yesterday. Yes, if he went away early, and was out of humor too, it must mean it.... He's been so long in love, and I'm very sorry for him."

"So that's it! ... I should imagine, though, she might reckon on a better match," said Vronsky, drawing himself up and walking about again, "though I don't know him, of course," he added. "Yes, that is a hateful position! That's why most fellows prefer to have to do with Klaras. If you don't succeed with them it only proves that you've not enough cash, but in this case one's dignity's at stake. But here's the train."

The engine had already whistled in the distance. A few instants later the platform was quivering, and with puffs of steam hanging low in the air from the frost, the engine rolled up, with the lever of the middle wheel rhythmically moving up and down, and the stooping figure of the engine-driver covered with frost. Behind the tender, setting the platform more and more slowly swaying, came the luggage-van with a dog whining in it. At last the passenger carriages rolled in, oscillating before coming to a standstill.

A smart guard jumped out, giving a whistle, and after him one by one the impatient passengers began to get down: an officer of the guards, holding himself erect, and looking severely about him; a nimble little merchant with a satchel, smiling gaily; a peasant with a sack over his shoulder.

Vronsky, standing beside Oblonsky, watched the carriages and the passengers, totally oblivious of his mother. What he had just heard about Kitty excited and delighted him. Unconsciously he arched his chest, and his eyes flashed. He felt himself a conqueror.

"Countess Vronskaya is in that compartment," said the smart guard, going up to Vronsky.

The guard's words roused him, and forced him to think of his mother and his approaching meeting with her. He did not in his heart respect his mother, and without acknowledging it to himself, he did not love her, though in accordance with the ideas of the set in which he lived, and with his own education, he could not have conceived of any behavior to his mother not in the highest degree respectful and obedient, and the more externally obedient and respectful his behavior, the less in his heart he respected and loved her.

CHAPTER XVIII

VRONSKY FOLLOWED THE GUARD TO THE CARRIAGE, AND AT THE DOOR OF the compartment he stopped short to make room for a lady who was getting out.

With the insight of a man of the world, from one glance at this lady's appearance Vronsky classified her as belonging to the best society. He begged pardon, and was getting into the carriage, but felt he must glance at her once more; not that she was very beautiful, not on account of the elegance and modest grace which were apparent in her whole figure, but because in the expression of her charming face, as she passed close by him, there was something peculiarly caressing and soft. As he looked round, she too turned her head. Her shining gray eyes, that looked dark from the thick lashes, rested with friendly attention on his face, as though she were recognizing him, and then promptly turned away to the passing crowd, as though seeking some one. In that brief look Vronsky had time to notice the suppressed eagerness which played over her face, and flitted between the brilliant eyes and the faint smile that curved her red lips. It was as though her nature were so brimming over with something that against her will it showed itself now in the flash of her eyes, and now in her smile. Deliberately she shrouded the light in her eyes, but it shone against her will in the faintly perceptible smile.

Vronsky stepped into the carriage. His mother, a dried-up old lady with black eyes and ringlets, screwed up her eyes, scanning her son, and smiled slightly with her thin lips. Getting up from the seat and handing her maid a bag, she gave her little wrinkled hand to her son to kiss, and lifting his head from her hand, kissed him on the cheek.

"You got my telegram? Quite well? Thank God."

"You had a good journey?" said her son, sitting down beside her, and involuntarily listening to a woman's voice outside the door. He knew it was the voice of the lady he had met at the door.

"All the same I don't agree with you," said the lady's voice.

"It's the Petersburg view, madame."

"Not Petersburg, but simply feminine," she responded.

"Well, well, allow me to kiss your hand."

"Good-bye, Ivan Petrovitch. And could you see if my brother is here, and send him to me?" said the lady in the doorway, and stepped back again into the compartment.

"Well, have you found your brother?" said Countess Vronskaya, addressing the lady.

Vronsky understood now that this was Madame Karenina.

"Your brother is here," he said, standing up. "Excuse me, I did not know you, and, indeed, our acquaintance was so slight," said Vronsky, bowing, "that no doubt you do not remember me."

"Oh, no," said she, "I should have known you because your mother and I have been talking, I think, of nothing but you all the way." As she spoke she let the eagerness that would insist on coming out show itself in her smile. "And still no sign of my brother."

"Do call him, Alexey," said the old countess. Vronsky stepped out onto the platform and shouted:

"Oblonsky! Here!"

Madame Karenina, however, did not wait for her brother, but catching sight of him she stepped out with her light, resolute step. And as soon as her brother had reached her, with a gesture that struck Vronsky by its decision and its grace, she flung her left arm around his neck, drew him rapidly to her, and kissed him warmly. Vronsky gazed, never taking his eyes from her, and smiled, he could not have said why. But recollecting that his mother was waiting for him, he went back again into the carriage.

"She's very sweet, isn't she?" said the countess of Madame Karenina. "Her husband put her with me, and I was delighted to have her. We've been talking all the way. And so you, I hear ... *vous filez le parfait amour. Tant mieux, mon cher, tant mieux.*"

"I don't know what you are referring to, maman," he answered coldly. "Come, maman, let us go."

Madame Karenina entered the carriage again to say good-bye to the countess.

"Well, countess, you have met your son, and I my brother," she said. "And all my gossip is exhausted. I should have nothing more to tell you."

"Oh, no," said the countess, taking her hand. "I could go all around the world with you and never be dull. You are one of those delightful women in whose company it's sweet to be silent as well as to talk. Now please don't fret over your son; you can't expect never to be parted."

Madame Karenina stood quite still, holding herself very erect, and her eyes were smiling.

"Anna Arkadyevna," the countess said in explanation to her son, "has a little son eight years old, I believe, and she has never been parted from him before, and she keeps fretting over leaving him."

"Yes, the countess and I have been talking all the time, I of my son and she of hers," said Madame Karenina, and again a smile lighted up her face, a caressing smile intended for him.

"I am afraid that you must have been dreadfully bored," he said, promptly catching the ball of coquetry she had flung him. But apparently she did not care to pursue the conversation in that strain, and she turned to the old countess.

"Thank you so much. The time has passed so quickly. Good-bye, countess."

"Good-bye, my love," answered the countess. "Let me have a kiss of your pretty face. I speak plainly, at my age, and I tell you simply that I've lost my heart to you."

Stereotyped as the phrase was, Madame Karenina obviously believed it and was delighted by it. She flushed, bent down slightly, and put her cheek to the countess's lips, drew herself up again, and with the same smile fluttering between her lips and her eyes, she gave her hand to Vronsky. He pressed the little hand she gave him, and was delighted, as though at something special, by the energetic squeeze with which she freely and vigorously shook his hand. She went out with the rapid step which bore her rather fully-developed figure with such strange lightness.

"Very charming," said the countess.

That was just what her son was thinking. His eyes followed her till her graceful figure was out of sight, and then the smile remained on his face. He saw out of the window how she went up to her brother, put her arm in his, and began telling him something eagerly, obviously something that had nothing to do with him, Vronsky, and at that he felt annoyed.

"Well, maman, are you perfectly well?" he repeated, turning to his mother.

"Everything has been delightful. Alexander has been very good, and Marie has grown very pretty. She's very interesting."

And she began telling him again of what interested her most—the christening of her grandson, for which she had been staying in Petersburg, and the special favor shown her elder son by the Tsar.

"Here's Lavrenty," said Vronsky, looking out of the window; "now we can go, if you like."

The old butler who had traveled with the countess, came to the carriage to announce that everything was ready, and the countess got up to go.

"Come; there's not such a crowd now," said Vronsky.

The maid took a hand-bag and the lap-dog, the butler and a porter the other baggage. Vronsky gave his mother his arm; but just as they were getting out of the carriage several men ran suddenly by with panic-stricken faces. The station-master, too, ran by in his extraordinary colored cap. Obviously something unusual had happened. The crowd who had left the train were running back again.

"What?... What?... Where?... Flung himself! ... Crushed! ..." was heard among the crowd. Stepan Arkadyevitch, with his sister on his arm, turned back. They too looked scared, and stopped at the carriage door to avoid the crowd.

The ladies got in, while Vronsky and Stepan Arkadyevitch followed the crowd to find out details of the disaster.

A guard, either drunk or too much muffled up in the bitter frost, had not heard the train moving back, and had been crushed.

Before Vronsky and Oblonsky came back the ladies heard the facts from the butler.

Oblonsky and Vronsky had both seen the mutilated corpse. Oblonsky was evidently upset. He frowned and seemed ready to cry.

"Ah, how awful! Ah, Anna, if you had seen it! Ah, how awful!" he said.

Vronsky did not speak; his handsome face was serious, but perfectly composed.

"Oh, if you had seen it, countess," said Stepan Arkadyevitch. "And his wife was there.... It was awful to see her! ... She flung herself on the body. They say he was the only support of an immense family. How awful!"

"Couldn't one do anything for her?" said Madame Karenina in an agitated whisper.

Vronsky glanced at her, and immediately got out of the carriage.

"I'll be back directly, maman," he remarked, turning round in the doorway.

When he came back a few minutes later, Stepan Arkadyevitch was already in conversation with the countess about the new singer, while the countess was impatiently looking towards the door, waiting for her son.

"Now let us be off," said Vronsky, coming in. They went out together; Vronsky was in front with his mother. Behind walked Madame Karenina with her brother. Just as they were going out of the station the station-master overtook Vronsky.

"You gave my assistant two hundred roubles. Would you kindly explain for whose benefit you intend them?"

"For the widow," said Vronsky, shrugging his shoulders. "I should have thought there was no need to ask."

"You gave that?" cried Oblonsky, behind, and, pressing his sister's hand, he added: "Very nice, very nice! Isn't he a splendid fellow? Good-bye, countess."

And he and his sister stood still, looking for her maid.

When they went out the Vronskys' carriage had already driven away. People coming in were still talking of what happened.

"What a horrible death!" said a gentleman, passing by. "They say he was cut in two pieces."

"On the contrary, I think it's the easiest—instantaneous," observed another.

"How is it they don't take proper precautions?" said a third.

Madame Karenina seated herself in the carriage, and Stepan Arkadyevitch saw with surprise that her lips were quivering, and she was with difficulty restraining her tears.

"What is it, Anna?" he asked, when they had driven a few hundred yards.

"It's an omen of evil," she said.

"What nonsense!" said Stepan Arkadyevitch. "You've come, that's the chief thing. You can't conceive how I'm resting my hopes on you."

"Have you known Vronsky long?" she asked.

"Yes. You know we're hoping he will marry Kitty."

"Yes?" said Anna softly. "Come now, let us talk of you," she added, tossing her head, as though she would physically shake off something superfluous oppressing her. "Let us talk of your affairs. I got your letter, and here I am."

"Yes, all my hopes are in you," said Stepan Arkadyevitch.

"Well, tell me all about it."

And Stepan Arkadyevitch began to tell his story.

On reaching home Oblonsky helped his sister out, sighed, pressed her hand, and set off to his office.

CHAPTER XIX

WHEN ANNA WENT INTO THE ROOM, DOLLY WAS SITTING IN THE little drawing-room with a white-headed fat little boy, already like his father, giving him a lesson in French reading. As the boy read, he kept twisting and trying to tear off a button that was nearly off his jacket. His mother had several times taken his hand from it, but the fat little hand went back to the button again. His mother pulled the button off and put it in her pocket.

"Keep your hands still, Grisha," she said, and she took up her work, a coverlet she had long been making. She always set to work on it at depressed moments, and now she knitted at it nervously, twitching her fingers and counting the stitches. Though she had sent word the day before to her husband that it was nothing to her whether his sister came or not, she had made everything ready for her arrival, and was expecting her sister-in-law with emotion.

Dolly was crushed by her sorrow, utterly swallowed up by it. Still she did not forget that Anna, her sister-in-law, was the wife of one of the most important personages in Petersburg, and was a Petersburg *grande dame*. And, thanks to this circumstance, she did not carry out her threat to her husband—that is to say, she remembered that her sister-in-law was coming. "And, after all, Anna is in no wise to blame," thought Dolly. "I know nothing of her except the very best, and I have seen nothing but kindness and affection from her towards myself." It was true that as far as she could recall her impressions at Petersburg at the Karenins', she did not like their household itself; there was something artificial in the whole framework of their family life. "But why should I not receive her? If only she doesn't take it into her head to console me!" thought Dolly. "All consolation and counsel and Christian forgiveness, all that I have thought over a thousand times, and it's all no use."

All these days Dolly had been alone with her children. She did not want to talk of her sorrow, but with that sorrow in her heart she could not talk of outside matters. She knew that in one way or another she would tell Anna everything, and she was alternately glad at the thought of speaking freely, and angry at the necessity of speaking of her humiliation with her, his sister, and of hearing her ready-made phrases of good advice and comfort. She had been on the lookout for her, glancing at her watch every minute, and, as so often happens, let slip just that minute when her visitor arrived, so that she did not hear the bell.

Catching a sound of skirts and light steps at the door, she looked round, and her care-worn face unconsciously expressed not gladness, but wonder. She got up and embraced her sister-in-law.

"What, here already!" she said as she kissed her.

"Dolly, how glad I am to see you!"

"I am glad, too," said Dolly, faintly smiling, and trying by the expression of Anna's face to find out whether she knew. "Most likely she knows," she thought, noticing the sympathy in Anna's face. "Well, come along, I'll take you to your room," she went on, trying to defer as long as possible the moment of confidences.

"Is this Grisha? Heavens, how he's grown!" said Anna; and kissing him, never taking her eyes off Dolly, she stood still and flushed a little. "No, please, let us stay here."

She took off her kerchief and her hat, and catching it in a lock of her black hair, which was a mass of curls, she tossed her head and shook her hair down.

"You are radiant with health and happiness!" said Dolly, almost with envy.

"I? ... Yes," said Anna. "Merciful heavens, Tanya! You're the same age as my Seryozha," she added, addressing the little girl as she ran in. She took her in her arms and kissed her. "Delightful child, delightful! Show me them all."

She mentioned them, not only remembering the names, but the years, months, characters, illnesses of all the children, and Dolly could not but appreciate that.

"Very well, we will go to them," she said. "It's a pity Vassya's asleep."

After seeing the children, they sat down, alone now, in the drawing-room, to coffee. Anna took the tray, and then pushed it away from her.

"Dolly," she said, "he has told me."

Dolly looked coldly at Anna; she was waiting now for phrases of conventional sympathy, but Anna said nothing of the sort.

"Dolly, dear," she said, "I don't want to speak for him to you, nor to try to comfort you; that's impossible. But, darling, I'm simply sorry, sorry from my heart for you!"

Under the thick lashes of her shining eyes tears suddenly glittered. She moved nearer to her sister-in-law and took her hand in her vigorous little hand. Dolly did not shrink away, but her face did not lose its frigid expression. She said:

"To comfort me's impossible. Everything's lost after what has happened, everything's over!"

And directly she had said this, her face suddenly softened. Anna lifted the wasted, thin hand of Dolly, kissed it and said:

"But, Dolly, what's to be done, what's to be done? How is it best to act in this awful position—that's what you must think of."

"All's over, and there's nothing more," said Dolly. "And the worst of it all is, you see, that I can't cast him off: there are the children, I am tied. And I can't live with him! it's a torture to me to see him."

"Dolly, darling, he has spoken to me, but I want to hear it from you: tell me all about it."

Dolly looked at her inquiringly.

Sympathy and love unfeigned were visible on Anna's face.

"Very well," she said all at once. "But I will tell you it from the beginning. You know how I was married. With the education mamma gave us I was more than innocent, I was stupid. I knew nothing. I know they say men tell their wives of their former lives, but Stiva"—she corrected herself—"Stepan Arkadyevitch told me nothing. You'll hardly believe it, but till now I imagined that I was the only woman he had known. So I lived eight years. You must understand that I was so far from suspecting infidelity, I regarded it as impossible, and then—try to imagine it—with such ideas, to find out suddenly all the horror, all the loathsomeness.... You must try and understand me. To be fully convinced of one's happiness, and all at once ..." continued Dolly, holding back her sobs, "to get a letter ... his letter to his mistress, my governess. No, it's too awful!" She hastily pulled out her handkerchief and hid her face in it. "I can understand being carried away by feeling," she went on after a brief silence, "but deliberately, slyly deceiving me ... and with whom? ... To go on being my husband together with her ... it's awful! You can't understand ..."

"Oh, yes, I understand! I understand! Dolly, dearest, I do understand," said Anna, pressing her hand.

"And do you imagine he realizes all the awfulness of my position?" Dolly resumed. "Not the slightest! He's happy and contented."

"Oh, no!" Anna interposed quickly. "He's to be pitied, he's weighed down by remorse …"

"Is he capable of remorse?" Dolly interrupted, gazing intently into her sister-in-law's face.

"Yes. I know him. I could not look at him without feeling sorry for him. We both know him. He's good-hearted, but he's proud, and now he's so humiliated. What touched me most …" (and here Anna guessed what would touch Dolly most) "he's tortured by two things: that he's ashamed for the children's sake, and that, loving you—yes, yes, loving you beyond everything on earth," she hurriedly interrupted Dolly, who would have answered—"he has hurt you, pierced you to the heart. 'No, no, she cannot forgive me,' he keeps saying."

Dolly looked dreamily away beyond her sister-in-law as she listened to her words.

"Yes, I can see that his position is awful; it's worse for the guilty than the innocent," she said, "if he feels that all the misery comes from his fault. But how am I to forgive him, how am I to be his wife again after her? For me to live with him now would be torture, just because I love my past love for him…."

And sobs cut short her words. But as though of set design, each time she was softened she began to speak again of what exasperated her.

"She's young, you see, she's pretty," she went on. "Do you know, Anna, my youth and my beauty are gone, taken by whom? By him and his children. I have worked for him, and all I had has gone in his service, and now of course any fresh, vulgar creature has more charm for him. No doubt they talked of me together, or, worse still, they were silent. Do you understand?"

Again her eyes glowed with hatred.

"And after that he will tell me … What! can I believe him? Never! No, everything is over, everything that once made my comfort, the reward of my work, and my sufferings…. Would you believe it, I was teaching Grisha just now: once this was a joy to me, now it is a torture. What have I to strive and toil for? Why are the children here? What's so awful is that all at once my heart's turned, and instead of love and tenderness, I have nothing but hatred for him; yes, hatred. I could kill him."

"Darling Dolly, I understand, but don't torture yourself. You are so distressed, so overwrought, that you look at many things mistakenly."

Dolly grew calmer, and for two minutes both were silent.

"What's to be done? Think for me, Anna, help me. I have thought over everything, and I see nothing."

Anna could think of nothing, but her heart responded instantly to each word, to each change of expression of her sister-in-law.

"One thing I would say," began Anna. "I am his sister, I know his character, that faculty of forgetting everything, everything" (she waved her hand before her forehead), "that faculty for being completely carried away, but for completely repenting too. He cannot believe it, he cannot comprehend now how he can have acted as he did."

"No; he understands, he understood!" Dolly broke in. "But I ... you are forgetting me ... does it make it easier for me?"

"Wait a minute. When he told me, I will own I did not realize all the awfulness of your position. I saw nothing but him, and that the family was broken up. I felt sorry for him, but after talking to you, I see it, as a woman, quite differently. I see your agony, and I can't tell you how sorry I am for you! But, Dolly, darling, I fully realize your sufferings, only there is one thing I don't know; I don't know ... I don't know how much love there is still in your heart for him. That you know—whether there is enough for you to be able to forgive him. If there is, forgive him!"

"No," Dolly was beginning, but Anna cut her short, kissing her hand once more.

"I know more of the world than you do," she said. "I know how men like Stiva look at it. You speak of his talking of you with her. That never happened. Such men are unfaithful, but their home and wife are sacred to them. Somehow or other these women are still looked on with contempt by them, and do not touch on their feeling for their family. They draw a sort of line that can't be crossed between them and their families. I don't understand it, but it is so."

"Yes, but he has kissed her ..."

"Dolly, hush, darling. I saw Stiva when he was in love with you. I remember the time when he came to me and cried, talking of you, and all the poetry and loftiness of his feeling for you, and I know that the longer he has lived with you the loftier you have been in his eyes. You know we have sometimes laughed at him for putting in at every word: 'Dolly's a marvelous woman.' You have always been a divinity for him, and you are that still, and this has not been an infidelity of the heart...."

"But if it is repeated?"

"It cannot be, as I understand it...."

"Yes, but could you forgive it?"

"I don't know, I can't judge.... Yes, I can," said Anna, thinking a moment; and grasping the position in her thought and weighing it in her inner balance, she added: "Yes, I can, I can, I can. Yes, I could forgive it. I could not be the same, no; but I could forgive it, and forgive it as though it had never been, never been at all...."

"Oh, of course," Dolly interposed quickly, as though saying what she had more than once thought, "else it would not be forgiveness. If one forgives, it must be completely, completely. Come, let us go; I'll take you to your room," she said, getting up, and on the way she embraced Anna. "My dear, how glad I am you came. It has made things better, ever so much better."

CHAPTER XX

THE WHOLE OF THAT DAY ANNA SPENT AT HOME, THAT'S TO SAY AT THE Oblonskys', and received no one, though some of her acquaintances had already heard of her arrival, and came to call the same day. Anna spent the whole morning with Dolly and the children. She merely sent a brief note to her brother to tell him that he must not fail to dine at home. "Come, God is merciful," she wrote.

Oblonsky did dine at home: the conversation was general, and his wife, speaking to him, addressed him as "Stiva," as she had not done before. In the relations of the husband and wife the same estrangement still remained, but there was no talk now of separation, and Stepan Arkadyevitch saw the possibility of explanation and reconciliation.

Immediately after dinner Kitty came in. She knew Anna Arkadyevna, but only very slightly, and she came now to her sister's with some trepidation at the prospect of meeting this fashionable Petersburg lady, whom every one spoke so highly of. But she made a favorable impression on Anna Arkadyevna—she saw that at once. Anna was unmistakably admiring her loveliness and her youth: before Kitty knew where she was she found herself not merely under Anna's sway, but in love with her, as young girls do fall in love with older and married women. Anna was not like a fashionable lady, nor the mother of a boy of eight years old. In the elasticity of her movements, the freshness and the unflagging eagerness which persisted in her face, and broke out in her smile and her glance, she would rather have passed for a girl of twenty, had it not been for a serious and at times mournful look in her eyes, which struck and attracted Kitty. Kitty felt that Anna was perfectly simple and was concealing nothing, but that she had another higher world of interests inaccessible to her, complex and poetic.

After dinner, when Dolly went away to her own room, Anna rose quickly and went up to her brother, who was just lighting a cigar.

"Stiva," she said to him, winking gaily, crossing him, and glancing towards the door, "go, and God help you."

He threw down the cigar, understanding her, and departed through the doorway.

When Stepan Arkadyevitch had disappeared, she went back to the sofa where she had been sitting, surrounded by the children. Either because the children saw that their mother was fond of this aunt, or that they felt a special charm in her themselves, the two elder ones, and the younger following their lead, as children so often do, had clung about their new aunt since before dinner, and would not leave her side. And it had become a sort of game among them to sit as close as possible to their aunt, to touch her, hold her little hand, kiss it, play with her ring, or even touch the flounce of her skirt.

"Come, come, as we were sitting before," said Anna Arkadyevna, sitting down in her place.

And again Grisha poked his little face under her arm, and nestled with his head on her gown, beaming with pride and happiness.

"And when is your next ball?" she asked Kitty.

"Next week, and a splendid ball. One of those balls where one always enjoys oneself."

"Why, are there balls where one always enjoys oneself?" Anna said, with tender irony.

"It's strange, but there are. At the Bobrishtchevs' one always enjoys oneself, and at the Nikitins' too, while at the Mezhkovs' it's always dull. Haven't you noticed it?"

"No, my dear, for me there are no balls now where one enjoys oneself," said Anna, and Kitty detected in her eyes that mysterious world which was not open to her. "For me there are some less dull and tiresome."

"How can *you* be dull at a ball?"

"Why should not *I* be dull at a ball?" inquired Anna.

Kitty perceived that Anna knew what answer would follow.

"Because you always look nicer than any one."

Anna had the faculty of blushing. She blushed a little, and said:

"In the first place it's never so; and secondly, if it were, what difference would it make to me?"

"Are you coming to this ball?" asked Kitty.

"I imagine it won't be possible to avoid going. Here, take it," she said to Tanya, who was pulling the loosely-fitting ring off her white, slender-tipped finger.

"I shall be so glad if you go. I should so like to see you at a ball."

"Anyway, if I do go, I shall comfort myself with the thought that it's a pleasure to you.... Grisha, don't pull my hair. It's untidy enough without that," she said, putting up a straying lock, which Grisha had been playing with.

"I imagine you at the ball in lilac."

"And why in lilac precisely?" asked Anna, smiling. "Now, children, run along, run along. Do you hear? Miss Hoole is calling you to tea," she said, tearing the children from her, and sending them off to the dining-room.

"I know why you press me to come to the ball. You expect a great deal of this ball, and you want every one to be there to take part in it."

"How do you know? Yes."

"Oh! what a happy time you are at," pursued Anna. "I remember, and I know that blue haze like the mist on the mountains in Switzerland. That mist which covers everything in that blissful time when childhood is just ending, and out of that vast circle, happy and gay, there is a path growing narrower and narrower, and it is delightful and alarming to enter the ballroom, bright and splendid as it is.... Who has not been through it?"

Kitty smiled without speaking. "But how did she go through it? How I should like to know all her love-story!" thought Kitty, recalling the unromantic appearance of Alexey Alexandrovitch, her husband.

"I know something. Stiva told me, and I congratulate you. I liked him so much," Anna continued. "I met Vronsky at the railway station."

"Oh, was he there?" asked Kitty, blushing. "What was it Stiva told you?"

"Stiva gossiped about it all. And I should be so glad.... I traveled yesterday with Vronsky's mother," she went on; "and his mother talked without a pause of him, he's her favorite. I know mothers are partial, but ..."

"What did his mother tell you?"

"Oh, a great deal! And I know that he's her favorite; still one can see how chivalrous he is ... Well, for instance, she told me that he had wanted to give up all his property to his brother, that he had done something extraordinary when he was quite a child, saved a woman out of the water. He's a hero, in fact," said Anna, smiling and recollecting the two hundred roubles he had given at the station.

But she did not tell Kitty about the two hundred roubles. For some reason it was disagreeable to her to think of it. She felt that there was something that had to do with her in it, and something that ought not to have been.

"She pressed me very much to go and see her," Anna went on; "and I shall be glad to go to see her to-morrow. Stiva is staying a long while in Dolly's room, thank God," Anna added, changing the subject, and getting up, Kitty fancied, displeased with something.

"No, I'm first! No, I!" screamed the children, who had finished tea, running up to their Aunt Anna.

"All together," said Anna, and she ran laughing to meet them, and embraced and swung round all the throng of swarming children, shrieking with delight.

CHAPTER XXI

DOLLY CAME OUT OF HER ROOM TO THE TEA OF THE GROWN-UP PEOPLE. Stepan Arkadyevitch did not come out. He must have left his wife's room by the other door.

"I am afraid you'll be cold up-stairs," observed Dolly, addressing Anna; "I want to move you down-stairs, and we shall be nearer."

"Oh, please, don't trouble about me," answered Anna, looking intently into Dolly's face, trying to make out whether there had been a reconciliation or not.

"It will be lighter for you here," answered her sister-in-law.

"I assure you that I sleep everywhere, and always like a marmot."

"What's the question?" inquired Stepan Arkadyevitch, coming out of his room and addressing his wife.

From his tone both Kitty and Anna knew that a reconciliation had taken place.

"I want to move Anna down-stairs, but we must hang up blinds. No one knows how to do it; I must see to it myself," answered Dolly addressing him.

"God knows whether they are fully reconciled," thought Anna, hearing her tone, cold and composed.

"Oh, nonsense, Dolly, always making difficulties," answered her husband. "Come, I'll do it all, if you like…."

"Yes, they must be reconciled," thought Anna.

"I know how you do everything," answered Dolly. "You tell Matvey to do what can't be done, and go away yourself, leaving him to make a muddle of everything," and her habitual, mocking smile curved the corners of Dolly's lips as she spoke.

"Full, full reconciliation, full," thought Anna; "thank God!" and rejoicing that she was the cause of it, she went up to Dolly and kissed her.

"Not at all. Why do you always look down on me and Matvey?" said Stepan Arkadyevitch, smiling hardly perceptibly, and addressing his wife.

The whole evening Dolly was, as always, a little mocking in her tone to her husband, while Stepan Arkadyevitch was happy and cheerful, but not so as to seem as though, having been forgiven, he had forgotten his offense.

At half-past nine o'clock a particularly joyful and pleasant family conversation over the tea-table at the Oblonskys' was broken up by an apparently simple incident. But this simple incident for some reason struck every one as strange. Talking about common acquaintances in Petersburg, Anna got up quickly.

"She is in my album," she said; "and, by the way, I'll show you my Seryozha," she added, with a mother's smile of pride.

Towards ten o'clock, when she usually said good-night to her son, and often before going to a ball put him to bed herself, she felt depressed at being so far from him; and whatever she was talking about, she kept coming back in thought to her curly-headed Seryozha. She longed to look at his photograph and talk of him. Seizing the first pretext, she got up, and with her light, resolute step went for her album. The stairs up to her room came out on the landing of the great warm main staircase.

Just as she was leaving the drawing-room, a ring was heard in the hall.

"Who can that be?" said Dolly.

"It's early for me to be fetched, and for anyone else it's late," observed Kitty.

"Sure to be some one with papers for me," put in Stepan Arkadyevitch. When Anna was passing the top of the staircase, a servant was running up to announce the visitor, while the visitor himself was standing under a lamp. Anna glancing down at once recognized Vronsky, and a strange feeling of pleasure and at the same time of dread of something stirred in her heart. He was standing still, not taking off his coat, pulling something out of his pocket. At the instant when she was just facing the stairs, he raised his eyes, caught sight of her, and into the expression of his face there passed a shade of embarrassment and dismay. With a slight inclination of her head she passed, hearing behind her Stepan Arkadyevitch's loud voice calling him to come up, and the quiet, soft, and composed voice of Vronsky refusing.

When Anna returned with the album, he was already gone, and Stepan Arkadyevitch was telling them that he had called to inquire about the dinner they were giving next day to a celebrity who had just arrived. "And nothing would induce him to come up. What a queer fellow he is!" added Stepan Arkadyevitch.

Kitty blushed. She thought that she was the only person who knew why he had come, and why he would not come up. "He has been at home," she thought, "and didn't find me, and thought I should be here, but he did not come up because he thought it late, and Anna's here."

All of them looked at each other, saying nothing, and began to look at Anna's album.

There was nothing either exceptional or strange in a man's calling at half-past nine on a friend to inquire details of a proposed dinner-party and not coming in, but it seemed strange to all of them. Above all, it seemed strange and not right to Anna.

CHAPTER XXII

THE BALL WAS ONLY JUST BEGINNING AS KITTY AND HER MOTHER WALKED UP the great staircase, flooded with light, and lined with flowers and footmen in powder and red coats. From the rooms came a constant, steady hum, as from a hive, and the rustle of movement; and while on the landing between plants they gave last touches to their hair and dresses before the mirror, they heard from the ballroom the careful, distinct notes of the fiddles of the orchestra beginning the first waltz. A little old man in civilian dress, arranging his gray curls before another mirror, and diffusing an odor of scent, stumbled against them on the stairs, and stood aside, evidently admiring Kitty, whom he did not know. A beardless youth, one of those society youths whom the old Prince Shtcherbatsky called "young bucks," in an exceedingly open waistcoat, straightening his white tie as he went, bowed to them, and after running by, came back to ask Kitty for a quadrille. As the first quadrille had already been given to Vronsky, she had to promise this youth the second. An officer, buttoning his glove, stood aside in the doorway, and stroking his mustache, admired rosy Kitty.

Although her dress, her coiffure, and all the preparations for the ball had cost Kitty great trouble and consideration, at this moment she walked into the ballroom in her elaborate tulle dress over a pink slip as easily and simply as though all the rosettes and lace, all the minute details of her attire, had not cost her or her family a moment's attention, as though she had been born in that tulle and lace, with her hair done up high on her head, and a rose and two leaves on the top of it.

When, just before entering the ballroom, the princess, her mother, tried to turn right side out of the ribbon of her sash, Kitty had drawn back a little. She felt that everything must be right of itself, and graceful, and nothing could need setting straight.

It was one of Kitty's best days. Her dress was not uncomfortable anywhere; her lace berthe did not droop anywhere; her rosettes were not crushed nor torn off; her pink slippers with high, hollowed-out heels did not pinch, but gladdened her feet; and the thick rolls of fair chignon kept up on her head as if they were her own hair. All the three buttons buttoned up without tearing on the long glove that covered her hand without concealing its lines. The black velvet of her locket nestled with special softness round her neck. That velvet was delicious; at home, looking at her neck in the looking-glass, Kitty had felt that that velvet was speaking. About all the rest there might be a doubt, but the velvet was delicious. Kitty smiled here too, at the ball, when she glanced at it in the glass. Her bare shoulders and arms gave Kitty a sense of chill marble, a feeling she particularly liked. Her eyes sparkled, and her rosy lips could not keep from smiling from the consciousness of her own attractiveness. She had scarcely entered the ballroom and reached the throng of ladies, all tulle, ribbons, lace, and flowers, waiting to be asked to dance—Kitty was never one of that throng—when she was asked for a waltz, and asked by the best partner, the first star in the hierarchy of the ballroom, a renowned director of dances, a married man, handsome and well-built, Yegorushka Korsunsky. He had only just left the Countess Bonina, with whom he had danced the first half of the waltz, and, scanning his kingdom—that is to say, a few couples who had started dancing—he caught sight of Kitty, entering, and flew up to her with that peculiar, easy amble which is confined to directors of balls. Without even asking her if she cared to dance, he put out his arm to encircle her slender waist. She looked round for someone to give her fan to, and their hostess, smiling to her, took it.

"How nice you've come in good time," he said to her, embracing her waist; "such a bad habit to be late." Bending her left hand, she laid it on his shoulder, and her little feet in their pink slippers began swiftly, lightly, and rhythmically moving over the slippery floor in time to the music.

"It's a rest to waltz with you," he said to her, as they fell into the first slow steps of the waltz. "It's exquisite—such lightness, precision." He said to her the same thing he said to almost all his partners whom he knew well.

She smiled at his praise, and continued to look about the room over his shoulder. She was not like a girl at her first ball, for whom all faces in the ballroom melt into one vision of fairyland. And she was not a girl who had gone the stale round of balls till every face in the ballroom was familiar and tiresome. But she was in the middle stage between these two; she was excited, and at the same time she had sufficient self-possession to be able to observe. In the left corner of the ballroom she saw the cream of society gathered together. There—incredibly naked—was the beauty Lidi, Korsunsky's wife; there was the lady of the house; there shone the bald head of Krivin, always to be found where the best people were. In that direction gazed the young men, not venturing to approach. There, too, she descried Stiva, and there she saw the exquisite figure and head of Anna in a black velvet gown. And *he* was there. Kitty had not seen him since the evening she refused Levin. With her long-sighted eyes, she knew him at once, and was even aware that he was looking at her.

"Another turn, eh? You're not tired?" said Korsunsky, a little out of breath.

"No, thank you!"

"Where shall I take you?"

"Madame Karenina's here, I think ... take me to her."

"Wherever you command."

And Korsunsky began waltzing with measured steps straight towards the group in the left corner, continually saying, "Pardon, mesdames, pardon, pardon, mesdames"; and steering his course through the sea of lace, tulle, and ribbon, and not disarranging a feather, he turned his partner sharply round, so that her slim ankles, in light transparent stockings, were exposed to view, and her train floated out in fan shape and covered Krivin's knees. Korsunsky bowed, set straight his open shirt-front, and gave her his arm to conduct her to Anna Arkadyevna. Kitty, flushed, took her train from Krivin's knees, and, a little giddy, looked round, seeking Anna. Anna was not in lilac, as Kitty had so urgently wished, but in a black, low-cut, velvet gown, showing her full throat and shoulders, that looked as though carved in old ivory, and her rounded arms, with tiny, slender wrists. The whole gown was trimmed with Venetian

guipure. On her head, among her black hair—her own, with no false addi-
tions—was a little wreath of pansies, and a bouquet of the same in the black
ribbon of her sash among white lace. Her coiffure was not striking. All that
was noticeable was the little wilful tendrils of her curly hair that would always
break free about her neck and temples. Round her well-cut, strong neck was
a thread of pearls.

Kitty had been seeing Anna every day; she adored her, and had pictured
her invariably in lilac. But now seeing her in black, she felt that she had not fully
seen her charm. She saw her now as some one quite new and surprising to her.
Now she understood that Anna could not have been in lilac, and that her charm
was just that she always stood out against her attire, that her dress could never
be noticeable on her. And her black dress, with its sumptuous lace, was not
noticeable on her; it was only the frame, and all that was seen was she—simple,
natural, elegant, and at the same time gay and eager.

She was standing holding herself, as always, very erect, and when Kitty
drew near the group she was speaking to the master of the house, her head
slightly turned towards him.

"No, I don't throw stones," she was saying, in answer to something,
"though I can't understand it," she went on, shrugging her shoulders, and she
turned at once with a soft smile of protection towards Kitty. With a flying,
feminine glance she scanned her attire, and made a movement of her head,
hardly perceptible, but understood by Kitty, signifying approval of her dress
and her looks. "You came into the room dancing," she added.

"This is one of my most faithful supporters," said Korsunsky, bowing to
Anna Arkadyevna, whom he had not yet seen. "The princess helps to make
balls happy and successful. Anna Arkadyevna, a waltz?" he said, bending down
to her.

"Why, have you met?" inquired their host.

"Is there any one we have not met? My wife and I are like white wolves—
every one knows us," answered Korsunsky. "A waltz, Anna Arkadyevna?"

"I don't dance when it's possible not to dance," she said.

"But to-night it's impossible," answered Korsunsky.

At that instant Vronsky came up.

"Well, since it's impossible to-night, let us start," she said, not noticing
Vronsky's bow, and she hastily put her hand on Korsunsky's shoulder.

"What is she vexed with him about?" thought Kitty, discerning that
Anna had intentionally not responded to Vronsky's bow. Vronsky went up to
Kitty reminding her of the first quadrille, and expressing his regret that he

had not seen her all this time. Kitty gazed in admiration at Anna waltzing, and listened to him. She expected him to ask her for a waltz, but he did not, and she glanced wonderingly at him. He flushed slightly, and hurriedly asked her to waltz, but he had only just put his arm round her waist and taken the first step when the music suddenly stopped. Kitty looked into his face, which was so close to her own, and long afterwards—for several years after—that look, full of love, to which he made no response, cut her to the heart with an agony of shame.

"*Pardon! pardon!* Waltz! waltz!" shouted Korsunsky from the other side of the room, and seizing the first young lady he came across he began dancing himself.

CHAPTER XXIII

V RONSKY AND KITTY WALTZED SEVERAL TIMES ROUND THE ROOM. AFTER the first waltz Kitty went to her mother, and she had hardly time to say a few words to Countess Nordston when Vronsky came up again for the first quadrille. During the quadrille nothing of any significance was said: there was disjointed talk between them of the Korsunskys, husband and wife, whom he described very amusingly, as delightful children at forty, and of the future town theater; and only once the conversation touched her to the quick, when he asked her about Levin, whether he was here, and added that he liked him so much. But Kitty did not expect much from the quadrille. She looked forward with a thrill at her heart to the mazurka. She fancied that in the mazurka everything must be decided. The fact that he did not during the quadrille ask her for the mazurka did not trouble her. She felt sure she would dance the mazurka with him as she had done at former balls, and refused five young men, saying she was engaged for the mazurka. The whole ball up to the last quadrille was for Kitty an enchanted vision of delightful colors, sounds, and motions. She only sat down when she felt too tired and begged for a rest. But as she was dancing the last quadrille with one of the tiresome young men whom she could not refuse, she chanced to be *vis-à-vis* with Vronsky and Anna. She had not been near Anna again since the beginning of the evening, and now again she saw her suddenly quite new and surprising. She saw in her the signs of that excitement of success she knew so well in herself; she saw that she was intoxicated with the delighted admiration she was exciting. She knew that feeling and knew its signs, and saw them in Anna; saw the quivering, flashing light in her eyes, and the smile of happiness and excitement unconsciously playing on her lips, and the deliberate grace, precision, and lightness of her movements.

"Who?" she asked herself. "All or one?" And not assisting the harassed young man she was dancing with in the conversation, the thread of which he had lost and could not pick up again, she obeyed with external liveliness the peremptory shouts of Korsunsky starting them all into the *grand rond*, and then into the *chaî ne*, and at the same time she kept watch with a growing pang at her heart. "No, it's not the admiration of the crowd has intoxicated her, but the adoration of one. And that one? can it be he?" Every time he spoke to Anna the joyous light flashed into her eyes, and the smile of happiness curved her red lips. She seemed to make an effort to control herself, to try not to show these signs of delight, but they came out on her face of themselves. "But what of him?" Kitty looked at him and was filled with terror. What was pictured so clearly to Kitty in the mirror of Anna's face she saw in him. What had become of his always self-possessed resolute manner, and the carelessly serene expression of his face? Now every time he turned to her, he bent his head, as though he would have fallen at her feet, and in his eyes there was nothing but humble submission and dread. "I would not offend you," his eyes seemed every time to be saying, "but I want to save myself, and I don't know how." On his face was a look such as Kitty had never seen before.

They were speaking of common acquaintances, keeping up the most trivial conversation, but to Kitty it seemed that every word they said was determining their fate and hers. And strange it was that they were actually talking of how absurd Ivan Ivanovitch was with his French, and how the Eletskaya girl might have made a better match, yet these words had all the while consequence for them, and they were feeling just as Kitty did. The whole ball, the whole world, everything seemed lost in fog in Kitty's soul. Nothing but the stern discipline of her bringing-up supported her and forced her to do what was expected of her, that is, to dance, to answer questions, to talk, even to smile. But before the mazurka, when they were beginning to rearrange the chairs and a few couples moved out of the smaller rooms into the big room, a moment of despair and horror came for Kitty. She had refused five partners, and now she was not dancing the mazurka. She had not even a hope of being asked for it, because she was so successful in society that the idea would never occur to anyone that she had remained disengaged till now. She would have to tell her mother she felt ill and go home, but she had not the strength to do this. She felt crushed. She went to the furthest end of the little drawing-room and sank into a low chair. Her light, transparent skirts rose like a cloud about her slender waist; one bare, thin, soft, girlish arm, hanging listlessly, was lost in the folds of her pink tunic; in the other she held her fan, and with rapid, short strokes fanned her burning face. But while she looked like a butterfly, clinging to a blade of grass, and just about to open its rainbow wings for fresh flight, her heart ached with a horrible despair.

"But perhaps I am wrong, perhaps it was not so?" And again she recalled all she had seen.

"Kitty, what is it?" said Countess Nordston, stepping noiselessly over the carpet towards her. "I don't understand it."

Kitty's lower lip began to quiver; she got up quickly.

"Kitty, you're not dancing the mazurka?"

"No, no," said Kitty in a voice shaking with tears.

"He asked her for the mazurka before me," said Countess Nordston, knowing Kitty would understand who were "he" and "her." "She said: 'Why, aren't you going to dance it with Princess Shtcherbatskaya?'"

"Oh, I don't care!" answered Kitty.

No one but she herself understood her position; no one knew that she had just refused the man whom perhaps she loved, and refused him because she had put her faith in another.

Countess Nordston found Korsunsky, with whom she was to dance the mazurka, and told him to ask Kitty.

Kitty danced in the first couple, and luckily for her she had not to talk, because Korsunsky was all the time running about directing the figure. Vronsky and Anna sat almost opposite her. She saw them with her long-sighted eyes, and saw them, too, close by, when they met in the figures, and the more she saw of them the more convinced was she that her unhappiness was complete. She saw that they felt themselves alone in that crowded room. And on Vronsky's face, always so firm and independent, she saw that look that had struck her, of bewilderment and humble submissiveness, like the expression of an intelligent dog when it has done wrong.

Anna smiled, and her smile was reflected by him. She grew thoughtful, and he became serious. Some supernatural force drew Kitty's eyes to Anna's face. She was fascinating in her simple black dress, fascinating were her round arms with their bracelets, fascinating was her firm neck with its thread of pearls, fascinating the straying curls of her loose hair, fascinating the graceful, light movements of her little feet and hands, fascinating was that lovely face in its eagerness, but there was something terrible and cruel in her fascination.

Kitty admired her more than ever, and more and more acute was her suffering. Kitty felt overwhelmed, and her face showed it. When Vronsky saw her, coming across her in the mazurka, he did not at once recognize her, she was so changed.

"Delightful ball!" he said to her, for the sake of saying something.

"Yes," she answered.

In the middle of the mazurka, repeating a complicated figure, newly invented by Korsunsky, Anna came forward into the center of the circle, chose two gentlemen, and summoned a lady and Kitty. Kitty gazed at her in dismay as she went up. Anna looked at her with drooping eyelids, and smiled, pressing her hand. But, noticing that Kitty only responded to her smile by a look of despair and amazement, she turned away from her, and began gaily talking to the other lady.

"Yes, there is something uncanny, devilish and fascinating in her," Kitty said to herself.

Anna did not mean to stay to supper, but the master of the house began to press her to do so.

"Nonsense, Anna Arkadyevna," said Korsunsky, drawing her bare arm under the sleeve of his dress coat, "I've such an idea for a *cotillon! Un bijou!*"

And he moved gradually on, trying to draw her along with him. Their host smiled approvingly.

"No, I am not going to stay," answered Anna, smiling, but in spite of her smile, both Korsunsky and the master of the house saw from her resolute tone that she would not stay.

"No; why, as it is, I have danced more at your ball in Moscow than I have all the winter in Petersburg," said Anna, looking round at Vronsky, who stood near her. "I must rest a little before my journey."

"Are you certainly going to-morrow then?" asked Vronsky.

"Yes, I suppose so," answered Anna, as it were wondering at the boldness of his question; but the irrepressible, quivering brilliance of her eyes and her smile set him on fire as she said it.

Anna Arkadyevna did not stay to supper, but went home.

CHAPTER XXIV

Y ES, THERE IS SOMETHING IN ME HATEFUL, REPULSIVE," THOUGHT LEVIN, AS
he came away from the Shtcherbatskys', and walked in the direction of
his brother's lodgings. "And I don't get on with other people. Pride,
they say. No, I have no pride. If I had any pride, I should not have put myself
in such a position." And he pictured to himself Vronsky, happy, good-natured,
clever, and self-possessed, certainly never placed in the awful position in which
he had been that evening. "Yes, she was bound to choose him. So it had to be,
and I cannot complain of any one or anything. I am myself to blame. What
right had I to imagine she would care to join her life to mine? Who am I and
what am I? A nobody, not wanted by any one, nor of use to anybody." And he
recalled his brother Nikolay, and dwelt with pleasure on the thought of him.
"Isn't he right that everything in the world is base and loathsome? And are we
fair in our judgment of brother Nikolay? Of course, from the point of view of
Prokofy, seeing him in a torn cloak and tipsy, he's a despicable person. But I
know him differently. I know his soul, and know that we are like him. And I,
instead of going to seek him out, went out to dinner, and came here." Levin
walked up to a lamp-post, read his brother's address, which was in his pocketbook, and called a sledge. All the long way to his brother's, Levin vividly recalled all the facts familiar to him of his brother Nikolay's life. He remembered
how his brother, while at the university, and for a year afterwards, had, in spite
of the jeers of his companions, lived like a monk, strictly observing all religious
rites, services, and fasts, and avoiding every sort of pleasure, especially women.
And afterwards, how he had all at once broken out: he had associated with
the most horrible people, and rushed into the most senseless debauchery. He
remembered later the scandal over a boy, whom he had taken from the country
to bring up, and, in a fit of rage, had so violently beaten that proceedings were
brought against him for unlawfully wounding. Then he recalled the scandal
with a sharper, to whom he had lost money, and given a promissory note, and
against whom he had himself lodged a complaint, asserting that he had cheated
him. (This was the money Sergey Ivanovitch had paid.) Then he remembered
how he had spent a night in the lockup for disorderly conduct in the street.
He remembered the shameful proceedings he had tried to get up against his
brother Sergey Ivanovitch, accusing him of not having paid him his share of his
mother's fortune, and the last scandal, when he had gone to a western province
in an official capacity, and there had got into trouble for assaulting a village

elder … It was all horribly disgusting, yet to Levin it appeared not at all in the same disgusting light as it inevitably would to those who did not know Nikolay, did not know all his story, did not know his heart.

Levin remembered that when Nikolay had been in the devout stage, the period of fasts and monks and church services, when he was seeking in religion a support and a curb for his passionate temperament, every one, far from encouraging him, had jeered at him, and he, too, with the others. They had teased him, called him Noah and Monk; and, when he had broken out, no one had helped him, but every one had turned away from him with horror and disgust.

Levin felt that, in spite of all the ugliness of his life, his brother Nikolay, in his soul, in the very depths of his soul, was no more in the wrong than the people who despised him. He was not to blame for having been born with his unbridled temperament and his somehow limited intelligence. But he had always wanted to be good. "I will tell him everything, without reserve, and I will make him speak without reserve, too, and I'll show him that I love him, and so understand him," Levin resolved to himself, as, towards eleven o'clock, he reached the hotel of which he had the address.

"At the top, 12 and 13," the porter answered Levin's inquiry.

"At home?"

"Sure to be at home."

The door of No. 12 was half open, and there came out into the streak of light thick fumes of cheap, poor tobacco, and the sound of a voice, unknown to Levin; but he knew at once that his brother was there; he heard his cough.

As he went in the door, the unknown voice was saying:

"It all depends with how much judgment and knowledge the thing's done."

Konstantin Levin looked in at the door, and saw that the speaker was a young man with an immense shock of hair, wearing a Russian jerkin, and that a pockmarked woman in a woolen gown, without collar or cuffs, was sitting on the sofa. His brother was not to be seen. Konstantin felt a sharp pang at his heart at the thought of the strange company in which his brother spent his life. No one had heard him, and Konstantin, taking off his goloshes, listened to what the gentleman in the jerkin was saying. He was speaking of some enterprise.

"Well, the devil flay them, the privileged classes," his brother's voice responded, with a cough. "Masha! get us some supper and some wine if there's any left; or else go and get some."

The woman rose, came out from behind the screen, and saw Konstantin.

"There's some gentleman, Nikolay Dmitrievitch," she said.

"Whom do you want?" said the voice of Nikolay Levin, angrily.

"It's I," answered Konstantin Levin, coming forward into the light.

"Who's *I*?" Nikolay's voice said again, still more angrily. He could be heard getting up hurriedly, stumbling against something, and Levin saw, facing him in the doorway, the big, scared eyes, and the huge, thin, stooping figure of his brother, so familiar, and yet astonishing in its weirdness and sickliness.

He was even thinner than three years before, when Konstantin Levin had seen him last. He was wearing a short coat, and his hands and big bones seemed huger than ever. His hair had grown thinner, the same straight mustaches hid his lips, the same eyes gazed strangely and naïvely at his visitor.

"Ah, Kostya!" he exclaimed suddenly, recognizing his brother, and his eyes lighted up with joy. But the same second he looked round at the young man, and gave the nervous jerk of his head and neck that Konstantin knew so well, as if his neckband hurt him; and a quite different expression, wild, suffering, and cruel, rested on his emaciated face.

"I wrote to you and Sergey Ivanovitch both that I don't know you and don't want to know you. What is it you want?"

He was not at all the same as Konstantin had been fancying him. The worst and most tiresome part of his character, what made all relations with him so difficult, had been forgotten by Konstantin Levin when he thought of him, and now, when he saw his face, and especially that nervous twitching of his head, he remembered it all.

"I didn't want to see you for anything," he answered timidly. "I've simply come to see you."

His brother's timidity obviously softened Nikolay. His lips twitched.

"Oh, so that's it?" he said. "Well, come in; sit down. Like some supper? Masha, bring supper for three. No, stop a minute. Do you know who this is?" he said, addressing his brother, and indicating the gentleman in the jerkin: "This is Mr. Kritsky, my friend from Kiev, a very remarkable man. He's persecuted by the police, of course, because he's not a scoundrel."

And he looked round in the way he always did at every one in the room. Seeing that the woman standing in the doorway was moving to go, he shouted to her, "Wait a minute, I said." And with the inability to express himself, the incoherence that Konstantin knew so well, he began, with another look round at every one, to tell his brother Kritsky's story: how he had been expelled from the university for starting a benefit society for the poor students and Sunday-schools; and how he had afterwards been a teacher in a peasant school, and how he had been driven out of that too, and had afterwards been condemned for something.

"You're of the Kiev university?" said Konstantin Levin to Kritsky, to break the awkward silence that followed.

"Yes, I was of Kiev," Kritsky replied angrily, his face darkening.

"And this woman," Nikolay Levin interrupted him, pointing to her, "is the partner of my life, Marya Nikolaevna. I took her out of a bad house," and he jerked his neck saying this; "but I love her and respect her, and any one who wants to know me," he added, raising his voice and knitting his brows, "I beg to love her and respect her. She's just the same as my wife, just the same. So now you know whom you've got to do with. And if you think you're lowering yourself, well, here's the floor, there's the door."

And again his eyes traveled inquiringly over all of them.

"Why I should be lowering myself, I don't understand."

"Then, Masha, tell them to bring supper; three portions, spirits and wine … No, wait a minute…. No, it doesn't matter…. Go along."

CHAPTER XXV

S O YOU SEE," PURSUED NIKOLAY LEVIN, PAINFULLY WRINKLING HIS FOREHEAD and twitching.

It was obviously difficult for him to think of what to say and do.

"Here, do you see?"… He pointed to some sort of iron bars, fastened together with strings, lying in a corner of the room. "Do you see that? That's the beginning of a new thing we're going into. It's a productive association…."

Konstantin scarcely heard him. He looked into his sickly, consumptive face, and he was more and more sorry for him, and he could not force himself to listen to what his brother was telling him about the association. He saw that this association was a mere anchor to save him from self-contempt. Nikolay Levin went on talking:

"You know that capital oppresses the laborer. The laborers with us, the peasants, bear all the burden of labor, and are so placed that however much they work they can't escape from their position of beasts of burden. All the profits of labor, on which they might improve their position, and gain leisure for themselves, and after that education, all the surplus values are taken from them by the capitalists. And society's so constituted that the harder they work, the greater the profit of the merchants and landowners, while they stay beasts of burden to the end. And that state of things must be changed," he finished up, and he looked questioningly at his brother.

"Yes, of course," said Konstantin, looking at the patch of red that had come out on his brother's projecting cheek-bones.

"And so we're founding a locksmiths' association, where all the production and profit and the chief instruments of production will be in common."

"Where is the association to be?" asked Konstantin Levin.

"In the village of Vozdrem, Kazan government."

"But why in a village? In the villages, I think, there is plenty of work as it is. Why a locksmiths' association in a village?"

"Why? Because the peasants are just as much slaves as they ever were, and that's why you and Sergey Ivanovitch don't like people to try and get them out of their slavery," said Nikolay Levin, exasperated by the objection.

Konstantin Levin sighed, looking meanwhile about the cheerless and dirty room. This sigh seemed to exasperate Nikolay still more.

"I know your and Sergey Ivanovitch's aristocratic views. I know that he applies all the power of his intellect to justify existing evils."

"No; and what do you talk of Sergey Ivanovitch for?" said Levin, smiling.

"Sergey Ivanovitch? I'll tell you what for!" Nikolay Levin shrieked suddenly at the name of Sergey Ivanovitch. "I'll tell you what for.... But what's the use of talking? There's only one thing.... What did you come to me for? You look down on this, and you're welcome to,—and go away, in God's name go away!" he shrieked, getting up from his chair. "And go away, and go away!"

"I don't look down on it at all," said Konstantin Levin timidly. "I don't even dispute it."

At that instant Marya Nikolaevna came back. Nikolay Levin looked round angrily at her. She went quickly to him, and whispered something.

"I'm not well; I've grown irritable," said Nikolay Levin, getting calmer and breathing painfully; "and then you talk to me of Sergey Ivanovitch and his article. It's such rubbish, such lying, such self-deception. What can a man write of justice who knows nothing of it? Have you read his article?" he asked Kritsky, sitting down again at the table, and moving back off half of it the scattered cigarettes, so as to clear a space.

"I've not read it," Kritsky responded gloomily, obviously not desiring to enter into the conversation.

"Why not?" said Nikolay Levin, now turning with exasperation upon Kritsky.

"Because I didn't see the use of wasting my time over it."

"Oh, but excuse me, how did you know it would be wasting your time? That article's too deep for many people—that's to say it's over their heads. But with me, it's another thing; I see through his ideas, and I know where its weakness lies."

Every one was mute. Kritsky got up deliberately and reached his cap.

"Won't you have supper? All right, good-bye! Come round to-morrow with the locksmith."

Kritsky had hardly gone out when Nikolay Levin smiled and winked.

"He's no good either," he said. "I see, of course ..."

But at that instant Kritsky, at the door, called him....

"What do you want now?" he said, and went out to him in the passage. Left alone with Marya Nikolaevna, Levin turned to her.

"Have you been long with my brother?" he said to her.

"Yes, more than a year. Nikolay Dmitrievitch's health has become very poor. Nikolay Dmitrievitch drinks a great deal," she said.

"That is ... how does he drink?"

"Drinks vodka, and it's bad for him."

"And a great deal?" whispered Levin.

"Yes," she said, looking timidly towards the doorway, where Nikolay Levin had reappeared.

"What were you talking about?" he said, knitting his brows, and turning his scared eyes from one to the other. "What was it?"

"Oh, nothing," Konstantin answered in confusion.

"Oh, if you don't want to say, don't. Only it's no good your talking to her. She's a wench, and you're a gentleman," he said with a jerk of the neck. "You understand everything, I see, and have taken stock of everything, and look with commiseration on my shortcomings," he began again, raising his voice.

"Nikolay Dmitrievitch, Nikolay Dmitrievitch," whispered Marya Niko-laevna, again going up to him.

"Oh, very well, very well! ... But where's the supper? Ah, here it is," he said, seeing a waiter with a tray. "Here, set it here," he added angrily, and promptly seizing the vodka, he poured out a glassful and drank it greedily. "Like a drink?" he turned to his brother, and at once became better humored.

"Well, enough of Sergey Ivanovitch. I'm glad to see you, anyway. After all's said and done, we're not strangers. Come, have a drink. Tell me what you're doing," he went on, greedily munching a piece of bread, and pouring out another glassful. "How are you living?"

"I live alone in the country, as I used to. I'm busy looking after the land," answered Konstantin, watching with horror the greediness with which his brother ate and drank, and trying to conceal that he noticed it.

"Why don't you get married?"

"It hasn't happened so," Konstantin answered, reddening a little.

"Why not? For me now … everything's at an end! I've made a mess of my life. But this I've said, and I say still, that if my share had been given me when I needed it, my whole life would have been different."

Konstantin made haste to change the conversation.

"Do you know your little Vanya's with me, a clerk in the counting-house at Pokrovskoe."

Nikolay jerked his neck, and sank into thought.

"Yes, tell me what's going on at Pokrovskoe. Is the house standing still, and the birch-trees, and our schoolroom? And Philip the gardener, is he living? How I remember the arbor and the seat! Now mind and don't alter anything in the house, but make haste and get married, and make everything as it used to be again. Then I'll come and see you, if your wife is nice."

"But come to me now," said Levin. "How nicely we would arrange it!"

"I'd come and see you if I were sure I should not find Sergey Ivanovitch."

"You wouldn't find him there. I live quite independently of him."

"Yes, but say what you like, you will have to choose between me and him," he said, looking timidly into his brother's face.

This timidity touched Konstantin.

"If you want to hear my confession of faith on the subject, I tell you that in your quarrel with Sergey Ivanovitch I take neither side. You're both wrong. You're more wrong externally, and he inwardly."

"Ah, ah! You see that, you see that!" Nikolay shouted joyfully.

"But I personally value friendly relations with you more because …"

"Why, why?"

Konstantin could not say that he valued it more because Nikolay was unhappy, and needed affection. But Nikolay knew that this was just what he meant to say, and scowling he took up the vodka again.

"Enough, Nikolay Dmitrievitch!" said Marya Nikolaevna, stretching out her plump, bare arm towards the decanter.

"Let it be! Don't insist! I'll beat you!" he shouted.

Marya Nikolaevna smiled a sweet and good-humored smile, which was at once reflected on Nikolay's face, and she took the bottle.

"And do you suppose she understands nothing?" said Nikolay. "She understands it all better than any of us. Isn't it true there's something good and sweet in her?"

"Were you never before in Moscow?" Konstantin said to her, for the sake of saying something.

"Only you mustn't be polite and stiff with her. It frightens her. No one ever spoke to her so but the justices of the peace who tried her for trying to get out of a house of ill-fame. Mercy on us, the senselessness in the world!" he cried suddenly. "These new institutions, these justices of the peace, rural councils, what hideousness it all is!"

And he began to enlarge on his encounters with the new institutions.

Konstantin Levin heard him, and the disbelief in the sense of all public institutions, which he shared with him, and often expressed, was distasteful to him now from his brother's lips.

"In another world we shall understand it all," he said lightly.

"In another world! Ah, I don't like that other world! I don't like it," he said, letting his scared eyes rest on his brother's eyes. "Here one would think that to get out of all the baseness and the mess, one's own and other people's, would be a good thing, and yet I'm afraid of death, awfully afraid of death." He shuddered. "But do drink something. Would you like some champagne? Or shall we go somewhere? Let's go to the Gypsies! Do you know I have got so fond of the Gypsies and Russian songs."

His speech had begun to falter, and he passed abruptly from one subject to another. Konstantin with the help of Masha persuaded him not to go out anywhere, and got him to bed hopelessly drunk.

Masha promised to write to Konstantin in case of need, and to persuade Nikolay Levin to go and stay with his brother.

CHAPTER XXVI

IN THE MORNING KONSTANTIN LEVIN LEFT MOSCOW, AND TOWARDS EVENING HE reached home. On the journey in the train he talked to his neighbors about politics and the new railways, and, just as in Moscow, he was overcome by a sense of confusion of ideas, dissatisfaction with himself, shame of something or other. But when he got out at his own station, when he saw his one-eyed coachman, Ignat, with the collar of his coat turned up; when, in the dim light reflected by the station fires, he saw his own sledge, his own horses with their tails tied up, in their harness trimmed with rings and tassels; when the coachman Ignat, as he put in his luggage, told him the village news, that the contractor had arrived, and that Pava had calved,—he felt that little by little the confusion was clearing up, and the shame and self-dissatisfaction were passing away. He felt this at the mere sight of Ignat and the horses; but when he had put on the sheepskin brought for him, had sat down wrapped up in the sledge, and had driven off pondering on the work that lay before him in the village, and staring at the side-horse, that had been his saddle-horse, past his prime now, but a spirited beast from the Don, he began to see what had happened to him in quite a different light. He felt himself, and did not want to be any one else. All he wanted now was to be better than before. In the first place he resolved that from that day he would give up hoping for any extraordinary happiness, such as marriage must have given him, and consequently he would not so disdain what he really had. Secondly, he would never again let himself give way to low passion, the memory of which had so tortured him when he had been making up his mind to make an offer. Then remembering his brother Nikolay, he resolved to himself that he would never allow himself to forget him, that he would follow him up, and not lose sight of him, so as to be ready to help when things should go ill with him. And that would be soon, he felt. Then, too, his brother's talk of communism, which he had treated so lightly at the time, now made him think. He considered a revolution in economic conditions nonsense. But he always felt the injustice of his own abundance in comparison with the poverty of the peasants, and now he determined that so as to feel quite in the right, though he had worked hard and lived by no means luxuriously before, he would now work still harder, and would allow himself even less luxury. And all this seemed to him so easy a conquest over himself that he spent the whole drive in the pleasantest day-dreams. With a resolute feeling of hope in a new, better life, he reached home before nine o'clock at night.

The snow of the little quadrangle before the house was lit up by a light in the bedroom windows of his old nurse, Agafea Mihalovna, who performed the duties of housekeeper in his house. She was not yet asleep. Kouzma, waked up by her, came sidling sleepily out onto the steps. A setter bitch, Laska, ran out too, almost upsetting Kouzma, and whining, turned round about Levin's knees, jumping up and longing, but not daring, to put her forepaws on his chest.

"You're soon back again, sir," said Agafea Mihalovna.

"I got tired of it, Agafea Mihalovna. With friends, one is well; but at home, one is better," he answered, and went into his study.

The study was slowly lit up as the candle was brought in. The familiar details came out: the stag's horns, the bookshelves, the looking-glass, the stove with its ventilator, which had long wanted mending, his father's sofa, a large table, on the table an open book, a broken ash-tray, a manuscript-book with his handwriting. As he saw all this, there came over him for an instant a doubt of the possibility of arranging the new life, of which he had been dreaming on the road. All these traces of his life seemed to clutch him, and to say to him: "No, you're not going to get away from us, and you're not going to be different, but you're going to be the same as you've always been; with doubts, everlasting dissatisfaction with yourself, vain efforts to amend, and falls, and everlasting expectation, of a happiness which you won't get, and which isn't possible for you."

This the things said to him, but another voice in his heart was telling him that he must not fall under the sway of the past, and that one can do anything with oneself. And hearing that voice, he went into the corner where stood his two heavy dumb-bells, and began brandishing them like a gymnast, trying to restore his confident temper. There was a creak of steps at the door. He hastily put down the dumb-bells.

The bailiff came in, and said everything, thank God, was doing well; but informed him that the buckwheat in the new drying-machine had been a little scorched. This piece of news irritated Levin. The new drying-machine had been constructed and partly invented by Levin. The bailiff had always been against the drying-machine, and now it was with suppressed triumph that he announced that the buckwheat had been scorched. Levin was firmly convinced that if the buckwheat had been scorched, it was only because the precautions had not been taken, for which he had hundreds of times given orders. He was annoyed, and reprimanded the bailiff. But there had been an important and joyful event: Pava, his best cow, an expensive beast, bought at a show, had calved.

"Kouzma, give me my sheepskin. And you tell them to take a lantern. I'll come and look at her," he said to the bailiff.

The cowhouse for the more valuable cows was just behind the house. Walking across the yard, passing a snowdrift by the lilac-tree, he went into the cowhouse. There was the warm, steamy smell of dung when the frozen door was opened, and the cows, astonished at the unfamiliar light of the lantern, stirred on the fresh straw. He caught a glimpse of the broad, smooth, black and piebald back of Hollandka. Berkoot, the bull, was lying down with his ring in his lip, and seemed about to get up, but thought better of it, and only gave two snorts as they passed by him. Pava, a perfect beauty, huge as a hippopotamus, with her back turned to them, prevented their seeing the calf, as she sniffed her all over.

Levin went into the pen, looked Pava over, and lifted the red and spotted calf onto her long, tottering legs. Pava, uneasy, began lowing, but when Levin put the calf close to her she was soothed, and, sighing heavily, began licking her with her rough tongue. The calf, fumbling, poked her nose under her mother's udder, and stiffened her tail out straight.

"Here, bring the light, Fyodor, this way," said Levin, examining the calf. "Like the mother! though the color takes after the father; but that's nothing. Very good. Long and broad in the haunch. Vassily Fedorovitch, isn't she splendid?" he said to the bailiff, quite forgiving him for the buckwheat under the influence of his delight in the calf.

"How could she fail to be? Oh, Semyon the contractor came the day after you left. You must settle with him, Konstantin Dmitrievitch," said the bailiff. "I did inform you about the machine."

This question was enough to take Levin back to all the details of his work on the estate, which was on a large scale, and complicated. He went straight from the cowhouse to the counting-house, and after a little conversation with the bailiff and Semyon the contractor, he went back to the house and straight up-stairs to the drawing-room.

CHAPTER XXVII

THE HOUSE WAS BIG AND OLD-FASHIONED, AND LEVIN, THOUGH HE LIVED alone, had the whole house heated and used. He knew that this was stupid, he knew that it was positively not right, and contrary to his present new plans, but this house was a whole world to Levin. It was the world in which his father and mother had lived and died. They had lived just the life that to Levin seemed the ideal of perfection, and that he had dreamed of beginning with his wife, his family.

Levin scarcely remembered his mother. His conception of her was for him a sacred memory, and his future wife was bound to be in his imagination a repetition of that exquisite, holy ideal of a woman that his mother had been.

He was so far from conceiving of love for woman apart from marriage that he positively pictured to himself first the family, and only secondarily the woman who would give him a family. His ideas of marriage were, consequently, quite unlike those of the great majority of his acquaintances, for whom getting married was one of the numerous facts of social life. For Levin it was the chief affair of life, on which its whole happiness turned. And now he had to give up that.

When he had gone into the little drawing-room, where he always had tea, and had settled himself in his armchair with a book, and Agafea Mihalovna had brought him tea, and with her usual, "Well, I'll stay a while, sir," had taken a chair in the window, he felt that, however strange it might be, he had not parted from his day-dreams, and that he could not live without them. Whether with her, or with another, still it would be. He was reading a book, and thinking of what he was reading, and stopping to listen to Agafea Mihalovna, who gossiped away without flagging, and yet with all that, all sorts of pictures of family life and work in the future rose disconnectedly before his imagination. He felt that in the depth of his soul something had been put in its place, settled down, and laid to rest.

He heard Agafea Mihalovna talking of how Prohor had forgotten his duty to God, and with the money Levin had given him to buy a horse, had been drinking without stopping, and had beaten his wife till he'd half killed her. He listened, and read his book, and recalled the whole train of ideas suggested by his reading. It was Tyndall's *Treatise on Heat*. He recalled his own criticisms of Tyndall for his complacent satisfaction in the cleverness of his experiments, and for his lack of philosophic insight. And suddenly there floated into his mind the joyful thought: "In two years' time I shall have two Dutch cows; Pava herself will perhaps still be alive, a dozen young daughters of Berkoot and the three others—how lovely!"

He took up his book again. "Very good, electricity and heat are the same thing; but is it possible to substitute the one quantity for the other in the equation for the solution of any problem? No. Well, then what of it? The connection between all the forces of nature is felt instinctively.... It's particulary nice if Pava's daughter should be a red-spotted cow, and all the herd will take after her, and the other three, too! Splendid! To go out with my wife and visitors to meet the herd.... My wife says, 'Kostya and I looked after that calf like a child.' 'How can it interest you so much?' says a visitor. 'Everything that interests him, interests me.' But who will she be?" And he remembered what had happened at Moscow.... "Well, there's nothing to be done.... It's not my fault. But now everything shall go on in a new way. It's nonsense to pretend that life won't let one, that the past won't let one. One must struggle to live better, much better."... He raised his head, and fell to dreaming. Old Laska, who had not yet fully digested her delight at his return, and had run out into the yard to bark, came back wagging her tail, and crept up to him, bringing in the scent of fresh air, put her head under his hand, and whined plaintively, asking to be stroked.

"There, who'd have thought it?" said Agafea Mihalovna. "The dog now ... why, she understands that her master's come home, and that he's low-spirited."

"Why low-spirited?"

"Do you suppose I don't see it, sir? It's high time I should know the gentry. Why, I've grown up from a little thing with them. It's nothing, sir, so long as there's health and a clear conscience."

Levin looked intently at her, surprised at how well she knew his thought.

"Shall I fetch you another cup?" said she, and taking his cup she went out.

Laska kept poking her head under his hand. He stroked her, and she promptly curled up at his feet, laying her head on a hindpaw. And in token of all now being well and satisfactory, she opened her mouth a little, smacked her lips, and settling her sticky lips more comfortably about her old teeth, she sank into blissful repose. Levin watched all her movements attentively.

"That's what I'll do," he said to himself; "that's what I'll do! Nothing's amiss.... All's well."

CHAPTER XXVIII

A FTER THE BALL, EARLY NEXT MORNING, ANNA ARKADYEVNA SENT HER husband a telegram that she was leaving Moscow the same day.

"No, I must go, I must go"; she explained to her sister-in-law the change in her plans in a tone that suggested that she had to remember so many things that there was no enumerating them: "no, it had really better be to-day!"

Stepan Arkadyevitch was not dining at home, but he promised to come and see his sister off at seven o'clock.

Kitty, too, did not come, sending a note that she had a headache. Dolly and Anna dined alone with the children and the English governess. Whether it was that the children were fickle, or that they had acute senses, and felt that Anna was quite different that day from what she had been when they had taken such a fancy to her, that she was not now interested in them,—but they had abruptly dropped their play with their aunt, and their love for her, and were quite indifferent that she was going away. Anna was absorbed the whole morning in preparations for her departure. She wrote notes to her Moscow acquaintances, put down her accounts, and packed. Altogether Dolly fancied she was not in a placid state of mind, but in that worried mood, which Dolly knew well with herself, and which does not come without cause, and for the most part covers dissatisfaction with self. After dinner, Anna went up to her room to dress, and Dolly followed her.

"How queer you are to-day!" Dolly said to her.

"I? Do you think so? I'm not queer, but I'm nasty. I am like that sometimes. I keep feeling as if I could cry. It's very stupid, but it'll pass off," said Anna quickly, and she bent her flushed face over a tiny bag in which she was packing a nightcap and some cambric handkerchiefs. Her eyes were particularly bright, and were continually swimming with tears. "In the same way I didn't want to leave Petersburg, and now I don't want to go away from here."

"You came here and did a good deed," said Dolly, looking intently at her.

Anna looked at her with eyes wet with tears.

"Don't say that, Dolly. I've done nothing, and could do nothing. I often wonder why people are all in league to spoil me. What have I done, and what could I do? In your heart there was found love enough to forgive...."

"If it had not been for you, God knows what would have happened! How happy you are, Anna!" said Dolly. "Everything is clear and good in your heart."

"Every heart has its own *skeletons*, as the English say."

"You have no sort of *skeleton*, have you? Everything is so clear in you."

"I have!" said Anna suddenly, and, unexpectedly after her tears, a sly, ironical smile curved her lips.

"Come, he's amusing, anyway, your *skeleton*, and not depressing," said Dolly, smiling.

"No, he's depressing. Do you know why I'm going to-day instead of to-morrow? It's a confession that weighs on me; I want to make it to you," said Anna, letting herself drop definitely into an armchair, and looking straight into Dolly's face.

And to her surprise Dolly saw that Anna was blushing up to her ears, up to the curly black ringlets on her neck.

"Yes," Anna went on. "Do you know why Kitty didn't come to dinner? She's jealous of me. I have spoiled ... I've been the cause of that ball being a torture to her instead of a pleasure. But truly, truly, it's not my fault, or only my fault a little bit," she said, daintily drawling the words "a little bit."

"Oh, how like Stiva you said that!" said Dolly, laughing.

Anna was hurt.

"Oh no, oh no! I'm not Stiva," she said, knitting her brows. "That's why I'm telling you, just because I could never let myself doubt myself for an instant," said Anna.

But at the very moment she was uttering the words, she felt that they were not true. She was not merely doubting herself, she felt emotion at the thought of Vronsky, and was going away sooner than she had meant, simply to avoid meeting him.

"Yes, Stiva told me you danced the mazurka with him, and that he ..."

"You can't imagine how absurdly it all came about. I only meant to be matchmaking, and all at once it turned out quite differently. Possibly against my own will ..."

She crimsoned and stopped.

"Oh, they feel it directly!" said Dolly.

"But I should be in despair if there were anything serious in it on his side," Anna interrupted her. "And I am certain it will all be forgotten, and Kitty will leave off hating me."

"All the same, Anna, to tell you the truth, I'm not very anxious for this marriage for Kitty. And it's better it should come to nothing, if he, Vronsky, is capable of falling in love with you in a single day."

"Oh, heavens, that would be too silly!" said Anna, and again a deep flush of pleasure came out on her face, when she heard the idea, that absorbed her, put into words. "And so here I am going away, having made an enemy of Kitty, whom I liked so much! Ah, how sweet she is! But you'll make it right, Dolly? Eh?"

Dolly could scarcely suppress a smile. She loved Anna, but she enjoyed seeing that she too had her weaknesses.

"An enemy? That can't be."

"I did so want you all to care for me, as I do for you, and now I care for you more than ever," said Anna, with tears in her eyes. "Ah, how silly I am to-day!"

She passed her handkerchief over her face and began dressing.

At the very moment of starting Stepan Arkadyevitch arrived, late, rosy and good-humored, smelling of wine and cigars.

Anna's emotionalism infected Dolly, and when she embraced her sister-in-law for the last time, she whispered: "Remember, Anna, what you've done for me—I shall never forget. And remember that I love you, and shall always love you as my dearest friend!"

"I don't know why," said Anna, kissing her and hiding her tears. "You understood me, and you understand. Good-bye, my darling!"

CHAPTER XXIX

COME, IT'S ALL OVER, AND THANK GOD!" WAS THE FIRST THOUGHT THAT came to Anna Arkadyevna, when she had said good-bye for the last time to her brother, who had stood blocking up the entrance to the carriage till the third bell rang. She sat down on her lounge beside Annushka, and looked about her in the twilight of the sleeping-carriage. "Thank God! to-morrow I shall see Seryozha and Alexey Alexandrovitch, and my life will go on in the old way, all nice and as usual."

Still in the same anxious frame of mind, as she had been all that day, Anna took pleasure in arranging herself for the journey with great care. With her little deft hands she opened and shut her little red bag, took out a cushion, laid it on her knees, and carefully wrapping up her feet, settled herself comfortably. An invalid lady had already lain down to sleep. Two other ladies began talking to Anna, and a stout elderly lady tucked up her feet, and made observations about the heating of the train. Anna answered a few words, but not foreseeing any entertainment from the conversation, she asked Annushka to get a lamp, hooked it onto the arm of her seat, and took from her bag a paper-knife and an English novel. At first her reading made no progress. The fuss and bustle were disturbing; then when the train had started, she could not help listening to the noises; then the snow beating on the left window and sticking to the pane, and the sight of the muffled guard passing by, covered with snow on one side, and the conversations about the terrible snowstorm raging outside, distracted her attention. Farther on, it was continually the same again and again: the same shaking and rattling, the same snow on the window, the same rapid transitions from steaming heat to cold, and back again to heat, the same passing glimpses of the same figures in the twilight, and the same voices, and Anna began to read and to understand what she read. Annushka was already dozing, the red bag on her lap, clutched by her broad hands, in gloves, of which one was torn. Anna Arkadyevna read and understood; but it was distasteful to her to read, that is, to follow the reflection of other people's lives. She had too great a desire to live herself. If she read that the heroine of the novel was nursing a sick man, she longed to move with noiseless steps about the room of a sick man; if she read of a member of Parliament making a speech, she longed to be delivering the speech; if she read of how Lady Mary had ridden after the hounds, and had provoked her sister-in-law, and had surprised every one by her boldness, she too wished to be doing the same. But there was no chance of doing anything; and twisting the smooth paper-knife in her little hands, she forced herself to read.

The hero of the novel was already almost reaching his English happiness, a baronetcy and an estate, and Anna was feeling a desire to go with him to the estate, when she suddenly felt that *he* ought to feel ashamed, and that she was ashamed of the same thing. But what had he to be ashamed of? "What have I to be ashamed of?" she asked herself in injured surprise. She laid down the book and sank against the back of the chair, tightly gripping the paper-cutter in both hands. There was nothing. She went over all her Moscow recollections. All were good, pleasant. She remembered the ball, remembered Vronsky and his face of slavish adoration, remembered all her conduct with him: there was nothing shameful. And for all that, at the same point in her memories, the feeling of shame was intensified, as though some inner voice, just at the point when she thought of Vronsky, were saying to her, "Warm, very warm, hot." "Well, what is it?" she said to herself resolutely, shifting her seat in the lounge. "What does it mean? Am I afraid to look it straight in the face? Why, what is it? Can it be that between me and this officer boy there exist, or can exist, any other relations than such as are common with every acquaintance?" She laughed contemptuously and took up her book again; but now she was definitely unable to follow what she read. She passed the paper-knife over the window-pane, then laid its smooth, cool surface to her cheek, and almost laughed aloud at the feeling of delight that all at once without cause came over her. She felt as though her nerves were strings being strained tighter and tighter on some sort of screwing peg. She felt her eyes opening wider and wider, her fingers and toes twitching nervously, something within oppressing her breathing, while all shapes and sounds seemed in the uncertain half-light to strike her with unaccustomed vividness. Moments of doubt were continually coming upon her, when she was uncertain whether the train were going forwards or backwards, or were standing still altogether; whether it were Annushka at her side or a stranger. "What's that on the arm of the chair, a fur cloak or some beast? And what am I myself? Myself or some other woman?" She was afraid of giving away to this delirium. But something drew her towards it, and she could yield to it or resist it at will. She got up to rouse herself, and slipped off her plaid and the cape of her warm dress. For a moment she regained her self-possession, and realized that the thin peasant who had come in wearing a long overcoat, with buttons missing from it, was the stoveheater, that he was looking at the thermometer, that it was the wind and snow bursting in after him at the door; but then everything grew blurred again…. That peasant with the long waist seemed to be gnawing something on the wall, the old lady began stretching her legs the whole length of the carriage, and filling it with a black cloud; then there was a fearful shrieking and banging, as though some one were being torn to pieces; then there was a blinding dazzle of red fire before her eyes and a wall seemed to rise up and hide everything. Anna felt as though she were sinking down. But it was not terrible, but delightful. The voice of a man muffled up and covered with snow shouted something in her ear. She got up and pulled herself together; she realized that they had reached a station and that this was the guard. She asked Annushka to hand her the cape she had taken off and her shawl, put them on and moved towards the door.

"Do you wish to get out?" asked Annushka.

"Yes, I want a little air. It's very hot in here." And she opened the door. The driving snow and the wind rushed to meet her and struggled with her over the door. But she enjoyed the struggle.

She opened the door and went out. The wind seemed as though lying in wait for her; with gleeful whistle it tried to snatch her up and bear her off, but she clung to the cold door-post, and holding her skirt got down onto the platform and under the shelter of the carriages. The wind had been powerful on the steps, but on the platform, under the lee of the carriages, there was a lull. With enjoyment she drew deep breaths of the frozen, snowy air, and standing near the carriage looked about the platform and the lighted station.

CHAPTER XXX

THE RAGING TEMPEST RUSHED WHISTLING BETWEEN THE WHEELS OF THE carriages, about the scaffolding, and round the corner of the station. The carriages, posts, people, everything that was to be seen was covered with snow on one side, and was getting more and more thickly covered. For a moment there would come a lull in the storm, but then it would swoop down again with such onslaughts that it seemed impossible to stand against it. Meanwhile men ran to and fro, talking merrily together, their steps crackling on the platform as they continually opened and closed the big doors. The bent shadow of a man glided by at her feet, and she heard sounds of a hammer upon iron. "Hand over that telegram!" came an angry voice out of the stormy darkness on the other side. "This way! No. 28!" several different voices shouted again, and muffled figures ran by covered with snow. Two gentlemen with lighted cigarettes passed by her. She drew one more deep breath of the fresh air, and had just put her hand out of her muff to take hold of the door-post and get back into the carriage, when another man in a military overcoat, quite close beside her, stepped between her and the flickering light of the lamp-post. She looked round, and the same instant recognized Vronsky's face. Putting his hand to the peak of his cap, he bowed to her and asked, Was there anything she wanted? Could he be of any service to her? She gazed rather a long while at him without answering, and, in spite of the shadow in which he was standing, she saw, or fancied she saw, both the expression of his face and his eyes. It was again that expression of reverential ecstasy which had so worked upon her the day before. More than once she had told herself during the past few days, and again only a few moments before, that Vronsky was for her only one of the hundreds of young men, forever exactly the same, that are met everywhere, that she would never allow herself to bestow a thought upon him. But now at the first instant of meeting him, she was seized by a feeling of joyful pride. She had no need to ask why he had come. She knew as certainly as if he had told her that he was here to be where she was.

"I didn't know you were going. What are you coming for?" she said, letting fall the hand with which she had grasped the door-post. And irrepressible delight and eagerness shone in her face.

"What am I coming for?" he repeated, looking straight into her eyes. "You know that I have come to be where you are," he said; "I can't help it."

At that moment the wind, as it were, surmounting all obstacles, sent the snow flying from the carriage roofs, and clanked some sheet of iron it had torn off, while the hoarse whistle of the engine roared in front, plaintively and gloomily. All the awfulness of the storm seemed to her more splendid now. He had said what her soul longed to hear, though she feared it with her reason. She made no answer, and in her face he saw conflict.

"Forgive me, if you dislike what I said," he said humbly.

He had spoken courteously, deferentially, yet so firmly, so stubbornly, that for a long while she could make no answer.

"It's wrong, what you say, and I beg you, if you're a good man, to forget what you've said, as I forget it," she said at last.

"Not one word, not one gesture of yours shall I, could I, ever forget...."

"Enough, enough!" she cried, trying assiduously to give a stern expression to her face, into which he was gazing greedily. And clutching at the cold door-post, she clambered up the steps and got rapidly into the corridor of the carriage. But in the little corridor she paused, going over in her imagination what had happened. Though she could not recall her own words or his, she realized instinctively that the momentary conversation had brought them fearfully closer; and she was panic-stricken and blissful at it. After standing still a few seconds, she went into the carriage and sat down in her place. The overstrained condition which had tormented her before did not only come back, but was intensified, and reached such a pitch that she was afraid every minute that something would snap within her from the excessive tension. She did not sleep all night. But in that nervous tension, and in the visions that filled her imagination, there was nothing disagreeable or gloomy: on the contrary there was something blissful, glowing, and exhilarating. Towards morning Anna sank into a doze, sitting in her place, and when she waked it was daylight and the train was near Petersburg. At once thoughts of home, of husband and of son, and the details of that day and the following came upon her.

At Petersburg, as soon as the train stopped and she got out, the first person that attracted her attention was her husband. "Oh, mercy! why do his ears look like that?" she thought, looking at his frigid and imposing figure, and especially the ears that struck her at the moment as propping up the brim of his round hat. Catching sight of her, he came to meet her, his lips falling into their habitual sarcastic smile, and his big, tired eyes looking straight at her. An unpleasant sensation gripped at her heart when she met his obstinate and weary glance, as though she had expected to see him different. She was especially struck by the feeling of dissatisfaction with herself that she experienced on meeting him. That feeling was an intimate, familiar feeling, like a consciousness of hypocrisy, which she experienced in her relations with her husband. But hitherto she had not taken note of the feeling, now she was clearly and painfully aware of it.

"Yes, as you see, your tender spouse, as devoted as the first year after marriage, burned with impatience to see you," he said in his deliberate, high-pitched voice, and in that tone which he almost always took with her, a tone of jeering at any one who should say in earnest what he said.

"Is Seryozha quite well?" she asked.

"And is this all the reward," said he, "for my ardor? He's quite well...."

CHAPTER XXXI

Vronsky had not even tried to sleep all that night. He sat in his armchair, looking straight before him or scanning the people who got in and out. If he had indeed on previous occasions struck and impressed people who did not know him by his air of unhesitating composure, he seemed now more haughty and self-possessed than ever. He looked at people as if they were things. A nervous young man, a clerk in a law-court, sitting opposite him, hated him for that look. The young man asked him for a light, and entered into conversation with him, and even pushed against him, to make him feel that he was not a thing, but a person. But Vronsky gazed at him exactly as he did at the lamp, and the young man made a wry face, feeling that he was losing his self-possession under the oppression of this refusal to recognize him as a person.

Vronsky saw nothing and no one. He felt himself a king, not because he believed that he had made an impression on Anna—he did not yet believe that—but because the impression she had made on him gave him happiness and pride.

What would come of it all he did not know, he did not even think. He felt that all his forces, hitherto dissipated, wasted, were centered on one thing, and bent with fearful energy on one blissful goal. And he was happy at it. He knew only that he had told her the truth, that he had come where she was, that all the happiness of his life, the only meaning in life for him, now lay in seeing and hearing her. And when he got out of the carriage at Bologova to get some seltzer water, and caught sight of Anna, involuntarily his first word had told her just what he thought. And he was glad he had told her it, that she knew it now and was thinking of it. He did not sleep all night. When he was back in the carriage, he kept unceasingly going over every position in which he had seen her, every word she had uttered, and before his fancy, making his heart faint with emotion, floated pictures of a possible future.

When he got out of the train at Petersburg, he felt after his sleepless night as keen and fresh as after a cold bath. He paused near his compartment, waiting for her to get out. "Once more," he said to himself, smiling unconsciously, "once more I shall see her walk, her face; she will say something, turn her head, glance, smile, maybe." But before he caught sight of her, he saw her husband, whom the station-master was deferentially escorting through the crowd. "Ah, yes! The husband." Only now for the first time did Vronsky realize clearly the fact that there was a person attached to her, a husband. He knew that she had a husband, but had hardly believed in his existence, and only now fully believed in him, with his head and shoulders, and his legs clad in black trousers; especially when he saw this husband calmly take her arm with a sense of property.

Seeing Alexey Alexandrovitch with his Petersburg face and severely self-confident figure, in his round hat, with his rather prominent spine, he believed in him, and was aware of a disagreeable sensation, such as a man might feel tortured by thirst, who, on reaching a spring, should find a dog, a sheep, or a pig, who has drunk of it and muddied the water. Alexey Alexandrovitch's manner of walking, with a swing of the hips and flat feet, particularly annoyed Vronsky. He could recognize in no one but himself an indubitable right to love her. But she was still the same, and the sight of her affected him the same way, physically reviving him, stirring him, and filling his soul with rapture. He told his German valet, who ran up to him from the second-class, to take his things and go on, and he himself went up to her. He saw the first meeting between the husband and wife, and noted with a lover's insight the signs of slight reserve with which she spoke to her husband. "No, she does not love him and cannot love him," he decided to himself.

At the moment when he was approaching Anna Arkadyevna he noticed too with joy that she was conscious of his being near, and looked round, and seeing him, turned again to her husband.

"Have you passed a good night?" he asked, bowing to her and her husband together, and leaving it up to Alexey Alexandrovitch to accept the bow on his own account, and to recognize it or not, as he might see fit.

"Thank you, very good," she answered.

Her face looked weary, and there was not that play of eagerness in it, peeping out in her smile and her eyes; but for a single instant, as she glanced at him, there was a flash of something in her eyes, and although the flash died away at once, he was happy for that moment. She glanced at her husband to find out whether he knew Vronsky. Alexey Alexandrovitch looked at Vronsky with displeasure, vaguely recalling who this was. Vronsky's composure and self-confidence here struck, like a scythe against a stone, upon the cold self-confidence of Alexey Alexandrovitch.

"Count Vronsky," said Anna.

"Ah! We are acquainted, I believe," said Alexey Alexandrovitch indifferently, giving his hand.

"You set off with the mother and you return with the son," he said, articulating each syllable, as though each were a separate favor he was bestowing.

"You're back from leave, I suppose?" he said, and without waiting for a reply, he turned to his wife in his jesting tone: "Well, were a great many tears shed at Moscow at parting?"

By addressing his wife like this he gave Vronsky to understand that he wished to be left alone, and, turning slightly towards him, he touched his hat; but Vronsky turned to Anna Arkadyevna.

"I hope I may have the honor of calling on you," he said.

Alexey Alexandrovitch glanced with his weary eyes at Vronsky.

"Delighted," he said coldly. "On Mondays we're at home. Most fortunate," he said to his wife, dismissing Vronsky altogether, "that I should just have half an hour to meet you, so that I can prove my devotion," he went on in the same jesting tone.

"You lay too much stress on your devotion for me to value it much," she responded in the same jesting tone, involuntarily listening to the sound of Vronsky's steps behind them. "But what has it to do with me?" she said to herself, and she began asking her husband how Seryozha had got on without her.

"Oh, capitally! Mariette says he has been very good, And ... I must disappoint you ... but he has not missed you as your husband has. But once more *merci*, my dear, for giving me a day. Our dear *Samovar* will be delighted." (He used to call the Countess Lidia Ivanovna, well known in society, a samovar, because she was always bubbling over with excitement.) "She has been continually asking after you. And, do you know, if I may venture to advise you, you should go and see her to-day. You know how she takes everything to heart. Just now, with all her own cares, she's anxious about the Oblonskys being brought together."

The Countess Lidia Ivanovna was a friend of her husband's, and the center of that one of the coteries of the Petersburg world with which Anna was, through her husband, in the closest relations.

"But you know I wrote to her?"

"Still she'll want to hear details. Go and see her, if you're not too tired, my dear. Well, Kondraty will take you in the carriage, while I go to my committee. I shall not be alone at dinner again," Alexey Alexandrovitch went on, no longer in a sarcastic tone. "You wouldn't believe how I've missed ..." And with a long pressure of her hand and a meaning smile, he put her in her carriage.

CHAPTER XXXII

THE FIRST PERSON TO MEET ANNA AT HOME WAS HER SON. HE DASHED DOWN the stairs to her, in spite of the governess's call, and with desperate joy shrieked: "Mother! mother!" Running up to her, he hung on her neck. "I told you it was mother!" he shouted to the governess. "I knew!"

And her son, like her husband, aroused in Anna a feeling akin to disappointment. She had imagined him better than he was in reality. She had to let herself drop down to the reality to enjoy him as he really was. But even as he was, he was charming, with his fair curls, his blue eyes, and his plump, graceful little legs in tightly pulled-up stockings. Anna experienced almost physical pleasure in the sensation of his nearness and his caresses, and moral soothing, when she met his simple, confiding, and loving glance, and heard his naïve questions. Anna took out the presents Dolly's children had sent him, and told her son what sort of little girl was Tanya at Moscow, and how Tanya could read, and even taught the other children.

"Why, am I not so nice as she?" asked Seryozha.

"To me you're nicer than anyone in the world."

"I know that," said Seryozha, smiling.

Anna had not had time to drink her coffee when the Countess Lidia Ivanovna was announced. The Countess Lidia Ivanovna was a tall, stout woman, with an unhealthily sallow face and splendid, pensive black eyes. Anna liked her, but to-day she seemed to be seeing her for the first time with all her defects.

"Well, my dear, so you took the olive branch?" inquired Countess Lidia Ivanovna, as soon as she came into the room.

"Yes, it's all over, but it was all much less serious than we had supposed," answered Anna. "My *belle-sœur* is in general too hasty."

But Countess Lidia Ivanovna, though she was interested in everything that did not concern her, had a habit of never listening to what interested her; she interrupted Anna:

"Yes, there's plenty of sorrow and evil in the world. I am so worried to-day."

"Oh, why?" asked Anna, trying to suppress a smile.

"I'm beginning to be weary of fruitlessly championing the truth, and sometimes I'm quite unhinged by it. The Society of the Little Sisters" (this was a religiously-patriotic, philanthropic institution) "was going splendidly, but with these gentlemen it's impossible to do anything," added Countess Lidia Ivanovna in a tone of ironical submission to destiny. "They pounce on the idea, and distort it, and then work it out so pettily and unworthily. Two or three people, your husband among them, understand all the importance of the thing, but the others simply drag it down. Yesterday Pravdin wrote to me ..."

Pravdin was a well-known Panslavist abroad, and Countess Lidia Ivanovna described the purport of his letter.

Then the countess told her of more disagreements and intrigues against the work of the unification of the churches, and departed in haste, as she had that day to be at the meeting of some society and also at the Slavonic committee.

"It was all the same before, of course; but why was it I didn't notice it before?" Anna asked herself. "Or has she been very much irritated to-day? It's really ludicrous; her object is doing good; she's a Christian, yet she's always angry; and she always has enemies, and always enemies in the name of Christianity and doing good."

After Countess Lidia Ivanovna another friend came, the wife of a chief secretary, who told her all the news of the town. At three o'clock she too went away, promising to come to dinner. Alexey Alexandrovitch was at the ministry. Anna, left alone, spent the time till dinner in assisting at her son's dinner (he dined apart from his parents) and in putting her things in order, and in reading and answering the notes and letters which had accumulated on her table.

The feeling of causeless shame, which she had felt on the journey, and her excitement, too, had completely vanished. In the habitual conditions of her life she felt again resolute and irreproachable.

She recalled with wonder her state of mind on the previous day. "What was it? Nothing. Vronsky said something silly, which it was easy to put a stop to, and I answered as I ought to have done. To speak of it to my husband would be unnecessary and out of the question. To speak of it would be to attach importance to what has no importance." She remembered how she had told her husband of what was almost a declaration made her at Petersburg by a young man, one of her husband's subordinates, and how Alexey Alexandrovitch had answered that every woman living in the world was exposed to such incidents, but that he had the fullest confidence in her tact, and could never lower her and himself by jealousy. "So then there's no reason to speak of it? And indeed, thank God, there's nothing to speak of," she told herself.

CHAPTER XXXIII

A LEXEY ALEXANDROVITCH CAME BACK FROM THE MEETING OF THE ministers at four o'clock, but as often happened, he had not time to come in to her. He went into his study to see the people waiting for him with petitions, and to sign some papers brought him by his chief secretary. At dinner-time (there were always a few people dining with the Karenins) there arrived an old lady, a cousin of Alexey Alexandrovitch, the chief secretary of the department and his wife, and a young man who had been recommended to Alexey Alexandrovitch for the service. Anna went into the drawing-room to receive these guests. Precisely at five o'clock, before the bronze Peter the First clock had struck the fifth stroke, Alexey Alexandrovitch came in, wearing a white tie and evening coat with two stars, as he had to go out directly after dinner. Every minute of Alexey Alexandrovitch's life was portioned out and occupied. And to make time to get through all that lay before him every day, he adhered to the strictest punctuality. "Unhasting and unresting," was his motto. He came into the dining-hall, greeted every one, and hurriedly sat down, smiling to his wife.

"Yes, my solitude is over. You wouldn't believe how uncomfortable" (he laid stress on the word *uncomfortable*) "it is to dine alone."

At dinner he talked a little to his wife about Moscow matters, and, with a sarcastic smile, asked her after Stepan Arkadyevitch; but the conversation was for the most part general, dealing with Petersburg official and public news. After dinner he spent half an hour with his guests, and again, with a smile, pressed his wife's hand, withdrew, and drove off to the council. Anna did not go out that evening either to the Princess Betsy Tverskaya, who, hearing of her return, had invited her, nor to the theater, where she had a box for that evening. She did not go out principally because the dress she had reckoned upon was not ready. Altogether, Anna, on turning, after the departure of her guests, to the consideration of her attire, was very much annoyed. She was generally a mistress of the art of dressing well without great expense, and be-fore leaving Moscow she had given her dressmaker three dresses to transform. The dresses had to be altered so that they could not be recognized, and they ought to have been ready three days before. It appeared that two dresses had not been done at all, while the other one had not been altered as Anna had intended. The dressmaker came to explain, declaring that it would be bet-ter as she had done it, and Anna was so furious that she felt ashamed when she thought of it afterwards. To regain her serenity completely she went into the nursery, and spent the whole evening with her son, put him to bed herself, signed him with the cross, and tucked him up. She was glad she had not gone out anywhere, and had spent the evening so well. She felt so light-hearted and serene, she saw so clearly that all that had seemed to her so important on her railway journey was only one of the common trivial incidents of fashionable life, and that she had no reason to feel ashamed before any one else or before herself. Anna sat down at the hearth with an English novel and waited for her husband. Exactly at half-past nine she heard his ring, and he came into the room.

"Here you are at last!" she observed, holding out her hand to him.

He kissed her hand and sat down beside her.

"Altogether then, I see your visit was a success," he said to her.

"Oh, yes," she said, and she began telling him about everything from the beginning: her journey with Countess Vronskaya, her arrival, the accident at the station. Then she described the pity she had felt, first for her brother, and afterwards for Dolly.

"I imagine one cannot exonerate such a man from blame, though he is your brother," said Alexey Alexandrovitch severely.

Anna smiled. She knew that he said that simply to show that family considerations could not prevent him from expressing his genuine opinion. She knew that characteristic in her husband, and liked it.

"I am glad it has all ended so satisfactorily, and that you are back again," he went on. "Come, what do they say about the new act I have got passed in the council?"

Anna had heard nothing of this act, and she felt conscience-stricken at having been able so readily to forget what was to him of such importance.

"Here, on the other hand, it has made a great sensation," he said, with a complacent smile.

She saw that Alexey Alexandrovitch wanted to tell her something pleasant to him about it, and she brought him by questions to telling it. With the same complacent smile he told her of the ovations he had received in consequence of the act he had passed.

"I was very, very glad. It shows that at last a reasonable and steady view of the matter is becoming prevalent among us."

Having drunk his second cup of tea with cream, and bread, Alexey Alexandrovitch got up, and was going towards his study.

"And you've not been anywhere this evening? You've been dull, I expect?" he said.

"Oh, no!" she answered, getting up after him and accompanying him across the room to his study. "What are you reading now?" she asked.

"Just now I'm reading Duc de Lille, *Poésie des Enfers*," he answered. "A very remarkable book."

Anna smiled, as people smile at the weaknesses of those they love, and, putting her hand under his, she escorted him to the door of the study. She knew his habit, that had grown into a necessity, of reading in the evening. She knew, too, that in spite of his official duties, which swallowed up almost the whole of his time, he considered it his duty to keep up with everything of note that appeared in the intellectual world. She knew, too, that he was really interested in books dealing with politics, philosophy, and theology, that art was utterly foreign to his nature; but, in spite of this, or rather, in consequence of it, Alexey Alexandrovitch never missed over anything in the world of art, but made it his duty to read everything. She knew that in politics, in philosophy, in theology, Alexey Alexandrovitch often had doubts, and made investigations; but on questions of art and poetry, and, above all, of music, of which he was totally devoid of understanding, he had the most distinct and decided opinions. He was fond of talking about Shakespeare, Raphael, Beethoven, of the significance of new schools of poetry and music, all of which were classified by him with very conspicuous consistency.

"Well, God be with you," she said at the door of the study, where a shaded candle and a decanter of water were already put by his armchair. "And I'll write to Moscow."

He pressed her hand, and again kissed it.

"All the same he's a good man; truthful, good-hearted, and remarkable in his own line," Anna said to herself going back to her room, as though she were defending him to some one who had attacked him and said that one could not love him. "But why is it his ears stick out so strangely? Or has he had his hair cut?"

Precisely at twelve o'clock, when Anna was still sitting at her writing-table, finishing a letter to Dolly, she heard the sound of measured steps in slippers, and Alexey Alexandrovitch, freshly washed and combed, with a book under his arm, came in to her.

"It's time, it's time," said he, with a meaning smile, and he went into their bedroom.

"And what right had he to look at him like that?" thought Anna, recalling Vronsky's glance at Alexey Alexandrovitch.

Undressing, she went into the bedroom; but her face had none of the eagerness which, during her stay in Moscow, had fairly flashed from her eyes and her smile; on the contrary, now the fire seemed quenched in her, hidden somewhere far away.

CHAPTER XXXIV

WHEN VRONSKY WENT TO MOSCOW FROM PETERSBURG, HE HAD LEFT his large set of rooms in Morskaia to his friend and favorite comrade Petritsky.

Petritsky was a young lieutenant, not particularly well-connected, and not merely not wealthy, but always hopelessly in debt. Towards evening he was always drunk, and he had often been locked up after all sorts of ludicrous and disgraceful scandals, but he was a favorite both of his comrades and his superior officers. On arriving at twelve o'clock from the station at his flat, Vronsky saw, at the outer door, a hired carriage familiar to him. While still outside his own door, as he rang, he heard masculine laughter, the lisp of a feminine voice, and Petritsky's voice. "If that's one of the villains, don't let him in!" Vronsky told the servant not to announce him, and slipped quietly into the first room. Baroness Shilton, a friend of Petritsky's, with a rosy little face and flaxen hair, resplendent in a lilac satin gown, and filling the whole room, like a canary, with her Parisian chatter, sat at the round table making coffee. Petritsky, in his overcoat, and the cavalry captain Kamerovsky, in full uniform, probably just come from duty, were sitting each side of her.

"Bravo! Vronsky!" shouted Petritsky, jumping up, scraping his chair. "Our host himself! Baroness, some coffee for him out of the new coffee-pot. Why, we didn't expect you! Hope you're satisfied with the ornament of your study," he said, indicating the baroness. "You know each other, of course?"

"I should think so," said Vronsky, with a bright smile, pressing the baroness's little hand. "What next! I'm an old friend."

"You're home after a journey," said the baroness, "so I'm flying. Oh, I'll be off this minute, if I'm in the way."

"You're home, wherever you are, baroness," said Vronsky. "How do you do, Kamerovsky?" he added, coldly shaking hands with Kamerovsky.

"There, you never know how to say such pretty things," said the baroness, turning to Petritsky.

"No; what's that for? After dinner I say things quite as good."

"After dinner there's no credit in them! Well, then, I'll make you some coffee, so go and wash and get ready," said the baroness, sitting down again, and anxiously turning the screw in the new coffee-pot. "Pierre, give me the coffee," she said, addressing Petritsky, whom she called Pierre as a contraction of his surname, making no secret of her relations with him. "I'll put it in."

"You'll spoil it!"

"No, I won't spoil it! Well, and your wife?" said the baroness suddenly, interrupting Vronsky's conversation with his comrade. "We've been marrying you here. Have you brought your wife?"

"No, baroness. I was born a Bohemian, and a Bohemian I shall die."

"So much the better, so much the better. Shake hands on it."

And the baroness, detaining Vronsky, began telling him, with many jokes, about her last new plans of life, asking his advice.

"He persists in refusing to give me a divorce! Well, what am I to do?" (*He* was her husband.) "Now I want to begin a suit against him. What do you advise? Kamerovsky, look after the coffee; it's boiling over. You see, I'm engrossed with business! I want a lawsuit, because I must have my property. Do you understand the folly of it, that on the pretext of my being unfaithful to him," she said contemptuously, "he wants to get the benefit of my fortune."

Vronsky heard with pleasure this light-hearted prattle of a pretty woman, agreed with her, gave her half-joking counsel, and altogether dropped at once into the tone habitual to him in talking to such women. In his Petersburg world all people were divided into utterly opposed classes. One, the lower class, vulgar, stupid, and, above all, ridiculous people, who believe that one husband ought to live with the one wife whom he has lawfully married; that a girl should be innocent, a woman modest, and a man manly, self-controlled, and strong; that one ought to bring up one's children, earn one's bread, and pay one's debts; and various similar absurdities. This was the class of old-fashioned and ridiculous people. But there was another class of people, the real people. To this class they all belonged, and in it the great thing was to be elegant, generous, plucky, gay, to abandon oneself without a blush to every passion, and to laugh at everything else.

For the first moment only, Vronsky was startled after the impressions of a quite different world that he had brought with him from Moscow. But immediately as though slipping his feet into old slippers, he dropped back into the light-hearted, pleasant world he had always lived in.

The coffee was never really made, but spluttered over every one, and boiled away, doing just what was required of it—that is, providing cause for much noise and laughter, and spoiling a costly rug and the baroness's gown.

"Well now, good-bye, or you'll never get washed, and I shall have on my conscience the worst sin a gentleman can commit. So you would advise a knife to his throat?"

"To be sure, and manage that your hand may not be far from his lips. He'll kiss your hand, and all will end satisfactorily," answered Vronsky.

"So at the Francais!" and, with a rustle of her skirts, she vanished.

Kamerovsky got up too, and Vronsky, not waiting for him to go, shook hands and went off to his dressing-room.

While he was washing, Petritsky described to him in brief outlines his position, as far as it had changed since Vronsky had left Petersburg. No money at all. His father said he wouldn't give him any and pay his debts. His tailor was trying to get him locked up, and another fellow, too, was threatening to get him locked up. The colonel of the regiment had announced that if these scandals did not cease he would have to leave. As for the baroness, he was sick to death of her, especially since she'd taken to offering continually to lend him money. But he had found a girl—he'd show her to Vronsky—a marvel, exquisite, in the strict Oriental style, "genre of the slave Rebecca, don't you know." He'd had a row, too, with Berkoshov, and was going to send seconds to him, but of course it would come to nothing. Altogether everything was supremely amusing and jolly. And, not letting his comrade enter into further details of his position, Petritsky proceeded to tell him all the interesting news. As he listened to Petritsky's familiar stories in the familiar setting of the rooms he had spent the last three years in, Vronsky felt a delightful sense of coming back to the careless Petersburg life that he was used to.

"Impossible!" he cried, letting down the pedal of the washing basin in which he had been sousing his healthy red neck. "Impossible!" he cried, at the news that Laura had flung over Fertinghof and had made up to Mileev. "And is he as stupid and pleased as ever? Well, and how's Buzulukov?"

"Oh, there is a tale about Buzulukov—simply lovely!" cried Petritsky. "You know his weakness for balls, and he never misses a single court ball. He went to a big ball in a new helmet. Have you seen the new helmets? Very nice, lighter. Well, so he's standing ... No, I say, do listen."

"I am listening," answered Vronsky, rubbing himself with a rough towel.

"Up comes the Grand-Duchess with some ambassador or other, and, as ill-luck would have it, she begins talking to him about the new helmets. The Grand-Duchess positively wanted to show the new helmet to the ambassador.

They see our friend standing there." (Petritsky mimicked how he was standing with the helmet.) "The Grand-Duchess asked him to give her the helmet; he doesn't give it her. What do you think of that? Well, every one's winking at him, nodding, frowning—give it to her, do! He doesn't give it to her. He's mute as a fish. Only picture it! ... Well, the ... what's his name, whatever he was ... tries to take the helmet from him ... he won't give it up! ... He pulls it from him, and hands it to the Grand-Duchess. 'Here, your Highness,' says he, 'is the new helmet.' She turned the helmet the other side up, And—just picture it!—plop went a pear and sweetmeats out of it, two pounds of sweetmeats! ... He'd been storing them up, the darling!"

Vronsky burst into roars of laughter. And long afterwards, when he was talking of other things, he broke out into his healthy laugh, showing his strong, close rows of teeth, when he thought of the helmet.

Having heard all the news, Vronsky, with the assistance of his valet, got into his uniform, and went off to report himself. He intended, when he had done that, to drive to his brother's, and to Betsy's, and to pay several visits with a view to beginning to go into that society where he might meet Madame Karenina. As he always did in Petersburg, he left home not meaning to return till late at night.

PART TWO

CHAPTER I

A T THE END OF THE WINTER, IN THE SHTCHERBATSKYS' HOUSE, A CONSUL-tation was being held, which was to pronounce on the state of Kitty's health and the measures to be taken to restore her failing strength. She had been ill, and as spring came on she grew worse. The family doctor gave her cod-liver oil, then iron, then nitrate of silver, but as the first and the second and the third were alike in doing no good, and as his advice when spring came was to go abroad, a celebrated physician was called in. The celebrated physician, a very handsome man, still youngish, asked to examine the patient. He maintained, with peculiar satisfaction, it seemed, that maiden modesty is a mere relic of barbarism, and that nothing could be more natural than for a man still youngish to handle a young girl naked. He thought it natural because he did it every day, and felt and thought, as it seemed to him, no harm as he did it and consequently he considered modesty in the girl not merely as a relic of barbarism, but also as an insult to himself.

There was nothing for it but to submit, since, although all the doctors had studied in the same school, had read the same books, and learned the same science, and though some people said this celebrated doctor was a bad doctor, in the princess's household and circle it was for some reason accepted that this celebrated doctor alone had some special knowledge, and that he alone could save Kitty. After a careful examination and sounding of the bewildered patient, dazed with shame, the celebrated doctor, having scrupulously washed his hands, was standing in the drawing-room talking to the prince. The prince frowned and coughed, listening to the doctor. As a man who had seen something of life, and neither a fool nor an invalid, he had no faith in medicine, and in his heart was furious at the whole farce, specially as he was perhaps the only one who fully comprehended the cause of Kitty's illness. "Conceited blockhead!" he thought, as he listened to the celebrated doctor's chatter about his daughter's symptoms. The doctor was meantime with difficulty restraining the expression of his contempt for this old gentleman, and with difficulty condescending to the level of his intelligence. He perceived that it was no good talking to the old man, and that the principal person in the house was the mother. Before her he decided to scatter his pearls. At that instant the princess came into the drawing-room with the family doctor. The prince withdrew, trying not to show how ridiculous he thought the whole performance. The princess was distracted, and did not know what to do. She felt she had sinned against Kitty.

"Well, doctor, decide our fate," said the princess. "Tell me everything."

"Is there hope?" she meant to say, but her lips quivered, and she could not utter the question. "Well, doctor?"

"Immediately, princess. I will talk it over with my colleague, and then I will have the honor of laying my opinion before you."

"So we had better leave you?"

"As you please."

The princess went out with a sigh.

When the doctors were left alone, the family doctor began timidly explaining his opinion, that there was a commencement of tuberculous trouble, but... and so on. The celebrated doctor listened to him, and in the middle of his sentence looked at his big gold watch.

"Yes," said he. "But ..."

The family doctor respectfully ceased in the middle of his observations.

"The commencement of the tuberculous process we are not, as you are aware, able to define; till there are cavities, there is nothing definite. But we may suspect it. And there are indications; malnutrition, nervous excitability, and so on. The question stands thus: in presence of indications of tuberculous process, what is to be done to maintain nutrition?"

"But, you know, there are always moral, spiritual causes at the back in these cases," the family doctor permitted himself to interpolate with a subtle smile.

"Yes, that's an understood thing," responded the celebrated physician, again glancing at his watch. "Beg pardon, is the Yausky bridge done yet, or shall I have to drive around?" he asked. "Ah! it is. Oh, well, then I can do it in twenty minutes. So we were saying the problem may be put thus: to maintain nutrition and to give tone to the nerves. The one is in close connection with the other, one must attack both sides at once."

"And how about a tour abroad?" asked the family doctor.

"I've no liking to foreign tours. And take note: if there is an early stage of tuberculous process, of which we cannot be certain, a foreign tour will be of no use. What is wanted is means of improving nutrition, and not for lowering it." And the celebrated doctor expounded his plan of treatment with Soden waters, a remedy obviously prescribed primarily on the ground that they could do no harm.

The family doctor listened attentively and respectfully.

"But in favor of foreign travel I would urge the change of habits, the removal from conditions calling up reminiscences. And then the mother wishes it," he added.

"Ah! Well, in that case, to be sure, let them go. Only, those German quacks are mischievous.... They ought to be persuaded....Well, let them go then."

He glanced once more at his watch.

"Oh! time's up already," And he went to the door. The celebrated doctor announced to the princess (a feeling of what was due from him dictated his doing so) that he ought to see the patient once more.

"What! another examination!" cried the mother, with horror.

"Oh, no, only a few details, princess."

"Come this way."

And the mother, accompanied by the doctor, went into the drawing-room to Kitty. Wasted and flushed, with a peculiar glitter in her eyes, left there by the agony of shame she had been put through, Kitty stood in the middle of the room. When the doctor came in she flushed crimson, and her eyes filled with tears. All her illness and treatment struck her as a thing so stupid, ludicrous even! Doctoring her seemed to her as absurd as putting together the pieces of a broken vase. Her heart was broken. Why would they try to cure her with pills and powders? But she could not grieve her mother, especially as her mother considered herself to blame.

"May I trouble you to sit down, princess?" the celebrated doctor said to her.

He sat down with a smile, facing her, felt her pulse, and again began asking her tiresome questions. She answered him, and all at once got up furious.

"Excuse me, doctor, but there is really no object in this. This is the third time you've asked me the same thing."

The celebrated doctor did not take offense.

"Nervous irritability," he said to the princess, when Kitty had left the room. "However, I had finished...."

And the doctor began scientifically explaining to the princess, as an exceptionally intelligent woman, the condition of the young princess, and concluded by insisting on the drinking of the waters, which were certainly harmless. At the question: Should they go abroad? the doctor plunged into deep meditation, as though resolving a weighty problem. Finally his decision was pronounced: they were to go abroad, but to put no faith in foreign quacks, and to apply to him in any need.

It seemed as though some piece of good fortune had come to pass after the doctor had gone. The mother was much more cheerful when she went back to her daughter, and Kitty pretended to be more cheerful. She had often, almost always, to be pretending now.

"Really, I'm quite well, mamma. But if you want to go abroad, let's go!" she said, and trying to appear interested in the proposed tour, she began talking of the preparations for the journey.

CHAPTER II

SOON AFTER THE DOCTOR, DOLLY HAD ARRIVED. SHE KNEW THAT THERE WAS TO be a consultation that day, and though she was only just up after her confinement (she had another baby, a little girl, born at the end of the winter), though she had trouble and anxiety enough of her own, she had left her tiny baby and a sick child, to come and hear Kitty's fate, which was to be decided that day.

"Well, well?" she said, coming into the drawing-room, without taking off her hat. "You're all in good spirits. Good news, then?"

They tried to tell her what the doctor had said, but it appeared that though the doctor had talked distinctly enough and at great length, it was utterly impossible to report what he had said. The only point of interest was that it was settled they should go abroad.

Dolly could not help sighing. Her dearest friend, her sister, was going away. And her life was not a cheerful one. Her relations with Stepan Arkadyevitch after their reconciliation had become humiliating. The union Anna had cemented turned out to be of no solid character, and family harmony was breaking down again at the same point. There had been nothing definite, but Stepan Arkadyevitch was hardly ever at home; money, too, was hardly ever forthcoming, and Dolly was continually tortured by suspicions of infidelity, which she tried to dismiss, dreading the agonies of jealousy she had been through, already. The first onslaught of jealousy, once lived through, could never come back again, and even the discovery of infidelities could never now affect her as it had the first time. Such a discovery now would only mean breaking up family habits, and she let herself be deceived, despising him and still more herself, for the weakness. Besides this, the care of her large family was a constant worry to her: first, the nursing of her young baby did not go well, then the nurse had gone away, now one of the children had fallen ill.

"Well, how are all of you?" asked her mother.

"Ah, mamma, we have plenty of troubles of our own. Lili is ill, and I'm afraid it's scarlatina. I have come here now to hear about Kitty, and then I shall shut myself up entirely, if—God forbid—it should be scarlatina."

The old prince too had come in from his study after the doctor's departure, and after presenting his cheek to Dolly, and saying a few words to her, he turned to his wife:

"How have you settled it? you're going? Well, and what do you mean to do with me?"

"I suppose you had better stay here, Alexander," said his wife.

"That's as you like."

"Mamma, why shouldn't father come with us?" said Kitty. "It would be nicer for him and for us as well."

The old prince got up and stroked Kitty's hair. She lifted her head and looked at him with a forced smile. It always seemed to her that he understood her better than any one in the family, though he did not say much about her. Being the youngest, she was her father's favorite, and she fancied that his love gave him insight. When now her glance met his blue kindly eyes looking intently at her, it seemed to her that he saw right through her, and understood all that was not good that was passing within her. Reddening, she stretched out towards him expecting a kiss, but he only patted her hair and said:

"These stupid chignons! There's no getting at the real daughter, one simply strokes the bristles of dead women. Well, Dolinka," he turned to his elder daughter, "what's your young buck about, hey?"

"Nothing, father," answered Dolly, understanding that her husband was meant. "He's always out; I scarcely ever see him," she could not resist adding with a sarcastic smile.

"Why, hasn't he gone into the country yet—to see about selling that forest?"

"No, he's still getting ready for the journey."

"Oh, that's it!" said the prince. "And so am I to be getting ready for a journey too? At your service," he said to his wife, sitting down. "And I tell you what, Katia," he went on to his younger daughter, "you must wake up one fine day and say to yourself: Why, I'm quite well, and merry, and going out again with father for an early morning walk in the frost. Hey?"

What her father said seemed simple enough, yet at these words Kitty became confused and overcome like a detected criminal. "Yes, he sees it all, he understands it all, and in these words he's telling me that though I'm ashamed, I must get over my shame." She could not pluck up spirit to make any answer. She tried to begin, and all at once burst into tears, and rushed out of the room.

"See what comes of your jokes!" the princess pounced down on her husband. "You're always ..." she began a string of reproaches.

The prince listened to the princess's scolding rather a long while without speaking, but his face was more and more frowning.

"She's so much to be pitied, poor child, so much to be pitied, and you don't feel how it hurts her to hear the slightest reference to the cause of it. Ah! to be so mistaken in people!" said the princess, and by the change in her tone both Dolly and the prince knew she was speaking of Vronsky. "I don't know why there aren't laws against such base, dishonorable people."

"Ah, I can't bear to hear you!" said the prince gloomily, getting up from his low chair, and seeming anxious to get away, yet stopping in the doorway. "There are laws, madam, and since you've challenged me to it, I'll tell you who's to blame for it all: you and you, you and nobody else. Laws against such young gallants there have always been, and there still are! Yes, if there has been nothing that ought not to have been, old as I am, I'd have called him out to the barrier, the young dandy. Yes, and now you physic her and call in these quacks."

The prince apparently had plenty more to say, but as soon as the princess heard his tone she subsided at once, and became penitent, as she always did on serious occasions.

"Alexander, Alexander," she whispered, moving to him and beginning to weep.

As soon as she began to cry the prince too calmed down. He went up to her.

"There, that's enough, that's enough! You're wretched too, I know. It can't be helped. There's no great harm done. God is merciful ... thanks ..." he said, not knowing what he was saying, as he responded to the tearful kiss of the princess that he felt on his hand. And the prince went out of the room.

Before this, as soon as Kitty went out of the room in tears, Dolly, with her motherly, family instincts, had promptly perceived that here a woman's work lay before her, and she prepared to do it. She took off her hat, and, morally speaking, tucked up her sleeves and prepared for action. While her mother was attacking her father, she tried to restrain her mother, so far as filial reverence would allow. During the prince's outburst she was silent; she felt ashamed for her mother, and tender towards her father for so quickly being kind again. But when her father left them she made ready for what was the chief thing needful—to go to Kitty and console her.

"I'd been meaning to tell you something for a long while, mamma: did you know that Levin meant to make Kitty an offer when he was here the last time? He told Stiva so."

"Well, what then? I don't understand...."

"So did Kitty perhaps refuse him? ... She didn't tell you so?"

"No, she has said nothing to me either of one or the other; she's too proud. But I know it's all on account of the other."

"Yes, but suppose she has refused Levin, and she wouldn't have refused him if it hadn't been for the other, I know. And then, he has deceived her so horribly."

It was too terrible for the princess to think how she had sinned against her daughter, and she broke out angrily.

"Oh, I really don't understand! Nowadays they will all go their own way, and mothers haven't a word to say in anything, and then ..."

"Mamma, I'll go up to her."

"Well, do. Did I tell you not to?" said her mother.

CHAPTER III

WHEN SHE WENT INTO KITTY'S LITTLE ROOM, A PRETTY, PINK LITTLE room, full of knick-knacks in *vieux saxe,* as fresh, and pink, and white, and gay as Kitty herself had been two months ago, Dolly remembered how they had decorated the room the year before together, with what love and gaiety. Her heart turned cold when she saw Kitty sitting on a low chair near the door, her eyes fixed immovably on a corner of the rug. Kitty glanced at her sister, and the cold, rather ill-tempered, expression of her face did not change.

"I'm just going now, and I shall have to keep in and you won't be able to come to see me," said Dolly, sitting down beside her. "I want to talk to you."

"What about?" Kitty asked swiftly, lifting her head in dismay.

"What should it be, but your trouble?"

"I have no trouble."

"Nonsense, Kitty. Do you suppose I could help knowing? I know all about it. And believe me, it's of so little consequence ... We've all been through it."

Kitty did not speak, and her face had a stern expression.

"He's not worth your grieving over him," pursued Darya Alexandrovna, coming straight to the point.

"No, because he has treated me with contempt," said Kitty, in a breaking voice. "Don't talk of it! Please, don't talk of it!"

"But who can have told you so? No one has said that. I'm certain he was in love with you, and would still be in love with you, if it hadn't ..."

"Oh, the most awful thing of all for me is this sympathizing!" shrieked Kitty, suddenly flying into a passion. She turned round on her chair, flushed crimson, and rapidly moving her fingers, pinched the clasp of her belt first with one hand and then with the other. Dolly knew this trick her sister had of clenching her hands when she was much excited; she knew, too, that in moments of excitement Kitty was capable of forgetting herself and saying a great deal too much, and Dolly would have soothed her, but it was too late.

"What, what is it you want to make me feel, eh?" said Kitty quickly. "That I've been in love with a man who didn't care a straw for me, and that I'm dying of love for him? And this is said to me by my own sister, who imagines that ... that ... that she's sympathizing with me! ... I don't want these condolences and humbug!"

"Kitty, you're unjust."

"Why are you tormenting me?"

"But I ... quite the contrary ... I see you're unhappy...."

But Kitty in her fury did not hear her.

"I've nothing to grieve over and be comforted about. I am too proud ever to allow myself to care for a man who does not love me."

"Yes, I don't say so either.... Only one thing. Tell me the truth," said Darya Alexandrovna, taking her by the hand: "tell me, did Levin speak to you? ..."

The mention of Levin's name seemed to deprive Kitty of the last vestige of self-control. She leaped up from her chair, and flinging her clasp on the ground, she gesticulated rapidly with her hands and said:

"Why bring Levin in too? I can't understand what you want to torment me for. I've told you, and I say it again, that I have some pride, and never, *never* would I do as you're doing—go back to a man who's deceived you, who has cared for another woman. I can't understand it! You may, but I can't!"

And saying these words she glanced at her sister, and seeing that Dolly sat silent, her head mournfully bowed, Kitty, instead of running out of the room, as she had meant to do, sat down near the door, and hid her face in her handkerchief.

The silence lasted for two minutes: Dolly was thinking of herself. That humiliation of which she was always conscious came back to her with a peculiar bitterness when her sister reminded her of it. She had not looked for such cruelty in her sister, and she was angry with her. But suddenly she heard the rustle of a skirt, and with it the sound of heart-rending, smothered sobbing, and felt arms about her neck. Kitty was on her knees before her.

"Dolinka, I am so, so wretched!" she whispered penitently. And the sweet face covered with tears hid itself in Darya Alexandrovna's skirt.

As though tears were the indispensable oil, without which the machinery of mutual confidence could not run smoothly between the two sisters, the sisters after their tears talked, not of what was uppermost in their minds, but, though they talked of outside matters, they understood each other. Kitty knew that the words she had uttered in anger about her husband's infidelity and her humiliating position had cut her poor sister to the heart, but that she had forgiven her. Dolly for her part knew all she had wanted to find out. She felt certain that her surmises were correct; that Kitty's misery, her inconsolable misery, was due precisely to the fact that Levin had made her an offer and she had refused him, and Vronsky had deceived her, and that she was fully prepared to love Levin and to detest Vronsky. Kitty said not a word of that; she talked of nothing but her spiritual condition.

"I have nothing to make me miserable," she said, getting calmer; "but can you understand that everything has become hateful, loathsome, coarse to me, and I myself most of all? You can't imagine what loathsome thoughts I have about everything."

"Why, whatever loathsome thoughts can you have?" asked Dolly, smiling.

"The most utterly loathsome and coarse: I can't tell you. It's not unhappiness, or low spirits, but much worse. As though everything that was good in me was all hidden away, and nothing was left but the most loathsome. Come, how am I to tell you?" she went on, seeing the puzzled look in her sister's eyes. "Father began saying something to me just now…. It seems to me he thinks all I want is to be married. Mother takes me to a ball: it seems to me she only takes me to get me married off as soon as may be, and be rid of me. I know it's not the truth, but I can't drive away such thoughts. Eligible suitors, as they call them—I can't bear to see them. It seems to me they're taking stock of me and summing me up. In old days to go anywhere in a ball-dress was a simple joy to me, I admired myself; now I feel ashamed and awkward. And then! The doctor … Then …" Kitty hesitated; she wanted to say further that ever since this change had taken place in her, Stepan Arkadyevitch had become insufferably repulsive to her, and that she could not see him without the grossest and most hideous conceptions rising before her imagination.

"Oh, well, everything presents itself to me, in the coarsest, most loathsome light," she went on. "That's my illness. Perhaps it will pass off."

"But you mustn't think about it."

"I can't help it. I'm never happy except with the children at your house."

"What a pity you can't be with me!"

"Oh, yes, I'm coming. I've had scarlatina, and I'll persuade mamma to let me."

Kitty insisted on having her way, and went to stay at her sister's and nursed the children all through the scarlatina, for scarlatina it turned out to be. The two sisters brought all the six children successfully through it, but Kitty was no better in health, and in Lent the Shtcherbatskys went abroad.

CHAPTER IV

THE HIGHEST PETERSBURG SOCIETY IS ESSENTIALLY ONE: IN IT EVERY ONE knows every one else, every one even visits every one else. But this great set has its subdivisions. Anna Arkadyevna Karenina had friends and close ties in three different circles of this highest society. One circle was her husband's government official set, consisting of his colleagues and subordinates, brought together in the most various and capricious manner, and belonging to different social strata. Anna found it difficult now to recall the feeling of almost awe-stricken reverence which she had at first entertained for these persons. Now she knew all of them as people know one another in a country town; she knew their habits and weaknesses, and where the shoe pinched each one of them. She knew their relations with one another and with the head authorities, knew who was for whom, and how each one maintained his position, and where they agreed and disagreed. But the circle of political, masculine interests had never interested her, in spite of countess Lidia Ivanovna's influence, and she avoided it.

Another little set with which Anna was in close relations was the one by means of which Alexey Alexandrovitch had made his career. The center of this circle was the Countess Lidia Ivanovna. It was a set made up of elderly, ugly, benevolent, and godly women, and clever, learned, and ambitious men. One of the clever people belonging to the set had called it "the conscience of Petersburg society." Alexey Alexandrovitch had the highest esteem for this circle, and Anna with her special gift for getting on with every one, had in the early days of her life in Petersburg made friends in this circle also. Now, since her return from Moscow, she had come to feel this set insufferable. It seemed to her that both she and all of them were insincere, and she felt so bored and ill at ease in that world that she went to see the Countess Lidia Ivanovna as little as possible.

The third circle with which Anna had ties was preëminently the fashionable world—the world of balls, of dinners, of sumptuous dresses, the world that hung on to the court with one hand, so as to avoid sinking to the level of the demi-monde. For the demi-monde the members of that fashionable world believed that they despised, though their tastes were not merely similar, but in fact identical. Her connection with this circle was kept up through Princess Betsy Tverskaya, her cousin's wife, who had an income of a hundred and twenty thousand roubles, and who had taken a great fancy to Anna ever since she first came out, showed her much attention, and drew her into her set, making fun of Countess Lidia Ivanovna's coterie.

"When I'm old and ugly I'll be the same," Betsy used to say; "but for a pretty young woman like you it's early days for that house of charity."

Anna had at first avoided as far as she could Princess Tverskaya's world, because it necessitated an expenditure beyond her means, and besides in her heart she preferred the first circle. But since her visit to Moscow she had done quite the contrary. She avoided her serious-minded friends, and went out into the fashionable world. There she met Vronsky, and experienced an agitating joy at those meetings. She met Vronsky specially often at Betsy's for Betsy was a Vronsky by birth and his cousin. Vronsky was everywhere where he had any chance of meeting Anna, and speaking to her, when he could, of his love. She gave him no encouragement, but every time she met him there surged up in her heart that same feeling of quickened life that had come upon her that day in the railway carriage when she saw him for the first time. She was conscious herself that her delight sparkled in her eyes and curved her lips into a smile, and she could not quench the expression of this delight.

At first Anna sincerely believed that she was displeased with him for daring to pursue her. Soon after her return from Moscow, on arriving at a soirée where she had expected to meet him, and not finding him there, she realized distinctly from the rush of disappointment that she had been deceiving herself, and that this pursuit was not merely not distasteful to her, but that it made the whole interest of her life.

A celebrated singer was singing for the second time, and all the fashionable world was in the theater. Vronsky, seeing his cousin from his stall in the front row, did not wait till the *entr'acte*, but went to her box.

"Why didn't you come to dinner?" she said to him. "I marvel at the second-sight of lovers," she added with a smile, so that no one but he could hear; "*she wasn't there*. But come after the opera."

Vronsky looked inquiringly at her. She nodded. He thanked her by a smile, and sat down beside her.

"But how I remember your jeers!" continued Princess Betsy, who took a peculiar pleasure in following up this passion to a successful issue. "What's become of all that? You're caught, my dear boy."

"That's my one desire, to be caught," answered Vronsky, with his serene, good-humored smile. "If I complain of anything it's only that I'm not caught enough, to tell the truth. I begin to lose hope."

"Why, whatever hope can you have?" said Betsy, offended on behalf of her friend. "*Entendons nous....*" But in her eyes there were gleams of light that betrayed that she understood perfectly and precisely as he did what hope he might have.

"None whatever," said Vronsky, laughing and showing his even rows of teeth. "Excuse me," he added, taking an opera-glass out of her hand, and proceeding to scrutinize, over her bare shoulder, the row of boxes facing them. "I'm afraid I'm becoming ridiculous."

He was very well aware that he ran no risk of being ridiculous in the eyes of Betsy or any other fashionable people. He was very well aware that in their eyes the position of an unsuccessful lover of a girl, or of any woman free to marry, might be ridiculous. But the position of a man pursuing a married woman, and, regardless of everything, staking his life on drawing her into adultery, has something fine and grand about it, and can never be ridiculous; and so it was with a proud and gay smile under his mustaches that he lowered the opera-glass and looked at his cousin.

"But why was it you didn't come to dinner?" she said, admiring him.

"I must tell you about that. I was busily employed, and doing what, do you suppose? I'll give you a hundred guesses, a thousand ... you'd never guess. I've been reconciling a husband with a man who'd insulted his wife. Yes, really!"

"Well, did you succeed?"

"Almost."

"You really must tell me about it," she said, getting up. "Come to me in the next *entr'acte*."

"I can't; I'm going to the French theater."

"From Nilsson?" Betsy queried in horror, though she could not herself have distinguished Nilsson's voice from any chorus girl's.

"Can't help it. I've an appointment there, all to do with my mission of peace."

"Blessed are the peacemakers; theirs is the kingdom of heaven,'" said Betsy, vaguely recollecting she had heard some similar saying from some one. "Very well, then, sit down, and tell me what it's all about."

And she sat down again.

CHAPTER V

THIS IS RATHER INDISCREET, BUT IT'S SO GOOD IT'S AN AWFUL TEMPTATION to tell the story," said Vronsky, looking at her with his laughing eyes. "I'm not going to mention any names."

"But I shall guess, so much the better."

"Well, listen: two festive young men were driving ..."

"Officers of your regiment, of course?"

"I didn't say they were officers,—two young men who had been lunching."

"In other words, drinking."

"Possibly. They were driving on their way to dinner with a friend in the most festive state of mind. And they beheld a pretty woman in a hired sledge; she overtakes them, looks round at them, and, so they fancy anyway, nods to them and laughs. They, of course, follow her. They gallop at full speed. To their amazement, the fair one alights at the entrance of the very house to which they were going. The fair one darts up-stairs to the top story. They get a glimpse of red lips under a short veil, and exquisite little feet."

"You describe it with such feeling that I fancy you must be one of the two."

"And after what you said, just now! Well, the young men go in to their comrade's; he was giving a farewell dinner. There they certainly did drink a little too much, as one always does at farewell dinners. And at dinner they inquire who lives at the top in that house. No one knows; only their host's valet, in answer to their inquiry whether any 'young ladies' are living on the top floor, answered that there were a great many of them about there. After dinner the two young men go into their host's study, and write a letter to the unknown fair one. They compose an ardent epistle, a declaration in fact, and they carry the letter up-stairs themselves, so as to elucidate whatever might appear not perfectly intelligible in the letter."

"Why are you telling me these horrible stories? Well?"

"They ring. A maid-servant opens the door, they hand her the letter, and assure the maid that they're both so in love that they'll die on the spot at the door. The maid, stupefied, carries in their messages. All at once a gentleman appears with whiskers like sausages, as red as a lobster, announces that there is no one living in the flat except his wife, and sends them both about their business."

"How do you know he had whiskers like sausages, as you say?"

"Ah, you shall hear. I've just been to make peace between them."

"Well, and what then?"

"That's the most interesting part of the story. It appears that it's a happy couple, a government clerk and his lady. The government clerk lodges a complaint, and I became a mediator, and such a mediator! ... I assure you Talleyrand couldn't hold a candle to me."

"Why, where was the difficulty?"

"Ah, you shall hear .... We apologize in due form: we are in despair, we entreat forgiveness for the unfortunate misunderstanding. The government clerk with the sausages begins to melt, but he, too, desires to express his sentiments, and as soon as ever he begins to express them, he begins to get hot and say nasty things, and again I'm obliged to trot out all my diplomatic talents. I allowed that their conduct was bad, but I urged him to take into consideration their heedlessness, their youth; then, too, the young men had only just been lunching together. 'You understand. They regret it deeply, and beg you to overlook their misbehavior.' The government clerk was softened once more. 'I consent, count, and am ready to overlook it; but you perceive that my wife—my wife's a respectable woman—has been exposed to the persecution, and insults, and effrontery of young upstarts, scoundrels....' And you must understand, the young upstarts are present all the while, and I have to keep the peace between them. Again I call out all my diplomacy, and again as soon as the thing was about at an end, our friend the government clerk gets hot and red, and his sausages stand on end with wrath, and once more I launch out into diplomatic wiles."

"Ah, he must tell you this story!" said Betsy, laughing, to a lady who came into her box. "He has been making me laugh so."

"Well, *bonne chance!*" she added, giving Vronsky one finger of the hand in which she held her fan, and with a shrug of her shoulders she twitched down the bodice of her gown that had worked up, so as to be duly naked as she moved forward towards the footlights into the light of the gas, and the sight of all eyes.

Vronsky drove to the French theater, where he really had to see the colonel of his regiment, who never missed a single performance there. He wanted to see him, to report on the result of his mediation, which had occupied and amused him for the last three days. Petritsky, whom he liked, was implicated in the affair, and the other culprit was a capital fellow and first-rate comrade, who had lately joined the regiment, the young Prince Kedrov. And what was most important, the interests of the regiment were involved in it too.

Both the young men were in Vronsky's company. The colonel of the regiment was waited upon by the government clerk, Venden, with a complaint against his officers, who had insulted his wife. His young wife, so Venden told the story—he had been married half a year—was at church with her mother, and suddenly overcome by indisposition, arising from her interesting condition, she could not remain standing, she drove home in the first sledge, a smart-looking one, she came across. On the spot the officers set off in pursuit of her; she was alarmed, and feeling still more unwell, ran up the staircase home. Venden himself, on returning from his office, heard a ring at their bell and voices, went out, and seeing the intoxicated officers with a letter, he had turned them out. He asked for exemplary punishment.

"Yes, it's all very well," said the colonel to Vronsky, whom he had invited to come and see him. "Petritsky's becoming impossible. Not a week goes by without some scandal. This government clerk won't let it drop, he'll go on with the thing."

Vronsky saw all the thanklessness of the business, and that there could be no question of a duel in it, that everything must be done to soften the government clerk, and hush the matter up. The colonel had called in Vronsky just because he knew him to be an honorable and intelligent man, and, more than all, a man who cared for the honor of the regiment. They talked it over, and decided that Petritsky and Kedrov must go with Vronsky to Venden's to apologize. The colonel and Vronsky were both fully aware that Vronsky's name and rank would be sure to contribute greatly to the softening of the injured husband's feelings.

And these two influences were not in fact without effect; though the result remained, as Vronsky had described, uncertain.

On reaching the French theater, Vronsky retired to the foyer with the colonel, and reported to him his success, or non-success. The colonel, thinking it all over, made up his mind not to pursue the matter further, but then for his own satisfaction proceeded to cross-examine Vronsky about his interview; and it was a long while before he could restrain his laughter, as Vronsky described how the government clerk, after subsiding for a while, would suddenly flare up again, as he recalled the details, and how Vronsky, at the last half word of conciliation, skillfully manœuvered a retreat, shoving Petritsky out before him.

"It's a disgraceful story, but killing. Kedrov really can't fight the gentleman! Was he so awfully hot?" he commented, laughing. "But what do you say to Claire to-day? She's marvelous," he went on, speaking of a new French actress. "However often you see her, every day she's different. It's only the French who can do that."

CHAPTER VI

PRINCESS BETSY DROVE HOME FROM THE THEATER, WITHOUT WAITING FOR the end of the last act. She had only just time to go into her dressing-room, sprinkle her long, pale face with powder, rub it, set her dress to rights, and order tea in the big drawing-room, when one after another carriages drove up to her huge house in Bolshaia Morskaia. Her guests stepped out at the wide entrance, and the stout porter, who used to read the newspapers in the mornings behind the glass door, to the edification of the passers-by, noiselessly opened the immense door, letting the visitors pass by him into the house.

Almost at the same instant the hostess, with freshly arranged coiffure and freshened face, walked in at one door and her guests at the other door of the drawing-room, a large room with dark walls, downy rugs, and a brightly lighted table, gleaming with the light of candles, white cloth, silver samovar, and transparent china tea-things.

The hostess sat down at the table and took off her gloves. Chairs were set with the aid of footmen, moving almost imperceptibly about the room; the party settled itself, divided into two groups: one round the samovar near the hostess, the other at the opposite end of the drawing-room, round the handsome wife of an ambassador, in black velvet, with sharply defined black eyebrows. In both groups conversation wavered, as it always does, for the first few minutes, broken up by meetings, greetings, offers of tea, and as it were, feeling about for something to rest upon.

"She's exceptionally good as an actress; one can see she's studied Kaulbach," said a diplomatic attaché in the group round the ambassador's wife. "Did you notice how she fell down? ..."

"Oh, please, don't let us talk about Nilsson! No one can possibly say anything new about her," said a fat, red-faced, flaxen-headed lady, without eyebrows and chignon, wearing an old silk dress. This was Princess Myakaya, noted for her simplicity and the roughness of her manners, and nicknamed *enfant terrible*. Princess Myakaya, sitting in the middle between the two groups, and listening to both, took part in the conversation first of one and then of the other. "Three people have used that very phrase about Kaulbach to me to-day already, just as though they had made a compact about it. And I can't see why they liked that remark so."

The conversation was cut short by this observation, and a new subject had to be thought of again.

"Do tell me something amusing but not spiteful," said the ambassador's wife, a great proficient in the art of that elegant conversation called by the English, *small-talk*. She addressed the attaché, who was at a loss now what to begin upon.

"They say that that's a difficult task, that nothing's amusing that isn't spiteful," he began with a smile. "But I'll try. Get me a subject. It all lies in the subject. If a subject's given me, it's easy to spin something round it. I often think that the celebrated talkers of the last century would have found it difficult to talk cleverly now. Everything clever is so stale ..."

"That has been said long ago," the ambassador's wife interrupted him, laughing.

The conversation began amiably, but just because it was too amiable, it came to a stop again. They had to have recourse to the sure, never-failing topic—gossip.

"Don't you think there's something Louis Quinze about Tushkevitch?" he said, glancing towards a handsome, fair-haired young man, standing at the table.

"Oh, yes! He's in the same style as the drawing-room and that's why it is he's so often here."

This conversation was maintained, since it rested on allusions to what could not be talked of in that room—that is to say, of the relations of Tushkevitch with their hostess.

Round the samovar and the hostess the conversation had been meanwhile vacillating in just the same way between three inevitable topics: the latest piece of public news, the theater, and scandal. It, too, came finally to rest on the last topic, that is, ill-natured gossip.

"Have you heard the Maltishtcheva woman—the mother, not the daughter—has ordered a costume in *diable rose* color?"

"Nonsense! No, that's too lovely!"

"I wonder that with her sense—for she's not a fool, you know— that she doesn't see how funny she is."

Every one had something to say in censure or ridicule of the luckless Madame Maltishtcheva, and the conversation crackled merrily, like a burning fagot-stack.

The husband of Princess Betsy, a good-natured fat man, an ardent collector of engravings, hearing that his wife had visitors, came into the drawing-room before going to his club. Stepping noiselessly over the thick rugs, he went up to Princess Myakaya.

"How did you like Nilsson?" he asked.

"Oh, how can you steal upon anyone like that! How you startled me!" she responded. "Please don't talk to me about the opera; you know nothing about music. I'd better meet you on your own ground, and talk about your majolica and engravings. Come now, what treasure have you been buying lately at the old curiosity shops?"

"Would you like me to show you? But you don't understand such things."

"Oh, do show me! I've been learning about them at those—what's their names? … the bankers … they've some splendid engravings. They showed them to us."

"Why, have you been at the Schützburgs?" asked the hostess from the samovar.

"Yes, *ma chère*. They asked my husband and me to dinner, and told us the sauce at that dinner cost a hundred pounds," Princess Myakaya said, speaking loudly, and conscious every one was listening; "and very nasty sauce it was, some green mess. We had to ask them, and I made them sauce for eighteen pence, and everybody was very much pleased with it. I can't run to hundred-pound sauces."

"She's unique!" said the lady of the house.

"Marvelous!" said some one.

The sensation produced by Princess Myakaya's speeches was always unique, and the secret of the sensation she produced lay in the fact that though she spoke not always appropriately, as now, she said simple things with some sense in them. In the society in which she lived such plain statements produced the effect of the wittiest epigram. Princess Myakaya could never see why it had that effect, but she knew it had, and took advantage of it.

As every one had been listening while Princess Myakaya spoke, and so the conversation around the ambassador's wife had dropped, Princess Betsy tried to bring the whole party together, and she turned to the ambassador's wife.

"Will you really not have tea? You should come over here by us."

"No, we're very happy here," the ambassador's wife responded with a smile, and she went on with the conversation that had been begun.

It was a very agreeable conversation. They were criticizing the Karenins, husband and wife.

"Anna is quite changed since her stay in Moscow. There's something strange about her," said her friend.

"The great change is that she brought back with her the shadow of Alexey Vronsky," said the ambassador's wife.

"Well, what of it? There's a fable of Grimm's about a man without a shadow, a man who's lost his shadow. And that's his punishment for something. I never could understand how it was a punishment. But a woman must dislike being without a shadow."

"Yes, but women with a shadow usually come to a bad end," said Anna's friend.

"Bad luck to your tongue!" said Princess Myakaya suddenly. "Madame Karenina's a splendid woman. I don't like her husband, but I like her very much."

"Why don't you like her husband? He's such a remarkable man," said the ambassador's wife. "My husband says there are few statesmen like him in Europe."

"And my husband tells me just the same, but I don't believe it," said Princess Myakaya. "If our husbands didn't talk to us, we should see the facts as they are. Alexey Alexandrovitch, to my thinking, is simply a fool. I say it in a whisper ... but doesn't it really make everything clear? Before, when I was told to consider him clever, I kept looking for his ability, and thought myself a fool for not seeing it; but directly I said, *he's a fool*, though only in a whisper, everything's explained, isn't it?"

"How spiteful you are to-day!"

"Not a bit. I'd no other way out of it. One of the two had to be a fool. And, well, you know one can't say that of oneself."

"'No one is satisfied with his fortune, and every one is satisfied with his wit.'" The attaché repeated the French saying.

"That's just it, just it," Princess Myakaya turned to him. "But the point is that I won't abandon Anna to your mercies. She's so nice, so charming. How can she help it if they're all in love with her, and follow her about like shadows?"

"Oh, I had no idea of blaming her for it," Anna's friend said in self-defense.

"If no one follows us about like a shadow, that's no proof that we've any right to blame her."

And having duly disposed of Anna's friend, the Princess Myakaya got up, and together with the ambassador's wife, joined the group at the table, where the conversation was dealing with the king of Prussia.

"What wicked gossip were you talking over there?" asked Betsy.

"About the Karenins. The princess gave us a sketch of Alexey Alexandrovitch," said the ambassador's wife with a smile, as she sat down at the table.

"Pity we didn't hear it!" said Princess Betsy, glancing towards the door. "Ah, here you are at last!" she said, turning with a smile to Vronsky, as he came in.

Vronsky was not merely acquainted with all the persons whom he was meeting here; he saw them all every day; and so he came in with the quiet manner with which one enters a room full of people from whom one has only just parted.

"Where do I come from?" he said, in answer to a question from the ambassador's wife. "Well, there's no help for it, I must confess. From the *opéra bouffe*. I do believe I've seen it a hundred times, and always with fresh enjoyment. It's exquisite! I know it's disgraceful, but I go to sleep at the opera, and I sit out the *opéra bouffe* to the last minute, and enjoy it. This evening …"

He mentioned a French actress, and was going to tell something about her; but the ambassador's wife, with playful horror, cut him short.

"Please don't tell us about that horror."

"All right, I won't, especially as every one knows those horrors."

"And we should all go to see them if it were accepted as the correct thing, like the opera," chimed in Princess Myakaya.

CHAPTER VII

STEPS WERE HEARD AT THE DOOR, AND PRINCESS BETSY, KNOWING IT WAS Madame Karenina, glanced at Vronsky. He was looking towards the door, and his face wore a strange new expression. Joyfully, intently, and at the same time timidly, he gazed at the approaching figure, and slowly he rose to his feet. Anna walked into the drawing-room. Holding herself extremely erect, as always, looking straight before her, and moving with her swift, resolute, and light step, that distinguished her from all other society women, she crossed the short space to her hostess, shook hands with her, smiled, and with the same smile looked around at Vronsky. Vronsky bowed low and pushed a chair up for her.

She acknowledged this only by a slight nod, flushed a little, and frowned. But immediately, while rapidly greeting her acquaintances, and shaking the hands proffered to her, she addressed Princess Betsy:

"I have been at Countess Lidia's, and meant to have come here earlier, but I stayed on. Sir John was there. He's very interesting."

"Oh, that's this missionary?"

"Yes; he told us about the life in India, most interesting things."

The conversation, interrupted by her coming in, flickered up again like the light of a lamp being blown out.

"Sir John! Yes, Sir John; I've seen him. He speaks well. The Vlassieva girl's quite in love with him."

"And is it true the younger Vlassieva girl's to marry Topov?"

"Yes, they say it's quite a settled thing."

"I wonder at the parents! They say it's a marriage for love."

"For love? What antediluvian notions you have! Can one talk of love in these days?" said the ambassador's wife.

"What's to be done? It's a foolish old fashion that's kept up still," said Vronsky.

"So much the worse for those who keep up the fashion. The only happy marriages I know are marriages of prudence."

"Yes, but then how often the happiness of these prudent marriages flies away like dust just because that passion turns up that they have refused to recognize," said Vronsky.

"But by marriages of prudence we mean those in which both parties have sown their wild oats already. That's like scarlatina—one has to go through it and get it over."

"Then they ought to find out how to vaccinate for love, like smallpox."

"I was in love in my young days with a deacon," said the Princess Myakaya. "I don't know that it did me any good."

"No; I imagine, joking apart, that to know love, one must make mistakes and then correct them," said Princess Betsy.

"Even after marriage?" said the ambassador's wife playfully.

"'It's never too late to mend.'" The attaché repeated the English proverb.

"Just so," Betsy agreed; "one must make mistakes and correct them. What do you think about it?" She turned to Anna, who, with a faintly perceptible resolute smile on her lips, was listening in silence to the conversation.

"I think," said Anna, playing with the glove she had taken off, "I think ... of so many men, so many minds, certainly so many hearts, so many kinds of love."

Vronsky was gazing at Anna, and with a fainting heart waiting for what she would say. He sighed as after a danger escaped when she uttered these words.

Anna suddenly turned to him.

"Oh, I have had a letter from Moscow. They write me that Kitty Shtcherbatskaya's very ill."

"Really?" said Vronsky, knitting his brows.

Anna looked sternly at him.

"That doesn't interest you?"

"On the contrary, it does, very much. What was it exactly they told you, if I may know?" he questioned.

Anna got up and went to Betsy.

"Give me a cup of tea," she said, standing at her table.

While Betsy was pouring out the tea, Vronsky went up to Anna.

"What is it they write to you?" he repeated.

"I often think men have no understanding of what's not honorable though they're always talking of it," said Anna, without answering him. "I've wanted to tell you so a long while," she added, and moving a few steps away, she sat down at a table in a corner covered with albums.

"I don't quite understand the meaning of your words," he said, handing her the cup.

She glanced towards the sofa beside her, and he instantly sat down.

"Yes, I have been wanting to tell you," she said, not looking at him. "You behaved wrongly, very wrongly."

"Do you suppose I don't know that I've acted wrongly? But who was the cause of my doing so?"

"What do you say that to me for?" she said, glancing severely at him.

"You know what for," he answered boldly and joyfully, meeting her glance and not dropping his eyes.

Not he, but she, was confused.

"That only shows you have no heart," she said. But her eyes said that she knew he had a heart, and that was why she was afraid of him.

"What you spoke of just now was a mistake, and not love."

"Remember that I have forbidden you to utter that word, that hateful word," said Anna, with a shudder. But at once she felt that by that very word "forbidden" she had shown that she acknowledged certain rights over him, and by that very fact was encouraging him to speak of love. "I have long meant to tell you this," she went on, looking resolutely into his eyes, and hot all over from the burning flush on her cheeks. "I've come on purpose this evening, knowing

I should meet you. I have come to tell you that this must end. I have never blushed before any one, and you force me to feel to blame for something."

He looked at her and was struck by a new spiritual beauty in her face.

"What do you wish of me?" he said simply and seriously.

"I want you to go to Moscow and ask for Kitty's forgiveness," she said.

"You don't wish that?" he said.

He saw she was saying what she forced herself to say, not what she wanted to say.

"If you love me, as you say," she whispered, "do so that I may be at peace."

His face grew radiant.

"Don't you know that you're all my life to me? But I know no peace, and I can't give it to you; all myself—and love … yes. I can't think of you and myself apart. You and I are one to me. And I see no chance before us of peace for me or for you. I see a chance of despair, of wretchedness … or I see a chance of bliss, what bliss! … Can it be there's no chance of it?" he murmured with his lips; but she heard.

She strained every effort of her mind to say what ought to be said. But instead of that she let her eyes rest on him, full of love, and made no answer.

"It's come!" he thought in ecstasy. "When I was beginning to despair, and it seemed there would be no end—it's come! She loves me! She owns it!"

"Then do this for me: never say such things to me, and let us be friends," she said in words; but her eyes spoke quite differently.

"Friends we shall never be, you know that yourself. Whether we shall be the happiest or the wretchedest of people—that's in your hands."

She would have said something, but he interrupted her.

"I ask one thing only: I ask for the right to hope, to suffer as I do. But if even that cannot be, command me to disappear, and I disappear. You shall not see me if my presence is distasteful to you."

"I don't want to drive you away."

"Only don't change anything, leave everything as it is," he said in a shaky voice. "Here's your husband."

At that instant Alexey Alexandrovitch did in fact walk into the room with his calm, awkward gait.

Glancing at his wife and Vronsky, he went up to the lady of the house, and sitting down for a cup of tea, began talking in his deliberate, always audible voice, in his habitual tone of banter, ridiculing some one.

"Your Rambouillet is in full conclave," he said, looking round at all the party; "the graces and the muses."

But Princess Betsy could not endure that tone of his—"sneering," as she called it, using the English word, and like a skillful hostess she at once brought him into a serious conversation on the subject of universal conscription. Alexey Alexandrovitch was immediately interested in the subject, and began seriously defending the new imperial decree against Princess Betsy, who had attacked it.

Vronsky and Anna still sat at the little table.

"This is getting indecorous," whispered one lady, with an expressive glance at Madame Karenina, Vronsky, and her husband.

"What did I tell you?" said Anna's friend.

But not only those ladies, almost every one in the room, even the Princess Myakaya and Betsy herself, looked several times in the direction of the two who had withdrawn from the general circle, as though that were a disturbing fact. Alexey Alexandrovitch was the only person who did not once look in that direction, and was not diverted from the interesting discussion he had entered upon.

Noticing the disagreeable impression that was being made on every one, Princess Betsy slipped someone else into her place to listen to Alexey Alexandrovitch, and went up to Anna.

"I'm always amazed at the clearness and precision of your husband's language," she said. "The most transcendental ideas seem to be within my grasp when he's speaking."

"Oh, yes!" said Anna, radiant with a smile of happiness, and not understanding a word of what Betsy had said. She crossed over to the big table and took part in the general conversation.

Alexey Alexandrovitch, after staying half an hour, went up to his wife and suggested that they should go home together. But she answered, not looking at him, that she was staying to supper. Alexey Alexandrovitch made his bows and withdrew.

The fat old Tatar, Madame Karenina's coachman, was with difficulty holding one of her pair of grays, chilled with the cold and rearing at the entrance. A footman stood opening the carriage door. The hall porter stood holding open the great door of the house. Anna Arkadyevna, with her quick little hand, was unfastening the lace of her sleeve, caught in the hook of her fur cloak, and with bent head listening to the words Vronsky murmured as he escorted her down.

"You've said nothing, of course, and I ask nothing," he was saying; "but you know that friendship's not what I want: that there's only one happiness in life for me, that word that you dislike so ... yes, love! ..."

"Love," she repeated slowly, in an inner voice, and suddenly, at the very instant she unhooked the lace, she added, "Why I don't like the word is that it means too much to me, far more than you can understand," and she glanced into his face. "*Au revoir!*"

She gave him her hand, and with her rapid, springy step she passed by the porter and vanished into the carriage.

Her glance, the touch of her hand, set him aflame. He kissed the palm of his hand where she had touched it, and went home, happy in the sense that he had got nearer to the attainment of his aims that evening than during the last two months.

CHAPTER VIII

ALEXEY ALEXANDROVITCH HAD SEEN NOTHING STRIKING OR IMPROPER IN the fact that his wife was sitting with Vronsky at a table apart, in eager conversation with him about something. But he noticed that to the rest of the party this appeared something striking and improper, and for that reason it seemed to him too to be improper. He made up his mind that he must speak of it to his wife.

On reaching home Alexey Alexandrovitch went to his study, as he usually did, seated himself in his low chair, opened a book on the Papacy at the place where he had laid the paper-knife in it, and read till one o'clock, just as he usually did. But from time to time he rubbed his high forehead and shook his head, as though to drive away something. At his usual time he got up and made his toilet for the night. Anna Arkadyevna had not yet come in. With a book under his arm he went up-stairs. But this evening, instead of his usual thoughts and meditations upon official details, his thoughts were absorbed by his wife and something disagreeable connected with her. Contrary to his usual habit, he did not get into bed, but fell to walking up and down the rooms with his hands clasped behind his back. He could not go to bed, feeling that it was absolutely needful for him first to think thoroughly over the position that had just arisen.

When Alexey Alexandrovitch had made up his mind that he must talk to his wife about it, it had seemed a very easy and simple matter. But now, when he began to think over the question that had just presented itself, it seemed to him very complicated and difficult.

Alexey Alexandrovitch was not jealous. Jealousy according to his notions was an insult to one's wife, and one ought to have confidence in one's wife.

Why one ought to have confidence—that is to say, complete conviction that his young wife would always love him—he did not ask himself. But he had no experience of lack of confidence, because he had confidence in her, and told himself that he ought to have it. Now, though his conviction, that jealousy was a shameful feeling and that one ought to feel confidence, had not broken down, he felt that he was standing face to face with something illogical and irrational, and did not know what was to be done. Alexey Alexandrovitch was standing face to face with life, with the possibility of his wife's loving some one other than himself, and this seemed to him very irrational and incomprehensible because it was life itself. All his life Alexey Alexandrovitch had lived and worked in official spheres, having to do with the reflection of life. And every time he had stumbled against life itself he had shrunk away from it. Now he experienced a feeling akin to that of a man who, while calmly crossing a precipice by a bridge, should suddenly discover that the bridge is broken, and that there is a chasm below. That chasm was life itself, the bridge that artificial life in which Alexey Alexandrovitch had lived. For the first time the question presented itself to him of the possibility of his wife's loving some one else, and he was horrified at it.

He did not undress, but walked up and down with his regular tread over the resounding parquet of the dining-room, where one lamp was burning, over the carpet of the dark drawing-room, in which the light was reflected on the big new portrait of himself hanging over the sofa, and across her boudoir, where two candles burned, lighting up the portraits of her parents and woman friends, and the pretty knick-knacks of her writing-table, that he knew so well. He walked across her boudoir to the bedroom door, and turned back again. At each turn in his walk, especially at the parquet of the lighted dining-room, he halted and said to himself, "Yes, this I must decide and put a stop to; I must express my view of it and my decision." And he turned back again. "But express what—what decision?" he said to himself in the drawing-room, and he found no reply. "But after all," he asked himself before turning into the boudoir, "what has occurred? Nothing. She was talking a long while with him. But what of that? Surely women in society can talk to whom they please. And then, jealousy means lowering both myself and her," he told himself as he went into her boudoir; but this dictum, which had always had such weight with him before, had now no weight and no meaning at all. And from the bedroom door he turned back again; but as he entered the dark drawing-room some inner voice told him that it was not so, and that if others noticed it that showed that there was something. And he said to himself again in the dining-room, "Yes, I must decide and put a stop to it, and express my view of it...." And again at the turn in the drawing-room he asked himself, "Decide how?" And again he asked himself, "What had occurred?" and answered, "Nothing," and recollected that jealousy was a feeling insulting to his wife; but again in the drawing-room he was convinced that something had happened. His thoughts, like his body, went round a complete circle, without coming upon anything new. He noticed this, rubbed his forehead, and sat down in her boudoir.

There, looking at her table, with the malachite blotting-case lying at the top and an unfinished letter, his thoughts suddenly changed. He began to think of her, of what she was thinking and feeling. For the first time he pictured vividly to himself her personal life, her ideas, her desires, and the idea that she could and should have a separate life of her own seemed to him so alarming that he made haste to dispel it. It was the chasm which he was afraid to peep into. To put himself in thought and feeling in another person's place was a spiritual exercise not natural to Alexey Alexandrovitch. He looked on this spiritual exercise as a harmful and dangerous abuse of the fancy.

"And the worst of it all," thought he, "is that just now, at the very moment when my great work is approaching completion" (he was thinking of the project he was bringing forward at the time), "when I stand in need of all my mental peace and all my energies, just now this stupid worry should fall foul of me. But what's to be done? I'm not one of those men who submit to uneasiness and worry without having the force of character to face them."

"I must think it over, come to a decision, and put it out of my mind," he said aloud.

"The question of her feelings, of what has passed and may be passing in her soul, that's not my affair; that's the affair of her conscience, and falls under the head of religion," he said to himself, feeling consolation in the sense that he had found to which division of regulating principles this new circumstance could be properly referred.

"And so," Alexey Alexandrovitch said to himself, "questions as to her feelings, and so on, are questions for her conscience, with which I can have nothing to do. My duty is clearly defined. As the head of the family, I am a person bound in duty to guide her, and consequently, in part the person responsible; I am bound to point out the danger I perceive, to warn her, even to use my authority. I ought to speak plainly to her." And everything that he would say to-night to his wife took clear shape in Alexey Alexandrovitch's head. Thinking over what he would say, he somewhat regretted that he should have to use his time and mental powers for domestic consumption, with so little to show for it, but, in spite of that, the form and contents of the speech before him shaped itself as clearly and distinctly in his head as a ministerial report.

"I must say and express fully the following points: first, exposition of the value to be attached to public opinion and to decorum; secondly, exposition of religious significance of marriage; thirdly, if need be, reference to the calamity possibly ensuing to our son; fourthly, reference to the unhappiness likely to result to herself." And, interlacing his fingers, Alexey Alexandrovitch stretched them, and the joints of the fingers cracked. This trick, a bad habit, the cracking of his fingers, always soothed him, and gave precision to his thoughts, so needful to him at this juncture.

There was the sound of a carriage driving up to the front door. Alexey Alexandrovitch halted in the middle of the room.

A woman's step was heard mounting the stairs. Alexey Alexandrovitch, ready for his speech, stood compressing his crossed fingers, waiting to see if the crack would not come again. One joint cracked.

Already, from the sound of light steps on the stairs, he was aware that she was close, and though he was satisfied with his speech, he felt frightened of the explanation confronting him.

CHAPTER IX

ANNA CAME IN WITH HANGING HEAD, PLAYING WITH THE TASSELS OF HER hood. Her face was brilliant and glowing; but this glow was not one of brightness; it suggested the fearful glow of a conflagration in the midst of a dark night. On seeing her husband, Anna raised her head and smiled, as though she had just waked up.

"You're not in bed? What a wonder!" she said, letting fall her hood, and without stopping, she went on into the dressing-room. "It's late, Alexey Alexandrovitch," she said, when she had gone through the doorway.

"Anna, it's necessary for me to have a talk with you."

"With me?" she said, wonderingly. She came out from behind the door of the dressing-room, and looked at him. "Why, what is it? What about?" she asked, sitting down. "Well, let's talk, if it's so necessary. But it would be better to get to sleep."

Anna said what came to her lips, and marveled, hearing herself, at her own capacity for lying. How simple and natural were her words, and how likely that she was simply sleepy! She felt herself clad in an impenetrable armor of falsehood. She felt that some unseen force had come to her aid and was supporting her.

"Anna, I must warn you," he began.

"Warn me?" she said. "Of what?"

She looked at him so simply, so brightly, that any one who did not know her as her husband knew her could not have noticed anything unnatural, either in the sound or the sense of her words. But to him, knowing her, knowing that whenever he went to bed five minutes later than usual, she noticed it, and asked him the reason; to him, knowing that every joy, every pleasure and pain that she felt she communicated to him at once; to him, now to see that she did not care to notice his state of mind, that she did not care to say a word about herself, meant a great deal. He saw that the inmost recesses of her soul, that had always hitherto lain open before him, were closed against him. More than that, he saw from her tone that she was not even perturbed at that, but as it were said straight out to him: "Yes, it's shut up, and so it must be, and will be in future." Now he experienced a feeling such as a man might have, returning home and finding his own house locked up. "But perhaps the key may yet be found," thought Alexey Alexandrovitch.

"I want to warn you," he said in a low voice, "that through thoughtlessness and lack of caution you may cause yourself to be talked about in society. Your too animated conversation this evening with Count Vronsky" (he enunciated the name firmly and with deliberate emphasis) "attracted attention."

He talked and looked at her laughing eyes, which frightened him now with their impenetrable look, and, as he talked, he felt all the uselessness and idleness of his words.

"You're always like that," she answered as though completely misapprehending him, and of all he had said only taking in the last phrase. "One time you don't like my being dull, and another time you don't like my being lively. I wasn't dull. Does that offend you?"

Alexey Alexandrovitch shivered, and bent his hands to make the joints crack.

"Oh, please, don't do that, I do so dislike it," she said.

"Anna, is this you?" said Alexey Alexandrovitch, quietly making an effort over himself, and restraining the motion of his fingers.

"But what is it all about?" she said, with such genuine and droll wonder. "What do you want of me?"

Alexey Alexandrovitch paused, and rubbed his forehead and his eyes. He saw that instead of doing as he had intended—that is to say, warning his wife against a mistake in the eyes of the world—he had unconsciously become agitated over what was the affair of her conscience, and was struggling against the barrier he fancied between them.

"This is what I meant to say to you," he went on coldly and composedly, "and I beg you to listen to it. I consider jealousy, as you know, a humiliating and degrading feeling, and I shall never allow myself to be influenced by it; but there are certain rules of decorum which cannot be disregarded with impunity. This evening it was not I observed it, but judging by the impression made on the company, every one observed that your conduct and deportment were not altogether what could be desired."

"I positively don't understand," said Anna, shrugging her shoulders.— "He doesn't care," she thought. "But other people noticed it, and that's what upsets him."—"You're not well, Alexey Alexandrovitch," she added, and she got up, and would have gone towards the door; but he moved forward as though he would stop her.

His face was ugly and forbidding, as Anna had never seen him. She stopped, and bending her head back and on one side, began with her rapid hand taking out her hairpins.

"Well, I'm listening to what's to come," she said, calmly and ironically; "and indeed I listen with interest, for I should like to understand what's the matter."

She spoke, and marveled at the confident, calm, and natural tone in which she was speaking, and the choice of the words she used.

"To enter into all the details of your feelings I have no right, and besides, I regard that as useless and even harmful," began Alexey Alexandrovitch. "Ferreting in one's soul, one often ferrets out something that might have lain there unnoticed. Your feelings are an affair of your own conscience; but I am in duty bound to you, to myself, and to God, to point out to you your duties. Our life has been joined, not by man, but by God. That union can only be severed by a crime, and a crime of that nature brings its own chastisement."

"I don't understand a word. And, oh dear! how sleepy I am, unluckily," she said, rapidly passing her hand through her hair, feeling for the remaining hairpins.

"Anna, for God's sake don't speak like that!" he said gently. "Perhaps I am mistaken, but believe me, what I say, I say as much for myself as for you. I am your husband, and I love you."

For an instant her face fell, and the mocking gleam in her eyes died away; but the word love threw her into revolt again. She thought: "Love? Can he love? If he hadn't heard there was such a thing as love, he would never have used the word. He doesn't even know what love is."

"Alexey Alexandrovitch, really I don't understand," she said. "Define what it is you find ..."

"Pardon, let me say all I have to say. I love you. But I am not speaking of myself; the most important persons in this matter are our son and yourself. It may very well be, I repeat, that my words seem to you utterly unnecessary and out of place; it may be that they are called forth by my mistaken impression. In that case, I beg you to forgive me. But if you are conscious yourself of even the smallest foundation for them, then I beg you to think a little, and if your heart prompts you, to speak out to me...."

Alexey Alexandrovitch was unconsciously saying something utterly unlike what he had prepared.

"I have nothing to say. And besides," she said hurriedly, with difficulty repressing a smile, "it's really time to be in bed."

Alexey Alexandrovitch sighed, and, without saying more, went into the bedroom.

When she came into the bedroom, he was already in bed. His lips were sternly compressed, and his eyes looked away from her. Anna got into her bed, and lay expecting every minute that he would begin to speak to her again. She both feared his speaking and wished for it. But he was silent. She waited for a long while without moving, and had forgotten about him. She thought of that other; she pictured him, and felt how her heart was flooded with emotion and guilty delight at the thought of him. Suddenly she heard an even, tranquil snore. For the first instant Alexey Alexandrovitch seemed, as it were, appalled at his own snoring, and ceased; but after an interval of two breathings the snore sounded again, with a new tranquil rhythm.

"It's late, it's late," she whispered with a smile. A long while she lay, not moving, with open eyes, whose brilliance she almost fancied she could herself see in the darkness.

CHAPTER X

FROM THAT TIME A NEW LIFE BEGAN FOR ALEXEY ALEXANDROVITCH AND FOR his wife. Nothing special happened. Anna went out into society, as she had always done, was particularly often at Princess Betsy's, and met Vronsky everywhere. Alexey Alexandrovitch saw this, but could do nothing. All his efforts to draw her into open discussion she confronted with a barrier which he could not penetrate, made up of a sort of amused perplexity. Outwardly everything was the same, but their inner relations were completely changed. Alexey Alexandrovitch, a man of great power in the world of politics, felt himself helpless in this. Like an ox with head bent, submissively he awaited the blow which he felt was lifted over him. Every time he began to think about it, he felt that he must try once more, that by kindness, tenderness, and persuasion there was still hope of saving her, of bringing her back to herself, and every day he made ready to talk to her. But every time he began talking to her, he felt that the spirit of evil and deceit, which had taken possession of her, had possession of him too, and he talked to her in a tone quite unlike that in which he had meant to talk. Involuntarily he talked to her in his habitual tone of jeering at any one who should say what he was saying. And in that tone it was impossible to say what needed to be said to her.

CHAPTER XI

THAT WHICH FOR VRONSKY HAD BEEN ALMOST A WHOLE YEAR THE ONE absorbing desire of his life, replacing all his old desires; that which for Anna had been an impossible, terrible, and even for that reason more entrancing dream of bliss, that desire had been fulfilled. He stood before her, pale, his lower jaw quivering, and besought her to be calm, not knowing how or why.

"Anna! Anna!" he said with a choking voice, "Anna, for pity's sake! ..."

But the louder he spoke, the lower she dropped her once proud and gay, now shame-stricken head, and she bowed down and sank from the sofa where she was sitting, down on the floor, at his feet; she would have fallen on the carpet if he had not held her.

"My God! Forgive me!" she said, sobbing, pressing his hands to her bosom.

She felt so sinful, so guilty, that nothing was left her but to humiliate herself and beg forgiveness; and as now there was no one in her life but him, to him she addressed her prayer for forgiveness. Looking at him, she had a physical sense of her humiliation, and she could say nothing more. He felt what a murderer must feel, when he sees the body he has robbed of life. That body, robbed by him of life, was their love, the first stage of their love. There was something awful and revolting in the memory of what had been bought at this fearful price of shame. Shame at their spiritual nakedness crushed her and infected him. But in spite of all the murderer's horror before the body of his victim, he must hack it to pieces, hide the body, must use what he has gained by his murder.

And with fury, as it were with passion, the murderer falls on the body, and drags it and hacks at it; so he covered her face and shoulders with kisses. She held his hand, and did not stir. "Yes, these kisses—that is what has been bought by this shame. Yes, and one hand, which will always be mine—the hand of my accomplice." She lifted up that hand and kissed it. He sank on his knees and tried to see her face; but she hid it, and said nothing. At last, as though making an effort over herself, she got up and pushed him away. Her face was still as beautiful, but it was only the more pitiful for that.

"All is over," she said; "I have nothing but you. Remember that."

"I can never forget what is my whole life. For one instant of this happiness ..."

"Happiness!" she said with horror and loathing and her horror unconsciously infected him. "For pity's sake, not a word, not a word more."

She rose quickly and moved away from him.

"Not a word more," she repeated, and with a look of chill despair, incomprehensible to him, she parted from him. She felt that at that moment she could not put into words the sense of shame, of rapture, and of horror at this stepping into a new life, and she did not want to speak of it, to vulgarize this feeling by inappropriate words. But later too, and the next day and the third day, she still found no words in which she could express the complexity of her feelings; indeed, she could not even find thoughts in which she could clearly think out all that was in her soul.

She said to herself: "No, just now I can't think of it, later on, when I am calmer." But this calm for thought never came; every time the thought rose of what she had done and what would happen to her, and what she ought to do, a horror came over her and she drove those thoughts away.

"Later, later," she said—"when I am calmer."

But in dreams, when she had no control over her thoughts, her position presented itself to her in all its hideous nakedness. One dream haunted her almost every night. She dreamed that both were her husbands at once, that both were lavishing caresses on her. Alexey Alexandrovitch was weeping, kissing her hands, and saying, "How happy we are now!" And Alexey Vronsky was there too, and he too was her husband. And she was marveling that it had once seemed impossible to her, was explaining to them, laughing, that this was ever so much simpler, and that now both of them were happy and contented. But this dream weighed on her like a nightmare, and she awoke from it in terror.

CHAPTER XII

IN THE EARLY DAYS AFTER HIS RETURN FROM MOSCOW, WHENEVER LEVIN shuddered and grew red, remembering the disgrace of his rejection, he said to himself: "This was just how I used to shudder and blush, thinking myself utterly lost, when I was plucked in physics and did not get my remove; and how I thought myself utterly ruined after I had mismanaged that affair of my sister's that was intrusted to me. And yet, now that years have passed, I recall it and wonder that it could distress me so much. It will be the same thing too with this trouble. Time will go by and I shall not mind about this either."

But three months had passed and he had not left off minding about it; and it was as painful for him to think of it as it had been those first days. He could not be at peace because after dreaming so long of family life, and feeling himself so ripe for it, he was still not married, and was further than ever from marriage. He was painfully conscious himself, as were all about him, that at his years it is not well for man to be alone. He remembered how before starting for Moscow he had once said to his cowman Nikolay, a simple-hearted peasant, whom he liked talking to: "Well, Nikolay! I mean to get married," and how Nikolay had promptly answered, as of a matter on which there could be no possible doubt: "And high time too, Konstantin Dmitrievitch." But marriage had now become further off than ever. The place was taken, and whenever he tried to imagine any of the girls he knew in that place, he felt that it was utterly impossible. Moreover, the recollection of the rejection and the part he had played in the affair tortured him with shame. However often he told himself that he was in no wise to blame in it, that recollection, like other humiliating reminiscences of a similar kind, made him twinge and blush. There had been in his past, as in every man's, actions, recognized by him as bad, for which his conscience ought to have tormented him; but the memory of these evil actions was far from causing him so much suffering as those trivial but humiliating reminiscences. These wounds never healed. And with these memories was now ranged his rejection and the pitiful position in which he must have appeared to others that evening. But time and work did their part. Bitter memories were more and more covered up by the incidents—paltry in his eyes, but really important—of his country life. Every week he thought less often of Kitty. He was impatiently looking forward to the news that she was married, or just going to be married, hoping that such news would, like having a tooth out, completely cure him.

Meanwhile spring came on, beautiful and kindly, without the delays and treacheries of spring,—one of those rare springs in which plants, beasts, and man rejoice alike. This lovely spring roused Levin still more, and strengthened him in his resolution of renouncing all his past and building up his lonely life firmly and independently. Though many of the plans with which he had returned to the country had not been carried out, still his most important resolution—that of purity—had been kept by him. He was free from that shame, which had usually harassed him after a fall; and he could look every one straight in the face. In February he had received a letter from Marya Nikolaevna telling him that his brother Nikolay's health was getting worse, but that he would not take advice, and in consequence of this letter Levin went to Moscow to his brother's and succeeded in persuading him to see a doctor and to go to a watering-place abroad. He succeeded so well in persuading his brother, and in lending him money for the journey without irritating him, that he was satisfied with himself in that matter. In addition to his farming, which called for special attention in spring, and in addition to reading, Levin had begun that winter a work on agriculture, the plan of which turned on taking into account the character of the laborer on the land as one of the unalterable data of the question, like the climate and the soil, and consequently deducing all the principles of scientific culture, not simply from the data of soil and climate, but from the data of soil, climate, and a certain unalterable character of the laborer. Thus, in spite of his solitude, or in consequence of his solitude, his life was exceedingly full. Only rarely he suffered from an unsatisfied desire to communicate his stray ideas to some one besides Agafea Mihalovna. With her indeed he not infrequently fell into discussion upon physics, the theory of agriculture, and especially philosophy; philosophy was Agafea Mihalovna's favorite subject.

Spring was slow in unfolding. For the last few weeks it had been steadily fine frosty weather. In the daytime it thawed in the sun, but at night there were even seven degrees of frost. There was such a frozen surface on the snow that they drove the wagons anywhere off the roads. Easter came in the snow. Then all of a sudden, on Easter Monday, a warm wind sprang up, storm-clouds swooped down, and for three days and three nights the warm, driving rain fell in streams. On Thursday the wind dropped, and a thick gray fog brooded over the land as though hiding the mysteries of the transformations that were being wrought in nature. Behind the fog there was the flowing of water, the cracking and floating of ice, the swift rush of turbid, foaming torrents; and on the following Monday, in the evening, the fog parted, the storm-clouds split up into little curling crests of cloud, the sky cleared, and the real spring had come. In the morning the sun rose brilliant and quickly wore away the thin layer of ice that covered the water, and all the warm air was quivering with the steam that rose up from the quickened earth. The old grass looked greener, and the young grass thrust up its tiny blades; the buds of the guelder-rose and of the currant and the sticky birch-buds were swollen with sap, and an exploring bee was humming about the golden blossoms that studded the willow. Larks trilled unseen above the velvety green fields and the ice-covered stubble-land; peewits wailed over the low lands and marshes flooded by the pools; cranes and wild geese flew high across the sky uttering their spring calls. The cattle, bald in patches where the new hair had not grown yet, lowed in the pastures; the bow-legged lambs frisked round their bleating mothers. Nimble children ran about the drying paths, covered with the prints of bare feet. There was a merry chatter of peasant women over their linen at the pond, and the ring of axes in the yard, where the peasants were repairing ploughs and harrows. The real spring had come.

CHAPTER XIII

LEVIN PUT ON HIS BIG BOOTS, AND, FOR THE FIRST TIME, A CLOTH JACKET, instead of his fur cloak, and went out to look after his farm, stepping over streams of water that flashed in the sunshine and dazzled his eyes, and treading one minute on ice and the next into sticky mud.

Spring is the time of plans and projects. And, as he came out into the farmyard, Levin, like a tree in spring that knows not what form will be taken by the young shoots and twigs imprisoned in its swelling buds, hardly knew what undertakings he was going to begin upon now in the farm-work that was so dear to him. But he felt that he was full of the most splendid plans and projects. First of all he went to the cattle. The cows had been let out into their paddock, and their smooth sides were already shining with their new, sleek, spring coats; they basked in the sunshine and lowed to go to the meadow. Levin gazed admiringly at the cows he knew so intimately to the minutest detail of their condition, and gave orders for them to be driven out into the meadow, and the calves to be let into the paddock. The herdsman ran gaily to get ready for the meadow. The cowherd girls, picking up their petticoats, ran splashing through the mud with bare legs, still white, not yet brown from the sun, waving brush-wood in their hands, chasing the calves that frolicked in the mirth of spring.

After admiring the young ones of that year, who were particularly fine—the early calves were the size of a peasant's cow, and Pava's daughter, at three months old, was as big as a yearling—Levin gave orders for a trough to be brought out and for them to be fed in the paddock. But it appeared that as the paddock had not been used during the winter, the hurdles made in the autumn for it were broken. He sent for the carpenter, who, according to his orders, ought to have been at work at the thrashing-machine. But it appeared that the carpenter was repairing the harrows, which ought to have been repaired before Lent. This was very annoying to Levin. It was annoying to come upon that everlasting slovenliness in the farm-work against which he had been striving with all his might for so many years. The hurdles, as he ascertained, being not wanted in winter, had been carried to the cart-horses' stable; and there broken, as they were of light construction, only meant for folding calves. Moreover, it was apparent also that the harrows and all the agricultural implements, which he had directed to be looked over and repaired in the winter, for which very purpose he had hired three carpenters, had not been put into repair, and the harrows were being repaired when they ought to have been harrowing the field. Levin sent for his bailiff, but immediately went off himself to look for him. The bailiff, beaming all over, like every one that day, in a sheepskin bordered with astrachan, came out of the barn, twisting a bit of straw in his hands.

"Why isn't the carpenter at the thrashing-machine?"

"Oh, I meant to tell you yesterday, the harrows want repairing. Here it's time they got to work in the fields."

"But what were they doing in the winter, then?"

"But what did you want the carpenter for?"

"Where are the hurdles for the calves' paddock?"

"I ordered them to be got ready. What would you have with those peasants!" said the bailiff, with a wave of his hand.

"It's not those peasants but this bailiff!" said Levin, getting angry. "Why, what do I keep you for?" he cried. But, bethinking himself that this would not help matters, he stopped short in the middle of a sentence, and merely sighed. "Well, what do you say? Can sowing begin?" he asked, after a pause.

"Behind Turkin to-morrow or the next day they might begin."

"And the clover?"

"I've sent Vassily and Mishka; they're sowing. Only I don't know if they'll manage to get through; it's so slushy."

"How many acres?"

"About fifteen."

"Why not sow all?" cried Levin.

That they were only sowing the clover on fifteen acres, not on all the forty-five, was still more annoying to him. Clover, as he knew, both from books and from his own experience, never did well except when it was sown as early as possible, almost in the snow. And yet Levin could never get this done.

"There's no one to send. What would you have with such a set of peasants? Three haven't turned up. And there's Semyon ..."

"Well, you should have taken some men from the thatching."

"And so I have, as it is."

"Where are the peasants, then?"

"Five are making *compôte*" (which meant compost), "four are shifting the oats for fear of a touch of mildew, Konstantin Dmitrievitch."

Levin knew very well that "a touch of mildew" meant that his English seed oats were already ruined. Again they had not done as he had ordered.

"Why, but I told you during Lent to put in pipes," he cried.

"Don't put yourself out; we shall get it all done in time."

Levin waved his hand angrily, went into the granary to glance at the oats, and then to the stable. The oats were not yet spoiled. But the peasants were carrying the oats in spades when they might simply let them slide down into the lower granary; and arranging for this to be done, and taking two workmen from there for sowing clover, Levin got over his vexation with the bailiff. Indeed, it was such a lovely day that one could not be angry.

"Ignat!" he called to the coachman, who, with his sleeves tucked up, was washing the carriage wheels, "saddle me ..."

"Which, sir?"

"Well, let it be Kolpik."

"Yes, sir."

While they were saddling his horse, Levin again called up the bailiff, who was hanging about in sight, to make it up with him, and began talking to him about the spring operations before them, and his plans for the farm.

The wagons were to begin carting manure earlier, so as to get all done before the early mowing. And the ploughing of the further land to go on without a break so as to let it ripen lying fallow. And the mowing to be all done by hired labor, not on half-profits. The bailiff listened attentively, and obviously made an effort to approve of his employer's projects. But still he had that look Levin knew so well that always irritated him, a look of hopelessness and despondency. That look said: "That's all very well, but as God wills."

Nothing mortified Levin so much as that tone. But it was the tone common to all the bailiffs he had ever had. They had all taken up that attitude to his plans, and so now he was not angered by it, but mortified, and felt all the more roused to struggle against this, as it seemed, elemental force continually ranged against him, for which he could find no other expression than "as God wills."

"If we can manage it, Konstantin Dmitrievitch," said the bailiff.

"Why ever shouldn't you manage it?"

"We positively must have another fifteen laborers. And they don't turn up. There were some here to-day asking seventy roubles for the summer."

Levin was silent. Again he was brought face to face with that opposing force. He knew that however much they tried, they could not hire more than forty—thirty-seven perhaps or thirty-eight—laborers for a reasonable sum. Some forty had been taken on, and there were no more. But still he could not help struggling against it.

"Send to Sury, to Tchefirovka; if they don't come we must look for them."

"Oh, I'll send, to be sure," said Vassily Fedorovitch despondently. "But there are the horses, too, they're not good for much."

"We'll get some more. I know, of course," Levin added laughing, "you always want to do with as little and as poor quality as possible; but this year I'm not going to let you have things your own way. I'll see to everything myself."

"Why, I don't think you take much rest as it is. It cheers us up to work under the master's eye...."

"So they're sowing clover behind the Birch Dale? I'll go and have a look at them," he said, getting on to the little bay cob, Kolpik, who was led up by the coachman.

"You can't get across the streams, Konstantin Dmitrievitch," the coachman shouted.

"All right, I'll go by the forest."

And Levin rode through the slush of the farmyard to the gate and out into the open country, his good little horse, after his long inactivity, stepping out gallantly, snorting over the pools, and asking, as it were, for guidance. If Levin had felt happy before in the cattle-pens and farmyard, he felt happier yet in the open country. Swaying rhythmically with the ambling paces of his good little cob, drinking in the warm yet fresh scent of the snow and the air, as he rode through his forest over the crumbling, wasted snow, still left in parts, and covered with dissolving tracks, he rejoiced over every tree, with the moss reviving on its bark and the buds swelling on its shoots. When he came out of the forest, in the immense plain before him, his grass fields stretched in an unbroken carpet of green, without one bare place or swamp, only spotted here and there in the hollows with patches of melting snow. He was not put out of temper even by the sight of the peasants' horses and colts trampling down his young grass (he told a peasant he met to drive them out), nor by the sarcastic and stupid reply of the peasant Ipat, whom he met on the way, and asked, "Well, Ipat, shall we soon be sowing?" "We must get the ploughing done first, Konstantin Dmitrievitch," answered Ipat. The further he rode, the happier he became, and plans for the land rose to his mind each better than the last; to plant all his fields with hedges along the southern borders, so that the snow should not lie under them; to divide them up into six fields of arable and three of pasture and hay; to build a cattle-yard at the further end of the estate, and to dig a pond and to construct movable pens for the cattle as a means of manuring the land. And then eight hundred acres of wheat, three hundred of potatoes, and four hundred of clover, and not one acre exhausted.

Absorbed in such dreams, carefully keeping his horse by the hedges, so as not to trample his young crops, he rode up to the laborers who had been sent to sow clover. A cart with the seed in it was standing, not at the edge, but in the middle of the crop, and the winter-corn had been torn up by the wheels and trampled by the horse. Both the laborers were sitting in the hedge, probably smoking a pipe together. The earth in the cart, with which the seed was mixed, was not crushed to powder, but crusted together or adhering in clods. Seeing the master, the laborer, Vassily, went towards the cart, while Mishka set to work sowing. This was not as it should be, but with the laborers Levin seldom lost his temper. When Vassily came up, Levin told him to lead the horse to the hedge.

"It's all right, sir, it'll spring up again," responded Vassily.

"Please don't argue," said Levin, "but do as you're told."

"Yes, sir," answered Vassily, and he took the horse's head. "What a sowing, Konstantin Dmitrievitch," he said, hesitating; "first rate. Only it's a work to get about! You drag a ton of earth on your shoes."

"Why is it you have earth that's not sifted?" said Levin.

"Well, we crumble it up," answered Vassily, taking up some seed and rolling the earth in his palms.

Vassily was not to blame for their having filled up his cart with unsifted earth, but still it was annoying.

Levin had more than once already tried a way he knew for stifling his anger, and turning all that seemed dark right again, and he tried that way now. He watched how Mishka strode along, swinging the huge clods of earth that clung to each foot; and getting off his horse, he took the sieve from Vassily and started sowing himself.

"Where did you stop?"

Vassily pointed to the mark with his foot, and Levin went forward as best he could, scattering the seed on the land. Walking was as difficult as on a bog, and by the time Levin had ended the row he was in a great heat, and he stopped and gave up the sieve to Vassily.

"Well, master, when summer's here, mind you don't scold me for these rows," said Vassily.

"Eh?" said Levin cheerily, already feeling the effect of his method.

"Why, you'll see in the summer-time. It'll look different. Look you where I sowed last spring. How I did work at it! I do my best, Konstantin Dmitrievitch, d'ye see, as I would for my own father. I don't like bad work myself, nor would I let another man do it. What's good for the master's good for us too. To look out yonder now," said Vassily, pointing, "it does one's heart good."

"It's a lovely spring, Vassily."

"Why, it's a spring such as the old men don't remember the like of. I was up home; an old man up there has sown wheat too, about an acre of it. He was saying you wouldn't know it from rye."

"Have you been sowing wheat long?"

"Why, sir, it was you taught us the year before last. You gave me two measures. We sold about eight bushels and sowed a rood."

"Well, mind you crumble up the clods," said Levin, going towards his horse, "and keep an eye on Mishka. And if there's a good crop you shall have half a rouble for every acre."

"Humbly thankful. We are very well content, sir, as it is."

Levin got on his horse and rode towards the field where was last year's clover, and the one which was ploughed ready for the spring corn.

The crop of clover coming up in the stubble was magnificent. It had survived everything, and stood up vividly green through the broken stalks of last year's wheat. The horse sank in up to the pasterns, and he drew each hoof with a sucking sound out of the half-thawed ground. Over the ploughland riding was utterly impossible; the horse could only keep a foothold where there was ice, and in the thawing furrows he sank deep in at each step. The ploughland was in splendid condition; in a couple of days it would be fit for harrowing and sowing. Everything was capital, everything was cheering. Levin rode back across the streams, hoping the water would have gone down. And he did in fact get across, and startled two ducks. "There must be snipe too," he thought, and just as he reached the turning homewards he met the forest-keeper, who confirmed his theory about the snipe.

Levin went home at a trot, so as to have time to eat his dinner and get his gun ready for the evening.

CHAPTER XIV

As HE RODE UP TO THE HOUSE IN THE HAPPIEST FRAME OF MIND, LEVIN heard the bell ring at the side of the principal entrance of the house.

"Yes, that's some one from the railway station," he thought, "just the time to be here from the Moscow train…. Who could it be? What if it's brother Nikolay? He did say: 'Maybe I'll go to the waters, or maybe I'll come down to you.'" He felt dismayed and vexed for the first minute, that his brother Nikolay's presence should come to disturb his happy mood of spring. But he felt ashamed of the feeling, and at once he opened, as it were, the arms of his soul, and with a softened feeling of joy and expectation, now he hoped with all his heart that it was his brother. He pricked up his horse, and riding out from behind the acacias he saw a hired three-horse sledge from the railway station, and a gentleman in a fur coat. It was not his brother. "Oh, if it were only some nice person one could talk to a little!" he thought.

"Ah," cried Levin joyfully, flinging up both his hands. "Here's a delightful visitor! Ah, how glad I am to see you!" he shouted, recognizing Stepan Arkadyevitch.

"I shall find out for certain whether she's married, or when she's going to be married," he thought. And on that delicious spring day he felt that the thought of her did not hurt him at all.

"Well, you didn't expect me, eh?" said Stepan Arkadyevitch, getting out of the sledge, splashed with mud on the bridge of his nose, on his cheek, and on his eyebrows, but radiant with health and good spirits. "I've come to see you in the first place," he said, embracing and kissing him, "to have some stand-shooting second, and to sell the forest at Ergushovo third."

"Delightful! What a spring we're having! How ever did you get along in a sledge?"

"In a cart it would have been worse still, Konstantin Dmitrievitch," answered the driver, who knew him.

"Well, I'm very, very glad to see you," said Levin, with a genuine smile of childlike delight.

Levin led his friend to the room set apart for visitors, where Stepan Arkadyevitch's things were carried also—a bag, a gun in a case, a satchel for cigars. Leaving him there to wash and change his clothes, Levin went off to the counting-house to speak about the ploughing and clover. Agafea Mihalovna, always very anxious for the credit of the house, met him in the hall with inquiries about dinner.

"Do just as you like, only let it be as soon as possible," he said, and went to the bailiff.

When he came back, Stepan Arkadyevitch, washed and combed, came out of his room with a beaming smile, and they went up-stairs together.

"Well, I am glad I managed to get away to you! Now I shall understand what the mysterious business is that you are always absorbed in here. No, really, I envy you. What a house, how nice it all is! So bright, so cheerful!" said Stepan Arkadyevitch, forgetting that it was not always spring and fine weather like that day. "And your nurse is simply charming! A pretty maid in an apron might be even more agreeable, perhaps; but for your severe monastic style it does very well."

Stepan Arkadyevitch told him many interesting pieces of news; especially interesting to Levin was the news that his brother, Sergey Ivanovitch, was intending to pay him a visit in the summer.

Not one word did Stepan Arkadyevitch say in reference to Kitty and the Shtcherbatskys; he merely gave him greetings from his wife. Levin was grateful to him for his delicacy and was very glad of his visitor. As always happened with him during his solitude, a mass of ideas and feelings had been accumulating within him, which he could not communicate to those about him.

And now he poured out upon Stepan Arkadyevitch his poetic joy in the spring, and his failures and plans for the land, and his thoughts and criticisms on the books he had been reading, and the idea of his own book, the basis of which really was, though he was unaware of it himself, a criticism of all the old books on agriculture. Stepan Arkadyevitch, always charming, understanding everything at the slightest reference, was particularly charming on this visit, and Levin noticed in him a special tenderness, as it were, and a new tone of respect that flattered him.

The efforts of Agafea Mihalovna and the cook, that the dinner should be particularly good, only ended in the two famished friends attacking the pre-liminary course, eating a great deal of bread-and-butter, salt goose and salted mushrooms, and in Levin's finally ordering the soup to be served without the accompaniment of little pies, with which the cook had particularly meant to impress their visitor. But though Stepan Arkadyevitch was accustomed to very different dinners, he thought everything excellent: the herb-brandy, and the bread, and the butter, and above all the salt goose and the mushrooms, and the nettle soup, and the chicken in white sauce, and the white Crimean wine— everything was superb and delicious.

"Splendid, splendid!" he said, lighting a fat cigar after the roast. "I feel as if, coming to you, I had landed on a peaceful shore after the noise and jolting of a steamer. And so you maintain that the laborer himself is an element to be studied and to regulate the choice of methods in agriculture. Of course, I'm an ignorant outsider; but I should fancy theory and its application will have its influence on the laborer too."

"Yes, but wait a bit. I'm not talking of political economy, I'm talking of the science of agriculture. It ought to be like the natural sciences, and to observe given phenomena and the laborer in his economic, ethnographical ..."

At that instant Agafea Mihalovna came in with jam.

"Oh, Agafea Mihalovna," said Stepan Arkadyevitch, kissing the tips of his plump fingers, "what salt goose, what herb-brandy! ...What do you think, isn't it time to start, Kostya?" he added.

Levin looked out of the window at the sun sinking behind the bare tree-tops of the forest.

"Yes, it's time," he said. "Kouzma, get ready the trap," and he ran down-stairs.

Stepan Arkadyevitch, going down, carefully took the canvas cover off his varnished gun-case with his own hands, and opening it, began to get ready his expensive new-fashioned gun. Kouzma, who already scented a big tip, never left Stepan Arkadyevitch's side, and put on him both his stockings and boots, a task which Stepan Arkadyevitch readily left him.

"Kostya, give orders that if the merchant Ryabinin comes … I told him to come to-day, he's to be brought in and to wait for me …"

"Why, do you mean to say you're selling the forest to Ryabinin?"

"Yes. Do you know him?"

"To be sure I do. I have had to do business with him, 'positively and conclusively.'"

Stepan Arkadyevitch laughed. "Positively and conclusively" were the merchant's favorite words.

"Yes, it's wonderfully funny the way he talks. She knows where her master's going!" he added, patting Laska, who hung about Levin, whining and licking his hands, his boots, and his gun.

The trap was already at the steps when they went out.

"I told them to bring the trap round; or would you rather walk?"

"No, we'd better drive," said Stepan Arkadyevitch, getting into the trap. He sat down, tucked the tiger-skin rug round him, and lighted a cigar. "How is it you don't smoke? A cigar is a sort of thing, not exactly a pleasure, but the crown and outward sign of pleasure. Come, this is life! How splendid it is! This is how I should like to live!"

"Why, who prevents you?" said Levin, smiling.

"No, you're a lucky man! You've got everything you like. You like horses— and you have them; dogs—you have them; shooting— you have it; farming you have it."

"Perhaps because I rejoice in what I have, and don't fret for what I haven't," said Levin, thinking of Kitty.

Stepan Arkadyevitch comprehended, looked at him, but said nothing.

Levin was grateful to Oblonsky for noticing, with his never-failing tact, that he dreaded conversation about the Shtcherbatskys, and so saying nothing about them. But now Levin was longing to find out what was tormenting him so, yet he had not the courage to begin.

"Come, tell me how things are going with you," said Levin, bethinking himself that it was not nice of him to think only of himself.

Stepan Arkadyevitch's eyes sparkled merrily.

"You don't admit, I know, that one can be fond of new rolls when one has had one's rations of bread—to your mind it's a crime; but I don't count life as life without love," he said, taking Levin's question his own way. "What am I to do? I'm made that way. And really, one does so little harm to any one, and gives oneself so much pleasure …"

"What! is there something new, then?" queried Levin.

"Yes, my boy, there is! There, do you see, you know the type of Ossian's women ... Women, such as one sees in dreams ... Well, these women are sometimes to be met in reality... and these women are terrible. Woman, don't you know, is such a subject that however much you study it, it's always perfectly new."

"Well, then, it would be better not to study it."

"No. Some mathematician has said that enjoyment lies in the search for truth, not in the finding it."

Levin listened in silence, and in spite of all the efforts he made, he could not in the least enter into the feelings of his friend and understand his sentiments and the charm of studying such women.

CHAPTER XV

T HE PLACE FIXED ON FOR THE STAND-SHOOTING WAS NOT FAR ABOVE A stream in a little aspen copse. On reaching the copse, Levin got out of the trap and led Oblonsky to a corner of a mossy, swampy glade, already quite free from snow. He went back himself to a double birch-tree on the other side, and leaning his gun on the fork of a dead lower branch, he took off his full overcoat, fastened his belt again, and worked his arms to see if they were free.

Gray old Laska, who had followed them, sat down warily opposite him and pricked up her ears. The sun was setting behind a thick forest, and in the glow of sunset the birch-trees, dotted about in the aspen copse, stood out clearly with their hanging twigs, and their buds swollen almost to bursting.

From the thickest parts of the copse, where the snow still remained, came the faint sound of narrow winding threads of water running away. Tiny birds twittered, and now and then fluttered from tree to tree.

In the pauses of complete stillness there came the rustle of last year's leaves, stirred by the thawing of the earth and the growth of the grass.

"Imagine! One can hear and see the grass growing!" Levin said to himself, noticing a wet, slate-colored aspen leaf moving beside a blade of young grass. He stood, listened, and gazed sometimes down at the wet mossy ground, sometimes at Laska listening all alert, sometimes at the sea of bare tree-tops that stretched on the slope below him, sometimes at the darkening sky, covered with white streaks of cloud.

A hawk flew high over a forest far away with slow sweep of its wings; another flew with exactly the same motion in the same direction and vanished. The birds twittered more and more loudly and busily in the thicket. An owl hooted not far off, and Laska, starting, stepped cautiously a few steps forward, and putting her head on one side, began to listen intently. Beyond the stream was heard the cuckoo. Twice she uttered her usual cuckoo-call, and then gave a hoarse, hurried call and broke down.

"Imagine! the cuckoo already!" said Stepan Arkadyevitch, coming out from behind a bush.

"Yes, I hear it," answered Levin, reluctantly breaking the stillness with his voice, which sounded disagreeable to himself. "Now it's coming!"

Stepan Arkadyevitch's figure again went behind the bush, and Levin saw nothing but the bright flash of a match, followed by the red glow and blue smoke of a cigarette.

"Tchk! tchk!" came the snapping sound of Stepan Arkadyevitch cocking his gun.

"What's that cry?" asked Oblonsky, drawing Levin's attention to a prolonged cry, as though a colt were whinnying in a high voice, in play.

"Oh, don't you know it? That's the hare. But enough talking! Listen, it's flying!" almost shrieked Levin, cocking his gun.

They heard a shrill whistle in the distance, and in the exact time, so well-known to the sportsman, two seconds later—another, a third, and after the third whistle the hoarse, guttural cry could be heard.

Levin looked about him to right and to left, and there, just facing him against the dusky blue sky above the confused mass of tender shoots of the aspens, he saw the flying bird. It was flying straight towards him; the guttural cry, like the even tearing of some strong stuff, sounded close to his ear; the long beak and neck of the bird could be seen, and at the very instant when Levin was taking aim, behind the bush where Oblonsky stood, there was a flash of red lightning: the bird dropped like an arrow, and darted upwards again. Again came the red flash and the sound of a blow, and fluttering its wings as though trying to keep up in the air, the bird halted, stopped still an instant, and fell with a heavy splash on the slushy ground.

"Can I have missed it?" shouted Stepan Arkadyevitch, who could not see for the smoke.

"Here it is!" said Levin, pointing to Laska, who with one ear raised, wagging the end of her shaggy tail, came slowly back as though she would prolong the pleasure, and as it were smiling, brought the dead bird to her master. "Well,

I'm glad you were successful," said Levin, who, at the same time, had a sense of envy that he had not succeeded in shooting the snipe.

"It was a bad shot from the right barrel," responded Stepan Arkadyevitch, loading his gun. "Sh … it's flying!"

The shrill whistles rapidly following one another were heard again. Two snipe, playing and chasing one another, and only whistling, not crying, flew straight at the very heads of the sportsmen. There was the report of four shots, and like swallows the snipe turned swift somersaults in the air and vanished from sight.

The stand-shooting was capital. Stepan Arkadyevitch shot two more birds and Levin two, of which one was not found. It began to get dark. Venus, bright and silvery, shone with her soft light low down in the west behind the birch-trees, and high up in the east twinkled the red lights of Arcturus. Over his head Levin made out the stars of the Great Bear and lost them again. The snipe had ceased flying; but Levin resolved to stay a little longer, till Venus, which he saw below a branch of birch, should be above it, and the stars of the Great Bear should be perfectly plain. Venus had risen above the branch, and the ear of the Great Bear with its shaft was now all plainly visible against the dark blue sky, yet still he waited.

"Isn't it time to go home?" said Stepan Arkadyevitch.

It was quite still now in the copse, and not a bird was stirring.

"Let's stay a little while," answered Levin.

"As you like."

They were standing now about fifteen paces from one another.

"Stiva!" said Levin unexpectedly; "how is it you don't tell me whether your sister-in-law's married yet, or when she's going to be?"

Levin felt so resolute and serene that no answer, he fancied, could affect him. But he had never dreamed of what Stepan Arkadyevitch replied.

"She's never thought of being married, and isn't thinking of it; but she's very ill, and the doctors have sent her abroad. They're positively afraid she may not live."

"What!" cried Levin. "Very ill? What is wrong with her? How has she … ?"

While they were saying this, Laska, with ears pricked up, was looking upwards at the sky, and reproachfully at them.

"They have chosen a time to talk," she was thinking. "It's on the wing … Here it is, yes, it is. They'll miss it," thought Laska.

But at that very instant both suddenly heard a shrill whistle which, as it were, smote on their ears, and both suddenly seized their guns and two flashes gleamed, and two bangs sounded at the very same instant. The snipe flying high above instantly folded its wings and fell into a thicket, bending down the delicate shoots.

"Splendid! Together!" cried Levin, and he ran with Laska into the thicket to look for the snipe.

"Oh, yes, what was it that was unpleasant?" he wondered. "Yes, Kitty's ill.... Well, it can't be helped; I'm very sorry," he thought.

"She's found it! Isn't she a clever thing?" he said, taking the warm bird from Laska's mouth and packing it into the almost full game-bag. "I've got it, Stiva!" he shouted.

CHAPTER XVI

ON THE WAY HOME LEVIN ASKED ALL DETAILS OF KITTY'S ILLNESS AND THE Shtcherbatskys' plans, and though he would have been ashamed to admit it, he was pleased at what he heard. He was pleased that there was still hope, and still more pleased that she should be suffering who had made him suffer so much. But when Stepan Arkadyevitch began to speak of the causes of Kitty's illness, and mentioned Vronsky's name, Levin cut him short.

"I have no right whatever to know family matters, and, to tell the truth, no interest in them either."

Stepan Arkadyevitch smiled hardly perceptibly, catching the instantaneous change he knew so well in Levin's face, which had become as gloomy as it had been bright a minute before.

"Have you quite settled about the forest with Ryabinin?" asked Levin.

"Yes, it's settled. The price is magnificent; thirty-eight thousand. Eight straight away, and the rest in six years. I've been bothering about it for ever so long. No one would give more."

"Then you've as good as given away your forest for nothing," said Levin gloomily.

"How do you mean for nothing?" said Stepan Arkadyevitch with a good-humored smile, knowing that nothing would be right in Levin's eyes now.

"Because the forest is worth at least a hundred and fifty roubles the acre," answered Levin.

"Oh, these farmers!" said Stepan Arkadyevitch playfully. "Your tone of contempt for us poor townsfolk! ... But when it comes to business, we do it better than anyone. I assure you I have reckoned it all out," he said, "and the forest is fetching a very good price—so much so that I'm afraid of this fellow's crying off, in fact. You know it's not 'timber,'" said Stepan Arkadyevitch, hoping by this distinction to convince Levin completely of the unfairness of his doubts. "And it won't run to more than twenty-five yards of fagots per acre, and he's giving me at the rate of seventy roubles the acre."

Levin smiled contemptuously. "I know," he thought, "that fashion not only in him, but in all city people, who, after being twice in ten years in the country, pick up two or three phrases and use them in season and out of season, firmly persuaded that they know all about it. '*Timber, run to so many yards the acre.*' He says those words without understanding them himself."

"I wouldn't attempt to teach you what you write about in your office," said he, "and if need arose, I should come to you to ask about it. But you're so positive you know all the lore of the forest. It's difficult. Have you counted the trees?"

"How count the trees?" said Stepan Arkadyevitch, laughing, still trying to draw his friend out of his ill-temper. "Count the sands of the sea, number the stars. Some higher power might do it."

"Oh, well, the higher power of Ryabinin can. Not a single merchant ever buys a forest without counting the trees, unless they get it given them for nothing, as you're doing now. I know your forest. I go there every year shooting, and your forest's worth a hundred and fifty roubles an acre paid down, while he's giving you sixty by installments. So that in fact you're making him a present of thirty thousand."

"Come, don't let your imagination run away with you," said Stepan Arkadyevitch piteously. "Why was it none would give it, then?"

"Why, because he has an understanding with the merchants; he's bought them off. I've had to do with all of them; I know them. They're not merchants, you know: they're speculators. He wouldn't look at a bargain that gave him ten, fifteen per cent profit, but holds back to buy a rouble's worth for twenty kopecks."

"Well, enough of it! You're out of temper."

"Not the least," said Levin gloomily, as they drove up to the house.

At the steps there stood a trap tightly covered with iron and leather, with a sleek horse tightly harnessed with broad collar-straps. In the trap sat the chubby, tightly belted clerk who served Ryabinin as coachman. Ryabinin himself was already in the house, and met the friends in the hall. Ryabinin was a tall, thinnish, middle-aged man, with mustache and a projecting clean-shaven chin, and prominent muddy-looking eyes. He was dressed in a long-skirted blue coat, with buttons below the waist at the back, and wore high boots wrinkled over the ankles and straight over the calf, with big galoshes drawn over them. He rubbed his face with his handkerchief, and wrapping round him his coat, which sat extremely well as it was, he greeted them with a smile, holding out his hand to Stepan Arkadyevitch, as though he wanted to catch something.

"So here you are," said Stepan Arkadyevitch, giving him his hand."That's capital."

"I did not venture to disregard your excellency's commands, though the road was extremely bad. I positively walked the whole way, but I am here at my time. Konstantin Dmitrievitch, my respects"; he turned to Levin, trying to seize his hand too. But Levin, scowling, made as though he did not notice his hand, and took out the snipe. "Your honors have been diverting yourselves with the chase? What kind of bird may it be, pray?" added Ryabinin, looking contemptuously at the snipe: "a great delicacy, I suppose." And he shook his head disapprovingly, as though he had grave doubts whether this game were worth the candle.

"Would you like to go into my study?" Levin said in French to Stepan Arkadyevitch, scowling morosely. "Go into my study; you can talk there."

"Quite so, where you please," said Ryabinin with contemptuous dignity, as though wishing to make it felt that others might be in difficulties as to how to behave, but that he could never be in any difficulty about anything.

On entering the study Ryabinin looked about, as his habit was, as though seeking the holy picture, but when he had found it, he did not cross himself. He scanned the bookcases and bookshelves, and with the same dubious air with which he had regarded the snipe, he smiled contemptuously and shook his head disapprovingly, as though by no means willing to allow that this game were worth the candle.

"Well, have you brought the money?" asked Oblonsky. "Sit down."

"Oh, don't trouble about the money. I've come to see you to talk it over."

"What is there to talk over? But do sit down."

"I don't mind if I do," said Ryabinin, sitting down and leaning his elbows on the back of his chair in a position of the most intense discomfort to himself. "You must knock it down a bit, prince. It would be too bad. The money is ready conclusively to the last farthing. As to paying the money down, there'll be no hitch there."

Levin, who had meanwhile been putting his gun away in the cupboard, was just going out of the door, but catching the merchant's words, he stopped.

"Why, you've got the forest for nothing as it is," he said. "He came to me too late, or I'd have fixed the price for him."

Ryabinin got up, and in silence, with a smile, he looked Levin down and up.

"Very close about money is Konstantin Dmitrievitch," he said with a smile, turning to Stepan Arkadyevitch; "there's positively no dealing with him. I was bargaining for some wheat of him, and a pretty price I offered too."

"Why should I give you my goods for nothing? I didn't pick it up on the ground, nor steal it either."

"Mercy on us! nowadays there's no chance at all of stealing. With the open courts and everything done in style, nowadays there's no question of stealing. We are just talking things over like gentlemen. His excellency's asking too much for the forest. I can't make both ends meet over it. I must ask for a little concession."

"But is the thing settled between you or not? If it's settled, it's useless haggling; but if it's not," said Levin, "I'll buy the forest."

The smile vanished at once from Ryabinin's face. A hawklike, greedy, cruel expression was left upon it. With rapid, bony fingers he unbuttoned his coat, revealing a shirt, bronze waistcoat buttons, and a watch-chain, and quickly pulled out a fat old pocketbook.

"Here you are, the forest is mine," he said, crossing himself quickly, and holding out his hand. "Take the money; it's my forest. That's Ryabinin's way of doing business; he doesn't haggle over every halfpenny," he added, scowling and waving the pocketbook.

"I wouldn't be in a hurry if I were you," said Levin.

"Come, really," said Oblonsky in surprise. "I've given my word, you know."

Levin went out of the room, slamming the door. Ryabinin looked towards the door and shook his head with a smile.

"It's all youthfulness—positively nothing but boyishness. Why, I'm buying it, upon my honor, simply, believe me, for the glory of it, that Ryabinin, and no one else, should have bought the copse of Oblonsky. And as to the profits, why, I must make what God gives. In God's name. If you would kindly sign the title-deed ..."

Within an hour the merchant, stroking his big overcoat neatly down, and hooking up his jacket, with the agreement in his pocket, seated himself in his tightly covered trap, and drove homewards.

"Ugh, these gentlefolks!" he said to the clerk. "They—they're a nice lot!"

"That's so," responded the clerk, handing him the reins and buttoning the leather apron. "But I can congratulate you on the purchase, Mihail Ignatitch?"

"Well, well...."

CHAPTER XVII

S TEPAN ARKADYEVITCH WENT UP-STAIRS WITH HIS POCKET BULGING WITH
notes, which the merchant had paid him for three months in advance. The
business of the forest was over, the money in his pocket; their shooting had
been excellent, and Stepan Arkadyevitch was in the happiest frame of mind, and
so he felt specially anxious to dissipate the ill-humor that had come upon Levin.
He wanted to finish the day at supper as pleasantly as it had been begun.

Levin certainly was out of humor, and in spite of all his desire to be affectionate and cordial to his charming visitor, he could not control his mood. The
intoxication of the news that Kitty was not married had gradually begun to work
upon him.

Kitty was not married, but ill, and ill from love for a man who had slighted
her. This slight, as it were, rebounded upon him. Vronsky had slighted her, and
she had slighted him, Levin. Consequently Vronsky had the right to despise
Levin, and therefore he was his enemy. But all this Levin did not think out.
He vaguely felt that there was something in it insulting to him, and he was not
angry now at what had disturbed him, but he fell foul of everything that presented itself. The stupid sale of the forest, the fraud practiced upon Oblonsky
and concluded in his house, exasperated him.

"Well, finished?" he said, meeting Stepan Arkadyevitch up-stairs. "Would
you like supper?"

"Well, I wouldn't say no to it. What an appetite I get in the country! Wonderful! Why didn't you offer Ryabinin something?"

"Oh, damn him!"

"Still, how you do treat him!" said Oblonsky. "You didn't even shake hands
with him. Why not shake hands with him?"

"Because I don't shake hands with a waiter, and a waiter's a hundred times
better than he is."

"What a reactionist you are, really! What about the amalgamation of
classes?" said Oblonsky.

"Anyone who likes amalgamating is welcome to it, but it sickens me."

"You're a regular reactionist, I see."

"Really, I have never considered what I am. I am Konstantin Levin, and
nothing else."

"And Konstantin Levin very much out of temper," said Stepan Arkadyevitch, smiling.

"Yes, I am out of temper, and do you know why? Because—excuse me—of your stupid sale...."

Stepan Arkadyevitch frowned good-humoredly, like one who feels himself teased and attacked for no fault of his own.

"Come, enough about it!" he said. "When did anybody ever sell anything without being told immediately after the sale, 'It was worth much more'? But when one wants to sell, no one will give anything.... No, I see you've a grudge against that unlucky Ryabinin."

"Maybe I have. And do you know why? You'll say again that I'm a reactionist, or some other terrible word; but all the same it does annoy and anger me to see on all sides the impoverishing of the nobility to which I belong, and, in spite of the amalgamation of classes, I'm glad to belong. And their impoverishment is not due to extravagance—that would be nothing; living in good style—that's the proper thing for noblemen; it's only the nobles who know how to do it. Now the peasants about us buy land, and I don't mind that. The gentleman does nothing, while the peasant works and supplants the idle man. That's as it ought to be. And I'm very glad for the peasant. But I do mind seeing the process of impoverishment from a sort of—I don't know what to call it— innocence. Here a Polish speculator bought for half its value a magnificent estate from a young lady who lives in Nice. And there a merchant will get three acres of land, worth ten roubles, as security for the loan of one rouble. Here, for no kind of reason, you've made that rascal a present of thirty thousand roubles."

"Well, what should I have done? Counted every tree?"

"Of course, they must be counted. You didn't count them, but Ryabinin did. Ryabinin's children will have means of livelihood and education, while yours maybe will not!"

"Well, you must excuse me, but there's something mean in this counting. We have our business and they have theirs, and they must make their profit. Anyway, the thing's done, and there's an end of it. And here come some poached eggs, my favorite dish. And Agafea Mihalovna will give us that marvelous herb-brandy..."

Stepan Arkadyevitch sat down at the table and began joking with Agafea Mihalovna, assuring her that it was long since he had tasted such a dinner and such a supper.

"Well, you do praise it, anyway," said Agafea Mihalovna, "but Konstantin Dmitrievitch, give him what you will—a crust of bread—he'll eat it and walk away."

Though Levin tried to control himself, he was gloomy and silent. He wanted to put one question to Stepan Arkadyevitch, but he could not bring himself to the point, and could not find the words or the moment in which to put it. Stepan Arkadyevitch had gone down to his room, undressed, again washed, and attired in a night-shirt with goffered frills, he had got into bed, but Levin still lingered in his room, talking of various trifling matters, and not daring to ask what he wanted to know.

"How wonderfully they make this soap," he said gazing at a piece of soap he was handling, which Agafea Mihalovna had put ready for the visitor but Oblonsky had not used. "Only look; why, it's a work of art."

"Yes, everything's brought to such a pitch of perfection nowadays," said Stepan Arkadyevitch, with a moist and blissful yawn. "The theater, for instance, and the entertainments ... a-a-a!" he yawned. "The electric light everywhere ... a-a-a!"

"Yes, the electric light," said Levin. "Yes. Oh, and where's Vronsky now?" he asked suddenly, laying down the soap.

"Vronsky?" said Stepan Arkadyevitch, checking his yawn; "he's in Petersburg. He left soon after you did, and he's not once been in Moscow since. And do you know, Kostya, I'll tell you the truth," he went on, leaning his elbow on the table, and propping on his hand his handsome ruddy face, in which his moist, good-natured, sleepy eyes shone like stars. "It's your own fault. You took fright at the sight of your rival. But, as I told you at the time, I couldn't say which had the better chance. Why didn't you fight it out? I told you at the time that ..." He yawned inwardly, without opening his mouth.

"Does he know, or doesn't he, that I did make an offer?" Levin wondered, gazing at him. "Yes, there's something humbugging, diplomatic in his face," and feeling he was blushing, he looked Stepan Arkadyevitch straight in the face without speaking.

"If there was anything on her side at the time, it was nothing but a superficial attraction," pursued Oblonsky. "His being such a perfect aristocrat, don't you know, and his future position in society, had an influence not with her, but with her mother."

Levin scowled. The humiliation of his rejection stung him to the heart, as though it were a fresh wound he had only just received. But he was at home, and the walls of home are a support.

"Stay, stay," he began, interrupting Oblonsky. "You talk of his being an aristocrat. But allow me to ask what it consists in, that aristocracy of Vronsky or of anybody else, beside which I can be looked down upon? You consider Vronsky an aristocrat, but I don't. A man whose father crawled up from nothing at all by intrigue, and whose mother—God knows whom she wasn't mixed up with.... No, excuse me, but I consider myself aristocratic, and people like me, who can point back in the past to three or four honorable generations of their family, of the highest degree of breeding (talent and intellect, of course that's another matter), and have never curried favor with any one, never depended on any one for anything, like my father and my grandfather. And I know many such. You think it mean of me to count the trees in my forest, while you make Ryabinin a present of thirty thousand; but you get rents from your lands and I don't know what, while I don't and so I prize what's come to me from my ancestors or been won by hard work.... We are aristocrats, and not those who can only exist by favor of the powerful of this world, and who can be bought for twopence halfpenny."

"Well, but whom are you attacking? I agree with you," said Stepan Arkadyevitch, sincerely and genially; though he was aware that in the class of those who could be bought for twopence halfpenny Levin was reckoning him too. Levin's warmth gave him genuine pleasure. "Whom are you attacking? Though a good deal is not true that you say about Vronsky, but I won't talk about that. I tell you straight out, if I were you, I should go back with me to Moscow, and ..."

"No; I don't know whether you know it or not, but I don't care. And I tell you—I did make an offer and was rejected, and Katerina Alexandrovna is nothing now to me but a painful and humiliating reminiscence."

"What ever for? What nonsense!"

"But we won't talk about it. Please forgive me, if I've been nasty," said Levin. Now that he had opened his heart, he became as he had been in the morning. "You're not angry with me, Stiva? Please don't be angry," he said, and smiling, he took his hand.

"Of course not; not a bit, and no reason to be. I'm glad we've spoken openly. And do you know, stand-shooting in the morning is usually good—why not go? I couldn't sleep the night anyway, but I might go straight from shooting to the station."

"Capital."

CHAPTER XVIII

ALTHOUGH ALL VRONSKY'S INNER LIFE WAS ABSORBED IN HIS PASSION, HIS external life unalterably and inevitably followed along the old accustomed lines of his social and regimental ties and interests.

The interests of his regiment took an important place in Vronsky's life, both because he was fond of the regiment, and because the regiment was fond of him. They were not only fond of Vronsky in his regiment, they respected him too, and were proud of him; proud that this man, with his immense wealth, his brilliant education and abilities, and the path open before him to every kind of success, distinction, and ambition, had disregarded all that, and of all the interests of life had the interests of his regiment and his comrades nearest to his heart. Vronsky was aware of his comrades' view of him, and in addition to his liking for the life, he felt bound to keep up that reputation.

It need not be said that he did not speak of his love to any of his comrades, nor did he betray his secret even in the wildest drinking bouts (though indeed he was never so drunk as to lose all control of himself). And he shut up any of his thoughtless comrades who attempted to allude to his connection. But in spite of that, his love was known to all the town; every one guessed with more or less confidence at his relations with Madame Karenina. The majority of the younger men envied him for just what was the most irksome factor in his love—the exalted position of Karenin, and the consequent publicity of their connection in society.

The greater number of the young women, who envied Anna and had long been weary of hearing her called *virtuous*, rejoiced at the fulfillment of their predictions, and were only waiting for a decisive turn in public opinion to fall upon her with all the weight of their scorn. They were already making ready their handfuls of mud to fling at her when the right moment arrived. The greater number of the middle-aged people and certain great personages were displeased at the prospect of the impending scandal in society.

Vronsky's mother, on hearing of his connection, was at first pleased at it, because nothing to her mind gave such a finishing-touch to a brilliant young man as a *liaison* in the highest society; she was pleased, too, that Madame Karenina, who had so taken her fancy, and had talked so much of her son, was, after all, just like all other pretty and well-bred women,—at least according to the Countess Vronskaya's ideas. But she had heard of late that her son had refused a position offered him of great importance to his career, simply in order to remain in the regiment, where he could be constantly seeing Madame Karenina. She learned that great personages were displeased with him on this account, and she changed her opinion. She was vexed, too, that from all she could learn of this connection it was not that brilliant, graceful, worldly *liaison* which she would have welcomed, but a sort of Wertherish, desperate passion, so she was told, which might well lead him into imprudence. She had not seen him since his abrupt departure from Moscow, and she sent her elder son to bid him come to see her.

This elder son, too, was displeased with his younger brother. He did not distinguish what sort of love his might be, big or little, passionate or passionless, lasting or passing (he kept a ballet-girl himself, though he was the father of a family, so he was lenient in these matters), but he knew that this love-affair was viewed with displeasure by those whom it was necessary to please, and therefore he did not approve of his brother's conduct.

Besides the service and society, Vronsky had another great interest—horses; he was passionately fond of horses.

That year races and a steeplechase had been arranged for the officers. Vronsky had put his name down, bought a thoroughbred English mare, and in spite of his love-affair, he was looking forward to the races with intense, though reserved, excitement....

These two passions did not interfere with one another. On the contrary, he needed occupation and distraction quite apart from his love, so as to recruit and rest himself from the violent emotions that agitated him.

CHAPTER XIX

ON THE DAY OF THE RACES AT KRASNOE SELO, VRONSKY HAD COME earlier than usual to eat beefsteak in the common mess-room of the regiment. He had no need to be strict with himself, as he had very quickly been brought down to the required light weight; but still he had to avoid gaining flesh, and so he eschewed farinaceous and sweet dishes. He sat with his coat unbuttoned over a white waistcoat, resting both elbows on the table, and while waiting for the steak he had ordered he looked at a French novel that lay open on his plate. He was only looking at the book to avoid conversation with the officers coming in and out; he was thinking.

He was thinking of Anna's promise to see him that day after the races. But he had not seen her for three days, and as her husband had just returned from abroad, he did not know whether she would be able to meet him to-day or not, and he did not know how to find out. He had had his last interview with her at his cousin Betsy's summer villa. He visited the Karenins' summer villa as rarely as possible. Now he wanted to go there, and he pondered the question how to do it.

"Of course I shall say Betsy has sent me to ask whether she's coming to the races. Of course, I'll go," he decided, lifting his head from the book. And as he vividly pictured the happiness of seeing her, his face lighted up.

"Send to my house, and tell them to have out the carriage and three horses as quick as they can," he said to the servant, who handed him the steak on a hot silver dish, and moving the dish up he began eating.

From the billiard-room next door came the sound of balls knocking, of talk and laughter. Two officers appeared at the entrance-door: one, a young fellow, with a feeble, delicate face, who had lately joined the regiment from the Corps of Pages; the other, a plump, elderly officer, with a bracelet on his wrist, and little eyes, lost in fat.

Vronsky glanced at them, frowned, and looking down at his book as though he had not noticed them, he proceeded to eat and read at the same time.

"What? Fortifying yourself for your work?" said the plump officer, sitting down beside him.

"As you see," responded Vronsky, knitting his brows, wiping his mouth, and not looking at the officer.

"So you're not afraid of getting fat?" said the latter, turning a chair round for the young officer.

"What?" said Vronsky angrily, making a wry face of disgust, and showing his even teeth.

"You're not afraid of getting fat?"

"Waiter, sherry!" said Vronsky, without replying, and moving the book to the other side of him, he went on reading.

The plump officer took up the list of wines and turned to the young officer.

"You choose what we're to drink," he said, handing him the card, and looking at him.

"Rhine wine, please," said the young officer, stealing a timid glance at Vronsky, and trying to pull his scarcely visible mustache. Seeing that Vronsky did not turn round, the young officer got up.

"Let's go into the billiard-room," he said.

The plump officer rose submissively, and they moved towards the door.

At that moment there walked into the room the tall and well-built Captain Yashvin. Nodding with an air of lofty contempt to the two officers, he went up to Vronsky.

"Ah! here he is!" he cried, bringing his big hand down heavily on his epaulet. Vronsky looked round angrily, but his face lighted up immediately with his characteristic expression of genial and manly serenity.

"That's it, Alexey," said the captain, in his loud baritone. "You must just eat a mouthful, now, and drink only one tiny glass."

"Oh, I'm not hungry."

"There go the inseparables," Yashvin dropped, glancing sarcastically at the two officers who were at that instant leaving the room. And he bent his long legs, swathed in tight riding-breeches, and sat down in the chair, too low for him, so that his knees were cramped up in a sharp angle.

"Why didn't you turn up at the Red Theater yesterday? Numerova wasn't at all bad. Where were you?"

"I was late at the Tverskoys'," said Vronsky.

"Ah!" responded Yashvin.

Yashvin, a gambler and a rake, a man not merely without moral principles, but of immoral principles, Yashvin was Vronsky's greatest friend in the regiment. Vronsky liked him both for his exceptional physical strength, which he showed for the most part by being able to drink like a fish, and do without sleep without being in the slightest degree affected by it; and for his great strength of character, which he showed in his relations with his comrades and superior officers, commanding both fear and respect, and also at cards, when he would play for tens of thousands and however much he might have drunk, always with such skill and decision that he was reckoned the best player in the English Club. Vronsky respected and liked Yashvin particularly because he felt Yashvin liked him, not for his name and his money, but for himself. And of all men he was the only one with whom Vronsky would have liked to speak of his love. He felt that Yashvin, in spite of his apparent contempt for every sort of feeling, was the only man who could, so he fancied, comprehend the intense passion which now filled his whole life. Moreover, he felt certain that Yashvin, as it was, took no delight in gossip and scandal, and interpreted his feeling rightly, that is to say, knew and believed that this passion was not a jest, not a pastime, but something more serious and important.

Vronsky had never spoken to him of his passion, but he was aware that he knew all about it, and that he put the right interpretation on it, and he was glad to see that in his eyes.

"Ah! yes," he said, to the announcement that Vronsky had been at the Tverskoys'; and his black eyes shining, he plucked at his left mustache, and began twisting it into his mouth, a bad habit he had.

"Well, and what did you do yesterday? Win anything?" asked Vronsky.

"Eight thousand. But three don't count; he won't pay up."

"Oh, then you can afford to lose over me," said Vronsky, laughing. (Yashvin had betted heavily on Vronsky in the races.)

"No chance of my losing. Mahotin's the only one that's risky."

And the conversation passed to forecasts of the coming race, the only thing Vronsky could think of just now.

"Come along, I've finished," said Vronsky, and getting up he went to the door. Yashvin got up too, stretching his long legs and his long back.

"It's too early for me to dine, but I must have a drink. I'll come along directly. Hi, wine!" he shouted, in his rich voice, that always rang out so loudly at drill, and set the windows shaking now.

"No, all right," he shouted again immediately after. "You're going home, so I'll go with you."

And he walked out with Vronsky.

CHAPTER XX

Vronsky was staying in a roomy, clean, Finnish hut, divided into two by a partition. Petritsky lived with him in camp too. Petritsky was asleep when Vronsky and Yashvin came into the hut.

"Get up, don't go on sleeping," said Yashvin, going behind the partition and giving Petritsky, who was lying with ruffled hair and with his nose in the pillow, a prod on the shoulder.

Petritsky jumped up suddenly onto his knees and looked round.

"Your brother's been here," he said to Vronsky. "He waked me up, damn him, and said he'd look in again." And pulling up the rug he flung himself back on the pillow. "Oh, do shut up, Yashvin!" he said, getting furious with Yashvin, who was pulling the rug off him. "Shut up!" He turned over and opened his eyes. "You'd better tell me what to drink; such a nasty taste in my mouth, that ..."

"Brandy's better than anything," boomed Yashvin. "Tereshtchenko! brandy for your master and cucumbers," he shouted, obviously taking pleasure in the sound of his own voice.

"Brandy, do you think? Eh?" queried Petritsky, blinking and rubbing his eyes. "And you'll drink something? All right then, we'll have a drink together!

Vronsky, have a drink?" said Petritsky, getting up and wrapping the tiger-skin rug round him. He went to the door of the partition wall, raised his hands, and hummed in French, "There was a king in Thule." "Vronsky, will you have a drink?"

"Go along," said Vronsky, putting on the coat his valet handed to him.

"Where are you off to?" asked Yashvin. "Oh, here are your three horses," he added, seeing the carriage drive up.

"To the stables, and I've got to see Bryansky, too, about the horses," said Vronsky.

Vronsky had as a fact promised to call at Bryansky's, some eight miles from Peterhof, and to bring him some money owing for some horses; and he hoped to have time to get that in too. But his comrades were at once aware that he was not only going there.

Petritsky, still humming, winked and made a pout with his lips, as though he would say: "Oh, yes, we know your Bryansky."

"Mind you're not late!" was Yashvin's only comment; and to change the conversation: "How's my roan? is he doing all right?" he inquired, looking out of the window at the middle one of the three horses, which he had sold Vronsky.

"Stop!" cried Petritsky to Vronsky as he was just going out. "Your brother left a letter and a note for you. Wait a bit; where are they?"

Vronsky stopped.

"Well, where are they?"

"Where are they? That's just the question!" said Petritsky solemnly, moving his forefinger upwards from his nose.

"Come, tell me; this is silly!" said Vronsky, smiling.

"I have not lighted the fire. Here somewhere about."

"Come, enough fooling! Where is the letter?"

"No, I've forgotten really. Or was it a dream? Wait a bit, wait a bit! But what's the use of getting in a rage. If you'd drunk four bottles yesterday as I did you'd forget where you were lying. Wait a bit, I'll remember!"

Petritsky went behind the partition and lay down on his bed.

"Wait a bit! This was how I was lying, and this was how he was standing. Yes—yes—yes…. Here it is!"—and Petritsky pulled a letter out from under the mattress, where he had hidden it.

Vronsky took the letter and his brother's note. It was the letter he was expecting—from his mother, reproaching him for not having been to see her—and the note was from his brother to say that he must have a little talk with him. Vronsky knew that it was all about the same thing. "What business is it of theirs!" thought Vronsky, and crumpling up the letters he thrust them between the buttons of his coat so as to read them carefully on the road. In the porch of the hut he was met by two officers; one of his regiment and one of another.

Vronsky's quarters were always a meeting-place for all the officers.

"Where are you off to?"

"I must go to Peterhof."

"Has the mare come from Tsarskoe?"

"Yes, but I've not seen her yet."

"They say Mahotin's Gladiator's lame."

"Nonsense! But however are you going to race in this mud?" said the other.

"Here are my saviors!" cried Petritsky, seeing them come in. Before him stood the orderly with a tray of brandy and salted cucumbers. "Here's Yashvin ordering me to drink a pick-me-up."

"Well, you did give it to us yesterday," said one of those who had come in; "you didn't let us get a wink of sleep all night."

"Oh, didn't we make a pretty finish!" said Petritsky. "Volkov climbed onto the roof and began telling us how sad he was. I said: 'Let's have music, the funeral march!' He fairly dropped asleep on the roof over the funeral march."

"Drink it up; you positively must drink the brandy, and then seltzer water and a lot of lemon," said Yashvin, standing over Petritsky like a mother making a child take medicine, "and then a little champagne—just a small bottle."

"Come, there's some sense in that. Stop a bit, Vronsky. We'll all have a drink."

"No; good-bye all of you. I'm not going to drink to-day."

"Why, are you gaining weight? All right, then we must have it alone. Give us the seltzer water and lemon."

"Vronsky!" shouted someone when he was already outside.

"Well?"

"You'd better get your hair cut, it'll weigh you down, especially at the top."

Vronsky was in fact beginning, prematurely, to get a little bald. He laughed gaily, showing his even teeth, and pulling his cap over the thin place, went out and got into his carriage.

"To the stables!" he said, and was just pulling out the letters to read them through, but he thought better of it, and put off reading them so as not to distract his attention before looking at the mare. "Later!"

CHAPTER XXI

THE TEMPORARY STABLE, A WOODEN SHED, HAD BEEN PUT UP CLOSE TO THE race-course, and there his mare was to have been taken the previous day. He had not yet seen her there.

During the last few days he had not ridden her out for exercise himself, but had put her in the charge of the trainer, and so now he positively did not know in what condition his mare had arrived yesterday and was to-day. He had scarcely got out of his carriage when his groom, the so-called "stable-boy," recognizing the carriage some way off, called the trainer. A dry-looking Englishman, in high boots and a short jacket, cleanshaven, except for a tuft below his chin, came to meet him, walking with the uncouth gait of jockey, turning his elbows out and swaying from side to side.

"Well, how's Frou-Frou?" Vronsky asked in English.

"All right, sir," the Englishman's voice responded somewhere in the inside of his throat. "Better not go in," he added, touching his hat. "I've put a muzzle on her, and the mare's fidgety. Better not go in, it'll excite the mare."

"No, I'm going in. I want to look at her."

"Come along, then," said the Englishman, frowning, and speaking with his mouth shut, and with swinging elbows, he went on in front with his disjointed gait.

They went into the little yard in front of the shed. A stable-boy, spruce and smart in his holiday attire, met them with a broom in his hand, and followed them. In the shed there were five horses in their separate stalls, and Vronsky knew that his chief rival, Gladiator, a very tall chestnut horse, had been brought there, and must be standing among them. Even more than his mare, Vronsky longed to see Gladiator, whom he had never seen. But he knew that by the etiquette of the race-course it was not merely impossible for him to see the horse, but improper even to ask questions about him. Just as he was passing along the passage, the boy opened the door into the second horse-box on the left, and Vronsky caught a glimpse of a big chestnut horse with white legs. He knew that this was Gladiator, but, with the feeling of a man turning away from the sight of another man's open letter, he turned round and went into Frou-Frou's stall.

"The horse is here belonging to Mak ... Mak ... I never can say the name," said the Englishman, over his shoulder, pointing his big finger and dirty nail towards Gladiator's stall.

"Mahotin? Yes, he's my most serious rival," said Vronsky.

"If you were riding him," said the Englishman, "I'd bet on you."

"Frou-Frou's more nervous; he's stronger," said Vronsky, smiling at the compliment to his riding.

"In a steeplechase it all depends on riding and on pluck," said the Englishman.

Of pluck—that is, energy and courage—Vronsky did not merely feel that he had enough; what was of far more importance, he was firmly convinced that no one in the world could have more of this "pluck" than he had.

"Don't you think I want more thinning down?"

"Oh, no," answered the Englishman. "Please, don't speak loud. The mare's fidgety," he added, nodding towards the horse-box, before which they were standing, and from which came the sound of restless stamping in the straw.

He opened the door, and Vronsky went into the horse-box, dimly lighted by one little window. In the horse-box stood a dark bay mare, with a muzzle on, picking at the fresh straw with her hoofs. Looking round him in the twilight of the horse-box, Vronsky unconsciously took in once more in a comprehensive glance all the points of his favorite mare. Frou-Frou was a beast of medium size, not altogether free from reproach, from a breeder's point of view. She was small-boned all over; though her chest was extremely prominent in front, it was narrow. Her hind-quarters were a little drooping, and in her fore-legs, and still more in her hind-legs, there was a noticeable curvature. The muscles of both hind- and fore-legs were not very thick; but across her shoulders the mare was exceptionally broad, a peculiarity specially striking now that she was lean from training. The bones of her legs below the knees looked no thicker than a finger from in front, but were extraordinarily thick seen from the side. She looked altogether, except across the shoulders, as it were, pinched in at the sides and pressed out in depth. But she had in the highest degree the quality that makes all defects forgotten: that quality was *blood*, the blood *that tells*, as the English expression has it. The muscles stood up sharply under the network of sinews, covered with the delicate, mobile skin, soft as satin, and they were hard as bone. Her clean-cut head, with prominent, bright, spirited eyes, broadened out at the open nostrils, that showed the red blood in the cartilage within. About all her figure, and especially her head, there was a certain expression of energy, and, at the same time, of softness. She was one of those creatures which seem only not to speak because the mechanism of their mouth does not allow them to.

To Vronsky, at any rate, it seemed that she understood all he felt at that moment, looking at her.

Directly Vronsky went towards her, she drew in a deep breath, and, turning back her prominent eye till the white looked bloodshot, she started at the approaching figures from the opposite side, shaking her muzzle, and shifting lightly from one leg to the other.

"There, you see how fidgety she is," said the Englishman.

"There, darling! There!" said Vronsky, going up to the mare and speaking soothingly to her.

But the nearer he came, the more excited she grew. Only when he stood by her head, she was suddenly quieter, while the muscles quivered under her soft, delicate coat. Vronsky patted her strong neck, straightened over her sharp withers a stray lock of her mane that had fallen on the other side, and moved his face near her dilated nostrils, transparent as a bat's wing. She drew a loud breath and snorted out through her tense nostrils, started, pricked up her sharp ear, and put out her strong, black lip towards Vronsky, as though she would nip hold of his sleeve. But remembering the muzzle, she shook it and again began restlessly stamping one after the other her shapely legs.

"Quiet, darling, quiet!" he said, patting her again over her hind-quarters; and with a glad sense that his mare was in the best possible condition, he went out of the horse-box.

The mare's excitement had infected Vronsky. He felt that his heart was throbbing, and that he, too, like the mare, longed to move, to bite; it was both dreadful and delicious.

"Well, I rely on you, then," he said to the Englishman; "half-past six on the ground."

"All right," said the Englishman. "Oh, where are you going, my lord?" he asked suddenly, using the title "my lord," which he had scarcely ever used before.

Vronsky in amazement raised his head, and stared, as he knew how to stare, not into the Englishman's eyes, but at his forehead, astounded at the impertinence of his question. But realizing that in asking this the Englishman had been looking at him not as an employer, but as a jockey, he answered:

"I've got to go to Bryansky's; I shall be home within an hour."

"How often I'm asked that question to-day!" he said to himself, and he blushed, a thing which rarely happened to him. The Englishman looked gravely at him; and, as though he, too, knew where Vronsky was going, he added:

"The great thing's to keep quiet before a race," said he; "don't get out of temper or upset about anything."

"All right," answered Vronsky, smiling; and jumping into his carriage, he told the man to drive to Peterhof.

Before he had driven many paces away, the dark clouds that had been threatening rain all day broke, and there was a heavy downpour of rain.

"What a pity!" thought Vronsky, putting up the roof of the carriage. "It was muddy before, now it will be a perfect swamp." As he sat in solitude in the closed carriage, he took out his mother's letter and his brother's note, and read them through.

Yes, it was the same thing over and over again. Every one, his mother, his brother, every one thought fit to interfere in the affairs of his heart. This interference aroused in him a feeling of angry hatred—a feeling he had rarely known before. "What business is it of theirs? Why does everybody feel called upon to concern himself about me? And why do they worry me so? Just because they see that this is something they can't understand. If it were a common, vulgar, worldly intrigue, they would have left me alone. They feel that this is something different, that this is not a mere pastime, that this woman is dearer to me than life. And this is incomprehensible, and that's why it annoys them. Whatever our destiny is or may be, we have made it ourselves, and we do not complain of it," he said, in the word *we* linking himself with Anna. "No, they must needs teach us how to live. They haven't an idea of what happiness is; they don't know that without our love, for us there is neither happiness nor unhappiness—no life at all," he thought.

He was angry with all of them for their interference just because he felt in his soul that they, all these people, were right. He felt that the love that bound him to Anna was not a momentary impulse, which would pass, as worldly intrigues do pass, leaving no other traces in the life of either but pleasant or unpleasant memories. He felt all the torture of his own and her position, all the difficulty there was for them, conspicuous as they were in the eye of all the world, in concealing their love, in lying and deceiving; and in lying, deceiving, feigning, and continually thinking of others, when the passion that united them was so intense that they were both oblivious of everything else but their love.

He vividly recalled all the constantly recurring instances of inevitable necessity for lying and deceit, which were so against his natural bent. He recalled particularly vividly the shame he had more than once detected in her at this necessity for lying and deceit. And he experienced the strange feeling that had sometimes come upon him since his secret love for Anna. This was a feeling of loathing for something—whether for Alexey Alexandrovitch, or for himself, or for the whole world, he could not have said. But he always drove away this strange feeling. Now, too, he shook it off and continued the thread of his thoughts.

"Yes, she was unhappy before, but proud and at peace; and now she cannot be at peace and feel secure in her dignity, though she does not show it. Yes, we must put an end to it," he decided.

And for the first time the idea clearly presented itself that it was essential to put an end to this false position, and the sooner the better. "Throw up everything, she and I, and hide ourselves somewhere alone with our love," he said to himself.

CHAPTER XXII

THE RAIN DID NOT LAST LONG, AND BY THE TIME VRONSKY ARRIVED, HIS shaft-horse trotting at full speed and dragging the trace-horses galloping through the mud, with their reins hanging loose, the sun had peeped out again, the roofs of the summer villas and the old lime-trees in the gardens on both sides of the principal streets sparkled with wet brilliance, and from the twigs came a pleasant drip and from the roofs rushing streams of water. He thought no more of the shower spoiling the race-course, but was rejoicing now that—thanks to the rain—he would be sure to find her at home and alone, as he knew that Alexey Alexandrovitch, who had lately returned from a foreign watering-place, had not moved from Petersburg.

Hoping to find her alone, Vronsky alighted, as he always did, to avoid attracting attention, before crossing the bridge, and walked to the house. He did not go up the steps to the street door, but went into the court.

"Has your master come?" he asked a gardener.

"No, sir. The mistress is at home. But will you please go to the front door; there are servants there," the gardener answered. "They'll open the door."

"No, I'll go in from the garden."

And feeling satisfied that she was alone, and wanting to take her by surprise, since he had not promised to be there to-day, and she would certainly not expect him to come before the races, he walked, holding his sword and stepping cautiously over the sandy path, bordered with flowers, to the terrace that looked out upon the garden. Vronsky forgot now all that he had thought on the way of the hardships and difficulties of their position. He thought of nothing but that he would see her directly, not in imagination, but living, all of her, as she was in reality. He was just going in, stepping on his whole foot so as not to creak, up the worn steps of the terrace, when he suddenly remembered what he always forgot, and what caused the most torturing side of his relations with her, her son with his questioning—hostile, as he fancied—eyes.

This boy was more often than anyone else a check upon their freedom. When he was present, both Vronsky and Anna did not merely avoid speaking of anything that they could not have repeated before every one; they did not even allow themselves to refer by hints to anything the boy did not understand. They had made no agreement about this, it had settled itself. They would have felt it wounding themselves to deceive the child. In his presence they talked like acquaintances. But in spite of this caution, Vronsky often saw the child's intent, bewildered glance fixed upon him, and a strange shyness, uncertainty, at one time friendliness, at another, coldness and reserve, in the boy's manner to him; as though the child felt that between this man and his mother there existed some important bond, the significance of which he could not understand.

As a fact, the boy did feel that he could not understand this relation, and he tried painfully, and was not able to make clear to himself what feeling he ought to have for this man. With a child's keen instinct for every manifestation of feeling, he saw distinctly that his father, his governess, his nurse,—all did not merely dislike Vronsky, but looked on him with horror and aversion, though they never said anything about him, while his mother looked on him as her greatest friend.

"What does it mean? Who is he? How ought I to love him? If I don't know, it's my fault; either I'm stupid or a naughty boy," thought the child. And this was what caused his dubious, inquiring, sometimes hostile, expression, and the shyness and uncertainty which Vronsky found so irksome. This child's presence always and infallibly called up in Vronsky that strange feeling of inexplicable loathing which he had experienced of late. This child's presence called up both in Vronsky and in Anna a feeling akin to the feeling of a sailor who sees by the compass that the direction in which he is swiftly moving is far from the right one, but that to arrest his motion is not in his power, that every instant is carrying him further and further away, and that to admit to himself his deviation from the right direction is the same as admitting his certain ruin.

This child, with his innocent outlook upon life, was the compass that showed them the point to which they had departed from what they knew, but did not want to know.

This time Seryozha was not at home, and she was completely alone. She was sitting on the terrace waiting for the return of her son, who had gone out for his walk and been caught in the rain. She had sent a manservant and a maid out to look for him. Dressed in a white gown, deeply embroidered, she was sitting in a corner of the terrace behind some flowers, and did not hear him. Bending her curly black head, she pressed her forehead against a cool watering-pot that stood on the parapet, and both her lovely hands, with the

you will never talk about this. When you talk about it—it's only then it worries me."

"I don't understand," he said.

"I know," she interrupted him, "how hard it is for your truthful nature to lie, and I grieve for you. I often think that you have ruined your whole life for me."

"I was just thinking the very same thing," he said; "how could you sacrifice everything for my sake? I can't forgive myself that you're unhappy!"

"I unhappy?" she said, coming closer to him, and looking at him with an ecstatic smile of love. "I am like a hungry man who has been given food. He may be cold, and dressed in rags, and ashamed, but he is not unhappy. I unhappy? No, this is my unhappiness...."

She could hear the sound of her son's voice coming towards them, and glancing swiftly round the terrace, she got up impulsively. Her eyes glowed with the fire he knew so well; with a rapid movement she raised her lovely hands, covered with rings, took his head, looked a long look into his face, and, putting up her face with smiling, parted lips, swiftly kissed his mouth and both eyes, and pushed him away. She would have gone, but he held her back.

"When?" he murmured in a whisper, gazing in ecstasy at her.

"To-night, at one o'clock," she whispered, and, with a heavy sigh, she walked with her light, swift step to meet her son.

Seryozha had been caught by the rain in the big garden, and he and his nurse had taken shelter in an arbor.

"Well, *au revoir*," she said to Vronsky. "I must soon be getting ready for the races. Betsy promised to fetch me."

Vronsky, looking at his watch, went away hurriedly.

CHAPTER XXIV

WHEN VRONSKY LOOKED AT HIS WATCH ON THE KARENINS' BALCONY, he was so greatly agitated and lost in his thoughts that he saw the figures on the watch's face, but could not take in what time it was. He came out on to the highroad and walked, picking his way carefully through the mud, to his carriage. He was so completely absorbed in his feeling for Anna, that he did not even think what o'clock it was, and whether he had time to go to Bryansky's. He had left him, as often happens, only the external faculty of memory, that points out each step one has to take, one after the other. He went up to his coachman, who was dozing on the box in the shadow, already lengthening, of a thick limetree; he admired the shifting clouds of midges circling over the hot horses, and, waking the coachman, he jumped into the carriage, and told him to drive to Bryansky's. It was only after driving nearly five miles that he had sufficiently recovered himself to look at his watch, and realize that it was half-past five, and he was late.

There were several races fixed for that day: the Mounted Guards' race, then the officers' mile-and-a-half race, then the three-mile race, and then the race for which he was entered. He could still be in time for his race, but if he went to Bryansky's he could only just be in time, and he would arrive when the whole of the court would be in their places. That would be a pity. But he had promised Bryansky to come, and so he decided to drive on, telling the coachman not to spare the horses.

He reached Bryansky's, spent five minutes there, and galloped back. This rapid drive calmed him. All that was painful in his relations with Anna, all the feeling of indefiniteness left by their conversation, had slipped out of his mind. He was thinking now with pleasure and excitement of the race, of his being anyhow, in time, and now and then the thought of the blissful interview awaiting him that night flashed across his imagination like a flaming light.

The excitement of the approaching race gained upon him as he drove further and further into the atmosphere of the races, overtaking carriages driving up from the summer villas or out of Petersburg.

At his quarters no one was left at home; all were at the races, and his valet was looking out for him at the gate. While he was changing his clothes, his valet told him that the second race had begun already, that a lot of gentlemen had been to ask for him, and a boy had twice run up from the stables. Dressing without hurry (he never hurried himself, and never lost his self-possession), Vronsky drove to the sheds. From the sheds he could see a perfect sea of carriages, and people on foot, soldiers surrounding the race-course, and pavilions swarming with people. The second race was apparently going on, for just as he went into the sheds he heard a bell ringing. Going towards the stable, he met the white-legged chestnut, Mahotin's Gladiator, being led to the race-course in a blue forage horsecloth, with what looked like huge ears edged with blue.

"Where's Cord?" he asked the stable-boy.

"In the stable, putting on the saddle."

In the open horse-box stood Frou-Frou, saddled ready. They were just going to lead her out.

"I'm not too late?"

"All right! All right!" said the Englishman; "don't upset yourself!"

Vronsky once more took in in one glance the exquisite lines of his favorite mare; who was quivering all over, and with an effort he tore himself from the sight of her, and went out of the stable. He went towards the pavilions at the most favorable moment for escaping attention. The mile-and-a-half race was just finishing, and all eyes were fixed on the horse-guard in front and the light hussar behind, urging their horses on with a last effort close to the winning-post. From the center and outside of the ring all were crowding to the winning-post, and a group of soldiers and officers of the horse-guards were shouting loudly their delight at the expected triumph of their officer and comrade. Vronsky moved into the middle of the crowd unnoticed, almost at the very moment when the bell rang at the finish of the race, and the tall, mud-spattered horse-guard who came in first, bending over the saddle, let go the reins of his panting gray horse that looked dark with sweat.

The horse, stiffening out its legs, with an effort stopped its rapid course, and the officer of the horse-guards looked round him like a man waking up from a heavy sleep, and just managed to smile. A crowd of friends and outsiders pressed round him.

Vronsky intentionally avoided that select crowd of the upper world, which was moving and talking with discreet freedom before the pavilions. He knew that Madame Karenina was there, and Betsy, and his brother's wife, and he purposely did not go near them for fear of something distracting his attention. But he was continually met and stopped by acquaintances, who told him about the previous races, and kept asking him why he was so late.

At the time when the racers had to go to the pavilion to receive the prizes, and all attention was directed to that point, Vronsky's elder brother, Alexander, a colonel with heavy fringed epaulets, came up to him. He was not tall, though as broadly built as Alexey, and handsomer and rosier than he; he had a red nose, and an open, drunken-looking face.

"Did you get my note?" he said. "There's never any finding you."

Alexander Vronsky, in spite of the dissolute life, and in especial the drunken habits, for which he was notorious, was quite one of the court circle.

Now, as he talked to his brother of a matter bound to be exceedingly disagreeable to him, knowing that the eyes of many people might be fixed upon him, he kept a smiling countenance, as though he were jesting with his brother about something of little moment.

"I got it, and I really can't make out what *you* are worrying yourself about," said Alexey.

"I'm worrying myself because the remark has just been made to me that you weren't here, and that you were seen in Peterhof on Monday."

"There are matters which only concern those directly interested in them, and the matter you are so worried about is ..."

"Yes, but if so, you may as well cut the service...."

"I beg you not to meddle, and that's all I have to say."

Alexey Vronsky's frowning face turned white, and his prominent lower jaw quivered, which happened rarely with him. Being a man of very warm heart, he was seldom angry; but when he was angry, and when his chin quivered, then, as Alexander Vronsky knew, he was dangerous. Alexander Vronsky smiled gaily.

"I only wanted to give you mother's letter. Answer it, and don't worry about anything just before the race. *Bonne chance*," he added, smiling and he moved away from him. But after him another friendly greeting brought Vronsky to a standstill.

"So you won't recognize your friends! How are you, *mon cher?*" said Stepan Arkadyevitch, as conspicuously brilliant in the midst of all the Petersburg brilliance as he was in Moscow, his face rosy, and his whiskers sleek and glossy. "I came up yesterday, and I'm delighted that I shall see your triumph. When shall we meet?"

"Come to-morrow to the mess-room," said Vronsky, and squeezing him by the sleeve of his coat, with apologies, he moved away to the center of the race-course, where the horses were being led for the great steeplechase.

The horses who had run in the last race were being led home, steaming and exhausted, by the stable-boys, and one after another the fresh horses for the coming race made their appearance, for the most part English racers, wearing horsecloths, and looking with their drawn-up bellies like strange, huge birds. On the right was led in Frou-Frou, lean and beautiful, lifting up her elastic, rather long pasterns, as though moved by springs. Not far from her they were taking the rug off the lop-eared Gladiator. The strong, exquisite, perfectly correct lines of the stallion, with his superb hind-quarters and excessively short pasterns almost over his hoofs, attracted Vronsky's attention in spite of himself. He would have gone up to his mare, but he was again detained by an acquaintance.

"Oh, there's Karenin!" said the acquaintance with whom he was chatting. "He's looking for his wife, and she's in the middle of the pavilion. Didn't you see her?"

"No," answered Vronsky, and without even glancing round towards the pavilion where his friend was pointing out Madame Karenina, he went up to his mare.

Vronsky had not had time to look at the saddle, about which he had to give some direction, when the competitors were summoned to the pavilion to receive their numbers and places in the row at starting. Seventeen officers, looking serious and severe, many with pale faces, met together in the pavilion and drew the numbers. Vronsky drew the number seven. The cry was heard: "Mount!"

Feeling that with the others riding in the race, he was the center upon which all eyes were fastened, Vronsky walked up to his mare in that state of nervous tension in which he usually became deliberate and composed in his movements. Cord, in honor of the races, had put on his best clothes, a black coat buttoned up, a stiffly starched collar, which propped up his cheeks, a round black hat, and top-boots. He was calm and dignified as ever, and was with his own hands holding Frou-Frou by both reins, standing straight in front of her. Frou-Frou was still trembling as though in a fever. Her eye, full of fire, glanced sideways at Vronsky. Vronsky slipped his finger under the saddle-girth. The mare glanced aslant at him, drew up her lip, and twitched her ear. The Englishman puckered up his lips, intending to indicate a smile that anyone should verify his saddling.

"Get up; you won't feel so excited."

Vronsky looked round for the last time at his rivals. He knew that he would not see them during the race. Two were already riding forward to the point from which they were to start. Galtsin, a friend of Vronsky's and one of his more formidable rivals, was moving round a bay horse that would not let him mount. A little light hussar in tight riding-breeches rode off at a gallop, crouched up like a cat on the saddle, in imitation of English jockeys. Prince Kuzovlev sat with a white face on his thoroughbred mare from the Grabovsky stud, while an English groom led her by the bridle. Vronsky and all his comrades knew Kuzovlev and his peculiarity of "weak nerves" and terrible vanity. They knew that he was afraid of everything, afraid of riding a spirited horse. But now, just because it was terrible, because people broke their necks, and there was a doctor standing at each obstacle, and an ambulance with a cross on it, and a sister of mercy, he had made up his mind to take part in the race. Their

be in the way. But Frou-Frou drew up her legs and back in the very act of leaping, like a falling cat, and, clearing the other mare, alighted beyond her.

"O the darling!" thought Vronsky.

After crossing the stream Vronsky had complete control of his mare, and began holding her in, intending to cross the great barrier behind Mahotin, and to try to overtake him in the clear ground of about five hundred yards that followed it.

The great barrier stood just in front of the imperial pavilion. The Tsar and the whole court and crowds of people were all gazing at them—at him, and Mahotin a length ahead of him, as they drew near the "devil," as the solid barrier was called. Vronsky was aware of those eyes fastened upon him from all sides, but he saw nothing except the ears and neck of his own mare, the ground racing to meet him, and the back and white legs of Gladiator beating time swiftly before him, and keeping always the same distance ahead. Gladiator rose, with no sound of knocking against anything. With a wave of his short tail he disappeared from Vronsky's sight.

"Bravo!" cried a voice.

At the same instant, under Vronsky's eyes, right before him flashed the palings of the barrier. Without the slightest change in her action his mare flew over it; the palings vanished, and he heard only a crash behind him. The mare, excited by Gladiator's keeping ahead, had risen too soon before the barrier, and grazed it with her hind hoofs. But her pace never changed, and Vronsky, feeling a spatter of mud in his face, realized that he was once more the same distance from Gladiator. Once more he perceived in front of him the same back and short tail, and again the same swiftly moving white legs that got no further away.

At the very moment when Vronsky thought that now was the time to overtake Mahotin, Frou-Frou herself, understanding his thoughts, without any incitement on his part, gained ground considerably, and began getting alongside of Mahotin on the most favorable side, close to the inner cord. Mahotin would not let her pass that side. Vronsky had hardly formed the thought that he could perhaps pass on the outer side, when Frou-Frou shifted her pace and began overtaking him on the other side. Frou-Frou's shoulder, beginning by now to be dark with sweat, was even with Gladiator's back. For a few lengths they moved evenly. But before the obstacle they were approaching, Vronsky began working at the reins, anxious to avoid having to take the outer circle, and swiftly passed Mahotin just upon the declivity. He caught a glimpse of his mud-stained face as he flashed by. He even fancied that he smiled. Vronsky passed Mahotin, but he was immediately aware of him close upon him, and he never ceased hearing the even-thudding hoofs and the rapid and still quite fresh breathing of Gladiator.

The next two obstacles, the water-course and the barrier, were easily crossed, but Vronsky began to hear the snorting and thud of Gladiator closer upon him. He urged on his mare, and to his delight felt that she easily quickened her pace, and the thud of Gladiator's hoofs was again heard at the same distance away.

Vronsky was at the head of the race, just as he wanted to be and as Cord had advised, and now he felt sure of being the winner. His excitement, his delight, and his tenderness for Frou-Frou grew keener and keener. He longed to look round again, but he did not dare do this, and tried to be cool and not to urge on his mare so to keep the same reserve of force in her as he felt that Gladiator still kept. There remained only one obstacle, the most difficult; if he could cross it ahead of the others he would come in first. He was flying towards the Irish barricade, Frou-Frou and he both together saw the barricade in the distance, and both the man and the mare had a moment's hesitation. He saw the uncertainty in the mare's ears and lifted the whip, but at the same time felt that his fears were groundless; the mare knew what was wanted. She quickened her pace and rose smoothly, just as he had fancied she would, and as she left the ground gave herself up to the force of her rush, which carried her far beyond the ditch; and with the same rhythm, without effort, with the same leg forward, Frou-Frou fell back into her pace again.

"Bravo, Vronsky!" he heard shouts from a knot of men—he knew they were his friends in the regiment—who were standing at the obstacle. He could not fail to recognize Yashvin's voice though he did not see him.

"O my sweet!" he said inwardly to Frou-Frou, as he listened for what was happening behind. "He's cleared it!" he thought, catching the thud of Gladiator's hoofs behind him. There remained only the last ditch, filled with water and five feet wide. Vronsky did not even look at it, but anxious to get in a long way first began sawing away at the reins, lifting the mare's head and letting it go in time with her paces. He felt that the mare was at her very last reserve of strength; not her neck and shoulders merely were wet, but the sweat was standing in drops on her mane, her head, her sharp ears, and her breath came in short, sharp gasps. But he knew that she had strength left more than enough for the remaining five hundred yards. It was only from feeling himself nearer the ground and from the peculiar smoothness of his motion that Vronsky knew how greatly the mare had quickened her pace. She flew over the ditch as though not noticing it. She flew over it like a bird; but at the same instant Vronsky, to

wife's health. Alexey Alexandrovitch did not want to think at all about his wife's behavior, and he actually succeeded in not thinking about it at all.

Alexey Alexandrovitch's permanent summer villa was in Peterhof, and the Countess Lidia Ivanovna used as a rule to spend the summer there, close to Anna, and constantly seeing her. That year Countess Lidia Ivanovna declined to settle in Peterhof, was not once at Anna Arkadyevna's, and in conversation with Alexey Alexandrovitch hinted at the unsuitability of Anna's close intimacy with Betsy and Vronsky. Alexey Alexandrovitch sternly cut her short, roundly declaring his wife to be above suspicion, and from that time began to avoid Countess Lidia Ivanovna. He did not want to see, and did not see, that many people in society cast dubious glances on his wife; he did not want to understand, and did not understand, why his wife had so particularly insisted on staying at Tsarskoe, where Betsy was staying, and not far from the camp of Vronsky's regiment. He did not allow himself to think about it, and he did not think about it; but all the same though he never admitted it to himself, and had no proofs, not even suspicious evidence, in the bottom of his heart he knew beyond all doubt that he was a deceived husband, and he was profoundly miserable about it.

How often during those eight years of happy life with his wife Alexey Alexandrovitch had looked at other men's faithless wives and other deceived husbands and asked himself: "How can people descend to that? how is it they don't put an end to such a hideous position?" But now, when the misfortune had come upon himself, he was so far from thinking of putting an end to the position that he would not recognize it at all, would not recognize it just because it was too awful, too unnatural.

Since his return from abroad Alexey Alexandrovitch had twice been at their country villa. Once he dined there, another time he spent the evening there with a party of friends, but he had not once stayed the night there, as it had been his habit to do in previous years.

The day of the races had been a very busy day for Alexey Alexandrovitch; but when mentally sketching out the day in the morning, he made up his mind to go to their country house to see his wife immediately after dinner, and from there to the races, which all the Court were to witness, and at which he was bound to be present. He was going to see his wife, because he had determined to see her once a week to keep up appearances. And besides, on that day, as it was the fifteenth, he had to give his wife some money for her expenses, according to their usual arrangement.

With his habitual control over his thoughts, though he thought all this about his wife, he did not let his thoughts stray further in regard to her.

That morning was a very full one for Alexey Alexandrovitch. The evening before, Countess Lidia Ivanovna had sent him a pamphlet by a celebrated traveler in China, who was staying in Petersburg, and with it she enclosed a note begging him to see the traveler himself, as he was an extremely interesting person from various points of view, and likely to be useful. Alexey Alexandrovitch had not had time to read the pamphlet through in the evening, and finished it in the morning. Then people began arriving with petitions, and there came the reports, interviews, appointments, dismissals, apportionment of rewards, pensions, grants, notes, the workaday round, as Alexey Alexandrovitch called it, that always took up so much time. Then there was private business of his own, a visit from the doctor and the steward who managed his property. The steward did not take up much time. He simply gave Alexey Alexandrovitch the money he needed together with a brief statement of the position of his affairs, which was not altogether satisfactory, as it had happened that during that year, owing to increased expenses, more had been paid out than usual, and there was a deficit. But the doctor, a celebrated Petersburg doctor, who was an intimate acquaintance of Alexey Alexandrovitch, took up a great deal of time. Alexey Alexandrovitch had not expected him that day, and was surprised at his visit, and still more so when the doctor questioned him very carefully about his health, listened to his breathing, and tapped at his liver. Alexey Alexandrovitch did not know that his friend Lidia Ivanovna, noticing that he was not as well as usual that year, had begged the doctor to go and examine him. "Do this for my sake," the Countess Lidia Ivanovna had said to him.

"I will do it for the sake of Russia, countess," replied the doctor.

"A priceless man!" said the Countess Lidia Ivanovna.

The doctor was extremely dissatisfied with Alexey Alexandrovitch. He found the liver considerably enlarged, and the digestive powers weakened, while the course of mineral waters had been quite without effect. He prescribed more physical exercise as far as possible, and as far as possible less mental strain, and above all no worry—in other words, just what was as much out of Alexey Alexandrovitch's power as abstaining from breathing. Then he withdrew, leaving in Alexey Alexandrovitch an unpleasant sense that something was wrong with him, and that there was no chance of curing it.

As he was coming away, the doctor chanced to meet on the staircase an acquaintance of his, Sludin, who was secretary of Alexey Alexandrovitch's department. They had been comrades at the university, and though they rarely met, they thought highly of each other and were excellent friends, and so there was no one to whom the doctor would have given his opinion of a patient so freely as to Sludin.

bore. And he answered simply, though jestingly. There was nothing remarkable in all this conversation, but never after could Anna recall this brief scene without an agonizing pang of shame.

Seryozha came in preceded by his governess. If Alexey Alexandrovitch had allowed himself to observe he would have noticed the timid and bewildered eyes with which Seryozha glanced first at his father and then at his mother. But he would not see anything, and he did not see it.

"Ah, the young man! He's grown. Really, he's getting quite a man. How are you, young man?"

And he gave his hand to the scared child. Seryozha had been shy of his father before, and now, ever since Alexey Alexandrovitch had taken to calling him young man, and since that insoluble question had occurred to him whether Vronsky were a friend or a foe, he avoided his father. He looked round towards his mother as though seeking shelter. It was only with his mother that he was at ease. Meanwhile, Alexey Alexandrovitch was holding his son by the shoulder while he was speaking to the governess, and Seryozha was so miserably uncomfortable that Anna saw he was on the point of tears.

Anna, who had flushed a little the instant her son came in, noticing that Seryozha was uncomfortable, got up hurriedly, took Alexey Alexandrovitch's hand from her son's shoulder, and kissing the boy, led him out onto the terrace, and quickly came back.

"It's time to start, though," said she, glancing at her watch. "How is it Betsy doesn't come? ..."

"Yes," said Alexey Alexandrovitch, and getting up, he folded his hands and cracked his fingers. "I've come to bring you some money, too, for nightingales, we know, can't live on fairy tales," he said. "You want it, I expect?"

"No, I don't ... yes, I do," she said, not looking at him, and crimsoning to the roots of her hair. "But you'll come back here after the races, I suppose?"

"Oh, yes!" answered Alexey Alexandrovitch. "And here's the glory of Peterhof, Princess Tverskaya," he added, looking out of the window at the elegant English carriage with the tiny seats placed extremely high. "What elegance! Charming! Well, let us be starting too, then."

Princess Tverskaya did not get out of her carriage, but her groom, in high boots, a cape, and block hat, darted out at the entrance.

"I'm going; good-bye!" said Anna, and kissing her son, she went up to Alexey Alexandrovitch and held out her hand to him. "It was ever so nice of you to come."

Alexey Alexandrovitch kissed her hand.

"Well, *au revoir*, then! You'll come back for some tea; that's delightful!" she said, and went out, gay and radiant. But as soon as she no longer saw him, she was aware of the spot on her hand that his lips had touched, and she shuddered with repulsion.

CHAPTER XXVIII

WHEN ALEXEY ALEXANDROVITCH REACHED THE RACE-COURSE, ANNA was already sitting in the pavilion beside Betsy, in that pavilion where all the highest society had gathered. She caught sight of her husband in the distance. Two men, her husband and her lover, were the two centers of her existence, and unaided by her external senses she was aware of their nearness. She was aware of her husband approaching a long way off, and she could not help following him in the surging crowd in the midst of which he was moving. She watched his progress towards the pavilion, saw him now responding condescendingly to an ingratiating bow, now exchanging friendly, nonchalant greetings with his equals, now asiduously trying to catch the eye of some great one of this world, and taking off his big round hat that squeezed the tips of his ears. All these ways of his she knew, and all were hateful to her. "Nothing but ambition, nothing but the desire to get on, that's all there is in his soul," she thought; "as for these lofty ideals, love of culture, religion, they are only so many tools for getting on."

From his glances towards the ladies' pavilion (he was staring straight at her, but did not distinguish his wife in the sea of muslin, ribbons, feathers, parasols and flowers) she saw that he was looking for her, but she purposely avoided noticing him.

"Alexey Alexandrovitch!" Princess Betsy called to him; "I'm sure you don't see your wife: here she is."

He smiled his chilly smile.

"There's so much splendor here that one's eyes are dazzled," he said, and he went into the pavilion. He smiled to his wife as a man should smile on meeting his wife after only just parting from her, and greeted the princess and other acquaintances, giving to each what was due—that is to say, jesting with the ladies and dealing out friendly greetings among the men. Below, near the pavilion, was standing an adjutant-general of whom Alexey Alexandrovitch

"But here's this lady too, and others very much moved as well; it's very natural," Alexey Alexandrovitch told himself. He tried not to look at her, but unconsciously his eyes were drawn to her. He examined that face again, trying not to read what was so plainly written on it, and against his own will, with horror read on it what he did not want to know.

The first fall—Kuzovlev's, at the stream—agitated every one, but Alexey Alexandrovitch saw distinctly on Anna's pale, triumphant face that the man she was watching had not fallen. When, after Mahotin and Vronsky had cleared the worst barrier, the next officer had been thrown straight on his head at it and fatally injured, and a shudder of horror passed over the whole public, Alexey Alexandrovitch saw that Anna did not even notice it, and had some difficulty in realizing what they were talking of about her. But more and more often, and with greater persistence, he watched her. Anna, wholly engrossed as she was with the race, became aware of her husband's cold eyes fixed upon her from one side.

She glanced round for an instant, looked inquiringly at him, and with a slight frown turned away again.

"Ah, I don't care!" she seemed to say to him, and she did not once glance at him again.

The race was an unlucky one, and of the seventeen officers who rode in it more than half were thrown and hurt. Towards the end of the race every one was in a state of agitation, which was intensified by the fact that the Tsar was displeased.

CHAPTER XXIX

EVERY ONE WAS LOUDLY EXPRESSING DISAPPROBATION, EVERY ONE WAS repeating a phrase some one had uttered—"The lions and gladiators will be the next thing," and every one was feeling horrified; so that when Vronsky fell to the ground, and Anna moaned aloud, there was nothing very out of the way in it. But afterwards a change came over Anna's face which really was beyond decorum. She utterly lost her head. She began fluttering like a caged bird, at one moment would have got up and moved away, at the next turned to Betsy.

"Let us go, let us go!" she said.

But Betsy did not hear her. She was bending down, talking to a general who had come up to her.

Alexey Alexandrovitch went up to Anna and courteously offered her his arm.

"Let us go, if you like," he said in French, but Anna was listening to the general and did not notice her husband.

"He's broken his leg too, so they say," the general was saying. "This is beyond everything."

Without answering her husband, Anna lifted her opera-glass and gazed towards the place where Vronsky had fallen; but it was so far off, and there was such a crowd of people about it, that she could make out nothing. She laid down the opera-glass, and would have moved away, but at that moment an officer galloped up and made some announcement to the Tsar. Anna craned forward, listening.

"Stiva! Stiva!" she cried to her brother.

But her brother did not hear her. Again she would have moved away.

"Once more I offer you my arm if you want to be going," said Alexey Alexandrovitch, reaching towards her hand.

She drew back from him with aversion, and without looking in his face answered:

"No, no, let me be, I'll stay."

She saw now that from the place of Vronsky's accident an officer was running across the course towards the pavilion. Betsy waved her handkerchief to him. The officer brought the news that the rider was not killed, but the horse had broken its back.

On hearing this Anna sat down hurriedly, and hid her face in her fan. Alexey Alexandrovitch saw that she was weeping, and could not control her tears, nor even the sobs that were shaking her bosom. Alexey Alexandrovitch stood so as to screen her, giving her time to recover herself.

"For the third time I offer you my arm," he said to her after a little time, turning to her. Anna gazed at him and did not know what to say. Princess Betsy came to her rescue.

"No, Alexey Alexandrovitch; I brought Anna and I promised to take her home," put in Betsy.

"I sent to Alexey to find out how he is, and he writes me he is quite well and unhurt, but in despair."

"So *he* will be here," she thought. "What a good thing I told him all!"

She glanced at her watch. She had still three hours to wait, and the memories of their last meeting set her blood in flame.

"My God, how light it is! It's dreadful, but I do love to see his face, and I do love this fantastic light.... My husband! Oh! yes ... Well, thank God! everything's over with him."

CHAPTER XXX

IN THE LITTLE GERMAN WATERING-PLACE TO WHICH THE SHTCHERBATSKYS HAD betaken themselves, as in all places indeed where people are gathered together, the usual process, as it were, of the crystallization of society went on, assigning to each member of that society a definite and unalterable place. Just as the particle of water in frost, definitely and unalterably, takes the special form of the crystal of snow, so each new person that arrived at the springs was at once placed in his special place.

Fürst Shtcherbatsky, *sammt Gemahlin und Tochter*, by the apartments they took, and from their name and from the friends they made, were immediately crystallized into a definite place marked out for them.

There was visiting the watering-place that year a real German Fürstin, in consequence of which the crystallizing process went on more vigorously than ever. Princess Shtcherbatskaya wished, above everything, to present her daughter to this German princess, and the day after their arrival she duly performed this rite. Kitty made a low and graceful curtsey in the *very simple*, that is to say, very elegant frock that had been ordered her from Paris. The German princess said, "I hope the roses will soon come back to this pretty little face," and for the Shtcherbatskys certain definite lines of existence were at once laid down from which there was no departing. The Shtcherbatskys made the acquaintance too of the family of an English Lady Somebody, and of a German countess and her son, wounded in the last war, and of a learned Swede, and of M. Canut and his sister. But yet inevitably the Shtcherbatskys were thrown most into the society of a Moscow lady, Marya Yevgenyevna Rtishtcheva and her daughter, whom Kitty disliked, because she had fallen ill, like herself, over a love affair, and a

Moscow colonel, whom Kitty had known from childhood, and always seen in uniform and epaulets, and who now, with his little eyes and his open neck and flowered cravat, was uncommonly ridiculous and tedious, because there was no getting rid of him. When all this was so firmly established, Kitty began to be very much bored, especially as the prince went away to Carlsbad and she was left alone with her mother. She took no interest in the people she knew, feeling that nothing fresh would come of them. Her chief mental interest in the watering-place consisted in watching and making theories about the people she did not know. It was characteristic of Kitty that she always imagined everything in people in the most favorable light possible, especially so in those she did not know. And now as she made surmises as to who people were, what were their relations to one another, and what they were like, Kitty endowed them with the most marvelous and noble characters, and found confirmation of her idea in her observations.

Of these people the one that attracted her most was a Russian girl who had come to the watering-place with an invalid Russian lady, Madame Stahl, as every one called her. Madame Stahl belonged to the highest society, but she was so ill that she could not walk, and only on exceptionally fine days made her appearance at the springs in an invalid carriage. But it was not so much from ill-health as from pride—so Princess Shtcherbatskaya interpreted it—that Madame Stahl had not made the acquaintance of any one among the Russians there. The Russian girl looked after Madame Stahl, and besides that, she was, as Kitty observed, on friendly terms with all the invalids who were seriously ill, and there were many of them at the springs, and looked after them in the most natural way. This Russian girl was not, as Kitty gathered, related to Madame Stahl, nor was she a paid attendant. Madame Stahl called her Varenka, and other people called her "Mademoiselle Varenka." Apart from the interest Kitty took in this girl's relations with Madame Stahl and with other unknown persons, Kitty, as often happened, felt an inexplicable attraction to Mademoiselle Varenka, and was aware when their eyes met that she too liked her.

Of Mademoiselle Varenka one would not say that she had passed her first youth, but she was, as it were, a creature without youth; she might have been taken for nineteen or for thirty. If her features were criticized separately, she was handsome rather than plain, in spite of the sickly hue of her face. She would have been a good figure, too, if it had not been for her extreme thinness and the size of her head, which was too large for her medium height. But she was not likely to be attractive to men. She was like a fine flower, already past its bloom

"Scandalous and disgraceful!" answered the colonel. "The one thing to be dreaded is meeting Russians abroad. That tall gentleman was abusing the doctor, flinging all sorts of insults at him because he wasn't treating him quite as he liked, and he began waving his stick at him. It's simply a scandal!"

"Oh, how unpleasant!" said the princess. "Well, and how did it end?"

"Luckily at that point that ... the one in the mushroom hat ... intervened. A Russian lady, I think she is," said the colonel.

"Mademoiselle Varenka?" asked Kitty.

"Yes, yes. She came to the rescue before any one; she took the man by the arm and led him away."

"There, mamma," said Kitty; "you wonder that I'm enthusiastic about her."

The next day, as she watched her unknown friend, Kitty noticed that Mademoiselle Varenka was already on the same terms with Levin and his companion as with her other protégés. She went up to them, entered into conversation with them, and served as interpreter for the woman, who could not speak any foreign language.

Kitty began to entreat her mother still more urgently to let her make friends with Varenka. And, disagreeable as it was to the princess to seem to take the first step in wishing to make the acquaintance of Madame Stahl, who thought fit to give herself airs, she made inquiries about Varenka, and, having ascertained particulars about her tending to prove that there could be no harm though little good in the acquaintance, she herself approached Varenka and made acquaintance with her.

Choosing a time when her daughter had gone to the spring, while Varenka had stopped outside the baker's, the princess went up to her.

"Allow me to make your acquaintance," she said, with her dignified smile. "My daughter has lost her heart to you," she said. "Possibly you do not know me. I am ..."

"That feeling is more than reciprocal, princess," Varenka answered hurriedly.

"What a good deed you did yesterday to our poor compatriot!" said the princess.

Varenka flushed a little. "I don't remember. I don't think I did anything," she said.

"Why, you saved that Levin from disagreeable consequences."

"Yes, *sa compagne* called me, and I tried to pacify him; he's very ill, and was dissatisfied with the doctor. I'm used to looking after such invalids."

"Yes, I've heard you live at Mentone with your aunt—I think—
Stahl: I used to know her *belle-sœur*."

"No, she's not my aunt. I call her mamma, but I am not related to her;
brought up by her," answered Varenka, flushing a little again.

This was so simply said, and so sweet was the truthful and candid expression
of her face, that the princess saw why Kitty had taken such a fancy to Varenka.

"Well, and what's this Levin going to do?" asked the princess.

"He's going away," answered Varenka.

At that instant Kitty came up from the spring beaming with delight that her
mother had become acquainted with her unknown friend.

"Well, see, Kitty, your intense desire to make friends with Mademoiselle . . ."

"Varenka," Varenka put in smiling, "that's what every one calls me."

Kitty blushed with pleasure, and slowly, without speaking, pressed her new
friend's hand, which did not respond to her pressure, but lay motionless in her
hand. The hand did not respond to her pressure, but the face of Mademoiselle
Varenka glowed with a soft, glad, though rather mournful smile, that showed
large but handsome teeth.

"I have long wished for this too," she said.

"But you are so busy."

"Oh, no, I'm not at all busy," answered Varenka, but at that moment she
had to leave her new friends because two little Russian girls, children of an
invalid, ran up to her.

"Varenka, mamma's calling!" they cried.

And Varenka went after them.

CHAPTER XXXII

THE PARTICULARS WHICH THE PRINCESS HAD LEARNED IN REGARD TO
Varenka's past and her relations with Madame Stahl were as fo's:
Madame Stahl, of whom some people said that she had ied
her husband out of his life, while others said it was he who had her
wretched by his immoral behavior, had always been a woman of w ealth
and enthusiastic temperament. When, after her separation from h band,
she gave birth to her only child, the child had died almost imm y, and
the family of Madame Stahl, knowing her sensibility, and fea news

…l her, had substituted another child, a baby born the same night and …ame house in Petersburg, the daughter of the chief cook of the Imperial …ehold. This was Varenka. Madame Stahl learned later on that Varenka … not her own child, but she went on bringing her up, especially as very …on afterwards Varenka had not a relation of her own living. Madame Stahl had now been living more than ten years continuously abroad, in the south, never leaving her couch. And some people said that Madame Stahl had made her social position as a philanthropic, highly religious woman; other people said she really was at heart the highly ethical being, living for nothing but the good of her fellow-creatures, which she represented herself to be. No one knew what her faith was—Catholic, Protestant, or Orthodox. But one fact was indubitable—she was in amicable relations with the highest dignitaries of all the churches and sects.

Varenka lived with her all the while abroad, and every one who knew Madame Stahl knew and liked Mademoiselle Varenka, as every one called her.

Having learned all these facts, the princess found nothing to object to in her daughter's intimacy with Varenka, more especially as Varenka's breeding and education were of the best—she spoke French and English extremely well—and what was of the most weight, brought a message from Madame Stahl expressing her regret that she was prevented by her ill-health from making the acquaintance of the princess.

After getting to know Varenka, Kitty became more and more fascinated by her friend, and every day she discovered new virtues in her.

The princess, hearing that Varenka had a good voice, asked her to come and sing to them in the evening.

"Kitty plays, and we have a piano; not a good one, it's true, but you will give us so much pleasure," said the princess with her affected smile, which Kitty disliked particularly just then, because she noticed that Varenka had no inclination to sing. Varenka came, however, in the evening and brought a roll of music with her. The princess had invited Marya Yevgenyevna and her daughter and the colonel.

Varenka seemed quite unaffected by there being persons present she did not know, and she went directly to the piano. She could not accompany herself, but she could sing music at sight very well. Kitty, who played well, accompanied her.

"You have an extraordinary talent," the princess said to her after Varenka had sung the first song extremely well.

Marya Yevgenyevna and her daughter expressed their thanks and admiration.

"Look," said the colonel, looking out of the window, "what an audience has collected to listen to you." There actually was quite a considerable crowd under the windows.

"I am very glad it gives you pleasure," Varenka answered simply.

Kitty looked with pride at her friend. She was enchanted by her talent, and her voice, and her face, but most of all by her manner, by the way Varenka obviously thought nothing of her singing and was quite unmoved by their praises. She seemed only to be asking: "Am I to sing again, or is that enough?"

"If it had been I," thought Kitty, "how proud I should have been! How delighted I should have been to see that crowd under the windows! But she's utterly unmoved by it. Her only motive is to avoid refusing and to please mamma. What is there in her? What is it gives her the power to look down on everything, to be calm independently of everything? How I should like to know it and to learn it of her!" thought Kitty, gazing into her serene face. The princess asked Varenka to sing again, and Varenka sang another song, also smoothly, distinctly, and well, standing erect at the piano and beating time on it with her thin, dark-skinned hand.

The next song in the book was an Italian one. Kitty played the opening bars, and looked round at Varenka.

"Let's skip that," said Varenka, flushing a little. Kitty let her eyes rest on Varenka's face, with a look of dismay and inquiry.

"Very well, the next one," she said hurriedly, turning over the pages, and at once feeling that there was something connected with the song.

"No," answered Varenka with a smile, laying her hand on the music, "no, let's have that one." And she sang it just as quietly, as coolly, and as well as the others.

When she had finished, they all thanked her again, and went off to tea. Kitty and Varenka went out into the little garden that adjoined the house.

"Am I right, that you have some reminiscences connected with that song?" said Kitty. "Don't tell me," she added hastily, "only say if I'm right."

"No, why not? I'll tell you simply," said Varenka, and, without waiting for a reply, she went on: "Yes, it brings up memories, once painful ones. I cared for some one once, and I used to sing him that song."

Kitty with big, wide-open eyes gazed silently, sympathetically at Varenka.

"I cared for him, and he cared for me; but his mother did not wish it, and he married another girl. He's living now not far from us, and I see him sometimes. You didn't think I had a love story too," she said, and there was a faint gleam in her handsome face of that fire which Kitty felt must once have glowed all over her.

"I didn't think so? Why, if I were a man, I could never care for any one else after knowing you. Only I can't understand how he could, to please his mother, forget you and make you unhappy; he had no heart."

"Oh, no, he's a very good man, and I'm not unhappy; quite the contrary, I'm very happy. Well, so we shan't be singing any more now," she added, turning towards the house.

"How good you are! how good you are!" cried Kitty, and stopping her, she kissed her. "If I could only be even a little like you!"

"Why should you be like any one? You're nice as you are," said Varenka, smiling her gentle, weary smile.

"No, I'm not nice at all. Come, tell me … Stop a minute, let's sit down," said Kitty, making her sit down again beside her. "Tell me, isn't it humiliating to think that a man has disdained your love, that he hasn't cared for it? …"

"But he didn't disdain it; I believe he cared for me, but he was a dutiful son …"

"Yes, but if it hadn't been on account of his mother, if it had been his own doing? …" said Kitty, feeling she was giving away her secret, and that her face, burning with the flush of shame, had betrayed her already.

"In that case he would have done wrong, and I should not have regretted him," answered Varenka, evidently realizing that they were now talking not of her, but of Kitty.

"But the humiliation," said Kitty, "the humiliation one can never forget, can never forget," she said, remembering her look at the last ball during the pause in the music.

"Where is the humiliation? Why, you did nothing wrong?"

"Worse than wrong—shameful."

Varenka shook her head and laid her hand on Kitty's hand.

"Why, what is there shameful?" she said. "You didn't tell a man, who didn't care for you, that you loved him, did you?"

"Of course not; I never said a word, but he knew it. No, no, there are looks, there are ways; I can't forget it, if I live a hundred years."

"Why so? I don't understand. The whole point is whether you love him now or not," said Varenka, who called everything by its name.

"I hate him; I can't forgive myself."

"Why, what for?"

"The shame, the humiliation!"

"Oh! if every one were as sensitive as you are!" said Varenka. "There isn't a girl who hasn't been through the same. And it's all so unimportant."

"Why, what is important?" said Kitty, looking into her face with inquisitive wonder.

"Oh, there's so much that's important," said Varenka, smiling.

"Why, what?"

"Oh, so much that's more important," answered Varenka, not knowing what to say. But at that instant they heard the princess's voice from the window. "Kitty, it's cold! Either get a shawl, or come indoors."

"It really is time to go in!" said Varenka, getting up. "I have to go on to Madame Berthe's; she asked me to."

Kitty held her by the hand, and with passionate curiosity and entreaty her eyes asked her: "What is it, what is this of such importance that gives you such tranquillity? You know, tell me!" But Varenka did not even know what Kitty's eyes were asking her. She merely thought that she had to go to see Madame Berthe too that evening, and to make haste home in time for *maman's* tea at twelve o'clock. She went indoors, collected her music, and saying good-bye to every one, was about to go.

"Allow me to see you home," said the colonel.

"Yes, how can you go alone at night like this?" chimed in the princess. "Anyway, I'll send Parasha."

Kitty saw that Varenka could hardly restrain a smile at the idea that she needed an escort.

"No, I always go about alone and nothing ever happens to me," she said, taking her hat. And kissing Kitty once more, without saying what was important, she stepped out courageously with the music under her arm and vanished into the twilight of the summer night, bearing away with her her secret of what was important and what gave her the calm and dignity so much to be envied.

CHAPTER XXXIII

K ITTY MADE THE ACQUAINTANCE OF MADAME STAHL TOO, AND THIS acquaintance, together with her friendship with Varenka, did not merely exercise a great influence on her, it also comforted her in her

"How is it Anna Pavlovna's not been to see us for so long?" the princess said one day of Madame Petrova. "I've asked her, but she seems put out about something."

"No, I've not noticed it, maman," said Kitty, flushing hotly.

"Is it long since you went to see them?"

"We're meaning to make an expedition to the mountains to-morrow," answered Kitty,

"Well, you can go," answered the princess, gazing at her daughter's embarrassed face and trying to guess the cause of her embarrassment.

That day Varenka came to dinner and told them that Anna Pavlovna had changed her mind and given up the expedition for the morrow. And the princess noticed again that Kitty reddened.

"Kitty, haven't you had some misunderstanding with the Petrovs?" said the princess, when they were left alone. "Why has she given up sending the children and coming to see us?"

Kitty answered that nothing had happened between them, and that she could not tell why Anna Pavlovna seemed displeased with her. Kitty answered perfectly truly. She did not know the reason Anna Pavlovna had changed to her, but she guessed it. She guessed at something which she could not tell her mother, which she did not put into words to herself. It was one of those things which one knows but which one can never speak of even to oneself, so terrible and shameful would it be to be mistaken.

Again and again she went over in her memory all her relations with the family. She remembered the simple delight expressed on the round, good-humored face of Anna Pavlovna at their meetings; she remembered their secret confabulations about the invalid, their plots to draw him away from the work which was forbidden him, and to get him out-of-doors; the devotion of the youngest boy, who used to call her "my Kitty," and would not go to bed without her. How nice it all was! Then she recalled the thin, terribly thin figure of Petrov, with his long neck, in his brown coat, his scant, curly hair, his questioning blue eyes that were so terrible to Kitty at first, and his painful attempts to seem hearty and lively in her presence. She recalled the efforts she had made at first to overcome the repugnance she felt for him, as for all consumptive people, and the pains it had cost her to think of things to say to him. She recalled the timid, softened look with which he gazed at her, and the strange feeling of compassion and awkwardness, and later of a sense of her own goodness, which she had felt at it. How nice it all was! But all that was at first. Now, a few days ago, everything was suddenly spoiled. Anna Pavlovna had met Kitty with affected cordiality, and had kept continual watch on her and on her husband.

Could that touching pleasure he showed when she came near be the cause of Anna Pavlovna's coolness?

"Yes," she mused, "there was something unnatural about Anna Pavlovna, and utterly unlike her good nature, when she said angrily the day before yesterday: 'There, he will keep waiting for you; he wouldn't drink his coffee without you, though he's grown so dreadfully weak.'"

"Yes, perhaps, too, she didn't like it when I gave him the rug. It was all so simple, but he took it so awkwardly, and was so long thanking me, that I felt awkward too. And then that portrait of me he did so well. And most of all that look of confusion and tenderness! Yes, yes, that's it!" Kitty repeated to herself with horror. "No, it can't be, it oughtn't to be! He's so much to be pitied!" she said to herself directly after.

This doubt poisoned the charm of her new life.

CHAPTER XXXIV

BEFORE THE END OF THE COURSE OF DRINKING THE WATERS, PRINCE Shtcherbatsky, who had gone on from Carlsbad to Baden and Kissingen to Russian friends—to get a breath of Russian air, as he said—came back to his wife and daughter.

The views of the prince and of the princess on life abroad were completely opposed. The princess thought everything delightful, and in spite of her established position in Russian society, she tried abroad to be like a European fashionable lady, which she was not—for the simple reason that she was a typical Russian gentlewoman; and so she was affected, which did not altogether suit her. The prince, on the contrary, thought everything foreign detestable, got sick of European life, kept to his Russian habits, and purposely tried to show himself abroad less European than he was in reality.

The prince returned thinner, with the skin hanging in loose bags on his cheeks, but in the most cheerful frame of mind. His good-humor was even greater when he saw Kitty completely recovered. The news of Kitty's friendship with Madame Stahl and Varenka, and the reports the princess gave him of some kind of change she had noticed in Kitty, troubled the prince and aroused his habitual feeling of jealousy of everything that drew his daughter away from him, and a dread that his daughter might have got out of the reach of his influence into regions inaccessible to him. But these unpleasant matters were all drowned in the sea of kindliness and good-humor which was always within him, and more so than ever since his course of Carlsbad waters.

The day after his arrival the prince, in his long overcoat, with his Russian wrinkles and baggy cheeks propped up by a starched collar, set off with his daughter to the spring in the greatest good-humor.

It was a lovely morning: the bright, cheerful houses with their little gardens, the sight of the red-faced, red-armed, beer-drinking German waitresses, working away merrily, did the heart good. But the nearer they got to the springs the oftener they met sick people; and their appearance seemed more pitiable than ever among the every day conditions of prosperous German life. Kitty was no longer struck by this contrast. The bright sun, the brilliant green of the foliage, the strains of the music were for her the natural setting of all these familiar faces, with their changes to greater emaciation or to convalescence, for which she watched. But to the prince the brightness and gaiety of the June morning, and the sound of the orchestra playing a gay waltz then in fashion, and above all, the appearance of the healthy attendants, seemed something unseemly and monstrous, in conjunction with these slowly moving, dying figures gathered together from all parts of Europe. In spite of his feeling of pride and, as it were, of the return of youth, with his favorite daughter on his arm, he felt awkward, and almost ashamed of his vigorous step and his sturdy, stout limbs. He felt almost like a man not dressed in a crowd.

"Present me to your new friends," he said to his daughter, squeezing her hand with his elbow. "I like even your horrid Soden for making you so well again. Only it's melancholy, very melancholy here. Who's that?"

Kitty mentioned the names of all the people they met, with some of whom she was acquainted and some not. At the entrance of the garden they met the blind lady, Madame Berthe, with her guide, and the prince was delighted to see the old Frenchwoman's face light up when she heard Kitty's voice. She at once began talking to him with French exaggerated politeness, applauding him for having such a delightful daughter, extolling Kitty to the skies before her face, and calling her a treasure, a pearl, and a consoling angel.

"Well, she's the second angel, then," said the prince, smiling. "she calls Mademoiselle Varenka angel number one."

"Oh! Mademoiselle Varenka, she's a real angel, allez," Madame Berthe assented.

In the arcade they met Varenka herself. She was walking rapidly towards them carrying an elegant red bag.

"Here is papa come," Kitty said to her.

Varenka made—simply and naturally as she did everything—a movement between a bow and a curtsey, and immediately began talking to the prince, without shyness, naturally, as she talked to every one.

"Of course I know you; I know you very well," the prince said to her with a smile, in which Kitty detected with joy that her father liked her friend. "Where are you off to in such haste?"

"Maman's here," she said, turning to Kitty. "She has not slept all night, and the doctor advised her to go out. I'm taking her her work."

"So that's angel number one?" said the prince when Varenka had gone on.

Kitty saw that her father had meant to make fun of Varenka, but that he could not do it because he liked her.

"Come, so we shall see all your friends," he went on, "even Madame Stahl, if she deigns to recognize me."

"Why, did you know her, papa?" Kitty asked apprehensively, catching the gleam of irony that kindled in the prince's eyes at the mention of Madame Stahl.

"I used to know her husband, and her too a little, before she'd joined the Pietists."

"What is a Pietist, papa?" asked Kitty, dismayed to find that what she prized so highly in Madame Stahl had a name.

"I don't quite know myself. I only know that she thanks God for everything, for every misfortune, and thanks God too that her husband died. And that's rather droll, as they didn't get on together."

"Who's that? What a piteous face!" he asked, noticing a sick man of medium height sitting on a bench, wearing a brown overcoat and white trousers that fell in strange folds about his long, fleshless legs. This man lifted his straw hat, showed his scanty curly hair and high forehead, painfully reddened by the pressure of the hat.

"That's Petrov, an artist," answered Kitty, blushing. "And that's his wife," she added, indicating Anna Pavlovna, who, as though on purpose, at the very instant they approached walked away after a child that had run off along a path.

"Poor fellow! and what a nice face he has!" said the prince. "Why don't you go up to him? He wanted to speak to you."

"Well, let us go, then," said Kitty, turning round resolutely. "How are you feeling to-day?" she asked Petrov.

Petrov got up, leaning on his stick, and looked shyly at the prince.

"This is my daughter," said the prince. "Let me introduce myself."

The painter bowed and smiled, showing his strangely dazzling white teeth.

"We expected you yesterday, princess," he said to Kitty. He staggered as he said this, and then repeated the motion, trying to make it seem as if it had been intentional.

"I meant to come, but Varenka said that Anna Pavlovna sent word you were not going."

"Not going!" said Petrov, blushing, and immediately beginning to cough, and his eyes sought his wife. "Anita! Anita!" he said loudly, and the swollen veins stood out like cords on his thin white neck.

Anna Pavlovna came up.

"So you sent word to the princess that we weren't going!" he whispered to her angrily, losing his voice.

"Good-morning, princess," said Anna Pavlovna, with an assumed smile utterly unlike her former manner. "Very glad to make your acquaintance," she said to the prince. "You've long been expected, prince."

"What did you send word to the princess that we weren't going for?" the artist whispered hoarsely once more, still more angrily, obviously exasperated that his voice failed him so that he could not give his words the expression he would have liked to.

"Oh, mercy on us! I thought we weren't going," his wife answered crossly.

"What, when …" He coughed and waved his hand. The prince took off his hat and moved away with his daughter.

"Ah! ah!" he sighed deeply. "Oh, poor things!"

"Yes, papa," answered Kitty. "And you must know they've three children, no servant, and scarcely any means. He gets something from the Academy," she went on briskly, trying to drown the distress that the queer change in Anna Pavlovna's manner to her had aroused in her.

"Oh, here's Madame Stahl," said Kitty, indicating an invalid carriage, where, propped on pillows, something in gray and blue was lying under a sunshade. This was Madame Stahl. Behind her stood the gloomy, healthy-looking German workman who pushed the carriage. Close by was standing a flaxenheaded Swedish count, whom Kitty knew by name. Several invalids were lingering near the low carriage, staring at the lady as though she were some curiosity.

The prince went up to her, and Kitty detected that disconcerting gleam of irony in his eyes. He went up to Madame Stahl, and addressed her with extreme courtesy and affability in that excellent French that so few speak nowadays.

"I don't know if you remember me, but I must recall myself to thank you for your kindness to my daughter," he said, taking off his hat and not putting it on again.

"Prince Alexander Shtcherbatsky," said Madame Stahl, lifting upon him her heavenly eyes, in which Kitty discerned a look of annoyance. "Delighted! I have taken a great fancy to your daughter."

"You are still in weak health?"

"Yes; I'm used to it," said Madame Stahl, and she introduced the prince to the Swedish count.

"You are scarcely changed at all," the prince said to her. "It's ten or eleven years since I had the honor of seeing you."

"Yes; God sends the cross and sends the strength to bear it. Often one wonders what is the goal of this life? ... The other side!" she said angrily to Varenka, who had rearranged the rug over her feet not to her satisfaction.

"To do good, probably," said the prince with a twinkle in his eye.

"That is not for us to judge," said Madame Stahl, perceiving the shade of expression on the prince's face. "So you will send me that book, dear count? I'm very grateful to you," she said to the young Swede.

"Ah!" cried the prince, catching sight of the Moscow colonel standing near, and with a bow to Madame Stahl he walked away with his daughter and the Moscow colonel, who joined them.

"That's our aristocracy, prince!" the Moscow colonel said with ironical intention. He cherished a grudge against Madame Stahl for not making his acquaintance.

"She's just the same," replied the prince.

"Did you know her before her illness, prince—that's to say before she took to her bed?"

"Yes. She took to her bed before my eyes," said the prince.

"They say it's ten years since she has stood on her feet."

"She doesn't stand up because her legs are too short. She's a very bad figure."

"Papa, it's not possible!" cried Kitty.

"That's what wicked tongues say, my darling. And your Varenka catches it too," he added. "Oh, these invalid ladies!"

"Oh, no, papa!" Kitty objected warmly. "Varenka worships her. And then she does so much good! Ask any one! Every one knows her and Aline Stahl."

"Perhaps so," said the prince, squeezing her hand with his elbow; "but it's better when one does good so that you may ask every one and no one knows."

Kitty did not answer, not because she had nothing to say, but because she did not care to reveal her secret thoughts even to her father. But, strange to say, although she had so made up her mind not to be influenced by her father's views, not to let him into her inmost sanctuary, she felt that the heavenly image of Madame Stahl, which she had carried for a whole month in her heart, had vanished, never to return, just as the fantastic figure made up of some clothes thrown down at random vanishes when one sees that it is only some garment lying there. All that was left was a woman with short legs, who lay down because she had a bad figure, and worried patient Varenka for not arranging her rug to her liking. And by no effort of the imagination could Kitty bring back the former Madame Stahl.

CHAPTER XXXV

THE PRINCE COMMUNICATED HIS GOOD-HUMOR TO HIS OWN FAMILY AND HIS friends, and even to the German landlord in whose rooms the Shtcherbatskys were staying.

On coming back with Kitty from the springs, the prince, who had asked the colonel, and Marya Yevgenyevna, and Varenka all to come and have coffee with them, gave orders for a table and chairs to be taken into the garden under the chestnut-tree, and lunch to be laid there. The landlord and the servants, too, grew brisker under the influence of his good spirits. They knew his open-handedness; and half an hour later the invalid doctor from Hamburg, who lived on the top floor, looked enviously out of the window at the merry party of healthy Russians assembled under the chestnut-tree. In the trembling circles of shadow cast by the leaves, at a table, covered with a white cloth, and set with coffeepot, bread-and-butter, cheese, and cold game, sat the princess in a high cap with lilac ribbons, distributing cups and bread-and-butter. At the other end sat the prince, eating heartily, and talking loudly and merrily. The prince had spread out near him his purchases, carved boxes, and knick-knacks, paper-knives of all sorts, of which he bought a heap at every watering-place, and bestowed them upon every one, including Lieschen, the servant girl, and the landlord, with whom he jested in his comically bad German, assuring him that it was not the water had cured Kitty, but his splendid cookery, especially his plum-soup. The princess laughed at her husband for his Russian ways, but she was more lively and good-humored than she had been all the while she had been at the waters. The colonel smiled, as he always did, at the prince's jokes, but as far as regards Europe, of which he believed himself to be making a careful study, he took the princess's side. The simple-hearted Marya Yevgenyevna simply roared with laughter at everything absurd the prince said, and his jokes made Varenka helpless with feeble but infectious laughter, which was something Kitty had never seen before.

Kitty was glad of all this, but she could not be light-hearted. She could not solve the problem her father had unconsciously set her by his good-humored view of her friends, and of the life that had so attracted her. To this doubt there was joined the change in her relations with the Petrovs, which had been so conspicuously and unpleasantly marked that morning. Every one was good-humored, but Kitty could not feel good-humored, and this increased her distress. She felt a feeling such as she had known in childhood, when she had been shut in her room as a punishment, and had heard her sisters' merry laughter outside.

"Well, but what did you buy this mass of things for?" said the princess, smiling, and handing her husband a cup of coffee.

"One goes for a walk, one looks in a shop, and they ask you to buy. '*Erlaucht, Durchlaucht?*' Directly they say '*Durchlaucht*,' I can't hold out. I lose ten thalers."

"It's simply from boredom," said the princess.

"Of course it is. Such boredom, my dear, that one doesn't know what to do with oneself."

"How can you be bored, prince? There's so much that's interesting now in Germany," said Marya Yevgenyevna.

"But I know everything that's interesting: the plum-soup I know, and the pea-sausages I know. I know everything."

"No, you may say what you like, prince, there's the interest of their institutions," said the colonel.

"But what is there interesting about it? They're all as pleased as brass halfpence. They've conquered everybody, and why am I to be pleased at that? I haven't conquered any one; and I'm obliged to take off my own boots, yes, and put them away too; in the morning, get up and dress at once, and go to the dining-room to drink bad tea! How different it is at home! You get up in no haste, you get cross, grumble a little, and come round again. You've time to think things over, and no hurry."

"But time's money, you forget that," said the colonel.

"Time, indeed, that depends! Why, there's time one would give a month of for sixpence, and time you wouldn't give half an hour of for any money. Isn't that so, Katinka? What is it? why are you so depressed?"

"I'm not depressed."

"Where are you off to? Stay a little longer," he said to Varenka.

"I must be going home," said Varenka, getting up, and again she went off into a giggle. When she had recovered, she said good-bye, and went into the house to get her hat.

Kitty followed her. Even Varenka struck her as different. She was not worse, but different from what she had fancied her before.

"Oh, dear! it's a long while since I've laughed so much!" said Varenka, gathering up her parasol and her bag. "How nice he is, your father!"

Kitty did not speak.

"When shall I see you again?" asked Varenka.

"Mamma meant to go and see the Petrovs. Won't you be there?" said Kitty, to try Varenka.

"Yes," answered Varenka. "They're getting ready to go away, so I promised to help them pack."

"Well, I'll come too, then."

"No, why should you?"

"Why not? why not? why not?" said Kitty, opening her eyes wide, and clutching at Varenka's parasol, so as not to let her go. "No, wait a minute; why not?"

"Oh, nothing; your father has come, and besides, they will feel awkward at your helping."

"No, tell me why you don't want me to be often at the Petrovs. You don't want me to—why not?"

"I didn't say that," said Varenka quietly.

"No, please tell me!"

"Tell you everything?" asked Varenka.

"Everything, everything!" Kitty assented.

"Well, there's really nothing of any consequence; only that Mihail Alexeyevitch" (that was the artist's name) "had meant to leave earlier, and now he doesn't want to go away," said Varenka, smiling.

"Well, well!" Kitty urged impatiently, looking darkly at Varenka.

"Well, and for some reason Anna Pavlovna told him that he didn't want to go because you are here. Of course, that was nonsense; but there was a dispute over it—over you. You know how irritable these sick people are."

Kitty, scowling more than ever, kept silent, and Varenka went on speaking alone, trying to soften or soothe her, and seeing a storm coming—she did not know whether of tears or of words.

"So you'd better not go…. You understand; you won't be offended? …"

"And it serves me right! And it serves me right!" Kitty cried quickly, snatching the parasol out of Varenka's hand, and looking past her friend's face.

Varenka felt inclined to smile, looking at her childish fury, but she was afraid of wounding her.

"How does it serve you right? I don't understand," she said.

"It serves me right, because it was all sham; because it was all done on purpose, and not from the heart. What business had I to interfere with outsiders? And so it's come about that I'm a cause of quarrel, and that I've done what nobody asked me to do. Because it was all a sham! a sham! a sham! ..."

"A sham! with what object?" said Varenka gently.

"Oh, it's so idiotic! so hateful! There was no need whatever for me.... Nothing but sham!" she said, opening and shutting the parasol.

"But with what object?"

"To seem better to people, to myself, to God; to deceive every one. No! now I won't descend to that. I'll be bad; but anyway not a liar, a cheat."

"But who is a cheat?" said Varenka reproachfully. "You speak as if ..."

But Kitty was in one of her gusts of fury, and she would not let her finish.

"I don't talk about you, not about you at all. You're perfection. Yes, yes, I know you're all perfection; but what am I to do if I'm bad? This would never have been if I weren't bad. So let me be what I am. I won't be a sham. What have I to do with Anna Pavlovna? Let them go their way, and me go mine. I can't be different.... And yet it's not that, it's not that."

"What is not that?" asked Varenka in bewilderment.

"Everything. I can't act except from the heart, and you act from principle. I liked you simply, but you most likely only wanted to save me, to improve me."

"You are unjust," said Varenka.

"But I'm not speaking of other people, I'm speaking of myself."

"Kitty," they heard her mother's voice, "come here, show papa your necklace."

Kitty, with a haughty air, without making peace with her friend, took the necklace in a little box from the table and went to her mother.

"What's the matter? Why are you so red?" her mother and father said to her with one voice.

"Nothing," she answered. "I'll be back directly," and she ran back.

"She's still here," she thought. "What am I to say to her? Oh, dear! what have I done, what have I said? Why was I rude to her? What am I to do? What am I to say to her?" thought Kitty, and she stopped in the doorway.

Varenka in her hat and with the parasol in her hands was sitting at the table examining the spring which Kitty had broken. She lifted her head.

"Varenka, forgive me, do forgive me," whispered Kitty, going up to her. "I don't remember what I said. I . . ."

"I really didn't mean to hurt you," said Varenka, smiling.

Peace was made. But with her father's coming all the world in which she had been living was transformed for Kitty. She did not give up everything she had learned, but she became aware that she had deceived herself in supposing she could be what she wanted to be. Her eyes were, it seemed, opened; she felt all the difficulty of maintaining herself without hypocrisy and self-conceit on the pinnacle to which she had wished to mount. Moreover, she became aware of all the dreariness of the world of sorrow, of sick and dying people, in which she had been living. The efforts she had made to like it seemed to her intolerable, and she felt a longing to get back quickly into the fresh air, to Russia, to Ergushovo, where, as she knew from letters, her sister Dolly had already gone with her children.

But her affection for Varenka did not wane. As she said good-bye, Kitty begged her to come to them in Russia.

"I'll come when you get married," said Varenka.

"I shall never marry."

"Well, then, I shall never come."

"Well, then, I shall be married simply for that. Mind now, remember your promise," said Kitty.

The doctor's prediction was fulfilled. Kitty returned home to Russia cured. She was not so gay and thoughtless as before, but she was serene. Her Moscow troubles had become a memory to her.

PART THREE

CHAPTER I

S ERGEY IVANOVITCH KOZNISHEV WANTED A REST FROM MENTAL WORK, AND IN-stead of going abroad as he usually did, he came towards the end of May to stay in the country with his brother. In his judgment the best sort of life was a country life. He had come now to enjoy such a life at his brother's. Konstantin Levin was very glad to have him, especially as he did not expect his brother Nikolay that summer. But in spite of his affection and respect for Sergey Ivanovitch, Konstantin Levin was uncomfortable with his brother in the country. It made him uncomfortable, and it positively annoyed him to see his brother's attitude to the country. To Konstantin Levin the country was the background of life, that is of pleasures, endeavors, labor. To Sergey Ivanovitch the country meant on one hand rest from work, on the other a valuable antidote to the cor-rupt influences of town, which he took with satisfaction and a sense of its utility. To Konstantin Levin the country was good first because it afforded a field for labor, of the usefulness of which there could be no doubt. To Sergey Ivanovitch the country was particularly good, because there it was possible and fitting to do nothing. Moreover, Sergey Ivanovitch's attitude to the peasants rather piqued Konstantin. Sergey Ivanovitch used to say that he knew and liked the peasantry, and he often talked to the peasants, which he knew how to do without affectation or condescension, and from every such conversation he would deduce general conclusions in favor of the peasantry and in confirmation of his knowing them. Konstantin Levin did not like such an attitude to the peasants. To Konstantin the peasant was simply the chief partner in their common labor, and in spite of all the respect and the love, almost like that of kinship, he had for the peasant—sucked in probably, as he said himself, with the milk of his peasant nurse—still as a fellow-worker with him, while sometimes enthusiastic over the vigor, gentleness, and justice of these men, he was very often, when their common labors called for other qualities, exasperated with the peasant for his carelessness, lack of meth-od, drunkenness, and lying. If he had been asked whether he liked or didn't like the peasants, Konstantin Levin would have been absolutely at a loss what to re-ply. He liked and did not like the peasants, just as he liked and did not like men in general. Of course, being a good-hearted man, he liked men rather than he disliked them, and so too with the peasants. But like or dislike "the people" as something apart he could not, not only because he lived with "the people," and all his interests were bound up with theirs, but also because he regarded himself as a part of "the people," did not see any special qualities or failings distinguishing himself and "the people," and could not contrast himself with them. Moreover, although he had lived so long in the closest relations with the peasants, as farmer and arbitrator, and what was more, as adviser (the peasants trusted him, and for thirty miles round they would come to ask his advice), he had no definite views of "the people," and would have been as much at a loss to answer the question whether he knew "the people" as the question whether he liked them. For him to say he knew the peasantry would have been the same as to say he knew men. He was continually watching and getting to know people of all sorts, and among them peasants, whom he regarded as good and interesting people, and he was continually observing new points in them, altering his former views of them and forming new ones. With Sergey Ivanovitch it was quite the contrary. Just as he liked and praised a country life in comparison with the life he did not like, so too he liked the peasantry in contradistinction to the class of men he did not like, and so too he knew the peasantry as something distinct from and opposed to men generally. In his methodical brain there were distinctly formulated certain aspects of peasant life, deduced partly from that life itself, but chiefly from contrast with other modes of life. He never changed his opinion of the peasantry and his sympathetic attitude towards them.

In the discussions that arose between the brothers on their views of the peasantry, Sergey Ivanovitch always got the better of his brother, precisely because Sergey Ivanovitch had definite ideas about the peasant—his character, his qualities, and his tastes. Konstantin Levin had no definite and unalterable idea on the subject, and so in their arguments Konstantin was readily convicted of contradicting himself.

In Sergey Ivanovitch's eyes his younger brother was a capital fellow, *with his heart in the right place* (as he expressed it in French), but with a mind which, though fairly quick, was too much influenced by the impressions of the moment, and consequently filled with contradictions. With all the condescension of an elder brother he sometimes explained to him the true import of things, but he derived little satisfaction from arguing with him because he got the better of him too easily.

Konstantin Levin regarded his brother as a man of immense intellect and culture, as generous in the highest sense of the word, and possessed of a special faculty for working for the public good. But in the depths of his heart, the older he became, and the more intimately he knew his brother, the more and more frequently the thought struck him that this faculty of working for the public good, of which he felt himself utterly devoid, was possibly not so much a quality as a lack of something—not a lack of good, honest, noble desires and tastes, but a lack of vital force, of what is called heart, of that impulse which drives a man to choose some one out of the innumerable paths of life, and to care only for that one. The better he knew his brother, the more he noticed that Sergey Ivanovitch, and many other people who worked for the public welfare, were not led by an impulse of the heart to care for the public good, but reasoned from intellectual considerations that it was a right thing to take interest in public affairs, and consequently took interest in them. Levin was confirmed in this generalization by observing that his brother did not take questions affecting the public welfare or the question of the immortality of the soul a bit more to heart than he did chess problems, or the ingenious construction of a new machine.

Besides this, Konstantin Levin was not at his ease with his brother, because in summer in the country Levin was continually busy with work on the land, and the long summer day was not long enough for him to get through all he had to do, while Sergey Ivanovitch was taking a holiday. But though he was taking a holiday now, that is to say, he was doing no writing, he was so used to intellectual activity that he liked to put into concise and eloquent shape the ideas that occurred to him, and liked to have some one to listen to him. His most usual and natural listener was his brother. And so in spite of the friendliness and directness of their relations, Konstantin felt an awkwardness in leaving him alone. Sergey Ivanovitch liked to stretch himself on the grass in the sun, and to lie so, basking and chatting lazily.

"You wouldn't believe," he would say to his brother, "what a pleasure this rural laziness is to me. Not an idea in one's brain, as empty as a drum!"

But Konstantin Levin found it dull sitting and listening to him, especially when he knew that while he was away they would be carting dung onto the fields not ploughed ready for it, and heaping it all up anyhow; and would not screw the shares in the ploughs, but would let them come off and then say that the new ploughs were a silly invention, and there was nothing like the old Andreevna plough, and so on.

"Come, you've done enough trudging about in the heat," Sergey Ivanovitch would say to him.

"No, I must just run round to the counting-house for a minute," Levin would answer, and he would run off to the fields.

with the doctor, he wanted to talk. Levin, on the other hand, would have liked to get home as soon as possible to give orders about getting together the mowers for next day, and to set at rest his doubts about the mowing, which greatly absorbed him.

"Well, let's be going," he said.

"Why be in such a hurry? Let's stay a little. But how wet you are! Even though one catches nothing, it's nice. That's the best thing about every part of sport, that one has to do with nature. How exquisite this steely water is!" said Sergey Ivanovitch. "These riverside banks always remind me of the riddle—do you know it? 'The grass says to the water: we quiver and we quiver.'"

"I don't know the riddle," answered Levin wearily.

CHAPTER III

Do you know, I've been thinking about you," said Sergey Ivanovitch. "It's beyond everything what's being done in the district, according to what this doctor tells me. He's a very intelligent fellow. And as I've told you before, I tell you again: it's not right for you not to go to the meetings, and altogether to keep out of the district business. If decent people won't go into it, of course it's bound to go all wrong. We pay the money, and it all goes in salaries, and there are no schools, nor district nurses, nor midwives, nor drug-stores—nothing."

"Well, I did try, you know," Levin said slowly and unwillingly. "I can't! and so there's no help for it."

"But why can't you? I must own I can't make it out. Indifference, incapacity—I won't admit; surely it's not simply laziness?"

"None of those things. I've tried, and I see I can do nothing," said Levin.

He had hardly grasped what his brother was saying. Looking towards the plough-land across the river, he made out something black, but he could not distinguish whether it was a horse or the bailiff on horseback.

"Why is it you can do nothing? You made an attempt and didn't succeed, as you think, and you give in. How can you have so little self-respect?"

"Self-respect!" said Levin, stung to the quick by his brother's words; "I don't understand. If they'd told me at college that other people understood the integral calculus, and I didn't, then pride would have come in. But in this case one wants first to be convinced that one has certain qualifications for this sort of business, and especially that all this business is of great importance."

"What! do you mean to say it's not of importance?" said Sergey Ivanovitch, stung to the quick too at his brother's considering anything of no importance that interested him, and still more at his obviously paying little attention to what he was saying.

"I don't think it important; it does not take hold of me, I can't help it," answered Levin, making out that what he saw was the bailiff, and that the bailiff seemed to be letting the peasants go off the ploughed land. They were turning the plough over. "Can they have finished ploughing?" he wondered.

"Come, really though," said the elder brother, with a frown on his handsome, clever face, "there's a limit to everything. It's very well to be original and genuine, and to dislike everything conventional—I know all about that; but really, what you're saying either has no meaning, or it has a very wrong meaning. How can you think it a matter of no importance whether the peasant, whom you love as you assert ..."

"I never did assert it," thought Konstantin Levin.

—"dies without help? The ignorant peasant-women starve the children, and the people stagnate in darkness, and are helpless in the hands of every village clerk, while you have at your disposal a means of helping them, and don't help them because to your mind it's of no importance."

And Sergey Ivanovitch put before him the alternative: either you are so undeveloped that you can't see all that you can do, or you won't sacrifice your ease, your vanity, or whatever it is, to do it.

Konstantin Levin felt that there was no course open to him but to submit, or to confess to a lack of zeal for the public good. And this mortified him and hurt his feelings.

"It's both," he said resolutely: "I don't see that it was possible ..."

"What! was it impossible, if the money were properly laid out, to provide medical aid?"

"Impossible, as it seems to me.... For the three thousand square miles of our district, what with our thaws, and the storms, and the work in the fields, I don't see how it is possible to provide medical aid all over. And besides, I don't believe in medicine."

"Oh, well, that's unfair....I can quote to you thousands of instances.... But the schools, anyway."

"Why have schools?"

"I simply mean to say that those rights that touch me … my interest, I shall always defend to the best of my ability; that when they made raids on us students, and the police read our letters, I was ready to defend those rights to the utmost, to defend my rights to education and freedom. I can understand compulsory military service, which affects my children, my brothers, and myself, I am ready to deliberate on what concerns me; but deliberating on how to spend forty thousand roubles of district council money, or judging the half-witted Alioshka—I don't understand, and I can't do it."

Konstantin Levin spoke as though the floodgates of his speech had burst open. Sergey Ivanovitch smiled.

"But to-morrow it'll be your turn to be tried; would it have suited your tastes better to be tried in the old criminal tribunal?"

"I'm not going to be tried. I shan't murder anybody, and I've no need of it. Well, I tell you what," he went on, flying off again to a subject quite beside the point, "our district self-government and all the rest of it—it's just like the birch-branches we stick in the ground on Trinity Day, for instance, to look like a copse which has grown up of itself in Europe, and I can't gush over these birch-branches and believe in them."

Sergey Ivanovitch merely shrugged his shoulders, as though to express his wonder how the birch-branches had come into their argument at that point, though he did really understand at once what his brother meant.

"Excuse me, but you know one really can't argue in that way," he observed.

But Konstantin Levin wanted to justify himself for the failing, of which he was conscious, of lack of zeal for the public welfare, and he went on.

"I imagine," he said, "that no sort of activity is likely to be lasting if it is not founded on self-interest, that's a universal principle, a philosophical principle," he said, repeating the word "philosophical" with determination, as though wishing to show that he had as much right as any one else to talk of philosophy.

Sergey Ivanovitch smiled. "He too has a philosophy of his own at the service of his natural tendencies," he thought.

"Come, you'd better let philosophy alone," he said. "The chief problem of the philosophy of all ages consists just in finding the indispensable connection which exists between individual and social interests. But that's not to the point; what is to the point is a correction I must make in your comparison. The birches are not simply stuck in, but some are sown and some are planted, and one must deal carefully with them. It's only those peoples that have an intuitive sense of what's of importance and significance in their institutions, and know how to value them, that have a future before them—it's only those peoples that one can truly call historical."

And Sergey Ivanovitch carried the subject into the regions of philosophical history where Konstantin Levin could not follow him, and showed him all the incorrectness of his view.

"As for your dislike of it, excuse my saying so, that's simply our Russian sloth and old serf-owner's ways, and I'm convinced that in you it's a temporary error and will pass."

Konstantin was silent. He felt himself vanquished on all sides, but he felt at the same time that what he wanted to say was unintelligible to his brother. Only he could not make up his mind whether it was unintelligible because he was not capable of expressing his meaning clearly, or because his brother would not or could not understand him. But he did not pursue the speculation, and without replying, he fell to musing on a quite different and personal matter.

Sergey Ivanovitch wound up the last line, untied the horse, and they drove off.

CHAPTER IV

THE PERSONAL MATTER THAT ABSORBED LEVIN DURING HIS CONVERSATION with his brother was this. Once in a previous year he had gone to look at the mowing, and being made very angry by the bailiff he had recourse to his favorite means for regaining his temper,— he took a scythe from a peasant and began mowing.

He liked the work so much that he had several times tried his hand at mowing since. He had cut the whole of the meadow in front of his house, and this year ever since the early spring he had cherished a plan for mowing for whole days together with the peasants. Ever since his brother's arrival, he had been in doubt whether to mow or not. He was loth to leave his brother alone all day long, and he was afraid his brother would laugh at him about it. But as he drove into the meadow, and recalled the sensations of mowing, he came near deciding that he would go mowing. After the irritating discussion with his brother, he pondered over this intention again.

"I must have physical exercise, or my temper'll certainly be ruined," he thought, and he determined he would go mowing, however awkward he might feel about it with his brother or the peasants.

Towards evening Konstantin Levin went to his counting-house, gave directions as to the work to be done, and sent about the village to summon the mowers for the morrow, to cut the hay in Kalinov meadow, the largest and best of his grass lands.

"And send my scythe, please, to Tit, for him to set it, and bring it round to-morrow. I shall maybe do some mowing myself too," he said trying not to be embarrassed.

The bailiff smiled and said: "Yes, sir."

At tea the same evening Levin said to his brother:

"I fancy the fine weather will last," said he. "To-morrow I shall start mowing."

"I'm so fond of that form of field labor," said Sergey Ivanovitch.

"I'm awfully fond of it. I sometimes mow myself with the peasants, and to-morrow I want to try mowing the whole day."

Sergey Ivanovitch lifted his head, and looked with interest at his brother.

"How do you mean? Just like one of the peasants, all day long?"

"Yes, it's very pleasant," said Levin.

"It's splendid as exercise, only you'll hardly be able to stand it," said Sergey Ivanovitch, without a shade of irony.

"I've tried it. It's hard work at first, but you get into it. I dare say I shall manage to keep it up...."

"Really! what an idea! But tell me, how do the peasants look at it? I suppose they laugh in their sleeves at their master's being such a queer fish?"

"No, I don't think so; but it's so delightful, and at the same time such hard work, that one has no time to think about it."

"But how will you do about dining with them? To send you a bottle of Lafitte and roast turkey out there would be a little awkward."

"No, I'll simply come home at the time of their noonday rest."

Next morning Konstantin Levin got up earlier than usual, but he was detained giving directions on the farm, and when he reached the mowing-grass the mowers were already at their second row.

From the uplands he could get a view of the shaded cut part of the meadow below, with its grayish ridges of cut grass, and the black heaps of coats, taken off by the mowers at the place from which they had started cutting.

Gradually, as he rode towards the meadow, the peasants came into sight, some in coats, some in their shirts mowing, one behind another in a long string, swinging their scythes differently. He counted forty-two of them.

They were mowing slowly over the uneven, low-lying parts of the meadow, where there had been an old dam. Levin recognized some of his own men. Here was old Yermil in a very long white smock, bending forward to swing a scythe; there was a young fellow, Vaska, who had been a coachman of Levin's, taking every row with a wide sweep. Here, too, was Tit, Levin's preceptor in the art of mowing, a thin little peasant. He was in front of all, and cut his wide row without bending, as though playing with the scythe.

Levin got off his mare, and fastening her up by the roadside went to meet Tit, who took a second scythe out of a bush and gave it to him.

"It's ready, sir; it's like a razor, cuts of itself," said Tit, taking off his cap with a smile and giving him the scythe.

Levin took the scythe, and began trying it. As they finished their rows, the mowers, hot and good-humored, came out into the road one after another, and, laughing a little, greeted the master. They all stared at him, but no one made any remark, till a tall old man, with a wrinkled, beardless face, wearing a short sheepskin jacket, came out into the road and accosted him.

"Look'ee now, master, once take hold of the rope there's no letting it go!" he said, and Levin heard smothered laughter among the mowers.

"I'll try not to let it go," he said, taking his stand behind Tit, and waiting for the time to begin.

"Mind'ee," repeated the old man.

Tit made room, and Levin started behind him. The grass was short close to the road, and Levin, who had not done any mowing for a long while, and was disconcerted by the eyes fastened upon him, cut badly for the first moments, though he swung his scythe vigorously. Behind him he heard voices:

"It's not set right; handle's too high; see how he has to stoop to it," said one.

"Press more on the heel," said another.

"Never mind, he'll get on all right," the old man resumed.

"He's made a start.... You swing it too wide, you'll tire yourself out.... The master, sure, does his best for himself! But see the grass missed out! For such work us fellows would catch it!"

The grass became softer, and Levin, listening without answering, followed Tit, trying to do the best he could. They moved a hundred paces. Tit kept moving on, without stopping, not showing the slightest weariness, but Levin was already beginning to be afraid he would not be able to keep it up: he was so tired.

He felt as he swung his scythe that he was at the very end of his strength, and was making up his mind to ask Tit to stop. But at that very moment Tit stopped of his own accord, and stooping down picked up some grass, rubbed his scythe, and began whetting it. Levin straightened himself, and drawing a deep breath looked round. Behind him came a peasant, and he too was evidently tired, for he stopped at once without waiting to mow up to Levin, and began whetting his scythe. Tit sharpened his scythe and Levin's, and they went on. The next time it was just the same. Tit moved on with sweep after sweep of his scythe, not stopping nor showing signs of weariness. Levin followed him, trying not to get left behind, and he found it harder and harder: the moment came when he felt he had no strength left, but at that very moment Tit stopped and whetted the scythes.

So they mowed the first row. And this long row seemed particularly hard work to Levin; but when the end was reached and Tit, shouldering his scythe, began with deliberate stride returning on the tracks left by his heels in the cut grass, and Levin walked back in the same way over the space he had cut, in spite of the sweat that ran in streams over his face and fell in drops down his nose, and drenched his back as though he had been soaked in water, he felt very happy. What delighted him particularly was that now he knew he would be able to hold out.

His pleasure was only disturbed by his row not being well cut. "I will swing less with my arm and more with my whole body," he thought, comparing Tit's row, which looked as if it had been cut with a line, with his own unevenly and irregularly lying grass.

The first row, as Levin noticed, Tit had mowed specially quickly, probably wishing to put his master to the test, and the row happened to be a long one. The next rows were easier, but still Levin had to strain every nerve not to drop behind the peasants.

He thought of nothing, wished for nothing, but not to be left behind the peasants, and to do his work as well as possible. He heard nothing but the swish of scythes, and saw before him Tit's upright figure mowing away, the crescent-shaped curve of the cut grass, the grass and flower heads slowly and rhythmically falling before the blade of his scythe, and ahead of him the end of the row, where would come the rest.

Suddenly, in the midst of his toil, without understanding what it was or whence it came, he felt a pleasant sensation of chill on his hot, moist shoulders. He glanced at the sky in the interval for whetting the scythes. A heavy, lowering storm-cloud had blown up, and big raindrops were falling. Some of the peasants went to their coats and put them on; others—just like Levin himself—merely shrugged their shoulders, enjoying the pleasant coolness of it.

Another row, and yet another row, followed—long rows and short rows, with good grass and with poor grass. Levin lost all sense of time, and could not have told whether it was late or early now. A change began to come over his work, which gave him immense satisfaction. In the midst of his toil there were moments during which he forgot what he was doing, and it came all easy to him, and at those same moments his row was almost as smooth and well cut as Tit's. But so soon as he recollected what he was doing, and began trying to do better, he was at once conscious of all the difficulty of his task, and the row was badly mown.

On finishing yet another row he would have gone back to the top of the meadow again to begin the next, but Tit stopped, and going up to the old man said something in a low voice to him. They both looked at the sun. "What are they talking about, and why doesn't he go back?" thought Levin, not guessing that the peasants had been mowing no less than four hours without stopping, and it was time for their lunch.

"Lunch, sir," said the old man.

"Is it really time? That's right; lunch, then."

Levin gave his scythe to Tit, and together with the peasants, who were crossing the long stretch of mown grass, slightly sprinkled with rain, to get their bread from the heap of coats, he went towards his house. Only then he suddenly awoke to the fact that he had been wrong about the weather and the rain was drenching his hay.

"The hay will be spoiled," he said.

"Not a bit of it, sir; mow in the rain, and you'll rake in fine weather!" said the old man.

Levin untied his horse and rode home to his coffee. Sergey Ivanovitch was only just getting up. When he had drunk his coffee, Levin rode back again to the mowing before Sergey Ivanovitch had had time to dress and come down to the dining-room.

CHAPTER V

AFTER LUNCH LEVIN WAS NOT IN THE SAME PLACE IN THE STRING OF MOW-ers as before, but stood between the old man who had accosted him jocosely, and now invited him to be his neighbor, and a young peasant, who had only been married in the autumn, and who was mowing this summer for the first time.

The old man, holding himself erect, moved in front, with his feet turned out, taking long, regular strides, and with a precise and regular action which seemed to cost him no more effort than swinging one's arms in walking, as though it were in play, he laid down the high, even row of grass. It was as though it were not he but the sharp scythe of itself swishing through the juicy grass.

Behind Levin came the lad Mishka. His pretty, boyish face, with a twist of fresh grass bound round his hair, was all working with effort; but whenever any one looked at him he smiled. He would clearly have died sooner than own it was hard work for him.

Levin kept between them. In the very heat of the day the mowing did not seem such hard work to him. The perspiration with which he was drenched cooled him, while the sun, that burned his back, his head, and his arms, bare to the elbow, gave a vigor and dogged energy to his labor; and more and more often now came those moments of unconsciousness, when it was possible not to think what one was doing. The scythe cut of itself. These were happy moments. Still more delightful were the moments when they reached the stream where the rows ended, and the old man rubbed his scythe with the wet, thick grass, rinsed its blade in the fresh water of the stream, ladled out a little in a tin dipper, and offered Levin a drink.

"What do you say to my home-brew, eh? Good, eh?" said he, winking.

And truly Levin had never drunk any liquor so good as this warm water with green bits floating in it, and a taste of rust from the tin dipper. And immediately after this came the delicious, slow saunter, with his hand on the scythe, during which he could wipe away the streaming sweat, take deep breaths of air, and look about at the long string of mowers and at what was happening around in the forest and the country.

The longer Levin mowed, the oftener he felt the moments of unconsciousness in which it seemed not his hands that swung the scythe, but the scythe mowing of itself, a body full of life and consciousness of its own, and as though by magic, without thinking of it, the work turned out regular and well-finished of itself. These were the most blissful moments.

It was only hard work when he had to break off the motion, which had become unconscious, and to think; when he had to mow round a hillock or a tuft of sorrel. The old man did this easily. When a hillock came he changed his action, and at one time with the heel, and at another with the tip of his scythe, clipped the hillock round both sides with short strokes. And while he did this he kept looking about and watching what came into his view: at one moment he picked a wild berry and ate it or offered it to Levin, then he flung away a twig with the blade of the scythe, then he looked at a quail's nest, from which the bird flew just under the scythe, or caught a snake that crossed his path, and lifting it on the scythe as though on a fork showed it to Levin and threw it away.

For both Levin and the young peasant behind him, such changes of position were difficult. Both of them, repeating over and over again the same strained movement, were in a perfect frenzy of toil, and were incapable of shifting their position and at the same time watching what was before them.

Levin did not notice how time was passing. If he had been asked how long he had been working he would have said half an hour—and it was getting on for dinner-time. As they were walking back over the cut grass, the old man called Levin's attention to the little girls and boys who were coming from different directions, hardly visible through the long grass, and along the road towards the mowers, carrying sacks of bread dragging at their little hands and pitchers of the sour rye-beer, with cloths wrapped round them.

"Look'ee, the little emmets crawling!" he said, pointing to them, and he shaded his eyes with his hand to look at the sun. They mowed two more rows; the old man stopped.

"Come, master, dinner-time!" he said briskly. And on reaching the stream the mowers moved off across the lines of cut grass towards their pile of coats, where the children who had brought their dinners were sitting waiting for them. The peasants gathered into groups—those further away under a cart, those nearer under a willow bush.

Levin sat down by them; he felt disinclined to go away.

All constraint with the master had disappeared long ago. The peasants got ready for dinner. Some washed, the young lads bathed in the stream, others made a place comfortable for a rest, untied their sacks of bread, and uncovered the pitchers of rye-beer. The old man crumbled up some bread in a cup, stirred it with the handle of a spoon, poured water on it from the dipper, broke up some more bread, and having seasoned it with salt, he turned to the east to say his prayer.

"Come, master, taste my sop," said he, kneeling down before the cup.

The sop was so good that Levin gave up the idea of going home. He dined with the old man, and talked to him about his family affairs, taking the keenest interest in them, and told him about his own affairs and all the circumstances that could be of interest to the old man. He felt much nearer to him than to his brother, and could not help smiling at the affection he felt for this man. When the old man got up again, said his prayer, and lay down under a bush, putting some grass under his head for a pillow, Levin did the same, and in spite of the clinging flies that were so persistent in the sunshine, and the midges that tickled his hot face and body, he fell asleep at once and only waked when the sun had passed to the other side of the bush and reached him. The old man had been awake a long while, and was sitting up whetting the scythes of the younger lads.

Levin looked about him and hardly recognized the place, everything was so changed. The immense stretch of meadow had been mown and was sparkling with a peculiar fresh brilliance, with its lines of already sweet-smelling grass in the slanting rays of the evening sun. And the bushes about the river had been cut down, and the river itself, not visible before, now gleaming like steel in its bends, and the moving, ascending peasants, and the sharp wall of grass of the unmown part of the meadow, and the hawks hovering over the stripped meadow—all was perfectly new. Raising himself, Levin began considering how much had been cut and how much more could still be done that day.

The work done was exceptionally much for forty-two men. They had cut the whole of the big meadow, which had, in the years of serf labor, taken thirty scythes two days to mow. Only the corners remained to do, where the rows were short. But Levin felt a longing to get as much mowing done that day as possible, and was vexed with the sun sinking so quickly in the sky. He felt no weariness; all he wanted was to get his work done more and more quickly and as much done as possible.

"Could you cut Mashkin Upland too?—what do you think?" he said to the old man.

"As God wills, the sun's not high. A little vodka for the lads?"

At the afternoon rest, when they were sitting down again, and those who smoked had lighted their pipes, the old man told the men that Mashkin Upland's to be cut—"there'll be some vodka."

"Why not cut it? Come on, Tit! We'll look sharp! We can eat at night. Come on!" cried voices, and eating up their bread, the mowers went back to work.

"Come, lads, keep it up!" said Tit, and ran on ahead almost at a trot.

"Get along, get along!" said the old man, hurrying after him and easily overtaking him, "I'll mow you down, look out!"

And young and old mowed away, as though they were racing with one another. But however fast they worked, they did not spoil the grass, and the rows were laid just as neatly and exactly. The little piece left uncut in the corner was mown in five minutes. The last of the mowers were just ending their rows while the foremost snatched up their coats onto their shoulders, and crossed the road towards Mashkin Upland.

The sun was already sinking into the trees when they went with their jingling dippers into the wooded ravine of Mashkin Upland. The grass was up to their waists in the middle of the hollow, soft, tender, and feathery, spotted here and there among the trees with wild heart's-ease.

After a brief consultation—whether to take the rows lengthwise or diagonally—Prohor Yermilin, also a renowned mower, a huge, black-haired peasant, went on ahead. He went up to the top, turned back again and started mowing, and they all proceeded to form in line behind him, going downhill through the hollow and uphill right up to the edge of the forest. The sun sank behind the forest. The dew was falling by now; the mowers were in the sun only on the hillside, but below, where a mist was rising, and on the opposite side, they mowed into the fresh, dewy shade. The work went rapidly. The grass cut with a juicy sound, and was at once laid in high, fragrant rows. The mowers from all sides, brought closer together in the short row, kept urging one another on to the sound of jingling dippers and clanging scythes, and the hiss of the whetstones sharpening them, and good-humored shouts.

Levin still kept between the young peasant and the old man. The old man, who had put on his short sheepskin jacket, was just as good-humored, jocose, and free in his movements. Among the trees they were continually cutting with their scythes the so-called "birch mushrooms," swollen fat in the succulent grass. But the old man bent down every time he came across a mushroom, picked it up and put it in his bosom. "Another present for my old woman," he said as he did so.

Easy as it was to mow the wet, soft grass, it was hard work going up and down the steep sides of the ravine. But this did not trouble the old man. Swinging his scythe just as ever, and moving his feet in their big, plaited shoes with firm, little steps, he climbed slowly up the steep place, and though his breeches hanging out below his smock, and his whole frame trembled with effort, he did not miss one blade of grass or one mushroom on his way, and kept making jokes with the peasants and Levin. Levin walked after him and often thought he must fall, as he climbed with a scythe up a steep cliff where it would have been hard work to clamber without anything. But he climbed up and did what he had to do. He felt as though some external force were moving him.

CHAPTER VI

MASHKIN UPLAND WAS MOWN, THE LAST ROW FINISHED, THE PEASANTS had put on their coats and were gaily trudging home. Levin got on his horse and, parting regretfully from the peasants, rode homewards. On the hillside he looked back; he could not see them in the mist that had risen from the valley; he could only hear rough, good-humored voices, laughter, and the sound of clanking scythes.

Sergey Ivanovitch had long ago finished dinner, and was drinking iced lemon and water in his own room, looking through the reviews and papers which he had only just received by post, when Levin rushed into the room, talking merrily, with his wet and matted hair sticking to his forehead, and his back and chest grimed and moist.

"We mowed the whole meadow! Oh, it is nice, delicious! And how have you been getting on?" said Levin, completely forgetting the disagreeable conversation of the previous day.

"Mercy! what do you look like!" said Sergey Ivanovitch, for the first moment looking round with some dissatisfaction. "And the door, do shut the door!" he cried. "You must have let in a dozen at least."

Sergey Ivanovitch could not endure flies, and in his own room he never opened the window except at night, and carefully kept the door shut.

"Not one, on my honor. But if I have, I'll catch them. You wouldn't believe what a pleasure it is! How have you spent the day?"

"Very well. But have you really been mowing the whole day? I expect you're as hungry as a wolf. Kouzma has got everything ready for you."

"No, I don't feel hungry even. I had something to eat there. But I'll go and wash."

"Yes, go along, go along, and I'll come to you directly," said Sergey Ivanovitch, shaking his head as he looked at his brother. "Go along, make haste," he added smiling, and gathering up his books, he prepared to go too. He, too, felt suddenly good-humored and disinclined to leave his brother's side. "But what did you do while it was raining?"

"Rain? Why, there was scarcely a drop. I'll come directly. So you had a nice day too? That's first-rate." And Levin went off to change his clothes.

Five minutes later the brothers met in the dining-room. Although it seemed to Levin that he was not hungry, and he sat down to dinner simply so as not to hurt Kouzma's feelings, yet when he began to eat the dinner struck him as extraordinarily good. Sergey Ivanovitch watched him with a smile.

"Oh, by the way, there's a letter for you," said he. "Kouzma, bring it down, please. And mind you shut the doors."

The letter was from Oblonsky. Levin read it aloud. Oblonsky wrote to him from Petersburg: "I have had a letter from Dolly; she's at Ergushovo, and everything seems going wrong there. Do ride over and see her, please; help her with advice; you know all about it. She will be so glad to see you. She's quite alone, poor thing. My mother-in-law and all of them are still abroad."

"That's capital! I will certainly ride over to her," said Levin. "Or we'll go together. She's such a splendid woman, isn't she?"

"They're not far from here, then?"

"Twenty-five miles. Or perhaps it is thirty. But a capital road. Capital, we'll drive over."

"I shall be delighted," said Sergey Ivanovitch, still smiling. The sight of his younger brother's appearance had immediately put him in a good humor.

"Well, you have an appetite!" he said, looking at his dark-red, sunburnt face and neck bent over the plate.

"Splendid! You can't imagine what an effectual remedy it is for every sort of foolishness. I want to enrich medicine with a new word: *Arbeitskur*."

"Well, but you don't need it, I should fancy."

"No, but for all sorts of nervous invalids."

"Yes, it ought to be tried. I had meant to come to the mowing to look at you, but it was so unbearably hot that I got no further than the forest. I sat there a little, and went on by the forest to the village, met your old nurse, and sounded her as to the peasants' view of you. As far as I can make out, they don't approve of this. She said: 'It's not a gentleman's work.' Altogether, I fancy that in the people's ideas there are very clear and definite notions of certain, as they call it, 'gentlemanly' lines of action. And they don't sanction the gentry's moving outside bounds clearly laid down in their ideas."

"Maybe so; but anyway it's a pleasure such as I have never known in my life. And there's no harm in it, you know. Is there?" answered Levin. "I can't help it if they don't like it. Though I do believe it's all right. Eh?"

"Altogether," pursued Sergey Ivanovitch, "you're satisfied with your day?"

"Quite satisfied. We cut the whole meadow. And such a splendid old man I made friends with there! You can't fancy how delightful he was!"

"Well, so you're content with your day. And so am I. First, I solved two chess problems, and one a very pretty one—a pawn opening. I'll show it you. And then—I thought over our conversation yesterday."

"Eh! our conversation yesterday?" said Levin, blissfully dropping his eyelids and drawing deep breaths after finishing his dinner, and absolutely incapable of recalling what their conversation yesterday was about.

"I think you are partly right. Our difference of opinion amounts to this, that you make the mainspring self-interest, while I suppose that interest in the common weal is bound to exist in every man of a certain degree of advancement. Possibly you are right too, that action founded on material interest would be more desirable. You are altogether, as the French say, too *primesautière* a nature; you must have intense, energetic action, or nothing."

Levin listened to his brother and did not understand a single word, and did not want to understand. He was only afraid his brother might ask him some question which would make it evident he had not heard.

"So that's what I think it is, my dear boy," said Sergey Ivanovitch, touching him on the shoulder.

"Yes, of course. But, do you know? I won't stand up for my view," answered Levin, with a guilty, childlike smile. "Whatever was it I was disputing about?" he wondered. "Of course, I'm right, and he's right, and it's all first-rate. Only I must go round to the counting-house and see to things." He got up, stretching and smiling. Sergey Ivanovitch smiled too.

"If you want to go out, let's go together," he said, disinclined to be parted from his brother, who seemed positively breathing out freshness and energy. "Come, we'll go to the counting-house, if you have to go there."

"Oh, heavens!" shouted Levin, so loudly that Sergey Ivanovitch was quite frightened.

"What, what is the matter?"

"How's Agafea Mihalovna's hand?" said Levin, slapping himself on the head. "I'd positively forgotten her even."

"It's much better."

"Well, anyway I'll run down to her. Before you've time to get your hat on, I'll be back."

And he ran down-stairs, clattering with his heels like a spring-rattle.

CHAPTER VII

S TEPAN ARKADYEVITCH HAD GONE TO PETERSBURG TO PERFORM THE MOST natural and essential official duty—so familiar to every one in the government service, though incomprehensible to outsiders—that duty, but for which one could hardly be in government service, of reminding the ministry of his existence—and having, for the due performance of this rite, taken all the available cash from home, was gaily and agreeably spending his days at the races and in the summer villas. Meanwhile Dolly and the children had moved into the country, to cut down expenses as much as possible. She had gone to Ergushovo, the estate that had been her dowry, and the one where in spring the forest had been sold. It was nearly forty miles from Levin's Pokrovskoe. The big, old house at Ergushovo had been pulled down long ago, and the old prince had had the lodge done up and built on to. Twenty years before, when Dolly was a child, the lodge had been roomy and comfortable, though, like all lodges, it stood sideways to the entrance avenue, and faced the south. But by now this lodge was old and dilapidated. When Stepan Arkadyevitch had gone down in the spring to sell the forest, Dolly had begged him to look over the house and order what repairs might be needed. Stepan Arkadyevitch, like all unfaithful husbands indeed, was very solicitous for his wife's comfort, and he had himself looked over the house, and given instructions about everything that he considered necessary. What he considered necessary was to cover all the furniture with cretonne, to put up curtains, to weed the garden, to make a little bridge on the pond, and to plant flowers. But he forgot many other essential matters, the want of which greatly distressed Darya Alexandrovna later on.

In spite of Stepan Arkadyevitch's efforts to be an attentive father and husband, he never could keep in his mind that he had a wife and children. He had bachelor tastes, and it was in accordance with them that he shaped his life. On his return to Moscow he informed his wife with pride that everything was ready, that the house would be a little paradise, and that he advised her most certainly to go. His wife's staying away in the country was very agreeable to Stepan Arkadyevitch from every point of view: it did the children good, it decreased expenses, and it left him more at liberty. Darya Alexandrovna regarded staying in the country for the summer as essential for the children, especially for the little girl, who had not succeeded in regaining her strength after the scarlatina, and also as a means of escaping the petty humiliations, the little bills owing to the wood-merchant, the fishmonger, the shoemaker, which made her miserable. Besides this, she was pleased to go away to the country because she was dreaming of getting her sister Kitty to stay with her there. Kitty was to be back from abroad in the middle of the summer, and bathing had been prescribed for her. Kitty wrote that no prospect was so alluring as to spend the summer with Dolly at Ergushovo, full of childish associations for both of them.

The first days of her existence in the country were very hard for Dolly. She used to stay in the country as a child, and the impression she had retained of it was that the country was a refuge from all the unpleasantness of the town, that life there, though not luxurious—Dolly could easily make up her mind to that—was cheap and comfortable; that there was plenty of everything, everything was cheap, everything could be got, and children were happy. But now coming to the country as the head of a family, she perceived that it was all utterly unlike what she had fancied.

The day after their arrival there was a heavy fall of rain and in the night the water came through in the corridor and in the nursery, so that the beds had to be carried into the drawing-room. There was no kitchenmaid to be found; of the nine cows, it appeared from the words of the cowherd-woman that some were about to calve, others had just calved, others were old, and others again hard-uddered; there was not butter nor milk enough even for the children. There were no eggs. They could get no fowls; old, purplish, stringy cocks were all they had for roasting and boiling. Impossible to get women to scrub the floors—all were potato-hoeing. Driving was out of the question, because one of the horses was restive, and bolted in the shafts. There was no place where they could bathe; the whole of the river-bank was trampled by the cattle and open to the road; even walks were impossible, for the cattle strayed into the garden through a gap in the hedge, and there was one terrible bull, who bellowed, and therefore might be expected to gore somebody. There were no proper cupboards for their clothes; what cupboards there were either would not close at all, or burst open whenever anyone passed by them. There were no pots and pans; there was no copper in the wash-house, nor even an ironing-board in the maids' room.

Finding instead of peace and rest all these, from her point of view, fearful calamities, Darya Alexandrovna was at first in despair. She exerted herself to the utmost, felt the hopelessness of the position, and was every instant suppressing the tears that started into her eyes. The bailiff, a retired quartermaster, whom Stepan Arkadyevitch had taken a fancy to and had appointed bailiff on account of his handsome and respectful appearance as a hall-porter, showed no sympathy for Darya Alexandrovna's woes. He said respectfully, "nothing can be done, the peasants are such a wretched lot," and did nothing to help her.

The position seemed hopeless. But in the Oblonskys' household, as in all families indeed, there was one inconspicuous but most valuable and useful person, Marya Philimonovna. She soothed her mistress, assured her that everything would *come round* (it was her expression, and Matvey had borrowed it from her), and without fuss or hurry proceeded to set to work herself. She had immediately made friends with the bailiff's wife, and on the very first day she drank tea with her and the bailiff under the acacias, and reviewed all the circumstances of the position. Very soon Marya Philimonovna had established her club, so to say, under the acacias, and there it was, in this club, consisting of the bailiff's wife, the village elder, and the counting-house clerk, that the difficulties of existence were gradually smoothed away, and in a week's time everything actually had come round. The roof was mended, a kitchenmaid was found—a crony of the village elder's—hens were bought, the cows began giving milk, the garden hedge was stopped up with stakes, the carpenter made a mangle, hooks were put in the cupboards, and they ceased to burst open spontaneously, and an ironing-board covered with army cloth was placed across from the arm of a chair to the chest of drawers, and there was a smell of flatirons in the maids' room.

"Just see, now, and you were quite in despair," said Marya Philimonovna, pointing to the ironing-board. They even rigged up a bathing-shed of straw hurdles. Lily began to bathe, and Darya Alexandrovna began to realize, if only in part, her expectations, if not of a peaceful, at least of a comfortable, life in the country. Peaceful with six children Darya Alexandrovna could not be. One would fall ill, another might easily become so, a third would be without something necessary, a fourth would show symptoms of a bad disposition, and so on. Rare indeed were the brief periods of peace. But these cares and anxieties were for Darya Alexandrovna the sole happiness possible. Had it not been for them, she would have been left alone to brood over her husband who did not love her. And besides, hard though it was for the mother to bear the dread of illness, the illnesses themselves, and the grief of seeing signs of evil propensities in her children—the children themselves were even now repaying her in small joys for her sufferings. Those joys were so small that they passed unnoticed, like gold in sand, and at bad moments she could see nothing but the pain, nothing but sand; but there were good moments too when she saw nothing but the joy, nothing but gold.

had whistled too, and he was not punished, and that he wasn't crying for the tart—he didn't care—but at being unjustly treated. This was really too tragic, and Darya Alexandrovna made up her mind to persuade the English governess to forgive Grisha, and she went to speak to her. But on the way, as she passed the drawing-room, she beheld a scene, filling her heart with such pleasure that the tears came into her eyes, and she forgave the delinquent herself.

The culprit was sitting at the window in the corner of the drawing-room; beside him was standing Tanya with a plate. On the pretext of wanting to give some dinner to her dolls, she had asked the governess's permission to take her share of tart to the nursery, and had taken it instead to her brother. While still weeping over the injustice of his punishment, he was eating the tart, and kept saying through his sobs, "Eat yourself; let's eat it together ... together."

Tanya had at first been under the influence of her pity for Grisha, then of a sense of her noble action, and tears were standing in her eyes too; but she did not refuse, and ate her share.

On catching sight of their mother they were dismayed, but, looking into her face, they saw they were not doing wrong. They burst out laughing, and, with their mouths full of tart, they began wiping their smiling lips with their hands, and smearing their radiant faces all over with tears and jam.

"Mercy! Your new white frock! Tanya! Grisha!" said their mother, trying to save the frock, but with tears in her eyes, smiling a blissful, rapturous smile.

The new frocks were taken off, and orders were given for the little girls to have their blouses put on, and the boys their old jackets, and the wagonette to be harnessed; with Brownie, to the bailiff's annoyance, again in the shafts, to drive out for mushroom-picking and bathing. A roar of delighted shrieks arose in the nursery, and never ceased till they had set off for the bathing-place.

They gathered a whole basketful of mushrooms; even Lily found a birch mushroom. It had always happened before that Miss Hoole found them and pointed them out to her; but this time she found a big one quite of herself, and there was a general scream of delight, "Lily has found a mushroom!"

Then they reached the river, put the horses under the birch-trees, and went to the bathing-place. The coachman, Terenty, fastened the horses, who kept whisking away the flies, to a tree, and, treading down the grass, lay down in the shade of a birch and smoked his shag, while the never-ceasing shrieks of delight of the children floated across to him from the bathing-place.

Though it was hard work to look after all the children and restrain their wild pranks, though it was difficult too to keep in one's head and not mix up all the stockings, little breeches, and shoes for the different legs, and to undo and to do up again all the tapes and buttons, Darya Alexandrovna, who had always liked bathing herself, and believed it to be very good for the children, enjoyed nothing so much as bathing with all the children. To go over all those fat little legs, pulling on their stockings, to take in her arms and dip those little naked bodies, and to hear their screams of delight and alarm, to see the breathless faces with wide-open, scared, and happy eyes of all her splashing cherubs, was a great pleasure to her.

When half the children had been dressed, some peasant women in holiday dress, out picking herbs, came up to the bathing-shed and stopped shyly. Marya Philimonovna called one of them and handed her a sheet and a shirt that had dropped into the water for her to dry them, and Darya Alexandrovna began to talk to the women. At first they laughed behind their hands and did not understand her questions, but soon they grew bolder and began to talk, winning Darya Alexandrovna's heart at once by the genuine admiration of the children that they showed.

"My, what a beauty! as white as sugar," said one, admiring Tanitchka, and shaking her head; "but thin ..."

"Yes, she has been ill."

"And so they've been bathing you too," said another to the baby.

"No; he's only three months old," answered Darya Alexandrovna with pride.

"You don't say so!"

"And have you any children?"

"I've had four; I've two living—a boy and a girl. I weaned her last carnival."

"How old is she?"

"Why, two years old."

"Why did you nurse her so long?"

"It's our custom; for three fasts...."

And the conversation became most interesting to Darya Alexandrovna. What sort of time did she have? What was the matter with the boy? Where was her husband? Did it often happen?

Darya Alexandrovna felt disinclined to leave the peasant women, so interesting to her was their conversation, so completely identical were all their interests. What pleased her most of all was that she saw clearly what all the women admired more than anything was her having so many children, and such fine ones. The peasant women even made Darya Alexandrovna laugh, and offended the English governess, because she was the cause of the laughter she did not understand. One of the younger women kept staring at the Englishwoman, who was dressing after all the rest, and when she put on her third petticoat she could

"Oh, well, then, I'll have a look at your cows, and if you'll allow me, I'll give directions about their food. Everything depends on their food."

And Levin, to turn the conversation, explained to Darya Alexandrovna the theory of cow-keeping, based on the principle that the cow is simply a machine for the transformation of food into milk, and so on.

He talked of this, and passionately longed to hear more of Kitty, and, at the same time, was afraid of hearing it. He dreaded the breaking up of the inward peace he had gained with such effort.

"Yes, but still all this has to be looked after, and who is there to look after it?" Darya Alexandrovna responded, without interest.

She had by now got her household matters so satisfactorily arranged, thanks to Marya Philimonovna, that she was disinclined to make any change in them; besides, she had no faith in Levin's knowledge of farming. General principles, as to the cow being a machine for the production of milk, she looked on with suspicion. It seemed to her that such principles could only be a hindrance in farm management. It all seemed to her a far simpler matter: all that was needed, as Marya Philimonovna had explained, was to give Brindle and Whitebreast more food and drink, and not to let the cook carry all the kitchen slops to the laundry-maid's cow. That was clear. But general propositions as to feeding on meal and on grass were doubtful and obscure. And, what was most important, she wanted to talk about Kitty.

CHAPTER X

K ITTY WRITES TO ME THAT THERE'S NOTHING SHE LONGS FOR SO MUCH AS quiet and solitude," Dolly said after the silence that had followed.

"And how is she—better?" Levin asked in agitation.

"Thank God, she's quite well again. I never believed her lungs were affected."

"Oh, I'm very glad!" said Levin, and Dolly fancied she saw something touching, helpless, in his face as he said this and looked silently into her face.

"Let me ask you, Konstantin Dmitrievitch," said Darya Alexandrovna, smiling her kindly and rather mocking smile, "why is it you are angry with Kitty?"

"I? I'm not angry with her," said Levin.

"Yes, you are angry. Why was it you did not come to see us nor them when you were in Moscow?"

"Darya Alexandrovna," he said, blushing up to the roots of his hair, "I wonder really that with your kind heart you don't feel this. How it is you feel no pity for me, if nothing else, when you know…"

"What do I know?"

"You know I made an offer and that I was refused," said Levin, and all the tenderness he had been feeling for Kitty a minute before was replaced by a feeling of anger for the slight he had suffered.

"What makes you suppose I know?"

"Because everybody knows it …"

"That's just where you are mistaken; I did not know it, though I had guessed it was so."

"Well, now you know it."

"All I knew was that something had happened that made her dreadfully miserable, and that she begged me never to speak of it. And if she would not tell me, she would certainly not speak of it to any one else. But what did pass between you? Tell me."

"I have told you."

"When was it?"

"When I was at their house the last time."

"Do you know that," said Darya Alexandrovna, "I am awfully, awfully sorry for her. You suffer only from pride…."

"Perhaps so," said Levin, "but …"

She interrupted him.

"But she, poor girl … I am awfully, awfully sorry for her. Now I see it all."

"Well, Darya Alexandrovna, you must excuse me," he said, getting up. "Good-bye, Darya Alexandrovna, till we meet again."

"No, wait a minute," she said, clutching him by the sleeve. "Wait a minute, sit down."

"Please, please, don't let us talk of this," he said, sitting down, and at the same time feeling rise up and stir within his heart a hope he had believed to be buried.

"If I did not like you," she said, and tears came into her eyes; "if I did not know you, as I do know you …"

The feeling that had seemed dead revived more and more, rose up and took possession of Levin's heart.

"Yes, I understand it all now," said Darya Alexandrovna. "You can't understand it; for you men, who are free and make your own choice, it's always clear whom you love. But a girl's in a position of suspense, with all a woman's

Levin saw she was unhappy and tried to comfort her, saying that it showed nothing bad, that all children fight; but, even as he said it, he was thinking in his heart: "No, I won't be artificial and talk French with my children; but my children won't be like that. All one has to do is not spoil children, not to distort their nature, and they'll be delightful. No, my children won't be like that."

He said good-bye and drove away, and she did not try to keep him.

CHAPTER XI

IN THE MIDDLE OF JULY THE ELDER OF THE VILLAGE ON LEVIN'S SISTER'S estate, about fifteen miles from Pokrovskoe, came to Levin to report on how things were going there and on the hay. The chief source of income on his sister's estate was from the riverside meadows. In former years the hay had been bought by the peasants for twenty roubles the three acres. When Levin took over the management of the estate, he thought on examining the grass-lands that they were worth more, and he fixed the price at twenty-five roubles the three acres. The peasants would not give that price, and, as Levin suspected, kept off other purchasers. Then Levin had driven over himself, and arranged to have the grass cut, partly by hired labor, partly at a payment of a certain proportion of the crop. His own peasants put every hindrance they could in the way of this new arrangement, but it was carried out, and the first year the meadows had yielded a profit almost double. The previous year—which was the third year—the peasants had maintained the same opposition to the arrangement, and the hay had been cut on the same system. This year the peasants were doing all the mowing for a third of the hay crop, and the village elder had come now to announce that the hay had been cut, and that, fearing rain, they had invited the counting-house clerk over, had divided the crop in his presence, and had raked together eleven stacks as the owner's share. From the vague answers to his question how much hay had been cut on the principal meadow, from the hurry of the village elder who had made the division, not asking leave, from the whole tone of the peasant, Levin perceived that there was something wrong in the division of the hay, and made up his mind to drive over himself to look into the matter.

Arriving to dinner at the village, and leaving his horse at the cottage of an old friend of his, the husband of his brother's wet-nurse, Levin went to see the old man in his bee-house, wanting to find out from him the truth about the hay.

Parmenitch, a talkative, comely old man, gave Levin a very warm welcome, showed him all he was doing, told him everything about his bees and the swarms of that year; but gave vague and unwilling answers to Levin's inquiries about the mowing. This confirmed Levin still more in his suspicions. He went to the hay-fields and examined the stacks. The haystacks could not possibly contain fifty wagon-loads each, and to convict the peasants Levin ordered the wagons that had carried the hay to be brought up directly, to lift one stack, and carry it into the barn. There turned out to be only thirty-two loads in the stack. In spite of the village elder's assertions about the compressibility of hay, and its having settled down in the stacks, and his swearing that everything had been done in the fear of God, Levin stuck to his point that the hay had been divided without his orders, and that, therefore, he would not accept that hay as fifty loads to a stack. After a prolonged dispute the matter was decided by the peasants taking these eleven stacks, reckoning them as fifty loads each. The arguments and the division of the haycocks lasted the whole afternoon. When the last of the hay had been divided, Levin, intrusting the superintendence of the rest to the counting-house clerk, sat down on a haycock marked off by a stake of willow, and looked admiringly at the meadow swarming with peasants.

In front of him, in the bend of the river beyond the marsh, moved a bright-colored line of peasant women, and the scattered hay was being rapidly formed into gray winding rows over the pale green stubble. After the women came the men with pitchforks, and from the gray rows there were growing up broad, high, soft haycocks. To the left, carts were rumbling over the meadow that had been already cleared, and one after another the haycocks vanished, flung up in huge forkfuls, and in their place there were rising heavy cartloads of fragrant hay hanging over the horses' hind-quarters.

"What weather for haying! What hay it'll be!" said an old man, squatting down beside Levin. "It's tea, not hay! It's like scattering grain to the ducks, the way they pick it up!" he added, pointing to the growing haycocks. "Since dinner-time they've carried a good half of it."

"The last load, eh?" he shouted to a young peasant, who drove by, standing in the front of an empty cart, shaking the cord reins.

"The last, dad!" the lad shouted back, pulling in the horse, and, smiling, he looked round at a bright, rosy-checked peasant girl who sat in the cart smiling too, and drove on.

"Who's that? Your son?" asked Levin.

"My baby," said the old man with a tender smile.

"What a fine fellow!"

All the long day of toil had left no trace in them but lightness of heart. Before the early dawn all was hushed. Nothing was to be heard but the night sounds of the frogs that never ceased in the marsh, and the horses snorting in the mist that rose over the meadow before the morning. Rousing himself, Levin got up from the haycock, and looking at the stars, he saw that the night was over.

"Well, what am I going to do? How am I to set about it?" he said to himself, trying to express to himself all the thoughts and feelings he had passed through in that brief night. All the thoughts and feelings he had passed through fell into three separate trains of thought. One was the renunciation of his old life, of his utterly useless education. This renunciation gave him satisfaction, and was easy and simple. Another series of thoughts and mental images related to the life he longed to live now. The simplicity, the purity, the sanity of this life he felt clearly, and he was convinced he would find in it the content, the peace, and the dignity, of the lack of which he was so miserably conscious. But a third series of ideas turned upon the question how to effect this transition from the old life to the new. And there nothing took clear shape for him. "Have a wife? Have work and the necessity of work? Leave Pokrovskoe? Buy land? Become a member of a peasant community? Marry a peasant girl? How am I to set about it?" he asked himself again, and could not find an answer. "I haven't slept all night, though, and I can't think it out clearly," he said to himself. "I'll work it out later. One thing's certain, this night has decided my fate. All my old dreams of home-life were absurd, not the real thing," he told himself. "It's all ever so much simpler and better...."

"How beautiful!" he thought, looking at the strange, as it were, mother-of-pearl shell of white fleecy cloudlets resting right over his head in the middle of the sky. "How exquisite it all is in this exquisite night! And when was there time for that cloud-shell to form? Just now I looked at the sky, and there was nothing in it—only two white streaks. Yes, and so imperceptibly too my views of life changed!"

He went out of the meadow and walked along the highroad towards the village. A slight wind arose, and the sky looked gray and sullen. The gloomy moment had come that usually precedes the dawn, the full triumph of light over darkness.

Shrinking from the cold, Levin walked rapidly, looking at the ground. "What's that? Some one coming," he thought, catching the tinkle of bells, and lifting his head. Forty paces from him a carriage with four horses harnessed abreast was driving towards him along the grassy highroad on which he was walking. The shaft-horses were tilted against the shafts by the ruts, but the dexterous driver sitting on the box held the shaft over the ruts, so that the wheels ran on the smooth part of the road.

This was all Levin noticed, and without wondering who it could be, he gazed absently at the coach.

In the coach was an old lady dozing in one corner, and at the window, evidently only just awake, sat a young girl holding in both hands the ribbons of a white cap. With a face full of light and thought, full of a subtle, complex inner life, that was remote from Levin, she was gazing beyond him at the glow of the sunrise.

At the very instant when this apparition was vanishing, the truthful eyes glanced at him. She recognized him, and her face lighted up with wondering delight.

He could not be mistaken. There were no other eyes like those in the world. There was only one creature in the world that could concentrate for him all the brightness and meaning of life. It was she. It was Kitty. He understood that she was driving to Ergushovo from the railway station. And everything that had been stirring Levin during that sleepless night, all the resolutions he had made, all vanished at once. He recalled with horror his dreams of marrying a peasant girl. There only, in the carriage that had crossed over to the other side of the road, and was rapidly disappearing, there only could he find the solution of the riddle of his life, which had weighed so agonizingly upon him of late.

She did not look out again. The sound of the carriage-springs was no longer audible, the bells could scarcely be heard. The barking of dogs showed the carriage had reached the village, and all that was left was the empty fields all round, the village in front, and he himself isolated and apart from it all, wandering lonely along the deserted highroad.

He glanced at the sky, expecting to find there the cloud-shell he had been admiring and taking as the symbol of the ideas and feelings of that night. There was nothing in the sky in the least like a shell. There, in the remote heights above, a mysterious change had been accomplished. There was no trace of shell, and there was stretched over fully half the sky an even cover of tiny and ever tinier cloudlets. The sky had grown blue and bright; and with the same softness, but with the same remoteness, it met his questioning gaze.

"No," he said to himself, "however good that life of simplicity and toil may be, I cannot go back to it. I love *her*."

"Daryalov fought a duel...."

The duel had particularly fascinated the thoughts of Alexey Alexandrovitch in his youth, just because he was physically a coward, and was himself well aware of the fact. Alexey Alexandrovitch could not without horror contemplate the idea of a pistol aimed at himself, and never made use of any weapon in his life. This horror had in his youth set him pondering on dueling, and picturing himself in a position in which he would have to expose his life to danger. Having attained success and an established position in the world, he had long ago forgotten this feeling; but the habitual bent of feeling reasserted itself, and dread of his own cowardice proved even now so strong that Alexey Alexandrovitch spent a long while thinking over the question of dueling in all its aspects, and hugging the idea of a duel, though he was fully aware beforehand that he would never under any circumstances fight one.

"There's no doubt our society is still so barbarous (it's not the same in England) that very many"—and among these were those whose opinion Alexey Alexandrovitch particularly valued—"look favorably on the duel; but what result is attained by it? Suppose I call him out," Alexey Alexandrovitch went on to himself, and vividly picturing the night he would spend after the challenge, and the pistol aimed at him, he shuddered, and knew that he never would do it—"suppose I call him out. Suppose I am taught," he went on musing, "to shoot; I press the trigger," he said to himself, closing his eyes, "and it turns out I have killed him," Alexey Alexandrovitch said to himself, and he shook his head as though to dispel such silly ideas. "What sense is there in murdering a man in order to define one's relation to a guilty wife and son? I should still just as much have to decide what I ought to do with her. But what is more probable and what would doubtless occur—I should be killed or wounded. I, the innocent person, should be the victim—killed or wounded. It's even more senseless. But apart from that, a challenge to fight would be an act hardly honest on my side. Don't I know perfectly well that my friends would never allow me to fight a duel—would never allow the life of a statesman, needed by Russia, to be exposed to danger? Knowing perfectly well beforehand that the matter would never come to real danger, it would amount to my simply trying to gain a certain sham reputation by such a challenge. That would be dishonest, that would be false, that would be deceiving myself and others. A duel is quite irrational, and no one expects it of me. My aim is simply to safeguard my reputation, which is essential for the uninterrupted pursuit of my public duties." Official duties, which had always been of great consequence in Alexey Alexandrovitch's eyes, seemed of special importance to his mind at this moment. Considering and rejecting the duel, Alexey Alexandrovitch turned to divorce—another solution selected by several of the husbands he remembered. Passing in mental review all the instances he knew of divorces (there were plenty of them in the very highest society with which he was very familiar), Alexey Alexandrovitch could not find a single example in which the object of divorce was that which he had in view. In all these instances the husband had practically ceded or sold his unfaithful wife, and the very party which, being in fault, had not the right to contract a fresh marriage, had formed counterfeit, pseudo-matrimonial ties with a self-styled husband. In his own case, Alexey Alexandrovitch saw that a legal divorce, that is to say, one in which only the guilty wife would be repudiated, was impossible of attainment. He saw that the complex conditions of the life they led made the coarse proofs of his wife's guilt, required by the law, out of the question; he saw that a certain refinement in that life would not admit of such proofs being brought forward, even if he had them, and that to bring forward such proofs would damage him in the public estimation more than it would her.

An attempt at divorce could lead to nothing but a public scandal, which would be a perfect godsend to his enemies for calumny and attacks on his high position in society. His chief object, to define the position with the least amount of disturbance possible, would not be attained by divorce either. Moreover, in the event of divorce, or even of an attempt to obtain a divorce, it was obvious that the wife broke off all relations with the husband and threw in her lot with the lover. And in spite of the complete, as he supposed, contempt and indifference he now felt for his wife, at the bottom of his heart, Alexey Alexandrovitch still had one feeling left in regard to her—a disinclination to see her free to throw in her lot with Vronsky, so that her crime would be to her advantage. The mere notion of this so exasperated Alexey Alexandrovitch, that directly it rose to his mind he groaned with inward agony, and got up and changed his place in the carriage, and for a long while after, he sat with scowling brows, wrapping his numbed and bony legs in the fleecy rug.

"Apart from formal divorce, one might still do like Karibanov, Paskudin, and that good fellow Dram—that is, separate from one's wife," he went on thinking, when he had regained his composure. But this step too presented the same drawback of public scandal as a divorce, and what was more, a separation, quite as much as a regular divorce, flung his wife into the arms of Vronsky. "No, it's out of the question, out of the question!" he said again, twisting his rug about him again. "I cannot be unhappy, but neither she nor he ought to be happy."

persuaded that you have repented and do repent of
what has called forth the present letter, and that you
will coöperate with me in eradicating the cause of
our estrangement, and forgetting the past. In the
contrary event, you can conjecture what awaits you
and your son. All this I hope to discuss more in detail
in a personal interview. As the season is drawing
to a close, I would beg you to return to Petersburg
as quickly as possible, not later than Tuesday. All
necessary preparations shall be made for your arrival
here. I beg you to note that I attach particular significance to compliance with this request.

A. KARENIN

"P.S.—I enclose the money which may be needed
for your expenses."

He read the letter through and felt pleased with it, and especially that he had
remembered to enclose money: there was not a harsh word, not a reproach in it,
nor was there undue indulgence. Most of all, it was a golden bridge for return.
Folding the letter and smoothing it with a massive ivory knife, and putting it
in an envelope with the money, he rang the bell with the gratification it always
afforded him to use the well-arranged appointments of his writing-table.

"Give this to the courier to be delivered to Anna Arkadyevna to-morrow
at the summer villa," he said, getting up.

"Certainly, your excellency; tea to be served in the study?"

Alexey Alexandrovitch ordered tea to be brought to the study, and playing
with the massive paper-knife, he moved to his easy-chair, near which there had
been placed ready for him a lamp and the French work on Egyptian hieroglyphics that he had begun. Over the easy-chair there hung in a gold frame an oval
portrait of Anna, a fine painting by a celebrated artist. Alexey Alexandrovitch
glanced at it. The unfathomable eyes gazed ironically and insolently at him.
Insufferably insolent and challenging was the effect in Alexey Alexandrovitch's
eyes of the black lace about the head, admirably touched in by the painter, the
black hair and handsome white hand with one finger lifted, covered with rings.
After looking at the portrait for a minute, Alexey Alexandrovitch shuddered
so that his lips quivered and he uttered the sound "brrr," and turned away. He
made haste to sit down in his easy-chair and opened the book. He tried to read,
but he could not revive the very vivid interest he had felt before in Egyptian

hieroglyphics. He looked at the book and thought of something else. He thought not of his wife, but of a complication that had arisen in his official life, which at the time constituted the chief interest of it. He felt that he had penetrated more deeply than ever before into this intricate affair, and that he had originated a leading idea—he could say it without self-flattery—calculated to clear up the whole business, to strengthen him in his official career, to discomfit his enemies, and thereby to be of the greatest benefit to the government. Directly the servant had set the tea and left the room, Alexey Alexandrovitch got up and went to the writing-table. Moving into the middle of the table a portfolio of papers, with a scarcely perceptible smile of self-satisfaction, he took a pencil from a rack and plunged into the perusal of a complex report relating to the present complication. The complication was of this nature: Alexey Alexandrovitch's characteristic quality as a politician, that special individual qualification that every rising functionary possesses, the qualification that with his unflagging ambition, his reserve, his honesty, and with his self-confidence had made his career, was his contempt for red tape, his cutting down of correspondence, his direct contact, wherever possible, with the living fact, and his economy. It happened that the famous Commission of the 2nd of June had set on foot an inquiry into the irrigation of lands in the Zaraisky province, which fell under Alexey Alexandrovitch's department, and was a glaring example of fruitless expenditure and paper reforms. Alexey Alexandrovitch was aware of the truth of this. The irrigation of these lands in the Zaraisky province had been initiated by the predecessor of Alexey Alexandrovitch's predecessor. And vast sums of money had actually been spent and were still being spent on this business, and utterly unproductively, and the whole business could obviously lead to nothing whatever. Alexey Alexandrovitch had perceived this at once on entering office, and would have liked to lay hands on the Board of Irrigation. But at first, when he did not yet feel secure in his position, he knew it would affect too many interests, and would be injudicious. Later on he had been engrossed in other questions, and had simply forgotten the Board of Irrigation. It went of itself, like all such boards, by the mere force of inertia. (Many people gained their livelihood by the Board of Irrigation, especially one highly conscientious and musical family: all the daughters played on stringed instruments, and Alexey Alexandrovitch knew the family and had stood godfather to one of the elder daughters.) The raising of this question by a hostile department was in Alexey Alexandrovitch's opinion a dishonorable proceeding, seeing that in every department there were things similar and worse, which no one inquired into, for well-known reasons of

to him, and she felt bitter against him for it. It seemed to her that the words that she had spoken to her husband, and had continually repeated in her imagination, she had said to every one, and every one had heard them. She could not bring herself to look those of her own household in the face. She could not bring herself to call her maid, and still less go down-stairs and see her son and his governess.

The maid, who had been listening at her door for a long while, came into her room of her own accord. Anna glanced inquiringly into her face, and blushed with a scared look. The maid begged her pardon for coming in, saying that she had fancied the bell rang. She brought her clothes and a note. The note was from Betsy. Betsy reminded her that Liza Merkalova and Baroness Shtoltz were coming to play croquet with her that morning with their adorers, Kaluzhsky and old Stremov. "Come, if only as a study in morals. I shall expect you," she finished.

Anna read the note and heaved a deep sigh.

"Nothing, I need nothing," she said to Annushka, who was rearranging the bottles and brushes on the dressing-table. "You can go. I'll dress at once and come down. I need nothing."

Annushka went out, but Anna did not begin dressing, and sat in the same position, her head and hands hanging listlessly, and every now and then she shivered all over, seemed as though she would make some gesture, utter some word, and sank back into lifelessness again. She repeated continually, "My God! my God!" But neither "God" nor "my" had any meaning to her. The idea of seeking help in her difficulty in religion was as remote from her as seeking help from Alexey Alexandrovitch himself, although she had never had doubts of the faith in which she had been brought up. She knew that the support of religion was possible only upon condition of renouncing what made up for her the whole meaning of life. She was not simply miserable, she began to feel alarm at the new spiritual condition, never experienced before, in which she found herself. She felt as though everything were beginning to be double in her soul, just as objects sometimes appear double to over-tired eyes. She hardly knew at times what it was she feared, and what she hoped for. Whether she feared or desired what had happened, or what was going to happen, and exactly what she longed for, she could not have said.

"Ah, what am I doing!" she said to herself, feeling a sudden thrill of pain in both sides of her head. When she came to herself, she saw that she was holding her hair in both hands, each side of her temples, and pulling it. She jumped up, and began walking about.

"The coffee is ready, and mademoiselle and Seryozha are waiting," said Annushka, coming back again and finding Anna in the same position.

"Seryozha? What about Seryozha?" Anna asked, with sudden eagerness, recollecting her son's existence for the first time that morning.

"He's been naughty, I think," answered Annushka with a smile.

"In what way?"

"Some peaches were lying on the table in the corner room. I think he slipped in and ate one of them on the sly."

The recollection of her son suddenly roused Anna from the helpless condition in which she found herself. She recalled the partly sincere, though greatly exaggerated, rôle of the mother living for her child, which she had taken up of late years, and she felt with joy that in the plight in which she found herself she had a support, quite apart from her relation to her husband or to Vronsky. This support was her son. In whatever position she might be placed, she could not lose her son. Her husband might put her to shame and turn her out, Vronsky might grow cold to her and go on living his own life apart (she thought of him again with bitterness and reproach); she could not leave her son. She had an aim in life. And she must act; act to secure this relation to her son, so that he might not be taken from her. Quickly indeed, as quickly as possible, she must take action before he was taken from her. She must take her son and go away. Here was the one thing she had to do now. She needed consolation. She must be calm, and get out of this insufferable position. The thought of immediate action binding her to her son, of going away somewhere with him, gave her this consolation.

She dressed quickly, went down-stairs, and with resolute steps walked into the drawing-room, where she found, as usual, waiting for her, the coffee, Seryozha, and his governess. Seryozha, all in white, with his back and head bent, was standing at a table under a looking-glass, and with an expression of intense concentration which she knew well, and in which he resembled his father, he was doing something to the flowers he carried.

The governess had a particularly severe expression. Seryozha screamed shrilly, as he often did, "Ah, mamma!" and stopped, hesitating whether to go to greet his mother and put down the flowers, or to finish making the wreath and go with the flowers.

The governess, after saying good-morning, began a long and detailed account of Seryozha's naughtiness, but Anna did not hear her; she was considering whether she would take her with her or not. "No, I won't take her," she decided. "I'll go alone with my child."

more read the letter all through again from the beginning. When she had finished, she felt that she was cold all over, and that a fearful calamity, such as she had not expected, had burst upon her.

In the morning she had regretted that she had spoken to her husband, and wished for nothing so much as that those words could be unspoken. And here this letter regarded them as unspoken, and gave her what she had wanted. But now this letter seemed to her more awful than anything she had been able to conceive.

"He's right!" she said; "of course, he's always right; he's a Christian, he's generous! Yes, vile, base creature! And no one understands it except me, and no one ever will; and I can't explain it. They say he's so religious, so high-principled, so upright, so clever; but they don't see what I've seen. They don't know how he has crushed my life for eight years, crushed everything that was living in me—he has not once even thought that I'm a live woman who must have love. They don't know how at every step he's humiliated me, and been just as pleased with himself. Haven't I striven, striven with all my strength, to find something to give meaning to my life? Haven't I struggled to love him, to love my son when I could not love my husband? But the time came when I knew that I couldn't cheat myself any longer, that I was alive, that I was not to blame, that God has made me so that I must love and live. And now what does he do? If he'd killed me, if he'd killed him, I could have borne anything, I could have forgiven anything; but, no, he … How was it I didn't guess what he would do? He's doing just what's characteristic of his mean character. He'll keep himself in the right, while me, in my ruin, he'll drive still lower to worse ruin yet…."

She recalled the words from the letter. "You can conjecture what awaits you and your son…." "That's a threat to take away my child, and most likely by their stupid law he can. But I know very well why he says it. He doesn't believe even in my love for my child, or he despises it (just as he always used to ridicule it). He despises that feeling in me, but he knows that I won't abandon my child, that I can't abandon my child, that there could be no life for me without my child, even with him whom I love; but that if I abandoned my child and ran away from him, I should be acting like the most infamous, basest of women. He knows that, and knows that I am incapable of doing that."

She recalled another sentence in the letter. "Our life must go on as it has done in the past…." "That life was miserable enough in the old days; it has been awful of late. What will it be now? And he knows all that; he knows that I can't repent that I breathe, that I love; he knows that it can lead to nothing but lying and deceit; but he wants to go on torturing me. I know him; I know that he's at home and is happy in deceit, like a fish swimming in the water. No, I won't give him that happiness. I'll break through the spiderweb of lies in which he wants to catch me, come what may. Anything's better than lying and deceit.

"But how? My God! my God! Was ever a woman so miserable as I am? ..."

"No; I will break through it, I will break through it!" she cried, jumping up and keeping back her tears. And she went to the writing-table to write him another letter. But at the bottom of her heart she felt that she was not strong enough to break through anything, that she was not strong enough to get out of her old position, however false and dishonorable it might be.

She sat down at the writing-table, but instead of writing she clasped her hands on the table, and, laying her head on them, burst into tears, with sobs and heaving breast like a child crying. She was weeping that her dream of her position being made clear and definite had been annihilated forever. She knew beforehand that everything would go on in the old way, and far worse, indeed, than in the old way. She felt that the position in the world that she enjoyed, and that had seemed to her of so little consequence in the morning, that this position was precious to her, that she would not have the strength to exchange it for the shameful position of a woman who has abandoned husband and child to join her lover; that however much she might struggle, she could not be stronger than herself. She would never know freedom in love, but would remain forever a guilty wife, with the menace of detection hanging over her at every instant; deceiving her husband for the sake of a shameful connection with a man living apart and away from her, whose life she could never share. She knew that this was how it would be, and at the same time it was so awful that she could not even conceive what it would end in. And she cried without restraint, as children cry when they are punished.

The sound of the footman's steps forced her to rouse herself, and, hiding her face from him, she pretended to be writing.

"The courier asks if there's an answer," the footman announced.

"An answer? Yes," said Anna. "Let him wait. I'll ring."

"What can I write?" she thought. "What can I decide upon alone? What do I know? What do I want? What is there I care for?" Again she felt that her soul was beginning to be split in two. She was terrified again at this feeling, and clutched at the first pretext for doing something which might divert her thoughts from herself. "I ought to see Alexey" (so she called Vronsky in her thoughts); "no one but he can tell me what I ought to do. I'll go to Betsy's, perhaps I shall see him there," she said to herself, completely forgetting that when she had

"No. I'm not going to let you go for anything," answered Betsy, looking intently into Anna's face. "Really, if I were not fond of you, I should feel offended. One would think you were afraid my society would compromise you. Tea in the little dining-room, please," she said, half closing her eyes, as she always did when addressing the footman.

Taking the note from him, she read it.

"Alexey's playing us false," she said in French; "he writes that he can't come," she added in a tone as simple and natural as though it could never enter her head that Vronsky could mean anything more to Anna than a game of croquet. Anna knew that Betsy knew everything, but, hearing how she spoke of Vronsky before her, she almost felt persuaded for a minute that she knew nothing.

"Ah!" said Anna indifferently, as though not greatly interested in the matter, and she went on smiling: "How can you or your friends compromise any one?"

This playing with words, this hiding of a secret, had a great fascination for Anna, as, indeed, it has for all women. And it was not the necessity of concealment, not the aim with which the concealment was contrived, but the process of concealment itself that attracted her.

"I can't be more Catholic than the Pope," she said. "Stremov and Liza Merkalova, why, they're the cream of the cream of society. Besides, they're received everywhere, and I"—she laid special stress on the I—"have never been strict and intolerant. It's simply that I haven't the time."

"No; you don't care, perhaps, to meet Stremov? Let him and Alexey Alexandrovitch tilt at each other in the committee—that's no affair of ours. But in the world, he's the most amiable man I know, and a devoted croquet-player. You shall see. And, in spite of his absurd position as Liza's lovesick swain at his age, you ought to see how he carries off the absurd position. He's very nice. Sappho Shtoltz you don't know? Oh, that's a new type, quite new."

Betsy said all this, and, at the same time, from her good-humored, shrewd glance, Anna felt that she partly guessed her plight, and was hatching something for her benefit. They were in the little boudoir.

"I must write to Alexey though," and Betsy sat down to the table, scribbled a few lines, and put the note in an envelope.

"I'm telling him to come to dinner. I've one lady extra to dinner with me, and no man to take her in. Look what I've said, will that persuade him? Excuse me, I must leave you for a minute. Would you seal it up, please, and send it off?" she said from the door; "I have to give some directions."

Without a moment's thought, Anna sat down to the table with Betsy's letter, and, without reading it, wrote below: "It's essential for me to see you. Come to the Vrede garden. I shall be there at six o'clock." She sealed it up, and, Betsy coming back, in her presence handed the note to be taken.

At tea, which was brought them on a little tea-table in the cool little drawing-room, the cozy chat promised by Princess Tverskaya before the arrival of her visitors really did come off between the two women. They criticized the people they were expecting, and the conversation fell upon Liza Merkalova.

"She's very sweet, and I always liked her," said Anna.

"You ought to like her. She raves about you. Yesterday she came up to me after the races and was in despair at not finding you. She says you're a real heroine of romance, and that if she were a man she would do all sorts of mad things for your sake. Stremov says she does that as it is."

"But do tell me, please, I never could make it out," said Anna, after being silent for some time, speaking in a tone that showed she was not asking an idle question, but that what she was asking was of more importance to her than it should have been; "do tell me, please, what are her relations with Prince Kaluzhsky, Mishka, as he's called? I've met them so little. What does it mean?"

Betsy smiled with her eyes, and looked intently at Anna.

"It's a new manner," she said. "They've all adopted that manner. They've flung their caps over the windmills. But there are ways and ways of flinging them."

"Yes, but what are her relations precisely with Kaluzhsky?"

Betsy broke into unexpectedly mirthful and irrepressible laughter, a thing which rarely happened with her.

"You're encroaching on Princess Myakaya's special domain now. That's the question of an *enfant terrible*," and Betsy obviously tried to restrain herself, but could not, and went off into peals of that infectious laughter that people laugh who do not laugh often. "You'd better ask them," she brought out, between tears of laughter.

"No; you laugh," said Anna, laughing too in spite of herself, "but I never could understand it. I can't understand the husband's rôle in it."

"The husband? Liza Merkalova's husband carries her shawl, and is always ready to be of use. But anything more than that in reality, no one cares to inquire. You know in decent society one doesn't talk or think even of certain details of the toilet. That's how it is with this."

"Will you be at Madame Rolandak's fête?" asked Anna, to change the conversation.

The weary, and at the same time passionate, glance of those eyes, encircled by dark rings, impressed one by its perfect sincerity. Every one looking into those eyes fancied he knew her wholly, and knowing her, could not but love her. At the sight of Anna, her whole face lighted up at once with a smile of delight.

"Ah, how glad I am to see you!" she said, going up to her. "Yesterday at the races all I wanted was to get to you, but you'd gone away. I did so want to see you, yesterday especially. Wasn't it awful?" she said, looking at Anna with eyes that seemed to lay bare all her soul.

"Yes; I had no idea it would be so thrilling," said Anna, blushing.

The company got up at this moment to go into the garden.

"I'm not going," said Liza, smiling and settling herself close to Anna. "You won't go either, will you? Who wants to play croquet?"

"Oh, I like it," said Anna.

"There, how do you manage never to be bored by things? It's delightful to look at you. You're alive, but I'm bored."

"How can you be bored? Why, you live in the liveliest set in Petersburg," said Anna.

"Possibly the people who are not of our set are even more bored; but we—I certainly—are not happy, but awfully, awfully bored."

Sappho smoking a cigarette went off into the garden with the two young men. Betsy and Stremov remained at the tea-table.

"What, bored!" said Betsy. "Sappho says they did enjoy themselves tremendously at your house last night."

"Ah, how dreary it all was!" said Liza Merkalova. "We all drove back to my place after the races. And always the same people, always the same. Always the same thing. We lounged about on sofas all the evening. What is there to enjoy in that? No; do tell me how you manage never to be bored?" she said, addressing Anna again. "One has but to look at you and one sees, here's a woman who may be happy or unhappy, but isn't bored. Tell me how you do it?"

"I do nothing," answered Anna, blushing at these searching questions.

"That's the best way," Stremov put in. Stremov was a man of fifty, partly gray, but still vigorous-looking, very ugly, but with a characteristic and intelligent face. Liza Merkalova was his wife's niece, and he spent all his leisure hours with her. On meeting Anna Karenina, as he was Alexey Alexandrovitch's enemy in the government, he tried, like a shrewd man and a man of the world, to be particularly cordial with her, the wife of his enemy.

"'Nothing,'" he put in with a subtle smile, "that's the very best way. I told you long ago," he said, turning to Liza Merkalova, "that if you don't want to be bored, you mustn't think you're going to be bored. It's just as you mustn't be afraid of not being able to fall asleep, if you're afraid of sleeplessness. That's just what Anna Arkadyevna has just said."

"I should be very glad if I had said it, for it's not only clever but true," said Anna, smiling.

"No, do tell me why it is one can't go to sleep, and one can't help being bored?"

"To sleep well one ought to work, and to enjoy oneself one ought to work too."

"What am I to work for when my work is no use to anybody? And I can't and won't knowingly make a pretense about it."

"You're incorrigible," said Stremov, not looking at her, and he spoke again to Anna. As he rarely met Anna, he could say nothing but commonplaces to her, but he said those commonplaces as to when she was returning to Petersburg, and how fond Countess Lidia Ivanovna was of her, with an expression which suggested that he longed with his whole soul to please her and show his regard for her and even more than that.

Tushkevitch came in, announcing that the party were awaiting the other players to begin croquet.

"No, don't go away, please don't," pleaded Liza Merkalova, hearing that Anna was going. Stremov joined in her entreaties.

"It's too violent a transition," he said, "to go from such company to old Madame Vrede. And besides, you will only give her a chance for talking scandal, while here you arouse none but such different feelings of the highest and most opposite kind," he said to her.

Anna pondered for an instant in uncertainty. This shrewd man's flattering words, the naïve, childlike affection shown her by Liza Merkalova, and all the social atmosphere she was used to,— it was all so easy, and what was in store for her was so difficult, that she was for a minute in uncertainty whether to remain, whether to put off a little longer the painful moment of explanation. But remembering what was in store for her alone at home, if she did not come to some decision, remembering that gesture—terrible even in memory—when she had clutched her hair in both hands—she said good-bye and went away.

not to lead a life which was a scandal to all good society. His mother's attempt to buy him stung him to the quick and made him feel colder than ever to her. But he could not draw back from the generous word when it was once uttered, even though he felt now, vaguely foreseeing certain eventualities in his intrigue with Madame Karenina, that this generous word had been spoken thoughtlessly, and that even though he were not married he might need all the hundred thousand of income. But it was impossible to draw back. He had only to recall his brother's wife, to remember how that sweet, delightful Varya sought, at every convenient opportunity, to remind him that she remembered his generosity and appreciated it, to grasp the impossibility of taking back his gift. It was as impossible as beating a woman, stealing, or lying. One thing only could and ought to be done, and Vronsky determined upon it without an instant's hesitation: to borrow money from a money-lender, ten thousand roubles, a proceeding which presented no difficulty, to cut down his expenses generally, and to sell his race-horses. Resolving on this, he promptly wrote a note to Rolandak, who had more than once sent to him with offers to buy horses from him. Then he sent for the Englishman and the money-lender, and divided what money he had according to the accounts he intended to pay. Having finished this business, he wrote a cold and cutting answer to his mother. Then he took out of his note-book three notes of Anna's, read them again, burned them, and remembering their conversation on the previous day, he sank into meditation.

CHAPTER XX

VRONSKY'S LIFE WAS PARTICULARLY HAPPY IN THAT HE HAD A CODE OF principles, which defined with unfailing certitude what he ought and what he ought not to do. This code of principles covered only a very small circle of contingencies, but then the principles were never doubtful, and Vronsky, as he never went outside that circle, had never had a moment's hesitation about doing what he ought to do. These principles laid down as invariable rules: that one must pay a cardsharper, but need not pay a tailor; that one must never tell a lie to a man, but one may to a woman; that one must never cheat any one, but one may a husband; that one must never pardon an insult, but one may give one and so on. These principles were possibly not reasonable and not good, but they were of unfailing certainty, and so long as he adhered to them, Vronsky felt that his heart was at peace and he could hold his head up. Only quite lately in regard to his relations with Anna, Vronsky had begun to feel that his code of principles did not fully cover all possible contingencies, and to foresee in the future difficulties and perplexities for which he could find no guiding clue.

His present relation to Anna and to her husband was to his mind clear and simple. It was clearly and precisely defined in the code of principles by which he was guided.

She was an honorable woman who had bestowed her love upon him, and he loved her, and therefore she was in his eyes a woman who had a right to the same, or even more, respect than a lawful wife. He would have had his hand chopped off before he would have allowed himself by a word, by a hint, to humiliate her, or even to fall short of the fullest respect a woman could look for.

His attitude to society, too, was clear. Every one might know, might suspect it, but no one might dare to speak of it. If any did so, he was ready to force all who might speak to be silent and to respect the non-existent honor of the woman he loved.

His attitude to the husband was the clearest of all. From the moment that Anna loved Vronsky, he had regarded his own right over her as the one thing unassailable. Her husband was simply a superfluous and tiresome person. No doubt he was in a pitiable position, but how could that be helped? The one thing the husband had a right to was to demand satisfaction with a weapon in his hand, and Vronsky was prepared for this at any minute.

But of late new inner relations had arisen between him and her, which frightened Vronsky by their indefiniteness. Only the day before she had told him that she was with child. And he felt that this fact and what she expected of him called for something not fully defined in that code of principles by which he had hitherto steered his course in life. And he had been indeed caught unawares, and at the first moment when she spoke to him of her position, his heart had prompted him to beg her to leave her husband. He had said that, but now thinking things over he saw clearly that it would be better to manage to avoid that; and at the same time, as he told himself so, he was afraid whether it was not wrong.

"If I told her to leave her husband, that must mean uniting her life with mine; am I prepared for that? How can I take her away now, when I have no money? Supposing I could arrange ... But how can I take her away while I'm in the service? If I say that—I ought to be prepared to do it, that is, I ought to have the money and to retire from the army."

barrel of vodka, and the robust, good-humored figure of the colonel surrounded by officers. He had gone out as far as the first step of the balcony and was loudly shouting across the band that played Offenbach's quadrille, waving his arms and giving some orders to a few soldiers standing on one side. A group of soldiers, a quartermaster, and several subalterns came up to the balcony with Vronsky. The colonel returned to the table, went out again onto the steps with a tumbler in his hand, and proposed the toast, "To the health of our former comrade, the gallant general, Prince Serpuhovskoy. Hurrah!"

The colonel was followed by Serpuhovskoy, who came out onto the steps smiling, with a glass in his hand.

"You always get younger, Bondarenko," he said to the rosy-checked, smart-looking quartermaster standing just before him, still youngish looking though doing his second term of service.

It was three years since Vronsky had seen Serpuhovskoy. He looked more robust, had let his whiskers grow, but was still the same graceful creature, whose face and figure were even more striking from their softness and nobility than their beauty. The only change Vronsky detected in him was that subdued, continual radiance of beaming content which settles on the faces of men who are successful and are sure of the recognition of their success by every one. Vronsky knew that radiant air, and immediately observed it in Serpuhovskoy.

As Serpuhovskoy came down the steps he saw Vronsky. A smile of pleasure lighted up his face. He tossed his head upwards and waved the glass in his hand, greeting Vronsky, and showing him by the gesture that he could not come to him before the quartermaster, who stood craning forward his lips ready to be kissed.

"Here he is!" shouted the colonel. "Yashvin told me you were in one of your gloomy tempers."

Serpuhovskoy kissed the moist, fresh lips of the gallant-looking quartermaster, and wiping his mouth with his handkerchief, went up to Vronsky.

"How glad I am!" he said, squeezing his hand and drawing him on one side.

"You look after him," the colonel shouted to Yashvin, pointing to Vronsky; and he went down below to the soldiers.

"Why weren't you at the races yesterday? I expected to see you there," said Vronsky, scrutinizing Serpuhovskoy.

"I did go, but late. I beg your pardon," he added, and he turned to the adjutant: "Please have this divided from me, each man as much as it runs to." And he hurriedly took notes for three hundred roubles from his pocketbook, blushing a little.

"Vronsky! Have anything to eat or drink?" asked Yashvin. "Hi, something for the count to eat! Ah, here it is: have a glass!"

The fête at the colonel's lasted a long while. There was a great deal of drinking. They tossed Serpuhovskoy in the air and caught him again several times. Then they did the same to the colonel. Then, to the accompaniment of the band, the colonel himself danced with Petritsky. Then the colonel, who began to show signs of feebleness, sat down on a bench in the courtyard and began demonstrating to Yashvin the superiority of Russia over Poland, especially in cavalry attack, and there was a lull in the revelry for a moment. Serpuhovskoy went into the house to the bathroom to wash his hands and found Vronsky there; Vronsky was drenching his head with water. He had taken off his coat and put his sunburnt, hairy neck under the tap, and was rubbing it and his head with his hands. When he had finished, Vronsky sat down by Serpuhovskoy. They both sat down in the bathroom on a lounge, and a conversation began which was very interesting to both of them.

"I've always been hearing about you through my wife," said Serpuhovskoy. "I'm glad you've been seeing her pretty often."

"She's friendly with Varya, and they're the only women in Petersburg I care about seeing," answered Vronsky, smiling. He smiled because he foresaw the topic the conversation would turn on, and he was glad of it.

"The only ones?" Serpuhovskoy queried, smiling.

"Yes; and I heard news of you, but not only through your wife," said Vronsky, checking his hint by a stern expression of face. "I was greatly delighted to hear of your success, but not a bit surprised. I expected even more."

Serpuhovskoy smiled. Such an opinion of him was obviously agreeable to him, and he did not think it necessary to conceal it.

"Well, I on the contrary expected less—I'll own frankly. But I'm glad, very glad. I'm ambitious; that's my weakness, and I confess to it."

"Perhaps you wouldn't confess to it if you hadn't been successful," said Vronsky.

"I don't suppose so," said Serpuhovskoy, smiling again. "I won't say life wouldn't be worth living without it, but it would be dull. Of course I may be mistaken, but I fancy I have a certain capacity for the line I've chosen, and that power of any sort in my hands, if it is to be, will be better than in the hands of a good many people I know," said Serpuhovskoy, with beaming consciousness of success; "and so the nearer I get to it, the better pleased I am."

"Perhaps that is true for you, but not for every one. I used to think so too, but here I live and think life worth living not only for that."

marriage. And that's what I felt when I was married. My hands were suddenly set free. But to drag that *fardeau* about with you without marriage, your hands will always be so full that you can do nothing. Look at Mazankov, at Krupov. They've ruined their careers for the sake of women."

"What women!" said Vronsky, recalling the Frenchwoman and the actress with whom the two men he had mentioned were connected.

"The firmer the woman's footing in society, the worse it is. That's much the same as—not merely carrying the *fardeau* in your arms—but tearing it away from some one else."

"You have never loved," Vronsky said softly, looking straight before him and thinking of Anna.

"Perhaps. But you remember what I've said to you. And another thing, women are all more materialistic than men. We make something immense out of love, but they are always *terre-à-terre*."

"Directly, directly!" he cried to a footman who came in. But the footman had not come to call them again, as he supposed. The footman brought Vronsky a note.

"A man brought it from Princess Tverskaya."

Vronsky opened the letter, and flushed crimson.

"My head's begun to ache; I'm going home," he said to Serpuhovskoy.

"Oh, good-bye then. You give me *carte blanche!*"

"We'll talk about it later on; I'll look you up in Petersburg."

CHAPTER XXII

IT WAS SIX O'CLOCK ALREADY, AND SO, IN ORDER TO BE THERE QUICKLY, AND AT the same time not to drive with his own horses, known to every one, Vronsky got into Yashvin's hired fly, and told the driver to drive as quickly as possible. It was a roomy, old-fashioned fly, with seats for four. He sat in one corner, stretched his legs out on the front seat, and sank into meditation.

A vague sense of the order into which his affairs had been brought, a vague recollection of the friendliness and flattery of Serpuhovskoy, who had considered him a man that was needed, and most of all, the anticipation of the interview before him—all blended into a general, joyous sense of life. This feeling was so strong that he could not help smiling. He dropped his legs, crossed one leg over the other knee, and taking it in his hand, felt the springy muscle of the calf, where it had been grazed the day before by his fall, and leaning back he drew several deep breaths.

"I'm happy, very happy!" he said to himself. He had often before had this sense of physical joy in his own body, but he had never felt so fond of himself, of his own body, as at that moment. He enjoyed the slight ache in his strong leg, he enjoyed the muscular sensation of movement in his chest as he breathed. The bright, cold August day, which had made Anna feel so hopeless, seemed to him keenly stimulating, and refreshed his face and neck that still tingled from the cold water. The scent of brilliantine on his whiskers struck him as particularly pleasant in the fresh air. Everything he saw from the carriage-window, everything in that cold pure air, in the pale light of the sunset, was as fresh, and gay, and strong as he was himself: the roofs of the houses shining in the rays of the setting sun, the sharp outlines of fences and angles of buildings, the figures of passers-by, the carriages that met him now and then, the motionless green of the trees and grass, the fields with evenly drawn furrows of potatoes, and the slanting shadows that fell from the houses, and trees, and bushes, and even from the rows of potatoes—everything was bright like a pretty landscape just finished and freshly varnished.

"Get on, get on!" he said to the driver, putting his head out of the window, and pulling a three-rouble note out of his pocket he handed it to the man as he looked round. The driver's hand fumbled with something at the lamp, the whip cracked, and the carriage rolled rapidly along the smooth highroad.

"I want nothing, nothing but this happiness," he thought, staring at the bone button of the bell in the space between the windows, and picturing to himself Anna just as he had seen her last time. "And as I go on, I love her more and more. Here's the garden of the Vrede Villa. Whereabouts will she be? Where? How? Why did she fix on this place to meet me, and why does she write in Betsy's letter?" he thought, wondering now for the first time at it. But there was now no time for wonder. He called to the driver to stop before reaching the avenue, and opening the door, jumped out of the carriage as it was moving, and went into the avenue that led up to the house. There was no one in the avenue; but looking round to the right he caught sight of her. Her face was hidden by a veil, but he drank in with glad eyes the special movement in walking, peculiar to her alone, the slope of the shoulders, and the setting of the head, and at once a sort of electric shock ran all over him. With fresh force, he felt conscious of himself from the springy motions of his legs to the movements of his lungs as he breathed, and something set his lips twitching.

Vronsky meant that after the duel—inevitable, he thought—things could not go on as before, but he said something different.

"It can't go on. I hope that now you will leave him. I hope"—he was confused, and reddened—"that you will let me arrange and plan our life. To-morrow..." he was beginning.

She did not let him go on.

"But my child!" she shrieked. "You see what he writes! I should have to leave him, and I can't and won't do that."

"But, for God's sake, which is better?—leave your child, or keep up this degrading position?"

"To whom is it degrading?"

"To all, and most of all to you."

"You say degrading ... don't say that. Those words have no meaning for me," she said in a shaking voice. She did not want him now to say what was untrue. She had nothing left her but his love, and she wanted to love him. "Don't you understand that from the day I loved you everything has changed for me? For me there is one thing, and one thing only—your love. If that's mine, I feel so exalted, so strong, that nothing can be humiliating to me. I am proud of my position, because ... proud of being ... proud ..." She could not say what she was proud of. Tears of shame and despair choked her utterance. She stood still and sobbed.

He felt, too, something swelling in his throat and twitching in his nose, and for the first time in his life he felt on the point of weeping. He could not have said exactly what it was touched him so. He felt sorry for her, and he felt he could not help her, and with that he knew that he was to blame for her wretchedness, and that he had done something wrong.

"Is not a divorce possible?" he said feebly. She shook her head, not answering. "Couldn't you take your son, and still leave him?"

"Yes; but it all depends on him. Now I must go to him," she said shortly. Her presentiment that all would again go on in the old way had not deceived her.

"On Tuesday I shall be in Petersburg, and everything can be settled."

"Yes," she said. "But don't let us talk any more of it."

Anna's carriage, which she had sent away, and ordered to come back to the little gate of the Vrede garden, drove up. Anna said good-bye to Vronsky, and drove home.

CHAPTER XXIII

O N MONDAY THERE WAS THE USUAL SITTING OF THE COMMISSION OF THE 2nd of June. Alexey Alexandrovitch walked into the hall where the sitting was held, greeted the members and the president, as usual, and sat down in his place, putting his hand on the papers laid ready before him. Among these papers lay the necessary evidence and a rough outline of the speech he intended to make. But he did not really need these documents. He remembered every point, and did not think it necessary to go over in his memory what he would say. He knew that when the time came, and when he saw his enemy facing him, and studiously endeavoring to assume an expression of indifference, his speech would flow of itself better than he could prepare it now. He felt that the import of his speech was of such magnitude that every word of it would have weight. Meantime, as he listened to the usual report, he had the most innocent and inoffensive air. No one, looking at his white hands, with their swollen veins and long fingers, so softly stroking the edges of the white paper that lay before him, and at the air of weariness with which his head drooped on one side, would have suspected that in a few minutes a torrent of words would flow from his lips that would arouse a fearful storm, set the members shouting and attacking one another, and force the president to call for order. When the report was over, Alexey Alexandrovitch announced in his subdued, delicate voice that he had several points to bring before the meeting in regard to the Commission for the Reorganization of the Native Tribes. All attention was turned upon him. Alexey Alexandrovitch cleared his throat, and not looking at his opponent, but selecting, as he always did while he was delivering his speeches, the first person sitting opposite him, an inoffensive little old man, who never had an opinion of any sort in the Commission, began to expound his views. When he reached the point about the fundamental and radical law, his opponent jumped up and began to protest. Stremov, who was also a member of the Commission, and also stung to the quick, began defending himself, and altogether a stormy sitting followed; but Alexey Alexandrovitch triumphed, and his motion was carried, three new commissions were appointed, and the next day in a certain Petersburg circle nothing else was talked of but this sitting. Alexey Alexandrovitch's success had been even greater than he had anticipated.

Next morning, Tuesday, Alexey Alexandrovitch, on waking up, recollected with pleasure his triumph of the previous day, and he could not help smiling, though he tried to appear indifferent, when the chief secretary of his department, anxious to flatter him, informed him of the rumors that had reached him concerning what had happened in the Commission.

Absorbed in business with the chief secretary, Alexey Alexandrovitch had completely forgotten that it was Tuesday, the day fixed by him for the return of Anna Arkadyevna, and he was surprised and received a shock of annoyance when a servant came in to inform him of her arrival.

Anna had arrived in Petersburg early in the morning; the carriage had been sent to meet her in accordance with her telegram, and so Alexey Alexandrovitch might have known of her arrival. But when she arrived, he did not meet her. She was told that he had not yet gone out, but was busy with his secretary. She sent word to her husband that she had come, went to her own room, and occupied herself in sorting out her things, expecting he would come to her. But an hour passed; he did not come. She went into the dining-room on the pretext of giving some directions, and spoke loudly on purpose, expecting him to come out there; but he did not come, though she heard him go to the door of his study as he parted from the chief secretary. She knew that he usually went out quickly to his office, and she wanted to see him before that, so that their attitude to one another might be defined.

She walked across the drawing-room and went resolutely to him. When she went into his study he was in official uniform, obviously ready to go out, sitting at a little table on which he rested his elbows, looking dejectedly before him. She saw him before he saw her, and she saw that he was thinking of her.

On seeing her, he would have risen, but changed his mind, then his face flushed hotly—a thing Anna had never seen before, and he got up quickly and went to meet her, looking not at her eyes, but above them at her forehead and hair. He went up to her, took her by the hand, and asked her to sit down.

"I am very glad you have come," he said, sitting down beside her, and obviously wishing to say something, he stuttered. Several times he tried to begin to speak, but stopped. In spite of the fact that, preparing herself for meeting him, she had schooled herself to despise and reproach him, she did not know what to say to him, and she felt sorry for him. And so the silence lasted for some time. "Is Seryozha quite well?" he said, and not waiting for an answer, he added: "I shan't be dining at home to-day, and I have got to go out directly."

"I had thought of going to Moscow," she said.

"No, you did quite, quite right to come," he said, and was silent again.

Seeing that he was powerless to begin the conversation, she began herself.

"Alexey Alexandrovitch," she said, looking at him and not dropping her eyes under his persistent gaze at her hair, "I'm a guilty woman, I'm a bad woman, but I am the same as I was, as I told you then, and I have come to tell you that I can change nothing."

"I have asked you no question about that," he said, all at once, resolutely and with hatred looking her straight in the face; "that was as I had supposed." Under the influence of anger he apparently regained complete possession of all his faculties. "But as I told you then, and have written to you," he said in a thin, shrill voice, "I repeat now, that I am not bound to know this. I ignore it. Not all wives are so kind as you, to be in such a hurry to communicate such agreeable news to their husbands." He laid special emphasis on the word "agreeable." "I shall ignore it so long as the world knows nothing of it, so long as my name is not disgraced. And so I simply inform you that our relations must be just as they have always been, and that only in the event of your compromising me I shall be obliged to take steps to secure my honor."

"But our relations cannot be the same as always," Anna began in a timid voice, looking at him with dismay.

When she saw once more those composed gestures, heard that shrill, childish, and sarcastic voice, her aversion for him extinguished her pity for him, and she felt only afraid, but at all costs she wanted to make clear her position.

"I cannot be your wife while I ..." she began.

He laughed a cold and malignant laugh.

"The manner of life you have chosen is reflected, I suppose, in your ideas. I have too much respect or contempt, or both ... I respect your past and despise your present ... that I was far from the interpretation you put on my words."

Anna sighed and bowed her head.

"Though indeed I fail to comprehend how, with the independence you show," he went on, getting hot, "—announcing your infidelity to your husband and seeing nothing reprehensible in it, apparently—you can see anything reprehensible in performing a wife's duties in relation to your husband."

"Alexey Alexandrovitch! What is it you want of me?"

"I want you not to meet that man here, and to conduct yourself so that neither the world nor the servants can reproach you...not to see him. That's not much, I think. And in return you will enjoy all the privileges of a faithful wife without fulfilling her duties. That's all I have to say to you. Now it's time for me to go. I'm not dining at home." He got up and moved towards the door.

Anna got up too. Bowing in silence, he let her pass before him.

To this now was joined the presence, only twenty-five miles off, of Kitty Shtcherbatskaya, whom he longed to see and could not see. Darya Alexandrovna Oblonskaya had invited him, when he was over there, to come; to come with the object of renewing his offer to her sister, who would, so she gave him to understand, accept him now. Levin himself had felt on seeing Kitty Shtcherbatskaya that he had never ceased to love her; but he could not go over to the Oblonskys', knowing she was there. The fact that he had made her an offer, and she had refused him, had placed an insuperable barrier between her and him. "I can't ask her to be my wife merely because she can't be the wife of the man she wanted to marry," he said to himself. The thought of this made him cold and hostile to her. "I should not be able to speak to her without a feeling of reproach; I could not look at her without resentment; and she will only hate me all the more, as she's bound to. And besides, how can I now, after what Darya Alexandrovna told me, go to see them? Can I help showing that I know what she told me? And me to go magnanimously to forgive her, and have pity on her! Me go through a performance before her of forgiving, and deigning to bestow my love on her! … What induced Darya Alexandrovna to tell me that? By chance I might have seen her, then everything would have happened of itself; but, as it is, it's out of the question, out of the question!"

Darya Alexandrovna sent him a letter, asking him for a side-saddle for Kitty's use. "I'm told you have a side-saddle," she wrote to him; "I hope you will bring it over yourself."

This was more than he could stand. How could a woman of any intelligence, of any delicacy, put her sister in such a humiliating position! He wrote ten notes, and tore them all up, and sent the saddle without any reply. To write that he would go was impossible, because he could not go; to write that he could not come because something prevented him, or that he would be away, that was still worse. He sent the saddle without an answer, and with a sense of having done something shameful; he handed over all the now revolting business of the estate to the bailiff, and set off next day to a remote district to see his friend Sviazhsky, who had splendid marshes for grouse in his neighborhood, and had lately written to ask him to keep a long-standing promise to stay with him. The grouse-marsh, in the Surovsky district, had long tempted Levin, but he had continually put off this visit on account of his work on the estate. Now he was glad to get away from the neighborhood of the Shtcherbatskys, and still more from his farm-work, especially on a shooting expedition, which always in trouble served as the best consolation.

CHAPTER XXV

IN THE SUROVSKY district there was no railway nor service of post-horses, and Levin drove there with his own horses in his big, old-fashioned carriage.

He stopped half-way at a well-to-do peasant's to feed his horses. A bald, well-preserved old man, with a broad, red beard, gray on his cheeks, opened the gate, squeezing against the gatepost to let the three horses pass. Directing the coachman to a place under the shed in the big, clean, tidy yard, with charred, old-fashioned ploughs in it, the old man asked Levin to come into the parlor. A cleanly dressed young woman, with clogs on her bare feet, was scrubbing the floor in the new outer room. She was frightened of the dog, that ran in after Levin, and uttered a shriek, but began laughing at her own fright at once when she was told the dog would not hurt her. Pointing Levin with her bare arm to the door into the parlor, she bent down again, hiding her handsome face, and went on scrubbing.

"Would you like the samovar?" she asked.

"Yes, please."

The parlor was a big room, with a Dutch stove, and a screen dividing it into two. Under the holy pictures stood a table painted in patterns, a bench, and two chairs. Near the entrance was a dresser full of crockery. The shutters were closed, there were few flies, and it was so clean that Levin was anxious that Laska, who had been running along the road and bathing in puddles, should not muddy the floor, and ordered her to a place in the corner by the door. After looking round the parlor, Levin went out in the back yard. The good-looking young woman in clogs, swinging the empty pails on the yoke, ran on before him to the well for water.

"Look sharp, my girl!" the old man shouted after her, good-humoredly, and he went up to Levin. "Well, sir, are you going to Nikolay Ivanovitch Sviazhsky? His honor comes to us too," he began, chatting, leaning his elbows on the railing of the steps. In the middle of the old man's account of his acquaintance with Sviazhsky, the gates creaked again, and laborers came into the yard from the fields, with wooden ploughs and harrows. The horses harnessed to the ploughs and harrows were sleek and fat. The laborers were obviously of the household: two were young men in cotton shirts and caps, the two others were hired laborers in homespun shirts, one an old man, the other a young fellow. Moving off from the steps, the old man went up to the horses and began unharnessing them.

with certainty, as so-called eligible young men always know it, though he could never have brought himself to speak of it to any one; and he knew too that, although he wanted to get married, and although by every token this very attractive girl would make an excellent wife, he could no more have married her, even if he had not been in love with Kitty Shtcherbatskaya, than he could have flown up to the sky. And this knowledge poisoned the pleasure he had hoped to find in the visit to Sviazhsky.

On getting Sviazhsky's letter with the invitation for shooting, Levin had immediately thought of this; but in spite of it he had made up his mind that Sviazhsky's having such views for him was simply his own groundless supposition, and so he would go, all the same. Besides, at the bottom of his heart he had a desire to try himself, put himself to the test in regard to this girl. The Sviazhskys' home-life was exceedingly pleasant, and Sviazhsky himself, the best type of man taking part in local affairs that Levin knew, was very interesting to him.

Sviazhsky was one of those people, always a source of wonder to Levin, whose convictions, very logical though never original, go one way by themselves, while their life, exceedingly definite and firm in its direction, goes its way quite apart and almost always in direct contradiction to their convictions. Sviazhsky was an extremely advanced man. He despised the nobility, and believed the mass of the nobility to be secretly in favor of serfdom, and only concealing their views from cowardice. He regarded Russia as a ruined country, rather after the style of Turkey, and the government of Russia as so bad that he never permitted himself to criticize its doings seriously, and yet he was a functionary of that government and a model marshal of nobility, and when he drove about he always wore the cockade of office and the cap with the red band. He considered human life tolerable only abroad, and went abroad to stay at every opportunity, and at the same time he carried on a complex and improved system of agriculture in Russia, and with extreme interest followed everything and knew everything that was being done in Russia. He considered the Russian peasant as occupying a stage of development intermediate between the ape and the man, and at the same time in the local assemblies no one was readier to shake hands with the peasants and listen to their opinion. He believed neither in God nor the devil, but was much concerned about the question of the improvement of the clergy and the maintenance of their revenues, and took special trouble to keep up the church in his village.

On the woman question he was on the side of the extreme advocates of complete liberty for women, and especially their right to labor. But he lived with his wife on such terms that their affectionate childless home-life was the admiration of every one, and arranged his wife's life so that she did nothing and could do nothing but share her husband's efforts that her time should pass as happily and as agreeably as possible.

If it had not been a characteristic of Levin's to put the most favorable interpretation on people, Sviazhsky's character would have presented no doubt or difficulty to him: he would have said to himself, "a fool or a knave," and everything would have seemed clear. But he could not say "a fool," because Sviazhsky was unmistakably clever, and moreover, a highly cultivated man, who was exceptionally modest over his culture. There was not a subject he knew nothing of. But he did not display his knowledge except when he was compelled to do so. Still less could Levin say that he was a knave, as Sviazhsky was unmistakably an honest, good-hearted, sensible man, who worked good-humoredly, keenly, and perseveringly at his work; he was held in high honor by every one about him, and certainly he had never consciously done, and was indeed incapable of doing, anything base.

Levin tried to understand him, and could not understand him, and looked at him and his life as at a living enigma.

Levin and he were very friendly, and so Levin used to venture to sound Sviazhsky, to try to get at the very foundation of his view of life; but it was always in vain. Every time Levin tried to penetrate beyond the outer chambers of Sviazhsky's mind, which were hospitably open to all, he noticed that Sviazhsky was slightly disconcerted; faint signs of alarm were visible in his eyes, as though he were afraid Levin would understand him, and he would give him a kindly, good-humored repulse.

Just now, since his disenchantment with farming, Levin was particularly glad to stay with Sviazhsky. Apart from the fact that the sight of this happy and affectionate couple, so pleased with themselves and every one else, and their well-ordered home had always a cheering effect on Levin, he felt a longing, now that he was so dissatisfied with his own life, to get at that secret in Sviazhsky that gave him such clearness, definiteness, and good courage in life. Moreover, Levin knew that at Sviazhsky's he should meet the landowners of the neighborhood, and it was particularly interesting for him just now to hear and take part in those rural conversations concerning crops, laborers' wages, and so on, which, he was aware, are conventionally regarded as something very low, but which seemed to him just now to constitute the one subject of importance. "It was not, perhaps, of importance in the days of serfdom, and it may not be of importance in England. In both cases the conditions of agriculture are firmly established; but among us now, when everything has

"The only gain is that I live in my own house, neither bought nor hired. Besides, one keeps hoping the people will learn sense. Though, instead of that, you'd never believe it—the drunkenness, the immorality! They keep chopping and changing their bits of land. Not a sight of a horse or a cow. The peasant's dying of hunger, but just go and take him on as a laborer, he'll do his best to do you a mischief, and then bring you up before the justice of the peace."

"But then you make complaints to the justice too," said Sviazhsky.

"I lodge complaints? Not for anything in the world! Such a talking, and such a to-do, that one would have cause to regret it. At the works, for instance, they pocketed the advance-money and made off. What did the justice do? Why, acquitted them. Nothing keeps them in order but their own communal court and their village elder. He'll flog them in the good old style! But for that there'd be nothing for it but to give it all up and run away."

Obviously the landowner was chaffing Sviazhsky, who, far from resenting it, was apparently amused by it.

"But you see we manage our land without such extreme measures," said he, smiling: "Levin and I and this gentleman."

He indicated the other landowner.

"Yes, the thing's done at Mihail Petrovitch's, but ask him how it's done. Do you call that a rational system?" said the landowner, obviously rather proud of the word "rational."

"My system's very simple," said Mihail Petrovitch, "thank God. All my management rests on getting the money ready for the autumn taxes, and the peasants come to me, 'Father, master, help us!' Well, the peasants are all one's neighbors; one feels for them. So one advances them a third, but one says: 'Remember, lads, I have helped you, and you must help me when I need it— whether it's the sowing of the oats, or the hay-cutting, or the harvest'; and well, one agrees, so much for each taxpayer—though there are dishonest ones among them too, it's true."

Levin, who had long been familiar with these patriarchal methods, exchanged glances with Sviazhsky and interrupted Mihail Petrovitch, turning again to the gentleman with the gray whiskers.

"Then what do you think?" he asked; "what system is one to adopt nowadays?"

"Why, manage like Mihail Petrovitch, or let the land for half the crop or for rent to the peasants; that one can do—only that's just how the general prosperity of the country is being ruined. Where the land with serf-labor and good management gave a yield of nine to one, on the half-crop system it yields three to one. Russia has been ruined by the emancipation!"

Sviazhsky looked with smiling eyes at Levin, and even made a faint gesture of irony to him; but Levin did not think the landowner's words absurd, he understood them better than he did Sviazhsky. A great deal more of what the gentleman with the gray whiskers said to show in what way Russia was ruined by the emancipation struck him indeed as very true, new to him, and quite incontestable. The landowner unmistakably spoke his own individual thought—a thing that very rarely happens—and a thought to which he had been brought not by a desire of finding some exercise for an idle brain, but a thought which had grown up out of the conditions of his life, which he had brooded over in the solitude of his village, and had considered in every aspect.

"The point is, don't you see, that progress of every sort is only made by the use of authority," he said, evidently wishing to show he was not without culture. "Take the reforms of Peter, of Catherine, of Alexander. Take European history. And progress in agriculture more than anything else—the potato, for instance, that was introduced among us by force. The wooden plough too wasn't always used. It was introduced maybe in the days before the Empire, but it was probably brought in by force. Now, in our own day, we landowners in the serf times used various improvements in our husbandry: drying machines and thrashing-machines, and carting manure and all the modern implements— all that we brought into use by our authority, and the peasants opposed it at first, and ended by imitating us. Now, by the abolition of serfdom we have been deprived of our authority; and so our husbandry, where it had been raised to a high level, is bound to sink to the most savage primitive condition. That's how I see it."

"But why so? If it's rational, you'll be able to keep up the same system with hired labor," said Sviazhsky.

"We've no power over them. With whom am I going to work the system, allow me to ask?"

"There it is—the labor force—the chief element in agriculture," thought Levin.

"With laborers."

"The laborers won't work well, and won't work with good implements. Our laborer can do nothing but get drunk like a pig, and when he's drunk he ruins everything you give him. He makes the horses ill with too much water, cuts good harness, barters the tires of the wheels for drink, drops bits of iron into the thrashing-machine, so as to break it. He loathes the sight of anything

out of his swinishness one must have authority, and there is none; one must have the stick, and we have become so liberal that we have all of a sudden replaced the stick that served us for a thousand years by lawyers and model prisons, where the worthless, stinking peasant is fed on good soup and has a fixed allowance of cubic feet of air.

"What makes you think," said Levin, trying to get back to the question, "that it's impossible to find some relation to the laborer in which the labor would become productive?"

"That never could be so with the Russian peasantry; we've no power over them," answered the landowner.

"How can new conditions be found?" said Sviazhsky. Having eaten some junket and lighted a cigarette, he came back to the discussion. "All possible relations to the labor force have been defined and studied," he said. "The relic of barbarism, the primitive commune with each guarantee for all, will disappear of itself; serfdom has been abolished—there remains nothing but free labor, and its forms are fixed and ready made, and must be adopted. Permanent hands, day-laborers, farmers—you can't get out of those forms."

"But Europe is dissatisfied with these forms."

"Dissatisfied, and seeking new ones. And will find them, in all probability."

"That's just what I was meaning," answered Levin. "Why shouldn't we seek them for ourselves?"

"Because it would be just like inventing afresh the means for constructing railways. They are ready, invented."

"But if they don't do for us, if they're stupid?" said Levin.

And again he detected the expression of alarm in the eyes of Sviazhsky.

"Oh, yes; we'll bury the world under our caps! We've found the secret Europe was seeking for! I've heard all that; but, excuse me, do you know all that's been done in Europe on the question of the organization of labor?"

"No, very little."

"That question is now absorbing the best minds in Europe. The Schulze-Delitsch movement.... And then all this enormous literature of the labor question, the most liberal Lassalle movement ... the Mulhausen experiment? That's a fact by now, as you're probably aware."

"I have some idea of it, but very vague."

"No, you only say that; no doubt you know all about it as well as I do. I'm not a professor of sociology, of course, but it interested me, and really, if it interests you, you ought to study it."

"But what conclusion have they come to?"

"Excuse me …"

The two neighbors had risen, and Sviazhsky, once more checking Levin in his inconvenient habit of peeping into what was beyond the outer chambers of his mind, went to see his guests out.

CHAPTER XXVIII

L EVIN WAS INSUFFERABLY BORED THAT EVENING WITH THE LADIES; HE WAS stirred as he had never been before by the idea that the dissatisfaction he was feeling with his system of managing his land was not an exceptional case, but the general condition of things in Russia; that the organization of some relation of the laborers to the soil in which they would work, as with the peasant he had met half-way to the Sviazhskys', was not a dream, but a problem which must be solved. And it seemed to him that the problem could be solved, and that he ought to try and solve it.

After saying good-night to the ladies, and promising to stay the whole of the next day, so as to make an expedition on horseback with them to see an interesting ruin in the crown forest, Levin went, before going to bed, into his host's study to get the books on the labor question that Sviazhsky had offered him. Sviazhsky's study was a huge room, surrounded by bookcases and with two tables in it—one a massive writing-table, standing in the middle of the room, and the other a round table, covered with recent numbers of reviews and journals in different languages, ranged like the rays of a star round the lamp. On the writing-table was a stand of drawers marked with gold lettering, and full of papers of various sorts.

Sviazhsky took out the books, and sat down in a rocking-chair.

"What are you looking at there?" he said to Levin, who was standing at the round table looking through the reviews.

"Oh, yes, there's a very interesting article here," said Sviazhsky of the review Levin was holding in his hand. "It appears," he went on, with eager interest, "that Friedrich was not, after all, the person chiefly responsible for the partition of Poland. It is proved …"

And with his characteristic clearness, he summed up those new, very important, and interesting revelations. Although Levin was engrossed at the moment by his ideas about the problem of the land, he wondered, as he heard

conceptions and ideas of the day, threw Levin into violent excitement. This dear good Sviazhsky, keeping a stock of ideas simply for social purposes, and obviously having some other principles hidden from Levin, while with the crowd, whose name is legion, he guided public opinion by ideas he did not share; that irascible country gentleman, perfectly correct in the conclusions that he had been worried into by life, but wrong in his exasperation against a whole class, and that the best class in Russia; his own dissatisfaction with the work he had been doing, and the vague hope of finding a remedy for all this—all was blended in a sense of inward turmoil, and anticipation of some solution near at hand.

Left alone in the room assigned him, lying on a spring mattress that yielded unexpectedly at every movement of his arm or his leg, Levin did not fall asleep for a long while. Not one conversation with Sviazhsky, though he had said a great deal that was clever, had interested Levin; but the conclusions of the irascible landowner required consideration. Levin could not help recalling every word he had said, and in imagination amending his own replies.

"Yes, I ought to have said to him: You say that our husbandry does not answer because the peasant hates improvements, and that they must be forced on him by authority. If no system of husbandry answered at all without these improvements, you would be quite right. But the only system that does answer is when the laborer is working in accordance with his habits, just as on the old peasant's land half-way here. Your and our general dissatisfaction with the system shows that either we are to blame or the laborers. We have gone our way— the European way—a long while, without asking ourselves about the qualities of our labor force. Let us try to look upon the labor force not as an abstract force, but as the *Russian peasant* with his instincts, and we shall arrange our system of culture in accordance with that. Imagine, I ought to have said to him, that you have the same system as the old peasant has, that you have found means of making your laborers take an interest in the success of the work, and have found the happy mean in the way of improvements which they will admit, and you will, without exhausting the soil, get twice or three times the yield you got before. Divide it in halves, give half as the share of labor, the surplus left you will be greater, and the share of labor will be greater too. And to do this one must lower the standard of husbandry and interest the laborers in its success. How to do this?—that's a matter of detail; but undoubtedly it can be done."

This idea threw Levin into a great excitement. He did not sleep half the night, thinking over in detail the putting of his idea into practice. He had not intended to go away next day, but he now determined to go home early in the morning. Besides, the sister-in-law with her low-necked bodice aroused in him a feeling akin to shame and remorse for some utterly base action. Most important of all—he must get back without delay: he would have to make haste to put his new project to the peasants before the sowing of the winter wheat, so that the sowing might be undertaken on a new basis. He had made up his mind to revolutionize his whole system.

CHAPTER XXIX

THE CARRYING OUT OF LEVIN'S PLAN PRESENTED MANY DIFFICULTIES; BUT he struggled on, doing his utmost, and attained a result which, though not what he desired, was enough to enable him, without self-deception, to believe that the attempt was worth the trouble. One of the chief difficulties was that the process of cultivating the land was in full swing, that it was impossible to stop everything and begin it all again from the beginning, and the machine had to be mended while in motion.

When on the evening that he arrived home he informed the bailiff of his plans, the latter with visible pleasure agreed with what he said so long as he was pointing out that all that had been done up to that time was stupid and useless. The bailiff said that he had said so a long while ago, but no heed had been paid him. But as for the proposal made by Levin—to take a part as shareholder with his laborers in each agricultural undertaking—at this the bailiff simply expressed a profound despondency, and offered no definite opinion, but began immediately talking of the urgent necessity of carrying the remaining sheaves of rye the next day, and of sending the men out for the second ploughing, so that Levin felt that this was not the time for discussing it.

On beginning to talk to the peasants about it, and making a proposition to cede them the land on new terms, he came into collision with the same great difficulty that they were so much absorbed by the current work of the day, that they had not time to consider the advantages and disadvantages of the proposed scheme.

The simple-hearted Ivan, the cowherd, seemed completely to grasp Levin's proposal—that he should with his family take a share of the profits of the cattle-yard—and he was in complete sympathy with the plan. But when Levin hinted

nothing bearing on the scheme he had undertaken. In the books on political economy—in Mill, for instance, whom he studied first with great ardor, hoping every minute to find an answer to the questions that were engrossing him—he found laws deduced from the condition of land culture in Europe; but he did not see why these laws, which did not apply in Russia, must be general. He saw just the same thing in the socialistic books: either they were the beautiful but impracticable fantasies which had fascinated him when he was a student, or they were attempts at improving, rectifying the economic position in which Europe was placed, with which the system of land tenure in Russia had nothing in common. Political economy told him that the laws by which the wealth of Europe had been developed, and was developing, were universal and unvarying. Socialism told him that development along these lines leads to ruin. And neither of them gave an answer, or even a hint, in reply to the question what he, Levin, and all the Russian peasants and landowners, were to do with their millions of hands and millions of acres, to make them as productive as possible for the common weal.

Having once taken the subject up, he read conscientiously everything bearing on it, and intended in the autumn to go abroad to study land systems on the spot, in order that he might not on this question be confronted with what so often met him on various subjects. Often, just as he was beginning to understand the idea in the mind of anyone he was talking to, and was beginning to explain his own, he would suddenly be told: "But Kauffmann, but Jones, but Dubois, but Michelli? You haven't read them: they've thrashed that question out thoroughly."

He saw now distinctly that Kauffmann and Michelli had nothing to tell him. He knew what he wanted. He saw that Russia has splendid land, splendid laborers, and that in certain cases, as at the peasant's on the way to Sviazhsky's, the produce raised by the laborers and the land is great—in the majority of cases when capital is applied in the European way the produce is small, and that this simply arises from the fact that the laborers want to work and work well only in their own peculiar way, and that this antagonism is not incidental but invariable, and has its roots in the national spirit. He thought that the Russian people whose task it was to colonize and cultivate vast tracts of unoccupied land, consciously adhered, till all their land was occupied, to the methods suitable to their purpose, and that their methods were by no means so bad as was generally supposed. And he wanted to prove this theoretically in his book and practically on his land.

CHAPTER XXX

A T THE END OF September the timber had been carted for building the cattle-yard on the land that had been allotted to the association of peasants, and the butter from the cows was sold and the profits divided. In practice the system worked capitally, or, at least, so it seemed to Levin. In order to work out the whole subject theoretically and to complete his book, which, in Levin's day-dreams, was not merely to effect a revolution in political economy, but to annihilate that science entirely and to lay the foundation of a new science of the relation of the people to the soil, all that was left to do was to make a tour abroad, and to study on the spot all that had been done in the same direction, and to collect conclusive evidence that all that had been done there was not what was wanted. Levin was only waiting for the delivery of his wheat to receive the money for it and go abroad. But the rains began, preventing the harvesting of the corn and potatoes left in the fields, and putting a stop to all work, even to the delivery of the wheat.

The mud was impassable along the roads; two mills were carried away, and the weather got worse and worse.

On the 30th of September the sun came out in the morning, and hoping for fine weather, Levin began making final preparations for his journey. He gave orders for the wheat to be delivered, sent the bailiff to the merchant to get the money owing him, and went out himself to give some final directions on the estate before setting off.

Having finished all his business, soaked through with the streams of water which kept running down the leather behind his neck and his gaiters, but in the keenest and most confident temper, Levin returned homewards in the evening. The weather had become worse than ever towards evening; the hail lashed the drenched mare so cruelly that she went along sideways, shaking her head and ears; but Levin was all right under his hood, and he looked cheerfully about him at the muddy streams running under the wheels, at the drops hanging on every bare twig, at the whiteness of the patch of unmelted hailstones on the planks of the bridge, at the thick layer of still juicy, fleshy leaves that lay heaped up about the stripped elm-tree. In spite of the gloominess of nature around him, he felt peculiarly eager. The talks he had been having with the peasants in the further village had shown that they were beginning to get used to their new position. The old servant to whose hut he had gone to get dry evidently approved of Levin's plan, and of his own accord proposed to enter the partnership by the purchase of cattle.

"I have only to go stubbornly on towards my aim, and I shall attain my end," thought Levin; "and it's something to work and take trouble for. This is not a matter of myself individually, the question of the public welfare comes into it. The whole system of culture, the chief element in the condition of the people, must be completely transformed. Instead of poverty, general prosperity and content; instead of hostility, harmony and unity of interests. In short, a bloodless revolution, but a revolution of the greatest magnitude, beginning in the little circle of our district, then the province, then Russia, the whole world. Because a just idea cannot but be fruitful. Yes, it's an aim worth working for. And it's being me, Kostya Levin, who went to a ball in a black tie, and was refused by the Shtcherbatskaya girl, and who was intrinsically such a pitiful, worthless creature—that proves nothing; I feel sure Franklin felt just as worthless, and he too had no faith in himself, thinking of himself as a whole. That means nothing. And he too, most likely, had an Agafea Mihalovna to whom he confided his secrets."

Musing on such thoughts Levin reached home in the darkness.

The bailiff, who had been to the merchant, had come back and brought part of the money for the wheat. An agreement had been made with the old servant, and on the road the bailiff had learned that everywhere the corn was still standing in the fields, so that his one hundred and sixty shocks that had not been carried were nothing in comparison with the losses of others.

After dinner Levin was sitting, as he usually did, in an easy-chair with a book, and as he read he went on thinking of the journey before him in connection with his book. To-day all the significance of his book rose before him with special distinctness, and whole periods ranged themselves in his mind in illustration of his theories. "I must write that down," he thought. "That ought to form a brief introduction, which I thought unnecessary before." He got up to go to his writing-table, and Laska, lying at his feet, got up too, stretching and looking at him as though to inquire where to go. But he had not time to write it down, for the head peasants had come round, and Levin went out into the hall to them.

After his levee, that is to say, giving directions about the labors of the next day, and seeing all the peasants who had business with him, Levin went back to his study and sat down to work.

Laska lay under the table; Agafea Mihalovna settled herself in her place with her stocking.

After writing for a little while, Levin suddenly thought with exceptional vividness of Kitty, her refusal, and their last meeting. He got up and began walking about the room.

"What's the use of being dreary?" said Agafea Mihalovna. "Come, why do you stay on at home? You ought to go to some warm springs, especially now you're ready for the journey."

"Well, I am going away the day after to-morrow, Agafea Mihalovna; I must finish my work."

"There, there, your work, you say! As if you hadn't done enough for the peasants! Why, as 'tis, they're saying, 'Your master will be getting some honor from the Tsar for it.' Indeed and it is a strange thing; why need you worry about the peasants?"

"I'm not worrying about them; I'm doing it for my own good."

Agafea Mihalovna knew every detail of Levin's plans for his land. Levin often put his views before her in all their complexity, and not uncommonly he argued with her and did not agree with her comments. But on this occasion she entirely misinterpreted what he had said.

"Of one's soul's salvation we all know and must think before all else," she said with a sigh. "Parfen Denisitch now, for all he was no scholar, he died a death that God grant every one of us the like," she said, referring to a servant who had died recently. "Took the sacrament and all."

"That's not what I mean," said he. "I mean that I'm acting for my own advantage. It's all the better for me if the peasants do their work better."

"Well, whatever you do, if he's a lazy good-for-nought, everything'll be at sixes and sevens. If he has a conscience, he'll work, and if not, there's no doing anything."

"Oh, come, you say yourself Ivan has begun looking after the cattle better."

"All I say is," answered Agafea Mihalovna, evidently not speaking at random, but in strict sequence of idea, "that you ought to get married, that's what I say."

Agafea Mihalovna's allusion to the very subject he had only just been thinking about, hurt and stung him. Levin scowled, and without answering her, he sat down again to his work, repeating to himself all that he had been thinking of the real significance of that work. Only at intervals he listened in the stillness to the click of Agafea Mihalovna's needles, and recollecting what he did not want to remember, he frowned again.

At nine o'clock they heard the bell and the faint vibration of a carriage over the mud.

"Well, here's visitors come to us, and you won't be dull," said Agafea Mihalovna, getting up and going to the door. But Levin overtook her. His work was not going well now, and he was glad of a visitor, whoever it might be.

CHAPTER XXXI

RUNNING HALF-WAY DOWN THE STAIRCASE, LEVIN CAUGHT A SOUND HE knew, a familiar cough in the hall. But he heard it indistinctly through the sound of his own footsteps, and hoped he was mistaken. Then he caught sight of a long, bony, familiar figure, and now it seemed there was no possibility of mistake; and yet he still went on hoping that this tall man taking off his fur cloak and coughing was not his brother Nikolay.

Levin loved his brother, but being with him was always a torture. Just now, when Levin, under the influence of the thoughts that had come to him, and Agafea Mihalovna's hint, was in a troubled and uncertain humor, the meeting with his brother that he had to face seemed particularly difficult. Instead of a lively, healthy visitor, some outsider who would, he hoped, cheer him up in his uncertain humor, he had to see his brother, who knew him through and through, who would call forth all the thoughts nearest his heart, would force him to show himself fully. And that he was not disposed to do.

Angry with himself for so base a feeling, Levin ran into the hall; as soon as he had seen his brother close, this feeling of selfish disappointment vanished instantly and was replaced by pity. Terrible as his brother Nikolay had been before in his emaciation and sickliness, now he looked still more emaciated, still more wasted. He was a skeleton covered with skin.

He stood in the hall, jerking his long thin neck, and pulling the scarf off it, and smiled a strange and pitiful smile. When he saw that smile, submissive and humble, Levin felt something clutching at his throat.

"You see, I've come to you," said Nikolay in a thick voice, never for one second taking his eyes off his brother's face. "I've been meaning to a long while, but I've been unwell all the time. Now I'm ever so much better," he said, rubbing his beard with his big thin hands.

"Yes, yes!" answered Levin. And he felt still more frightened when, kissing him, he felt with his lips the dryness of his brother's skin and saw close to him his big eyes, full of a strange light.

A few weeks before, Konstantin Levin had written to his brother that through the sale of the small part of the property, that had remained undivided, there was a sum of about two thousand roubles to come to him as his share.

Nikolay said that he had come now to take this money and, what was more important, to stay a while in the old nest, to get in touch with the earth, so as to renew his strength like the heroes of old for the work that lay before him. In spite of his exaggerated stoop, and the emaciation that was so striking from his height, his movements were as rapid and abrupt as ever. Levin led him into his study.

His brother dressed with particular care—a thing he never used to do—combed his scanty, lank hair, and, smiling, went up-stairs.

He was in the most affectionate and good-humored mood, just as Levin often remembered him in childhood. He even referred to Sergey Ivanovitch without rancor. When he saw Agafea Mihalovna, he made jokes with her and asked after the old servants. The news of the death of Parfen Denisitch made a painful impression on him. A look of fear crossed his face, but he regained his serenity immediately.

"Of course he was quite old," he said, and changed the subject. "Well, I'll spend a month or two with you, and then I'm off to Moscow. Do you know, Myakov has promised me a place there, and I'm going into the service. Now I'm going to arrange my life quite differently," he went on. "You know I got rid of that woman."

"Marya Nikolaevna? Why, what for?"

"Oh, she was a horrid woman! She caused me all sorts of worries." But he did not say what the annoyances were. He could not say that he had cast off Marya Nikolaevna because the tea was weak, and, above all, because she would look after him, as though he were an invalid.

"Besides, I want to turn over a new leaf completely now. I've done silly things, of course, like every one else, but money's the last consideration; I don't regret it. So long as there's health, and my health, thank God, is quite restored."

Levin listened and racked his brains, but could think of nothing to say. Nikolay probably felt the same; he began questioning his brother about his affairs; and Levin was glad to talk about himself, because then he could speak without hypocrisy. He told his brother of his plans and his doings.

His brother listened, but evidently he was not interested by it.

These two men were so akin, so near each other, that the slightest gesture, the tone of voice, told both more than could be said in words.

Both of them now had only one thought—the illness of Nikolay and the nearness of his death—which stifled all else. But neither of them dared to speak

people knew so well how to do it, and without it there was no living at all. He tried to say what he was not thinking, but he felt continually that it had a ring of falsehood, that his brother detected him in it, and was exasperated at it.

The third day Nikolay induced his brother to explain his plan to him again, and began not merely attacking it, but intentionally confounding it with communism.

"You've simply borrowed an idea that's not your own, but you've distorted it, and are trying to apply it where it's not applicable."

"But I tell you it's nothing to do with it. They deny the justice of property, of capital, of inheritance, while I do not deny this chief stimulus." (Levin felt disgusted himself at using such expressions, but ever since he had been engrossed by his work, he had unconsciously come more and more frequently to use words not Russian.) "All I want is to regulate labor."

"Which means, you've borrowed an idea, stripped it of all that gave it its force, and want to make believe that it's something new," said Nikolay, angrily tugging at his necktie.

"But my idea has nothing in common ..."

"That, anyway," said Nikolay Levin, with an ironical smile, his eyes flashing malignantly, "has the charm of—what's one to call it?—geometrical symmetry, of clearness, of definiteness. It may be a Utopia. But if once one allows the possibility of making of all the past a *tabula rasa*—no property, no family—then labor would organize itself. But you gain nothing ..."

"Why do you mix things up? I've never been a communist."

"But I have, and I consider it's premature, but rational, and it has a future, just like Christianity in its first ages."

"All that I maintain is that the labor force ought to be investigated from the point of view of natural science; that is to say, it ought to be studied, its qualities ascertained ..."

"But that's utter waste of time. That force finds a certain form of activity of itself, according to the stage of its development. There have been slaves first everywhere, then metayers; and we have the half-crop system, rent, and day-laborers. What are you trying to find?"

Levin suddenly lost his temper at these words, because at the bottom of his heart he was afraid that it was true—true that he was trying to hold the balance even between communism and the familiar forms, and that this was hardly possible.

"I am trying to find means of working productively for myself and for the laborers. I want to organize ..." he answered hotly.

"You don't want to organize anything; it's simply just as you've been all your life, that you want to be original to pose as not exploiting the peasants simply, but with some idea in view."

"Oh, all right, that's what you think—and let me alone!" answered Levin, feeling the muscles of his left cheek twitching uncontrollably.

"You've never had, and never have, convictions; all you want is to please your vanity."

"Oh, very well; then let me alone!"

"And I will let you alone! and it's high time I did, and go to the devil with you! and I'm very sorry I ever came!"

In spite of all Levin's efforts to soothe his brother afterwards, Nikolay would listen to nothing he said, declaring that it was better to part, and Konstantin saw that it simply was that life was unbearable to him.

Nikolay was just getting ready to go, when Konstantin went in to him again and begged him, rather unnaturally, to forgive him if he had hurt his feelings in any way.

"Ah, generosity!" said Nikolay, and he smiled. "If you want to be right, I can give you that satisfaction. You're in the right; but I'm going all the same."

It was only just at parting that Nikolay kissed him, and said, looking with sudden strangeness and seriousness at his brother:

"Anyway, don't remember evil against me, Kostya!" and his voice quivered. These were the only words that had been spoken sincerely between them. Levin knew that those words meant, "You see, and you know, that I'm in a bad way, and maybe we shall not see each other again." Levin knew this, and the tears gushed from his eyes. He kissed his brother once more, but he could not speak, and knew not what to say.

Three days after his brother's departure, Levin too set off for his foreign tour. Happening to meet Shtcherbatsky, Kitty's cousin, in the railway train, Levin greatly astonished him by his depression.

"What's the matter with you?" Shtcherbatsky asked him.

"Oh, nothing; there's not much happiness in life."

"Not much? You come with me to Paris instead of to Mulhausen. You shall see how to be happy."

"No, I've done with it all. It's time I was dead."

"Well, that's a good one!" said Shtcherbatsky, laughing; "why, I'm only just getting ready to begin."

"Yes, I thought the same not long ago, but now I know I shall soon be dead."

Levin said what he had genuinely been thinking of late. He saw nothing but death or the advance towards death in everything. But his cherished scheme only engrossed him the more. Life had to be got through somehow till death did come. Darkness had fallen upon everything for him; but just because of this darkness he felt that the one guiding clue in the darkness was his work, and he clutched it and clung to it with all his strength.

PART FOUR

CHAPTER I

THE KARENINS, HUSBAND AND WIFE, CONTINUED LIVING IN THE SAME HOUSE, met every day, but were complete strangers to one another. Alexey Alexandrovitch made it a rule to see his wife every day, so that the servants might have no grounds for suppositions, but avoided dining at home. Vronsky was never at Alexey Alexandrovitch's house, but Anna saw him away from home, and her husband was aware of it.

The position was one of misery for all three; and not one of them would have been equal to enduring this position for a single day, if it had not been for the expectation that it would change, that it was merely a temporary painful ordeal which would pass over. Alexey Alexandrovitch hoped that this passion would pass, as everything does pass, that every one would forget about it, and his name would remain unsullied. Anna, on whom the position depended, and for whom it was more miserable than for any one, endured it because she not merely hoped, but firmly believed, that it would all very soon be settled and come right. She had not the least idea what would settle the position, but she firmly believed that something would very soon turn up now. Vronsky, against his own will or wishes, followed her lead, hoped too that something, apart from his own action, would be sure to solve all difficulties.

In the middle of the winter Vronsky spent a very tiresome week. A foreign prince, who had come on a visit to Petersburg, was put under his charge, and he had to show him the sights worth seeing. Vronsky was of distinguished appearance; he possessed, moreover, the art of behaving with respectful dignity, and was used to having to do with such grand personages—that was how he came to be put in charge of the prince. But he felt his duties very irksome. The prince was anxious to miss nothing of which he would be asked at home, had he seen that in Russia? And on his own account he was anxious to enjoy to the utmost all Russian forms of amusement. Vronsky was obliged to be his guide in satisfying both these inclinations. The mornings they spent driving to look at places of interest; the evenings they passed enjoying the national entertainments. The prince rejoiced in health exceptional even among princes. By gymnastics and careful attention to his health he had brought himself to such a point that in spite of his excess in pleasure he looked as fresh as a big glossy green Dutch cucumber. The prince had traveled a great deal, and considered one of the chief advantages of modern facilities of communication was the accessibility of the pleasures of all nations.

He had been in Spain, and there had indulged in serenades and had made friends with a Spanish girl who played the mandolin. In Switzerland he had killed chamois. In England he had galloped in a red coat over hedges and killed two hundred pheasants for a bet. In Turkey he had got into a harem; in India he had hunted on an elephant, and now in Russia he wished to taste all the specially Russian forms of pleasure.

Vronsky, who was, as it were, chief master of the ceremonies to him, was at great pains to arrange all the Russian amusements suggested by various persons to the prince. They had race-horses, and Russian pancakes and bear hunts and three-horse sledges, and gypsies and drinking feasts, with the Russian accompaniment of broken crockery. And the prince with surprising ease fell in with the Russian spirit, smashed trays full of crockery, sat with a gypsy girl on his knee, and seemed to be asking—what more, and does the whole Russian spirit consist in just this?

In reality, of all the Russian entertainments the prince liked best French actresses and ballet-dancers and white-seal champagne. Vronsky was used to princes, but, either because he had himself changed of late, or that he was in too close proximity to the prince, that week seemed fearfully wearisome to him. The whole of that week he experienced a sensation such as a man might have set in charge of a dangerous madman, afraid of the madman, and at the same time, from being with him, fearing for his own reason. Vronsky was continually conscious of the necessity of never for a second relaxing the tone of stern official respectfulness, that he might not himself be insulted. The prince's manner of treating the very people who, to Vronsky's surprise, were ready to descend to any depths to provide him with Russian amusements, was contemptuous. His criticisms of Russian women, whom he wished to study, more than once made Vronsky crimson with indignation. The chief reason why the prince was so particularly disagreeable to Vronsky was that he could not help seeing himself in him. And what he saw in this mirror did not gratify his self-esteem. He was a very stupid and very self-satisfied and very healthy and very well-washed man, and nothing else. He was a gentleman—that was true, and Vronsky could not deny it. He was equable and not cringing with his superiors, was free and ingratiating in his behavior with his equals, and was contemptuously indulgent with his inferiors. Vronsky was himself the same, and regarded it as a great merit to be so. But for this prince he was an inferior, and his contemptuous and indulgent attitude to him revolted him.

"Brainless beef! can I be like that?" he thought.

Be that as it might, when, on the seventh day, he parted from the prince, who was starting for Moscow, and received his thanks, he was happy to be rid of his uncomfortable position and the unpleasant reflection of himself. He said good-bye to him at the station on their return from a bear-hunt, at which they had had a display of Russian prowess kept up all night.

CHAPTER II

WHEN HE GOT HOME, VRONSKY FOUND THERE A NOTE FROM ANNA. SHE wrote, "I am ill and unhappy. I cannot come out, but cannot go on longer without seeing you. Come in this evening. Alexey Alexandrovitch goes to the council at seven and will be there till ten." Thinking for an instant of the strangeness of her bidding him come straight to her, in spite of her husband's insisting on her not receiving him, he decided to go.

Vronsky had that winter got his promotion, was now a colonel, had left the regimental quarters, and was living alone. After having some lunch, he lay down on the sofa immediately, and in five minutes memories of the hideous scenes he had witnessed during the last few days were confused together and joined on to a mental image of Anna and of the peasant who had played an important part in the bear-hunt, and Vronsky fell asleep. He woke up in the dark, trembling with horror, and made haste to light a candle. "What was it? What? What was the dreadful thing I dreamed? Yes, yes; I think a little dirty man with a disheveled beard was stooping down doing something, and all of a sudden he began saying some strange words in French. Yes, there was nothing else in the dream," he said to himself. "But why was it so awful?" He vividly recalled the peasant again and those incomprehensible French words the peasant had uttered, and a chill of horror ran down his spine.

"What nonsense!" thought Vronsky, and glanced at his watch.

It was half-past eight already. He rang up his servant, dressed in haste, and went out onto the steps, completely forgetting the dream and only worried at being late. As he drove up to the Karenins' entrance he looked at his watch and saw it was ten minutes to nine. A high, narrow carriage with a pair of grays

"How disgusting you are, you men! How is it you can't understand that a woman can never forget that," she said, getting more and more angry, and so letting him see the cause of her irritation, "especially a woman who cannot know your life? What do I know? What have I ever known?" she said; "what you tell me. And how do I know whether you tell me the truth? ..."

"Anna, you hurt me. Don't you trust me? Haven't I told you that I haven't a thought I wouldn't lay bare to you?"

"Yes, yes," she said, evidently trying to suppress her jealous thoughts. "But if only you knew how wretched I am! I believe you, I believe you.... What were you saying?"

But he could not at once recall what he had been going to say. These fits of jealousy, which of late had been more and more frequent with her, horrified him, and however much he tried to disguise the fact, made him feel cold to her, although he knew the cause of her jealousy was her love for him. How often he had told himself that her love was happiness; and now she loved him as a woman can love when love has outweighed for her all the good things of life—and he was much further from happiness than when he had followed her from Moscow. Then he had thought himself unhappy, but happiness was before him; now he felt that the best happiness was already left behind. She was utterly unlike what she had been when he first saw her. Both morally and physically she had changed for the worse. She had broadened out all over, and in her face at the time when she was speaking of the actress there was an evil expression of hatred that distorted it. He looked at her as a man looks at a faded flower he has gathered, with difficulty recognizing in it the beauty for which he picked and ruined it. And in spite of this he felt that then, when his love was stronger, he could, if he had greatly wished it, have torn that love out of his heart; but now, when as at that moment it seemed to him he felt no love for her, he knew that what bound him to her could not be broken.

"Well, well, what was it you were going to say about the prince? I have driven away the fiend," she added. The fiend was the name they had given her jealousy. "What did you begin to tell me about the prince? Why did you find it so tiresome?"

"Oh, it was intolerable!" he said, trying to pick up the thread of his interrupted thought. "He does not improve on closer acquaintance. If you want him defined, here he is: a prime, well-fed beast such as takes medals at the cattle-shows, and nothing more," he said, with a tone of vexation that interested her.

"No; how so?" she replied. "He's seen a great deal, anyway; he's cultured?"

"It's an utterly different culture—their culture. He's cultivated, one sees, simply to be able to despise culture, as they despise everything but animal pleasures."

"But don't you all care for these animal pleasures?" she said, and again he noticed a dark look in her eyes that avoided him.

"How is it you're defending him?" he said, smiling.

"I'm not defending him, it's nothing to me; but I imagine, if you had not cared for those pleasures yourself, you might have got out of them. But if it affords you satisfaction to gaze at Thérèse in the attire of Eve …"

"Again, the devil again," Vronsky said, taking the hand she had laid on the table and kissing it.

"Yes; but I can't help it. You don't know what I have suffered waiting for you. I believe I'm not jealous. I'm not jealous: I believe you when you're here; but when you're away somewhere leading your life, so incomprehensible to me …"

She turned away from him, pulled the hook at last out of the crochet-work, and rapidly, with the help of her forefinger, began working loop after loop of the wool that was dazzling white in the lamplight, while the slender wrist moved swiftly, nervously in the embroidered cuff.

"How was it, then? Where did you meet Alexey Alexandrovitch?" Her voice sounded in an unnatural and jarring tone.

"We ran up against each other in the doorway."

"And he bowed to you like this?"

She drew a long face, and half-closing her eyes, quickly transformed her expression, folded her hands, and Vronsky suddenly saw in her beautiful face the very expression with which Alexey Alexandrovitch had bowed to him. He smiled, while she laughed gaily, with that sweet, deep laugh, which was one of her greatest charms.

"I don't understand him in the least," said Vronsky. "If after your avowal to him at your country house he had broken with you, if he had called me out—but this I can't understand. How can he put up with such a position? He feels it, that's evident."

"He?" she said sneeringly. "He's perfectly satisfied."

"What are we all miserable for, when everything might be so happy?"

"Only not he. Don't I know him, the falsity in which he's utterly steeped? … Could one, with any feeling, live as he is living with me? He understands nothing, and feels nothing. Could a man of any feeling live in the same house with his unfaithful wife? Could he talk to her, call her 'my dear'?"

CHAPTER IV

LEXEY ALEXANDROVITCH, AFTER MEETING VRONSKY ON HIS OWN STEPS, drove, as he had intended, to the Italian opera. He sat through two acts there, and saw every one he had wanted to see. On returning home, he carefully scrutinized the hat-stand, and noticing that there was not a military overcoat there, he went, as usual, to his own room. But, contrary to his usual habits, he did not go to bed, he walked up and down his study till three o'clock in the morning. The feeling of furious anger with his wife, who would not observe the proprieties and keep to the one stipulation he had laid on her, not to receive her lover in her own home, gave him no peace. She had not complied with his request, and he was bound to punish her and carry out his threat—obtain a divorce and take away his son. He knew all the difficulties connected with this course, but he had said he would do it, and now he must carry out his threat. Countess Lidia Ivanovna had hinted that this was the best way out of his position, and of late the obtaining of divorces had been brought to such perfection that Alexey Alexandrovitch saw a possibility of overcoming the formal difficulties. Misfortunes never come singly, and the affairs of the reorganization of the native tribes, and of the irrigation of the lands of the Zaraisky province, had brought such official worries upon Alexey Alexandrovitch that he had been of late in a continual condition of extreme irritability.

He did not sleep the whole night, and his fury, growing in a sort of vast, arithmetical progression, reached its highest limits in the morning. He dressed in haste, and as though carrying his cup full of wrath, and fearing to spill any over, fearing to lose with his wrath the energy necessary for the interview with his wife, he went into her room directly he heard she was up.

Anna, who had thought she knew her husband so well, was amazed at his appearance when he went in to her. His brow was lowering, and his eyes stared darkly before him, avoiding her eyes; his mouth was tightly and contemptuously shut. In his walk, in his gestures, in the sound of his voice there was a determination and firmness such as his wife had never seen in him. He went into her room, and without greeting her, walked straight up to her writing-table, and taking her keys, opened a drawer.

"What do you want?" she cried.

"Your lover's letters," he said.

"They're not here," she said, shutting the drawer; but from that action he saw he had guessed right, and roughly pushing away her hand, he quickly snatched a portfolio in which he knew she used to put her most important papers. She tried to pull the portfolio away, but he pushed her back.

"Sit down! I have to speak to you," he said, putting the portfolio under his arm, and squeezing it so tightly with his elbow that his shoulder stood up. Amazed and intimidated, she gazed at him in silence.

"I told you that I would not allow you to receive your lover in this house."

"I had to see him to…"

She stopped, not finding a reason.

"I do not enter into the details of why a woman wants to see her lover."

"I meant, I only …" she said, flushing hotly. This coarseness of his angered her, and gave her courage. "Surely you must feel how easy it is for you to insult me?" she said.

"An honest man and an honest woman may be insulted, but to tell a thief he's a thief is simply *la constatation d'un fait*."

"This cruelty is something new I did not know in you."

"You call it cruelty for a husband to give his wife liberty, giving her the honorable protection of his name, simply on the condition of observing the proprieties: is that cruelty?"

"It's worse than cruel—it's base, if you want to know!" Anna cried, in a rush of hatred, and getting up, she was going away.

"No!" he shrieked, in his shrill voice, which pitched a note higher than usual even, and his big hands clutching her by the arm so violently that red marks were left from the bracelet he was squeezing, he forcibly sat her down in her place.

"Base! If you care to use that word, what is base is to forsake husband and child for a lover, while you eat your husband's bread!"

She bowed her head. She did not say what she had said the evening before to her lover, that *he* was her husband, and her husband was superfluous; she did not even think that. She felt all the justice of his words, and only said softly:

"You cannot describe my position as worse than I feel it to be myself; but what are you saying all this for?"

"What am I saying it for? what for?" he went on, as angrily. "That you may know that since you have not carried out my wishes in regard to observing outward decorum, I will take measures to put an end to this state of things."

"Soon, very soon, it will end, anyway," she said; and again, at the thought of death near at hand and now desired, tears came into her eyes.

"It will end sooner than you and your lover have planned! If you must have the satisfaction of animal passion … "

The lawyer was a little, squat, bald man, with a dark, reddish beard, light-colored long eyebrows, and an overhanging brow. He was attired as though for a wedding, from his cravat to his double watch-chain and varnished boots. His face was clever and manly, but his dress was dandified and in bad taste.

"Pray walk in," said the lawyer, addressing Alexey Alexandrovitch; and, gloomily ushering Karenin in before him, he closed the door.

"Won't you sit down?" He indicated an armchair at a writing-table covered with papers. He sat down himself, and, rubbing his little hands with short fingers covered with white hairs, he bent his head on one side. But as soon as he was settled in this position a moth flew over the table. The lawyer, with a swiftness that could never have been expected of him, opened his hands, caught the moth, and resumed his former attitude.

"Before beginning to speak of my business," said Alexey Alexandrovitch, following the lawyer's movements with wondering eyes, "I ought to observe that the business about which I have to speak to you is to be strictly private."

The lawyer's overhanging reddish mustaches were parted in a scarcely perceptible smile.

"I should not be a lawyer if I could not keep the secrets confided to me. But if you would like proof ..."

Alexey Alexandrovitch glanced at his face, and saw that the shrewd, gray eyes were laughing, and seemed to know all about it already.

"You know my name?" Alexey Alexandrovitch resumed.

"I know you and the good"—again he caught a moth—"work you are doing, like every Russian," said the lawyer, bowing.

Alexey Alexandrovitch sighed, plucking up his courage. But having once made up his mind he went on in his shrill voice, without timidity or hesitation, accentuating here and there a word.

"I have the misfortune," Alexey Alexandrovitch began, "to have been deceived in my married life, and I desire to break off all relations with my wife by legal means—that is, to be divorced, but to do this so that my son may not remain with his mother."

The lawyer's gray eyes tried not to laugh, but they were dancing with irrepressible glee, and Alexey Alexandrovitch saw that it was not simply the delight of a man who has just got a profitable job: there was triumph and joy, there was a gleam like the malignant gleam he saw in his wife's eyes.

"You desire my assistance in securing a divorce?"

"Yes, precisely so; but I ought to warn you that I may be wasting your time and attention. I have come simply to consult you as a preliminary step. I want a divorce, but the form in which it is possible is of great consequence to me. It is very possible that if that form does not correspond with my requirements I may give up a legal divorce."

"Oh, that's always the case," said the lawyer, "and that's always for you to decide."

He let his eyes rest on Alexey Alexandrovitch's feet, feeling that he might offend his client by the sight of his irrepressible amusement. He looked at a moth that flew before his nose, and moved his hands, but did not catch it from regard for Alexey Alexandrovitch's position.

"Though in their general features our laws on this subject are known to me," pursued Alexey Alexandrovitch, "I should be glad to have an idea of the forms in which such things are done in practice."

"You would be glad," the lawyer, without lifting his eyes, responded, adopting, with a certain satisfaction, the tone of his client's remarks, "for me to lay before you all the methods by which you could secure what you desire?"

And on receiving an assuring nod from Alexey Alexandrovitch, he went on, stealing a glance now and then at Alexey Alexandrovitch's face, which was growing red in patches.

"Divorce by our laws," he said, with a slight shade of disapprobation of our laws, "is possible, as you are aware, in the following cases ... Wait a little!" he called to a clerk who put his head in at the door, but he got up all the same, said a few words to him, and sat down again. "... In the following cases: physical defect in the married parties, desertion without communication for five years," he said, crooking a short finger covered with hair, "adultery" (this word he pronounced with obvious satisfaction), "subdivided as follows" (he continued to crook his fat fingers, though the three cases and their sub-divisions could obviously not be classified together): "physical defect of the husband or of the wife, adultery of the husband or of the wife." As by now all his fingers were used up, he uncrooked all his fingers and went on: "This is the theoretical view; but I imagine you have done me the honor to apply to me in order to learn its application in practice. And therefore, guided by precedents, I must inform you that in practice cases of divorce may all be reduced to the following—there's no physical defect, I may assume, nor desertion? ..."

Alexey Alexandrovitch bowed his head in assent.

"—May be reduced to the following: adultery of one of the married parties, and the detection in the fact of the guilty party by mutual agreement, and failing such agreement, accidental detection. It must be admitted that the latter case is rarely met with in practice," said the lawyer, and stealing a glance at

commission's report, resorted to tactics which Alexey Alexandrovitch had not anticipated. Stremov, carrying with him several members, went over to Alexey Alexandrovitch's side, and not contenting himself with warmly defending the measure proposed by Karenin, proposed other more extreme measures in the same direction. These measures, still further exaggerated in opposition to what was Alexey Alexandrovitch's fundamental idea, were passed by the commission, and then the aim of Stremov's tactics became apparent. Carried to an extreme, the measures seemed at once to be so absurd that the highest authorities, and public opinion, and intellectual ladies, and the newspapers, all at the same time fell foul of them, expressing their indignation both with the measures and their nominal father, Alexey Alexandrovitch. Stremov drew back, affecting to have blindly followed Karenin, and to be astounded and distressed at what had been done. This meant the defeat of Alexey Alexandrovitch. But in spite of failing health, in spite of his domestic griefs, he did not give in. There was a split in the commission. Some members, with Stremov at their head, justified their mistake on the ground that they had put faith in the commission of revision, instituted by Alexey Alexandrovitch, and maintained that the report of the commission was rubbish, and simply so much waste paper. Alexey Alexandrovitch, with a following of those who saw the danger of so revolutionary an attitude to official documents, persisted in upholding the statements obtained by the revising commission. In consequence of this, in the higher spheres, and even in society, all was chaos, and although every one was interested, no one could tell whether the native tribes really were becoming impoverished and ruined, or whether they were in a flourishing condition. The position of Alexey Alexandrovitch, owing to this, and partly owing to the contempt lavished on him for his wife's infidelity, became very precarious. And in this position he took an important resolution. To the astonishment of the commission, he announced that he should ask permission to go himself to investigate the question on the spot. And having obtained permission, Alexey Alexandrovitch prepared to set off to these remote provinces.

Alexey Alexandrovitch's departure made a great sensation, the more so as just before he started he officially returned the posting-fares allowed him for twelve horses, to drive to his destination.

"I think it very noble," Betsy said about this to the Princess Myakaya. "Why take money for posting-horses when every one knows that there are railways everywhere now?"

But Princess Myakaya did not agree, and the Princess Tverskaya's opinion annoyed her indeed.

"It's all very well for you to talk," said she, "when you have I don't know how many millions; but I am very glad when my husband goes on a revising tour in the summer. It's very good for him and pleasant traveling about, and it's a settled arrangement for me to keep a carriage and coachman on the money."

On his way to the remote provinces Alexey Alexandrovitch stopped for three days at Moscow.

The day after his arrival he was driving back from calling on the governor-general. At the cross-roads by Gazetny Place, where there are always crowds of carriages and sledges, Alexey Alexandrovitch suddenly heard his name called out in such a loud and cheerful voice that he could not help looking round. At the corner of the pavement, in a short, stylish overcoat and a low-crowned fashionable hat, jauntily askew, with a smile that showed a gleam of white teeth and red lips, stood Stepan Arkadyevitch, radiant, young, and beaming. He called him vigorously and urgently, and insisted on his stopping. He had one arm on the window of a carriage that was stopping at the corner, and out of the window were thrust the heads of a lady in a velvet hat, and two children. Stepan Arkadyevitch was smiling and beckoning to his brother-in-law. The lady smiled a kindly smile too, and she too waved her hand to Alexey Alexandrovitch. It was Dolly with her children.

Alexey Alexandrovitch did not want to see any one in Moscow, and least of all his wife's brother. He raised his hat and would have driven on, but Stepan Arkadyevitch told his coachman to stop, and ran across the snow to him.

"Well, what a shame not to have let us know! Been here long? I was at Dussot's yesterday and saw 'Karenin' on the visitors' list, but it never entered my head that it was you," said Stepan Arkadyevitch, sticking his head in at the window of the carriage, "or I should have looked you up. I am glad to see you!" he said, knocking one foot against the other to shake the snow off. "What a shame of you not to let us know!" he repeated.

"I had no time; I am very busy," Alexey Alexandrovitch responded dryly.

"Come to my wife, she does so want to see you."

Alexey Alexandrovitch unfolded the rug in which his frozen feet were wrapped, and getting out of his carriage made his way over the snow to Darya Alexandrovna.

"Why, Alexey Alexandrovitch, what are you cutting us like this for?" said Dolly, smiling.

"I was very busy. Delighted to see you!" he said in a tone clearly indicating that he was annoyed by it. "How are you?"

"Tell me, how is my darling Anna?"

had hitherto belonged himself. On the previous day Stepan Arkadyevitch had appeared at the office in a uniform, and the new chief had been very affable and had talked to him as to an acquaintance. Consequently Stepan Arkadyevitch deemed it his duty to call upon him in his non-official dress. The thought that the new chief might not tender him a warm reception was the other unpleasant thing. But Stepan Arkadyevitch instinctively felt that everything would *come round* all right. "They're all people, all men, like us poor sinners; why be nasty and quarrelsome?" he thought as he went into the hotel.

"Good-day, Vassily," he said, walking into the corridor with his hat cocked on one side, and addressing a footman he knew; "why, you've let your whiskers grow! Levin, number seven, eh? Take me up, please. And find out whether Count Anitchkin" (this was the new head) "is receiving."

"Yes, sir," Vassily responded, smiling. "You've not been to see us for a long while."

"I was here yesterday, but at the other entrance. Is this number seven?"

Levin was standing with a peasant from Tver in the middle of the room, measuring a fresh bearskin, when Stepan Arkadyevitch went in.

"What! you killed him?" cried Stepan Arkadyevitch. "Well done! A she-bear? How are you, Arhip!"

He shook hands with the peasant and sat down on the edge of a chair, without taking off his coat and hat.

"Come, take off your coat and stay a little," said Levin, taking his hat.

"No, I haven't time; I've only looked in for a tiny second," answered Stepan Arkadyevitch. He threw open his coat, but afterwards did take it off, and sat on for a whole hour, talking to Levin about hunting and the most intimate subjects.

"Come, tell me, please, what you did abroad? Where have you been?" said Stepan Arkadyevitch, when the peasant had gone.

"Oh, I stayed in Germany, in Prussia, in France, and in England—not in the capitals, but in the manufacturing towns, and saw a great deal that was new to me. And I'm glad I went."

"Yes, I knew your idea of the solution of the labor question."

"Not a bit: in Russia there can be no labor question. In Russia the question is that of the relation of the working people to the land; though the question exists there too—but there it's a matter of repairing what's been ruined, while with us …"

Stepan Arkadyevitch listened attentively to Levin.

"Yes, yes!" he said, "it's very possible you're right. But I'm glad you're in good spirits, and are hunting bears, and working, and interested. Shtcherbatsky told me another story—he met you—that you were in such a depressed state, talking of nothing but death...."

"Well, what of it? I've not given up thinking of death," said Levin. "It's true that it's high time I was dead; and that all this is nonsense. It's the truth I'm telling you. I do value my idea and my work awfully; but in reality only consider this: all this world of ours is nothing but a speck of mildew, which has grown up on a tiny planet. And for us to suppose we can have something great—ideas, work—it's all dust and ashes."

"But all that's as old as the hills, my boy!"

"It is old; but do you know, when you grasp this fully, then somehow everything becomes of no consequence. When you understand that you will die to-morrow, if not to-day, and nothing will be left, then everything is so unimportant! And I consider my idea very important, but it turns out really to be as unimportant too, even if it were carried out, as doing for that bear. So one goes on living, amusing oneself with hunting, with work—anything so as not to think of death!"

Stepan Arkadyevitch smiled a subtle affectionate smile as he listened to Levin.

"Well, of course! Here you've come round to my point. Do you remember you attacked me for seeking enjoyment in life? Don't be so severe, O moralist!"

"No; all the same, what's fine in life is ..." Levin hesitated— "oh, I don't know. All I know is that we shall soon be dead."

"Why so soon?"

"And do you know, there's less charm in life, when one thinks of death, but there's more peace."

"On the contrary, the finish is always the best. But I must be going," said Stepan Arkadyevitch, getting up for the tenth time.

"Oh, no, stay a bit!" said Levin, keeping him. "Now, when shall we see each other again? I'm going to-morrow."

"I'm a nice person! Why, that's just what I came for! You simply must come to dinner with us to-day. Your brother's coming, and Karenin, my brother-in-law."

"You don't mean to say he's here?" said Levin, and he wanted to inquire about Kitty. He had heard at the beginning of the winter that she was at Petersburg with her sister, the wife of the diplomat, and he did not know whether she had come back or not; but he changed his mind and did not ask. "Whether she's coming or not, I don't care," he said to himself.

"So you'll come?"

"Excuse me, I can't, I can't believe it!"

Alexey Alexandrovitch sat down, feeling that his words had not had the effect he anticipated, and that it would be unavoidable for him to explain his position, and that, whatever explanations he might make, his relations with his brother-in-law would remain unchanged.

"Yes, I am brought to the painful necessity of seeking a divorce," he said.

"I will say one thing, Alexey Alexandrovitch. I know you for an excellent, upright man; I know Anna—excuse me, I can't change my opinion of her—for a good, an excellent woman; and so, excuse me, I cannot believe it. There is some misunderstanding," said he.

"Oh, if it were merely a misunderstanding! ..."

"Pardon, I understand," interposed Stepan Arkadyevitch. "But of course ... One thing: you must not act in haste. You must not, you must not act in haste!"

"I am not acting in haste," Alexey Alexandrovitch said coldly, "but one cannot ask advice of anyone in such a matter. I have quite made up my mind."

"This is awful!" said Stepan Arkadyevitch. "I would do one thing, Alexey Alexandrovitch. I beseech you, do it!" he said. "No action has yet been taken, if I understand rightly. Before you take advice, see my wife, talk to her. She loves Anna like a sister, she loves you, and she's a wonderful woman. For God's sake, talk to her! Do me that favor, I beseech you!"

Alexey Alexandrovitch pondered, and Stepan Arkadyevitch looked at him sympathetically, without interrupting his silence.

"You will go to see her?"

"I don't know. That was just why I have not been to see you. I imagine our relations must change."

"Why so? I don't see that. Allow me to believe that apart from our connection you have for me, at least in part, the same friendly feeling I have always had for you ... and sincere esteem," said Stepan Arkadyevitch, pressing his hand. "Even if your worst suppositions were correct, I don't—and never would—take on myself to judge either side, and I see no reason why our relations should be affected. But now, do this, come and see my wife."

"Well, we look at the matter differently," said Alexey Alexandrovitch coldly. "However, we won't discuss it."

"No; why shouldn't you come to-day to dine, anyway? My wife's expecting you. Please, do come. And, above all, talk it over with her. She's a wonderful woman. For God's sake, on my knees, I implore you!"

"If you so much wish it, I will come," said Alexey Alexandrovitch, sighing.

And, anxious to change the conversation, he inquired about what interested them both—the new head of Stepan Arkadyevitch's department, a man not yet old, who had suddenly been promoted to so high a position.

Alexey Alexandrovitch had previously felt no liking for Count Anitchkin, and had always differed from him in his opinions. But now, from a feeling readily comprehensible to officials—that hatred felt by one who has suffered a defeat in the service for one who has received a promotion, he could not endure him.

"Well, have you seen him?" said Alexey Alexandrovitch with a malignant smile.

"Of course; he was at our sitting yesterday. He seems to know his work capitally, and to be very energetic."

"Yes, but what is his energy directed to?" said Alexey Alexandrovitch. "Is he aiming at doing anything, or simply undoing what's been done? It's the great misfortune of our government—this paper administration, of which he's a worthy representative."

"Really, I don't know what fault one could find with him. His policy I don't know, but one thing—he's a very nice fellow," answered Stepan Arkadyevitch. "I've just been seeing him, and he's really a capital fellow. We lunched together, and I taught him how to make, you know that drink, wine and oranges. It's so cooling. And it's a wonder he didn't know it. He liked it awfully. No, really he's a capital fellow."

Stepan Arkadyevitch glanced at his watch.

"Why, good heavens, it's four already, and I've still to go to Dolgovushin's! So please come round to dinner. You can't imagine how you will grieve my wife and me."

The way in which Alexey Alexandrovitch saw his brother-in-law out was very different from the manner in which he had met him.

"I've promised, and I'll come," he answered wearily.

"Believe me, I appreciate it, and I hope you won't regret it," answered Stepan Arkadyevitch, smiling.

And, putting on his coat as he went, he patted the footman on the head, chuckled, and went out.

"At five o'clock, and not evening dress, please," he shouted once more, turning at the door.

"Oh, please, introduce me to Karenin," he brought out with an effort, and with a desperately determined step he walked into the drawing-room and beheld her.

She was not the same as she used to be, nor was she as she had been in the carriage; she was quite different.

She was scared, shy, shame-faced, and still more charming from it. She saw him the very instant he walked into the room. She had been expecting him. She was delighted, and so confused at her own delight that there was a moment, the moment when he went up to her sister and glanced again at her, when she, and he, and Dolly, who saw it all, thought she would break down and would begin to cry. She crimsoned, turned white, crimsoned again, and grew faint, waiting with quivering lips for him to come to her. He went up to her, bowed, and held out his hand without speaking. Except for the slight quiver of her lips and the moisture in her eyes that made them brighter, her smile was almost calm as she said:

"How long it is since we've seen each other!" and with desperate determination she pressed his hand with her cold hand.

"You've not seen me, but I've seen you," said Levin, with a radiant smile of happiness. "I saw you when you were driving from the railway station to Ergushovo."

"When?" she asked, wondering.

"You were driving to Ergushovo," said Levin, feeling as if he would sob with the rapture that was flooding his heart. "And how dared I associate a thought of anything not innocent with this touching creature? And, yes, I do believe it's true what Darya Alexandrovna told me," he thought.

Stepan Arkadyevitch took him by the arm and led him away to Karenin.

"Let me introduce you." He mentioned their names.

"Very glad to meet you again," said Alexey Alexandrovitch coldly, shaking hands with Levin.

"You are acquainted?" Stepan Arkadyevitch asked in surprise.

"We spent three hours together in the train," said Levin smiling, "but got out, just as in a masquerade, quite mystified—at least I was."

"Nonsense! Come along, please," said Stepan Arkadyevitch, pointing in the direction of the dining-room.

The men went into the dining-room and went up to a table, laid with six sorts of spirits and as many kinds of cheese, some with little silver spades and some without, caviar, herrings, preserves of various kinds, and plates with slices of French bread.

The men stood round the strong-smelling spirits and salt delicacies, and the discussion of the Russification of Poland between Koznishev, Karenin, and Pestsov died down in anticipation of dinner.

Sergey Ivanovitch was unequaled in his skill in winding up the most heated and serious argument by some unexpected pinch of Attic salt that changed the disposition of his opponent. He did this now.

Alexey Alexandrovitch had been maintaining that the Russification of Poland could only be accomplished as a result of larger measures which ought to be introduced by the Russian government.

Pestsov insisted that one country can only absorb another when it is the more densely populated.

Koznishev admitted both points, but with limitations. As they were going out of the drawing-room to conclude the argument, Koznishev said, smiling:

"So, then, for the Russification of our foreign populations there is but one method—to bring up as many children as one can. My brother and I are terribly in fault, I see. You married men, especially you, Stepan Arkadyevitch, are the real patriots: what number have you reached?" he said, smiling genially at their host and holding out a tiny wine-glass to him.

Every one laughed, and Stepan Arkadyevitch with particular good-humor.

"Oh, yes, that's the best method!" he said, munching cheese and filling the wine-glass with a special sort of spirit. The conversation dropped at the jest.

"This cheese is not bad. Shall I give you some?" said the master of the house. "Why, have you been going in for gymnastics again?" he asked Levin, pinching his muscle with his left hand. Levin smiled, bent his arm, and under Stepan Arkadyevitch's fingers the muscles swelled up like a sound cheese, hard as a knob of iron, through the fine cloth of the coat.

"What biceps! A perfect Samson!"

"I imagine great strength is needed for hunting bears," observed Alexey Alexandrovitch, who had the mistiest notions about the chase. He cut off and spread with cheese a wafer of bread fine as a spider-web.

Levin smiled.

"Not at all. Quite the contrary; a child can kill a bear," he said, with a slight bow moving aside for the ladies, who were approaching the table.

"You have killed a bear, I've been told!" said Kitty, trying assiduously to catch with her fork a perverse mushroom that would slip away, and setting the lace quivering over her white arm. "Are there bears on your place?" she added, turning her charming little head to him and smiling.

There was apparently nothing extraordinary in what she said, but what unutterable meaning there was for him in every sound, in every turn of her lips,

"I am not expressing my own opinion of either form of culture," Sergey Ivanovitch said, holding out his glass with a smile of condescension, as to a child. "I only say that both sides have strong arguments to support them," he went on, addressing Alexey Alexandrovitch. "My sympathies are classical from education, but in this discussion I am personally unable to arrive at a conclusion. I see no distinct grounds for classical studies being given a preëminence over scientific studies."

"The natural sciences have just as great an educational value," put in Pestsov. "Take astronomy, take botany, or zoology with its system of general principles."

"I cannot quite agree with that," responded Alexey Alexandrovitch "It seems to me that one must admit that the very process of studying the forms of language has a peculiarly favorable influence on intellectual development. Moreover, it cannot be denied that the influence of the classical authors is in the highest degree moral, while, unfortunately, with the study of the natural sciences are associated the false and noxious doctrines which are the curse of our day."

Sergey Ivanovitch would have said something, but Pestsov interrupted him in his rich bass. He began warmly contesting the justice of this view. Sergey Ivanovitch waited serenely to speak, obviously with a convincing reply ready.

"But," said Sergey Ivanovitch, smiling subtly, and addressing Karenin, "One must allow that to weigh all the advantages and disadvantages of classical and scientific studies is a difficult task, and the question which form of education was to be preferred would not have been so quickly and conclusively decided if there had not been in favor of classical education, as you expressed it just now, its moral—*disons le mot*—anti-nihilist influence."

"Undoubtedly."

"If it had not been for the distinctive property of anti-nihilistic influence on the side of classical studies, we should have considered the subject more, have weighed the arguments on both sides," said Sergey Ivanovitch with a subtle smile, "we should have given elbow-room to both tendencies. But now we know that these little pills of classical learning possess the medicinal property of anti-nihilism, and we boldly prescribe them to our patients.... But what if they had no such medicinal property?" he wound up humorously.

At Sergey Ivanovitch's little pills, every one laughed; Turovtsin in especial roared loudly and jovially, glad at last to have found something to laugh at, all he ever looked for in listening to conversation.

Stepan Arkadyevitch had not made a mistake in inviting Pestsov. With Pestsov intellectual conversation never flagged for an instant. Directly Sergey Ivanovitch had concluded the conversation with his jest, Pestsov promptly started a new one.

"I can't agree even," said he, "that the government had that aim. The government obviously is guided by abstract considerations, and remains indifferent to the influence its measures may exercise. The education of women, for instance, would naturally be regarded as likely to be harmful, but the government opens schools and universities for women."

And the conversation at once passed to the new subject of the education of women.

Alexey Alexandrovitch expressed the idea that the education of women is apt to be confounded with the emancipation of women, and that it is only so that it can be considered dangerous.

"I consider, on the contrary, that the two questions are inseparably connected together," said Pestsov; "it is a vicious circle. Woman is deprived of rights from lack of education, and the lack of education results from the absence of rights. We must not forget that the subjection of women is so complete, and dates from such ages back that we are often unwilling to recognize the gulf that separates them from us," said he.

"You said rights," said Sergey Ivanovitch, waiting till Pestsov had finished, "meaning the right of sitting on juries, of voting, of presiding at official meetings, the right of entering the civil service, of sitting in parliament ..."

"Undoubtedly."

"But if women, as a rare exception, can occupy such positions, it seems to me you are wrong in using the expression 'rights.' It would be more correct to say duties. Every man will agree that in doing the duty of a juryman, a witness, a telegraph clerk, we feel we are performing duties. And therefore it would be correct to say that women are seeking duties, and quite legitimately. And one can but sympathize with this desire to assist in the general labor of man."

"Quite so," Alexey Alexandrovitch assented. "The question, I imagine, is simply whether they are fitted for such duties."

"They will most likely be perfectly fitted," said Stepan Arkadyevitch, "when education has become general among them. We see this ..."

"How about the proverb?" said the prince, who had a long while been intent on the conversation, his little comical eyes twinkling. "I can say it before my daughter: her hair is long, because her wit is ..."

"Just what they thought of the negroes before their emancipation!" said Pestsov angrily.

"What seems strange to me is that women should seek fresh duties," said Sergey Ivanovitch, "while we see, unhappily, that men usually try to avoid them."

began to help her look after the children. Yes, and for three weeks he stopped with them, and looked after the children like a nurse."

"I am telling Konstantin Dmitrievitch about Turovtsin in the scarlet fever," she said, bending over to her sister.

"Yes, it was wonderful, noble!" said Dolly, glancing towards Turovtsin, who had become aware they were talking of him, and smiling gently to him. Levin glanced once more at Turovtsin, and wondered how it was he had not realized all this man's goodness before.

"I'm sorry, I'm sorry, and I'll never think ill of people again!" he said gaily, genuinely expressing what he felt at the moment.

CHAPTER XII

CONNECTED WITH THE CONVERSATION THAT HAD SPRUNG UP ON THE RIGHTS of women there were certain questions as to the inequality of rights in marriage improper to discuss before the ladies. Pestsov had several times during dinner touched upon these questions, but Sergey Ivanovitch and Stepan Arkadyevitch carefully drew him off them.

When they rose from the table and the ladies had gone out, Pestsov did not follow them, but addressing Alexey Alexandrovitch, began to expound the chief ground of inequality. The inequality in marriage, in his opinion, lay in the fact that the infidelity of the wife and the infidelity of the husband are punished unequally, both by the law and by public opinion. Stepan Arkadyevitch went hurriedly up to Alexey Alexandrovitch and offered him a cigar.

"No, I don't smoke," Alexey Alexandrovitch answered calmly, and as though purposely wishing to show that he was not afraid of the subject, he turned to Pestsov with a chilly smile.

"I imagine that such a view has a foundation in the very nature of things," he said, and would have gone on to the drawing-room. But at this point Turovtsin broke suddenly and unexpectedly into the conversation, addressing Alexey Alexandrovitch.

"You heard, perhaps, about Pryatchnikov?" said Turovtsin, warmed up by the champagne he had drunk, and long waiting for an opportunity to break the silence that had weighed on him. "Vasya Pryatchnikov," he said, with a good-natured smile on his damp, red lips, addressing himself principally to the most important guest, Alexey Alexandrovitch, "they told me to-day he fought a duel with Kvitsky at Tver, and has killed him."

Just as it always seems that one bruises oneself on a sore place, so Stepan Arkadyevitch felt now that the conversation would by ill luck fall every moment on Alexey Alexandrovitch's sore spot. He would again have got his brother-in-law away, but Alexey Alexandrovitch himself inquired, with curiosity:

"What did Pryatchnikov fight about?"

"His wife. Acted like a man, he did! Called him out and shot him!"

"Ah!" said Alexey Alexandrovitch indifferently, and lifting his eyebrows, he went into the drawing-room.

"How glad I am you have come," Dolly said with a frightened smile, meeting him in the outer drawing-room. "I must talk to you. Let's sit here."

Alexey Alexandrovitch, with the same expression of indifference, given him by his lifted eyebrows, sat down beside Darya Alexandrovna, and smiled affectedly.

"It's fortunate," said he, "especially as I was meaning to ask you to excuse me, and to be taking leave. I have to start to-morrow."

Darya Alexandrovna was firmly convinced of Anna's innocence, and she felt herself growing pale and her lips quivering with anger at this frigid, unfeeling man, who was so calmly intending to ruin her innocent friend.

"Alexey Alexandrovitch," she said, with desperate resolution looking him in the face, "I asked you about Anna; you made me no answer. How is she?"

"She is, I believe, quite well, Darya Alexandrovna," replied Alexey Alexandrovitch, not looking at her.

"Alexey Alexandrovitch, forgive me, I have no right … but I love Anna as a sister, and esteem her; I beg, I beseech you to tell me what is wrong between you? what fault do you find with her?"

Alexey Alexandrovitch frowned, and almost closing his eyes, dropped his head.

"I presume that your husband has told you the grounds on which I consider it necessary to change my attitude to Anna Arkadyevna?" he said, not looking her in the face, but eyeing with displeasure Shtcherbatsky, who was walking across the drawing-room.

"I don't believe it, I don't believe it, I can't believe it!" Dolly said, clasping her bony hands before her with a vigorous gesture. She rose quickly, and laid her hand on Alexey Alexandrovitch's sleeve. "We shall be disturbed here. Come this way, please."

Dolly's agitation had an effect on Alexey Alexandrovitch. He got up and submissively followed her to the schoolroom. They sat down to a table covered with an oilcloth cut in slits by penknives.

grief!" And regaining his self-possession, Alexey Alexandrovitch quietly took leave and went away.

CHAPTER XIII

WHEN THEY ROSE FROM TABLE, LEVIN WOULD HAVE LIKED TO FOLLOW Kitty into the drawing-room; but he was afraid she might dislike this, as too obviously paying her attention. He remained in the little ring of men, taking part in the general conversation, and without looking at Kitty, he was aware of her movements, her looks, and the place where she was in the drawing-room.

He did at once, and without the smallest effort, keep the promise he had made her—always to think well of all men, and to like every one always. The conversation fell on the village commune, in which Pestsov saw a sort of special principle, called by him the choral principle. Levin did not agree with Pestsov, nor with his brother, who had a special attitude of his own, both admitting and not admitting the significance of the Russian commune. But he talked to them, simply trying to reconcile and soften their differences. He was not in the least interested in what he said himself, and even less so in what they said; all he wanted was that they and every one should be happy and contented. He knew now the one thing of importance; and that one was at first there, in the drawing-room, and then began moving across and came to a standstill at the door. Without turning round he felt the eyes fixed on him, and the smile, and he could not help turning round. She was standing in the doorway with Shtcherbatsky, looking at him.

"I thought you were going towards the piano," said he, going up to her. "That's something I miss in the country—music."

"No; we only came to fetch you and thank you," she said, rewarding him with a smile that was like a gift, "for coming. What do they want to argue for? No one ever convinces any one, you know."

"Yes; that's true," said Levin; "it generally happens that one argues warmly simply because one can't make out what one's opponent wants to prove."

Levin had often noticed in discussions between the most intelligent people that after enormous efforts, and an enormous expenditure of logical subtleties and words, the disputants finally arrived at being aware that what they had so long been struggling to prove to one another had long ago, from the beginning of the argument, been known to both, but that they liked different things, and would not define what they liked for fear of its being attacked. He had often had the experience of suddenly in a discussion grasping what it was his opponent liked and at once liking it too, and immediately he found himself agreeing, and then all arguments fell away as useless. Sometimes, too, he had experienced the opposite, expressing at last what he liked himself, which he was devising arguments to defend, and, chancing to express it well and genuinely, he had found his opponent at once agreeing and ceasing to dispute his position. He tried to say this.

She knitted her brow, trying to understand. But directly he began to illustrate his meaning, she understood at once.

"I know: one must find out what he is arguing for, what is precious to him, then one can ..."

She had completely guessed and expressed his badly expressed idea. Levin smiled joyfully; he was struck by this transition from the confused, verbose discussion with Pestsov and his brother to this laconic, clear, almost wordless communication of the most complex ideas.

Shtcherbatsky moved away from them, and Kitty, going up to a card-table, sat down, and, taking up the chalk, began drawing diverging circles over the new green cloth.

They began again on the subject that had been started at dinner—the liberty and occupations of women. Levin was of the opinion of Darya Alexandrovna that a girl who did not marry should find a woman's duties in a family. He supported this view by the fact that no family can get on without women to help; that in every family, poor or rich, there are and must be nurses, either relations or hired.

"No," said Kitty, blushing, but looking at him all the more boldly with her truthful eyes; "a girl may be so circumstanced that she cannot live in the family without humiliation, while she herself ..."

At the hint he understood her.

"Oh, yes," he said. "Yes, yes, yes—you're right; you're right!"

And he saw all that Pestsov had been maintaining at dinner of the liberty of woman, simply from getting a glimpse of the terror of an old maid's existence and its humiliation in Kitty's heart; and loving her, he felt that terror and humiliation, and at once gave up his arguments.

A silence followed. She was still drawing with the chalk on the table. Her eyes were shining with a soft light. Under the influence of her mood he felt in all his being a continually growing tension of happiness.

"Ah! I've scribbled all over the table!" she said, and, laying down the chalk, she made a movement as though to get up.

"I'm going to a meeting."

"Well, I'll come with you. Can I?"

"What for? Yes, come along," said Sergey Ivanovitch, smiling. "What is the matter with you to-day?"

"With me? Happiness is the matter with me!" said Levin, letting down the window of the carriage they were driving in. "You don't mind?—it's so stifling. It's happiness is the matter with me! Why is it you have never married?"

Sergey Ivanovitch smiled.

"I am very glad, she seems a nice gi ..." Sergey Ivanovitch was beginning.

"Don't say it! don't say it!" shouted Levin, clutching at the collar of his fur coat with both hands, and muffling him up in it. "She's a nice girl" were such simple, humble words, so out of harmony with his feeling.

Sergey Ivanovitch laughed outright a merry laugh, which was rare with him. "Well, anyway, I may say that I'm very glad of it."

"That you may do to-morrow, to-morrow and nothing more! Nothing, nothing, silence," said Levin, and muffling him once more in his fur coat, he added: "I do like you so! Well, is it possible for me to be present at the meeting?"

"Of course it is."

"What is your discussion about to-day?" asked Levin, never ceasing smiling.

They arrived at the meeting. Levin heard the secretary hesitatingly read the minutes which he obviously did not himself understand; but Levin saw from this secretary's face what a good, nice, kind-hearted person he was. This was evident from his confusion and embarrassment in reading the minutes. Then the discussion began. They were disputing about the misappropriation of certain sums and the laying of certain pipes, and Sergey Ivanovitch was very cutting to two members, and said something at great length with an air of triumph; and another member, scribbling something on a bit of paper, began timidly at first, but afterwards answered him very viciously and delightfully. And then Sviazhsky (he was there too) said something too, very handsomely and nobly. Levin listened to them, and saw clearly that these missing sums and these pipes were not anything real, and that they were not at all angry, but were all the nicest, kindest people, and everything was as happy and charming as possible among them. They did no harm to any one, and were all enjoying it. What struck Levin was that he could see through them all to-day, and from little, almost imperceptible signs knew the soul of each, and saw distinctly that they were all good at heart. And Levin himself in particular they were all extremely fond of that day. That was evident from the way they spoke to him, from the friendly, affectionate way even those he did not know looked at him.

"Well, did you like it?" Sergey Ivanovitch asked him.

"Very much. I never supposed it was so interesting! Capital! Splendid!"

Sviazhsky went up to Levin and invited him to come round to tea with him. Levin was utterly at a loss to comprehend or recall what it was he had disliked in Sviazhsky, what he had failed to find in him. He was a clever and wonderfully good-hearted man.

"Most delighted," he said, and asked after his wife and sister-in-law. And from a queer association of ideas, because in his imagination the idea of Sviazhsky's sister-in-law was connected with marriage, it occurred to him that there was no one to whom he could more suitably speak of his happiness, and he was very glad to go and see them.

Sviazhsky questioned him about his improvements on his estate, presupposing, as he always did, that there was no possibility of doing anything not done already in Europe, and now this did not in the least annoy Levin. On the contrary, he felt that Sviazhsky was right, that the whole business was of little value, and he saw the wonderful softness and consideration with which Sviazhsky avoided fully expressing his correct view. The ladies of the Sviazhsky household were particularly delightful. It seemed to Levin that they knew all about it already and sympathized with him, saying nothing merely from delicacy. He stayed with them one hour, two, three, talking of all sorts of subjects but the one thing that filled his heart, and did not observe that he was boring them dreadfully, and that it was long past their bedtime.

Sviazhsky went with him into the hall, yawning and wondering at the strange humor his friend was in. It was past one o'clock. Levin went back to his hotel, and was dismayed at the thought that all alone now with his impatience he had ten hours still left to get through. The servant, whose turn it was to be up all night, lighted his candles, and would have gone away, but Levin stopped him. This servant, Yegor, whom Levin had noticed before, struck him as a very intelligent, excellent, and, above all, good-hearted man.

"Well, Yegor, it's hard work not sleeping, isn't it?"

"One's got to put up with it! It's part of our work, you see. In a gentleman's house it's easier; but then here one makes more."

It appeared that Yegor had a family, three boys and a daughter, a sempstress, whom he wanted to marry to a cashier in a saddler's shop.

Levin, on hearing this, informed Yegor that, in his opinion, in marriage the great thing was love, and that with love one would always be happy, for happiness rests only on oneself.

other sledge-drivers, and promising to drive with them too, Levin took one and told him to drive to the Shtcherbatskys'. The sledge-driver was splendid in a white shirt-collar sticking out over his overcoat and into his strong, full-blooded red neck. The sledge was high and comfortable, and altogether such a one as Levin never drove in after, and the horse was a good one, and tried to gallop but didn't seem to move. The driver knew the Shtcherbatskys' house, and drew up at the entrance with a curve of his arm and a "Wo!" especially indicative of respect for his fare. The Shtcherbatskys' hall-porter certainly knew all about it. This was evident from the smile in his eyes and the way he said:

"Well, it's a long while since you've been to see us, Konstantin Demitrievitch!"

Not only he knew all about it, but he was unmistakably delighted and making efforts to conceal his joy. Looking into his kindly old eyes, Levin realized even something new in his happiness.

"Are they up?"

"Pray walk in! Leave it here," said he, smiling, as Levin would have come back to take his hat. That meant something.

"To whom shall I announce your honor?" asked the footman.

The footman, though a young man, and one of the new school of footmen, a dandy, was a very kind-hearted, good fellow, and he too knew all about it.

"The princess ... the prince ... the young princess ..." said Levin.

The first person he saw was Mademoiselle Linon. She walked across the room, and her ringlets and her face were beaming. He had only just spoken to her, when suddenly he heard the rustle of a skirt at the door, and Mademoiselle Linon vanished from Levin's eyes, and a joyful terror came over him at the nearness of his happiness. Mademoiselle Linon was in great haste, and leaving him, went out at the other door. Directly she had gone out, swift, swift light steps sounded on the parquet, and his bliss, his life, himself—what was best in himself, what he had so long sought and longed for—was quickly, so quickly approaching him. She did not walk, but seemed, by some unseen force, to float to him. He saw nothing but her clear, truthful eyes, frightened by the same bliss of love that flooded his heart. Those eyes were shining nearer and nearer, blinding him with their light of love. She stopped still close to him, touching him. Her hands rose and dropped onto his shoulders.

She had done all she could—she had run up to him and given herself up entirely, shy and happy. He put his arms round her and pressed his lips to her mouth that sought his kiss.

She too had not slept all night, and had been expecting him all the morning.

Her mother and father had consented without demur, and were happy in her happiness. She had been waiting for him. She wanted to be the first to tell him her happiness and his. She had got ready to see him alone, and had been delighted at the idea, and had been shy and ashamed, and did not know herself what she was doing. She had heard his steps and voice, and had waited at the door for Mademoiselle Linon to go. Mademoiselle Linon had gone away. Without thinking, without asking herself how and what, she had gone up to him, and did as she was doing.

"Let us go to mamma!" she said, taking him by the hand. For a long while he could say nothing, not so much because he was afraid of desecrating the loftiness of his emotion by a word, as that every time he tried to say something, instead of words he felt that tears of happiness were welling up. He took her hand and kissed it.

"Can it be true?" he said at last in a choked voice. "I can't believe you love me, dear!"

She smiled at that "dear," and at the timidity with which he glanced at her.

"Yes!" she said significantly, deliberately. "I am so happy!"

Not letting go his hands, she went into the drawing-room. The princess, seeing them, breathed quickly, and immediately began to cry and then immediately began to laugh, and with a vigorous step Levin had not expected, ran up to him, and hugging his head, kissed him, wetting his cheeks with her tears.

"So it is all settled! I am glad. Love her. I am glad.... Kitty!"

"You've not been long settling things," said the old prince, trying to seem unmoved; but Levin noticed that his eyes were wet when he turned to him.

"I've long, always wished for this!" said the prince, taking Levin by the arm and drawing him towards himself. "Even when this little feather-head fancied ..."

"Papa!" shrieked Kitty, and shut his mouth with her hands.

"Well, I won't!" he said. "I'm very, very ... plea ... Oh, what a fool I am ..."

He embraced Kitty, kissed her face, her hand, her face again, and made the sign of the cross over her.

And there came over Levin a new feeling of love for this man, till then so little known to him, when he saw how slowly and tenderly Kitty kissed his muscular hand.

"Oh, are presents wanted?" And he galloped to Foulde's.

And at the confectioner's, and at Fomin's, and at Foulde's he saw that he was expected; that they were pleased to see him, and prided themselves on his happiness, just as every one whom he had to do with during those days. What was extraordinary was that every one not only liked him, but even people previously unsympathetic, cold, and callous, were enthusiastic over him, gave way to him in everything, treated his feeling with tenderness and delicacy, and shared his conviction that he was the happiest man in the world because his betrothed was beyond perfection. Kitty too felt the same thing. When Countess Nordston ventured to hint that she had hoped for something better, Kitty was so angry and proved so conclusively that nothing in the world could be better than Levin, that Countess Nordston had to admit it, and in Kitty's presence never met Levin without a smile of ecstatic admiration.

The confession he had promised was the one painful incident of this time. He consulted the old prince, and with his sanction gave Kitty his diary, in which there was written the confession that tortured him. He had written this diary at the time with a view to his future wife. Two things caused him anguish: his lack of purity and his lack of faith. His confession of unbelief passed unnoticed. She was religious, had never doubted the truths of religion, but his external unbelief did not affect her in the least. Through love she knew all his soul, and in his soul she saw what she wanted, and that such a state of soul should be called unbelieving was to her a matter of no account. The other confession set her weeping bitterly.

Levin, not without an inner struggle, handed her his diary. He knew that between him and her there could not be, and should not be, secrets, and so he had decided that so it must be. But he had not realized what an effect it would have on her, he had not put himself in her place. It was only when the same evening he came to their house before the theater, went into her room and saw her tear-stained, pitiful, sweet face, miserable with suffering he had caused and nothing could undo, he felt the abyss that separated his shameful past from her dovelike purity, and was appalled at what he had done.

"Take them, take these dreadful books!" she said, pushing away the notebooks lying before her on the table. "Why did you give them me? No, it was better anyway," she added, touched by his despairing face. "But it's awful, awful!"

His head sank, and he was silent. He could say nothing.

"You can't forgive me," he whispered.

"Yes, I forgive you; but it's terrible!"

But his happiness was so immense that this confession did not shatter it, it only added another shade to it. She forgave him; but from that time more than ever he considered himself unworthy of her, morally bowed down lower than ever before her, and prized more highly than ever his undeserved happiness.

CHAPTER XVII

UNCONSCIOUSLY GOING OVER IN HIS MEMORY THE CONVERSATIONS THAT had taken place during and after dinner, Alexey Alexandrovitch returned to his solitary room. Darya Alexandrovna's words about forgiveness had aroused in him nothing but annoyance. The applicability or non-applicability of the Christian precept to his own case was too difficult a question to be discussed lightly, and this question had long ago been answered by Alexey Alexandrovitch in the negative. Of all that had been said, what stuck most in his memory was the phrase of stupid, good-natured Turovtsin— *"Acted like a man, he did! Called him out and shot him!"* Every one had apparently shared this feeling, though from politeness they had not expressed it.

"But the matter is settled, it's useless thinking about it," Alexey Alexandrovitch told himself. And thinking of nothing but the journey before him, and the revision work he had to do, he went into his room and asked the porter who escorted him where his man was. The porter said that the man had only just gone out. Alexey Alexandrovitch ordered tea to be sent him, sat down to the table, and taking the guide-book, began considering the route of his journey.

"Two telegrams," said his manservant, coming into the room. "I beg your pardon, your excellency; I'd only just that minute gone out."

Alexey Alexandrovitch took the telegrams and opened them. The first telegram was the announcement of Stremov's appointment to the very post Karenin had coveted. Alexey Alexandrovitch flung the telegram down, and flushing a little, got up and began to pace up and down the room. "*Quos vult perdere dementat*," he said, meaning by *quos* the persons responsible for this appointment. He was not so much annoyed that he had not received the post, that he had been conspicuously passed over; but it was incomprehensible, amazing to him that they did not see that the wordy phrase-monger Stremov was the last man fit for it. How could they fail to see how they were ruining themselves, lowering their *prestige* by this appointment?

as though she were not only well and blooming, but in the happiest frame of mind. She was talking rapidly, musically, and with exceptionally correct articulation and expressive intonation.

"For Alexey—I am speaking of Alexey Alexandrovitch (what a strange and awful thing that both are Alexey, isn't it?)—Alexey would not refuse me. I should forget, he would forgive ... But why doesn't he come? He's so good he doesn't know himself how good he is. Ah, my God, what agony! Give me some water, quick! Oh, that will be bad for her, my little girl! Oh, very well then, give her to a nurse. Yes, I agree, it's better in fact. He'll be coming; it will hurt him to see her. Give her to the nurse."

"Anna Arkadyevna, he has come. Here he is!" said the midwife, trying to attract her attention to Alexey Alexandrovitch.

"Oh, what nonsense!" Anna went on, not seeing her husband. "No, give her to me; give me my little one! He has not come yet. You say he won't forgive me, because you don't know him. No one knows him. I'm the only one, and it was hard for me even. His eyes I ought to know—Seryozha has just the same eyes—and I can't bear to see them because of it. Has Seryozha had his dinner? I know every one will forget him. He would not forget. Seryozha must be moved into the corner room, and Mariette must be asked to sleep with him."

All of a sudden she shrank back, was silent; and in terror, as though expecting a blow, as though to defend herself, she raised her hands to her face. She had seen her husband.

"No, no!" she began. "I am not afraid of him; I am afraid of death. Alexey, come here. I am in a hurry, because I've no time, I've not long left to live; the fever will begin directly and I shall understand nothing more. Now I understand, I understand it all, I see it all!"

Alexey Alexandrovitch's wrinkled face wore an expression of agony; he took her by the hand and tried to say something, but he could not utter it; his lower lip quivered, but he still went on struggling with his emotion, and only now and then glanced at her. And each time he glanced at her, he saw her eyes gazing at him with such passionate and triumphant tenderness as he had never seen in them.

"Wait a minute, you don't know ... stay a little, stay! ..." She stopped, as though collecting her ideas. "Yes," she began; "yes, yes, yes. This is what I wanted to say. Don't be surprised at me. I'm still the same ... But there is another woman in me, I'm afraid of her: she loved that man, and I tried to hate you, and could not forget about her that used to be. I'm not that woman. Now I'm my real self, all myself. I'm dying now, I know I shall die, ask him. Even now I feel—see here, the weights on my feet, on my hands, on my fingers. My fingers—see how huge they are! But this will soon all be over ... Only one thing I want: forgive me, forgive me quite. I'm terrible, but my nurse used to tell me; the holy martyr—what was her name? She was worse. And I'll go to Rome; there's a wilderness, and there I shall be no trouble to any one, only I'll take Seryozha and the little one.... No, you can't forgive me! I know, it can't be forgiven! No, no, go away, you're too good!" She held his hand in one burning hand, while she pushed him away with the other.

The nervous agitation of Alexey Alexandrovitch kept increasing, and had by now reached such a point that he ceased to struggle with it. He suddenly felt that what he had regarded as nervous agitation was on the contrary a blissful spiritual condition that gave him all at once a new happiness he had never known. He did not think that the Christian law that he had been all his life trying to follow, enjoined on him to forgive and love his enemies; but a glad feeling of love and forgiveness for his enemies filled his heart. He knelt down, and laying his head in the curve of her arm, which burned him as with fire through the sleeve, he sobbed like a little child. She put her arm around his head, moved towards him, and with defiant pride lifted up her eyes.

"That is he. I knew him! Now, forgive me, every one, forgive me! ... They've come again; why don't they go away? ... Oh, take these cloaks off me!"

The doctor unloosed her hands, carefully laying her on the pillow, and covered her up to the shoulders. She lay back submissively, and looked before her with beaming eyes.

"Remember one thing, that I needed nothing but forgiveness, and I want nothing more.... Why doesn't *he* come?" she said, turning to the door towards Vronsky. "Do come, do come! Give him your hand."

Vronsky came to the side of the bed, and seeing Anna, again hid his face in his hands.

"Uncover your face—look at him! He's a saint," she said. "Oh! uncover your face, do uncover it!" she said angrily. "Alexey Alexandrovitch, do uncover his face! I want to see him."

Alexey Alexandrovitch took Vronsky's hands and drew them away from his face, which was awful with the expression of agony and shame upon it.

"Give him your hand. Forgive him."

Alexey Alexandrovitch gave him his hand, not attempting to restrain the tears that streamed from his eyes.

"Thank God, thank God!" she said, "now everything is ready. Only to stretch my legs a little. There, that's capital. How badly these flowers are

"A sledge, sir?" asked the porter.

"Yes, a sledge."

On getting home, after three sleepless nights, Vronsky, without undressing, lay down flat on the sofa, clasping his hands and laying his head on them. His head was heavy. Images, memories, and ideas of the strangest description followed one another with extraordinary rapidity and vividness. First it was the medicine he had poured out for the patient and spilt over the spoon, then the midwife's white hands, then the queer posture of Alexey Alexandrovitch on the floor beside the bed.

"To sleep! To forget!" he said to himself with the serene confidence of a healthy man that if he is tired and sleepy, he will go to sleep at once. And the same instant his head did begin to feel drowsy and he began to drop off into forgetfulness. The waves of the sea of unconsciousness had begun to meet over his head, when all at once—it was as though a violent shock of electricity had passed over him. He started so that he leaped up on the springs of the sofa, and leaning on his arms got in a panic onto his knees. His eyes were wide open as though he had never been asleep. The heaviness in his head and the weariness in his limbs that he had felt a minute before had suddenly gone.

"You may trample me in the mud," he heard Alexey Alexandrovitch's words and saw him standing before him, and saw Anna's face with its burning flush and glittering eyes, gazing with love and tenderness not at him but at Alexey Alexandrovitch; he saw his own, as he fancied, foolish and ludicrous figure when Alexey Alexandrovitch took his hands away from his face. He stretched out his legs again and flung himself on the sofa in the same position and shut his eyes.

"To sleep! To forget!" he repeated to himself. But with his eyes shut he saw more distinctly than ever Anna's face as it had been on the memorable evening before the races.

"That is not and will not be, and she wants to wipe it out of her memory. But I cannot live without it. How can we be reconciled? how can we be reconciled?" he said aloud, and unconsciously began to repeat these words. This repetition checked the rising up of fresh images and memories, which he felt were thronging in his brain. But repeating words did not check his imagination for long. Again in extraordinarily rapid succession his best moments rose before his mind, and then his recent humiliation. "Take away his hands," Anna's voice says. He takes away his hands and feels the shamestruck and idiotic expression of his face.

He still lay down, trying to sleep, though he felt there was not the smallest hope of it, and kept repeating stray words from some chain of thought, trying by this to check the rising flood of fresh images. He listened, and heard in a strange, mad whisper words repeated: "I did not appreciate it, did not make enough of it. I did not appreciate it, did not make enough of it."

"What's this? Am I going out of my mind?" he said to himself. "Perhaps. What makes men go out of their minds; what makes men shoot themselves?" he answered himself, and opening his eyes, he saw with wonder an embroidered cushion beside him, worked by Varya, his brother's wife. He touched the tassel of the cushion, and tried to think of Varya, of when he had seen her last. But to think of anything extraneous was an agonizing effort. "No, I must sleep!" He moved the cushion up, and pressed his head into it, but he had to make an effort to keep his eyes shut. He jumped up and sat down. "That's all over for me," he said to himself. "I must think what to do. What is left?" His mind rapidly ran through his life apart from his love of Anna.

"Ambition? Serpuhovskoy? Society? The court?" He could not come to a pause anywhere. All of it had had meaning before, but now there was no reality in it. He got up from the sofa, took off his coat, undid his belt, and uncovering his hairy chest to breathe more freely, walked up and down the room. "This is how people go mad," he repeated, "and how they shoot themselves ... to escape humiliation," he added slowly.

He went to the door and closed it, then with fixed eyes and clenched teeth he went up to the table, took a revolver, looked round him, turned it to a loaded barrel, and sank into thought. For two minutes, his head bent forward with an expression of an intense effort of thought, he stood with the revolver in his hand, motionless, thinking.

"Of course," he said to himself, as though a logical, continuous, and clear chain of reasoning had brought him to an indubitable conclusion. In reality this "of course," that seemed convincing to him, was simply the result of exactly the same circle of memories and images through which he had passed ten times already during the last hour—memories of happiness lost forever. There was the same conception of the senselessness of everything to come in life, the same consciousness of humiliation. Even the sequence of these images and emotions was the same.

"Of course," he repeated, when for the third time his thought passed again round the same spellbound circle of memories and images, and pulling the revolver to the left side of his chest, and clutching it vigorously with his whole hand, as it were, squeezing it in his fist, he pulled the trigger. He did not hear the sound of the shot, but a violent blow on his chest sent him reeling. He tried to clutch at the edge of the table, dropped the revolver, staggered,

"Princess Elizaveta Federovna Tverskaya," the groom answered, and it seemed to Alexey Alexandrovitch that he grinned.

During all this difficult time Alexey Alexandrovitch had noticed that his worldly acquaintances, especially women, took a peculiar interest in him and his wife. All these acquaintances he observed with difficulty concealing their mirth at something; the same mirth that he had perceived in the lawyer's eyes, and just now in the eyes of this groom. Every one seemed, somehow, hugely delighted, as though they had just been at a wedding. When they met him, with ill-disguised enjoyment they inquired after his wife's health. The presence of Princess Tverskaya was unpleasant to Alexey Alexandrovitch from the memories associated with her, and also because he disliked her, and he went straight to the nursery. In the day-nursery Seryozha, leaning on the table with his legs on a chair, was drawing and chatting away merrily. The English governess, who had during Anna's illness replaced the French one, was sitting near the boy knitting a shawl. She hurriedly got up, curtseyed, and pulled Seryozha.

Alexey Alexandrovitch stroked his son's hair, answered the governess's inquiries about his wife, and asked what the doctor had said of the baby.

"The doctor said it was nothing serious, and he ordered a bath, sir."

"But she is still in pain," said Alexey Alexandrovitch, listening to the baby's screaming in the next room.

"I think it's the wet-nurse, sir," the Englishwoman said firmly.

"What makes you think so?" he asked, stopping short.

"It's just as it was at Countess Paul's, sir. They gave the baby medicine, and it turned out that the baby was simply hungry: the nurse had no milk, sir."

Alexey Alexandrovitch pondered, and after standing still a few seconds he went in at the other door. The baby was lying with its head thrown back, stiffening itself in the nurse's arms, and would not take the plump breast offered it; and it never ceased screaming in spite of the double hushing of the wet-nurse and the other nurse, who was bending over her.

"Still no better?" said Alexey Alexandrovitch.

"She's very restless," answered the nurse in a whisper.

"Miss Edwarde says that perhaps the wet-nurse has no milk," he said.

"I think so too, Alexey Alexandrovitch."

"Then why didn't you say so?"

"Who's one to say it to? Anna Arkadyevna still ill ..." said the nurse discontentedly.

The nurse was an old servant of the family. And in her simple words there seemed to Alexey Alexandrovitch an allusion to his position.

The baby screamed louder than ever, struggling and sobbing. The nurse, with a gesture of despair, went to it, took it from the wet-nurse's arms, and began walking up and down, rocking it.

"You must ask the doctor to examine the wet-nurse," said Alexey Alexandrovitch. The smartly dressed and healthy-looking nurse, frightened at the idea of losing her place, muttered something to herself, and covering her bosom, smiled contemptuously at the idea of doubts being cast on her abundance of milk. In that smile, too, Alexey Alexandrovitch saw a sneer at his position.

"Luckless child!" said the nurse, hushing the baby, and still walking up and down with it.

Alexey Alexandrovitch sat down, and with a despondent and suffering face watched the nurse walking to and fro.

When the child at last was still, and had been put in a deep bed, and the nurse, after smoothing the little pillow, had left her, Alexey Alexandrovitch got up, and walking awkwardly on tiptoe, approached the baby. For a minute he was still, and with the same despondent face gazed at the baby; but all at once a smile, that moved his hair and the skin of his forehead, came out on his face, and he went as softly out of the room.

In the dining-room he rang the bell, and told the servant who came in to send again for the doctor. He felt vexed with his wife for not being anxious about this exquisite baby, and in this vexed humor he had no wish to go to her; he had no wish, either, to see Princess Betsy. But his wife might wonder why he did not go to her as usual; and so, overcoming his disinclination, he went towards the bedroom. As he walked over the soft rug towards the door, he could not help overhearing a conversation he did not want to hear.

"If he hadn't been going away, I could have understood your answer and his too. But your husband ought to be above that," Betsy was saying.

"It's not for my husband; for myself I don't wish it. Don't say that!" answered Anna's excited voice.

"Yes, but you must care to say good-bye to a man who has shot himself on your account...."

"That's just why I don't want to."

With a dismayed and guilty expression, Alexey Alexandrovitch stopped and would have gone back unobserved. But reflecting that this would be undignified, he turned back again, and clearing his throat, he went up to the bedroom. The voices were silent, and he went in.

Anna, in a gray dressing-gown, with a crop of short clustering black curls on her round head, was sitting on a settee. The eagerness died out of her face,

cannot live without him. No sort of necessity!" she compressed her lips, and dropped her burning eyes to his hands with their swollen veins. They were rubbing each other.

"Let us never speak of it," she added more calmly.

"I have left this question to you to decide, and I am very glad to see ..." Alexey Alexandrovitch was beginning.

"That my wish coincides with your own," she finished quickly, exasperated at his talking so slowly while she knew beforehand all he would say.

"Yes," he assented; "and Princess Tverskaya's interference in the most difficult private affairs is utterly uncalled for. She especially ..."

"I don't believe a word of what's said about her," said Anna quickly. "I know she really cares for me."

Alexey Alexandrovitch sighed and said nothing. She played nervously with the tassel of her dressing-gown, glancing at him with that torturing sensation of physical repulsion for which she blamed herself, though she could not control it. Her only desire now was to be rid of his oppressive presence.

"I have just sent for the doctor," said Alexey Alexandrovitch.

"I am very well; what do I want the doctor for?"

"No, the little one cries, and they say the nurse hasn't enough milk."

"Why didn't you let me nurse her, when I begged to? Anyway" (Alexey Alexandrovitch knew what was meant by that "anyway"), "she's a baby, and they're killing her." She rang the bell and ordered the baby to be brought her. "I begged to nurse her, I wasn't allowed to, and now I'm blamed for it."

"I don't blame ..."

"Yes, you do blame me! My God! why didn't I die!" And she broke into sobs. "Forgive me, I'm nervous, I'm unjust," she said, controlling herself, "but do go away ..."

"No, it can't go on like this," Alexey Alexandrovitch said to himself decidedly as he left his wife's room.

Never had the impossibility of his position in the world's eyes, and his wife's hatred of him, and altogether the might of that mysterious brutal force that guided his life against his spiritual inclinations, and exacted conformity with its decrees and change in his attitude to his wife, been presented to him with such distinctness as that day. He saw clearly that all the world and his wife expected of him something, but what exactly, he could not make out. He felt that this was rousing in his soul a feeling of anger destructive of his peace of mind and of all the good of his achievement. He believed that for Anna herself it would be better to break off all relations with Vronsky; but if they all thought this out of the question, he was even ready to allow these relations to be renewed, so long as the children were not disgraced, and he was not deprived of them nor forced to change his position. Bad as this might be, it was anyway better than a rupture, which would put her in a hopeless and shameful position, and deprive him of everything he cared for. But he felt helpless; he knew beforehand that every one was against him, and that he would not be allowed to do what seemed to him now so natural and right, but would be forced to do what was wrong, though it seemed the proper thing to them.

CHAPTER XXI

BEFORE BETSY HAD TIME TO WALK OUT OF THE DRAWING-ROOM, SHE WAS met in the doorway by Stepan Arkadyevitch, who had just come from Yeliseev's, where a consignment of fresh oysters had been received.

"Ah! princess! what a delightful meeting!" he began. "I've been to see you."

"A meeting for one minute, for I'm going," said Betsy, smiling and putting on her glove.

"Don't put on your glove yet, princess; let me kiss your hand. There's nothing I'm so thankful to the revival of the old fashions for as the kissing the hand." He kissed Betsy's hand. "When shall we see each other?"

"You don't deserve it," answered Betsy, smiling.

"Oh, yes, I deserve a great deal, for I've become a most serious person. I don't only manage my own affairs, but other people's too," he said, with a significant expression.

"Oh, I'm so glad!" answered Betsy, at once understanding that he was speaking of Anna. And going back into the drawing-room, they stood in a corner. "He's killing her," said Betsy in a whisper full of meaning. "It's impossible, impossible ..."

"I'm so glad you think so," said Stepan Arkadyevitch, shaking his head with a serious and sympathetically distressed expression, "that's what I've come to Petersburg for."

"The whole town's talking of it," she said. "It's an impossible position. She pines and pines away. He doesn't understand that she's one of those women who can't trifle with their feelings. One of two things: either let him take her away, act with energy, or give her a divorce. This is stifling her."

CHAPTER XXII

S TEPAN ARKADYEVITCH, WITH THE SAME SOMEWHAT SOLEMN EXPRESSION WITH which he used to take his presidential chair at his board, walked into Alexey Alexandrovitch's room. Alexey Alexandrovitch was walking about his room with his hands behind his back, thinking of just what Stepan Arkadyevitch had been discussing with his wife.

"I'm not interrupting you?" said Stepan Arkadyevitch, on the sight of his brother-in-law becoming suddenly aware of a sense of embarrassment unusual with him. To conceal this embarrassment he took out a cigarette-case he had just bought that opened in a new way, and sniffing the leather, took a cigarette out of it.

"No. Do you want anything?" Alexey Alexandrovitch asked without eagerness.

"Yes, I wished ... I wanted ... yes, I wanted to talk to you," said Stepan Arkadyevitch, with surprise aware of an unaccustomed timidity.

This feeling was so unexpected and so strange that he did not believe it was the voice of conscience telling him that what he was meaning to do was wrong.

Stepan Arkadyevitch made an effort and struggled with the timidity that had come over him.

"I hope you believe in my love for my sister and my sincere affection and respect for you," he said, reddening.

Alexey Alexandrovitch stood still and said nothing, but his face struck Stepan Arkadyevitch by its expression of an unresisting sacrifice.

"I intended ... I wanted to have a little talk with you about my sister and your mutual position," he said, still struggling with an unaccustomed constraint.

Alexey Alexandrovitch smiled mournfully, looked at his brother-in-law, and without answering went up to the table, took from it an unfinished letter, and handed it to his brother-in-law.

"I think unceasingly of the same thing. And here is what I had begun writing, thinking I could say it better by letter, and that my presence irritates her," he said, as he gave him the letter.

Stepan Arkadyevitch took the letter, looked with incredulous surprise at the lusterless eyes fixed so immovably on him, and began to read.

"I see that my presence is irksome to you. Painful as it is to me to believe it, I see that it is so, and cannot be otherwise. I don't blame you, and God is my witness that on seeing you at the time of your illness I resolved with my whole heart to forget all that had passed between us and to begin a new life. I do not regret, and shall never regret, what I have done; but I have desired one thing—your good, the good of your soul—and now I see I have not attained that. Tell me yourself what will give you true happiness and peace to your soul. I put myself entirely in your hands, and trust to your feeling of what's right."

Stepan Arkadyevitch handed back the letter, and with the same surprise continued looking at his brother-in-law, not knowing what to say. This silence was so awkward for both of them that Stepan Arkadyevitch's lips began twitching nervously, while he still gazed without speaking at Karenin's face.

"That's what I wanted to say to her," said Alexey Alexandrovitch, turning away.

"Yes, yes …" said Stepan Arkadyevitch, not able to answer for the tears that were choking him.

"Yes, yes, I understand you," he brought out at last.

"I want to know what she would like," said Alexey Alexandrovitch.

"I am afraid she does not understand her own position. She is not a judge," said Stepan Arkadyevitch, recovering himself. "She is crushed, simply crushed by your generosity. If she were to read this letter, she would be incapable of saying anything, she would only hang her head lower than ever."

"Yes, but what's to be done in that case? how explain, how find out her wishes?"

"If you will allow me to give my opinion, I think that it lies with you to point out directly the steps you consider necessary to end the position."

"So you consider it must be ended?" Alexey Alexandrovitch interrupted him. "But how?" he added, with a gesture of his hands before his eyes not usual with him. "I see no possible way out of it."

"There is some way of getting out of every position," said Stepan Arkadyevitch, standing up and becoming more cheerful. "There was a time when you thought of breaking off…. If you are convinced now that you cannot make each other happy …"

"Happiness may be variously understood. But suppose that I agree to everything, that I want nothing: what way is there of getting out of our position?"

"If you care to know my opinion," said Stepan Arkadyevitch with the same smile of softening, almond-oil tenderness with which he had been talking to Anna. His kindly smile was so winning that Alexey Alexandrovitch, feeling his own weakness and unconsciously swayed by it, was ready to believe what Stepan Arkadyevitch was saying.

When he went out of his brother-in-law's room he was touched, but that did not prevent him from being glad he had successfully brought the matter to a conclusion, for he felt certain Alexey Alexandrovitch would not go back on his words. To this satisfaction was added the fact that an idea had just struck him for a riddle turning on his successful achievement, that when the affair was over he would ask his wife and most intimate friends. He put this riddle into two or three different ways. "But I'll work it out better than that," he said to himself with a smile.

CHAPTER XXIII

VRONSKY'S WOUND HAD BEEN A DANGEROUS ONE, THOUGH IT DID NOT touch the heart, and for several days he had lain between life and death. The first time he was able to speak, Varya, his brother's wife, was alone in the room.

"Varya," he said, looking sternly at her, "I shot myself by accident. And please never speak of it, and tell every one so. Or else it's too ridiculous."

Without answering his words, Varya bent over him, and with a delighted smile gazed into his face. His eyes were clear, not feverish; but their expression was stern.

"Thank God!" she said. "You're not in pain?"

"A little here." He pointed to his breast.

"Then let me change your bandages."

In silence, stiffening his broad jaws, he looked at her while she bandaged him up. When she had finished he said:

"I'm not delirious. Please manage that there may be no talk of my having shot myself on purpose."

"No one does say so. Only I hope you won't shoot yourself by accident any more," she said, with a questioning smile.

"Of course I won't, but it would have been better ..."

And he smiled gloomily.

In spite of these words and this smile, which so frightened Varya, when the inflammation was over and he began to recover, he felt that he was completely free from one part of his misery. By his action he had, as it were, washed away the shame and humiliation he had felt before. He could now think calmly of

Alexey Alexandrovitch. He recognized all his magnanimity, but he did not now feel himself humiliated by it. Besides, he got back again into the beaten track of his life. He saw the possibility of looking men in the face again without shame, and he could live in accordance with his own habits. One thing he could not pluck out of his heart, though he never ceased struggling with it, was the regret, amounting to despair, that he had lost her forever. That now, having expiated his sin against the husband, he was bound to renounce her, and never in future to stand between her with her repentance and her husband, he had firmly decided in his heart; but he could not tear out of his heart his regret at the loss of her love, he could not erase from his memory those moments of happiness that he had so little prized at the time, and that haunted him in all their charm.

Serpuhovskoy had planned his appointment at Tashkend, and Vronsky agreed to the proposition without the slightest hesitation. But the nearer the time of departure came, the bitterer was the sacrifice he was making to what he thought his duty.

His wound had healed, and he was driving about making preparations for his departure for Tashkend.

"To see her once and then to bury myself, to die," he thought, and as he was paying farewell visits, he uttered this thought to Betsy. Charged with this commission, Betsy had gone to Anna, and brought him back a negative reply.

"So much the better," thought Vronsky, when he received the news. "It was a weakness, which would have shattered what strength I have left."

Next day Betsy herself came to him in the morning, and announced that she had heard through Oblonsky as a positive fact that Alexey Alexandrovitch had agreed to a divorce, and that therefore Vronsky could see Anna.

Without even troubling himself to see Betsy out of his flat, forgetting all his resolutions, without asking when he could see her, where her husband was, Vronsky drove straight to the Karenins'. He ran up the stairs seeing no one and nothing, and with a rapid step, almost breaking into a run, he went into her room. And without considering, without noticing whether there was any one in the room or not, he flung his arms round her, and began to cover her face, her hands, her neck with kisses.

Anna had been preparing herself for this meeting, had thought what she would say to him, but she did not succeed in saying anything of it; his passion mastered her. She tried to calm him, to calm herself, but it was too late. His feeling infected her. Her lips trembled so that for a long while she could say nothing.

"Yes, you have conquered me, and I am yours," she said at last, pressing his hands to her bosom.

"So it had to be," he said. "So long as we live, it must be so. I know it now."

"That's true," she said, getting whiter and whiter, and embracing his head. "Still there is something terrible in it after all that has happened."

"It will all pass, it will all pass; we shall be so happy. Our love, if it could be stronger, will be strengthened by there being something terrible in it," he said, lifting his head and parting his strong teeth in a smile.

And she could not but respond with a smile—not to his words, but to the love in his eyes. She took his hand and stroked her chilled cheeks and cropped head with it.

"I don't know you with this short hair. You've grown so pretty. A boy. But how pale you are!"

"Yes, I'm very weak," she said, smiling. And her lips began trembling again.

"We'll go to Italy; you will get strong," he said.

"Can it be possible we could be like husband and wife, alone, your family with you?" she said, looking close into his eyes.

"It only seems strange to me that it can ever have been otherwise."

"Stiva says that *he* has agreed to everything, but I can't accept *his* generosity," she said, looking dreamily past Vronsky's face. "I don't want a divorce; it's all the same to me now. Only I don't know what he will decide about Seryozha."

He could not conceive how at this moment of their meeting she could remember and think of her son, of divorce. What did it all matter?

"Don't speak of that, don't think of it," he said, turning her hand in his, and trying to draw her attention to him; but still she did not look at him.

"Oh, why didn't I die! it would have been better," she said, and silent tears flowed down both her cheeks; but she tried to smile, so as not to wound him.

To decline the flattering and dangerous appointment at Tashkend would have been, Vronsky had till then considered, disgraceful and impossible. But now, without an instant's consideration, he declined it, and observing dissatisfaction in the most exalted quarters at this step, he immediately retired from the army.

A month later Alexey Alexandrovitch was left alone with his son in his house at Petersburg, while Anna and Vronsky had gone abroad, not having obtained a divorce, but having absolutely declined all idea of one.

PART FIVE

CHAPTER I

PRINCESS SHTCHERBATSKAYA CONSIDERED THAT IT WAS OUT OF THE question for the wedding to take place before Lent, just five weeks off, since not half the trousseau could possibly be ready by that time. But she could not but agree with Levin that to fix it for after Lent would be putting it off too late, as an old aunt of Prince Shtcherbatsky's was seriously ill and might die, and then the mourning would delay the wedding still longer. And therefore, deciding to divide the trousseau into two parts—a larger and smaller trousseau—the princess consented to have the wedding before Lent. She determined that she would get the smaller part of the trousseau all ready now, and the larger part should be made later, and she was much vexed with Levin because he was incapable of giving her a serious answer to the question whether he agreed to this arrangement or not. The arrangement was the more suitable as, immediately after the wedding, the young people were to go to the country, where the more important part of the trousseau would not be wanted.

Levin still continued in the same delirious condition in which it seemed to him that he and his happiness constituted the chief and sole aim of all existence, and that he need not now think or care about anything, that everything was being done and would be done for him by others. He had not even plans and aims for the future, he left its arrangement to others, knowing that everything would be delightful. His brother Sergey Ivanovitch, Stepan Arkadyevitch, and the princess guided him in doing what he had to do. All he did was to agree entirely with everything suggested to him. His brother raised money for him, the princess advised him to leave Moscow after the wedding. Stepan Arkadyevitch advised him to go abroad. He agreed to everything. "Do what you choose, if it amuses you. I'm happy, and my happiness can be no greater and no less for anything you do," he thought. When he told Kitty of Stepan Arkadyevitch's advice that they should go abroad, he was much surprised that she did not agree to this, and had some definite requirements of her own in regard to their future. She knew Levin had work he loved in the country. She did not, as he saw, understand this work, she did not even care to understand it. But that did not prevent her from regarding it as a matter of great importance.

And then she knew their home would be in the country, and she wanted to go, not abroad where she was not going to live, but to the place where their home would be. This definitely expressed purpose astonished Levin. But since he did not care either way, he immediately asked Stepan Arkadyevitch, as though it were his duty, to go down to the country and to arrange everything there to the best of his ability with the taste of which he had so much.

"But I say," Stepan Arkadyevitch said to him one day after he had come back from the country, where he had got everything ready for the young people's arrival, "have you a certificate of having been at confession?"

"No. But what of it?"

"You can't be married without it."

"*Aïe, aïe, aïe!*" cried Levin. "Why, I believe it's nine years since I've taken the sacrament! I never thought of it."

"You're a pretty fellow!" said Stepan Arkadyevitch laughing, "and you call me a Nihilist! But this won't do, you know. You must take the sacrament."

"When? There are four days left now."

Stepan Arkadyevitch arranged this also, and Levin had to go to confession. To Levin, as to any unbeliever who respects the beliefs of others, it was exceedingly disagreeable to be present at and take part in church ceremonies. At this moment, in his present softened state of feeling, sensitive to everything, this inevitable act of hypocrisy was not merely painful to Levin, it seemed to him utterly impossible. Now, in the heyday of his highest glory, his fullest flower, he would have to be a liar or a scoffer. He felt incapable of being either. But though he repeatedly plied Stepan Arkadyevitch with questions as to the possibility of obtaining a certificate without actually communicating, Stepan Arkadyevitch maintained that it was out of the question.

"Besides, what is it to you—two days? And he's an awfully nice clever old fellow. He'll pull the tooth out for you so gently, you won't notice it."

Standing at the first litany, Levin attempted to revive in himself his youthful recollections of the intense religious emotion he had passed through between the ages of sixteen and seventeen.

But he was at once convinced that it was utterly impossible to him. He attempted to look at it all as an empty custom, having no sort of meaning, like the custom of paying calls. But he felt that he could not do that either. Levin found himself, like the majority of his contemporaries, in the vaguest position in regard to religion. Believe he could not, and at the same time he had no firm conviction that it was all wrong. And consequently, not being able to believe in the significance of what he was doing nor to regard it with indifference as an empty formality, during the whole period of preparing for the sacrament he was conscious of a feeling of discomfort and shame at doing what he did not himself understand, and what, as an inner voice told him, was therefore false and wrong.

During the service he would first listen to the prayers, trying to attach some meaning to them not discordant with his own views; then feeling that he could not understand and must condemn them, he tried not to listen to them, but to attend to the thoughts, observations, and memories which floated through his brain with extreme vividness during this idle time of standing in church.

He had stood through the litany, the evening service and the midnight service, and the next day he got up earlier than usual, and without having tea went at eight o'clock in the morning to the church for the morning service and the confession.

There was no one in the church but a beggar soldier, two old women, and the church officials. A young deacon, whose long back showed in two distinct halves through his thin undercassock, met him, and at once going to a little table at the wall read the exhortation. During the reading, especially at the frequent and rapid repetition of the same words, "Lord, have mercy on us!" which resounded with an echo, Levin felt that thought was shut and sealed up, and that it must not be touched or stirred now or confusion would be the result; and so standing behind the deacon he went on thinking of his own affairs, neither listening nor examining what was said. "It's wonderful what expression there is in her hand," he thought, remembering how they had been sitting the day before at a corner table. They had nothing to talk about, as was almost always the case at this time, and laying her hand on the table she kept opening and shutting it, and laughed herself as she watched her action. He remembered how he had kissed it and then had examined the lines on the pink palm. "Have mercy on us again!" thought Levin, crossing himself, bowing, and looking at the supple spring of the deacon's back bowing before him. "She took my hand then and examined the lines 'You've got a splendid hand,' she said." And he looked at his own hand and the short hand of the deacon. "Yes, now it will soon be over," he thought. "No, it seems to be beginning again," he thought, listening to the prayers. "No, it's just ending: there he is bowing down to the ground. That's always at the end."

The deacon's hand in a plush cuff accepted a three-rouble note unobtrusively, and the deacon said he would put it down in the register, and his new boots creaking jauntily over the flagstones of the empty church, he went to the altar. A moment later he peeped out thence and beckoned to Levin.

abundance and riches of His loving-kindness, forgives this child ..." and, finishing the prayer of absolution, the priest blessed him and dismissed him.

On getting home that day, Levin had a delightful sense of relief at the awkward position being over and having been got through without his having to tell a lie. Apart from this, there remained a vague memory that what the kind, nice old fellow had said had not been at all so stupid as he had fancied at first, and that there was something in it that must be cleared up.

"Of course, not now," thought Levin, "but some day later on." Levin felt more than ever now that there was something not clear and not clean in his soul, and that, in regard to religion, he was in the same position which he perceived so clearly and disliked in others, and for which he blamed his friend Sviazhsky.

Levin spent that evening with his betrothed at Dolly's, and was in very high spirits. To explain to Stepan Arkadyevitch the state of excitement in which he found himself, he said that he was happy like a dog being trained to jump through a hoop, who, having at last caught the idea, and done what was required of him, whines and wags its tail, and jumps up to the table and the windows in its delight.

CHAPTER II

ON THE DAY OF THE WEDDING, ACCORDING TO THE RUSSIAN CUSTOM (the princess and Darya Alexandrovna insisted on strictly keeping all the customs), Levin did not see his betrothed, and dined at his hotel with three bachelor friends, casually brought together at his rooms. These were Sergey Ivanovitch, Katavasov, a university friend, now professor of natural science, whom Levin had met in the street and insisted on taking home with him, and Tchirikov, his best man, a Moscow conciliation-board judge, Levin's companion in his bear-hunts. The dinner was a very merry one: Sergey Ivanovitch was in his happiest mood, and was much amused by Katavasov's originality. Katavasov, feeling his originality was appreciated and understood, made the most of it. Tchirikov always gave a lively and good-humored support to conversation of any sort.

"See, now," said Katavasov, drawling his words from a habit acquired in the lecture-room, "what a capable fellow was our friend Konstantin Dmitrievitch. I'm not speaking of present company, for he's absent. At the time he left the university he was fond of science, took an interest in humanity; now one-half of his abilities is devoted to deceiving himself, and the other to justifying the deceit."

"A more determined enemy of matrimony than you I never saw," said Sergey Ivanovitch.

"Oh, no, I'm not an enemy of matrimony. I'm in favor of division of labor. People who can do nothing else ought to rear people while the rest work for their happiness and enlightenment. That's how I look at it. To muddle up two trades is the error of the amateur; I'm not one of their number."

"How happy I shall be when I hear that you're in love!" said Levin. "Please invite me to the wedding."

"I'm in love now."

"Yes, with a cuttlefish! You know," Levin turned to his brother, "Mihail Semyonovitch is writing a work on the digestive organs of the ..."

"Now, make a muddle of it! It doesn't matter what about. And the fact is, I certainly do love cuttlefish."

"But that's no hindrance to your loving your wife."

"The cuttlefish is no hindrance. The wife is the hindrance."

"Why so?"

"Oh, you'll see! You care about farming, hunting,—well, you'd better look out!"

"Arhip was here to-day; he said there were a lot of elks in Prudno, and two bears," said Tchirikov.

"Well, you must go and get them without me."

"Ah, that's the truth," said Sergey Ivanovitch. "And you may say good-bye to bear-hunting for the future—your wife won't allow it!"

Levin smiled. The picture of his wife not letting him go was so pleasant that he was ready to renounce the delights of looking upon bears forever.

"Still, it's a pity they should get those two bears without you. Do you remember last time at Hapilovo? That was a delightful hunt!" said Tchirikov.

Levin had not the heart to disillusion him of the notion that there could be something delightful apart from her, and so said nothing.

"There's some sense in this custom of saying good-bye to bachelor life," said Sergey Ivanovitch. "However happy you may be, you must regret your freedom."

"And confess there is a feeling that you want to jump out of the window, like Gogol's bridegroom?"

"Of course there is, but it isn't confessed," said Katavasov, and he broke into loud laughter.

him completely, because she knew what he would like, and because everything he liked was good. And this seemed to him perfectly clear. When the princess came to them, they were sitting side by side on the chest, sorting the dresses and disputing over Kitty's wanting to give Dunyasha the brown dress she had been wearing when Levin proposed to her, while he insisted that that dress must never be given away, but Dunyasha must have the blue one.

"How is it you don't see? She's a brunette, and it won't suit her.... I've worked it all out."

Hearing why he had come, the princess was half humorously, half seriously angry with him, and sent him home to dress and not to hinder Kitty's hair-dressing, as Charles the hair-dresser was just coming.

"As it is, she's been eating nothing lately and is losing her looks, and then you must come and upset her with your nonsense," she said to him. "Get along with you, my dear!"

Levin, guilty and shamefaced, but pacified, went back to his hotel. His brother, Darya Alexandrovna, and Stepan Arkadyevitch, all in full dress, were waiting for him to bless him with the holy picture. There was no time to lose. Darya Alexandrovna had to drive home again to fetch her curled and pomaded son, who was to carry the holy pictures after the bride. Then a carriage had to be sent for the best man, and another that would take Sergey Ivanovitch away would have to be sent back.... Altogether there were a great many most complicated matters to be considered and arranged. One thing was unmistakable, that there must be no delay, as it was already half-past six.

Nothing special happened at the ceremony of benediction with the holy picture. Stepan Arkadyevitch stood in a comically solemn pose beside his wife, took the holy picture, and telling Levin to bow down to the ground, he blessed him with his kindly, ironical smile, and kissed him three times; Darya Alexandrovna did the same, and immediately was in a hurry to get off, and again plunged into the intricate question of the destinations of the various carriages.

"Come, I'll tell you how we'll manage: you drive in our carriage to fetch him, and Sergey Ivanovitch, if he'll be so good, will drive there and then send his carriage."

"Of course; I shall be delighted."

"We'll come on directly with him. Are your things sent off?" said Stepan Arkadyevitch.

"Yes," answered Levin, and he told Kouzma to put out his clothes for him to dress.

CHAPTER III

A CROWD OF PEOPLE, PRINCIPALLY WOMEN, WAS THRONGING ROUND THE church lighted up for the wedding. Those who had not succeeded in getting into the main entrance were crowding about the windows, pushing, wrangling, and peeping through the gratings.

More than twenty carriages had already been drawn up in ranks along the street by the police. A police officer, regardless of the frost, stood at the entrance, gorgeous in his uniform. More carriages were continually driving up, and ladies wearing flowers and carrying their trains, and men taking off their helmets or black hats kept walking into the church. Inside the church both lusters were already lighted, and all the candles before the holy pictures. The gilt on the red ground of the holy picture-stand, and the gilt relief on the pictures, and the silver of the lusters and candlesticks, and the stones of the floor, and the rugs, and the banners above in the choir, and the steps of the altar, and the old blackened books, and the cassocks and surplices—all were flooded with light. On the right side of the warm church, in the crowd of frock coats and white ties, uniforms and broadcloth, velvet, satin, hair and flowers, bare shoulders and arms and long gloves, there was discreet but lively conversation that echoed strangely in the high cupola. Every time there was heard the creak of the opened door the conversation in the crowd died away, and everybody looked round expecting to see the bride and bridegroom come in. But the door had opened more than ten times, and each time it was either a belated guest or guests, who joined the circle of the invited on the right, or a spectator, who had eluded or softened the police officer, and went to join the crowd of outsiders on the left. Both the guests and the outside public had by now passed through all the phases of anticipation.

At first they imagined that the bride and bridegroom would arrive immediately, and attached no importance at all to their being late. Then they began to look more and more often towards the door, and to talk of whether anything could have happened. Then the long delay began to be positively discomforting, and relations and guests tried to look as if they were not thinking of the bridegroom but were engrossed in conversation.

The head deacon, as though to remind them of the value of his time, coughed impatiently, making the window-panes quiver in their frames. In the choir the bored choristers could be heard trying their voices and blowing their noses. The priest was continually sending first the beadle and then the deacon to find out

"It's so stupid, what happened to me, I'm ashamed to speak of it!" he said, reddening, and he was obliged to turn to Sergey Ivanovitch, who came up to him.

"This is a pretty story of yours about the shirt!" said Sergey Ivanovitch, shaking his head and smiling.

"Yes, yes!" answered Levin, without an idea of what they were talking about.

"Now, Kostya, you have to decide," said Stepan Arkadyevitch with an air of mock dismay, "a weighty question. You are at this moment just in the humor to appreciate all its gravity. They ask me, are they to light the candles that have been lighted before or candles that have never been lighted? It's a matter of ten roubles," he added, relaxing his lips into a smile. "I have decided, but I was afraid you might not agree."

Levin saw it was a joke, but he could not smile.

"Well, how's it to be then?—unlighted or lighted candles? that's the question."

"Yes, yes, unlighted."

"Oh, I'm very glad. The question's decided!" said Stepan Arkadyevitch, smiling. "How silly men are, though, in this position," he said to Tchirikov, when Levin, after looking absently at him, had moved back to his bride.

"Kitty, mind you're the first to step on the carpet," said Countess Nordston, coming up. "You're a nice person!" she said to Levin.

"Aren't you frightened, eh?" said Marya Dmitrievna, an old aunt.

"Are you cold? You're pale. Stop a minute, stoop down," said Kitty's sister, Madame Lvova, and with her plump, handsome arms she smilingly set straight the flowers on her head.

Dolly came up, tried to say something, but could not speak, cried, and then laughed unnaturally.

Kitty looked at all of them with the same absent eyes as Levin.

Meanwhile the officiating clergy had got into their vestments, and the priest and deacon came out to the lectern, which stood in the forepart of the church. The priest turned to Levin saying something. Levin did not hear what the priest said.

"Take the bride's hand and lead her up," the best man said to Levin.

It was a long while before Levin could make out what was expected of him. For a long time they tried to set him right and made him begin again—because he kept taking Kitty by the wrong arm or with the wrong arm—till he understood at last that what he had to do was, without changing his position, to take her right hand in his right hand. When at last he had taken the bride's hand in the correct way, the priest walked a few paces in front of them and stopped at the lectern. The crowd of friends and relations moved after them, with a buzz of talk and a rustle of skirts. Some one stooped down and pulled out the bride's train. The church became so still that the drops of wax could be heard falling from the candles.

The little old priest in his ecclesiastical cap, with his long silvery-gray locks of hair parted behind his ears, was fumbling with something at the lectern, putting out his little old hands from under the heavy silver vestment with the gold cross on the back of it.

Stepan Arkadyevitch approached him cautiously, whispered something, and making a sign to Levin, walked back again.

The priest lighted two candles, wreathed with flowers, and holding them sideways so that the wax dropped slowly from them he turned, facing the bridal pair. The priest was the same old man that had confessed Levin. He looked with weary and melancholy eyes at the bride and bridegroom, sighed, and putting his right hand out from his vestment, blessed the bridegroom with it, and also with a shade of solicitous tenderness laid the crossed fingers on the bowed head of Kitty. Then he gave them the candles, and taking the censer, moved slowly away from them.

"Can it be true?" thought Levin, and he looked round at his bride. Looking down at her he saw her face in profile, and from the scarcely perceptible quiver of her lips and eyelashes he knew she was aware of his eyes upon her. She did not look round, but the high scalloped collar, that reached her little pink ear, trembled faintly. He saw that a sigh was held back in her throat, and the little hand in the long glove shook as it held the candle.

All the fuss of the shirt, of being late, all the talk of friends and relations, their annoyance, his ludicrous position—all suddenly passed away and he was filled with joy and dread.

The handsome, stately head-deacon wearing a silver robe and his curly locks standing out at each side of his head, stepped smartly forward, and lifting his stole on two fingers, stood opposite the priest.

"Blessed be the name of the Lord," the solemn syllables rang out slowly one after another, setting the air quivering with waves of sound.

"Blessed is the name of our God, from the beginning, is now, and ever shall be," the little old priest answered in a submissive, piping voice, still fingering something at the lectern. And the full chorus of the unseen choir rose up, filling the whole church, from the windows to the vaulted roof, with broad waves of melody. It grew stronger, rested for an instant, and slowly died away.

Levin felt more and more that all his ideas of marriage, all his dreams of how he would order his life, were mere childishness, and that it was something he had not understood hitherto, and now understood less than ever, though it was being performed upon him. The lump in his throat rose higher and higher, tears that would not be checked came into his eyes.

CHAPTER V

IN THE CHURCH THERE WAS ALL MOSCOW, ALL THE FRIENDS AND RELATIONS; and during the ceremony of plighting troth, in the brilliantly lighted church, there was an incessant flow of discreetly subdued talk in the circle of gaily dressed women and girls, and men in white ties, frock-coats, and uniforms. The talk was principally kept up by the men, while the women were absorbed in watching every detail of the ceremony, which always means so much to them.

In the little group nearest to the bride were her two sisters: Dolly, and the other one, the self-possessed beauty, Madame Lvova, who had just arrived from abroad.

"Why is it Marie's in lilac, as bad as black, at a wedding?" said Madame Korsunskaya.

"With her complexion, it's the one salvation," responded Madame Trubetskaya. "I wonder why they had the wedding in the evening? It's like shop-people …"

"So much prettier. I was married in the evening too …" answered Madame Korsunskaya, and she sighed, remembering how charming she had been that day, and how absurdly in love her husband was, and how different it all was now.

"They say if any one's best man more than ten times, he'll never be married. I wanted to be for the tenth time, but the post was taken," said Count Siniavin to the pretty Princess Tcharskaya, who had designs on him.

Princess Tcharskaya only answered with a smile. She looked at Kitty, thinking how and when she would stand with Count Siniavin in Kitty's place, and how she would remind him then of his joke to-day.

Shtcherbatsky told the old maid of honor, Madame Nikolaeva, that he meant to put the crown on Kitty's chignon for luck.

"She ought not to have worn a chignon," answered Madame Nikolaeva, who had long ago made up her mind that if the elderly widower she was angling for married her, the wedding should be of the simplest. "I don't like such grandeur."

Sergey Ivanovitch was talking to Darya Alexandrovna, jestingly assuring her that the custom of going away after the wedding was becoming common because newly married people always felt a little ashamed of themselves.

"Your brother may feel proud of himself. She's a marvel of sweetness. I believe you're envious."

"Oh, I've got over that, Darya Alexandrovna," he answered, and a melancholy and serious expression suddenly came over his face.

Stepan Arkadyevitch was telling his sister-in-law his joke about divorce.

"The wreath wants setting straight," she answered, not hearing him.

"What a pity she's lost her looks so," Countess Nordston said to Madame Lvova. "Still he's not worth her little finger, is he?"

"Oh, I like him so—not because he's my future *beau-frère*," answered Madame Lvova. "And how well he's behaving! It's so difficult, too, to look well in such a position, not to be ridiculous. And he's not ridiculous, and not affected; one can see he's moved."

"You expected it, I suppose?"

"Almost. She always cared for him."

"Well, we shall see which of them will step on the rug first. I warned Kitty."

"It will make no difference," said Madame Lvova; "we're all obedient wives; it's in our family."

"Oh, I stepped on the rug before Vassily on purpose. And you, Dolly?"

Dolly stood beside them; she heard them, but she did not answer. She was deeply moved. The tears stood in her eyes, and she could not have spoken without crying. She was rejoicing over Kitty and Levin; going back in thought to her own wedding, she glanced at the radiant figure of Stepan Arkadyevitch, forgot all the present, and remembered only her own innocent love. She recalled not herself only, but all her women-friends and acquaintances. She thought of them on the one day of their triumph, when they had stood like Kitty under the wedding crown, with love and hope and dread in their hearts, renouncing the past, and stepping forward into the mysterious future. Among the brides that came back to her memory, she thought too of her darling Anna, of whose proposed divorce she had just been hearing. And she had stood just as innocent in orange flowers and bridal veil. And now? "It's terribly strange," she said to herself. It was not merely the sisters, the

in her face. Levin longed to say something to her, but he did not know whether it was all over. The priest got him out of his difficulty. He smiled his kindly smile and said gently, "Kiss your wife, and you kiss your husband," and took the candles out of their hands.

Levin kissed her smiling lips with timid care, gave her his arm, and with a new strange sense of closeness, walked out of the church. He did not believe, he could not believe, that it was true. It was only when their wondering and timid eyes met that he believed in it, because he felt that they were one.

After supper, the same night, the young people left for the country.

CHAPTER VII

VRONSKY AND ANNA HAD BEEN TRAVELING FOR THREE MONTHS TOGETHER IN Europe. They had visited Venice, Rome, and Naples, and had just arrived at a small Italian town where they meant to stay some time. A handsome head waiter, with thick pomaded hair parted from the neck upwards, an evening coat, a broad white cambric shirt-front, and a bunch of trinkets hanging above his rounded stomach, stood with his hands in the full curve of his pockets, looking contemptuously from under his eyelids while he gave some frigid reply to a gentleman who had stopped him. Catching the sound of footsteps coming from the other side of the entry towards the stair-case, the head waiter turned round, and seeing the Russian count, who had taken their best rooms, he took his hands out of his pockets deferentially, and with a bow informed him that a courier had been, and that the business about the palazzo had been arranged. The steward was prepared to sign the agreement.

"Ah! I'm glad to hear it," said Vronsky. "Is madame at home or not?"

"Madame has been out for a walk but has returned now," answered the waiter.

Vronsky took off his soft, wide-brimmed hat and passed his handkerchief over his heated brow and hair, which had grown half over his ears, and was brushed back covering the bald patch on his head. And glancing casually at the gentleman, who still stood there gazing intently at him, he would have gone on.

"This gentleman is a Russian, and was inquiring after you," said the head waiter.

With mingled feelings of annoyance at never being able to get away from acquaintances anywhere, and longing to find some sort of diversion from the monotony of his life, Vronsky looked once more at the gentleman, who had retreated and stood still again, and at the same moment a light came into the eyes of both.

"Golenishtchev!"

"Vronsky!"

It really was Golenishtchev, a comrade of Vronsky's in the Corps of Pages. In the corps Golenishtchev had belonged to the liberal party; he left the corps without entering the army, and had never taken office under the government. Vronsky and he had gone completely different ways on leaving the corps, and had only met once since.

At that meeting Vronsky perceived that Golenishtchev had taken up a sort of lofty, intellectually liberal line, and was consequently disposed to look down upon Vronsky's interests and calling in life. Hence Vronsky had met him with the chilling and haughty manner he so well knew how to assume, the meaning of which was: "You may like or dislike my way of life, that's a matter of the most perfect indifference to me; you will have to treat me with respect if you want to know me." Golenishtchev had been contemptuously indifferent to the tone taken by Vronsky. This second meeting might have been expected, one would have supposed, to estrange them still more. But now they beamed and exclaimed with delight on recognizing one another. Vronsky would never have expected to be so pleased to see Golenishtchev, but probably he was not himself aware how bored he was. He forgot the disagreeable impression of their last meeting, and with a face of frank delight held out his hand to his old comrade. The same expression of delight replaced the look of uneasiness on Golenishtchev's face.

"How glad I am to meet you!" said Vronsky, showing his strong white teeth in a friendly smile.

"I heard the name Vronsky, but I didn't know which one. I'm very, very glad!"

"Let's go in. Come, tell me what you're doing."

"I've been living here for two years. I'm working."

"Ah!" said Vronsky, with sympathy; "let's go in." And with the habit common with Russians, instead of saying in Russian what he wanted to keep from the servants, he began to speak in French.

"Do you know Madame Karenina? We are traveling together. I am going to see her now," he said in French, carefully scrutinizing Golenishtchev's face.

"Ah! I did not know" (though he did know), Golenishtchev answered carelessly. "Have you been here long?" he added.

fellows, with whom he was irritated and angry. Was it worth it? Vronsky disliked it, yet he felt that Golenishtchev was unhappy, and was sorry for him. Unhappiness, almost mental derangement, was visible on his mobile, rather handsome face, while without even noticing Anna's coming in, he went on hurriedly and hotly expressing his views.

When Anna came in in her hat and cape, and her lovely hand rapidly swinging her parasol, and stood beside him, it was with a feeling of relief that Vronsky broke away from the plaintive eyes of Golenishtchev which fastened persistently upon him, and with a fresh rush of love looked at his charming companion, full of life and happiness. Golenishtchev recovered himself with an effort, and at first was dejected and gloomy, but Anna, disposed to feel friendly with every one as she was at that time, soon revived his spirits by her direct and lively manner. After trying various subjects of conversation, she got him upon painting, of which he talked very well, and she listened to him attentively. They walked to the house they had taken, and looked over it.

"I am very glad of one thing," said Anna to Golenishtchev when they were on their way back, "Alexey will have a capital *atelier*. You must certainly take that room," she said to Vronsky in Russian, using the affectionately familiar form as though she saw that Golenishtchev would become intimate with them in their isolation, and that there was no need of reserve before him.

"Do you paint?" said Golenishtchev, turning round quickly to Vronsky.

"Yes, I used to study long ago, and now I have begun to do a little," said Vronsky, reddening.

"He has great talent," said Anna with a delighted smile. "I'm no judge, of course. But good judges have said the same."

CHAPTER VIII

A NNA, IN THAT FIRST PERIOD OF HER EMANCIPATION AND RAPID RETURN TO health, felt herself unpardonably happy and full of the joy of life. The thought of her husband's unhappiness did not poison her happiness. On one side that memory was too awful to be thought of. On the other side her husband's unhappiness had given her too much happiness to be regretted. The memory of all that had happened after her illness: her reconciliation with her husband, its breakdown, the news of Vronsky's wound, his visit, the preparations for divorce, the departure from her husband's house, the parting from her son—all that seemed to her like a delirious dream, from which she had waked up alone with Vronsky abroad. The thought of the harm caused to her husband aroused in her a feeling like repulsion, and akin to what a drowning man might feel who has shaken off another man clinging to him. That man did drown. It was an evil action, of course, but it was the sole means of escape, and better not to brood over these fearful facts.

One consolatory reflection upon her conduct had occurred to her at the first moment of the final rupture, and when now she recalled all the past, she remembered that one reflection. "I have inevitably made that man wretched," she thought; "but I don't want to profit by his misery. I too am suffering, and shall suffer; I am losing what I prized above everything—I am losing my good name and my son. I have done wrong, and so I don't want happiness, I don't want a divorce, and shall suffer from my shame and the separation from my child." But, however sincerely Anna had meant to suffer, she was not suffering. Shame there was not. With the tact of which both had such a large share, they had succeeded in avoiding Russian ladies abroad, and so had never placed themselves in a false position, and everywhere they had met people who pretended that they perfectly understood their position, far better indeed than they did themselves. Separation from the son she loved—even that did not cause her anguish in these early days. The baby girl—*his* child—was so sweet, and had so won Anna's heart, since she was all that was left her, that Anna rarely thought of her son.

The desire for life, waxing stronger with recovered health, was so intense, and the conditions of life were so new and pleasant, that Anna felt unpardonably happy. The more she got to know Vronsky, the more she loved him. She loved him for himself, and for his love for her. Her complete ownership of him was a continual joy to her. His presence was always sweet to her. All the traits of his character, which she learned to know better and better, were unutterably dear to her. His appearance, changed by his civilian dress, was as fascinating to her as though she were some young girl in love. In everything he said, thought, and did, she saw something particularly noble and elevated. Her adoration of him alarmed her indeed; she sought and could not find in him anything not fine. She dared not show him her sense of her own insignificance beside him. It seemed to her that, knowing this, he might sooner cease to love her; and she dreaded nothing now so much as losing his love, though she had no grounds for fearing it. But she could not help being grateful to him for his attitude to her, and showing that she appreciated it. He, who had in her

picture?" he said, handing him a Russian gazette he had received that morning, and pointing to an article on a Russian artist, living in the very same town, and just finishing a picture which had long been talked about, and had been bought beforehand. The article reproached the government and the academy for letting so remarkable an artist be left without encouragement and support.

"I've seen it," answered Golenishtchev. "Of course, he's not without talent, but it's all in a wrong direction. It's all the Ivanov-Strauss-Renan attitude to Christ and to religious painting."

"What is the subject of the picture?" asked Anna.

"Christ before Pilate. Christ is represented as a Jew with all the realism of the new school."

And the question of the subject of the picture having brought him to one of his favorite theories, Golenishtchev launched forth into a disquisition on it.

"I can't understand how they can fall into such a gross mistake. Christ always has His definite embodiment in the art of the great masters. And therefore, if they want to depict, not God, but a revolutionist or a sage, let them take from history a Socrates, a Franklin, a Charlotte Corday, but not Christ. They take the very figure which cannot be taken for their art, and then ..."

"And is it true that this Mihailov is in such poverty?" asked Vronsky, thinking that, as a Russian Mæcenas, it was his duty to assist the artist regardless of whether the picture were good or bad.

"I should say not. He's a remarkable portrait-painter. Have you ever seen his portrait of Madame Vassiltchikova? But I believe he doesn't care about painting any more portraits, and so very likely he is in want. I maintain that ..."

"Couldn't we ask him to paint a portrait of Anna Arkadyevna?" said Vronsky.

"Why mine?" said Anna. "After yours I don't want another portrait. Better have one of Annie" (so she called her baby girl). "Here she is," she added, looking out of the window at the handsome Italian nurse, who was carrying the child out into the garden, and immediately glancing unnoticed at Vronsky. The handsome nurse, from whom Vronsky was painting a head for his picture, was the one hidden grief in Anna's life. He painted with her as his model, admired her beauty and mediævalism, and Anna dared not confess to herself that she was afraid of becoming jealous of this nurse, and was for that reason particularly gracious and condescending both to her and her little son. Vronsky, too, glanced out of the window and into Anna's eyes, and, turning at once to Golenishtchev, he said:

"Do you know this Mihailov?"

"I have met him. But he's a queer fish, and quite without breeding. You know, one of those uncouth new people one's so often coming across nowadays, one of those free-thinkers you know, who are reared *d'emblée* in theories of atheism, scepticism, and materialism. In former days," said Golenishtchev, not observing, or not willing to observe, that both Anna and Vronsky wanted to speak, "in former days the free-thinker was a man who had been brought up in ideas of religion, law, and morality, and only through conflict and struggle came to free-thought; but now there has sprung up a new type of born free-thinkers who grow up without even having heard of principles of morality or of religion, of the existence of authorities, who grow up directly in ideas of negation in everything, that is to say, savages. Well, he's of that class. He's the son, it appears, of some Moscow butler, and has never had any sort of bringing-up. When he got into the academy and made his reputation he tried, as he's no fool, to educate himself. And he turned to what seemed to him the very source of culture— the magazines. In old times, you see, a man who wanted to educate himself—a Frenchman, for instance—would have set to work to study all the classics and theologians and tragedians and historians and philosophers, and, you know, all the intellectual work that came in his way. But in our day he goes straight for the literature of negation, very quickly assimilates all the extracts of the science of negation, and he's ready. And that's not all—twenty years ago he would have found in that literature traces of conflict with authorities, with the creeds of the ages; he would have perceived from this conflict that there was something else; but now he comes at once upon a literature in which the old creeds do not even furnish matter for discussion, but it is stated baldly that there is nothing else—evolution, natural selection, struggle for existence—and that's all. In my article I've ..."

"I tell you what," said Anna, who had for a long while been exchanging wary glances with Vronsky, and knew that he was not in the least interested in the education of this artist, but was simply absorbed by the idea of assisting him, and ordering a portrait of him; "I tell you what," she said, resolutely interrupting Golenishtchev, who was still talking away, "let's go and see him!"

Golenishtchev recovered his self-possession and readily agreed. But as the artist lived in a remote suburb, it was decided to take the carriage.

An hour later Anna, with Golenishtchev by her side and Vronsky on the front seat of the carriage, facing them, drove up to a new ugly house in the remote suburb. On learning from the porter's wife, who came out to them, that Mihailov saw visitors at his studio, but that at that moment he was in his lodging only a couple of steps off, they sent her to him with their cards, asking permission to see his picture.

his broad face, and the combined expression of timidity and anxiety to keep up his dignity, Mihailov made an unpleasant impression.

"Please step in," he said, trying to look indifferent, and going into the passage he took a key out of his pocket and opened the door.

CHAPTER XI

ON ENTERING THE STUDIO, MIHAILOV ONCE MORE SCANNED HIS VISITORS and noted down in his imagination Vronsky's expression too, and especially his jaws. Although his artistic sense was unceasingly at work collecting materials, although he felt a continually increasing excitement as the moment of criticizing his work drew nearer, he rapidly and subtly formed, from imperceptible signs, a mental image of these three persons.

That fellow (Golenishtchev) was a Russian living here. Mihailov did not remember his surname nor where he had met him, nor what he had said to him. He only remembered his face as he remembered all the faces he had ever seen; but he remembered, too, that it was one of the faces laid by in his memory in the immense class of the falsely consequential and poor in expression. The abundant hair and very open forehead gave an appearance of consequence to the face, which had only one expression—a petty, childish, peevish expression, concentrated just above the bridge of the narrow nose. Vronsky and Madame Karenina must be, Mihailov supposed, distinguished and wealthy Russians, knowing nothing about art, like all those wealthy Russians, but posing as amateurs and connoisseurs. "Most likely they've already looked at all the antiques, and now they're making the round of the studios of the new people, the German humbug, and the cracked Pre-Raphaelite English fellow, and have only come to me to make the point of view complete," he thought. He was well acquainted with the way dilettanti have (the cleverer they were the worse he found them) of looking at the works of contemporary artists with the sole object of being in a position to say that art is a thing of the past, and that the more one sees of the new men the more one sees how inimitable the works of the great old masters have remained. He expected all this; he saw it all in their faces, he saw it in the careless indifference with which they talked among themselves, stared at the lay figures and busts, and walked about in leisurely fashion, waiting for him to uncover his picture. But in spite of this, while he was turning over his studies, pulling up the blinds and taking off the sheet, he was in intense excitement, especially as, in spite of his conviction that all distinguished and wealthy Russians were certain to be beasts and fools, he liked Vronsky, and still more Anna.

"Here, if you please," he said, moving on one side with his nimble gait and pointing to his picture, "it's the exhortation to Pilate. Matthew, chapter xxvii," he said, feeling his lips were beginning to tremble with emotion. He moved away and stood behind them.

For the few seconds during which the visitors were gazing at the picture in silence Mihailov too gazed at it with the indifferent eye of an outsider. For those few seconds he was sure in anticipation that a higher, juster criticism would be uttered by them, by those very visitors whom he had been so despising a moment before. He forgot all he had thought about his picture before during the three years he had been painting it; he forgot all its qualities which had been absolutely certain to him—he saw the picture with their indifferent, new, outside eyes, and saw nothing good in it. He saw in the foreground Pilate's irritated face and the serene face of Christ, and in the background the figures of Pilate's retinue and the face of John watching what was happening. Every face that, with such agony, such blunders and corrections had grown up within him with its special character, every face that had given him such torments and such raptures, and all these faces so many times transposed for the sake of the harmony of the whole, all the shades of color and tones that he had attained with such labor—all of this together seemed to him now, looking at it with their eyes, the merest vulgarity, something that had been done a thousand times over. The face dearest to him, the face of Christ, the center of the picture, which had given him such ecstasy as it unfolded itself to him, was utterly lost to him when he glanced at the picture with their eyes. He saw a well-painted (no, not even that—he distinctly saw now a mass of defects) repetition of those endless Christs of Titian, Raphael, Rubens, and the same soldiers and Pilate. It was all common, poor, and stale, and positively badly painted—weak and unequal. They would be justified in repeating hypocritically civil speeches in the presence of the painter, and pitying him and laughing at him when they were alone again.

The silence (though it lasted no more than a minute) became too intolerable to him. To break it, and to show he was not agitated, he made an effort and addressed Golenishtchev.

"I think I've had the pleasure of meeting you," he said, looking uneasily first at Anna, then at Vronsky, in fear of losing any shade of their expression.

"Yes; but in that case, if you will allow me to say what I think … Your picture is so fine that my observation cannot detract from it, and, besides, it is only my personal opinion. With you it is different. Your very motive is different. But let us take Ivanov. I imagine that if Christ is brought down to the level of an historical character, it would have been better for Ivanov to select some other historical subject, fresh, untouched."

"But if this is the greatest subject presented to art?"

"If one looked one would find others. But the point is that art cannot suffer doubt and discussion. And before the picture of Ivanov the question arises for the believer and the unbeliever alike, 'Is it God, or is it not God?' and the unity of the impression is destroyed."

"Why so? I think that for educated people," said Mihailov, "the question cannot exist."

Golenishtchev did not agree with this, and confounded Mihailov by his support of his first idea of the unity of the impression being essential to art.

Mihailov was greatly perturbed, but he could say nothing in defense of his own idea.

CHAPTER XII

A NNA AND VRONSKY HAD LONG BEEN EXCHANGING GLANCES, REGRETTING their friend's flow of cleverness. At last Vronsky, without waiting for the artist, walked away to another small picture.

"Oh, how exquisite! What a lovely thing! A gem! How exquisite!" they cried with one voice.

"What is it they're so pleased with?" thought Mihailov. He had positively forgotten that picture he had painted three years ago. He had forgotten all the agonies and the ecstasies he had lived through with that picture when for several months it had been the one thought haunting him day and night. He had forgotten, as he always forgot, the pictures he had finished. He did not even like to look at it, and had only brought it out because he was expecting an Englishman who wanted to buy it.

"Oh, that's only an old study," he said.

"How fine!" said Golenishtchev, he too, with unmistakable sincerity, falling under the spell of the picture.

Two boys were angling in the shade of a willow-tree. The elder had just dropped in the hook, and was carefully pulling the float from behind a bush, entirely absorbed in what he was doing. The other, a little younger, was lying in the grass leaning on his elbows, with his tangled, flaxen head in his hands, staring at the water with his dreamy blue eyes. What was he thinking of?

The enthusiasm over this picture stirred some of the old feeling for it in Mihailov, but he feared and disliked this waste of feeling for things past, and so, even though this praise was grateful to him, he tried to draw his visitors away to a third picture.

But Vronsky asked whether the picture was for sale. To Mihailov at that moment, excited by visitors, it was extremely distasteful to speak of money matters.

"It is put up there to be sold," he answered, scowling gloomily.

When the visitors had gone, Mihailov sat down opposite the picture of Pilate and Christ, and in his mind went over what had been said, and what, though not said, had been implied by those visitors. And, strange to say, what had had such weight with him, while they were there and while he mentally put himself at their point of view, suddenly lost all importance for him. He began to look at his picture with all his own full artist vision, and was soon in that mood of conviction of the perfectibility, and so of the significance, of his picture—a conviction essential to the most intense fervor, excluding all other interests—in which alone he could work.

Christ's foreshortened leg was not right, though. He took his palette and began to work. As he corrected the leg he looked continually at the figure of John in the background, which his visitors had not even noticed, but which he knew was beyond perfection. When he had finished the leg he wanted to touch that figure, but he felt too much excited for it. He was equally unable to work when he was cold and when he was too much affected and saw everything too much. There was only one stage in the transition from coldness to inspiration, at which work was possible. To-day he was too much agitated. He would have covered the picture, but he stopped, holding the cloth in his hand, and, smiling blissfully, gazed a long while at the figure of John. At last, as it were regretfully tearing himself away, he dropped the cloth, and, exhausted but happy, went home.

Vronsky, Anna, and Golenishtchev, on their way home, were particularly lively and cheerful. They talked of Mihailov and his pictures. The word *talent*, by which they meant an inborn, almost physical, aptitude apart from brain and heart, and in which they tried to find an expression for all the artist had gained from life, recurred particularly often in their talk, as though it were necessary to the lover. Just such a distasteful sensation was what Mihailov felt at the sight of Vronsky's painting: he felt it both ludicrous and irritating, both pitiable and offensive.

Vronsky's interest in painting and the Middle Ages did not last long. He had enough taste for painting to be unable to finish his picture. The picture came to a standstill. He was vaguely aware that its defects, inconspicuous at first, would be glaring if he were to go on with it. The same experience befell him as Golenishtchev, who felt that he had nothing to say, and continually deceived himself with the theory that his idea was not yet mature, that he was working it out and collecting materials. This exasperated and tortured Golenishtchev, but Vronsky was incapable of deceiving and torturing himself, and even more incapable of exasperation. With his characteristic decision, without explanation or apology, he simply ceased working at painting.

But without this occupation, the life of Vronsky and of Anna, who wondered at his loss of interest in it, struck them as intolerably tedious in an Italian town. The palazzo suddenly seemed so obtrusively old and dirty, the spots on the curtains, the cracks in the floors, the broken plaster on the cornices became so disagreeably obvious, and the everlasting sameness of Golenishtchev, and the Italian professor and the German traveler became so wearisome, that they had to make some change. They resolved to go to Russia, to the country. In Petersburg Vronsky intended to arrange a partition of the land with his brother, while Anna meant to see her son. The summer they intended to spend on Vronsky's great family estate.

CHAPTER XIV

L EVIN HAD BEEN MARRIED THREE MONTHS. HE WAS HAPPY, BUT NOT AT ALL IN the way he had expected to be. At every step he found his former dreams disappointed, and new, unexpected surprises of happiness. He was happy; but on entering upon family life he saw at every step that it was utterly different from what he had imagined. At every step he experienced what a man would experience who, after admiring the smooth, happy course of a little boat on a lake, should get himself into that little boat. He saw that it was not all sitting still, floating smoothly; that one had to think too, not for an instant to forget where one was floating; and that there was water under one, and that one must row; and that his unaccustomed hands would be sore; and that it was only to look at it that was easy; but that doing it, though very delightful, was very difficult.

As a bachelor, when he had watched other people's married life, seen the petty cares, the squabbles, the jealousy, he had only smiled contemptuously in his heart. In his future married life there could be, he was convinced, nothing of that sort; even the external forms, indeed, he fancied, must be utterly unlike the life of others in everything. And all of a sudden, instead of his life with his wife being made on an individual pattern, it was, on the contrary, entirely made up of the pettiest details, which he had so despised before, but which now, by no will of his own, had gained an extraordinary importance that it was useless to contend against. And Levin saw that the organization of all these details was by no means so easy as he had fancied before. Although Levin believed himself to have the most exact conceptions of domestic life, unconsciously, like all men, he pictured domestic life as the happiest enjoyment of love, with nothing to hinder and no petty cares to distract. He ought, as he conceived the position, to do his work, and to find repose from it in the happiness of love. She ought to be beloved, and nothing more. But, like all men, he forgot that she too would want work. And he was surprised that she, his poetic, exquisite Kitty, could, not merely in the first weeks, but even in the first days of their married life, think, remember, and busy herself about table-cloths, and furniture, about mattresses for visitors, about a tray, about the cook, and the dinner, and so on. While they were still engaged, he had been struck by the definiteness with which she had declined the tour abroad and decided to go into the country, as though she knew of something she wanted, and could still think of something outside her love. This had jarred upon him then, and now her trivial cares and anxieties jarred upon him several times. But he saw that this was essential for her. And, loving her as he did, though he did not understand the reason of them, and jeered at these domestic pursuits, he could not help admiring them. He jeered at the way in which she arranged the furniture they had brought from Moscow; rearranged their room; hung up curtains; prepared rooms for visitors; a room for Dolly; saw after an abode for her new maid; ordered dinner of the old cook; came into collision with Agafea Mihalovna, taking from her the charge of the stores. He saw how the old cook smiled, admiring her, and listening to her inexperienced, impossible orders, how mournfully and tenderly Agafea Mihalovna shook her head over the young mistress's new arrangements. He saw that Kitty was extraordinarily sweet when, laughing and crying, she came to tell him that her maid, Masha, was used to looking upon her as her young lady, and so no

period, when both were rarely in a normal frame of mind, both were rarely quite themselves.

It was only in the third month of their married life, after their return from Moscow, where they had been staying for a month, that their life began to go more smoothly.

CHAPTER XV

THEY HAD JUST COME BACK FROM MOSCOW, AND WERE GLAD TO BE ALONE. He was sitting at the writing-table in his study, writing. She, wearing the dark lilac dress she had worn during the first days of their married life, and put on again to-day, a dress particularly remembered and loved by him, was sitting on the sofa, the same old-fashioned leather sofa which had always stood in the study in Levin's father's and grandfather's days. She was sewing at *broderie anglaise*. He thought and wrote, never losing the happy consciousness of her presence. His work, both on the land and on the book, in which the principles of the new land system were to be laid down, had not been abandoned; but just as formerly these pursuits and ideas had seemed to him petty and trivial in comparison with the darkness that overspread all life, now they seemed as unimportant and petty in comparison with the life that lay before him suffused with the brilliant light of happiness. He went on with his work, but he felt now that the center of gravity of his attention had passed to something else, and that consequently he looked at his work quite differently and more clearly. Formerly this work had been for him an escape from life. Formerly he had felt that without this work his life would be too gloomy. Now these pursuits were necessary for him that life might not be too uniformly bright. Taking up his manuscript, reading through what he had written, he found with pleasure that the work was worth his working at. Many of his old ideas seemed to him superfluous and extreme, but many blanks became distinct to him when he reviewed the whole thing in his memory. He was writing now a new chapter on the causes of the present disastrous condition of agriculture in Russia. He maintained that the poverty of Russia arises not merely from the anomalous distribution of landed property and misdirected reforms, but that what had contributed of late years to this result was the civilization from without abnormally grafted upon Russia, especially facilities of communication, as railways, leading to centralization in towns, the development of luxury, and the consequent development of manufactures, credit and its accompaniment of speculation—all to the detriment of agriculture. It seemed to him that in a normal development of wealth in a state all these phenomena would arise only when a considerable amount of labor had been put into agriculture, when it had come under regular, or at least definite, conditions; that the wealth of a country ought to increase proportionally, and especially in such a way that other sources of wealth should not outstrip agriculture; that in harmony with a certain stage of agriculture there should be means of communication corresponding to it, and that in our unsettled condition of the land, railways, called into being by political and not by economic needs, were premature, and instead of promoting agriculture, as was expected of them, they were competing with agriculture and promoting the development of manufactures and credit, and so arresting its progress; and that just as the one-sided and premature development of one organ in an animal would hinder its general development, so in the general development of wealth in Russia, credit, facilities of communication, manufacturing activity, indubitably necessary in Europe, where they had arisen in their proper time, had with us only done harm, by throwing into the background the chief question calling for settlement—the question of the organization of agriculture.

While he was writing his ideas she was thinking how unnaturally cordial her husband had been to young Prince Tcharsky, who had, with great want of tact, flirted with her the day before they left Moscow. "He's jealous," she thought. "Goodness! how sweet and silly he is! He's jealous of me! If he knew that I think no more of them than of Piotr the cook," she thought, looking at his head and red neck with a feeling of possession strange to herself. "Though it's a pity to take him from his work (but he has plenty of time!), I must look at his face; will he feel I'm looking at him? I wish he'd turn round ... I'll *will* him to!" and she opened her eyes wide, as though to intensify the influence of her gaze.

"Yes, they draw away all the sap and give a false appearance of prosperity," he muttered, stopping to write, and, feeling that she was looking at him and smiling, he looked round.

"Well?" he queried, smiling, and getting up.

"He looked round," she thought.

"It's nothing; I wanted you to look round," she said, watching him, and trying to guess whether he was vexed at being interrupted or not.

"How happy we are alone together!—I am, that is," he said, going up to her with a radiant smile of happiness.

But Levin did not hear her. Flushing, he took the letter from Marya Nikolaevna, his brother's former mistress, and began to read it. This was the second letter he had received from Marya Nikolaevna. In the first letter, Marya Nikolaevna wrote that his brother had sent her away for no fault of hers, and, with touching simplicity, added that though she was in want again, she asked for nothing, and wished for nothing, but was only tormented by the thought that Nikolay Dmitrievitch would come to grief without her, owing to the weak state of his health, and begged his brother to look after him. Now she wrote quite differently. She had found Nikolay Dmitrievitch, had again made it up with him in Moscow, and had moved with him to a provincial town, where he had received a post in the government service. But that he had quarreled with the head official, and was on his way back to Moscow, only he had been taken so ill on the road that it was doubtful if he would ever leave his bed again, she wrote. "It's always of you he has talked, and, besides, he has no more money left."

"Read this; Dolly writes about you," Kitty was beginning, with a smile; but she stopped suddenly, noticing the changed expression on her husband's face.

"What is it? What's the matter?"

"She writes to me that Nikolay, my brother, is at death's door. I shall go to him."

Kitty's face changed at once. Thoughts of Tanya as a marquise, of Dolly, all had vanished.

"When are you going?" she said.

"To-morrow."

"And I will go with you, can I?" she said.

"Kitty! What are you thinking of?" he said reproachfully.

"How do you mean?" offended that he should seem to take her suggestion unwillingly and with vexation. "Why shouldn't I go? I shan't be in your way. I ..."

"I'm going because my brother is dying," said Levin. "Why should you ..."

"Why? For the same reason as you."

"And, at a moment of such gravity for me, she only thinks of her being dull by herself," thought Levin. And this lack of candor in a matter of such gravity infuriated him.

"It's out of the question," he said sternly.

Agafea Mihalovna, seeing that it was coming to a quarrel, gently put down her cup and withdrew. Kitty did not even notice her. The tone in which her husband had said the last words wounded her, especially because he evidently did not believe what she had said.

"I tell you, that if you go, I shall come with you; I shall certainly come," she said hastily and wrathfully. "Why out of the question? Why do you say it's out of the question?"

"Because it'll be going God knows where, by all sorts of roads and to all sorts of hotels. You would be a hindrance to me," said Levin, trying to be cool.

"Not at all. I don't want anything. Where you can go, I can...."

"Well, for one thing then, because this woman's there whom you can't meet."

"I don't know and don't care to know who's there and what. I know that my husband's brother is dying and my husband is going to him, and I go with my husband too...."

"Kitty! Don't get angry. But just think a little: this is a matter of such importance that I can't bear to think that you should bring in a feeling of weakness, of dislike to being left alone. Come, you'll be dull alone, so go and stay at Moscow a little."

"There, you always ascribe base, vile motives to me," she said with tears of wounded pride and fury. "I didn't mean, it wasn't weakness, it wasn't ... I feel that it's my duty to be with my husband when he's in trouble, but you try on purpose to hurt me, you try on purpose not to understand...."

"No; this is awful! To be such a slave!" cried Levin, getting up, and unable to restrain his anger any longer. But at the same second he felt that he was beating himself.

"Then why did you marry? You could have been free. Why did you, if you regret it?" she said, getting up and running away into the drawing-room.

When he went to her, she was sobbing.

He began to speak, trying to find words not to dissuade but simply to soothe her. But she did not heed him, and would not agree to anything. He bent down to her and took her hand, which resisted him. He kissed her hand, kissed her hair, kissed her hand again—still she was silent. But when he took her face in both his hands and said "Kitty!" she suddenly recovered herself, and began to cry, and they were reconciled.

It was decided that they should go together the next day. Levin told his wife that he believed she wanted to go simply in order to be of use, agreed that Marya Nikolaevna's being with his brother did not make her going improper, but he set off at the bottom of his heart dissatisfied both with her and with himself. He was dissatisfied with her for being unable to make up her mind to let him go when it was necessary (and how strange it was for him to think that he, so lately hardly daring to believe in such happiness as that she could love him—now was unhappy because she loved him too much!), and he was

condition of things. He had expected himself to feel the same distress at the loss of the brother he loved and the same horror in face of death as he had felt then, only in a greater degree. And he had prepared himself for this; but he found something utterly different.

In a little dirty room with the painted panels of its walls filthy with spittle, and conversation audible through the thin partition from the next room, in a stifling atmosphere saturated with impurities, on a bedstead moved away from the wall, there lay covered with a quilt, a body. One arm of this body was above the quilt, and the wrist, huge as a rake-handle, was attached, inconceivably it seemed, to the thin, long bone of the arm smooth from the beginning to the middle. The head lay sideways on the pillow. Levin could see the scanty locks wet with sweat on the temples and tense, transparent-looking forehead.

"It cannot be that that fearful body was my brother Nikolay?" thought Levin. But he went closer, saw the face, and doubt became impossible. In spite of the terrible change in the face, Levin had only to glance at those eager eyes raised at his approach, only to catch the faint movement of the mouth under the sticky mustache, to realize the terrible truth that this death-like body was his living brother.

The glittering eyes looked sternly and reproachfully at his brother as he drew near. And immediately this glance established a living relationship between living men. Levin immediately felt the reproach in the eyes fixed on him, and felt remorse at his own happiness.

When Konstantin took him by the hand, Nikolay smiled. The smile was faint, scarcely perceptible, and in spite of the smile the stern expression of the eyes was unchanged.

"You did not expect to find me like this," he articulated with effort.

"Yes ... no," said Levin, hesitating over his words. "How was it you didn't let me know before, that is, at the time of my wedding? I made inquiries in all directions."

He had to talk so as not to be silent, and he did not know what to say, especially as his brother made no reply, and simply stared without dropping his eyes, and evidently penetrated to the inner meaning of each word. Levin told his brother that his wife had come with him. Nikolay expressed pleasure, but said he was afraid of frightening her by his condition. A silence followed. Suddenly Nikolay stirred, and began to say something. Levin expected something of peculiar gravity and importance from the expression of his face, but Nikolay began speaking of his health. He found fault with the doctor, regretting he had not a celebrated Moscow doctor. Levin saw that he still hoped.

Seizing the first moment of silence, Levin got up, anxious to escape, if only for an instant, from his agonizing emotion, and said that he would go and fetch his wife.

"Very well, and I'll tell her to tidy up here. It's dirty and stinking here, I expect. Marya! clear up the room," the sick man said with effort. "Oh, and when you've cleared up, go away yourself," he added, looking inquiringly at his brother.

Levin made no answer. Going out into the corridor, he stopped short. He had said he would fetch his wife, but now, taking stock of the emotion he was feeling, he decided that he would try on the contrary to persuade her not to go in to the sick man. "Why should she suffer as I am suffering?" he thought.

"Well, how is he?" Kitty asked with a frightened face.

"Oh, it's awful, it's awful! What did you come for?" said Levin.

Kitty was silent for a few seconds, looking timidly and ruefully at her husband; then she went up and took him by the elbow with both hands.

"Kostya! take me to him; it will be easier for us to bear it together. You only take me, take me to him, please, and go away," she said. "You must understand that for me to see you, and not to see him, is far more painful. There I might be a help to you and to him. Please, let me!" she besought her husband, as though the happiness of her life depended on it.

Levin was obliged to agree, and regaining his composure, and completely forgetting about Marya Nikolaevna by now, he went again in to his brother with Kitty.

Stepping lightly, and continually glancing at her husband, showing him a valorous and sympathetic face, Kitty went into the sick-room, and, turning without haste, noiselessly closed the door. With inaudible steps she went quickly to the sick man's bedside, and going up so that he had not to turn his head, she immediately clasped in her fresh young hand the skeleton of his huge hand, pressed it, and began speaking with that soft eagerness, sympathetic and not jarring, which is peculiar to women.

"We have met, though we were not acquainted, at Soden," she said. "You never thought I was to be your sister?"

"You would not have recognized me?" he said, with a radiant smile at her entrance.

"Yes, I should. What a good thing you let us know! Not a day has passed that Kostya has not mentioned you, and been anxious."

But the sick man's interest did not last long.

The doctor brought by Levin, and found by him at the club, was not the one who had been attending Nikolay Levin, as the patient was dissatisfied with him. The new doctor took up a stethoscope and sounded the patient, shook his head, prescribed medicine, and with extreme minuteness explained first how to take the medicine and then what diet was to be kept to. He advised eggs, raw or hardly cooked, and seltzer water, with warm milk at a certain temperature. When the doctor had gone away the sick man said something to his brother, of which Levin could distinguish only the last words: "Your Katya." By the expression with which he gazed at her, Levin saw that he was praising her. He called indeed to Katya, as he called her.

"I'm much better already," he said. "Why, with you I should have got well long ago. How nice it is!" he took her hand and drew it towards his lips, but as though afraid she would dislike it he changed his mind, let it go, and only stroked it. Kitty took his hand in both hers and pressed it.

"Now turn me over on the left side and go to bed," he said.

No one could make out what he said but Kitty; she alone understood. She understood because she was all the while mentally keeping watch on what he needed.

"On the other side," she said to her husband, "he always sleeps on that side. Turn him over, it's so disagreeable calling the servants. I'm not strong enough. Can you?" she said to Marya Nikolaevna.

"I'm afraid not," answered Marya Nikolaevna.

Terrible as it was to Levin to put his arms round that terrible body, to take hold of that under the quilt, of which he preferred to know nothing, under his wife's influence he made his resolute face that she knew so well, and putting his arms into the bed took hold of the body, but in spite of his own strength he was struck by the strange heaviness of those powerless limbs. While he was turning him over, conscious of the huge emaciated arm about his neck, Kitty swiftly and noiselessly turned the pillow, beat it up and settled in it the sick man's head, smoothing back his hair, which was sticking again to his moist brow.

The sick man kept his brother's hand in his own. Levin felt that he meant to do something with his hand and was pulling it somewhere. Levin yielded with a sinking heart: yes, he drew it to his mouth and kissed it. Levin, shaking with sobs and unable to articulate a word, went out of the room.

CHAPTER XIX

T HOU HAST HID THESE THINGS FROM THE WISE AND PRUDENT, AND HAST
revealed them unto babes." So Levin thought about his wife as he talked to her that evening.

Levin thought of the text, not because he considered himself "wise and
prudent." He did not so consider himself, but he could not help knowing that
he had more intellect than his wife and Agafea Mihalovna, and he could not
help knowing that when he thought of death, he thought with all the force of
his intellect. He knew too that the brains of many great men, whose thoughts
he had read, had brooded over death and yet knew not a hundredth part of
what his wife and Agafea Mihalovna knew about it. Different as those two
women were, Agafea Mihalovna and Katya, as his brother Nikolay had called
her, and as Levin particularly liked to call her now, they were quite alike in
this. Both knew, without a shade of doubt, what sort of thing life was and what
was death, and though neither of them could have answered, and would even
not have understood the questions that presented themselves to Levin, both
had no doubt of the significance of this event, and were precisely alike in their
way of looking at it, which they shared with millions of people. The proof
that they knew for a certainty the nature of death lay in the fact that they knew
without a second of hesitation how to deal with the dying, and were not frightened of them. Levin and other men like him, though they could have said a
great deal about death, obviously did not know this since they were afraid of
death, and were absolutely at a loss what to do when people were dying. If
Levin had been alone now with his brother Nikolay, he would have looked at
him with terror, and with still greater terror waited, and would not have known
what else to do.

More than that, he did not know what to say, how to look, how to move.
To talk of outside things seemed to him shocking, impossible, to talk of death
and depressing subjects—also impossible. To be silent, also impossible. "If
I look at him he will think I am studying him, I am afraid; if I don't look at
him, he'll think I'm thinking of other things. If I walk on tiptoe, he will be
vexed; to tread firmly, I'm ashamed." Kitty evidently did not think of herself,
and had no time to think about herself: she was thinking about him because she
knew something, and all went well. She told him about herself even and about
her wedding, and smiled and sympathized with him and petted him, and talked
of cases of recovery and all went well; so then she must know. The proof that

CHAPTER XX

THE NEXT DAY THE SICK MAN RECEIVED THE SACRAMENT AND EXTREME unction. During the ceremony Nikolay Levin prayed fervently. His great eyes, fastened on the holy image that was set out on a card-table covered with a colored napkin, expressed such passionate prayer and hope that it was awful to Levin to see it. Levin knew that this passionate prayer and hope would only make him feel more bitterly parting from the life he so loved. Levin knew his brother and the workings of his intellect: he knew that his unbelief came not from life being easier for him without faith, but had grown up because step by step the contemporary scientific interpretation of natural phenomena crushed out the possibility of faith; and so he knew that his present return was not a legitimate one, brought about by way of the same working of his intellect, but simply a temporary, interested return to faith in a desperate hope of recovery. Levin knew too that Kitty had strengthened his hope by accounts of the marvelous recoveries she had heard of. Levin knew all this; and it was agonizingly painful to him to behold the supplicating, hopeful eyes and the emaciated wrist, lifted with difficulty, making the sign of the cross on the tense brow, and the prominent shoulders and hollow, gasping chest, which one could not feel consistent with the life the sick man was praying for. During the sacrament Levin did what he, an unbeliever, had done a thousand times. He said, addressing God, "If Thou dost exist, make this man to recover" (of course this same thing has been repeated many times), "and Thou wilt save him and me."

After extreme unction the sick man became suddenly much better. He did not cough once in the course of an hour, smiled, kissed Kitty's hand, thanking her with tears, and said he was comfortable, free from pain, and that he felt strong and had an appetite. He even raised himself when his soup was brought, and asked for a cutlet as well. Hopelessly ill as he was, obvious as it was at the first glance that he could not recover, Levin and Kitty were for that hour both in the same state of excitement, happy, though fearful of being mistaken.

"Is he better?"

"Yes, much."

"It's wonderful."

"There's nothing wonderful in it."

"Anyway, he's better," they said in a whisper, smiling to one another.

This self-deception was not of long duration. The sick man fell into a quiet sleep, but he was waked up half an hour later by his cough. And all at once every hope vanished in those about him and in himself. The reality of his suffering crushed all hopes in Levin and Kitty and in the sick man himself, leaving no doubt, no memory even of past hopes.

Without referring to what he had believed in half an hour before, as though ashamed even to recall it, he asked for iodine to inhale in a bottle covered with perforated paper. Levin gave him the bottle, and the same look of passionate hope with which he had taken the sacrament was now fastened on his brother, demanding from him the confirmation of the doctor's words that inhaling iodine worked wonders.

"Is Katya not here?" he gasped, looking round while Levin reluctantly assented to the doctor's words. "No; so I can say it … It was for her sake I went through that farce. She's so sweet; but you and I can't deceive ourselves. This is what I believe in," he said, and, squeezing the bottle in his bony hand, he began breathing over it.

At eight o'clock in the evening Levin and his wife were drinking tea in their room when Marya Nikolaevna ran in to them breathlessly. She was pale, and her lips were quivering. "He is dying!" she whispered. "I'm afraid he will die this minute."

Both of them ran to him. He was sitting raised up with one elbow on the bed, his long back bent, and his head hanging low.

"How do you feel?" Levin asked in a whisper, after a silence.

"I feel I'm setting off," Nikolay said with difficulty, but with extreme distinctness, screwing the words out of himself. He did not raise his head, but simply turned his eyes upwards, without their reaching his brother's face. "Katya, go away!" he added.

Levin jumped up, and with a peremptory whisper made her go out.

"I'm setting off," he said again.

"Why do you think so?" said Levin, so as to say something.

"Because I'm setting off," he repeated, as though he had a liking for the phrase. "It's the end."

Marya Nikolaevna went up to him.

"You had better lie down; you'd be easier," she said.

"I shall lie down soon enough," he pronounced slowly, "when I'm dead," he said sarcastically, wrathfully. "Well, you can lay me down if you like."

Levin laid his brother on his back, sat down beside him, and gazed at his face, holding his breath. The dying man lay with closed eyes, but the muscles twitched from time to time on his forehead, as with one thinking deeply and intensely. Levin involuntarily thought with him of what it was that was

His sufferings, steadily growing more intense, did their work and prepared him for death. There was no position in which he was not in pain, there was not a minute in which he was unconscious of it, not a limb, not a part of his body that did not ache and cause him agony. Even the memories, the impressions, the thoughts of this body awakened in him now the same aversion as the body itself. The sight of other people, their remarks, his own reminiscences, everything was for him a source of agony. Those about him felt this, and instinctively did not allow themselves to move freely, to talk, to express their wishes before him. All his life was merged in the one feeling of suffering and desire to be rid of it.

There was evidently coming over him that revulsion that would make him look upon death as the goal of his desires, as happiness. Hitherto each individual desire, aroused by suffering or privation, such as hunger, fatigue, thirst, had been satisfied by some bodily function giving pleasure. But now no physical craving or suffering received relief, and the effort to relieve them only caused fresh suffering. And so all desires were merged in one—the desire to be rid of all his sufferings and their source, the body. But he had no words to express this desire of deliverance, and so he did not speak of it, and from habit asked for the satisfaction of desires which could not now be satisfied. "Turn me over on the other side," he would say, and immediately after he would ask to be turned back again as before. "Give me some broth. Take away the broth. Talk of something: why are you silent?" And directly they began to talk he would close his eyes, and would show weariness, indifference, and loathing.

On the tenth day from their arrival at the town, Kitty was unwell. She suffered from headache and sickness, and she could not get up all the morning.

The doctor opined that the indisposition arose from fatigue and excitement, and prescribed rest.

After dinner, however, Kitty got up and went as usual with her work to the sick man. He looked at her sternly when she came in, and smiled contemptuously when she said she had been unwell. That day he was continually blowing his nose, and groaning piteously.

"How do you feel?" she asked him.

"Worse," he articulated with difficulty. "In pain!"

"In pain, where?"

"Everywhere."

"It will be over to-day, you will see," said Marya Nikolaevna. Though it was said in a whisper, the sick man, whose hearing Levin had noticed was very keen, must have heard. Levin said hush to her, and looked round at the sick man. Nikolay had heard; but these words produced no effect on him. His eyes had still the same intense, reproachful look.

"Why do you think so?" Levin asked her, when she had followed him into the corridor.

"He has begun picking at himself," said Marya Nikolaevna.

"How do you mean?"

"Like this," she said, tugging at the folds of her woolen skirt. Levin noticed, indeed, that all that day the patient pulled at himself, as it were, trying to snatch something away.

Marya Nikolaevna's prediction came true. Towards night the sick man was not able to lift his hands, and could only gaze before him with the same intensely concentrated expression in his eyes. Even when his brother or Kitty bent over him, so that he could see them, he looked just the same. Kitty sent for the priest to read the prayer for the dying.

While the priest was reading it, the dying man did not show any sign of life; his eyes were closed. Levin, Kitty, and Marya Nikolaevna stood at the bedside. The priest had not quite finished reading the prayer when the dying man stretched, sighed, and opened his eyes. The priest, on finishing the prayer, put the cross to the cold forehead, then slowly returned it to the stand, and after standing for two minutes more in silence, he touched the huge, bloodless hand that was turning cold.

"He is gone," said the priest, and would have moved away; but suddenly there was a faint stir in the mustaches of the dead man that seemed glued together, and quite distinctly in the hush they heard from the bottom of the chest the sharply defined sounds:

"Not quite ... soon."

And a minute later the face brightened, a smile came out under the mustaches, and the women who had gathered round began carefully laying out the corpse.

The sight of his brother, and the nearness of death, revived in Levin that sense of horror in face of the insoluble enigma, together with the nearness and inevitability of death, that had come upon him that autumn evening when his brother had come to him. This feeling was now even stronger than before; even less than before did he feel capable of apprehending the meaning of death, and its inevitability rose up before him more terrible than ever. But now, thanks to his wife's presence, that feeling did not reduce him to despair. In spite of death, he felt the need of life and love. He felt that love saved him from despair, and that this love, under the menace of despair, had become still stronger and purer.

On completing his high school and university courses with medals, Alexey Alexandrovitch had, with his uncle's aid, immediately started in a prominent position in the service, and from that time forward he had devoted himself exclusively to political ambition. In the high school and the university, and afterwards in the service, Alexey Alexandrovitch had never formed a close friendship with any one. His brother had been the person nearest to his heart, but he had a post in the Ministry of Foreign Affairs, and was always abroad, where he had died shortly after Alexey Alexandrovitch's marriage.

While he was governor of a province, Anna's aunt, a wealthy provincial lady, had thrown him—middle-aged as he was, though young for a governor—with her niece, and had succeeded in putting him in such a position that he had either to declare himself or to leave the town. Alexey Alexandrovitch was not long in hesitation. There were at the time as many reasons for the step as against it, and there was no over-balancing consideration to outweigh his invariable rule of abstaining when in doubt. But Anna's aunt had through a common acquaintance insinuated that he had already compromised the girl, and that he was in honor bound to make her an offer. He made the offer, and concentrated on his betrothed and his wife all the feeling of which he was capable.

The attachment he felt to Anna precluded in his heart every need of intimate relations with others. And now among all his acquaintances he had not one friend. He had plenty of so-called connections, but no friendships. Alexey Alexandrovitch had plenty of people whom he could invite to dinner, to whose sympathy he could appeal in any public affair he was concerned about, whose interest he could reckon upon for any one he wished to help, with whom he could candidly discuss other people's business and affairs of state. But his relations with these people were confined to one clearly defined channel, and had a certain routine from which it was impossible to depart. There was one man, a comrade of his at the university, with whom he had made friends later, and with whom he could have spoken of a personal sorrow; but this friend had a post in the Department of Education in a remote part of Russia. Of the people in Petersburg the most intimate and most possible were his chief secretary and his doctor.

Mihail Vassilievitch Sludin, the chief secretary, was a straightforward, intelligent, good-hearted, and conscientious man, and Alexey Alexandrovitch was aware of his personal good will. But their five years of official work together seemed to have put a barrier between them that cut off warmer relations.

After signing the papers brought him, Alexey Alexandrovitch had sat for a long while in silence, glancing at Mihail Vassilievitch, and several times he attempted to speak, but could not. He had already prepared the phrase: "You have heard of my trouble?" But he ended by saying, as usual: "So you'll get this ready for me?" and with that dismissed him.

The other person was the doctor, who had also a kindly feeling for him; but there had long existed a taciturn understanding between them that both were weighed down by work, and always in a hurry.

Of his women-friends, foremost amongst them Countess Lidia Ivanovna, Alexey Alexandrovitch never thought. All women, simply as women, were terrible and distasteful to him.

CHAPTER XXII

ALEXEY ALEXANDROVITCH HAD FORGOTTEN THE COUNTESS LIDIA IVA-novna, but she had not forgotten him. At the bitterest moment of his lonely despair she came to him, and without waiting to be announced, walked straight into his study. She found him as he was sitting with his head in both hands.

"*J'ai forcé la consigne*," she said, walking in with rapid steps and breathing hard with excitement and rapid exercise. "I have heard all! Alexey Alexandrovitch! Dear friend!" she went on, warmly squeezing his hand in both of hers and gazing with her fine pensive eyes into his.

Alexey Alexandrovitch, frowning, got up, and disengaging his hand, moved her a chair.

"Won't you sit down, countess? I'm seeing no one because I'm unwell, countess," he said, and his lips twitched.

"Dear friend!" repeated Countess Lidia Ivanovna, never taking her eyes off his, and suddenly her eyebrows rose at the inner corners, describing a triangle on her forehead, her ugly yellow face became still uglier, but Alexey Alexandrovitch felt that she was sorry for him and was preparing to cry. And he too was softened; he snatched her plump hand and proceeded to kiss it.

"Dear friend!" she said in a voice breaking with emotion. "You ought not to give way to grief. Your sorrow is a great one, but you ought to find consolation."

"I am crushed, I am annihilated, I am no longer a man!" said Alexey Alexandrovitch, letting go her hand, but still gazing into her brimming eyes. "My position is so awful because I can find nowhere, I cannot find within me strength to support me."

while he was dressing all it was necessary for him to know. But Lidia Ivanovna's help was none the less real; she gave Alexey Alexandrovitch moral support in the consciousness of her love and respect for him, and still more, as it was soothing to her to believe, in that she almost turned him to Christianity—that is, from an indifferent and apathetic believer she turned him into an ardent and steadfast adherent of the new interpretation of Christian doctrine, which had been gaining ground of late in Petersburg. It was easy for Alexey Alexandrovitch to believe in this teaching. Alexey Alexandrovitch, like Lidia Ivanovna indeed, and others who shared their views, was completely devoid of vividness of imagination, that spiritual faculty in virtue of which the conceptions evoked by the imagination become so vivid that they must needs be in harmony with other conceptions, and with actual fact. He saw nothing impossible and inconceivable in the idea that death, though existing for unbelievers, did not exist for him, and that, as he was possessed of the most perfect faith, of the measure of which he was himself the judge, therefore there was no sin in his soul, and he was experiencing complete salvation here on earth.

It is true that the erroneousness and shallowness of this conception of his faith was dimly perceptible to Alexey Alexandrovitch, and he knew that when, without the slightest idea that his forgiveness was the action of a higher power, he had surrendered directly to the feeling of forgiveness, he had felt more happiness than now when he was thinking every instant that Christ was in his heart, and that in signing official papers he was doing His will. But for Alexey Alexandrovitch it was a necessity to think in that way; it was such a necessity for him in his humiliation to have some elevated standpoint, however imaginary, from which, looked down upon by all, he could look down on others, that he clung, as to his one salvation, to his delusion of salvation.

CHAPTER XXIII

THE COUNTESS LIDIA IVANOVNA HAD, AS A VERY YOUNG AND SENTIMENTAL girl, been married to a wealthy man of high rank, an extremely good-natured, jovial, and extremely dissipated rake. Two months after marriage her husband abandoned her, and her impassioned protestations of affection he met with a sarcasm and even hostility that people knowing the count's good heart, and seeing no defects in the sentimental Lidia, were at a loss to explain. Though they were divorced and lived apart, yet whenever the husband met the wife, he invariably behaved to her with the same malignant irony, the cause of which was incomprehensible.

Countess Lidia Ivanovna had long given up being in love with her husband, but from that time she had never given up being in love with some one. She was in love with several people at once, both men and women; she had been in love with almost every one who had been particularly distinguished in any way. She was in love with all the new princes and princesses who married into the imperial family; she had been in love with a high dignitary of the Church, a vicar, and a parish priest; she had been in love with a journalist, three Slavophils, with Komissarov, with a minister, a doctor, an English missionary and Karenin. All these passions constantly waning or growing more ardent, did not prevent her from keeping up the most extended and complicated relations with the court and fashionable society. But from the time that after Karenin's trouble she took him under her special protection, from the time that she set to work in Karenin's household looking after his welfare, she felt that all her other attachments were not the real thing, and that she was now genuinely in love, and with no one but Karenin. The feeling she now experienced for him seemed to her stronger than any of her former feelings. Analyzing her feeling, and comparing it with former passions, she distinctly perceived that she would not have been in love with Komissarov if he had not saved the life of the Tsar, that she would not have been in love with Ristitch-Kudzhitsky if there had been no Slavonic question, but that she loved Karenin for himself, for his lofty, uncomprehended soul, for the sweet—to her—high notes of his voice, for his drawling intonation, his weary eyes, his character, and his soft white hands with their swollen veins. She was not simply overjoyed at meeting him, but she sought in his face signs of the impression she was making on him. She tried to please him, not by her words only, but in her whole person. For his sake it was that she now lavished more care on her dress than before. She caught herself in reveries on what might have been, if she had not been married and he had been free. She blushed with emotion when he came into the room, she could not repress a smile of rapture when he said anything amiable to her.

For several days now Countess Lidia Ivanovna had been in a state of intense excitement. She had learned that Anna and Vronsky were in Petersburg. Alexey Alexandrovitch must be saved from seeing her, he must be saved even from the torturing knowledge that that awful woman was in the same town with him, and that he might meet her any minute.

"Looking older, did you say? *Il fait des passions*. I believe Countess Lidia Ivanovna's jealous now of his wife."

"Oh, come now, please don't say any harm of Countess Lidia Ivanovna."

"Why, is there any harm in her being in love with Karenin?"

"But is it true Madame Karenina's here?"

"Well, not here in the palace, but in Petersburg. I met her yesterday with Alexey Vronsky, *bras dessus, bras dessous*, in the Morsky."

"*C'est un homme qui n'a pas …*" the gentleman of the bedchamber was beginning, but he stopped to make room, bowing, for a member of the Imperial family to pass.

Thus people talked incessantly of Alexey Alexandrovitch, finding fault with him and laughing at him, while he, blocking up the way of the member of the Imperial Council he had captured, was explaining to him point by point his new financial project, never interrupting his discourse for an instant for fear he should escape.

Almost at the same time that his wife left Alexey Alexandrovitch there had come to him that bitterest moment in the life of an official—the moment when his upward career comes to a full stop. This full stop had arrived and every one perceived it, but Alexey Alexandrovitch himself was not yet aware that his career was over. Whether it was due to his feud with Stremov, or his misfortune with his wife, or simply that Alexey Alexandrovitch had reached his destined limits, it had become evident to every one in the course of that year that his career was at an end. He still filled a position of consequence, he sat on many commissions and committees, but he was a man whose day was over, and from whom nothing was expected. Whatever he said, whatever he proposed, was heard as though it were something long familiar, and the very thing that was not needed. But Alexey Alexandrovitch was not aware of this, and, on the contrary, being cut off from direct participation in governmental activity, he saw more clearly than ever the errors and defects in the action of others, and thought it his duty to point out means for their correction. Shortly after his separation from his wife, he began writing his first note on the new judicial procedure, the first of the endless series of notes he was destined to write in the future.

Alexey Alexandrovitch did not merely fail to observe his hopeless position in the official world, he was not merely free from anxiety on this head, he was positively more satisfied than ever with his own activity.

"He that is unmarried careth for the things that belong to the Lord, how he may please the Lord: But he that is married careth for the things that are of the world, how he may please his wife," says the Apostle Paul, and

Alexey Alexandrovitch, who was now guided in every action by Scripture, often recalled this text. It seemed to him that ever since he had been left without a wife, he had in these very projects of reform been serving the Lord more zealously than before.

The unmistakable impatience of the member of the Council trying to get away from him did not trouble Alexey Alexandrovitch; he gave up his exposition only when the member of the Council, seizing his chance when one of the Imperial family was passing, slipped away from him.

Left alone, Alexey Alexandrovitch looked down, collecting his thoughts, then looked casually about him and walked towards the door, where he hoped to meet Countess Lidia Ivanovna.

"And how strong they all are, how sound physically," thought Alexey Alexandrovitch, looking at the powerfully built gentleman of the bedchamber with his well-combed, perfumed whiskers, and at the red neck of the prince, pinched by his tight uniform. He had to pass them on his way. "Truly is it said that all the world is evil," he thought, with another sidelong glance at the calves of the gentleman of the bedchamber.

Moving forward deliberately, Alexey Alexandrovitch bowed with his customary air of weariness and dignity to the gentleman who had been talking about him, and looking towards the door, his eyes sought Countess Lidia Ivanovna.

"Ah! Alexey Alexandrovitch!" said the little old man, with a malicious light in his eyes, at the moment when Karenin was on a level with them, and was nodding with a frigid gesture, "I haven't congratulated you yet," said the old man, pointing to his newly received ribbon.

"Thank you," answered Alexey Alexandrovitch. "What an *exquisite* day to-day," he added, laying emphasis in his peculiar way on the word *exquisite*.

That they laughed at him he was well aware, but he did not expect anything but hostility from them; he was used to that by now.

Catching sight of the yellow shoulders of Lidia Ivanovna jutting out above her corset, and her fine pensive eyes bidding him to her, Alexey Alexandrovitch smiled, revealing untarnished white teeth, and went towards her.

Lidia Ivanovna's dress had cost her great pains, as indeed all her dresses had done of late. Her aim in dress was now quite the reverse of that she had pursued thirty years before. Then her desire had been to adorn herself with something, and the more adorned the better. Now, on the contrary, she was perforce decked out in a way so inconsistent with her age and her figure, that her one anxiety was to contrive that the contrast between these adornments and her own exterior should not be too appalling. And as far as Alexey Alexandrovitch was

"But is that love, my friend? Is it sincere? Admitting that you have for-given—that you forgive—have we the right to work on the feelings of that angel? He looks on her as dead. He prays for her, and beseeches God to have mercy on her sins. And it is better so. But now what will he think?"

"I had not thought of that," said Alexey Alexandrovitch, evidently agreeing.

Countess Lidia Ivanovna hid her face in her hands and was silent. she was praying.

"If you ask my advice," she said, having finished her prayer and uncov-ered her face, "I do not advise you to do this. Do you suppose I don't see how you are suffering, how this has torn open your wounds? But supposing that, as always, you don't think of yourself, what can it lead to?—to fresh suffering for you, to torture for the child. If there were a trace of humanity left in her, she ought not to wish for it herself. No, I have no hesitation in saying I advise not, and if you will intrust it to me, I will write to her."

And Alexey Alexandrovitch consented, and Countess Lidia Ivanovna sent the following letter in French:

> Dear Madame,
> "To be reminded of you might have results for your
> son in leading to questions on his part which could
> not be answered without implanting in the child's
> soul a spirit of censure towards what should be for
> him sacred, and therefore I beg you to interpret your
> husband's refusal in the spirit of Christian love. I
> pray to Almighty God to have mercy on you.
>
> Countess Lidia.

This letter attained the secret object which Countess Lidia Ivanovna had concealed from herself. It wounded Anna to the quick.

For his part, Alexey Alexandrovitch, on returning home from Lidia Ivanovna's, could not all that day concentrate himself on his usual pursuits, and find that spiritual peace of one saved and believing which he had felt of late.

The thought of his wife, who had so greatly sinned against him, and towards whom he had been so saintly, as Countess Lidia Ivanovna had so justly told him, ought not to have troubled him; but he was not easy; he could not understand the book he was reading; he could not drive away harassing recol-lections of his relations with her, of the mistake which, as it now seemed, he had made in regard to her. The memory of how he had received her confession of infidelity on their way home from the races (especially that he had insisted only on the observance of external decorum, and had not sent a challenge) tortured him like a remorse. He was tortured too by the thought of the letter he had written her; and most of all, his forgiveness, which nobody wanted, and his care of the other man's child made his heart burn with shame and remorse.

And just the same feeling of shame and regret he felt now, as he reviewed all his past with her, recalling the awkward words in which, after long wavering, he had made her an offer.

"But how have I been to blame?" he said to himself. And this question always excited another question in him—whether they felt differently, did their loving and marrying differently, these Vronskys and Oblonskys … these gentlemen of the bedchamber, with their fine calves. And there passed before his mind a whole series of these mettlesome, vigorous, self-confident men, who always and everywhere drew his inquisitive attention in spite of himself. He tried to dispel these thoughts, he tried to persuade himself that he was not living for this transient life, but for the life of eternity, and that there was peace and love in his heart.

But the fact that he had in this transient, trivial life made, as it seemed to him, a few trivial mistakes tortured him as though the eternal salvation in which he believed had no existence. But this temptation did not last long, and soon there was reëstablished once more in Alexey Alexandrovitch's soul the peace and the elevation by virtue of which he could forget what he did not want to remember.

CHAPTER XXVI

WELL, Kapitonitch?" said Seryozha, coming back rosy and good-humored from his walk the day before his birthday, and giving his overcoat to the tall old hall-porter, who smiled down at the little person from the height of his long figure. "Well, has the bandaged clerk been here to-day? Did papa see him?"

"He saw him. The minute the chief secretary came out, I announced him," said the hall-porter with a good-humored wink. "Here, I'll take it off."

"Seryozha!" said the tutor, stopping in the doorway leading to the inner rooms. "Take it off yourself." But Seryozha, though he heard his tutor's feeble

to him, he believed him and seemed to comprehend, but as soon as he was left alone, he was positively unable to recollect and to understand that the short and familiar word "suddenly" is an adverb of manner of action. Still he was sorry that he had disappointed the teacher.

He chose a moment when the teacher was looking in silence at the book.

"Mihail Ivanitch, when is your birthday?" he asked all, of a sudden.

"You'd much better be thinking about your work. Birthdays are of no importance to a rational being. It's a day like any other on which one has to do one's work."

Seryozha looked intently at the teacher, at his scanty beard, at his spectacles, which had slipped down below the ridge on his nose, and fell into so deep a reverie that he heard nothing of what the teacher was explaining to him. He knew that the teacher did not think what he said; he felt it from the tone in which it was said. "But why have they all agreed to speak just in the same manner always the dreariest and most useless stuff? Why does he keep me off; why doesn't he love me?" he asked himself mournfully, and could not think of an answer.

CHAPTER XXVII

AFTER THE LESSON WITH THE GRAMMAR TEACHER CAME HIS FATHER'S LESSON. While waiting for his father, Seryozha sat at the table playing with a penknife, and fell to dreaming. Among Seryozha's favorite occupations was searching for his mother during his walks. He did not believe in death generally, and in her death in particular, in spite of what Lidia Ivanovna had told him and his father had confirmed, and it was just because of that, and after he had been told she was dead, that he had begun looking for her when out for a walk. Every woman of full, graceful figure with dark hair was his mother. At the sight of such a woman such a feeling of tenderness was stirred within him that his breath failed him, and tears came into his eyes. And he was on the tiptoe of expectation that she would come up to him, would lift her veil. All her face would be visible, she would smile, she would hug him, he would sniff her fragrance, feel the softness of her arms, and cry with happiness, just as he had one evening lain on her lap while she tickled him, and he laughed and bit her white, ring-covered fingers. Later, when he accidentally learned from his old nurse that his mother was not dead, and his father and Lidia Ivanovna had explained to him that she was dead to him because she was wicked (which he could not possibly believe, because he loved her), he went on seeking her and expecting her in the same way. That day in the public gardens there had been a lady in a lilac veil, whom he had watched with a throbbing heart, believing it to be she as she came towards them along the path. The lady had not come up to them, but had disappeared somewhere. That day, more intensely than ever, Seryozha felt a rush of love for her, and now, waiting for his father, he forgot everything, and cut all round the edge of the table with his penknife, staring straight before him with sparkling eyes and dreaming of her.

"Here is your papa!" said Vassily Lukitch, rousing him.

Seryozha jumped up and went up to his father, and kissing his hand, looked at him intently, trying to discover signs of his joy at receiving the Alexander Nevsky.

"Did you have a nice walk?" said Alexey Alexandrovitch, sitting down in his easy-chair, pulling the volume of the Old Testament to him and opening it. Although Alexey Alexandrovitch had more than once told Seryozha that every Christian ought to know Scripture history thoroughly, he often referred to the Bible himself during the lesson, and Seryozha observed this.

"Yes, it was very nice indeed, papa," said Seryozha, sitting sideways on his chair and rocking it, which was forbidden. "I saw Nadinka" (Nadinka was a niece of Lidia Ivanovna's who was being brought up in her house). "She told me you'd been given a new star. Are you glad, papa?"

"First of all, don't rock your chair, please," said Alexey Alexandrovitch. "And secondly, it's not the reward that's precious, but the work itself. And I could have wished you understood that. If you now are going to work, to study in order to win a reward, then the work will seem hard to you; but when you work" (Alexey Alexandrovitch, as he spoke, thought of how he had been sustained by a sense of duty through the wearisome labor of the morning, consisting of signing one hundred and eighty papers), "loving your work, you will find your reward in it."

Seryozha's eyes, that had been shining with gaiety and tenderness, grew dull and dropped before his father's gaze. This was the same long-familiar tone his father always took with him, and Seryozha had learned by now to fall in with it. His father always talked to him—so Seryozha felt—as though he were addressing some boy of his own imagination, one of those boys that exist in books, utterly unlike himself. And Seryozha always tried with his father to act being the story-book boy.

"Without the candle I can see better what I see and what I prayed for. There! I was almost telling the secret!" said Seryozha, laughing gaily.

When the candle was taken away, Seryozha heard and felt his mother. She stood over him, and with loving eyes caressed him. But then came windmills, a knife, everything began to be mixed up, and he fell asleep.

CHAPTER XXVIII

ON ARRIVING IN PETERSBURG, VRONSKY AND ANNA STAYED AT ONE OF THE best hotels; Vronsky apart in a lower story, Anna above with her child, its nurse, and her maid, in a large suite of four rooms.

On the day of his arrival Vronsky went to his brother's. There he found his mother, who had come from Moscow on business. His mother and sister-in-law greeted him as usual: they asked him about his stay abroad, and talked of their common acquaintances, but did not let drop a single word in allusion to his connection with Anna. His brother came the next morning to see Vronsky, and of his own accord asked him about her, and Alexey Vronsky told him directly that he looked upon his connection with Madame Karenina as marriage; that he hoped to arrange a divorce, and then to marry her, and until then he considered her as much a wife as any other wife, and he begged him to tell their mother and his wife so.

"If the world disapproves, I don't care," said Vronsky; "but if my relations want to be on terms of relationship with me, they will have to be on the same terms with my wife."

The elder brother, who had always a respect for his younger brother's judgment, could not well tell whether he was right or not till the world had decided the question; for his part he had nothing against it, and with Alexey he went up to see Anna.

Before his brother, as before every one, Vronsky addressed Anna with a certain formality, treating her as he might a very intimate friend, but it was understood that his brother knew their real relations, and they talked about Anna's going to Vronsky's estate.

In spite of all his social experience Vronsky was, in consequence of the new position in which he was placed, laboring under a strange misapprehension. One would have thought he must have understood that society was closed for him and Anna; but now some vague ideas had sprung up in his brain that this was only the case in old-fashioned days, and that now with the rapidity of modern progress (he had unconsciously become by now a partisan of every sort of progress) the views of society had changed, and that the question whether they would be received in society was not a foregone conclusion. "Of course," he thought, "she would not be received at court, but intimate friends can and must look at it in the proper light." One may sit for several hours at a stretch with one's legs crossed in the same position, if one knows that there's nothing to prevent one's changing one's position; but if a man knows that he must remain sitting so with crossed legs, then cramps come on, the legs begin to twitch and to strain towards the spot to which one would like to draw them. This was what Vronsky was experiencing in regard to the world. Though at the bottom of his heart he knew that the world was shut on them, he put it to the test whether the world had not changed by now and would not receive them. But he very quickly perceived that though the world was open for him personally, it was closed for Anna. Just as in the game of cat and mouse, the hands raised for him were dropped to bar the way for Anna.

One of the first ladies of Petersburg society whom Vronsky saw was his cousin Betsy.

"At last!" she greeted him joyfully. "And Anna? How glad I am! Where are you stopping? I can fancy after your delightful travels you must find our poor Petersburg horrid. I can fancy your honeymoon in Rome. How about the divorce? Is that all over?"

Vronsky noticed that Betsy's enthusiasm waned when she learned that no divorce had as yet taken place.

"People will throw stones at me, I know," she said, "but I shall come and see Anna; yes, I shall certainly come. You won't be here long, I suppose?"

And she did certainly come to see Anna the same day, but her tone was not at all the same as in former days. She unmistakably prided herself on her courage, and wished Anna to appreciate the fidelity of her friendship. She only stayed ten minutes, talking of society gossip, and on leaving she said:

"You've never told me when the divorce is to be? Supposing I'm ready to fling my cap over the mill, other starchy people will give you the cold shoulder until you're married. And that's so simple nowadays. *Ça se fait.* So you're going on Friday? Sorry we shan't see each other again."

From Betsy's tone Vronsky might have grasped what he had to expect from the world; but he made another effort in his own family. His mother he did not reckon upon. He knew that his mother, who had been so enthusiastic over

were shown to her husband, he would keep up his character of magnanimity, and would not refuse her request.

The commissionaire who took the letter had brought her back the most cruel and unexpected answer, that there was no answer. She had never felt so humiliated as at the moment when, sending for the commissionaire, she heard from him the exact account of how he had waited, and how afterwards he had been told there was no answer. Anna felt humiliated, insulted, but she saw that from her point of view Countess Lidia Ivanovna was right. Her suffering was the more poignant that she had to bear it in solitude. She could not and would not share it with Vronsky. She knew that to him, although he was the primary cause of her distress, the question of her seeing her son would seem a matter of very little consequence. She knew that he would never be capable of understanding all the depth of her suffering, that for his cool tone at any allusion to it she would begin to hate him. And she dreaded that more than anything in the world, and so she hid from him everything that related to her son. Spending the whole day at home she considered ways of seeing her son, and had reached a decision to write to her husband. She was just composing this letter when she was handed the letter from Lidia Ivanovna. The countess's silence had subdued and depressed her, but the letter, all that she read between the lines in it, so exasperated her, this malice was so revolting beside her passionate, legitimate tenderness for her son, that she turned against other people and left off blaming herself.

"This coldness—this pretense of feeling!" she said to herself. "They must needs insult me and torture the child, and I am to submit to it! Not on any consideration! She is worse than I am. I don't lie, anyway." And she decided on the spot that next day, Seryozha's birthday, she would go straight to her husband's house, bribe or deceive the servants, but at any cost see her son and overturn the hideous deception with which they were encompassing the unhappy child.

She went to a toy shop, bought toys and thought over a plan of action. She would go early in the morning at eight o'clock, when Alexey Alexandrovitch would be certain not to be up. She would have money in her hand to give the hall-porter and the footman, so that they should let her in, and not raising her veil, she would say that she had come from Seryozha's godfather to congratulate him, and that she had been charged to leave the toys at his bedside. She had prepared everything but the words she should say to her son. Often as she had dreamed of it, she could never think of anything.

The next day, at eight o'clock in the morning, Anna got out of a hired sledge and rang at the front entrance of her former home.

"Run and see what's wanted. Some lady," said Kapitonitch, who, not yet dressed, in his overcoat and goloshes, had peeped out of the window and seen a lady in a veil standing close up to the door. His assistant, a lad Anna did not know, had no sooner opened the door to her than she came in, and pulling a three-rouble note out of her muff put it hurriedly into his hand.

"Seryozha—Sergey Alexeitch," she said, and was going on. Scrutinizing the note, the porter's assistant stopped her at the second glass-door.

"Whom do you want?" he asked.

She did not hear his words and made no answer.

Noticing the embarrassment of the unknown lady, Kapitonitch went out to her, opened the second door for her, and asked her what she was pleased to want.

"From Prince Skorodumov for Sergey Alexeitch," she said.

"His honor's not up yet," said the porter, looking at her attentively.

Anna had not anticipated that the absolutely unchanged hall of the house where she had lived for nine years would so greatly affect her. Memories sweet and painful rose one after another in her heart, and for a moment she forgot what she was here for.

"Would you kindly wait?" said Kapitonitch, taking off her fur cloak.

As he took off the cloak, Kapitonitch glanced at her face, recognized her, and made her a low bow in silence.

"Please walk in, your excellency," he said to her.

She tried to say something, but her voice refused to utter any sound; with a guilty and imploring glance at the old man she went with light, swift steps up the stairs. Bent double, and his goloshes catching in the steps, Kapitonitch ran after her, trying to overtake her.

"The tutor's there; maybe he's not dressed. I'll let him know."

Anna still mounted the familiar staircase, not understanding what the old man was saying.

"This way, to the left, if you please. Excuse its not being tidy. His honor's in the old parlor now," the hall-porter said, panting. "Excuse me, wait a little, your excellency; I'll just see," he said, and overtaking her, he opened the high door and disappeared behind it. Anna stood still waiting. "He's only just awake," said the hall-porter, coming out. And at the very instant the porter said this, Anna caught the sound of a childish yawn. From the sound of this yawn alone she knew her son and seemed to see him living before her eyes.

"Let me in; go away!" she said, and went in through the high doorway. On the right of the door stood a bed, and sitting up in the bed was the boy. His little

went in person to the nursery at nine o'clock, and every one fully comprehended that it was impossible for the husband and wife to meet, and that they must prevent it. Korney, the valet, going down to the hall-porter's room, asked who had let her in, and how it was he had done so, and ascertaining that Kapitonitch had admitted her and shown her up, he gave the old man a talking-to. The hall-porter was doggedly silent, but when Korney told him he ought to be sent away, Kapitonitch darted up to him, and waving his hands in Korney's face, began:

"Oh yes, to be sure you'd not have let her in! After ten years' service, and never a word but of kindness, and there you'd up and say, 'Be off, go along, get away with you!' Oh yes, you're a shrewd one at politics, I dare say! You don't need to be taught how to swindle the master, and to filch fur coats!"

"Soldier!" said Korney contemptuously, and he turned to the nurse who was coming in. "Here, what do you think, Marya Efimovna: he let her in without a word to any one," Korney said addressing her. "Alexey Alexandrovitch will be down immediately—and go into the nursery!"

"A pretty business, a pretty business!" said the nurse. "You, Korney Vassilievitch, you'd best keep him some way or other, the master, while I'll run and get her away somehow. A pretty business!"

When the nurse went into the nursery, Seryozha was telling his mother how he and Nadinka had had a fall in sledging downhill, and had turned over three times. She was listening to the sound of his voice, watching his face and the play of expression on it, touching his hand, but she did not follow what he was saying. She must go, she must leave him,—this was the only thing she was thinking and feeling. She heard the steps of Vassily Lukitch coming up to the door and coughing; she heard, too, the steps of the nurse as she came near; but she sat like one turned to stone, incapable of beginning to speak or to get up.

"Mistress, darling!" began the nurse, going up to Anna and kissing her hands and shoulders. "God has brought joy indeed to our boy on his birthday. You aren't changed one bit."

"Oh, nurse dear, I didn't know you were in the house," said Anna, rousing herself for a moment.

"I'm not living here, I'm living with my daughter. I came for the birthday, Anna Arkadyevna, darling!"

The nurse suddenly burst into tears, and began kissing her hand again.

Seryozha, with radiant eyes and smiles, holding his mother by one hand and his nurse by the other, pattered on the rug with his fat little bare feet. The tenderness shown by his beloved nurse to his mother threw him into an ecstasy.

"Mother! She often comes to see me, and when she comes …" he was beginning, but he stopped, noticing that the nurse was saying something in a whisper to his mother, and that in his mother's face there was a look of dread and something like shame, which was so strangely unbecoming to her.

She went up to him.

"My sweet!" she said.

She could not say *good-bye*, but the expression on her face said it, and he understood. "Darling, darling Kootik!" she used the name by which she had called him when he was little, "you won't forget me? You …" but she could not say more.

How often afterwards she thought of words she might have said. But now she did not know how to say it, and could say nothing. But Seryozha knew all she wanted to say to him. He understood that she was unhappy and loved him. He understood even what the nurse had whispered. He had caught the words "always at nine o'clock," and he knew that this was said of his father, and that his father and mother could not meet. That he understood, but one thing he could not understand—why there should be a look of dread and shame in her face? … She was not in fault, but she was afraid of him and ashamed of something. He would have liked to put a question that would have set at rest this doubt, but he did not dare; he saw that she was miserable, and he felt for her. Silently he pressed close to her and whispered, "Don't go yet. He won't come just yet."

The mother held him away from her to see what he was thinking, what to say to him, and in his frightened face she read not only that he was speaking of his father, but, as it were, asking her what he ought to think about his father.

"Seryozha, my darling," she said, "love him; he's better and kinder than I am, and I have done him wrong. When you grow up you will judge."

"There's no one better than you! …" he cried in despair through his tears, and, clutching her by the shoulders, he began squeezing her with all his force to him, his arms trembling with the strain.

"My sweet, my little one!" said Anna, and she cried as weakly and childishly as he.

At that moment the door opened. Vassily Lukitch came in.

At the other door there was the sound of steps, and the nurse in a scared whisper said, "He's coming," and gave Anna her hat.

Seryozha sank onto the bed and sobbed, hiding his face in his hands. Anna removed his hands, once more kissed his wet face, and with rapid steps went to the door. Alexey Alexandrovitch walked in, meeting her. Seeing her, he stopped short and bowed his head.

at home yesterday, and the fact that he had insisted on their taking separate sets of rooms at Petersburg, and that even now he was not coming to her alone, as though he were trying to avoid meeting her face to face.

"But he ought to tell me so. I must know that it is so. If I knew it, then I know what I should do," she said to herself, utterly unable to picture to herself the position she would be in if she were convinced of his not caring for her. She thought he had ceased to love her, she felt close upon despair, and consequently she felt exceptionally alert. She rang for her maid and went to her dressing-room. As she dressed, she took more care over her appearance than she had done all those days, as though he might, if he had grown cold to her, fall in love with her again because she had dressed and arranged her hair in the way most becoming to her.

She heard the bell ring before she was ready. When she went into the drawing-room it was not he, but Yashvin, who met her eyes. Vronsky was looking through the photographs of her son, which she had forgotten on the table, and he made no haste to look round at her.

"We have met already," she said, putting her little hand into the huge hand of Yashvin, whose bashfulness was so queerly out of keeping with his immense frame and coarse face. "We met last year at the races. Give them to me," she said, with a rapid movement snatching from Vronsky the photographs of her son, and glancing significantly at him with flashing eyes. "Were the races good this year? Instead of them I saw the races in the Corso in Rome. But you don't care for life abroad," she said with a cordial smile. "I know you and all your tastes, though I have seen so little of you."

"I'm awfully sorry for that, for my tastes are mostly bad," said Yashvin, gnawing at his left mustache.

Having talked a little while, and noticing that Vronsky glanced at the clock, Yashvin asked her whether she would be staying much longer in Petersburg, and unbending his huge figure reached after his cap.

"Not long, I think," she said hesitatingly, glancing at Vronsky.

"So then we shan't meet again?"

"Come and dine with me," said Anna resolutely, angry it seemed with herself for her embarrassment, but flushing as she always did when she defined her position before a fresh person. "The dinner here is not good, but at least you will see him. There is no one of his old friends in the regiment Alexey cares for as he does for you."

"Delighted," said Yashvin with a smile, from which Vronsky could see that he liked Anna very much.

Yashvin said good-bye and went away; Vronsky stayed behind.

"Are you going too?" she said to him.

"I'm late already," he answered. "Run along! I'll catch you up in a moment," he called to Yashvin.

She took him by the hand, and without taking her eyes off him, gazed at him while she ransacked her mind for the words to say that would keep him.

"Wait a minute, there's something I want to say to you," and taking his broad hand she pressed it on her neck. "Oh, was it right my asking him to dinner?"

"You did quite right," he said with a serene smile that showed his even teeth, and he kissed her hand.

"Alexey, you have not changed to me?" she said, pressing his hand in both of hers. "Alexey, I am miserable here. When are we going away?"

"Soon, soon. You wouldn't believe how disagreeable our way of living here is to me too," he said, and he drew away his hand.

"Well, go, go!" she said in a tone of offense, and she walked quickly away from him.

CHAPTER XXXII

WHEN VRONSKY RETURNED HOME, ANNA WAS NOT YET HOME. SOON after he had left, some lady, so they told him, had come to see her, and she had gone out with her. That she had gone out without leaving word where she was going, that she had not yet come back, and that all the morning she had been going about somewhere without a word to him—all this, together with the strange look of excitement in her face in the morning, and the recollection of the hostile tone with which she had before Yashvin almost snatched her son's photographs out of his hands, made him serious. He decided he absolutely must speak openly with her. And he waited for her in her drawing-room. But Anna did not return alone, but brought with her her old unmarried aunt, Princess Oblonskaya. This was the lady who had come in the morning, and with whom Anna had gone out shopping. Anna appeared not to notice Vronsky's worried and inquiring expression, and began a lively account of her morning's shopping. He saw that there was something working within her; in her flashing eyes, when they rested for a moment on him, there was

CHAPTER XXXIII

VRONSKY FOR THE FIRST TIME EXPERIENCED A FEELING OF ANGER AGAINST Anna, almost a hatred for her willfully refusing to understand her own position. This feeling was aggravated by his being unable to tell her plainly the cause of his anger. If he had told her directly what he was thinking, he would have said:

"In that dress, with a princess only too well known to every one, to show yourself at the theater is equivalent not merely to acknowledging your position as a fallen woman, but is flinging down a challenge to society, that is to say, cutting yourself off from it forever."

He could not say that to her. "But how can she fail to see it, and what is going on in her?" he said to himself. He felt at the same time that his respect for her was diminished while his sense of her beauty was intensified.

He went back scowling to his rooms, and sitting down beside Yashvin, who, with his long legs stretched out on a chair, was drinking brandy and seltzer water, he ordered a glass of the same for himself.

"You were talking of Lankovsky's Powerful. That's a fine horse, and I would advise you to buy him," said Yashvin, glancing at his comrade's gloomy face. "His hind-quarters aren't quite first-rate, but the legs and head—one couldn't wish for anything better."

"I think I will take him," answered Vronsky.

Their conversation about horses interested him, but he did not for an instant forget Anna, and could not help listening to the sound of steps in the corridor and looking at the clock on the chimney-piece.

"Anna Arkadyevna gave orders to announce that she has gone to the theater."

Yashvin, tipping another glass of brandy into the bubbling water, drank it and got up, buttoning his coat.

"Well, let's go," he said, faintly smiling under his mustache, and showing by this smile that he knew the cause of Vronsky's gloominess, and did not attach any significance to it.

"I'm not going," Vronsky answered gloomily.

"Well, I must, I promised to. Good-bye, then. If you do, come to the stalls; you can take Kruzin's stall," added Yashvin as he went out.

"No, I'm busy."

"A wife is a care, but it's worse when she's not a wife," thought Yashvin, as he walked out of the hotel.

Vronsky, left alone, got up from his chair and began pacing up and down the room.

"And what's to-day? The fourth night…. Yegor and his wife are there, and my mother, most likely. Of course all Petersburg's there. Now she's gone in, taken off her cloak and come into the light. Tushkevitch, Yashvin, Princess Varvara," he pictured them to himself…. "What about me? Either that I'm frightened or have given up to Tushkevitch the right to protect her? From every point of view—stupid, stupid! … And why is she putting me in such a position?" he said with a gesture of despair.

With that gesture he knocked against the table, on which there was standing the seltzer water and the decanter of brandy, and almost upset it. He tried to catch it, let it slip, and angrily kicked the table over and rang.

"If you care to be in my service," he said to the valet who came in, "you had better remember your duties. This shouldn't be here. You ought to have cleared away."

The valet, conscious of his own innocence, would have defended himself, but glancing at his master, he saw from his face that the only thing to do was to be silent, and hurriedly threading his way in and out, dropped down on the carpet and began gathering up the whole and broken glasses and bottles.

"That's not your duty; send the waiter to clear away, and get my dress-coat out."

Vronsky went into the theater at half-past eight. The performance was in full swing. The little old box-keeper, recognizing Vronsky as he helped him off with his fur coat, called him "Your Excellency," and suggested he should not take a number but should simply call Fyodor. In the brightly lighted corridor there was no one but the box-opener and two attendants with fur cloaks on their arms listening at the doors. Through the closed doors came the sounds of the discreet *staccato* accompaniment of the orchestra, and a single female voice rendering distinctly a musical phrase. The door opened to let the box-opener slip through, and the phrase drawing to the end reached Vronsky's hearing clearly. But the doors were closed again at once, and Vronsky did not hear the end of the phrase and the cadence of the accompaniment, though he knew from the thunder of applause that it was over. When he entered the hall, brilliantly lighted with chandeliers and gas jets, the noise was still going on. On the stage the singer, bowing and smiling, with bare shoulders flashing with diamonds, was, with the help of the tenor who had given her his arm, gathering up the bouquets that were flying awkwardly over the footlights. Then she

Knowing that something had happened, but not knowing precisely what, Vronsky felt a thrill of agonizing anxiety, and hoping to find out something, he went towards his brother's box. Purposely choosing the way round furthest from Anna's box, he jostled as he came out against the colonel of his old regiment talking to two acquaintances. Vronsky heard the name of Madame Karenina, and noticed how the colonel hastened to address Vronsky loudly by name, with a meaning glance at his companions.

"Ah, Vronsky! When are you coming to the regiment? We can't let you off without a supper. You're one of the old set," said the colonel of his regiment.

"I can't stop, awfully sorry, another time," said Vronsky, and he ran up-stairs towards his brother's box.

The old countess, Vronsky's mother, with her steel-gray curls, was in his brother's box. Varya with the young Princess Sorokina met him in the corridor.

Leaving the Princess Sorokina with her mother, Varya held out her hand to her brother-in-law, and began immediately to speak of what interested him. She was more excited than he had ever seen her.

"I think it's mean and hateful, and Madame Kartasova had no right to do it. Madame Karenina …" she began.

"But what is it? I don't know."

"What? you've not heard?"

"You know I should be the last person to hear of it."

"There isn't a more spiteful creature than that Madame Kartasova!"

"But what did she do?"

"My husband told me…. She has insulted Madame Karenina. Her husband began talking to her across the box, and Madame Kartasova made a scene. She said something aloud, he says, something insulting, and went away."

"Count, your maman is asking for you," said the young Princess Sorokina, peeping out of the door of the box.

"I've been expecting you all the while," said his mother, smiling sarcastically. "You were nowhere to be seen."

Her son saw that she could not suppress a smile of delight.

"Good-evening, maman. I have come to you," he said coldly.

"Why aren't you going to *faire la cour à Madame Karenina*?" she went on, when Princess Sorokina had moved away. "*Elle fait sensation. On oublie la Patti pour elle.*"

"Maman, I have asked you not to say anything to me of that," he answered, scowling.

"I'm only saying what every one's saying."

Vronsky made no reply, and saying a few words to Princess Sorokina, he went away. At the door he met his brother.

"Ah, Alexey!" said his brother. "How disgusting! Idiot of a woman, nothing else.... I wanted to go straight to her. Let's go together."

Vronsky did not hear him. With rapid steps he went down-stairs; he felt that he must do something, but he did not know what. Anger with her for having put herself and him in such a false position, together with pity for her suffering, filled his heart. He went down, and made straight for Anna's box. At her box stood Stremov, talking to her.

"There are no more tenors. *Le moule en est brisé!*"

Vronsky bowed to her and stopped to greet Stremov.

"You came in late, I think, and have missed the best song," Anna said to Vronsky, glancing ironically, he thought, at him.

"I am a poor judge of music," he said, looking sternly at her.

"Like Prince Yashvin," she said smiling, "who considers that Patti sings too loud."

"Thank you," she said, her little hand in its long glove taking the playbill Vronsky picked up, and suddenly at that instant her lovely face quivered. She got up and went into the interior of the box.

Noticing in the next act that her box was empty, Vronsky, rousing indignant "hushes" in the silent audience, went out in the middle of a solo and drove home.

Anna was already at home. When Vronsky went up to her, she was in the same dress as she had worn at the theater. She was sitting in the first armchair against the wall, looking straight before her. She looked at him, and at once resumed her former position.

"Anna," he said.

"You, you are to blame for everything!" she cried, with tears of despair and hatred in her voice, getting up.

"I begged, I implored you not to go; I knew it would be unpleasant...."

"Unpleasant!" she cried—"hideous! As long as I live I shall never forget it. She said it was a disgrace to sit beside me."

"A silly woman's chatter," he said: "but why risk it, why provoke? ..."

"I hate your calm. You ought not to have brought me to this. If you had loved me ..."

"Anna! How does the question of my love come in?"

"Oh, if you loved me, as I love, if you were tortured as I am! ..." she said, looking at him with an expression of terror.

"Oh, we shall be delighted," answered Varenka, coloring a little. Kitty exchanged meaningful glances with Dolly. The proposal of the learned and intellectual Sergey Ivanovitch to go looking for mushrooms with Varenka confirmed certain theories of Kitty's with which her mind had been very busy of late. She made haste to address some remark to her mother, so that her look should not be noticed. After dinner Sergey Ivanovitch sat with his cup of coffee at the drawing-room window, and while he took part in a conversation he had begun with his brother, he watched the door through which the children would start on the mushroom-picking expedition. Levin was sitting in the window near his brother.

Kitty stood beside her husband, evidently awaiting the end of a conversation that had no interest for her, in order to tell him something.

"You have changed in many respects since your marriage, and for the better," said Sergey Ivanovitch, smiling to Kitty, and obviously little interested in the conversation, "but you have remained true to your passion for defending the most paradoxical theories."

"Katya, it's not good for you to stand," her husband said to her, putting a chair for her and looking significantly at her.

"Oh, and there's no time either," added Sergey Ivanovitch, seeing the children running out.

At the head of them all Tanya galloped sideways, in her tightly-drawn stockings, and waving a basket and Sergey Ivanovitch's hat, she ran straight up to him.

Boldly running up to Sergey Ivanovitch with shining eyes, so like her father's fine eyes, she handed him his hat and made as though she would put it on for him, softening her freedom by a shy and friendly smile.

"Varenka's waiting," she said, carefully putting his hat on, seeing from Sergey Ivanovitch's smile that she might do so.

Varenka was standing at the door, dressed in a yellow print gown, with a white kerchief on her head.

"I'm coming, I'm coming, Varvara Andreevna," said Sergey Ivanovitch, finishing his cup of coffee, and putting into their separate pockets his handkerchief and cigar-case.

"And how sweet my Varenka is! eh?" said Kitty to her husband, as soon as Sergey Ivanovitch rose. She spoke so that Sergey Ivanovitch could hear, and it was clear that she meant him to do so. "And how good-looking she is—such a refined beauty! Varenka!" Kitty shouted. "Shall you be in the mill copse? We'll come out to you."

"You certainly forget your condition, Kitty," said the old princess, hurriedly coming out at the door. "You mustn't shout like that."

Varenka, hearing Kitty's voice and her mother's reprimand, went with light, rapid steps up to Kitty. The rapidity of her movement, her flushed and eager face, everything betrayed that something out of the common was going on in her. Kitty knew what this was, and had been watching her intently. She called Varenka at that moment merely in order mentally to give her a blessing for the important event which, as Kitty fancied, was bound to come to pass that day after dinner in the wood.

"Varenka, I should be very happy if a certain something were to happen," she whispered as she kissed her.

"And are you coming with us?" Varenka said to Levin in confusion, pretending not to have heard what had been said.

"I am coming, but only as far as the threshing-floor, and there I shall stop."

"Why, what do you want there?" said Kitty.

"I must go to have a look at the new wagons, and to check the invoice," said Levin; "and where will you be?"

"On the terrace."

CHAPTER II

ON THE TERRACE WERE ASSEMBLED ALL THE LADIES OF THE PARTY. They always liked sitting there after dinner, and that day they had work to do there too. Besides the sewing and knitting of baby-clothes, with which all of them were busy, that afternoon jam was being made on the terrace by a method new to Agafea Mihalovna, without the addition of water. Kitty had introduced this new method, which had been in use in her home. Agafea Mihalovna, to whom the task of jam-making had always been intrusted, considering that what had been done in the Levin household could not be amiss, had nevertheless put water with the strawberries, maintaining that the jam could not be made without it. She had been caught in the act, and was now making jam before every one, and it was to be proved to her conclusively that jam could be very well made without water.

Agafea Mihalovna, her face heated and angry, her hair untidy, and her thin arms bare to the elbows, was turning the preserving-pan over the charcoal

"But what words did he say?"

"What did Kostya say to you?"

"He wrote it in chalk. It was wonderful.... How long ago it seems!" she said.

And the three women all fell to musing on the same thing. Kitty was the first to break the silence. She remembered all that last winter before her marriage, and her passion for Vronsky.

"There's one thing ... that old love-affair of Varenka's," she said, a natural chain of ideas bringing her to this point. "I should have liked to say something to Sergey Ivanovitch, to prepare him. They're all—all men, I mean," she added, "awfully jealous over our past."

"Not all," said Dolly. "You judge by your own husband. It makes him miserable even now to remember Vronsky. Eh? that's true, isn't it?"

"Yes," Kitty answered, a pensive smile in her eyes.

"But I really don't know," the mother put in in defense of her motherly care of her daughter, "what there was in your past that could worry him? That Vronsky paid you attentions—that happens to every girl."

"Oh, yes, but we didn't mean that," Kitty said, flushing a little.

"No, let me speak," her mother went on, "why, you yourself would not let me have a talk to Vronsky. Don't you remember?"

"Oh, mamma!" said Kitty, with an expression of suffering.

"There's no keeping you young people in check nowadays.... Your friendship could not have gone beyond what was suitable. I should myself have called upon him to explain himself. But, my darling, it's not right for you to be agitated. Please remember that, and calm yourself."

"I'm perfectly calm, maman."

"How happy it was for Kitty that Anna came then," said Dolly, "and how unhappy for her. It turned out quite the opposite," she said, struck by her own ideas. "Then Anna was so happy, and Kitty thought herself unhappy. Now it is just the opposite. I often think of her."

"A nice person to think about! Horrid, repulsive woman—no heart," said her mother, who could not forget that Kitty had married not Vronsky, but Levin.

"What do you want to talk of it for?" Kitty said with annoyance. "I never think about it, and I don't want to think of it.... And I don't want to think of it," she said, catching the sound of her husband's well-known step on the steps of the terrace.

"What's that you don't want to think about?" inquired Levin, coming onto the terrace.

But no one answered him, and he did not repeat the question.

"I'm sorry I've broken in on your feminine parliament," he said, looking round on every one discontentedly, and perceiving that they had been talking of something which they would not talk about before him.

For a second he felt that he was sharing the feeling of Agafea Mihalovna, vexation at their making jam without water, and altogether at the outside Shtcherbatsky element. He smiled, however, and went up to Kitty.

"Well, how are you?" he asked her, looking at her with the expression with which every one looked at her now.

"Oh, very well," said Kitty, smiling, "and how have things gone with you?"

"The wagons held three times as much as the old carts did. Well, are we going for the children? I've ordered the horses to be put in."

"What! you want to take Kitty in the wagonette?" her mother said reproachfully.

"Yes, at a walking-pace, princess."

Levin never called the princess "maman" as men often do call their mothers-in-law, and the princess disliked his not doing so. But though he liked and respected the princess, Levin could not call her so without a sense of profaning his feeling for his dead mother.

"Come with us, maman," said Kitty.

"I don't like to see such imprudence."

"Well, I'll walk then, I'm so well." Kitty got up and went to her husband and took his hand.

"You may be well, but everything in moderation," said the princess.

"Well, Agafea Mihalovna, is the jam done?" said Levin, smiling to Agafea Mihalovna, and trying to cheer her up. "Is it all right in the new way?"

"I suppose it's all right. For our notions it's boiled too long."

"It'll be all the better, Agafea Mihalovna, it won't mildew, even though our ice has begun to thaw already, so that we've no cool cellar to store it," said Kitty, at once divining her husband's motive, and addressing the old house-keeper with the same feeling; "but your pickle's so good, that mamma says she never tasted any like it," she added, smiling, and putting her kerchief straight.

Agafea Mihalovna looked angrily at Kitty.

"You needn't try to console me, mistress. I need only to look at you with him, and I feel happy," she said, and something in the rough familiarity of that *with him* touched Kitty.

"Come along with us to look for mushrooms, you will show us the best places." Agafea Mihalovna smiled and shook her head, as though to say: "I should like to be angry with you too, but I can't."

love for his brother, from his sense of shame at being too happy, and above all from his unflagging craving to be better—she loved it in him, and so she smiled.

"And you? What are you dissatisfied with?" she asked, with the same smile.

Her disbelief in his self-dissatisfaction delighted him, and unconsciously he tried to draw her into giving utterance to the grounds of her disbelief.

"I am happy, but dissatisfied with myself...." he said.

"Why, how can you be dissatisfied with yourself if you are happy?"

"Well, how shall I say? ... In my heart I really care for nothing whatever but that you should not stumble—see? Oh, but really you mustn't skip about like that!" he cried, breaking off to scold her for too agile a movement in stepping over a branch that lay in the path. "But when I think about myself, and compare myself with others, especially with my brother, I feel I'm a poor creature."

"But in what way?" Kitty pursued with the same smile. "Don't you too work for others? What about your co-operative settlement, and your work on the estate, and your book? ..."

"Oh, but I feel, and particularly just now—it's your fault," he said, pressing her hand—"that all that doesn't count. I do it in a way half-heartedly. If I could care for all that as I care for you! ... Instead of that, I do it in these days like a task that is set me."

"Well, what would you say about papa?" asked Kitty. "Is he a poor creature then, as he does nothing for the public good?"

"He?—no! But then one must have the simplicity, the straightforwardness, the goodness of your father: and I haven't got that. I do nothing, and I fret about it. It's all your doing. Before there was you—and *this* too," he added with a glance towards her waist that she understood—"I put all my energies into work; now I can't, and I'm ashamed; I do it just as though it were a task set me, I'm pretending...."

"Well, but would you like to change this minute with Sergey Ivanovitch?" said Kitty. "Would you like to do this work for the general good, and to love the task set you, as he does, and nothing else?"

"Of course not," said Levin. "But I'm so happy that I don't understand anything. So you think he'll make her an offer to-day?" he added after a brief silence.

"I think so, and I don't think so. Only, I'm awfully anxious for it. Here, wait a minute." She stooped down and picked a wild camomile at the edge of the path. "Come, count: he does propose, he doesn't," she said, giving him the flower.

"He does, he doesn't," said Levin, tearing off the white petals.

"No, no!" Kitty, snatching at his hand, stopped him. She had been watching his fingers with interest. "You picked off two."

"Oh, but see, this little one shan't count to make up," said Levin, tearing off a little half-grown petal. "Here's the wagonette overtaking us."

"Aren't you tired, Kitty?" called the princess.

"Not in the least."

"If you are you can get in, as the horses are quiet and walking."

But it was not worth while to get in, they were quite near the place, and all walked on together.

CHAPTER IV

VARENKA, WITH HER WHITE KERCHIEF ON HER BLACK HAIR, SURROUNDED BY the children, gaily and good-humoredly looking after them, and at the same time visibly excited at the possibility of receiving a declaration from the man she cared for, was very attractive. Sergey Ivanovitch walked beside her, and never left off admiring her. Looking at her, he recalled all the delightful things he had heard from her lips, all the good he knew about her, and became more and more conscious that the feeling he had for her was something special that he had felt long, long ago, and only once, in his early youth. The feeling of happiness in being near her continually grew, and at last reached such a point that, as he put a huge, slender-stalked agaric fungus in her basket, he looked straight into her face, and noticing the flush of glad and alarmed excitement that overspread her face, he was confused himself, and smiled to her in silence a smile that said too much.

"If so," he said to himself, "I ought to think it over and make up my mind, and not give way like a boy to the impulse of a moment."

"I'm going to pick by myself apart from all the rest, or else my efforts will make no show," he said, and he left the edge of the forest where they were walking on low silky grass between old birch-trees standing far apart, and went more into the heart of the wood, where between the white birch-trunks there were gray trunks of aspen and dark bushes of hazel. Walking some forty paces away, Sergey Ivanovitch, knowing he was out of sight, stood still behind a bushy spindle-tree in full flower with its rosy red catkins. It was perfectly still all round him. Only overhead in the birches under which he stood, the

"Well, did you find some?" she asked from under the white kerchief, turning her handsome, gently smiling face to him.

"Not one," said Sergey Ivanovitch. "Did you?"

She did not answer, busy with the children who thronged about her.

"That one too, near the twig," she pointed out to little Masha a little fungus, split in half across its rosy cap by the dry grass from under which it thrust itself. Varenka got up while Masha picked the fungus, breaking it into two white halves. "This brings back my childhood," she added, moving apart from the children beside Sergey Ivanovitch.

They walked on for some steps in silence. Varenka saw that he wanted to speak; she guessed of what, and felt faint with joy and panic. They had walked so far away that no one could hear them now, but still he did not begin to speak. It would have been better for Varenka to be silent. After a silence it would have been easier for them to say what they wanted to say than after talking about mushrooms. But against her own will, as it were accidentally, Varenka said:

"So you found nothing? In the middle of the wood there are always fewer, though." Sergey Ivanovitch sighed and made no answer. He was annoyed that she had spoken about the mushrooms. He wanted to bring her back to the first words she had uttered about her childhood; but after a pause of some length, as though against his own will, he made an observation in response to her last words.

"I have heard that the white edible funguses are found principally at the edge of the wood, though I can't tell them apart."

Some minutes more passed, they moved still further away from the children, and were quite alone. Varenka's heart throbbed so that she heard it beating, and felt that she was turning red and pale and red again.

To be the wife of a man like Koznishev, after her position with Madame Stahl, was to her imagination the height of happiness. Besides, she was almost certain that she was in love with him. And this moment it would have to be decided. She felt frightened. She dreaded both his speaking and his not speaking.

Now or never it must be said—that Sergey Ivanovitch felt too. Everything in the expression, the flushed cheeks and the downcast eyes of Varenka betrayed a painful suspense. Sergey Ivanovitch saw it and felt sorry for her. He felt even that to say nothing now would be a slight to her. Rapidly in his own mind he ran over all the arguments in support of his decision. He even said over to himself the words in which he meant to put his offer, but instead of those words, some utterly unexpected reflection that occurred to him made him ask:

"What is the difference between the 'birch' mushroom and the 'white' mushroom?"

Varenka's lips quivered with emotion as she answered:

"In the top part there is scarcely any difference, it's in the stalk."

And as soon as these words were uttered, both he and she felt that it was over, that what was to have been said would not be said; and their emotion, which had up to then been continually growing more intense, began to subside.

"The birch mushroom's stalk suggests a dark man's chin after two days without shaving," said Sergey Ivanovitch, speaking quite calmly now.

"Yes, that's true," answered Varenka smiling, and unconsciously the direction of their walk changed. They began to turn towards the children. Varenka felt both sore and ashamed; at the same time she had a sense of relief.

When he had got home again and went over the whole subject, Sergey Ivanovitch thought his previous decision had been a mistaken one. He could not be false to the memory of Marie.

"Gently, children, gently!" Levin shouted quite angrily to the children, standing before his wife to protect her when the crowd of children flew with shrieks of delight to meet them.

Behind the children Sergey Ivanovitch and Varenka walked out of the wood. Kitty had no need to ask Varenka; she saw from the calm and somewhat crestfallen faces of both that her plans had not come off.

"Well?" her husband questioned her as they were going home again.

"It doesn't bite," said Kitty, her smile and manner of speaking recalling her father, a likeness Levin often noticed with pleasure.

"How doesn't bite?"

"I'll show you," she said, taking her husband's hand, lifting it to her mouth, and just faintly brushing it with closed lips. "Like a kiss on a priest's hand."

"Which didn't it bite with?" he said, laughing.

"Both. But it should have been like this ..."

"There are some peasants coming ..."

"Oh, they didn't see."

"Maman, he'll do everything; he has agreed to everything," Kitty said, angry with her mother for appealing to Sergey Ivanovitch to judge in such a matter.

In the middle of their conversation they heard the snorting of horses and the sound of wheels on the gravel. Dolly had not time to get up to go and meet her husband, when from the window of the room below, where Grisha was having his lesson, Levin leaped out and helped Grisha out after him.

"It's Stiva!" Levin shouted from under the balcony. "We've finished, Dolly, don't be afraid!" he added, and started running like a boy to meet the carriage.

"*Is ea id, ejus, ejus, ejus!*" shouted Grisha, skipping along the avenue.

"And some one else too! Papa, of course!" cried Levin, stopping at the entrance of the avenue. "Kitty, don't come down the steep staircase, go round."

But Levin had been mistaken in taking the person sitting in the carriage for the old prince. As he got nearer to the carriage he saw beside Stepan Arkadyevitch not the prince but a handsome, stout young man in a Scotch cap, with long ends of ribbon behind. This was Vassenka Veslovsky, a distant cousin of the Shtcherbatskys, a brilliant young gentleman in Petersburg and Moscow society. "A capital fellow, and a keen sportsman," as Stepan Arkadyevitch said, introducing him.

Not a whit abashed by the disappointment caused by his having come in place of the old prince, Veslovsky greeted Levin gaily, claiming acquaintance with him in the past, and snatching up Grisha into the carriage, lifted him over the pointer that Stepan Arkadyevitch had brought with him.

Levin did not get into the carriage, but walked behind. He was rather vexed at the non-arrival of the old prince, whom he liked more and more the more he saw of him, and also at the arrival of this Vassenka Veslovsky, a quite uncongenial and superfluous person. He seemed to him still more uncongenial and superfluous when, on approaching the steps where the whole party, children and grown-up, were gathered together in much excitement, Levin saw Vassenka Veslovsky, with a particularly warm and gallant air, kissing Kitty's hand.

"Your wife and I are cousins and very old friends," said Vassenka Veslovsky, once more shaking Levin's hand with great warmth.

"Well, are there plenty of birds?" Stepan Arkadyevitch said to Levin, hardly leaving time for every one to utter their greetings. "We've come with the most savage intentions. Why, maman, they've not been in Moscow since! Look, Tanya, here's something for you! Get it, please, it's in the carriage, behind!" he talked in all directions. "How pretty you've grown, Dolly," he said to his wife, once more kissing her hand, holding it in one of his, and patting it with the other.

Levin, who a minute before had been in the happiest frame of mind, now looked darkly at every one, and everything displeased him.

"Who was it he kissed yesterday with those lips?" he thought, looking at Stepan Arkadyevitch's tender demonstrations to his wife. He looked at Dolly, and he did not like her either.

"She doesn't believe in his love. So what is she so pleased about? Revolting!" thought Levin.

He looked at the princess, who had been so dear to him a minute before, and he did not like the manner in which she welcomed this Vassenka, with his ribbons, just as though she were in her own house.

Even Sergey Ivanovitch, who had come out too onto the steps, seemed to him unpleasant with the show of cordiality with which he met Stepan Arkadyevitch, though Levin knew that his brother neither liked nor respected Oblonsky.

And Varenka, even she seemed hateful, with her air *sainte nitouche* making the acquaintance of this gentleman, while all the while she was thinking of nothing but getting married.

And more hateful than anyone was Kitty for falling in with the tone of gaiety with which this gentleman regarded his visit in the country, as though it were a holiday for himself and every one else. And, above all, unpleasant was that particular smile with which she responded to his smile.

Noisily talking, they all went into the house; but as soon as they were all seated, Levin turned and went out.

Kitty saw something was wrong with her husband. She tried to seize a moment to speak to him alone, but he made haste to get away from her, saying he was wanted at the counting-house. It was long since his own work on the estate had seemed to him so important as at that moment. "It's all holiday for them," he thought; "but these are no holiday matters, they won't wait, and there's no living without them."

CHAPTER VII

L EVIN CAME BACK TO THE HOUSE ONLY WHEN THEY SENT TO SUMMON HIM TO supper. On the stairs were standing Kitty and Agafea Mihalovna, consulting about wines for supper.

Levin saw that look. He turned white, and for a minute he could hardly breathe. "How dare he look at my wife like that!" was the feeling that boiled within him.

"To-morrow, then? Do, please, let us go," said Vassenka, sitting down on a chair, and again crossing his leg as his habit was.

Levin's jealousy went further still. Already he saw himself a deceived husband, looked upon by his wife and her lover as simply necessary to provide them with the conveniences and pleasures of life.... But in spite of that he made polite and hospitable inquiries of Vassenka about his shooting, his gun, and his boots, and agreed to go shooting next day.

Happily for Levin, the old princess cut short his agonies by getting up herself and advising Kitty to go to bed. But even at this point Levin could not escape another agony. As he said good-night to his hostess, Vassenka would again have kissed her hand, but Kitty, reddening, drew back her hand and said with a naïve bluntness, for which the old princess scolded her afterwards:

"We don't like that fashion."

In Levin's eyes she was to blame for having allowed such relations to arise, and still more to blame for showing so awkwardly that she did not like them.

"Why, how can one want to go to bed!" said Stepan Arkadyevitch, who, after drinking several glasses of wine at supper, was now in his most charming and sentimental humor. "Look, Kitty," he said, pointing to the moon, which had just risen behind the lime-trees —"how exquisite! Veslovsky, this is the time for a serenade. You know, he has a splendid voice; we practiced songs together along the road. He has brought some lovely songs with him, two new ones. Varvara Andreevna and he must sing some duets."

When the party had broken up, Stepan Arkadyevitch walked a long while about the avenue with Veslovsky; their voices could be heard singing one of the new songs.

Levin hearing these voices sat scowling in an easy-chair in his wife's bedroom, and maintained an obstinate silence when she asked him what was wrong. But when at last with a timid glance she hazarded the question: "Was there perhaps something you disliked about Veslovsky?"—it all burst out, and he told her all. He was humiliated himself at what he was saying, and that exasperated him all the more.

He stood facing her with his eyes glittering menacingly under his scowling brows, and he squeezed his strong arms across his chest, as though he were straining every nerve to hold himself in. The expression of his face would have been grim, and even cruel, if it had not at the same time had a look of suffering which touched her. His jaws were twitching, and his voice kept breaking.

"You must understand that I'm not jealous, that's a nasty word. I can't be jealous, and believe that.... I can't say what I feel, but this is awful.... I'm not jealous, but I'm wounded, humiliated that anybody dare think, that anybody dare look at you with eyes like that."

"Eyes like what?" said Kitty, trying as conscientiously as possible to recall every word and gesture of that evening and every shade implied in them.

At the very bottom of her heart she did think there had been something precisely at the moment when he had crossed over after her to the other end of the table; but she dared not own it even to herself, and would have been even more unable to bring herself to say so to him, and so increase his suffering.

"And what can there possibly be attractive about me as I am now?..."

"Ah!" he cried, clutching at his head, "you shouldn't say that! ... If you had been attractive then ..."

"Oh, no, Kostya, oh, wait a minute, oh, do listen!" she said, looking at him with an expression of pained commiseration. "Why, what can you be thinking about! When for me there's no one in the world, no one, no one! ... Would you like me never to see any one?"

For the first minute she had been offended at his jealousy; she was angry that the slightest amusement, even the most innocent, should be forbidden her; but now she would readily have sacrificed, not merely such trifles, but everything, for his peace of mind, to save him from the agony he was suffering.

"You must understand the horror and comedy of my position," he went on in a desperate whisper; "that he's in my house, that he's done nothing improper positively except his free and easy airs and the way he sits on his legs. He thinks it's the best possible form, and so I'm obliged to be civil to him."

"But, Kostya, you're exaggerating," said Kitty, at the bottom of her heart rejoicing at the depth of his love for her, shown now in his jealousy.

"The most awful part of it all is that you're just as you always are, and especially now when to me you're something sacred, and we're so happy, so particularly happy—and all of a sudden a little wretch ... He's not a little wretch; why should I abuse him? I have nothing to do with him. But why should my, and your, happiness ..."

"Do you know, I understand now what it's all come from," Kitty was beginning.

"Well, what? what?"

"I saw how you looked while we were talking at supper."

The point was that in the lodge that was being built the carpenter had spoiled the staircase, fitting it together without calculating the space it was to fill, so that the steps were all sloping when it was put in place. Now the carpenter wanted, keeping the same staircase, to add three steps.

"It will be much better."

"But where's your staircase coming out with its three steps?"

"Why, upon my word, sir," the carpenter said with a contemptuous smile. "It comes out right at the very spot. It starts, so to speak," he said, with a persuasive gesture; "it comes down, and comes down, and comes out."

"But three steps will add to the length too ... where is it to come out?"

"Why, to be sure, it'll start from the bottom and go up and go up, and come out so," the carpenter said obstinately and convincingly.

"It'll reach the ceiling and the wall."

"Upon my word! Why, it'll go up, and up, and come out like this."

Levin took out a ramrod and began sketching him the staircase in the dust.

"There, do you see?"

"As your honor likes," said the carpenter, with a sudden gleam in his eyes, obviously understanding the thing at last. "It seems it'll be best to make a new one."

"Well, then, do it as you're told," Levin shouted, seating himself in the wagonette. "Down! Hold the dogs, Philip!"

Levin felt now at leaving behind all his family and household cares such an eager sense of joy in life and expectation that he was not disposed to talk. Besides that, he had that feeling of concentrated excitement that every sportsman experiences as he approaches the scene of action. If he had anything on his mind at that moment, it was only the doubt whether they would start anything in the Kolpensky marsh, whether Laska would show to advantage in comparison with Krak, and whether he would shoot well that day himself. Not to disgrace himself before a new spectator—not to be outdone by Oblonsky—that too was a thought that crossed his brain.

Oblonsky was feeling the same, and he too was not talkative. Vassenka Veslovsky kept up alone a ceaseless flow of cheerful chatter. As he listened to him now, Levin felt ashamed to think how unfair he had been to him the day before. Vassenka was really a nice fellow, simple, good-hearted, and very good-humored. If Levin had met him before he was married, he would have made friends with him. Levin rather disliked his holiday attitude to life and a sort of free and easy assumption of elegance. It was as though he assumed a high degree of importance in himself that could not be disputed, because he had long nails and a stylish cap, and everything else to correspond; but this could be forgiven for the sake of his good nature and good breeding. Levin liked him for his good education, for speaking French and English with such an excellent accent, and for being a man of his world.

Vassenka was extremely delighted with the left horse, a horse of the Don steppes. He kept praising him enthusiastically. "How fine it must be galloping over the steppes on a steppe horse! Eh? isn't it?" he said. He had imagined riding on a steppe horse as something wild and romantic, and it turned out nothing of the sort. But his simplicity, particularly in conjunction with his good looks, his amiable smile, and the grace of his movements, was very attractive. Either because his nature was sympathetic to Levin, or because Levin was trying to atone for his sins of the previous evening by seeing nothing but what was good in him, anyway he liked his society.

After they had driven over two miles from home, Veslovsky all at once felt for a cigar and his pocketbook, and did not know whether he had lost them or left them on the table. In the pocketbook there were thirty-seven pounds, and so the matter could not be left in uncertainty.

"Do you know what, Levin, I'll gallop home on that left trace-horse. That will be splendid. Eh?" he said, preparing to get out.

"No, why should you?" answered Levin, calculating that Vassenka could hardly weigh less than seventeen stone. "I'll send the coachman."

The coachman rode back on the trace-horse, and Levin himself drove the remaining pair.

CHAPTER IX

WELL, NOW WHAT'S OUR PLAN OF CAMPAIGN? TELL US ALL ABOUT IT," said Stepan Arkadyevitch.

"Our plan is this. Now we're driving to Gvozdyov. In Gvozdyov there's a grouse marsh on this side, and beyond Gvozdyov come some magnificent snipe marshes where there are grouse too. It's hot now, and we'll get there—it's fifteen miles or so—towards evening and have some evening shooting; we'll spend the night there and go on to-morrow to the bigger moors."

"And is there nothing on the way?"

grew louder, came closer, and was joined with the sound of Veslovsky's voice, shouting something with strange loudness. Levin saw he had his gun pointed behind the snipe, but still he fired.

When he had made sure he had missed, Levin looked round and saw the horses and the wagonette not on the road but in the marsh.

Veslovsky, eager to see the shooting, had driven into the marsh, and got the horses stuck in the mud.

"Damn the fellow!" Levin said to himself, as he went back to the carriage that had sunk in the mire. "What did you drive in for?" he said to him dryly, and calling the coachman, he began pulling the horses out.

Levin was vexed both at being hindered from shooting and at his horses getting stuck in the mud, and still more at the fact that neither Stepan Arkadyevitch nor Veslovsky helped him and the coachman to unharness the horses and get them out, since neither of them had the slightest notion of harnessing. Without vouchsafing a syllable in reply to Vassenka's protestations that it had been quite dry there, Levin worked in silence with the coachman at extricating the horses. But then, as he got warm at the work and saw how assiduously Veslovsky was tugging at the wagonette by one of the mud-guards, so that he broke it indeed, Levin blamed himself for having under the influence of yesterday's feelings been too cold to Veslovsky, and tried to be particularly genial so as to smooth over his chilliness. When everything had been put right, and the carriage had been brought back to the road, Levin had the lunch served.

"*Bon appétit—bonne conscience! Ce poulet va tomber jusqu'au fond de mes bottes*," Vassenka, who had recovered his spirits, quoted the French saying as he finished his second chicken. "Well, now our troubles are over, now everything's going to go well. Only, to atone for my sins, I'm bound to sit on the box. That's so? eh? No, no! I'll be your Automedon. You shall see how I'll get you along," he answered, not letting go the rein, when Levin begged him to let the coachman drive. "No, I must atone for my sins, and I'm very comfortable on the box." And he drove.

Levin was a little afraid he would exhaust the horses, especially the chestnut, whom he did not know how to hold in; but unconsciously he fell under the influence of his gaiety and listened to the songs he sang all the way on the box, or the descriptions and representations he gave of driving in the English fashion, four-in-hand; and it was in the very best of spirits that after lunch they drove to the Gvozdyov marsh.

CHAPTER X

VASSENKA DROVE THE HORSES SO SMARTLY THAT THEY REACHED THE MARSH too early, while it was still hot.

As they drew near this more important marsh, the chief aim of their expedition, Levin could not help considering how he could get rid of Vassenka and be free in his movements. Stepan Arkadyevitch evidently had the same desire, and on his face Levin saw the look of anxiety always present in a true sportsman when beginning shooting, together with a certain good-humored slyness peculiar to him.

"How shall we go? It's a splendid marsh, I see, and there are hawks," said Stepan Arkadyevitch, pointing to two great birds hovering over the reeds. "Where there are hawks, there is sure to be game."

"Now, gentlemen," said Levin, pulling up his boots and examining the lock of his gun with rather a gloomy expression, "do you see those reeds?" He pointed to an oasis of blackish green in the huge half-mown wet meadow that stretched along the right bank of the river. "The marsh begins here, straight in front of us, do you see—where it is greener? From here it runs to the right where the horses are; there are breeding-places there, and grouse, and all round those reeds as far as that alder, and right up to the mill. Over there, do you see, where the pools are? That's the best place. There I once shot seventeen snipe. We'll separate with the dogs and go in different directions, and then meet over there at the mill."

"Well, which shall go to left and which to right?" asked Stepan Arkadyevitch. "It's wider to the right; you two go that way and I'll take the left," he said with apparent carelessness.

"Capital! we'll make the bigger bag! Yes, come along, come along!" Vassenka exclaimed.

Levin could do nothing but agree, and they divided.

As soon as they entered the marsh, the two dogs began hunting about together and made towards the green, slime-covered pool. Levin knew Laska's method, wary and indefinite; he knew the place too and expected a whole covey of snipe.

"Veslovsky, beside me, walk beside me!" he said in a faint voice to his companion splashing in the water behind him. Levin could not help feeling an interest in the direction his gun was pointed, after that casual shot near the Kolpensky marsh.

mire, and for a minute he hesitated. But Laska was setting. And immediately all his weariness vanished, and he walked lightly through the swamp towards the dog. A snipe flew up at his feet; he fired and killed it. Laska still pointed.— "Fetch it!" Another bird flew up close to the dog. Levin fired. But it was an unlucky day for him; he missed it, and when he went to look for the one he had shot, he could not find that either. He wandered all about the reeds, but Laska did not believe he had shot it, and when he sent her to find it, she pretended to hunt for it, but did not really. And in the absence of Vassenka, on whom Levin threw the blame of his failure, things went no better. There were plenty of snipe still, but Levin made one miss after another.

The slanting rays of the sun were still hot; his clothes, soaked through with perspiration, stuck to his body; his left boot full of water weighed heavily on his leg and squeaked at every step; the sweat ran in drops down his powder-grimed face, his mouth was full of the bitter taste, his nose of the smell of powder and stagnant water, his ears were ringing with the incessant whir of the snipe; he could not touch the stock of his gun, it was so hot; his heart beat with short, rapid throbs; his hands shook with excitement, and his weary legs stumbled and staggered over the hillocks and in the swamp, but still he walked on and still he shot. At last, after a disgraceful miss, he flung his gun and his hat on the ground.

"No, I must control myself," he said to himself. Picking up his gun and his hat, he called Laska, and went out of the swamp. When he got on to dry ground he sat down, pulled off his boot and emptied it, then walked to the marsh, drank some stagnant-tasting water, moistened his burning hot gun, and washed his face and hands. Feeling refreshed, he went back to the spot where a snipe had settled, firmly resolved to keep cool.

He tried to be calm, but it was the same again. His finger pressed the cock before he had taken a good aim at the bird. It got worse and worse.

He had only five birds in his game-bag when he walked out of the marsh towards the alders where he was to rejoin Stepan Arkadyevitch.

Before he caught sight of Stepan Arkadyevitch he saw his dog. Krak darted out from behind the twisted root of an alder, black all over with the stinking mire of the marsh, and with the air of a conqueror sniffed at Laska. Behind Krak there came into view in the shade of the alder-tree the shapely figure of Stepan Arkadyevitch. He came to meet him, red and perspiring, with unbuttoned neckband, still limping in the same way.

"Well? You have been popping away!" he said, smiling good-humoredly.

"How have you got on?" queried Levin. But there was no need to ask, for he had already seen the full game-bag.

"Oh, pretty fair."

He had fourteen birds.

"A splendid marsh! I've no doubt Veslovsky got in your way. It's awkward too, shooting with one dog," said Stepan Arkadyevitch, to soften his triumph.

CHAPTER XI

WHEN LEVIN AND STEPAN ARKADYEVITCH REACHED THE PEASANT'S hut where Levin always used to stay, Veslovsky was already there. He was sitting in the middle of the hut, clinging with both hands to the bench from which he was being pulled by a soldier, the brother of the peasant's wife, who was helping him off with his miry boots. Veslovsky was laughing his infectious, good-humored laugh.

"I've only just come. *Ils ont été charmants.* Just fancy, they gave me drink, fed me! Such bread, it was exquisite! *Délicieux!* And the vodka, I never tasted any better. And they would not take a penny for anything. And they kept saying: 'Excuse our homely ways.'"

"What should they take anything for? They were entertaining you, to be sure. Do you suppose they keep vodka for sale?" said the soldier, succeeding at last in pulling the soaked boot off the blackened stocking.

In spite of the dirtiness of the hut, which was all muddied by their boots and the filthy dogs licking themselves clean, and the smell of marsh mud and powder that filled the room, and the absence of knives and forks, the party drank their tea and ate their supper with a relish only known to sportsmen. Washed and clean, they went into a hay-barn swept ready for them, where the coachman had been making up beds for the gentlemen.

Though it was dusk, not one of them wanted to go to sleep.

After wavering among reminiscences and anecdotes of guns, of dogs, and of former shooting-parties, the conversation rested on a topic that interested all of them. After Vassenka had several times over expressed his appreciation of this delightful sleeping-place among the fragrant hay, this delightful broken cart (he supposed it to be broken because the shafts had been taken out), of the good-nature of the peasants that had treated him to vodka, of the dogs who lay at the feet of their respective masters, Oblonsky began telling them of a delightful shooting-party at Malthus's, where he had stayed the previous summer.

"No, excuse me, that's a paradox."

"Yes, there's something of a sophistry about that," Veslovsky agreed. "Ah! our host; so you're not asleep yet?" he said to the peasant who came into the barn, opening the creaking door. "How is it you're not asleep?"

"No, how's one to sleep! I thought our gentlemen would be asleep, but I heard them chattering. I want to get a hook from here. She won't bite?" he added, stepping cautiously with his bare feet.

"And where are you going to sleep?"

"We are going out for the night with the beasts."

"Ah, what a night!" said Veslovsky, looking out at the edge of the hut and the unharnessed wagonette that could be seen in the faint light of the evening glow in the great frame of the open doors. "But listen, there are women's voices singing, and, on my word, not badly too. Who's that singing, my friend?"

"That's the maids from hard by here."

"Let's go, let's have a walk! We shan't go to sleep, you know. Oblonsky, come along!"

"If one could only do both, lie here and go," answered Oblonsky, stretching. "It's capital lying here."

"Well, I shall go by myself," said Veslovsky, getting up eagerly, and putting on his shoes and stockings. "Good-bye, gentlemen. If it's fun, I'll fetch you. You've treated me to some good sport, and I won't forget you."

"He really is a capital fellow, isn't he?" said Stepan Arkadyevitch, when Veslovsky had gone out and the peasant had closed the door after him.

"Yes, capital," answered Levin, still thinking of the subject of their conversation just before. It seemed to him that he had clearly expressed his thoughts and feelings to the best of his capacity, and yet both of them, straightforward men and not fools, had said with one voice that he was comforting himself with sophistries. This disconcerted him.

"It's just this, my dear boy. One must do one of two things: either admit that the existing order of society is just, and then stick up for one's rights in it; or acknowledge that you are enjoying unjust privileges, as I do, and then enjoy them and be satisfied."

"No, if it were unjust, you could not enjoy these advantages and be satisfied—at least I could not. The great thing for me is to feel that I'm not to blame."

"What do you say, why not go after all?" said Stepan Arkadyevitch, evidently weary of the strain of thought. "We shan't go to sleep, you know. Come, let's go!"

Levin did not answer. What they had said in the conversation, that he acted justly only in a negative sense, absorbed his thoughts. "Can it be that it's only possible to be just negatively?" he was asking himself.

"How strong the smell of the fresh hay is, though," said Stepan Arkady-evitch, getting up. "There's not a chance of sleeping. Vassenka has been getting up some fun there. Do you hear the laughing and his voice? Hadn't we better go? Come along!"

"No, I'm not coming," answered Levin.

"Surely that's not a matter of principle too," said Stepan Arkadyevitch, smiling, as he felt about in the dark for his cap.

"It's not a matter of principle, but why should I go?"

"But do you know you are preparing trouble for yourself," said Stepan Arkadyevitch, finding his cap and getting up.

"How so?"

"Do you suppose I don't see the line you've taken up with your wife? I heard how it's a question of the greatest consequence, whether or not you're to be away for a couple of days' shooting. That's all very well as an idyllic episode, but for your whole life that won't answer. A man must be independent; he has his masculine interests. A man has to be manly," said Oblonsky, opening the door.

"In what way? To go running after servant-girls?" said Levin.

"Why not, if it amuses him? *Ça ne tire pas à conséquence.* It won't do my wife any harm, and it'll amuse me. The great thing is to respect the sanctity of the home. There should be nothing in the home. But don't tie your own hands."

"Perhaps so," said Levin dryly, and he turned on his side. "To-morrow, early, I want to go shooting, and I won't wake any one, and shall set off at daybreak."

"*Messieurs, venez vite!*" they heard the voice of Veslovsky coming back. "*Charmante!* I've made such a discovery. *Charmante!* a perfect Gretchen, and I've already made friends with her. Really, exceedingly pretty," he declared in a tone of approval, as though she had been made pretty entirely on his account, and he was expressing his satisfaction with the entertainment that had been provided for him.

Levin pretended to be asleep, while Oblonsky, putting on his slippers, and lighting a cigar, walked out of the barn, and soon their voices were lost.

For a long while Levin could not get to sleep. He heard the horses munch-ing hay, then he heard the peasant and his elder boy getting ready for the night,

Laska ran joyfully and anxiously through the slush that swayed under her.

Running into the marsh among the familiar scents of roots, marsh plants, and slime, and the extraneous smell of horse dung, Laska detected at once a smell that pervaded the whole marsh, the scent of that strong-smelling bird that always excited her more than any other. Here and there among the moss and marsh plants this scent was very strong, but it was impossible to determine in which direction it grew stronger or fainter. To find the direction, she had to go further away from the wind. Not feeling the motion of her legs, Laska bounded with a stiff gallop, so that at each bound she could stop short, to the right, away from the wind that blew from the east before sunrise, and turned facing the wind. Sniffing in the air with dilated nostrils, she felt at once that not their tracks only but they themselves were here before her, and not one, but many. Laska slackened her speed. They were here, but where precisely she could not yet determine. To find the very spot, she began to make a circle, when suddenly her master's voice drew her off. "Laska! here?" he asked, pointing her to a different direction. She stopped, asking him if she had better not go on doing as she had begun. But he repeated his command in an angry voice, pointing to a spot covered with water, where there could not be anything. She obeyed him, pretending she was looking, so as to please him, went round it, and went back to her former position, and was at once aware of the scent again. Now when he was not hindering her, she knew what to do, and without looking at what was under her feet, and to her vexation stumbling over a high stump into the water, but righting herself with her strong, supple legs, she began making the circle which was to make all clear to her. The scent of them reached her, stronger and stronger, and more and more defined, and all at once it became perfectly clear to her that one of them was here, behind this tuft of reeds, five paces in front of her; she stopped, and her whole body was still and rigid. On her short legs she could see nothing in front of her, but by the scent she knew it was sitting not more than five paces off. She stood still, feeling more and more conscious of it, and enjoying it in anticipation. Her tail was stretched straight and tense, and only wagging at the extreme end. Her mouth was slightly open, her ears raised. One ear had been turned wrong side out as she ran up, and she breathed heavily but warily, and still more warily looked round, but more with her eyes than her head, to her master. He was coming along with the face she knew so well, though the eyes were always terrible to her. He stumbled over the stump as he came, and moved, as she thought, extraordinarily slowly. She thought he came slowly, but he was running.

Noticing Laska's special attitude as she crouched on the ground, as it were, scratching big prints with her hind paws, and with her mouth slightly open,

Levin knew she was pointing at grouse, and with an inward prayer for luck, especially with the first bird, he ran up to her. Coming quite close up to her, he could from his height look beyond her, and he saw with his eyes what she was seeing with her nose. In a space between two little thickets, to a couple of yards' distance, he could see a grouse. Turning its head, it was listening. Then lightly preening and folding its wings, it disappeared round a corner with a clumsy wag of its tail.

"Fetch it, fetch it!" shouted Levin, giving Laska a shove from behind.

"But I can't go," thought Laska. "Where am I to go? From here I feel them, but if I move forward I shall know nothing of where they are or who they are." But then he shoved her with his knee, and in an excited whisper said, "Fetch it, Laska."

"Well, if that's what he wishes, I'll do it, but I can't answer for myself now," she thought, and darted forward as fast as her legs would carry her between the thick bushes. She scented nothing now; she could only see and hear, without understanding anything.

Ten paces from her former place a grouse rose with a guttural cry and the peculiar round sound of its wings. And immediately after the shot it splashed heavily with its white breast on the wet mire. Another bird did not linger, but rose behind Levin without the dog. When Levin turned towards it, it was already some way off. But his shot caught it. Flying twenty paces further, the second grouse rose upwards, and whirling round like a ball, dropped heavily on a dry place.

"Come, this is going to be some good!" thought Levin, packing the warm and fat grouse into his game-bag. "Eh, Laska, will it be good?"

When Levin, after loading his gun, moved on, the sun had fully risen, though unseen behind the storm-clouds. The moon had lost all of its luster, and was like a white cloud in the sky. Not a single star could be seen. The sedge, silvery with dew before, now shone like gold. The stagnant pools were all like amber. The blue of the grass had changed to yellow-green. The marsh birds twittered and swarmed about the brook and upon the bushes that glittered with dew and cast long shadows. A hawk woke up and settled on a haycock, turning its head from side to side and looking discontentedly at the marsh. Crows were flying about the field, and a bare-legged boy was driving the horses to an old man, who had got up from under his long coat and was combing his hair. The smoke from the gun was white as milk over the green of the grass.

One of the boys ran up to Levin.

"Uncle, there were ducks here yesterday!" he shouted to him, and he walked a little way off behind him.

CHAPTER XIV

NEXT DAY AT TEN O'CLOCK LEVIN, WHO HAD ALREADY GONE HIS ROUNDS, knocked at the room where Vassenka had been put for the night.

"*Entrez!*" Veslovsky called to him. "Excuse me, I've only just finished my ablutions," he said, smiling, standing before him in his underclothes only.

"Don't mind me, please." Levin sat down in the window. "Have you slept well?"

"Like the dead. What sort of day is it for shooting?"

"What will you take, tea or coffee?"

"Neither. I'll wait till lunch. I'm really ashamed. I suppose the ladies are down? A walk now would be capital. You show me your horses."

After walking about the garden, visiting the stable, and even doing some gymnastic exercises together on the parallel bars, Levin returned to the house with his guest, and went with him into the drawing-room.

"We had splendid shooting, and so many delightful experiences!" said Veslovsky, going up to Kitty, who was sitting at the samovar. "What a pity ladies are cut off from these delights!"

"Well, I suppose he must say something to the lady of the house," Levin said to himself. Again he fancied something in the smile, in the all-conquering air with which their guest addressed Kitty....

The princess, sitting on the other side of the table with Marya Vlasyevna and Stepan Arkadyevitch, called Levin to her side, and began to talk to him about moving to Moscow for Kitty's confinement, and getting ready rooms for them. Just as Levin had disliked all the trivial preparations for his wedding, as derogatory to the grandeur of the event, now he felt still more offensive the preparations for the approaching birth, the date of which they reckoned, it seemed, on their fingers. He tried to turn a deaf ear to these discussions of the best patterns of long clothes for the coming baby; tried to turn away and avoid seeing the mysterious, endless strips of knitting, the triangles of linen, and so on, to which Dolly attached special importance. The birth of a son (he was certain it would be a son) which was promised him, but which he still could not believe in—so marvelous it seemed—presented itself to his mind, on one hand, as a happiness so immense, and therefore so incredible; on the other, as an event so mysterious, that this assumption of a definite knowledge of what would be, and consequent preparation for it, as for something ordinary that did happen to people, jarred on him as confusing and humiliating.

But the princess did not understand his feelings, and put down his reluctance to think and talk about it to carelessness and indifference, and so she gave him no peace. She had commissioned Stepan Arkadyevitch to look at a flat, and now she called Levin up.

"I know nothing about it, princess. Do as you think fit," he said.

"You must decide when you will move."

"I really don't know. I know millions of children are born away from Moscow, and doctors ... why ..."

"But if so ..."

"Oh, no, as Kitty wishes."

"We can't talk to Kitty about it! Do you want me to frighten her? Why, this spring Natalia Golitzina died from having an ignorant doctor."

"I will do just what you say," he said gloomily.

The princess began talking to him, but he did not hear her. Though the conversation with the princess had indeed jarred upon him, he was gloomy, not on account of that conversation, but from what he saw at the samovar.

"No, it's impossible," he thought, glancing now and then at Vassenka bending over Kitty, telling her something with his charming smile, and at her, flushed and disturbed.

There was something not nice in Vassenka's attitude, in his eyes, in his smile. Levin even saw something not nice in Kitty's attitude and look. And again the light died away in his eyes. Again, as before, all of a sudden, without the slightest transition, he felt cast down from a pinnacle of happiness, peace, and dignity, into an abyss of despair, rage, and humiliation. Again everything and every one had become hateful to him.

"You do just as you think best, princess," he said again, looking round.

"Heavy is the cap of Monomach," Stepan Arkadyevitch said playfully, hinting, evidently, not simply at the princess's conversation, but at the cause of Levin's agitation, which he had noticed.

"How late you are to-day, Dolly!"

Every one got up to greet Darya Alexandrovna. Vassenka only rose for an instant, and with the lack of courtesy to ladies characteristic of the modern young man, he scarcely bowed, and resumed his conversation again, laughing at something.

"I've been worried about Masha. She did not sleep well, and is dreadfully tiresome to-day," said Dolly.

"Why, what has she done?" Levin said without much interest, for he had wanted to ask her advice, and so was annoyed that he had come at an unlucky moment.

"Grisha and she went into the raspberries, and there ... I can't tell you really what she did. It's a thousand pities Miss Elliot's not with us. This one sees to nothing—she's a machine ... *Figurez-vous que la petite?* ..."

And Darya Alexandrovna described Masha's crime.

"That proves nothing; it's not a question of evil propensities at all, it's simply mischief," Levin assured her.

"But you are upset about something? What have you come for?" asked Dolly. "What's going on there?"

And in the tone of her question Levin heard that it would be easy for him to say what he had meant to say.

"I've not been in there, I've been alone in the garden with Kitty. We've had a quarrel for the second time since ... Stiva came."

Dolly looked at him with her shrewd, comprehending eyes.

"Come, tell me, honor bright, has there been ... not in Kitty, but in that gentleman's behavior, a tone which might be unpleasant—not unpleasant, but horrible, offensive to a husband?"

"You mean, how shall I say ... Stay, stay in the corner!" she said to Masha, who, detecting a faint smile in her mother's face, had been turning round. "The opinion of the world would be that he is behaving as young men do behave. *Il fait la cour à une jeune et jolie femme*, and a husband who's a man of the world should only be flattered by it."

"Yes, yes," said Levin gloomily; "but you noticed it?"

"Not only I, but Stiva noticed it. Just after breakfast he said to me in so many words, *Je crois que Veslovsky fait un petit brin de cour à Kitty*."

"Well, that's all right then; now I'm satisfied. I'll send him away," said Levin.

"What do you mean! Are you crazy?" Dolly cried in horror; "nonsense, Kostya, only think!" she said, laughing. "You can go now to Fanny," she said to Masha. "No, if you wish it, I'll speak to Stiva. He'll take him away. He can say you're expecting visitors. Altogether he doesn't fit into the house."

"No, no, I'll do it myself."

"But you'll quarrel with him?"

"Not a bit. I shall so enjoy it," Levin said, his eyes flashing with real enjoyment. "Come, forgive her, Dolly, she won't do it again," he said of the little sinner, who had not gone to Fanny, but was standing irresolutely before her mother, waiting and looking up from under her brows to catch her mother's eye.

The mother glanced at her. The child broke into sobs, hid her face on her mother's lap, and Dolly laid her thin, tender hand on her head.

"And what is there in common between us and him?" thought Levin, and he went off to look for Veslovsky.

As he passed through the passage he gave orders for the carriage to be got ready to drive to the station.

"The spring was broken yesterday," said the footman.

"Well, the covered trap, then, and make haste. Where's the visitor?"

"The gentleman's gone to his room."

Levin came upon Veslovsky at the moment when the latter, having unpacked his things from his trunk, and laid out some new songs, was putting on his gaiters to go out riding.

Whether there was something exceptional in Levin's face, or that Vassenka was himself conscious that *ce petit brin de cour* he was making was out of place in this family, but he was somewhat (as much as a young man in society can be) disconcerted at Levin's entrance.

"You ride in gaiters?"

"Yes, it's much cleaner," said Vassenka, putting his fat leg on a chair, fastening the bottom hook, and smiling with simple-hearted good-humor.

He was undoubtedly a good-natured fellow, and Levin felt sorry for him and ashamed of himself, as his host, when he saw the shy look on Vassenka's face.

On the table lay a piece of stick which they had broken together that morning, trying their strength. Levin took the fragment in his hands and began smashing it up, breaking bits off the stick, not knowing how to begin.

"I wanted …" He paused, but suddenly, remembering Kitty and everything that had happened, he said, looking him resolutely in the face: "I have ordered the horses to be put-to for you."

"How so?" Vassenka began in surprise. "To drive where?"

"For you to drive to the station," Levin said gloomily.

"Are you going away, or has something happened?"

"It happens that I expect visitors," said Levin, his strong fingers more and more rapidly breaking off the ends of the split stick. "And I'm not expecting visitors, and nothing has happened, but I beg you to go away. You can explain my rudeness as you like."

Vassenka drew himself up.

"I beg you to explain …" he said with dignity, understanding at last.

"I can't explain," Levin said softly and deliberately, trying to control the trembling of his jaw; "and you'd better not ask."

taking Darya Alexandrovna the whole distance in a single day. At that moment, when horses were wanted for the princess, who was going, and for the midwife, it was a difficult matter for Levin to make up the number, but the duties of hospitality would not let him allow Darya Alexandrovna to hire horses when staying in his house. Moreover, he was well aware that the twenty roubles that would be asked for the journey were a serious matter for her; Darya Alexandrovna's pecuniary affairs, which were in a very unsatisfactory state, were taken to heart by the Levins as if they were their own.

Darya Alexandrovna, by Levin's advice, started before daybreak. The road was good, the carriage comfortable, the horses trotted along merrily, and on the box, besides the coachman, sat the counting-house clerk, whom Levin was sending instead of a groom for greater security. Darya Alexandrovna dozed and waked up only on reaching the inn where the horses were to be changed.

After drinking tea at the same well-to-do peasant's with whom Levin had stayed on the way to Sviazhsky's, and chatting with the women about their children, and with the old man about Count Vronsky, whom the latter praised very highly, Darya Alexandrovna, at ten o'clock, went on again. At home, looking after her children, she had no time to think. So now, after this journey of four hours, all the thoughts she had suppressed before rushed swarming into her brain, and she thought over all her life as she never had before, and from the most different points of view. Her thoughts seemed strange even to herself. At first she thought about the children, about whom she was uneasy, although the princess and Kitty (she reckoned more upon her) had promised to look after them. "If only Masha does not begin her naughty tricks, if Grisha isn't kicked by a horse, and Lily's stomach isn't upset again!" she thought. But these questions of the present were succeeded by questions of the immediate future. She began thinking how she had to get a new flat in Moscow for the coming winter, to renew the drawing-room furniture, and to make her elder girl a cloak. Then questions of the more remote future occurred to her: how she was to place her children in the world. "The girls are all right," she thought; "but the boys?"

"It's very well that I'm teaching Grisha, but of course that's only because I am free myself now, I'm not with child. Stiva, of course, there's no counting on. And with the help of good-natured friends I can bring them up; but if there's another baby coming? ..." And the thought struck her how untruly it was said that the curse laid on woman was that in sorrow she should bring forth children.

"The birth itself, that's nothing; but the months of carrying the child— that's what's so intolerable," she thought, picturing to herself her last pregnancy, and the death of the last baby. And she recalled the conversation she had just had with the young woman at the inn. On being asked whether she had any children, the handsome young woman had answered cheerfully:

"I had a girl baby, but God set me free; I buried her last Lent."

"Well, did you grieve very much for her?" asked Darya Alexandrovna.

"Why grieve? The old man has grandchildren enough as it is. It was only a trouble. No working, nor nothing. Only a tie."

This answer had struck Darya Alexandrovna as revolting in spite of the good-natured and pleasing face of the young woman; but now she could not help recalling these words. In those cynical words there was indeed a grain of truth.

"Yes, altogether," thought Darya Alexandrovna, looking back over her whole existence during those fifteen years of her married life, "pregnancy, sickness, mental incapacity, indifference to everything, and most of all— hideousness. Kitty, young and pretty as she is, even Kitty has lost her looks; and I when I'm with child become hideous, I know it. The birth, the agony, the hideous agonies, that last moment … then the nursing, the sleepless nights, the fearful pains…."

Darya Alexandrovna shuddered at the mere recollection of the pain from sore breasts which she had suffered with almost every child. "Then the children's illnesses, that everlasting apprehension; then bringing them up; evil propensities" (she thought of little Masha's crime among the raspberries), "education, Latin—it's all so incomprehensible and difficult. And on the top of it all, the death of these children." And there rose again before her imagination the cruel memory, that always tore her mother's heart, of the death of her last little baby, who had died of croup; his funeral, the callous indifference of all at the little pink coffin, and her own torn heart, and her lonely anguish at the sight of the pale little brow with its projecting temples, and the open, wondering little mouth seen in the coffin at the moment when it was being covered with the little pink lid with a cross braided on it.

"And all this, what's it for? What is to come of it all? That I'm wasting my life, never having a moment's peace, either with child, or nursing a child, forever irritable, peevish, wretched myself and worrying others, repulsive to my husband, while the children are growing up unhappy, badly educated, and penniless. Even now, if it weren't for spending the summer at the Levins', I don't know how we should be managing to live. Of course Kostya and Kitty have so much tact that we don't feel it; but it can't go on. They'll have children, they won't be able to keep us; it's a drag on them as it is. How is

"Vozdvizhenskoe, the manor-house? the count's?" he repeated; "go on to the end of this track. Then turn to the left. Straight along the avenue and you'll come right upon it. But whom do you want? The count himself?"

"Well, are they at home, my good man?" Darya Alexandrovna said vaguely, not knowing how to ask about Anna, even of this peasant.

"At home for sure," said the peasant, shifting from one bare foot to the other, and leaving a distinct print of five toes and a heel in the dust. "Sure to be at home," he repeated, evidently eager to talk. "Only yesterday visitors arrived. There's a sight of visitors come. What do you want?" He turned round and called to a lad, who was shouting something to him from the cart. "Oh! They all rode by here not long since, to look at a reaping-machine. They'll be home by now. And who will you be belonging to? ..."

"We've come a long way," said the coachman, climbing onto the box. "So it's not far?"

"I tell you, it's just here. As soon as you get out ..." he said, keeping hold all the while of the carriage.

A healthy-looking, broad-shouldered young fellow came up too.

"What, is it laborers they want for the harvest?" he asked.

"I don't know, my boy."

"So you keep to the left, and you'll come right on it," said the peasant, unmistakably loth to let the travelers go, and eager to converse.

The coachman started the horses, but they were only just turning off when the peasant shouted: "Stop! Hi, friend! Stop!" called the two voices. The coachman stopped.

"They're coming! They're yonder!" shouted the peasant. "See what a turn-out!" he said, pointing to four persons on horseback, and two in a *char-à-banc*, coming along the road.

They were Vronsky with a jockey, Veslovsky and Anna on horseback, and Princess Varvara and Sviazhsky in the *char-à-banc*. They had gone out to look at the working of a new reaping-machine.

When the carriage stopped, the party on horseback were coming at a walking-pace. Anna was in front beside Veslovsky. Anna, quietly walking her horse, a sturdy English cob with cropped mane and short tail, her beautiful head with her black hair straying loose under her high hat, her full shoulders, her slender waist in her black riding-habit, and all the ease and grace of her deportment, impressed Dolly.

For the first minute it seemed to her unsuitable for Anna to be on horseback. The conception of riding on horseback for a lady was, in Darya

Alexandrovna's mind, associated with ideas of youthful flirtation and frivol-
ity, which, in her opinion, was unbecoming in Anna's position. But when she
had scrutinized her, seeing her closer, she was at once reconciled to her riding.
In spite of her elegance, everything was so simple, quiet, and dignified in the
attitude, the dress and the movements of Anna, that nothing could have been
more natural.

Beside Anna, on a hot-looking gray cavalry-horse, was Vassenka Veslovsky
in his Scotch cap with floating ribbons, his stout legs stretched out in front, obviously pleased with his own appearance. Darya Alexandrovna could not suppress
a good-humored smile as she recognized him. Behind rode Vronsky on a dark
bay mare, obviously heated from galloping. He was holding her in, pulling at
the reins.

After him rode a little man in the dress of a jockey. Sviazhsky and Princess
Varvara in a new *char-à-banc* with a big, raven-black trotting-horse, overtook
the party on horseback.

Anna's face suddenly beamed with a joyful smile at the instant when, in the
little figure huddled in a corner of the old carriage, she recognized Dolly. She
uttered a cry, started in the saddle, and set her horse into a gallop. On reaching
the carriage she jumped off without assistance, and holding up her riding-habit,
she ran up to greet Dolly.

"I thought it was you and dared not think it. How delightful! You can't
fancy how glad I am!" she said, at one moment pressing her face against Dolly
and kissing her, and at the next holding her off and examining her with a smile.

"Here's a delightful surprise, Alexey!" she said, looking round at Vronsky,
who had dismounted, and was walking towards them.

Vronsky, taking off his tall gray hat, went up to Dolly.

"You wouldn't believe how glad we are to see you," he said, giving peculiar significance to the words, and showing his strong white teeth in a smile.

Vassenka Veslovsky, without getting off his horse, took off his cap and
greeted the visitor by gleefully waving the ribbons over his head.

"That's Princess Varvara," Anna said in reply to a glance of inquiry from
Dolly as the *char-à-banc* drove up.

"Ah!" said Darya Alexandrovna, and unconsciously her face betrayed her
dissatisfaction.

Princess Varvara was her husband's aunt, and she had long known her, and
did not respect her. She knew that Princess Varvara had passed her whole life
toadying on her rich relations, but that she should now be sponging on Vronsky,
a man who was nothing to her, mortified Dolly on account of her kinship with

green roofs that came into view behind the green hedges of acacia and lilac. "Quite a little town."

But Anna did not answer.

"No, no! How do you look at my position, what do you think of it?" she asked.

"I consider ..." Darya Alexandrovna was beginning, but at that instant Vassenka Veslovsky, having brought the cob to gallop with the right leg foremost, galloped past them, bumping heavily up and down in his short jacket on the chamois leather of the side-saddle. "He's doing it, Anna Arkadyevna!" he shouted.

Anna did not even glance at him; but again it seemed to Darya Alexandrovna out of place to enter upon such a long conversation in the carriage, and so she cut short her thought.

"I don't think anything," she said, "but I always loved you, and if one loves any one, one loves the whole person, just as they are and not as one would like them to be...."

Anna, taking her eyes off her friend's face and dropping her eyelids (this was a new habit Dolly had not seen in her before), pondered, trying to penetrate the full significance of the words. And obviously interpreting them as she would have wished, she glanced at Dolly.

"If you had any sins," she said, "they would all be forgiven you for your coming to see me and these words."

And Dolly saw that tears stood in her eyes. She pressed Anna's hand in silence.

"Well, what are these buildings? How many there are of them!" After a moment's silence she repeated her question.

"These are the servants' houses, barns, and stables," answered Anna. "And there the park begins. It had all gone to ruin, but Alexey had everything renewed. He is very fond of this place, and, what I never expected, he has become intensely interested in looking after it. But his is such a rich nature! Whatever he takes up, he does splendidly. So far from being bored by it, he works with passionate interest. He—with his temperament as I know it—he has become careful and businesslike, a first-rate manager, he positively reckons every penny in his management of the land. But only in that. When it's a question of tens of thousands, he doesn't think of money." She spoke with that gleefully sly smile with which women often talk of the secret characteristics only known to them—of those they love. "Do you see that big building? that's the new hospital. I believe it will cost over a hundred thousand; that's his hobby just now. And do you know how it all came about? The peasants asked him for some meadowland, I think it was, at a cheaper rate, and he refused, and I accused him of being miserly. Of course it was not really because of that, but everything together, he began this hospital to prove, do you see, that he was not miserly about money. *C'est une petitesse*, if you like, but I love him all the more for it. And now you'll see the house in a moment. It was his grandfather's house, and he has had nothing changed outside."

"How beautiful!" said Dolly, looking with involuntary admiration at the handsome house with columns, standing out among the different-colored greens of the old trees in the garden.

"Isn't it fine? And from the house, from the top, the view is wonderful."

They drove into a courtyard strewn with gravel and bright with flowers, in which two laborers were at work putting an edging of stones round the light mould of a flower-bed, and drew up in a covered entry.

"Ah, they're here already!" said Anna, looking at the saddle-horses, which were just being led away from the steps. "It is a nice horse, isn't it? It's my cob; my favorite. Lead him here and bring me some sugar. Where is the count?" she inquired of two smart footmen who darted out. "Ah, there he is!" she said, seeing Vronsky coming to meet her with Veslovsky.

"Where are you going to put the princess?" said Vronsky in French, addressing Anna, and without waiting for a reply, he once more greeted Darya Alexandrovna, and this time he kissed her hand. "I think the big balcony room."

"Oh, no, that's too far off! Better in the corner room, we shall see each other more. Come, let's go up," said Anna, as she gave her favorite horse the sugar the footman had brought her.

"*Et vous oubliez votre devoir*," she said to Veslovsky, who came out too on the steps.

"*Pardon, j'en ai tout plein les poches*," he answered, smiling, putting his fingers in his waistcoat pocket.

"*Mais vous venez trop tard*," she said, rubbing her handkerchief on her hand, which the horse had made wet in taking the sugar.

Anna turned to Dolly. "You can stay some time? For one day only? That's impossible!"

"I promised to be back, and the children ..." said Dolly, feeling embarrassed both because she had to get her bag out of the carriage, and because she knew her face must be covered with dust.

"No, Dolly, darling! ... Well, we'll see. Come along, come along!" and Anna led Dolly to her room.

That room was not the smart guest-chamber Vronsky had suggested, but the one of which Anna had said that Dolly would excuse it. And this room, for

"Annie?" (This was what she called her little daughter Anna.) "Very well. She has got on wonderfully. Would you like to see her? Come, I'll show her to you. We had a terrible bother," she began telling her, "over nurses. We had an Italian wet-nurse. A good creature, but so stupid! We wanted to get rid of her, but the baby is so used to her that we've gone on keeping her still."

"But how have you managed? …" Dolly was beginning a question as to what name the little girl would have; but noticing a sudden frown on Anna's face, she changed the drift of her question.

"How did you manage? have you weaned her yet?"

But Anna had understood.

"You didn't mean to ask that? You meant to ask about her surname. Yes? That worries Alexey. She has no name—that is, she's a Karenin," said Anna, dropping her eyelids till nothing could be seen but the eyelashes meeting. "But we'll talk about all that later," her face suddenly brightening. "Come, I'll show you her. *Elle est très gentille*. She crawls now."

In the nursery the luxury which had impressed Dolly in the whole house struck her still more. There were little go-carts ordered from England, and appliances for learning to walk, and a sofa after the fashion of a billiard-table, purposely constructed for crawling, and swings and baths, all of special pattern, and modern. They were all English, solid, and of good make, and obviously very expensive. The room was large, and very light and lofty.

When they went in, the baby, with nothing on but her little smock, was sitting in a little elbow-chair at the table, having her dinner of broth, which she was spilling all over her little chest. The baby was being fed, and the Russian nursery-maid was evidently sharing her meal. Neither the wet-nurse nor the head-nurse were there; they were in the next room, from which came the sound of their conversation in the queer French which was their only means of communication.

Hearing Anna's voice, a smart, tall, English nurse with a disagreeable face and a dissolute expression walked in at the door, hurriedly shaking her fair curls, and immediately began to defend herself though Anna had not found fault with her. At every word Anna said the English nurse said hurriedly several times, "Yes, my lady."

The rosy baby with her black eyebrows and hair, her sturdy red little body with tight goose-flesh skin, delighted Darya Alexandrovna in spite of the cross expression with which she stared at the stranger. She positively envied the baby's healthy appearance. She was delighted, too, at the baby's crawling. Not one of her own children had crawled like that. When the baby was put on the carpet and its little dress tucked up behind, it was wonderfully charming. Looking round like some little wild animal at the grown-up big people with her bright black eyes, she smiled, unmistakably pleased at their admiring her, and holding her legs sideways, she pressed vigorously on her arms, and rapidly drew her whole back up after, and then made another step forward with her little arms.

But the whole atmosphere of the nursery, and especially the English nurse, Darya Alexandrovna did not like at all. It was only on the supposition that no good nurse would have entered so irregular a household as Anna's that Darya Alexandrovna could explain to herself how Anna with her insight into people could take such an unprepossessing, disreputable-looking woman as nurse to her child.

Besides, from a few words that were dropped, Darya Alexandrovna saw at once that Anna, the two nurses, and the child had no common existence, and that the mother's visit was something exceptional. Anna wanted to get the baby her plaything, and could not find it.

Most amazing of all was the fact that on being asked how many teeth the baby had, Anna answered wrong, and knew nothing about the two last teeth.

"I sometimes feel sorry I'm so superfluous here," said Anna, going out of the nursery and holding up her skirt so as to escape the plaything standing in the doorway. "It was very different with my first child."

"I expected it to be the other way," said Darya Alexandrovna shyly.

"Oh, no! By the way, do you know I saw Seryozha?" said Anna, screwing up her eyes, as though looking at something far away. "But we'll talk about that later. You wouldn't believe it, I'm like a hungry beggar-woman when a full dinner is set before her, and she does not know what to begin on first. The dinner is you, and the talks I have before me with you, which I could never have with any one else; and I don't know which subject to begin upon first. *Mais je ne vous ferai grâce de rien.* I must have everything out with you."

"Oh, I ought to give you a sketch of the company you will meet with us," she went on. "I'll begin with the ladies. Princess Varvara—you know her, and I know your opinion and Stiva's about her. Stiva says the whole aim of her existence is to prove her superiority over Auntie Katerina Pavlovna: that's all true; but she's a good-natured woman, and I am so grateful to her. In Petersburg there was a moment when a chaperon was absolutely essential for me. Then she turned up. But really she is good-natured. She did a great deal to alleviate my position. I see you don't understand all the difficulty of my position … there in Petersburg," she added. "Here I'm perfectly at ease and happy. Well, of that later on, though. Then Sviazhsky—he's the marshal of the district, and he's

saw nothing in him of which he could be proud except his wealth. But against her own will, here in his own house, he overawed her more than ever, and she could not be at ease with him. She felt with him the same feeling she had had with the maid about her dressing-jacket. Just as with the maid she had felt not exactly ashamed, but embarrassed at her darns, so she felt with him not exactly ashamed, but embarrassed at herself.

Dolly was ill at ease, and tried to find a subject of conversation. Even though she supposed that, through his pride, praise of his house and garden would be sure to be disagreeable to him, she did all the same tell him how much she liked his house.

"Yes, it's a very fine building, and in the good old-fashioned style," he said.

"I like so much the court in front of the steps. Was that always so?"

"Oh, no!" he said, and his face beamed with pleasure. "If you could only have seen that court last spring!"

And he began, at first rather diffidently, but more and more carried away by the subject as he went on, to draw her attention to the various details of the decoration of his house and garden. It was evident that, having devoted a great deal of trouble to improve and beautify his home, Vronsky felt a need to show off the improvements to a new person, and was genuinely delighted at Darya Alexandrovna's praise.

"If you would care to look at the hospital, and are not tired, indeed, it's not far. Shall we go?" he said, glancing into her face to convince himself that she was not bored. "Are you coming, Anna?" he turned to her.

"We will come, won't we?" she said, addressing Sviazhsky. "*Mais il ne faut pas laisser le pauvre Veslovsky et Tushkevitch se morfondre là dans le bateau.* We must send and tell them."

"Yes, this is a monument he is setting up here," said Anna, turning to Dolly with that sly smile of comprehension with which she had previously talked about the hospital.

"Oh, it's a work of real importance!" said Sviazhsky. But to show he was not trying to ingratiate himself with Vronsky, he promptly added some slightly critical remarks.

"I wonder, though, count," he said, "that while you do so much for the health of the peasants, you take so little interest in the schools."

"*C'est devenu tellement commun les écoles,*" said Vronsky. "You understand it's not on that account, but it just happens so, my interest has been diverted elsewhere. This way then to the hospital," he said to Darya Alexandrovna, pointing to a turning out of the avenue.

The ladies put up their parasols and turned into the sidepath. After going down several turnings, and going through a little gate, Darya Alexandrovna saw standing on rising ground before her a large pretentious-looking red building, almost finished. The iron roof, which was not yet painted, shone with dazzling brightness in the sunshine. Beside the finished building another had been begun, surrounded by scaffolding. Workmen in aprons, standing on scaffolds, were laying bricks, pouring mortar out of vats, and smoothing it with trowels.

"How quickly work gets done with you!" said Sviazhsky. "When I was here last time the roof was not on."

"By the autumn it will all be ready. Inside almost everything is done," said Anna.

"And what's this new building?"

"That's the house for the doctor and the dispensary," answered Vronsky, seeing the architect in a short jacket coming towards him; and excusing himself to the ladies, he went to meet him.

Going round a hole where the workmen were slaking lime, he stood still with the architect and began talking rather warmly.

"The front is still too low," he said to Anna, who had asked what was the matter.

"I said the foundation ought to be raised," said Anna.

"Yes, of course it would have been much better, Anna Arkadyevna," said the architect, "but now it's too late."

"Yes, I take a great interest in it," Anna answered Sviazhsky, who was expressing his surprise at her knowledge of architecture. "This new building ought to have been in harmony with the hospital. It was an afterthought, and was begun without a plan."

Vronsky, having finished his talk with the architect, joined the ladies, and led them inside the hospital.

Although they were still at work on the cornices outside and were painting on the ground-floor, up-stairs almost all the rooms were finished. Going up the broad cast-iron staircase to the landing, they walked into the first large room. The walls were stuccoed to look like marble, the huge plate-glass windows were already in, only the parquet floor was not yet finished, and the carpenters, who were planing a block of it, left their work, taking off the bands that fastened their hair, to greet the gentry.

"This is the reception-room," said Vronsky. "Here there will be a desk, tables, and benches, and nothing more."

difficulty of Anna's position; and that you may well understand, if you do me the honor of supposing I have any heart. I am to blame for that position, and that is why I feel it."

"I understand," said Darya Alexandrovna, involuntarily admiring the sincerity and firmness with which he said this. "But just because you feel yourself responsible, you exaggerate it, I am afraid," she said. "Her position in the world is difficult, I can well understand."

"In the world it is hell!" he brought out quickly, frowning darkly. "You can't imagine moral sufferings greater than what she went through in Petersburg in that fortnight ... and I beg you to believe it."

"Yes, but here, so long as neither Anna ... nor you miss society ..."

"Society!" he said contemptuously, "how could I miss society?"

"So far—and it may be so always—you are happy and at peace. I see in Anna that she is happy, perfectly happy, she has had time to tell me so much already," said Darya Alexandrovna, smiling; and involuntarily, as she said this, at the same moment a doubt entered her mind whether Anna really were happy.

But Vronsky, it appeared, had no doubts on that score.

"Yes, yes," he said, "I know that she has revived after all her sufferings; she is happy. She is happy in the present. But I? ... I am afraid of what is before us ... I beg your pardon, you would like to walk on?"

"No, I don't mind."

"Well, then, let us sit here."

Darya Alexandrovna sat down on a garden-seat in a corner of the avenue. He stood up facing her.

"I see that she is happy," he repeated, and the doubt whether she were happy sank more deeply into Darya Alexandrovna's mind. "But can it last? Whether we have acted rightly or wrongly is another question, but the die is cast," he said, passing from Russian to French, "and we are bound together for life. We are united by all the ties of love that we hold most sacred. We have a child, we may have other children. But the law and all the conditions of our position are such that thousands of complications arise which she does not see and does not want to see. And that one can well understand. But I can't help seeing them. My daughter is by law not my daughter, but Karenin's. I cannot bear this falsity!" he said, with a vigorous gesture of refusal, and he looked with gloomy inquiry towards Darya Alexandrovna.

She made no answer, but simply gazed at him. He went on:

"One day a son may be born, my son, and he will be legally a Karenin; he will not be the heir of my name nor of my property, and however happy we may be in our home life and however many children we may have, there will be no real tie between us. They will be Karenins. You can understand the bitterness and horror of this position! I have tried to speak of this to Anna. It irritates her. She does not understand, and to her I cannot speak plainly of all this. Now look at another side. I am happy, happy in her love, but I must have occupation. I have found occupation, and am proud of what I am doing and consider it nobler than the pursuits of my former companions at court and in the army. And most certainly I would not change the work I am doing for theirs. I am working here, settled in my own place, and I am happy and contented, and we need nothing more to make us happy. I love my work here. *Ce n'est pas un pis-aller,* on the contrary …"

Darya Alexandrovna noticed that at this point in his explanation he grew confused, and she did not quite understand this digression, but she felt that having once begun to speak of matters near his heart, of which he could not speak to Anna, he was now making a clean breast of everything, and that the question of his pursuits in the country fell into the same category of matters near his heart, as the question of his relations with Anna.

"Well, I will go on," he said, collecting himself. "The great thing is that as I work I want to have a conviction that what I am doing will not die with me, that I shall have heirs to come after me,—and this I have not. Conceive the position of a man who knows that his children, the children of the woman he loves, will not be his, but will belong to some one who hates them and cares nothing about them! It is awful!"

He paused, evidently much moved.

"Yes, indeed, I see that. But what can Anna do?" queried Darya Alexandrovna.

"Yes, that brings me to the object of my conversation," he said, calming himself with an effort. "Anna can, it depends on her…. Even to petition the Tsar for legitimization, a divorce is essential. And that depends on Anna. Her husband agreed to a divorce—at that time your husband had arranged it completely. And now, I know, he would not refuse it. It is only a matter of writing to him. He said plainly at that time that if she expressed the desire, he would not refuse. Of course," he said gloomily, "it is one of those Pharisaical cruelties of which only such heartless men are capable. He knows what agony any recollection of him must give her, and knowing her, he must have a letter from her. I can understand that it is agony to her. But the matter is of such importance, that one must *passer par-dessus toutes ces finesses de sentiment. Il y va du bonheur et de l'existence d'Anne et de ses enfants.* I won't speak of myself, though it's hard for

indeed she did so with actual enjoyment, as Darya Alexandrovna observed. The conversation began about the row Tushkevitch and Veslovsky had taken alone together in the boat, and Tushkevitch began describing the last boat-races in Petersburg at the Yacht Club. But Anna, seizing the first pause, at once turned to the architect to draw him out of his silence.

"Nikolay Ivanitch was struck," she said, meaning Sviazhsky, "at the progress the new building had made since he was here last; but I am there every day, and every day I wonder at the rate at which it grows."

"It's first-rate working with his excellency," said the architect with a smile (he was respectful and composed, though with a sense of his own dignity). "It's a very different matter to have to do with the district authorities. Where one would have to write out sheaves of papers, here I call upon the count, and in three words we settle the business."

"The American way of doing business," said Sviazhsky, with a smile.

"Yes, there they build in a rational fashion …"

The conversation passed to the misuse of political power in the United States, but Anna quickly brought it round to another topic, so as to draw the steward into talk.

"Have you ever seen a reaping-machine?" she said, addressing Darya Alexandrovna. "We had just ridden over to look at one when we met. It's the first time I ever saw one."

"How do they work?" asked Dolly.

"Exactly like little scissors. A plank and a lot of little scissors. Like this."

Anna took a knife and fork in her beautiful white hands covered with rings, and began showing how the machine worked. It was clear that she saw nothing would be understood from her explanation; but aware that her talk was pleasant and her hands beautiful she went on explaining.

"More like little penknives," Veslovsky said playfully, never taking his eyes off her.

Anna gave a just perceptible smile, but made no answer. "Isn't it true, Karl Fedoritch, that it's just like little scissors?" she said to the steward.

"*Oh, ja,*" answered the German. "*Es it ein ganz einfaches Ding,*" and he began to explain the construction of the machine.

"It's a pity it doesn't bind too. I saw one at the Vienna exhibition, which binds with a wire," said Sviazhsky. "They would be more profitable in use."

"*Es kommt drauf an … Der Preis vom Draht muss ausgerechnet werden.*" And the German, roused from his taciturnity, turned to Vronsky. "*Das lässt sich ausrechnen, Erlaucht.*" The German was just feeling in the pocket where were his pencil and the note-book he always wrote in, but recollecting that he was at a dinner, and observing Vronsky's chilly glance, he checked himself. *"Zu compliziert, macht zu viel Klopot, "* he concluded.

"Wünscht man Dochots, so hat man auch Klopots, " said Vassenka Veslovsky, mimicking the German. *"J'adore l'allemand, "* he addressed Anna again with the same smile.

"Cessez, " she said with playful severity.

"We expected to find you in the fields, Vassily Semyonitch," she said to the doctor, a sickly-looking man; "have you been there?"

"I went there, but I had taken flight," the doctor answered with gloomy jocoseness.

"Then you've taken a good constitutional?"

"Splendid!"

"Well, and how was the old woman? I hope it's not typhus?"

"Typhus it is not, but it's taking a bad turn."

"What a pity!" said Anna, and having thus paid the dues of civility to her domestic circle, she turned to her own friends.

"It would be a hard task, though, to construct a machine from your description, Anna Arkadyevna," Sviazhsky said jestingly.

"Oh, no, why so?" said Anna with a smile that betrayed that she knew there was something charming in her disquisitions upon the machine that had been noticed by Sviazhsky. This new trait of girlish coquettishness made an unpleasant impression on Dolly.

"But Anna Arkadyevna's knowledge of architecture is marvelous," said Tushkevitch.

"To be sure, I heard Anna Arkadyevna talking yesterday about plinths and damp-courses," said Veslovsky. "Have I got it right?"

"There's nothing marvelous about it, when one sees and hears so much of it," said Anna. "But, I dare say, you don't even know what houses are made of?"

Darya Alexandrovna saw that Anna disliked the tone of raillery that existed between her and Veslovsky, but fell in with it against her will.

Vronsky acted in this matter quite differently from Levin. He obviously attached no significance to Veslovsky's chattering; on the contrary, he encouraged his jests.

"Come now, tell us, Veslovsky, how are the stones held together?"

"By cement, of course."

"Bravo! And what is cement?"

"Oh, some sort of paste ... no, putty," said Veslovsky, raising a general laugh.

the others. He was too eager, but he kept the players lively with his high spirits. His laughter and outcries never paused. Like the other men of the party, with the ladies' permission, he took off his coat, and his solid, comely figure in his white shirt-sleeves, with his red perspiring face and his impulsive movements, made a picture that imprinted itself vividly on the memory.

When Darya Alexandrovna lay in bed that night, as soon as she closed her eyes, she saw Vassenka Veslovsky flying about the croquet-ground.

During the game Darya Alexandrovna was not enjoying herself. She did not like the light tone of raillery that was kept up all the time between Vassenka Veslovsky and Anna, and the unnaturalness altogether of grown-up people, all alone without children, playing at a child's game. But to avoid breaking up the party and to get through the time somehow, after a rest she joined the game again, and pretended to be enjoying it. All that day it seemed to her as though she were acting in a theater with actors cleverer than she, and that her bad acting was spoiling the whole performance. She had come with the intention of staying two days, if all went well. But in the evening, during the game, she made up her mind that she would go home next day. The maternal cares and worries, which she had so hated on the way, now, after a day spent without them, struck her in quite another light, and tempted her back to them.

When, after evening tea and a row by night in the boat, Darya Alexandrovna went alone to her room, took off her dress, and began arranging her thin hair for the night, she had a great sense of relief.

It was positively disagreeable to her to think that Anna was coming to see her immediately. She longed to be alone with her own thoughts.

CHAPTER XXIII

DOLLY WAS WANTING TO GO TO BED WHEN ANNA CAME IN TO SEE HER, AT-tired for the night. In the course of the day Anna had several times begun to speak of matters near her heart, and every time after a few words she had stopped: "Afterwards, by ourselves, we'll talk about everything. I've got so much I want to tell you," she said.

Now they were by themselves, and Anna did not know what to talk about. She sat in the window looking at Dolly, and going over in her own mind all the stores of intimate talk which had seemed so inexhaustible beforehand, and she found nothing. At that moment it seemed to her that everything had been said already.

"Well, what of Kitty?" she said with a heavy sigh, looking penitently at Dolly. "Tell me the truth, Dolly: isn't she angry with me?"

"Angry? Oh, no!" said Darya Alexandrovna, smiling.

"But she hates me, despises me?"

"Oh, no! But you know that sort of thing isn't forgiven."

"Yes, yes," said Anna, turning away and looking out of the open window. "But I was not to blame. And who is to blame? What's the meaning of being to blame? Could it have been otherwise? What do you think? Could it possibly have happened that you didn't become the wife of Stiva?"

"Really, I don't know. But this is what I want you to tell me ..."

"Yes, yes, but we've not finished about Kitty. Is she happy? He's a very nice man, they say."

"He's much more than very nice. I don't know a better man."

"Ah, how glad I am! I'm so glad! Much more than very nice," she repeated. Dolly smiled.

"But tell me about yourself. We've a great deal to talk about. And I've had a talk with ..." Dolly did not know what to call him. She felt it awkward to call him either the count or Alexey Kirillovitch.

"With Alexey," said Anna, "I know what you talked about. But I wanted to ask you directly what you think of me, of my life?"

"How am I to say like that straight off? I really don't know."

"No, tell me all the same.... You see my life. But you mustn't forget that you're seeing us in the summer, when you have come to us and we are not alone.... But we came here early in the spring, lived quite alone, and shall be alone again, and I desire nothing better. But imagine me living alone without him, alone, and that will be ... I see by everything that it will often be repeated, that he will be half the time away from home," she said, getting up and sitting down close by Dolly.

"Of course," she interrupted Dolly, who would have answered, "of course I won't try to keep him by force. I don't keep him indeed. The races are just coming, his horses are running, he will go. I'm very glad. But think of me, fancy my position.... But what's the use of talking about it?" She smiled. "Well, what did he talk about with you?"

"He spoke of what I want to speak about of myself, and it's easy for me to be his advocate; of whether there is not a possibility ... whether you could not ..." (Darya Alexandrovna hesitated) "correct, improve your position....

"I should always feel I had wronged these unhappy children," she said. "If they are not, at any rate they are not unhappy; while if they are unhappy, I alone should be to blame for it."

These were the very arguments Darya Alexandrovna had used in her own reflections; but she heard them without understanding them. "How can one wrong creatures that don't exist?" she thought. And all at once the idea struck her: could it possibly, under any circumstances, have been better for her favorite Grisha if he had never existed? And this seemed to her so wild, so strange, that she shook her head to drive away this tangle of whirling, mad ideas.

"No, I don't know; it's not right," was all she said, with an expression of disgust on her face.

"Yes, but you mustn't forget that you and I ... And besides that," added Anna, in spite of the wealth of her arguments and the poverty of Dolly's objections, seeming still to admit that it was not right, "don't forget the chief point, that I am not now in the same position as you. For you the question is: do you desire not to have any more children; while for me it is: do I desire to have them? And that's a great difference. You must see that I can't desire it in my position."

Darya Alexandrovna made no reply. She suddenly felt that she had got far away from Anna; that there lay between them a barrier of questions on which they could never agree, and about which it was better not to speak.

CHAPTER XXIV

T HEN THERE IS ALL THE MORE REASON FOR YOU TO LEGALIZE YOUR position, if possible," said Dolly.

"Yes, if possible," said Anna, speaking all at once in an utterly different tone, subdued and mournful.

"Surely you don't mean a divorce is impossible? I was told your husband had consented to it."

"Dolly, I don't want to talk about that."

"Oh, we won't then," Darya Alexandrovna hastened to say, noticing the expression of suffering on Anna's face. "All I see is that you take too gloomy a view of things."

"I? Not at all! I'm always bright and happy. You see, *je fais des passions.* Veslovsky ..."

"Yes, to tell the truth, I don't like Veslovsky's tone," said Darya Alexandrovna, anxious to change the subject.

"Oh, that's nonsense! It amuses Alexey, and that's all; but he's a boy, and quite under my control. You know, I turn him as I please. It's just as it might be with your Grisha.... Dolly!"— she suddenly changed the subject—"you say I take too gloomy a view of things. You can't understand. It's too awful! I try not to take any view of it at all."

"But I think you ought to. You ought to do all you can."

"But what can I do? Nothing. You tell me to marry Alexey, and say I don't think about it. I don't think about it!" she repeated, and a flush rose into her face. She got up, straightening her chest, and sighed heavily. With her light step she began pacing up and down the room, stopping now and then. "I don't think of it? Not a day, not an hour passes that I don't think of it, and blame myself for thinking of it ... because thinking of that may drive me mad. Drive me mad!" she repeated. "When I think of it, I can't sleep without morphine. But never mind. Let us talk quietly. They tell me, divorce. In the first place, he won't give me a divorce. He's under the influence of Countess Lidia Ivanovna now."

Darya Alexandrovna, sitting erect on a chair, turned her head, following Anna with a face of sympathetic suffering.

"You ought to make the attempt," she said softly.

"Suppose I make the attempt. What does it mean?" she said, evidently giving utterance to a thought, a thousand times thought over and learned by heart. "It means that I, hating him, but still recognizing that I have wronged him—and I consider him magnanimous—that I humiliate myself to write to him ... Well, suppose I make the effort; I do it. Either I receive a humiliating refusal or consent ... Well, I have received his consent, say ..." Anna was at that moment at the furthest end of the room, and she stopped there, doing something to the curtain at the window. "I receive his consent, but my ... my son? They won't give him up to me. He will grow up despising me, with his father, whom I've abandoned. Do you see, I love ... equally, I think, but both more than myself—two creatures, Seryozha and Alexey."

She came out into the middle of the room and stood facing Dolly, with her arms pressed tightly across her chest. In her white dressing-gown her figure seemed more than usually grand and broad. She bent her head, and with shining, wet eyes looked from under her brows at Dolly, a thin little pitiful figure in her patched dressing-jacket and night-cap, shaking all over with emotion.

"It is only those two creatures that I love, and one excludes the other. I can't have them together, and that's the only thing I want. And since I can't have that,

CHAPTER XXV

VRONSKY AND ANNA SPENT THE WHOLE SUMMER AND PART OF THE WINTER in the country, living in just the same condition, and still taking no steps to obtain a divorce. It was an understood thing between them that they should not go away anywhere; but both felt, the longer they lived alone, especially in the autumn, without guests in the house, that they could not stand this existence, and that they would have to alter it.

Their life was apparently such that nothing better could be desired. They had the fullest abundance of everything; they had a child, and both had occupation. Anna devoted just as much care to her appearance when they had no visitors, and she did a great deal of reading, both of novels and of what serious literature was in fashion. She ordered all the books that were praised in the foreign papers and reviews she received, and read them with that concentrated attention which is only given to what is read in seclusion. Moreover, every subject that was of interest to Vronsky, she studied in books and special journals, so that he often went straight to her with questions relating to agriculture or architecture, sometimes even with questions relating to horse-breeding or sport. He was amazed at her knowledge, her memory, and at first was disposed to doubt it, to ask for confirmation of her facts; and she would find what he asked for in some book, and show it to him.

The building of the hospital, too, interested her. She did not merely assist, but planned and suggested a great deal herself. But her chief thought was still of herself—how far she was dear to Vronsky, how far she could make up to him for all he had given up. Vronsky appreciated this desire not only to please, but to serve him, which had become the sole aim of her existence, but at the same time he wearied of the loving snares in which she tried to hold him fast. As time went on, and he saw himself more and more often held fast in these snares, he had an ever-growing desire, not so much to escape from them, as to try whether they hindered his freedom. Had it not been for this growing desire to be free, not to have scenes every time he wanted to go to the town to a meeting or a race, Vronsky would have been perfectly satisfied with his life. The rôle he had taken up, the rôle of a wealthy landowner, one of that class which ought to be the very heart of the Russian aristocracy, was entirely to his taste; and now, after spending six months in that character, he derived even greater satisfaction from it. And his management of his estate, which occupied and absorbed him more and more, was most successful. In spite of the immense sums cost him by the hospital, by machinery, by cows ordered from Switzerland, and many other things, he was convinced that he was not wasting, but increasing his substance. In all matters affecting income, the sales of timber, wheat, and wool, the letting of lands, Vronsky was hard as a rock, and knew well how to keep up prices. In all operations on a large scale on this and his other estates, he kept to the simplest methods involving no risk, and in trifling details he was careful and exacting to an extreme degree. In spite of all the cunning and ingenuity of the German steward, who would try to tempt him into purchases by making his original estimate always far larger than really required, and then representing to Vronsky that he might get the thing cheaper, and so make a profit, Vronsky did not give in. He listened to his steward, cross-examined him, and only agreed to his suggestions when the implement to be ordered or constructed was the very newest, not yet known in Russia, and likely to excite wonder. Apart from such exceptions, he resolved upon an increased outlay only where there was a surplus, and in making such an outlay he went into the minutest details, and insisted on getting the very best for his money; so that by the method on which he managed his affairs, it was clear that he was not wasting, but increasing his substance.

In October there were the provincial elections in the Kashinsky province, where were the estates of Vronsky, Sviazhsky, Koznishev, Oblonsky, and a small part of Levin's land.

These elections were attracting public attention from several circumstances connected with them, and also from the people taking part in them. There had been a great deal of talk about them, and great preparations were being made for them. Persons who never attended the elections were coming from Moscow, from Petersburg, and from abroad to attend these. Vronsky had long before promised Sviazhsky to go to them. Before the elections Sviazhsky, who often visited Vozdvizhenskoe, drove over to fetch Vronsky. On the day before there had been almost a quarrel between Vronsky and Anna over this proposed expedition. It was the very dullest autumn weather, which is so dreary in the country, and so, preparing himself for a struggle, Vronsky, with a hard and cold expression, informed Anna of his departure as he had never spoken to her before. But, to his surprise, Anna accepted the information with great composure, and merely asked when he would be back. He looked intently at her, at a loss to explain this composure. She smiled at his look. He knew that way she had of withdrawing into herself, and knew that it only happened when she had determined upon something without letting him know her plans. He was afraid of this; but he was so anxious to avoid a scene

of the province, the high schools, female, male, and military, and popular instruction on the new model, and finally, the district council—the marshal of the province, Snetkov, was a nobleman of the old school,—dissipating an immense fortune, a good-hearted man, honest after his own fashion, but utterly without any comprehension of the needs of modern days. He always took, in every question, the side of the nobility; he was positively antagonistic to the spread of popular education, and he succeeded in giving a purely party character to the district council which ought by rights to be of such an immense importance. What was needed was to put in his place a fresh, capable, perfectly modern man, of contemporary ideas, and to frame their policy so as from the rights conferred upon the nobles, not as the nobility, but as an element of the district council, to extract all the powers of self-government that could possibly be derived from them. In the wealthy Kashinsky province, which always took the lead of other provinces in everything, there was now such a preponderance of forces that this policy, once carried through properly there, might serve as a model for other provinces for all Russia. And hence the whole question was of the greatest importance. It was proposed to elect as marshal in place of Snetkov either Sviazhsky, or, better still, Nevyedovsky, a former university professor, a man of remarkable intelligence and a great friend of Sergey Ivanovitch.

The meeting was opened by the governor, who made a speech to the nobles, urging them to elect the public functionaries, not from regard for persons, but for the service and welfare of their fatherland, and hoping that the honorable nobility of the Kashinsky province would, as at all former elections, hold their duty as sacred, and vindicate the exalted confidence of the monarch.

When he had finished with his speech, the governor walked out of the hall, and the noblemen noisily and eagerly—some even enthusiastically—followed him and thronged round him while he put on his fur coat and conversed amicably with the marshal of the province. Levin, anxious to see into everything and not to miss anything, stood there too in the crowd, and heard the governor say: "Please tell Marya Ivanovna my wife is very sorry she couldn't come to the Home." And thereupon the nobles in high good-humor sorted out their fur coats and all drove off to the cathedral.

In the cathedral Levin, lifting his hand like the rest and repeating the words of the archdeacon, swore with most terrible oaths to do all the governor had hoped they would do. Church services always affected Levin, and as he uttered the words "I kiss the cross," and glanced round at the crowd of young and old men repeating the same, he felt touched.

On the second and third days there was business relating to the finances of the nobility and the female high school, of no importance whatever, as Sergey Ivanovitch explained, and Levin, busy seeing after his own affairs, did not attend the meetings. On the fourth day the auditing of the marshal's accounts took place at the high table of the marshal of the province. And then there occurred the first skirmish between the new party and the old. The committee who had been deputed to verify the accounts reported to the meeting that all was in order. The marshal of the province got up, thanked the nobility for their confidence, and shed tears. The nobles gave him a loud welcome, and shook hands with him. But at that instant a nobleman of Sergey Ivanovitch's party said that he had heard that the committee had not verified the accounts, considering such a verification an insult to the marshal of the province. One of the members of the committee incautiously admitted this. Then a small gentleman, very young-looking but very malignant, began to say that it would probably be agreeable to the marshal of the province to give an account of his expenditures of the public moneys, and that the misplaced delicacy of the members of the committee was depriving him of this moral satisfaction. Then the members of the committee tried to withdraw their admission, and Sergey Ivanovitch began to prove that they must logically admit either that they had verified the accounts or that they had not, and he developed this dilemma in detail. Sergey Ivanovitch was answered by the spokesman of the opposite party. Then Sviazhsky spoke, and then the malignant gentleman again. The discussion lasted a long time and ended in nothing. Levin was surprised that they should dispute upon this subject so long, especially as, when he asked Sergey Ivanovitch whether he supposed that money had been misappropriated, Sergey Ivanovitch answered:

"Oh, no! He's an honest man. But those old-fashioned methods of paternal family arrangements in the management of provincial affairs must be broken down."

On the fifth day came the elections of the district marshals. It was rather a stormy day in several districts. In the Seleznevsky district Sviazhsky was elected unanimously without a ballot, and he gave a dinner that evening.

CHAPTER XXVIII

L EVIN WAS STANDING RATHER FAR OFF. A NOBLEMAN BREATHING HEAVILY and hoarsely at his side, and another whose thick boots were creaking, prevented him from hearing distinctly. He could only hear the soft voice of the marshal faintly, then the shrill voice of the malignant gentleman, and then the voice of Sviazhsky. They were disputing, as far as he could make out, as to the interpretation to be put on the act and the exact meaning of the words: "liable to be called up for trial."

The crowd parted to make way for Sergey Ivanovitch approaching the table. Sergey Ivanovitch, waiting till the malignant gentleman had finished speaking, said that he thought the best solution would be to refer to the act itself, and asked the secretary to find the act. The act said that in case of difference of opinion, there must be a ballot.

Sergey Ivanovitch read the act and began to explain its meaning, but at that point a tall, stout, round-shouldered landowner, with dyed whiskers, in a tight uniform that cut the back of his neck, interrupted him. He went up to the table, and striking it with his finger-ring, he shouted loudly: "A ballot! Put it to the vote! No need for more talking!" Then several voices began to talk all at once, and the tall nobleman with the ring, getting more and more exasperated, shouted more and more loudly. But it was impossible to make out what he said.

He was shouting for the very course Sergey Ivanovitch had proposed; but it was evident that he hated him and all his party, and this feeling of hatred spread through the whole party and roused in opposition to it the same vindictiveness, though in a more seemly form, on the other side. Shouts were raised, and for a moment all was confusion, so that the marshal of the province had to call for order.

"A ballot! A ballot! Every nobleman sees it! We shed our blood for our country! ... The confidence of the monarch.... No checking the accounts of the marshal; he's not a cashier ... But that's not the point.... Votes, please! Beastly! ..." shouted furious and violent voices on all sides. Looks and faces were even more violent and furious than their words. They expressed the most implacable hatred. Levin did not in the least understand what was the matter, and he marveled at the passion with which it was disputed whether or not the decision about Flerov should be put to the vote. He forgot, as Sergey Ivanovitch explained to him afterwards, this syllogism: that it was necessary for the public good to get rid of the marshal of the province; that to get rid of the marshal it was necessary to have a majority of votes; that to get a majority of votes it was necessary to secure Flerov's right to vote; that to secure the recognition of Flerov's right to vote they must decide on the interpretation to be put on the act.

"And one vote may decide the whole question, and one must be serious and consecutive, if one wants to be of use in public life," concluded Sergey Ivanovitch. But Levin forgot all that, and it was painful to him to see all these excellent persons, for whom he had a respect, in such an unpleasant and vicious state of excitement. To escape from this painful feeling he went away into the other room where there was nobody except the waiters at the refreshment-bar. Seeing the waiters busy over washing up the crockery and setting in order their plates and wine-glasses, seeing their calm and cheerful faces, Levin felt an unexpected sense of relief as though he had come out of a stuffy room into the fresh air. He began walking up and down, looking with pleasure at the waiters. He particularly liked the way one gray-whiskered waiter, who showed his scorn for the other younger ones and was jeered at by them, was teaching them how to fold up napkins properly. Levin was just about to enter into conversation with the old waiter, when the secretary of the court of wardship, a little old man whose specialty it was to know all the noblemen of the province by name and patronymic, drew him away.

"Please come, Konstantin Dmitrievitch," he said, "your brother's looking for you. They are voting on the legal point."

Levin walked into the room, received a white ball, and followed his brother, Sergey Ivanovitch, to the table where Sviazhsky was standing with a significant and ironical face, holding his beard in his fist and sniffing at it. Sergey Ivanovitch put his hand into the box, put the ball somewhere, and making room for Levin, stopped. Levin advanced, but utterly forgetting what he was to do, and much embarrassed, he turned to Sergey Ivanovitch with the question, "Where am I to put it?" He asked this softly, at a moment when there was talking going on near, so that he had hoped his question would not be overheard. But the persons speaking paused, and his improper question was overheard. Sergey Ivanovitch frowned.

"That is a matter for each man's own decision," he said severely.

Several people smiled. Levin crimsoned, hurriedly thrust his hand under the cloth, and put the ball to the right as it was in his right hand. Having put it in, he recollected that he ought to have thrust his left hand too, and so he thrust it in though too late, and, still more overcome with confusion, he beat a hasty retreat into the background.

"A hundred and twenty-six for admission! Ninety-eight against!" sang out the voice of the secretary, who could not pronounce the letter *r*. Then there

day, and he had studiously avoided him, not caring to greet him. He went to the window and sat down, scanning the groups, and listening to what was being said around him. He felt depressed, especially because every one else was, as he saw, eager, anxious, and interested, and he alone, with an old, toothless little man with mumbling lips wearing a naval uniform, sitting beside him, had no interest in it and nothing to do.

"He's such a blackguard! I have told him so, but it makes no difference. Only think of it! He couldn't collect it in three years!" he heard vigorously uttered by a round-shouldered, short, country gentleman, who had pomaded hair hanging on his embroidered collar, and new boots obviously put on for the occasion, with heels that tapped energetically as he spoke. Casting a displeased glance at Levin, this gentleman sharply turned his back.

"Yes, it's a dirty business, there's no denying," a small gentleman assented in a high voice.

Next, a whole crowd of country gentlemen, surrounding a stout general, hurriedly came near Levin. These persons were unmistakably seeking a place where they could talk without being overheard.

"How dare he say I had his breeches stolen! Pawned them for drink, I expect. Damn the fellow, prince indeed! He'd better not say it, the beast!"

"But excuse me! They take their stand on the act," was being said in another group; "the wife must be registered as noble."

"Oh, damn your acts! I speak from my heart. We're all gentlemen, aren't we? Above suspicion."

"Shall we go on, your excellency, *fine champagne?*"

Another group was following a nobleman, who was shouting something in a loud voice; it was one of the three intoxicated gentlemen.

"I always advised Marya Semyonovna to let for a fair rent, for she can never save a profit," he heard a pleasant voice say. The speaker was a country gentleman with gray whiskers, wearing the regimental uniform of an old general staff-officer. It was the very landowner Levin had met at Sviazhsky's. He knew him at once. The landowner too stared at Levin, and they exchanged greetings.

"Very glad to see you! To be sure! I remember you very well. Last year at our district marshal, Nikolay Ivanovitch's."

"Well, and how is your land doing?" asked Levin.

"Oh, still just the same, always at a loss," the landowner answered with a resigned smile, but with an expression of serenity and conviction that so it must be. "And how do you come to be in our province?" he asked. "Come to take part in our *coup d'etat?*" he said, confidently pronouncing the French words with a bad accent. "All Russia's here—gentlemen of the bedchamber, and everything short of the ministry." He pointed to the imposing figure of Stepan Arkady-evitch in white trousers and his court uniform, walking by with a general.

"I ought to own that I don't very well understand the drift of the provincial elections," said Levin.

The landowner looked at him.

"Why, what is there to understand? There's no meaning in it at all. It's a decaying institution that goes on running only by the force of inertia. Just look, the very uniforms tell you that it's an assembly of justices of the peace, perma-nent members of the court, and so on, but not of noblemen."

"Then why do you come?" asked Levin.

"From habit, nothing else. Then, too, one must keep up connections. It's a moral obligation of a sort. And then, to tell the truth, there's one's own interests. My son-in-law wants to stand as a permanent member; they're not rich people, and he must be brought forward. These gentlemen, now, what do they come for?" he said, pointing to the malignant gentleman, who was talking at the high table.

"That's the new generation of nobility."

"New it may be, but nobility it isn't. They're proprietors of a sort, but we're the landowners. As noblemen, they're cutting their own throats."

"But you say it's an institution that's served its time."

"That it may be, but still it ought to be treated a little more respectfully. Snetkov, now … We may be of use, or we may not, but we're the growth of a thousand years. If we're laying out a garden, planning one before the house, you know, and there you've a tree that's stood for centuries in the very spot … Old and gnarled it may be, and yet you don't cut down the old fellow to make room for the flowerbeds, but lay out your beds so as to take advantage of the tree. You won't grow him again in a year," he said cautiously, and he immedi-ately changed the conversation. "Well, and how is your land doing?"

"Oh, not very well. I make five per cent."

"Yes, but you don't reckon your own work. Aren't you worth something too? I'll tell you my own case. Before I took to seeing after the land, I had a salary of three hundred pounds from the service. Now I do more work than I did in the service, and like you I get five per cent on the land, and thank God for that. But one's work is thrown in for nothing."

"Then why do you do it, if it's a clear loss?"

"Oh, well, one does it! What would you have? It's habit, and one knows it's how it should be. And what's more," the landowner went on, leaning his

648 ❖ Anna Karenina

"Well, you find it exciting too?" said Stepan Arkadyevitch, winking at Vronsky. "It's something like a race. One might bet on it."

"Yes, it is keenly exciting," said Vronsky. "And once taking the thing up, one's eager to see it through. It's a fight!" he said, scowling and setting his powerful jaws.

"What a capable fellow Sviazhsky is! Sees it all so clearly."

"Oh, yes!" Vronsky assented indifferently.

A silence followed, during which Vronsky—since he had to look at something—looked at Levin, at his feet, at his uniform, then at his face, and noticing his gloomy eyes fixed upon him, he said, in order to say something:

"How is it that you, living constantly in the country, are not a justice of the peace? You are not in the uniform of one."

"It's because I consider that the justice of the peace is a silly institution," Levin answered gloomily. He had been all the time looking for an opportunity to enter into conversation with Vronsky, so as to smooth over his rudeness at their first meeting.

"I don't think so, quite the contrary," Vronsky said, with quiet surprise.

"It's a plaything," Levin cut him short. "We don't want justices of the peace. I've never had a single thing to do with them during eight years. And what I have had was decided wrongly by them. The justice of the peace is over thirty miles from me. For some matter of two roubles I should have to send a lawyer, who costs me fifteen."

And he related how a peasant had stolen some flour from the miller, and when the miller told him of it, had lodged a complaint for slander. All this was utterly uncalled for and stupid, and Levin felt it himself as he said it.

"Oh, this is such an original fellow!" said Stepan Arkadyevitch with his most soothing, almond-oil smile. "But come along; I think they're voting...."

And they separated.

"I can't understand," said Sergey Ivanovitch, who had observed his brother's clumsiness, "I can't understand how any one can be so absolutely devoid of political tact. That's where we Russians are so deficient. The marshal of the province is our opponent, and with him you're *ami cochon*, and you beg him to stand. Count Vronsky, now ... I'm not making a friend of him; he's asked me to dinner, and I'm not going; but he's one of our side—why make an enemy of him? Then you ask Nevyedovsky if he's going to stand. That's not a thing to do."

"Oh, I don't understand it at all! And it's all such nonsense," Levin answered gloomily.

"You say it's all such nonsense, but as soon as you have anything to do with it, you make a muddle."

Levin did not answer, and they walked together into the big room.

The marshal of the province, though he was vaguely conscious in the air of some trap being prepared for him, and though he had not been called upon by all to stand, had still made up his mind to stand. All was silence in the room. The secretary announced in a loud voice that the captain of the guards, Mihail Stepanovitch Snetkov, would now be balloted for as marshal of the province.

The district marshals walked carrying plates, on which were balls, from their tables to the high table, and the election began.

"Put it in the right side," whispered Stepan Arkadyevitch, as with his brother Levin followed the marshal of his district to the table. But Levin had forgotten by now the calculations that had been explained to him, and was afraid Stepan Arkadyevitch might be mistaken in saying "the right side." Surely Snetkov was the enemy. As he went up, he held the ball in his right hand, but thinking he was wrong, just at the box he changed to the left hand, and undoubtedly put the ball to the left. An adept in the business, standing at the box and seeing by the mere action of the elbow where each put his ball, scowled with annoyance. It was no good for him to use his insight.

Everything was still, and the counting of the balls was heard. Then a single voice rose and proclaimed the numbers for and against. The marshal had been voted for by a considerable majority. All was noise and eager movement towards the doors. Snetkov came in, and the nobles thronged round him, congratulating him.

"Well, now is it over?" Levin asked Sergey Ivanovitch.

"It's only just beginning," Sviazhsky said, replying for Sergey Ivanovitch with a smile. "Some other candidate may receive more votes than the marshal."

Levin had quite forgotten about that. Now he could only remember that there was some sort of trickery in it, but he was too bored to think what it was exactly. He felt depressed, and longed to get out of the crowd.

As no one was paying any attention to him, and no one apparently needed him, he quietly slipped away into the little room where the refreshments were, and again had a great sense of comfort when he saw the waiters. The little old waiter pressed him to have something, and Levin agreed. After eating a cutlet with beans and talking to the waiters of their former masters, Levin, not wishing to go back to the hall, where it was all so distasteful to him, proceeded to walk through the galleries. The galleries were full of fashionably dressed ladies, leaning over the balustrade and trying not to lose a single word of what was being

direct, equable manner with every one, which very quickly made the majority of the noblemen reverse the current opinion of his supposed haughtiness. He was himself conscious that, except that whimsical gentleman married to Kitty Shtcherbatskaya, who had *à propos de bottes* poured out a stream of irrelevant absurdities with such spiteful fury, every nobleman with whom he had made acquaintance had become his adherent. He saw clearly, and other people recognized it, too, that he had done a great deal to secure the success of Nevyedovsky. And now at his own table, celebrating Nevyedovsky's election, he was experiencing an agreeable sense of triumph over the success of his candidate. The election itself had so fascinated him that, if he could succeed in getting married during the next three years, he began to think of standing himself—much as after winning a race ridden by a jockey, he had longed to ride a race himself.

To-day he was celebrating the success of his jockey. Vronsky sat at the head of the table, on his right hand sat the young governor, a general of high rank. To all the rest he was the chief man in the province, who had solemnly opened the elections with his speech, and aroused a feeling of respect and even of awe in many people, as Vronsky saw; to Vronsky he was little Katka Maslov—that had been his nickname in the Pages' Corps—whom he felt to be shy and tried to *mettre à son aise*. On the left hand sat Nevyedovsky with his youthful, stubborn, and malignant face. With him Vronsky was simple and deferential.

Sviazhsky took his failure very light-heartedly. It was indeed no failure in his eyes, as he said himself, turning, glass in hand, to Nevyedovsky; they could not have found a better representative of the new movement, which the nobility ought to follow. And so every honest person, as he said, was on the side of to-day's success and was rejoicing over it.

Stepan Arkadyevitch was glad, too, that he was having a good time, and that every one was pleased. The episode of the elections served as a good occasion for a capital dinner. Sviazhsky comically imitated the tearful discourse of the marshal, and observed, addressing Nevyedovsky, that his excellency would have to select another more complicated method of auditing the accounts than tears. Another nobleman jocosely described how footmen in stockings had been ordered for the marshal's ball, and how now they would have to be sent back unless the new marshal would give a ball with footmen in stockings.

Continually during dinner they said of Nevyedovsky: "Our marshal," and "your excellency."

This was said with the same pleasure with which a bride is called "Madame" and her husband's name. Nevyedovsky affected to be not merely indifferent but scornful of this appellation, but it was obvious that he was highly delighted, and had to keep a curb on himself not to betray the triumph which was unsuitable to their new liberal tone.

After dinner several telegrams were sent to people interested in the result of the election. And Stepan Arkadyevitch, who was in high good-humor, sent Darya Alexandrovna a telegram: "Nevyedovsky elected by twenty votes. Congratulations. Tell people." He dictated it aloud, saying: "We must let them share our rejoicing." Darya Alexandrovna, getting the message, simply sighed over the rouble wasted on it, and understood that it was an after-dinner affair. She knew Stiva had a weakness after dining for *faire jouer le télégraphe*.

Everything, together with the excellent dinner and the wine, not from Russian merchants, but imported direct from abroad, was extremely dignified, simple, and enjoyable. The party—some twenty—had been selected by Sviazhsky from among the more active new liberals, all of the same way of thinking, who were at the same time clever and well bred. They drank, also half in jest, to the health of the new marshal of the province, of the governor, of the bank director, and of "our amiable host."

Vronsky was satisfied. He had never expected to find so pleasant a tone in the provinces.

Towards the end of dinner it was still more lively. The governor asked Vronsky to come to a concert for the benefit of the Servians which his wife, who was anxious to make his acquaintance, had been getting up.

"There'll be a ball, and you'll see the belle of the province. Worth seeing, really."

"Not in my line," Vronsky answered. He liked that English phrase. But he smiled, and promised to come.

Before they rose from the table, when all of them were smoking, Vronsky's valet went up to him with a letter on a tray.

"From Vozdvizhenskoe by special messenger," he said with a significant expression.

"Astonishing! how like he is to the deputy prosecutor Sventitsky," said one of the guests in French of the valet, while Vronsky, frowning, read the letter.

The letter was from Anna. Before he read the letter, he knew its contents. Expecting the elections to be over in five days, he had promised to be back on Friday. To-day was Saturday, and he knew that the letter contained reproaches for not being back at the time fixed. The letter he had sent the previous evening had probably not reached her yet.

The letter was what he had expected, but the form of it was unexpected, and particularly disagreeable to him. "Annie is very ill, the doctor says it may

"Well, how is Annie?" he said timidly from below, looking up to Anna as she ran down to him.

He was sitting on a chair, and a footman was pulling off his warm over-boot.

"Oh, she is better."

"And you?" he said, shaking himself.

She took his hand in both of hers, and drew it to her waist, never taking her eyes off him.

"Well, I'm glad," he said, coldly scanning her, her hair, her dress, which he knew she had put on for him. All was charming, but how many times it had charmed him! And the stern, stony expression that she so dreaded settled upon his face.

"Well, I'm glad. And are you well?" he said, wiping his damp beard with his handkerchief and kissing her hand.

"Never mind," she thought, "only let him be here, and so long as he's here he cannot, he dare not, cease to love me."

The evening was spent happily and gaily in the presence of Princess Varvara, who complained to him that Anna had been taking morphine in his absence.

"What am I to do? I couldn't sleep ... My thoughts prevented me. When he's here I never take it—hardly ever."

He told her about the election, and Anna knew how by adroit questions to bring him to what gave him most pleasure—his own success. She told him of everything that interested him at home; and all that she told him was of the most cheerful description.

But late in the evening, when they were alone, Anna, seeing that she had regained complete possession of him, wanted to erase the painful impression of the glance he had given her for her letter. She said:

"Tell me frankly, you were vexed at getting my letter, and you didn't believe me?"

As soon as she had said it, she felt that however warm his feelings were to her, he had not forgiven her for that.

"Yes," he said, "the letter was so strange. First, Annie ill, and then you thought of coming yourself."

"It was all the truth."

"Oh, I don't doubt it."

"Yes, you do doubt it. You are vexed, I see."

"Not for one moment. I'm only vexed, that's true, that you seem somehow unwilling to admit that there are duties ..."

"The duty of going to a concert ..."

"But we won't talk about it," he said.

"Why not talk about it?" she said.

"I only meant to say that matters of real importance may turn up. Now, for instance, I shall have to go to Moscow to arrange about the house.... Oh, Anna, why are you so irritable? Don't you know that I can't live without you?"

"If so," said Anna, her voice suddenly changing, "it means that you are sick of this life ... Yes, you will come for a day and go away, as men do ..."

"Anna, that's cruel. I am ready to give up my whole life."

But she did not hear him.

"If you go to Moscow, I will go too. I will not stay here. Either we must separate or else live together."

"Why, you know, that's my one desire. But for that ..."

"We must get a divorce. I will write to him. I see I cannot go on like this ... But I will come with you to Moscow."

"You talk as if you were threatening me. But I desire nothing so much as never to be parted from you," said Vronsky, smiling.

But as he said these words there gleamed in his eyes not merely a cold look, but the vindictive look of a man persecuted and made cruel.

She saw the look and correctly divined its meaning.

"If so, it's a calamity!" that glance told her. It was a moment's impression, but she never forgot it.

Anna wrote to her husband asking him about a divorce, and towards the end of November, taking leave of Princess Varvara, who wanted to go to Petersburg, she went with Vronsky to Moscow. Expecting every day an answer from Alexey Alexandrovitch, and after that the divorce, they now established themselves together like married people.

necessary, exactly as she spoke to Princess Marya Borissovna, and more than that, to do so in such a way that everything to the faintest intonation and smile would have been approved by her husband, whose unseen presence she seemed to feel about her at that instant.

She said a few words to him, even smiled serenely at his joke about the elections, which he called "our parliament." (She had to smile to show she saw the joke.) But she turned away immediately to Princess Marya Borissovna, and did not once glance at him till he got up to go; then she looked at him, but evidently only because it would be uncivil not to look at a man when he is saying good-bye.

She was grateful to her father for saying nothing to her about their meeting Vronsky, but she saw by his special warmth to her after the visit during their usual walk that he was pleased with her. She was pleased with herself. She had not expected she would have had the power, while keeping somewhere in the bottom of her heart all the memories of her old feeling for Vronsky, not only to seem but to be perfectly indifferent and composed with him.

Levin flushed a great deal more than she when she told him she had met Vronsky at Princess Marya Borissovna's. It was very hard for her to tell him this, but still harder to go on speaking of the details of the meeting, as he did not question her, but simply gazed at her with a frown.

"I am very sorry you weren't there," she said. "Not that you weren't in the room ... I couldn't have been so natural in your presence...I am blushing now much more, much, much more," she said, blushing till the tears came into her eyes. "But that you couldn't see through a crack."

The truthful eyes told Levin that she was satisfied with herself, and in spite of her blushing he was quickly reassured and began questioning her, which was all she wanted. When he had heard everything, even to the detail that for the first second she could not help flushing, but that afterwards she was just as direct and as much at her ease as with any chance acquaintance, Levin was quite happy again and said he was glad of it, and would not now behave as stupidly as he had done at the election, but would try the first time he met Vronsky to be as friendly as possible.

"It's so wretched to feel that there's a man almost an enemy whom it's painful to meet," said Levin. "I'm very, very glad."

CHAPTER II

D
O, PLEASE, GO THEN AND CALL ON THE BOLS," KITTY SAID TO HER
husband, when he came in to see her at eleven o'clock before going
out. "I know you are dining at the club; papa put down your name.
But what are you going to do in the morning?"

"I am only going to Katavasov," answered Levin.

"Why so early?"

"He promised to introduce me to Metrov. I wanted to talk to him about my
work. He's a distinguished scientific man from Petersburg," said Levin.

"Yes; wasn't it his article you were praising so? Well, and after that?" said
Kitty.

"I shall go to the court, perhaps, about my sister's business."

"And the concert?" she queried.

"I shan't go there all alone."

"No? do go; there are going to be some new things…. That interested you
so. I should certainly go."

"Well, anyway, I shall come home before dinner," he said, looking at his
watch.

"Put on your frock-coat, so that you can go straight to call on Countess
Bola."

"But is it absolutely necessary?"

"Oh, absolutely! He has been to see us. Come, what is it? You go in, sit
down, talk for five minutes of the weather, get up and go away."

"Oh, you wouldn't believe it! I've got so out of the way of all this that it
makes me feel positively ashamed. It's such a horrible thing to do! A complete
outsider walks in, sits down, stays on with nothing to do, wastes their time and
worries himself, and walks away!"

Kitty laughed.

"Why, I suppose you used to pay calls before you were married, didn't
you?"

"Yes, I did, but I always felt ashamed, and now I'm so out of the way of it
that, by Jove! I'd sooner go two days running without my dinner than pay this
call! One's so ashamed! I feel all the while that they're annoyed, that they're
saying, 'What has he come for?'"

"No, they won't. I'll answer for that," said Kitty, looking into his face with
a laugh. She took his hand. "Well, good-bye…. Do go, please."

he could not help reflecting that these liveries were of no use to anyone—but they were indubitably necessary, to judge by the amazement of the princess and Kitty when he suggested that they might do without liveries,—that these liveries would cost the wages of two laborers for the summer, that is, would pay for about three hundred working days from Easter to Ash Wednesday, and each a day of hard work from early morning to late evening—and that hundred-rouble note did stick in his throat. But the next note, changed to pay for providing a dinner for their relations, that cost twenty-eight roubles, though it did excite in Levin the reflection that twenty-eight roubles meant nine measures of oats, which men would with groans and sweat have reaped and bound and thrashed and winnowed and sifted and sown,—this next one he parted with more easily. And now the notes he changed no longer aroused such reflections, and they flew off like little birds. Whether the labor devoted to obtaining the money corresponded to the pleasure given by what was bought with it, was a consideration he had long ago dismissed. His business calculation that there was a certain price below which he could not sell certain grain was forgotten too. The rye, for the price of which he had so long held out, had been sold for fifty kopecks a measure cheaper than it had been fetching a month ago. Even the consideration that with such an expenditure he could not go on living for a year without debt, that even had no force. Only one thing was essential: to have money in the bank, without inquiring where it came from, so as to know that one had the wherewithal to buy meat for to-morrow. And this condition had hitherto been fulfilled; he had always had the money in the bank. But now the money in the bank had gone, and he could not quite tell where to get the next installment. And this it was which, at the moment when Kitty had mentioned money, had disturbed him; but he had no time to think about it. He drove off, thinking of Katavasov and the meeting with Metrov that was before him.

CHAPTER III

L EVIN HAD ON THIS VISIT TO TOWN SEEN A GREAT DEAL OF HIS OLD FRIEND AT the university, Professor Katavasov, whom he had not seen since his marriage. He liked in Katavasov the clearness and simplicity of his conception of life. Levin thought that the clearness of Katavasov's conception of life was due to the poverty of his nature; Katavasov thought that the disconnectedness of Levin's ideas was due to his lack of intellectual discipline; but Levin enjoyed Katavasov's clearness, and Katavasov enjoyed the abundance of Levin's untrained ideas, and they liked to meet and to discuss.

Levin had read Katavasov some parts of his book, and he had liked them. On the previous day Katavasov had met Levin at a public lecture and told him that the celebrated Metrov, whose article Levin had so much liked, was in Moscow, that he had been much interested by what Katavasov had told him about Levin's work, and that he was coming to see him to-morrow at eleven, and would be very glad to make Levin's acquaintance.

"You're positively a reformed character, I'm glad to see," said Katavasov, meeting Levin in the little drawing-room. "I heard the bell and thought: Impossible that it can be he at the exact time! ... Well, what do you say to the Montenegrins now? They're a race of warriors."

"Why, what's happened?" asked Levin.

Katavasov in a few words told him the last piece of news from the war, and going into his study, introduced Levin to a short, thick-set man of pleasant appearance. This was Metrov. The conversation touched for a brief space on politics and on how recent events were looked at in the higher spheres in Petersburg. Metrov repeated a saying that had reached him through a most trustworthy source, reported as having been uttered on this subject by the Tsar and one of the ministers. Katavasov had heard also on excellent authority that the Tsar had said something quite different. Levin tried to imagine circumstances in which both sayings might have been uttered, and the conversation on that topic dropped.

"Yes, here he's written almost a book on the natural conditions of the laborer in relation to the land," said Katavasov; "I'm not a specialist, but I, as a natural science man, was pleased at his not taking mankind as something outside biological laws; but, on the contrary, seeing his dependence on his surroundings, and in that dependence seeking the laws of his development."

"That's very interesting," said Metrov.

"What I began precisely was to write a book on agriculture; but studying the chief instrument of agriculture, the laborer," said Levin, reddening, "I could not help coming to quite unexpected results."

And Levin began carefully, as it were, feeling his ground, to expound his views. He knew Metrov had written an article against the generally accepted theory of political economy, but to what extent he could reckon on his sympathy with his own new views he did not know and could not guess from the clever and serene face of the learned man.

When the reader had finished, the chairman thanked him and read some verses of the poet Ment sent him on the jubilee, and said a few words by way of thanks to the poet. Then Katavasov in his loud, ringing voice read his address on the scientific labors of the man whose jubilee was being kept.

When Katavasov had finished, Levin looked at his watch, saw it was past one, and thought that there would not be time before the concert to read Metrov his book, and indeed, he did not now care to do so. During the reading he had thought over their conversation. He saw distinctly now that though Metrov's ideas might perhaps have value, his own ideas had a value too, and their ideas could only be made clear and lead to something if each worked separately in his chosen path, and that nothing would be gained by putting their ideas together. And having made up his mind to refuse Metrov's invitation, Levin went up to him at the end of the meeting. Metrov introduced Levin to the chairman, with whom he was talking of the political news. Metrov told the chairman what he had already told Levin, and Levin made the same remarks on his news that he had already made that morning, but for the sake of variety he expressed also a new opinion which had only just struck him. After that the conversation turned again on the university question. As Levin had already heard it all, he made haste to tell Metrov that he was sorry he could not take advantage of his invitation, took leave, and drove to Lvov's.

CHAPTER IV

LVOV, THE HUSBAND OF NATALIA, KITTY'S SISTER, HAD SPENT ALL HIS LIFE IN foreign capitals, where he had been educated, and had been in the diplomatic service.

During the previous year he had left the diplomatic service, not owing to any "unpleasantness" (he never had any "unpleasantness" with any one), and was transferred to the department of the court of the palace in Moscow, in order to give his two boys the best education possible.

In spite of the striking contrast in their habits and views and the fact that Lvov was older than Levin, they had seen a great deal of one another that winter, and had taken a great liking to each other.

Lvov was at home, and Levin went in to him unannounced.

Lvov, in a house coat with a belt and in chamois leather shoes, was sitting in an armchair, and with a pince-nez with blue glasses he was reading a book that stood on a reading-desk, while in his beautiful hand he held a half-burned cigarette daintily away from him.

His handsome, delicate, and still youthful-looking face, to which his curly, glistening silvery hair gave a still more aristocratic air, lighted up with a smile when he saw Levin.

"Capital! I was meaning to send to you. How's Kitty? Sit here, it's more comfortable." He got up and pushed up a rocking-chair. "Have you read the last circular in the *Journal de St. Pétersburg?* I think it's excellent," he said, with a slight French accent.

Levin told him what he had heard from Katavasov was being said in Petersburg, and after talking a little about politics, he told him of his interview with Metrov, and the learned society's meeting. To Lvov it was very interesting.

"That's what I envy you, that you are able to mix in these interesting scientific circles," he said. And as he talked, he passed as usual into French, which was easier to him. "It's true I haven't the time for it. My official work and the children leave me no time; and then I'm not ashamed to own that my education has been too defective."

"That I don't believe," said Levin with a smile, feeling, as he always did, touched at Lvov's low opinion of himself, which was not in the least put on from a desire to seem or to be modest, but was absolutely sincere.

"Oh, yes, indeed! I feel now how badly educated I am. To educate my children I positively have to look up a great deal, and in fact simply to study myself. For it's not enough to have teachers, there must be some one to look after them, just as on your land you want laborers and an overseer. See what I'm reading"—he pointed to Buslaev's *Grammar* on the desk—"it's expected of Misha, and it's so difficult ... Come, explain to me ... Here he says ..."

Levin tried to explain to him that it couldn't be understood, but that it had to be taught; but Lvov would not agree with him.

"Oh, you're laughing at it!"

"On the contrary, you can't imagine how, when I look at you, I'm always learning the task that lies before me, that is the education of one's children."

"Well, there's nothing for you to learn," said Lvov.

"All I know," said Levin, "is that I have never seen better brought-up children than yours, and I wouldn't wish for children better than yours."

But the more he listened to the fantasia of *King Lear* the further he felt from forming any definite opinion of it. There was, as it were, a continual beginning, a preparation of the musical expression of some feeling, but it fell to pieces again directly, breaking into new musical motives, or simply nothing but the whims of the composer, exceedingly complex but disconnected sounds. And these fragmentary musical expressions, though sometimes beautiful, were disagreeable, because they were utterly unexpected and not led up to by anything. Gaiety and grief and despair and tenderness and triumph followed one another without any connection, like the emotions of a madman. And those emotions, like a madman's, sprang up quite unexpectedly.

During the whole of the performance Levin felt like a deaf man watching people dancing, and was in a state of complete bewilderment when the fantasia was over, and felt a great weariness from the fruitless strain on his attention. Loud applause resounded on all sides. Every one got up, moved about, and began talking. Anxious to throw some light on his own perplexity from the impressions of others, Levin began to walk about, looking for connoisseurs, and was glad to see a well-known musical amateur in conversation with Pestsov, whom he knew.

"Marvelous!" Pestsov was saying in his mellow bass. "How are you, Konstantin Dmitrievitch? Particularly sculpturesque and plastic, so to say, and richly colored is that passage where you feel Cordelia's approach, where woman, *das ewig Weibliche*, enters into conflict with fate. Isn't it?"

"You mean ... what has Cordelia to do with it?" Levin asked timidly, forgetting that the fantasia was supposed to represent King Lear.

"Cordelia comes in ... see here!" said Pestsov, tapping his finger on the satiny surface of the program he held in his hand and passing it to Levin.

Only then Levin recollected the title of the fantasia, and made haste to read in the Russian translation the lines from Shakespeare that were printed on the back of the program.

"You can't follow it without that," said Pestsov, addressing Levin, as the person he had been speaking to had gone away, and he had no one to talk to.

In the *entr'acte* Levin and Pestsov fell into an argument upon the merits and defects of music of the Wagner school. Levin maintained that the mistake of Wagner and all his followers lay in their trying to take music into the sphere of another art, just as poetry goes wrong when it tries to paint a face as the art of painting ought to do, and as an instance of this mistake he cited the sculptor who carved in marble certain poetic phantasms flitting round the figure of the poet on the pedestal. "These phantoms were so far from being phantoms that they were positively clinging on the ladder," said Levin. The comparison pleased him, but he could not remember whether he had not used the same phrase before, and to Pestsov, too, and as he said it he felt confused.

Pestsov maintained that art is one, and that it can attain its highest manifestations only by conjunction with all kinds of art.

The second piece that was performed Levin could not hear. Pestsov, who was standing beside him, was talking to him almost all the time, condemning the music for its excessive affected assumption of simplicity, and comparing it with the simplicity of the Pre-Raphaelites in painting. As he went out Levin met many more acquaintances, with whom he talked of politics, of music, and of common acquaintances. Among others he met Count Bol, whom he had utterly forgotten to call upon.

"Well, go at once then," Madame Lvova said, when he told her; "perhaps they'll not be at home, and then you can come to the meeting to fetch me. You'll find me still there."

CHAPTER VI

P ERHAPS THEY'RE NOT AT HOME?" SAID LEVIN, AS HE WENT INTO THE HALL of Countess Bola's house.

"At home; please walk in," said the porter, resolutely removing his overcoat.

"How annoying!" thought Levin with a sigh, taking off one glove and stroking his hat. "What did I come for? What have I to say to them?"

As he passed through the first drawing-room Levin met in the doorway Countess Bola, giving some order to a servant with a care-worn and severe face. On seeing Levin she smiled, and asked him to come into the little drawing-room, where he heard voices. In this room there were sitting in armchairs the two daughters of the countess, and a Moscow colonel, whom Levin knew. Levin went up, greeted them, and sat down beside the sofa with his hat on his knees.

"How is your wife? Have you been at the concert? We couldn't go. Mamma had to be at the funeral service."

"Yes, I heard … What a sudden death!" said Levin.

The countess came in, sat down on the sofa, and she too asked after his wife and inquired about the concert.

The porter did not only know Levin, but also all his ties and relationships, and so immediately mentioned his intimate friends.

Passing through the outer hall, divided up by screens, and the room partitioned on the right, where a man sits at the fruit-buffet, Levin overtook an old man walking slowly in, and entered the dining-room full of noise and people.

He walked along the tables, almost all full, and looked at the visitors. He saw people of all sorts, old and young; some he knew a little, some intimate friends. There was not a single cross or worried-looking face. All seemed to have left their cares and anxieties in the porter's room with their hats, and were all deliberately getting ready to enjoy the material blessings of life. Sviazhsky was here and Shtcherbatsky, Nevyedovsky and the old prince, and Vronsky and Sergey Ivanovitch.

"Ah! why are you late?" the prince said smiling, and giving him his hand over his own shoulder. "How's Kitty?" he added, smoothing out the napkin he had tucked in at his waistcoat buttons.

"All right; they are dining at home, all the three of them."

"Ah, 'Aline-Nadine,' to be sure! There's no room with us. Go to that table, and make haste and take a seat," said the prince, and turning away he carefully took a plate of eel soup.

"Levin, this way!" a good-natured voice shouted a little further on. It was Turovtsin. He was sitting with a young officer, and beside them were two chairs turned upside down. Levin gladly went up to them. He had always liked the good-hearted rake, Turovtsin—he was associated in his mind with memories of his courtship—and at that moment, after the strain of intellectual conversation, the sight of Turovtsin's good-natured face was particularly welcome.

"For you and Oblonsky. He'll be here directly."

The young man, holding himself very erect, with eyes forever twinkling with enjoyment, was an officer from Petersburg, Gagin. Turovtsin introduced them.

"Oblonsky's always late."

"Ah, here he is!"

"Have you only just come?" said Oblonsky, coming quickly towards them. "Good-day. Had some vodka? Well, come along then."

Levin got up and went with him to the big table spread with spirits and appetizers of the most various kinds. One would have thought that out of two dozen delicacies one might find something to one's taste, but Stepan Arkadyevitch asked for something special, and one of the liveried waiters standing by immediately brought what was required. They drank a wine-glassful and returned to their table.

At once, while they were still at the soup, Gagin was served with champagne, and told the waiter to fill four glasses. Levin did not refuse the wine, and asked for a second bottle. He was very hungry, and ate and drank with great enjoyment, and with still greater enjoyment took part in the lively and simple conversation of his companions. Gagin, dropping his voice, told the last good story from Petersburg, and the story, though improper and stupid, was so ludicrous that Levin broke into roars of laughter so loud that those near looked round.

"That's in the same style as, 'that's a thing I can't endure!' You know the story?" said Stepan Arkadyevitch. "Ah, that's exquisite! Another bottle," he said to the waiter, and he began to relate his good story.

"Pyotr Illyitch Vinovsky invites you to drink with him," a little old waiter interrupted Stepan Arkadyevitch, bringing two delicate glasses of sparkling champagne, and addressing Stepan Arkadyevitch and Levin. Stepan Arkadyevitch took the glass, and looking towards a bald man with red mustaches at the other end of the table, he nodded to him, smiling.

"Who's that?" asked Levin.

"You met him once at my place, don't you remember? A good-natured fellow."

Levin did the same as Stepan Arkadyevitch and took the glass.

Stepan Arkadyevitch's anecdote too was very amusing. Levin told his story, and that too was successful. Then they talked of horses, of the races, of what they had been doing that day, and of how smartly Vronsky's Atlas had won the first prize. Levin did not notice how the time passed at dinner.

"Ah! and here they are!" Stepan Arkadyevitch said towards the end of dinner, leaning over the back of his chair and holding out his hand to Vronsky, who came up with a tall officer of the Guards. Vronsky's face too beamed with the look of good-humored enjoyment that was general in the club. He propped his elbow playfully on Stepan Arkadyevitch's shoulder, whispering something to him, and he held out his hand to Levin with the same good-humored smile.

"Very glad to meet you," he said. "I looked out for you at the election, but I was told you had gone away."

"Yes, I left the same day. We've just been talking of your horse. I congratulate you," said Levin. "It was very rapidly run."

"Yes; you've race-horses too, haven't you?"

"No, my father had; but I remember and know something about it."

don't go," he said, and he warmly squeezed his arm above the elbow, obviously not at all wishing to let him go.

"This is a true friend of mine—almost my greatest friend," he said to Vronsky. "You have become even closer and dearer to me. And I want you, and I know you ought, to be friends, and great friends, because you're both splendid fellows."

"Well, there's nothing for us now but to kiss and be friends," Vronsky said, with good-natured playfulness, holding out his hand.

Levin quickly took the offered hand, and pressed it warmly.

"I'm very, very glad," said Levin.

"Waiter, a bottle of champagne," said Stepan Arkadyevitch.

"And I'm very glad," said Vronsky.

But in spite of Stepan Arkadyevitch's desire, and their own desire, they had nothing to talk about, and both felt it.

"Do you know, he has never met Anna?" Stepan Arkadyevitch said to Vronsky. "And I want above everything to take him to see her. Let us go, Levin!"

"Really?" said Vronsky. "She will be very glad to see you. I should be going home at once," he added, "but I'm worried about Yashvin, and I want to stay on till he finishes."

"Why, is he losing?"

"He keeps losing, and I'm the only friend that can restrain him."

"Well, what do you say to pyramids? Levin, will you play? Capital!" said Stepan Arkadyevitch. "Get the table ready," he said to the marker.

"It has been ready a long while," answered the marker, who had already set the balls in a triangle, and was knocking the red one about for his own diversion.

"Well, let us begin."

After the game Vronsky and Levin sat down at Gagin's table, and at Stepan Arkadyevitch's suggestion Levin took a hand in the game.

Vronsky sat down at the table, surrounded by friends, who were incessantly coming up to him. Every now and then he went to the "infernal" to keep an eye on Yashvin. Levin was enjoying a delightful sense of repose after the mental fatigue of the morning. He was glad that all hostility was at an end with Vronsky, and the sense of peace, decorum, and comfort never left him.

When the game was over, Stepan Arkadyevitch took Levin's arm.

"Well, let us go to Anna's, then. At once? Eh? She is at home. I promised her long ago to bring you. Where were you meaning to spend the evening?"

"Oh, nowhere specially. I promised Sviazhsky to go to the Society of Agriculture. By all means, let us go," said Levin.

"Very good; come along. Find out if my carriage is here," Stepan Arkady-evitch said to the waiter.

Levin went up to the table, paid the forty roubles he had lost; paid his bill, the amount of which was in some mysterious way ascertained by the little old waiter who stood at the counter, and swinging his arms he walked through all the rooms to the way out.

CHAPTER IX

OBLONSKY'S CARRIAGE!" THE PORTER SHOUTED IN AN ANGRY BASS. The carriage drove up and both got in. It was only for the first few moments, while the carriage was driving out of the clubhouse gates, that Levin was still under the influence of the club atmosphere of repose, comfort, and unimpeachable good form. But as soon as the carriage drove out into the street, and he felt it jolting over the uneven road, heard the angry shout of a sledge-driver coming towards them, saw in the uncertain light the red blind of a tavern and the shops, this impression was dissipated, and he began to think over his actions, and to wonder whether he was doing right in going to see Anna. What would Kitty say? But Stepan Arkadyevitch gave him no time for reflection, and, as though divining his doubts, he scattered them.

"How glad I am," he said, "that you should know her! You know Dolly has long wished for it. And Lvov's been to see her, and often goes. Though she is my sister," Stepan Arkadyevitch pursued, "I don't hesitate to say that she's a remarkable woman. But you will see. Her position is very painful, especially now."

"Why especially now?"

"We are carrying on negotiations with her husband about a divorce. And he's agreed; but there are difficulties in regard to the son, and the business, which ought to have been arranged long ago, has been dragging on for three months past. As soon as the divorce is over, she will marry Vronsky. How stupid these old ceremonies are, that no one believes in, and which only prevent people being comfortable!" Stepan Arkadyevitch put in. "Well, then their position will be as regular as mine, as yours."

"What is the difficulty?" said Levin.

"Oh, it's a long and tedious story! The whole business is in such an anomalous position with us. But the point is she has been for three months in Moscow,

"I am delighted, delighted," she repeated, and on her lips these simple words took for Levin's ears a special significance. "I have known you and liked you for a long while, both from your friendship with Stiva and for your wife's sake…. I knew her for a very short time, but she left on me the impression of an exquisite flower, simply a flower. And to think she will soon be a mother!"

She spoke easily and without haste, looking now and then from Levin to her brother, and Levin felt that the impression he was making was good, and he felt immediately at home, simple and happy with her, as though he had known her from childhood.

"Ivan Petrovitch and I settled in Alexey's study," she said in answer to Stepan Arkadyevitch's question whether he might smoke, "just so as to be able to smoke"—and glancing at Levin, instead of asking whether he would smoke, she pulled closer a tortoise-shell cigar-case and took a cigarette.

"How are you feeling to-day?" her brother asked her.

"Oh, nothing. Nerves, as usual."

"Yes, isn't it extraordinarily fine?" said Stepan Arkadyevitch, noticing that Levin was scrutinizing the picture.

"I have never seen a better portrait."

"And extraordinarily like, isn't it?" said Vorkuev.

Levin looked from the portrait to the original. A peculiar brilliance lighted up Anna's face when she felt his eyes on her. Levin flushed, and to cover his confusion would have asked whether she had seen Darya Alexandrovna lately; but at that moment Anna spoke. "We were just talking, Ivan Petrovitch and I, of Vashtchenkov's last pictures. Have you seen them?"

"Yes, I have seen them," answered Levin.

"But, I beg your pardon, I interrupted you … you were saying? …"

Levin asked if she had seen Dolly lately.

"She was here yesterday. She was very indignant with the high school people on Grisha's account. The Latin teacher, it seems, had been unfair to him."

"Yes, I have seen his pictures. I didn't care for them very much," Levin went back to the subject she had started.

Levin talked now not at all with that purely businesslike attitude to the subject with which he had been talking all the morning. Every word in his conversation with her had a special significance. And talking to her was pleasant; still pleasanter it was to listen to her.

Anna talked not merely naturally and cleverly, but cleverly and carelessly, attaching no value to her own ideas and giving great weight to the ideas of the person she was talking to.

The conversation turned on the new movement in art, on the new illustrations of the Bible by a French artist. Vorkuev attacked the artist for a realism carried to the point of coarseness.

Levin said that the French had carried conventionality further than any one, and that consequently they see a great merit in the return to realism. In the fact of not lying they see poetry.

Never had anything clever said by Levin given him so much pleasure as this remark. Anna's face lighted up at once, as at once she appreciated the thought. She laughed.

"I laugh," she said, "as one laughs when one sees a very true portrait. What you said so perfectly hits off French art now, painting and literature too, indeed—Zola, Daudet. But perhaps it is always so, that men form their conceptions from fictitious, conventional types, and then—all the *combinaisons* made—they are tired of the fictitious figures and begin to invent more natural, true figures."

"That's perfectly true," said Vorkuev.

"So you've been at the club?" she said to her brother.

"Yes, yes, this is a woman!" Levin thought, forgetting himself and staring persistently at her lovely, mobile face, which at that moment was all at once completely transformed. Levin did not hear what she was talking of as she leaned over to her brother, but he was struck by the change of her expression. Her face—so handsome a moment before in its repose—suddenly wore a look of strange curiosity, anger, and pride. But this lasted only an instant. She dropped her eyelids, as though recollecting something.

"Oh, well, but that's of no interest to any one," she said, and she turned to the English girl.

"Please order the tea in the drawing-room," she said in English.

The girl got up and went out.

"Well, how did she get through her examination?" asked Stepan Arkadyevitch.

"Splendidly! She's a very gifted child and a sweet character."

"It will end in your loving her more than your own."

"There a man speaks. In love there's no more nor less. I love my daughter with one love, and her with another."

"I was just telling Anna Arkadyevna," said Vorkuev, "that if she were to put a hundredth part of the energy she devotes to this English girl to the public question of the education of Russian children, she would be doing a great and useful work."

CHAPTER XI

W HAT A MARVELOUS, SWEET AND UNHAPPY WOMAN!" HE WAS THINKING, as he stepped out into the frosty air with Stepan Arkadyevitch. "Well, didn't I tell you?" said Stepan Arkadyevitch, seeing that Levin had been completely won over.

"Yes," said Levin dreamily, "an extraordinary woman! It's not her cleverness, but she has such wonderful depth of feeling. I'm awfully sorry for her!"

"Now, please God, everything will soon be settled. Well, well, don't be hard on people in future," said Stepan Arkadyevitch, opening the carriage door. "Good-bye; we don't go the same way."

Still thinking of Anna, of everything, even the simplest phrase in their conversation with her, and recalling the most minute changes in her expression, entering more and more into her position, and feeling sympathy for her, Levin reached home.

At home Kouzma told Levin that Katerina Alexandrovna was quite well, and that her sisters had not long been gone, and he handed him two letters. Levin read them at once in the hall, that he might not overlook them later. One was from Sokolov, his bailiff. Sokolov wrote that the corn could not be sold, that it was fetching only five and a half roubles, and that more than that could not be got for it. The other letter was from his sister. She scolded him for her business being still unsettled.

"Well, we must sell it at five and a half if we can't get more," Levin decided the first question, which had always before seemed such a weighty one, with extraordinary facility on the spot. "It's extraordinary how all one's time is taken up here," he thought, considering the second letter. He felt himself to blame for not having got done what his sister had asked him to do for her. "To-day, again, I've not been to the court, but to-day I've certainly not had time." And resolving that he would not fail to do it next day, he went up to his wife. As he went in, Levin rapidly ran through mentally the day he had spent. All the events of the day were conversations, conversations he had heard and taken part in. All the conversations were upon subjects which, if he had been alone at home, he would never have taken up, but here they were very interesting. And all these conversations were right enough, only in two places there was something not quite right. One was what he had said about the carp, the other was something not "quite the thing" in the tender sympathy he was feeling for Anna.

Levin found his wife low-spirited and dull. The dinner of the three sisters had gone off very well, but then they had waited and waited for him, all of them had felt dull, the sisters had departed, and she had been left alone.

"Well, and what have you been doing?" she asked him, looking straight into his eyes, which shone with rather a suspicious brightness. But that she might not prevent his telling her everything, she concealed her close scrutiny of him, and with an approving smile listened to his account of how he had spent the evening.

"Well, I'm very glad I met Vronsky. I felt quite at ease and natural with him. You understand, I shall try not to see him, but I'm glad that this awkwardness is all over," he said, and remembering that by way of trying not to see him, he had immediately gone to call on Anna, he blushed. "We talk about the peasants drinking; I don't know which drinks most, the peasantry or our own class; the peasants do on holidays, but …"

But Kitty took not the slightest interest in discussing the drinking habits of the peasants. She saw that he blushed, and she wanted to know why.

"Well, and then where did you go?"

"Stiva urged me awfully to go and see Anna Arkadyevna."

And as he said this, Levin blushed even more, and his doubts as to whether he had done right in going to see Anna were settled once for all. He knew now that he ought not to have done so.

Kitty's eyes opened in a curious way and gleamed at Anna's name, but controlling herself with an effort, she concealed her emotion and deceived him.

"Oh!" was all she said.

"I'm sure you won't be angry at my going. Stiva begged me to, and Dolly wished it," Levin went on.

"Oh, no!" she said, but he saw in her eyes a constraint that boded him no good.

"She is a very sweet, very, very unhappy, good woman," he said, telling her about Anna, her occupations, and what she had told him to say to her.

"Yes, of course, she is very much to be pitied," said Kitty, when he had finished. "Whom was your letter from?"

He told her, and believing in her calm tone, he went to change his coat.

Coming back, he found Kitty in the same easy-chair. When he went up to her, she glanced at him and broke into sobs.

"What? what is it?" he asked, knowing beforehand what.

"You're in love with that hateful woman; she has bewitched you! I saw it in your eyes. Yes, yes! What can it all lead to? You were drinking at the club,

His hand closed, he turned away, and his face wore a still more obstinate expression.

"For you it's a matter of obstinacy," she said, watching him intently and suddenly finding the right word for that expression that irritated her, "simply obstinacy. For you it's a question of whether you keep the upper hand of me, while for me ..." Again she felt sorry for herself, and she almost burst into tears. "If you knew what it is for me! When I feel as I do now that you are hostile, yes, hostile to me, if you knew what this means for me! If you knew how I feel on the brink of calamity at this instant, how afraid I am of myself!" And she turned away, hiding her sobs.

"But what are you talking about?" he said, horrified at her expression of despair, and again bending over her, he took her hand and kissed it. "What is it for? Do I seek amusements outside our home? Don't I avoid the society of women?"

"Well, yes! If that were all!" she said.

"Come, tell me what I ought to do to give you peace of mind? I am ready to do anything to make you happy," he said, touched by her expression of despair; "what wouldn't I do to save you from distress of any sort, as now, Anna!" he said.

"It's nothing, nothing!" she said. "I don't know myself whether it's the solitary life, my nerves ... Come, don't let us talk of it. What about the race? You haven't told me!" she inquired, trying to conceal her triumph at the victory, which had anyway been on her side.

He asked for supper, and began telling her about the races; but in his tone, in his eyes, which became more and more cold, she saw that he did not forgive her for her victory, that the feeling of obstinacy with which she had been struggling had asserted itself again in him. He was colder to her than before, as though he were regretting his surrender. And she, remembering the words that had given her the victory, "how I feel on the brink of calamity, how afraid I am of myself," saw that this weapon was a dangerous one, and that it could not be used a second time. And she felt that beside the love that bound them together there had grown up between them some evil spirit of strife, which she could not exorcise from his, and still less from her own heart.

CHAPTER XIII

THERE ARE NO CONDITIONS TO WHICH A MAN CANNOT BECOME USED, especially if he sees that all around him are living in the same way. Levin could not have believed three months before that he could have gone quietly to sleep in the condition in which he was that day, that leading an aimless, irrational life, living too beyond his means, after drinking to excess (he could not call what happened at the club anything else), forming inappropriately friendly relations with a man with whom his wife had once been in love, and a still more inappropriate call upon a woman who could only be called a lost woman, after being fascinated by that woman and causing his wife distress—he could still go quietly to sleep. But under the influence of fatigue, a sleepless night, and the wine he had drunk, his sleep was sound and untroubled.

At five o'clock the creak of a door opening waked him. He jumped up and looked round. Kitty was not in bed beside him. But there was a light moving behind the screen, and he heard her steps.

"What is it? ... what is it?" he said, half-asleep. "Kitty! What is it?"

"Nothing," she said, coming from behind the screen with a candle in her hand. "I felt unwell," she said, smiling a particularly sweet and meaning smile.

"What? has it begun?" he said in terror. "We ought to send ..." and hurriedly he reached after his clothes.

"No, no," she said, smiling and holding his hand. "It's sure to be nothing. I was rather unwell, only a little. It's all over now."

And getting into bed, she blew out the candle, lay down and was still. Though he thought her stillness suspicious, as though she were holding her breath, and still more suspicious the expression of peculiar tenderness and excitement with which, as she came from behind the screen, she said "nothing," he was so sleepy that he fell asleep at once. Only later he remembered the stillness of her breathing, and understood all that must have been passing in her sweet, precious heart while she lay beside him, not stirring, in anticipation of the greatest event in a woman's life. At seven o'clock he was waked by the touch of her hand on his shoulder, and a gentle whisper. She seemed struggling between regret at waking him, and the desire to talk to him.

"Kostya, don't be frightened. It's all right. But I fancy ... We ought to send for Lizaveta Petrovna."

The candle was lighted again. She was sitting up in bed, holding some knitting, which she had been busy upon during the last few days.

CHAPTER XIV

THE DOCTOR WAS NOT YET UP, AND THE FOOTMAN SAID THAT HE HAD BEEN up late, and had given orders not to be waked, but would get up soon. The footman was cleaning the lamp-chimneys, and seemed very busy about them. This concentration of the footman upon his lamps, and his indifference to what was passing in Levin, at first astounded him, but immediately on considering the question he realized that no one knew or was bound to know his feelings, and that it was all the more necessary to act calmly, sensibly, and resolutely to get through this wall of indifference and attain his aim.

"Don't be in a hurry or let anything slip," Levin said to himself, feeling a greater and greater flow of physical energy and attention to all that lay before him to do.

Having ascertained that the doctor was not getting up, Levin considered various plans, and decided on the following one: that Kouzma should go for another doctor, while he himself should go to the chemist's for opium, and if when he came back the doctor had not yet begun to get up, he would either by tipping the footman, or by force, wake the doctor at all hazards.

At the chemist's the lank shopman sealed up a packet of powders for a coachman who stood waiting, and refused him opium with the same callousness with which the doctor's footman had cleaned his lamp-chimneys. Trying not to get flurried or out of temper, Levin mentioned the names of the doctor and midwife, and explaining what the opium was needed for, tried to persuade him. The assistant inquired in German whether he should give it, and receiving an affirmative reply from behind the partition, he took out a bottle and a funnel, deliberately poured the opium from a bigger bottle into a little one, stuck on a label, sealed it up, in spite of Levin's request that he would not do so, and was about to wrap it up too. This was more than Levin could stand; he took the bottle firmly out of his hands, and ran to the big glass doors. The doctor was not even now getting up, and the footman, busy now in putting down the rugs, refused to wake him. Levin deliberately took out a ten-rouble note, and, careful to speak slowly, though losing no time over the business, he handed him the note, and explained that Pyotr Dmitrievitch (what a great and important personage he seemed to Levin now, this Pyotr Dmitrievitch, who had been of so little consequence in his eyes before!) had promised to come at any time; that he would certainly not be angry! and that he must therefore wake him at once.

The footman agreed, and went up-stairs, taking Levin into the waiting-room.

Levin could hear through the door the doctor coughing, moving about, washing, and saying something. Three minutes passed; it seemed to Levin that more than an hour had gone by. He could not wait any longer.

"Pyotr Dmitrievitch, Pyotr Dmitrievitch!" he said in an imploring voice at the open door. "For God's sake, forgive me! See me as you are. It's been going on more than two hours already."

"In a minute; in a minute!" answered a voice, and to his amazement Levin heard that the doctor was smiling as he spoke.

"For one instant."

"In a minute."

Two minutes more passed while the doctor was putting on his boots, and two minutes more while the doctor put on his coat and combed his hair.

"Pyotr Dmitrievitch!" Levin was beginning again in a plaintive voice, just as the doctor came in dressed and ready. "These people have no conscience," thought Levin. "Combing his hair, while we're dying!"

"Good-morning!" the doctor said to him, shaking hands, and, as it were, teasing him with his composure. "There's no hurry. Well now?"

Trying to be as accurate as possible, Levin began to tell him every unnecessary detail of his wife's condition, interrupting his account repeatedly with entreaties that the doctor would come with him at once.

"Oh, you needn't be in any hurry. You don't understand, you know. I'm certain I'm not wanted, still I've promised, and if you like, I'll come. But there's no hurry. Please sit down; won't you have some coffee?"

Levin stared at him with eyes that asked whether he was laughing at him; but the doctor had no notion of making fun of him.

"I know, I know," the doctor said, smiling; "I'm a married man myself; and at these moments we husbands are very much to be pitied. I've a patient whose husband always takes refuge in the stables on such occasions."

"But what do you think, Pyotr Dmitrievitch? Do you suppose it may go all right?"

"Everything points to a favorable issue."

"So you'll come immediately?" said Levin, looking wrathfully at the servant who was bringing in the coffee.

"In an hour's time."

"Oh, for mercy's sake!"

"Well, let me drink my coffee, anyway."

The doctor started upon his coffee. Both were silent.

childhood and first youth.

All this time he had two distinct spiritual conditions. One was away from her, with the doctor, who kept smoking one fat cigarette after another and extinguishing them on the edge of a full ash-tray, with Dolly, and with the old prince, where there was talk about dinner, about politics, about Marya Petrovna's illness, and where Levin suddenly forgot for a minute what was happening, and felt as though he had waked up from sleep; the other was in her presence, at her pillow, where his heart seemed breaking and still did not break from sympathetic suffering, and he prayed to God without ceasing. And every time he was brought back from a moment of oblivion by a scream reaching him from the bedroom, he fell into the same strange terror that had come upon him the first minute. Every time he heard a shriek, he jumped up, ran to justify himself, remembered on the way that he was not to blame, and he longed to defend her, to help her. But as he looked at her, he saw again that help was impossible, and he was filled with terror and prayed: "Lord, have mercy on us, and help us!" And as time went on, both these conditions became more intense; the calmer he became away from her, completely forgetting her, the more agonizing became both her sufferings and his feeling of helplessness before them. He jumped up, would have liked to run away, but ran to her.

Sometimes, when again and again she called upon him, he blamed her; but seeing her patient, smiling face, and hearing the words, "I am worrying you," he threw the blame on God; but thinking of God, at once he fell to beseeching God to forgive him and have mercy.

CHAPTER XV

H E DID NOT KNOW WHETHER IT WAS LATE OR EARLY. THE CANDLES HAD ALL burned out. Dolly had just been in the study and had suggested to the doctor that he should lie down. Levin sat listening to the doctor's stories of a quack mesmerizer and looking at the ashes of his cigarette. There had been a period of repose, and he had sunk into oblivion. He had completely forgotten what was going on now. He heard the doctor's chat and understood it. Suddenly there came an unearthly shriek. The shriek was so awful that Levin did not even jump up, but holding his breath, gazed in terrified inquiry at the doctor. The doctor put his head on one side, listened, and smiled approvingly. Everything was so extraordinary that nothing could strike Levin as strange. "I suppose it must be so," he thought, and still sat where he was. Whose scream was this? He jumped up, ran on tiptoe to the bedroom, edged round Lizaveta Petrovna and the princess, and took up his position at Kitty's pillow. The scream had subsided, but there was some change now. What it was he did not see and did not comprehend, and he had no wish to see or comprehend. But he saw it by the face of Lizaveta Petrovna. Lizaveta Petrovna's face was stern and pale, and still as resolute, though her jaws were twitching, and her eyes were fixed intently on Kitty. Kitty's swollen and agonized face, a tress of hair clinging to her moist brow, was turned to him and sought his eyes. Her lifted hands asked for his hands. Clutching his chill hands in her moist ones, she began squeezing them to her face.

"Don't go, don't go! I'm not afraid, I'm not afraid!" she said rapidly. "Mamma, take my earrings. They bother me. You're not afraid? Quick, quick, Lizaveta Petrovna ..."

She spoke quickly, very quickly, and tried to smile. But suddenly her face was drawn, she pushed him away.

"Oh, this is awful! I'm dying, I'm dying! Go away!" she shrieked, and again he heard that unearthly scream.

Levin clutched at his head and ran out of the room.

"It's nothing, it's nothing, it's all right," Dolly called after him.

But they might say what they liked, he knew now that all was over. He stood in the next room, his head leaning against the door-post, and heard shrieks, howls such as he had never heard before, and he knew that what had been Kitty was uttering these shrieks. He had long ago ceased to wish for the child. By now he loathed this child. He did not even wish for her life now, all he longed for was the end of this awful anguish.

"Doctor! What is it? what is it? By God!" he said, snatching at the doctor's hand as he came up.

"It's the end," said the doctor. And the doctor's face was so grave as he said it that Levin took *the end* as meaning her death.

Beside himself, he ran into the bedroom. The first thing he saw was the face of Lizaveta Petrovna. It was even more frowning and stern. Kitty's face he did not know. In the place where it had been was something that was fearful in its strained distortion and in the sounds that came from it. He fell down with his head on the wooden framework of the bed, feeling that his heart was bursting. The awful scream never paused, it became still more awful, and as though it had reached the utmost limit of terror, suddenly it ceased. Levin could not be-

make him tidy first," and Lizaveta Petrovna laid the red wobbling thing on the bed, began untrussing and trussing up the baby, lifting it up and turning it over with one finger and powdering it with something.

Levin, looking at the tiny, pitiful creature, made strenuous efforts to discover in his heart some traces of fatherly feeling for it. He felt nothing towards it but disgust. But when it was undressed and he caught a glimpse of wee, wee, little hands, little feet, saffron-colored, with little toes, too, and positively with a little big toe different from the rest, and when he saw Lizaveta Petrovna closing the wide-open little hands, as though they were soft springs, and putting them into linen garments, such pity for the little creature came upon him, and such terror that she would hurt it, that he held her hand back.

Lizaveta Petrovna laughed.

"Don't be frightened, don't be frightened!"

When the baby had been put to rights and transformed into a firm doll, Lizaveta Petrovna dandled it as though proud of her handiwork, and stood a little away so that Levin might see his son in all his glory.

Kitty looked sideways in the same direction, never taking her eyes off the baby. "Give him to me! give him to me!" she said, and even made as though she would sit up.

"What are you thinking of, Katerina Alexandrovna, you mustn't move like that! Wait a minute. I'll give him to you. Here we're showing papa what a fine fellow we are!"

And Lizaveta Petrovna, with one hand supporting the wobbling head, lifted up on the other arm the strange, limp, red creature, whose head was lost in its swaddling-clothes. But it had a nose, too, and slanting eyes and smacking lips.

"A splendid baby!" said Lizaveta Petrovna.

Levin sighed with mortification. This splendid baby excited in him no feeling but disgust and compassion. It was not at all the feeling he had looked forward to.

He turned away while Lizaveta Petrovna put the baby to the unaccustomed breast.

Suddenly laughter made him look round. The baby had taken the breast.

"Come, that's enough, that's enough!" said Lizaveta Petrovna, but Kitty would not let the baby go. He fell asleep in her arms.

"Look, now," said Kitty, turning the baby so that he could see it. The aged-looking little face suddenly puckered up still more and the baby sneezed.

Smiling, hardly able to restrain his tears, Levin kissed his wife and went out of the dark room. What he felt towards this little creature was utterly unlike what he had expected. There was nothing cheerful and joyous in the feeling; on the contrary, it was a new torture of apprehension. It was the consciousness of a new sphere of liability to pain. And this sense was so painful at first, the apprehension lest this helpless creature should suffer was so intense, that it prevented him from noticing the strange thrill of senseless joy and even pride that he had felt when the baby sneezed.

CHAPTER XVII

STEPAN ARKADYEVITCH'S AFFAIRS WERE IN A VERY BAD WAY. The money for two-thirds of the forest had all been spent already, and he had borrowed from the merchant in advance at ten per cent discount, almost all the remaining third. The merchant would not give more, especially as Darya Alexandrovna, for the first time that winter insisting on her right to her own property, had refused to sign the receipt for the payment of the last third of the forest. All his salary went on household expenses and in payment of petty debts that could not be put off. There was positively no money.

This was unpleasant and awkward, and in Stepan Arkadyevitch's opinion things could not go on like this. The explanation of the position was, in his view, to be found in the fact that his salary was too small. The post he filled had been unmistakably very good five years ago, but it was so no longer.

Petrov, the bank director, had twelve thousand; Sventitsky, a company director, had seventeen thousand; Mitin, who had founded a bank, received fifty thousand.

"Clearly I've been napping, and they've overlooked me," Stepan Arkadyevitch thought about himself. And he began keeping his eyes and ears open, and towards the end of the winter he had discovered a very good berth and had formed a plan of attack upon it, at first from Moscow through aunts, uncles, and friends, and then, when the matter was well advanced, in the spring, he went himself to Petersburg. It was one of those snug, lucrative berths of which there are so many more nowadays than there used to be, with incomes ranging from one thousand to fifty thousand roubles. It was the post of secretary of the committee of the amalgamated agency of the Southern Railways, and of certain banking companies. This position, like all such appointments, called for such immense energy and such varied qualifications, that it was difficult

Stepan Arkadyevitch made haste to interrupt his brother-in-law.

"Yes; but you must agree that it's a new institution of undoubted utility that's being started. After all, you know, it's a growing thing! What they lay particular stress on is the thing being carried on honestly," said Stepan Arkadyevitch with emphasis.

But the Moscow significance of the word "honest" was lost on Alexey Alexandrovitch.

"Honesty is only a negative qualification," he said.

"Well, you'll do me a great service, anyway," said Stepan Arkadyevitch, "by putting in a word to Pomorsky—just in the way of conversation ..."

"But I fancy it's more in Volgarinov's hands," said Alexey Alexandrovitch.

"Volgarinov has fully assented, as far as he's concerned," said Stepan Arkadyevitch, turning red. Stepan Arkadyevitch reddened at the mention of that name, because he had been that morning at the Jew Volgarinov's, and the visit had left an unpleasant recollection.

Stepan Arkadyevitch believed most positively that the committee in which he was trying to get an appointment was a new, genuine, and honest public body, but that morning when Volgarinov had—intentionally, beyond a doubt—kept him two hours waiting with other petitioners in his waiting-room, he had suddenly felt uneasy.

Whether he was uncomfortable that he, a descendant of Rurik, Prince Oblonsky, had been kept for two hours waiting to see a Jew, or that for the first time in his life he was not following the example of his ancestors in serving the government, but was turning off into a new career, anyway he was very uncomfortable. During those two hours in Volgarinov's waiting-room Stepan Arkadyevitch, stepping jauntily about the room, pulling his whiskers, entering into conversation with the other petitioners, and inventing an epigram on his position, assiduously concealed from others, and even from himself, the feeling he was experiencing.

But all the time he was uncomfortable and angry, he could not have said why—whether because he could not get his epigram just right, or from some other reason. When at last Volgarinov had received him with exaggerated politeness and unmistakable triumph at his humiliation, and had all but refused the favor asked of him, Stepan Arkadyevitch had made haste to forget it all as soon as possible. And now, at the mere recollection, he blushed.

CHAPTER XVIII

NOW THERE IS SOMETHING I WANT TO TALK ABOUT, AND YOU KNOW WHAT it is. About Anna," Stepan Arkadyevitch said, pausing for a brief space, and shaking off the unpleasant impression.

As soon as Oblonsky uttered Anna's name, the face of Alexey Alexandrovitch was completely transformed; all the life was gone out of it, and it looked weary and dead.

"What is it exactly that you want from me?" he said, moving in his chair and snapping his pince-nez.

"A definite settlement, Alexey Alexandrovitch, some settlement of the position. I'm appealing to you" ("not as an injured husband," Stepan Arkadyevitch was going to say, but afraid of wrecking his negotiation by this, he changed the words) "not as a statesman" (which did not sound *à propos*), "but simply as a man, and a good-hearted man and a Christian. You must have pity on her," he said.

"That is, in what way precisely?" Karenin said softly.

"Yes, pity on her. If you had seen her as I have!—I have been spending all the winter with her—you would have pity on her. Her position is awful, simply awful!"

"I had imagined," answered Alexey Alexandrovitch in a higher, almost shrill voice, "that Anna Arkadyevna had everything she had desired for herself."

"Oh, Alexey Alexandrovitch, for heaven's sake, don't let us indulge in recriminations! What is past is past, and you know what she wants and is waiting for—divorce."

"But I believe Anna Arkadyevna refuses a divorce, if I make it a condition to leave me my son. I replied in that sense, and supposed that the matter was ended. I consider it at an end," shrieked Alexey Alexandrovitch.

"But, for heaven's sake, don't get hot!" said Stepan Arkadyevitch, touching his brother-in-law's knee. "The matter is not ended. If you will allow me to recapitulate, it was like this: when you parted, you were as magnanimous as could possibly be; you were ready to give her everything—freedom, divorce even. She appreciated that. No, don't think that. She did appreciate it—to such a degree that at the first moment, feeling how she had wronged you, she did not consider and could not consider everything. She gave up everything. But experience, time, have shown that her position is unbearable, impossible."

it were possible to arrange the divorce so as to let her have her son.... Stepan Arkadyevitch saw now that it was no good to dream of that, but still he was glad to see his nephew.

Alexey Alexandrovitch reminded his brother-in-law that they never spoke to the boy of his mother, and he begged him not to mention a single word about her.

"He was very ill after that interview with his mother, which we had not foreseen," said Alexey Alexandrovitch. "Indeed, we feared for his life. But with rational treatment, and sea-bathing in the summer, he regained his strength, and now, by the doctor's advice, I have let him go to school. And certainly the companionship of school has had a good effect on him, and he is perfectly well, and making good progress."

"What a fine fellow he's grown! He's not Seryozha now, but quite full-fledged Sergey Alexyevitch!" said Stepan Arkadyevitch, smiling, as he looked at the handsome, broad-shouldered lad in blue coat and long trousers, who walked in alertly and confidently. The boy looked healthy and good-humored. He bowed to his uncle as to a stranger, but recognizing him, he blushed and turned hurriedly away from him, as though offended and irritated at something. The boy went up to his father and handed him a note of the marks he had gained in school.

"Well, that's very fair," said his father, "you can go."

"He's thinner and taller, and has grown out of being a child into a boy; I like that," said Stepan Arkadyevitch. "Do you remember me?"

The boy looked back quickly at his uncle.

"Yes, *mon oncle*," he answered, glancing at his father, and again he looked downcast.

His uncle called him to him, and took his hand.

"Well, and how are you getting on?" he said, wanting to talk to him, and not knowing what to say.

The boy, blushing and making no answer, cautiously drew his hand away. As soon as Stepan Arkadyevitch let go his hand, he glanced doubtfully at his father, and like a bird set free, he darted out of the room.

A year had passed since the last time Seryozha had seen his mother. Since then he had heard nothing more of her. And in the course of that year he had gone to school, and made friends among his schoolfellows. The dreams and memories of his mother, which had made him ill after seeing her, did not occupy his thoughts now. When they came back to him, he studiously drove them away, regarding them as shameful and girlish, below the dignity of a boy and a schoolboy. He knew that his father and mother were separated by some quarrel, he knew that he had to remain with his father, and he tried to get used to that idea.

He disliked seeing his uncle, so like his mother, for it called up those memories of which he was ashamed. He disliked it all the more as from some words he had caught as he waited at the study door, and still more from the faces of his father and uncle, he guessed that they must have been talking of his mother. And to avoid condemning the father with whom he lived and on whom he was dependent, and, above all, to avoid giving way to sentimentality, which he considered so degrading, Seryozha tried not to look at his uncle who had come to disturb his peace of mind, and not to think of what he recalled to him.

But when Stepan Arkadyevitch, going out after him, saw him on the stairs, and calling to him, asked him how he spent his playtime at school, Seryozha talked more freely to him away from his father's presence.

"We have a railway now," he said in answer to his uncle's question. "It's like this, do you see: two sit on a bench—they're the passengers; and one stands up straight on the bench. And all are harnessed to it by their arms or by their belts, and they run through all the rooms—the doors are left open beforehand. Well, and it's pretty hard work being the conductor!"

"That's the one that stands?" Stepan Arkadyevitch inquired, smiling.

"Yes, you want pluck for it, and cleverness too, especially when they stop all of a sudden, or some one falls down."

"Yes, that must be a serious matter," said Stepan Arkadyevitch, watching with mournful interest the eager eyes, like his mother's; not childish now—no longer fully innocent. And though he had promised Alexey Alexandrovitch not to speak of Anna, he could not restrain himself.

"Do you remember your mother?" he asked suddenly.

"No, I don't," Seryozha said quickly. He blushed crimson, and his face clouded over. And his uncle could get nothing more out of him. His tutor found his pupil on the staircase half an hour later, and for a long while he could not make out whether he was ill-tempered or crying.

"What is it? I expect you hurt yourself when you fell down?" said the tutor. "I told you it was a dangerous game. And we shall have to speak to the director."

"If I had hurt myself, nobody should have found it out, that's certain."

"Well, what is it, then?"

"Leave me alone! If I remember, or if I don't remember? … what business is it of his? Why should I remember? Leave me in peace!" he said, addressing not his tutor, but the whole world.

believe it, in a fortnight I'd got into a dressing-gown and given up dressing for dinner. Needn't say I had no thoughts left for pretty women. I became quite an old gentleman. There was nothing left for me but to think of my eternal salvation. I went off to Paris—I was as right as could be at once."

Stepan Arkadyevitch felt exactly the difference that Pyotr Oblonsky described. In Moscow he degenerated so much that if he had had to be there for long together, he might in good earnest have come to considering his salvation; in Petersburg he felt himself a man of the world again.

Between Princess Betsy Tverskaya and Stepan Arkadyevitch there had long existed rather curious relations. Stepan Arkadyevitch always flirted with her in jest, and used to say to her, also in jest, the most unseemly things, knowing that nothing delighted her so much. The day after his conversation with Karenin, Stepan Arkadyevitch went to see her, and felt so youthful that in this jesting flirtation and nonsense he recklessly went so far that he did not know how to extricate himself, as unluckily he was so far from being attracted by her that he thought her positively disagreeable. What made it hard to change the conversation was the fact that he was very attractive to her. So that he was considerably relieved at the arrival of Princess Myakaya, which cut short their tête-à-tête.

"Ah, so you're here!" said she when she saw him. "Well, and what news of your poor sister? You needn't look at me like that," she added. "Ever since they've all turned against her, all those who're a thousand times worse than she, I've thought she did a very fine thing. I can't forgive Vronsky for not letting me know when she was in Petersburg. I'd have gone to see her and gone about with her everywhere. Please give her my love. Come, tell me about her."

"Yes, her position is very difficult; she ..." began Stepan Arkadyevitch, in the simplicity of his heart accepting as sterling coin Princess Myakaya's words "tell me about her." Princess Myakaya interrupted him immediately, as she always did, and began talking herself.

"She's done what they all do, except me—only they hide it. But she wouldn't be deceitful, and she did a fine thing. And she did better still in throwing up that crazy brother-in-law of yours. You must excuse me. Everybody used to say he was so clever, so very clever; I was the only one that said he was a fool. Now that he's so thick with Lidia Ivanovna and Landau, they all say he's crazy, and I should prefer not to agree with everybody, but this time I can't help it."

"Oh, do please explain," said Stepan Arkadyevitch; "what does it mean? Yesterday I was seeing him on my sister's behalf, and I asked him to give me a final answer. He gave me no answer, and said he would think it over. But this morning, instead of an answer, I received an invitation from Countess Lidia Ivanovna for this evening."

"Ah, so that's it, that's it!" said Princess Myakaya gleefully, "they're going to ask Landau what he's to say."

"Ask Landau? What for? Who or what's Landau?"

"What! you don't know Jules Landau, *le fameux Jules Landau*, *le clairvoyant*? He's crazy too, but on him your sister's fate depends. See what comes of living in the provinces—you know nothing about anything. Landau, do you see, was a *commis* in a shop in Paris, and he went to a doctor's; and in the doctor's waiting-room he fell asleep, and in his sleep he began giving advice to all the patients. And wonderful advice it was! Then the wife of Yury Meledinsky—you know, the invalid?—heard of this Landau, and had him to see her husband. And he cured her husband, though I can't say that I see he did him much good, for he's just as feeble a creature as ever he was, but they believed in him, and took him along with them and brought him to Russia. Here there's been a general rush to him, and he's begun doctoring every one. He cured Countess Bezzubova, and she took such a fancy to him that she adopted him."

"Adopted him?"

"Yes, as her son. He's not Landau any more now, but Count Bezzubov. That's neither here nor there, though; but Lidia—I'm very fond of her, but she has a screw loose somewhere—has lost her heart to this Landau now, and nothing is settled now in her house or Alexey Alexandrovitch's without him, and so your sister's fate is now in the hands of Landau, *alias* Count Bezzubov."

CHAPTER XXI

AFTER A CAPITAL DINNER AND A GREAT DEAL OF COGNAC DRUNK AT Bartnyansky's, Stepan Arkadyevitch, only a little later than the appointed time, went in to Countess Lidia Ivanovna's.

"Who else is with the countess?—a Frenchman?" Stepan Arkadyevitch asked the hall-porter, as he glanced at the familiar overcoat of Alexey Alexandrovitch and a queer, rather artless-looking overcoat with clasps.

"Alexey Alexandrovitch Karenin and Count Bezzubov," the porter answered severely.

all eyes were turned on him he raised his head and smiled a smile of childlike artlessness.

"Don't take any notice," said Lidia Ivanovna, and she lightly moved a chair up for Alexey Alexandrovitch. "I have observed ..." she was beginning, when a footman came into the room with a letter. Lidia Ivanovna rapidly ran her eyes over the note, and excusing herself, wrote an answer with extraordinary rapidity, handed it to the man, and came back to the table. "I have observed," she went on, "that Moscow people, especially the men, are more indifferent to religion than any one."

"Oh, no, countess, I thought Moscow people had the reputation of being the firmest in the faith," answered Stepan Arkadyevitch.

"But as far as I can make out, you are unfortunately one of the indifferent ones," said Alexey Alexandrovitch, turning to him with a weary smile.

"How anyone can be indifferent!" said Lidia Ivanovna.

"I am not so much indifferent on that subject as I am waiting in suspense," said Stepan Arkadyevitch, with his most deprecating smile. "I hardly think that the time for such questions has come yet for me."

Alexey Alexandrovitch and Lidia Ivanovna looked at each other.

"We can never tell whether the time has come for us or not," said Alexey Alexandrovitch severely. "We ought not to think whether we are ready or not ready. God's grace is not guided by human considerations: sometimes it comes not to those that strive for it, and comes to those that are unprepared, like Saul."

"No, I believe it won't be just yet," said Lidia Ivanovna, who had been meanwhile watching the movements of the Frenchman. Landau got up and came to them.

"Do you allow me to listen?" he asked.

"Oh, yes; I did not want to disturb you," said Lidia Ivanovna, gazing tenderly at him; "sit here with us."

"One has only not to close one's eyes to shut out the light," Alexey Alexandrovitch went on.

"Ah, if you knew the happiness we know, feeling His presence ever in our hearts!" said Countess Lidia Ivanovna with a rapturous smile.

"But a man may feel himself unworthy sometimes to rise to that height," said Stepan Arkadyevitch, conscious of hypocrisy in admitting this religious height, but at the same time unable to bring himself to acknowledge his free-thinking views before a person who, by a single word to Pomorsky, might procure him the coveted appointment.

"That is, you mean that sin keeps him back?" said Lidia Ivanovna. "But that is a false idea. There is no sin for believers, their sin has been atoned for. *Pardon*," she added, looking at the footman, who came in again with another letter. She read it and gave a verbal answer: "To-morrow at the Grand Duchess's, say." "For the believer sin is not," she went on.

"Yes, but faith without works is dead," said Stepan Arkadyevitch, recalling the phrase from the catechism, and only by his smile clinging to his independence.

"There you have it—from the epistle of St. James," said Alexey Alexandrovitch, addressing Lidia Ivanovna, with a certain reproachfulness in his tone. It was unmistakably a subject they had discussed more than once before. "What harm has been done by the false interpretation of that passage! Nothing holds men back from belief like that misinterpretation. 'I have not works, so I cannot believe,' though all the while that is not said. But the very opposite is said."

"Striving for God, saving the soul by fasting," said Countess Lidia Ivanovna, with disgusted contempt, "those are the crude ideas of our monks.... Yet that is nowhere said. It is far simpler and easier," she added, looking at Oblonsky with the same encouraging smile with which at court she encouraged youthful maids of honor, disconcerted by the new surroundings of the court.

"We are saved by Christ who suffered for us. We are saved by faith," Alexey Alexandrovitch chimed in, with a glance of approval at her words.

"*Vous comprenez l'anglais?*" asked Lidia Ivanovna, and receiving a reply in the affirmative, she got up and began looking through a shelf of books.

"I want to read him 'Safe and Happy,' or 'Under the Wing,'" she said, looking inquiringly at Karenin. And finding the book, and sitting down again in her place, she opened it. "It's very short. In it is described the way by which faith can be reached, and the happiness, above all earthly bliss, with which it fills the soul. The believer cannot be unhappy because he is not alone. But you will see." She was just settling herself to read when the footman came in again. "Madame Borozdina? Tell her, to-morrow at two o'clock. Yes," she said, putting her finger in the place in the book, and gazing before her with her fine pensive eyes, "that is how true faith acts. You know Marie Sanina? You know about her trouble? She lost her only child. She was in despair. And what happened? She found this comforter, and she thanks God now for the death of her child. Such is the happiness faith brings!"

"Oh, yes, that is most ..." said Stepan Arkadyevitch, glad they were going to read, and let him have a chance to collect his faculties. "No, I see I'd better not ask her about anything to-day," he thought. "If only I can get out of this without putting my foot in it!"

"It will be dull for you," said Countess Lidia Ivanovna, addressing Landau; "you don't know English, but it's short."

"Oh, I shall understand," said Landau, with the same smile, and he closed his eyes. Alexey Alexandrovitch and Lidia Ivanovna exchanged meaningful glances, and the reading began.

CHAPTER XXII

STEPAN ARKADYEVITCH FELT COMPLETELY NONPLUSSED BY THE STRANGE TALK which he was hearing for the first time. The complexity of Petersburg, as a rule, had a stimulating effect on him, rousing him out of his Moscow stagnation. But he liked these complications, and understood them only in the circles he knew and was at home in. In these unfamiliar surroundings he was puzzled and disconcerted, and could not get his bearings. As he listened to Countess Lidia Ivanovna, aware of the beautiful, artless—or perhaps artful, he could not decide which—eyes of Landau fixed upon him, Stepan Arkadyevitch began to be conscious of a peculiar heaviness in his head.

The most incongruous ideas were in confusion in his head. "Marie Sanina is glad her child's dead ... How good a smoke would be now! ... To be saved, one need only believe, and the monks don't know how the thing's to be done, but Countess Lidia Ivanovna does know ... And why is my head so heavy? Is it the cognac, or all this being so queer? Anyway, I fancy I've done nothing unsuitable so far. But anyway, it won't do to ask her now. They say they make one say one's prayers. I only hope they won't make me! That'll be too imbecile. And what stuff it is she's reading! but she has a good accent. Landau—Bezzubov—what's he Bezzubov for?" All at once Stepan Arkadyevitch became aware that his lower jaw was uncontrollably forming a yawn. He pulled his whiskers to cover the yawn, and shook himself together. But soon after he became aware that he was dropping asleep and on the very point of snoring. He recovered himself at the very moment when the voice of Countess Lidia Ivanovna was saying "he's asleep." Stepan Arkadyevitch started with dismay, feeling guilty and caught. But he was reassured at once by seeing that the words "he's asleep" referred not to him, but to Landau. The Frenchman was asleep as well as Stepan Arkadyevitch. But Stepan Arkadyevitch's being asleep would have offended them, as he thought (though even this, he thought, might not be so, as everything seemed so queer), while Landau's being asleep delighted them extremely, especially Countess Lidia Ivanovna.

"*Mon ami,*" said Lidia Ivanovna, carefully holding the folds of her silk gown so as not to rustle, and in her excitement calling Karenin not Alexey Alexandrovitch, but "*mon ami,*" "*donnez-lui la main. Vous voyez?* Sh!" she hissed at the footman as he came in again. "Not at home."

The Frenchman was asleep, or pretending to be asleep, with his head on the back of his chair, and his moist hand, as it lay on his knee, made faint movements, as though trying to catch something. Alexey Alexandrovitch got up, tried to move carefully, but stumbled against the table, went up and laid his hand in the Frenchman's hand. Stepan Arkadyevitch got up too, and opening his eyes wide, trying to wake himself up if he was asleep, he looked first at one and then at the other. It was all real. Stepan Arkadyevitch felt that his head was getting worse and worse.

"*Que la personne qui est arrivée la dernière, celle qui demande, qu'elle sorte! Qu'elle sorte!*" articulated the Frenchman, without opening his eyes.

"*Vous m'excuserez, mais vous voyez ... Revenez vers dix heures, encore mieux demain.*"

"*Qu'elle sorte!*" repeated the Frenchman impatiently.

"*C'est moi, n'est-ce pas?*" And receiving an answer in the affirmative, Stepan Arkadyevitch, forgetting the favor he had meant to ask of Lidia Ivanovna, and forgetting his sister's affairs, caring for nothing, but filled with the sole desire to get away as soon as possible, went out on tiptoe and ran out into the street as though from a plague-stricken house. For a long while he chatted and joked with his cab-driver, trying to recover his spirits.

At the French theater where he arrived for the last act, and afterwards at the Tatar restaurant after his champagne, Stepan Arkadyevitch felt a little refreshed in the atmosphere he was used to. But still he felt quite unlike himself all that evening.

On getting home to Pyotr Oblonsky's, where he was staying, Stepan Arkadyevitch found a note from Betsy. She wrote to him that she was very anxious to finish their interrupted conversation, and begged him to come next day. He had scarcely read this note, and frowned at its contents, when he heard below the ponderous tramp of the servants, carrying something heavy.

Stepan Arkadyevitch went out to look. It was the rejuvenated Pyotr Oblonsky. He was so drunk that he could not walk up-stairs; but he told them to set him on his legs when he saw Stepan Arkadyevitch, and clinging to him,

walked with him into his room and there began telling him how he had spent
the evening, and fell asleep doing so.

Stepan Arkadyevitch was in very low spirits, which happened rarely with
him, and for a long while he could not go to sleep. Everything he could recall
to his mind, everything was disgusting; but most disgusting of all, as if it were
something shameful, was the memory of the evening he had spent at Countess
Lidia Ivanovna's.

Next day he received from Alexey Alexandrovitch a final answer, refusing
to grant Anna's divorce, and he understood that this decision was based on
what the Frenchman had said in his real or pretended trance.

CHAPTER XXIII

I N ORDER TO CARRY THROUGH ANY UNDERTAKING IN FAMILY LIFE, THERE MUST
necessarily be either complete division between the husband and wife,
or loving agreement. When the relations of a couple are vacillating and
neither one thing nor the other, no sort of enterprise can be undertaken.

Many families remain for years in the same place, though both husband and
wife are sick of it, simply because there is neither complete division nor agreement between them.

Both Vronsky and Anna felt life in Moscow insupportable in the heat and
dust, when the spring sunshine was followed by the glare of summer, and all
the trees in the boulevards had long since been in full leaf, and the leaves were
covered with dust. But they did not go back to Vozdvizhenskoe, as they had
arranged to do long before; they went on staying in Moscow, though they both
loathed it, because of late there had been no agreement between them.

The irritability that kept them apart had no external cause, and all efforts to
come to an understanding intensified it, instead of removing it. It was an inner
irritation, grounded in her mind on the conviction that his love had grown less;
in his, on regret that he had put himself for her sake in a difficult position, which
she, instead of lightening, made still more difficult. Neither of them gave full
utterance to their sense of grievance, but they considered each other in the
wrong, and tried on every pretext to prove this to one another.

In her eyes the whole of him, with all his habits, ideas, desires, with all his spiritual and physical temperament, was one thing—love for women, and that love,

she felt, ought to be entirely concentrated on her alone. That love was less; consequently, as she reasoned, he must have transferred part of his love to other women or to another woman—and she was jealous. She was jealous not of any particular woman but of the decrease of his love. Not having got an object for her jealousy, she was on the lookout for it. At the slightest hint she transferred her jealousy from one object to another. At one time she was jealous of those low women with whom he might so easily renew his old bachelor ties; then she was jealous of the society women he might meet; then she was jealous of the imaginary girl whom he might want to marry, for whose sake he would break with her. And this last form of jealousy tortured her most of all, especially as he had unwarily told her, in a moment of frankness, that his mother knew him so little that she had had the audacity to try and persuade him to marry the young Princess Sorokina.

And being jealous of him, Anna was indignant against him and found grounds for indignation in everything. For everything that was difficult in her position she blamed him. The agonizing condition of suspense she had passed at Moscow, the tardiness and indecision of Alexey Alexandrovitch, her solitude—she put it all down to him. If he had loved her he would have seen all the bitterness of her position, and would have rescued her from it. For her being in Moscow and not in the country, he was to blame too. He could not live buried in the country as she would have liked to do. He must have society, and he had put her in this awful position, the bitterness of which he would not see. And again, it was his fault that she was forever separated from her son.

Even the rare moments of tenderness that came from time to time did not soothe her; in his tenderness now she saw a shade of complacency, of self-confidence, which had not been of old, and which exasperated her.

It was dusk. Anna was alone, and waiting for him to come back from a bachelor dinner. She walked up and down in his study (the room where the noise from the street was least heard), and thought over every detail of their yesterday's quarrel. Going back from the well-remembered, offensive words of the quarrel to what had been the ground of it, she arrived at last at its origin. For a long while she could hardly believe that their dissension had arisen from a conversation so inoffensive, of so little moment to either. But so it actually had been. It all arose from his laughing at the girls' high schools, declaring they were useless, while she defended them. He had spoken slightingly of women's education in general, and had said that Hannah, Anna's English protégée, had not the slightest need to know anything of physics.

This irritated Anna. She saw in this a contemptuous reference to her occupations. And she bethought her of a phrase to pay him back for the pain he had

"What an absurd fancy! Why, did she swim in some special way, then?" said Anna, not answering.

"There was absolutely nothing in it. That's just what I say, it was awfully stupid. Well, then, when do you think of going?"

Anna shook her head as though trying to drive away some unpleasant idea.

"When? Why, the sooner the better! By to-morrow we shan't be ready. The day after to-morrow."

"Yes ... oh, no, wait a minute! The day after to-morrow's Sunday, I have to be at maman's," said Vronsky, embarrassed, because as soon as he uttered his mother's name he was aware of her intent, suspicious eyes. His embarrassment confirmed her suspicion. She flushed hotly and drew away from him. It was now not the Queen of Sweden's swimming-mistress who filled Anna's imagination, but the young Princess Sorokina. She was staying in a village near Moscow with Countess Vronskaya.

"Can't you go to-morrow?" she said.

"Well, no! The deeds and the money for the business I'm going there for I can't get by to-morrow," he answered.

"If so, we won't go at all."

"But why so?"

"I shall not go later. Monday or never!"

"What for?" said Vronsky, as though in amazement. "Why, there's no meaning in it!"

"There's no meaning in it to you, because you care nothing for me. You don't care to understand my life. The one thing that I cared for here was Hannah. You say it's affectation. Why, you said yesterday that I don't love my daughter, that I love this English girl, that it's unnatural. I should like to know what life there is for me that could be natural!"

For an instant she had a clear vision of what she was doing, and was horrified at how she had fallen away from her resolution. But even though she knew it was her own ruin, she could not restrain herself, could not keep herself from proving to him that he was wrong, could not give way to him.

"I never said that; I said I did not sympathize with this sudden passion."

"How is it, though you boast of your straightforwardness, you don't tell the truth?"

"I never boast, and I never tell lies," he said slowly, restraining his rising anger. "It's a great pity if you can't respect ..."

"Respect was invented to cover the empty place where love should be. And if you don't love me any more, it would be better and more honest to say so."

"No, this is becoming unbearable!" cried Vronsky, getting up from his chair; and stopping short, facing her, he said, speaking deliberately: "What do you try my patience for?" looking as though he might have said much more, but was restraining himself. "It has limits."

"What do you mean by that?" she cried, looking with terror at the undisguised hatred in his whole face, and especially in his cruel, menacing eyes.

"I mean to say ..." he was beginning, but he checked himself. "I must ask what it is you want of me?"

"What can I want? All I can want is that you should not desert me, as you think of doing," she said, understanding all he had not uttered. "But that I don't want; that's secondary. I want love, and there is none. So then all is over."

She turned towards the door.

"Stop! sto—op!" said Vronsky, with no change in the gloomy lines of his brows, though he held her by the hand. "What is it all about? I said that we must put off going for three days, and on that you told me I was lying, that I was not an honorable man."

"Yes, and I repeat that the man who reproaches me with having sacrificed everything for me," she said, recalling the words of a still earlier quarrel, "that he's worse than a dishonorable man—he's a heartless man."

"Oh, there are limits to endurance!" he cried, and hastily let go her hand.

"He hates me, that's clear," she thought, and in silence, without looking round, she walked with faltering steps out of the room. "He loves another woman, that's even clearer," she said to herself as she went into her own room. "I want love, and there is none. So, then, all is over." She repeated the words she had said, "and it must be ended."

"But how?" she asked herself, and she sat down in a low chair before the looking-glass.

Thoughts of where she would go now, whether to the aunt who had brought her up, to Dolly, or simply alone abroad, and of what *he* was doing now alone in his study; whether this was the final quarrel, or whether reconciliation were still possible; and of what all her old friends at Petersburg would say of her now; and of how Alexey Alexandrovitch would look at it, and many other ideas of what would happen now after this rupture, came into her head; but she did not give herself up to them with all her heart. At the bottom of her heart was some obscure idea that alone interested her, but she could not get clear sight of it. Thinking once more of Alexey Alexandrovitch, she recalled the time of her illness after her confinement, and the feeling which never left her at that time. "Why didn't I die?" and the words and the feeling of that time came back to her. And all at once she knew what was in her soul. Yes, it was that idea which alone solved all. "Yes, to die! ... And the shame and disgrace of Alexey Alexandrovitch and of Seryozha, and my awful shame, it will all be saved by death. To die! and he will feel remorse; will be sorry; will love me; he will suffer on my account." With the trace of a smile of commiseration for herself she sat down in the armchair, taking off and putting on the rings on her left hand, vividly picturing from different sides his feelings after her death.

Approaching footsteps—his steps—distracted her attention. As though absorbed in the arrangement of her rings, she did not even turn to him.

He went up to her, and taking her by the hand, said softly:

"Anna, we'll go the day after to-morrow, if you like. I agree to everything." She did not speak.

"What is it?" he urged.

"You know," she said, and at the same instant, unable to restrain herself any longer, she burst into sobs.

"Cast me off!" she articulated between her sobs. "I'll go away to-morrow ... I'll do more. What am I? An immoral woman! A stone round your neck. I don't want to make you wretched, I don't want to! I'll set you free. You don't love me; you love some one else!"

Vronsky besought her to be calm, and declared that there was no trace of foundation for her jealousy; that he had never ceased, and never would cease, to love her; that he loved her more than ever.

"Anna, why distress yourself and me so?" he said to her, kissing her hands. There was tenderness now in his face, and she fancied she caught the sound of tears in his voice, and she felt them wet on her hand. And instantly Anna's despairing jealousy changed to a despairing passion of tenderness. She put her arms round him, and covered with kisses his head, his neck, his hands.

CHAPTER XXV

FEELING THAT THE RECONCILIATION WAS COMPLETE, ANNA SET EAGERLY TO work in the morning preparing for their departure. Though it was not settled whether they should go on Monday or Tuesday, as they had each given way to the other, Anna packed busily, feeling absolutely indifferent whether they went a day earlier or later. She was standing in her room over an open box, taking things out of it, when he came in to see her earlier than usual, dressed to go out.

"I'm going off at once to see maman; she can send me the money by Yegorov. And I shall be ready to go to-morrow," he said.

Though she was in such a good mood, the thought of his visit to his mother's gave her a pang.

"No, I shan't be ready by then myself," she said; and at once reflected, "so then it was possible to arrange to do as I wished." "No, do as you meant to do. Go into the dining-room, I'm coming directly. It's only to turn out those things that aren't wanted," she said, putting something more on the heap of frippery that lay in Annushka's arms.

Vronsky was eating his beefsteak when she came into the dining-room.

"You wouldn't believe how distasteful these rooms have become to me," she said, sitting down beside him to her coffee. "There's nothing more awful than these *chambres garnies*. There's no individuality in them, no soul. These clocks, and curtains, and, worst of all, the wall-papers—they're a nightmare. I think of Vozdvizhenskoe as the promised land. You're not sending the horses off yet?"

"No, they will come after us. Where are you going to?"

"I wanted to go to Wilson's to take some dresses to her. So it's really to be to-morrow?" she said in a cheerful voice; but suddenly her face changed.

Vronsky's valet came in to ask him to sign a receipt for a telegram from Petersburg. There was nothing out of the way in Vronsky's getting a telegram, but he said, as though anxious to conceal something from her, that the receipt was in his study, and he turned hurriedly to her.

"By to-morrow, without fail, I will finish it all."

"From whom is the telegram?" she asked, not hearing him.

"From Stiva," he answered reluctantly.

"Why didn't you show it to me? What secret can there be between Stiva and me?"

Vronsky called the valet back, and told him to bring the telegram.

"I didn't want to show it to you, because Stiva has such a passion for telegraphing: why telegraph when nothing is settled?"

"About the divorce?"

"Yes; but he says he has not been able to come at anything yet. He has promised a decisive answer in a day or two. But here it is; read it."

With trembling hands Anna took the telegram, and read what Vronsky had told her. At the end was added: "Little hope; but I will do everything possible and impossible."

"Don't you feel sorry for that unlucky Pyevtsov?" she went on, talking to Yashvin.

"I've never asked myself the question, Anna Arkadyevna, whether I'm sorry for him or not. You see, all my fortune's here"—he touched his breast-pocket—"and just now I'm a wealthy man. But to-day I'm going to the club, and I may come out a beggar. You see, whoever sits down to play with me—he wants to leave me without a shirt to my back, and so do I him. And so we fight it out, and that's the pleasure of it."

"Well, but suppose you were married," said Anna, "how would it be for your wife?"

Yashvin laughed.

"That's why I'm not married, and never mean to be."

"And Helsingfors?" said Vronsky, entering into the conversation and glancing at Anna's smiling face. Meeting his eyes, Anna's face instantly took a coldly severe expression as though she were saying to him: "It's not forgotten. It's all the same."

"Were you really in love?" she said to Yashvin.

"Oh heavens! ever so many times! But you see, some men can play but only so that they can always lay down their cards when the hour comes of a *rendez-vous*, while I can take up love, but only so as not to be late for my cards in the evening. That's how I manage things."

"No, I didn't mean that, but the real thing." She would have said *Helsingfors*, but would not repeat the word used by Vronsky.

Voytov, who was buying the horse, came in. Anna got up and went out of the room.

Before leaving the house, Vronsky went into her room. She would have pretended to be looking for something on the table, but ashamed of making a pretense, she looked straight in his face with cold eyes.

"What do you want?" she asked in French.

"To get the guarantee for Gambetta, I've sold him," he said, in a tone which said more clearly than words, "I've no time for discussing things, and it would lead to nothing."

"I'm not to blame in any way," he thought. "If she will punish herself, *tant pis pour elle*." But as he was going he fancied that she said something, and his heart suddenly ached with pity for her.

"Eh, Anna?" he queried.

"I said nothing," she answered just as coldly and calmly.

"Oh, nothing, *tant pis* then," he thought, feeling cold again, and he turned and went out. As he was going out he caught a glimpse in the looking-glass of her face, white, with quivering lips. He even wanted to stop and to say some comforting word to her, but his legs carried him out of the room before he could think what to say. The whole of that day he spent away from home, and when he came in late in the evening the maid told him that Anna Arkadyevna had a headache and begged him not to go in to her.

CHAPTER XXVI

NEVER BEFORE HAD A DAY BEEN PASSED IN QUARREL. TO-DAY WAS THE FIRST time. And this was not a quarrel. It was the open acknowledgment of complete coldness. Was it possible to glance at her as he had glanced when he came into the room for the guarantee?—to look at her, see her heart was breaking with despair, and go out without a word with that face of callous composure? He was not merely cold to her, he hated her because he loved another woman—that was clear.

And remembering all the cruel words he had said, Anna supplied, too, the words that he had unmistakably wished to say and could have said to her, and she grew more and more exasperated.

"I won't prevent you," he might say. "You can go where you like. You were unwilling to be divorced from your husband, no doubt so that you might go back to him. Go back to him. If you want money, I'll give it to you. How many roubles do you want?"

All the most cruel words that a brutal man could say, he said to her in her imagination, and she could not forgive him for them, as though he had actually said them.

"But didn't he only yesterday swear he loved me, he, a truthful and sincere man? Haven't I despaired for nothing many times already?" she said to herself afterwards.

All that day, except for the visit to Wilson's, which occupied two hours, Anna spent in doubts whether everything were over or whether there were still hope of reconciliation, whether she should go away at once or see him once more. She was expecting him the whole day, and in the evening, as she went to her own room, leaving a message for him that her head ached, she said to herself, "If he comes in spite of what the maid says, it means that

"Oh, by the way," he said at the very moment she was in the doorway, "we're going to-morrow for certain, aren't we?"

"You, but not I," she said, turning round to him.

"Anna, we can't go on like this ..."

"You, but not I," she repeated.

"This is getting unbearable!"

"You ... you will be sorry for this," she said, and went out.

Frightened by the desperate expression with which these words were uttered, he jumped up and would have run after her, but on second thoughts he sat down and scowled, setting his teeth. This vulgar—as he thought it—threat of something vague exasperated him. "I've tried everything," he thought; "the only thing left is not to pay attention," and he began to get ready to drive into town, and again to his mother's to get her signature to the deeds.

She heard the sound of his steps about the study and the dining-room. At the drawing-room he stood still. But he did not turn in to see her, he merely gave an order that the horse should be given to Voytov if he came while he was away. Then she heard the carriage brought round, the door opened, and he came out again. But he went back into the porch again, and some one was running up-stairs. It was the valet running up for his gloves that had been forgotten. She went to the window and saw him take the gloves without looking, and touching the coachman on the back he said something to him. Then without looking up at the window he settled himself in his usual attitude in the carriage, with his legs crossed, and drawing on his gloves he vanished round the corner.

CHAPTER XXVII

H E HAS GONE! IT IS OVER!" ANNA SAID TO HERSELF, STANDING AT THE WINdow; and in answer to this statement the impression of the darkness when the candle had flickered out, and of her fearful dream mingling into one, filled her heart with cold terror.

"No, that cannot be!" she cried, and crossing the room she rang the bell. She was so afraid now of being alone, that without waiting for the servant to come in, she went out to meet him.

"Inquire where the count has gone," she said. The servant answered that the count had gone to the stable.

"His honor left word that if you cared to drive out, the carriage would be back immediately."

"Very good. Wait a minute. I'll write a note at once. Send Mihail with the note to the stables. Make haste."

She sat down and wrote:

"I was wrong. Come back home; I must explain. For God's sake come! I'm afraid."

She sealed it up and gave it to the servant.

She was afraid of being left alone now; she followed the servant out of the room, and went to the nursery.

"Why, this isn't it, this isn't he! Where are his blue eyes, his sweet, shy smile?" was her first thought when she saw her chubby, rosy little girl with her black, curly hair instead of Seryozha, whom in the tangle of her ideas she had expected to see in the nursery. The little girl sitting at the table was obstinately and violently battering on it with a cork, and staring aimlessly at her mother with her pitch-black eyes. Answering the English nurse that she was quite well, and that she was going to the country to-morrow, Anna sat down by the little girl and began spinning the cork to show her. But the child's loud, ringing laugh, and the motion of her eyebrows, recalled Vronsky so vividly that she got up hurriedly, restraining her sobs, and went away. "Can it be all over? No, it cannot be!" she thought. "He will come back. But how can he explain that smile, that excitement after he had been talking to her? But even if he doesn't explain, I will believe. If I don't believe, there's only one thing left for me, and I can't."

She looked at her watch. Twenty minutes had passed. "By now he has received the note and is coming back. Not long, ten minutes more.... But what if he doesn't come? No, that cannot be. He mustn't see me with tear-stained eyes. I'll go and wash. Yes, yes; did I do my hair or not?" she asked herself. And she could not remember. She felt her head with her hand. "Yes, my hair has been done, but when I did it I can't in the least remember." She could not believe the evidence of her hand, and went up to the pier-glass to see whether she really had done her hair. She certainly had, but she could not think when she had done it. "Who's that?" she thought, looking in the looking-glass at the swollen face with strangely glittering eyes, that looked in a scared way at her. "Why, it's I!" she suddenly understood, and looking round, she seemed all at once to feel his kisses on her, and twitched her shoulders, shuddering. Then she lifted her hand to her lips and kissed it.

building? *Modes et robes,*" she read. A man bowed to her. It was Annushka's husband. "Our parasites"; she remembered how Vronsky had said that. "Our? Why our? What's so awful is that one can't tear up the past by its roots. One can't tear it out, but one can hide one's memory of it. And I'll hide it." And then she thought of her past with Alexey Alexandrovitch, of how she had blotted the memory of it out of her life. "Dolly will think I'm leaving my second husband, and so I certainly must be in the wrong. As if I cared to be right! I can't help it!" she said, and she wanted to cry. But at once she fell to wondering what those two girls could be smiling about. "Love, most likely. They don't know how dreary it is, how low … The boulevard and the children. Three boys running, playing at horses. Seryozha! And I'm losing everything and not getting him back. Yes, I'm losing everything, if he doesn't return. Perhaps he was late for the train and has come back by now. Longing for humiliation again!" she said to herself. "No, I'll go to Dolly, and say straight out to her, I'm unhappy, I deserve this, I'm to blame, but still I'm unhappy, help me. These horses, this carriage—how loathsome I am to myself in this carriage— all his; but I won't see them again."

Thinking over the words in which she would tell Dolly, and mentally working her heart up to great bitterness, Anna went up-stairs.

"Is there anyone with her?" she asked in the hall.

"Katerina Alexandrovna Levin," answered the footman.

"Kitty! Kitty, whom Vronsky was in love with!" thought Anna, "the girl he thinks of with love. He's sorry he didn't marry her. But me he thinks of with hatred, and is sorry he had anything to do with me."

The sisters were having a consultation about nursing when Anna called. Dolly went down alone to see the visitor who had interrupted their conversation.

"Well, so you've not gone away yet? I meant to have come to you," she said; "I had a letter from Stiva to-day."

"We had a telegram too," answered Anna, looking round for Kitty.

"He writes that he can't make out quite what Alexey Alexandrovitch wants, but he won't go away without a decisive answer."

"I thought you had some one with you. Can I see the letter?"

"Yes; Kitty," said Dolly, embarrassed. "She stayed in the nursery. She has been very ill."

"So I heard. May I see the letter?"

"I'll get it directly. But he doesn't refuse; on the contrary, Stiva has hopes," said Dolly, stopping in the doorway.

"I haven't, and indeed I don't wish it," said Anna.

"What's this? Does Kitty consider it degrading to meet me?" thought Anna when she was alone. "Perhaps she's right, too. But it's not for her, the girl who was in love with Vronsky, it's not for her to show me that, even if it is true. I know that in my position I can't be received by any decent woman. I knew that from the first moment I sacrificed everything to him. And this is my reward! Oh, how I hate him! And what did I come here for? I'm worse here, more miserable." She heard from the next room the sisters' voices in consultation. "And what am I going to say to Dolly now? Amuse Kitty by the sight of my wretchedness, submit to her patronizing? No; and besides, Dolly wouldn't understand. And it would be no good my telling her. It would only be interesting to see Kitty, to show her how I despise every one and everything, how nothing matters to me now."

Dolly came in with the letter. Anna read it and handed it back in silence.

"I knew all that," she said, "and it doesn't interest me in the least."

"Oh, why so? On the contrary, I have hopes," said Dolly, looking inquisitively at Anna. She had never seen her in such a strangely irritable condition. "When are you going away?" she asked.

Anna, half-closing her eyes, looked straight before her and did not answer.

"Why does Kitty shrink from me?" she said, looking at the door and flushing red.

"Oh, what nonsense! She's nursing, and things aren't going right with her, and I've been advising her…. She's delighted. She'll be here in a minute," said Dolly awkwardly, not clever at lying. "Yes, here she is."

Hearing that Anna had called, Kitty had wanted not to appear, but Dolly persuaded her. Rallying her forces, Kitty went in, walked up to her, blushing, and shook hands.

"I am so glad to see you," she said with a trembling voice.

Kitty had been thrown into confusion by the inward conflict between her antagonism to this bad woman and her desire to be nice to her. But as soon as she saw Anna's lovely and attractive face, all feeling of antagonism disappeared.

"I should not have been surprised if you had not cared to meet me. I'm used to everything. You have been ill? Yes, you are changed," said Anna.

Kitty felt that Anna was looking at her with hostile eyes. She ascribed this hostility to the awkward position in which Anna, who had once patronized her, must feel with her now, and she felt sorry for her.

They talked of Kitty's illness, of the baby, of Stiva, but it was obvious that nothing interested Anna.

"I came to say good-bye to you," she said, getting up.

was going. She longed to get away as quickly as possible from the feelings she had gone through in that awful house. The servants, the walls, the things in that house—all aroused repulsion and hatred in her and lay like a weight upon her.

"Yes, I must go to the railway station, and if he's not there, then go there and catch him." Anna looked at the railway timetable in the newspapers. An evening train went at two minutes past eight. "Yes, I shall be in time." She gave orders for the other horses to be put in the carriage, and packed in a traveling-bag the things needed for a few days. She knew she would never come back here again.

Among the plans that came into her head she vaguely determined that after what would happen at the station or at the countess's house, she would go as far as the first town on the Nizhni road and stop there.

Dinner was on the table; she went up, but the smell of the bread and cheese was enough to make her feel that all food was disgusting. She ordered the carriage and went out. The house threw a shadow now right across the street, but it was a bright evening and still warm in the sunshine. Annushka, who came down with her things, and Pyotr, who put the things in the carriage, and the coachman, evidently out of humor, were all hateful to her, and irritated her by their words and actions.

"I don't want you, Pyotr."

"But how about the ticket?"

"Well, as you like, it doesn't matter," she said crossly.

Pyotr jumped on the box, and putting his arms akimbo, told the coachman to drive to the booking-office.

CHAPTER XXX

HERE IT IS AGAIN! AGAIN I UNDERSTAND IT ALL!" ANNA SAID TO HERSELF, as soon as the carriage had started and swaying lightly, rumbled over the tiny cobbles of the paved road, and again one impression followed rapidly upon another.

"Yes; what was the last thing I thought of so clearly?" she tried to recall it. "*Tiutkin, coiffeur?*'—no, not that. Yes, of what Yashvin says, the struggle for existence and hatred is the one thing that holds men together. No, it's a useless journey you're making," she said, mentally addressing a party in a coach and four, evidently going for an excursion into the country. "And the dog you're taking with you will be no help to you. You can't get away from yourselves." Turning her eyes in the direction Pyotr had turned to look, she saw a factory-hand almost dead-drunk, with hanging head, being led away by a policeman. "Come, he's found a quicker way," she thought. "Count Vronsky and I did not find that happiness either, though we expected so much from it." And now for the first time Anna turned that glaring light in which she was seeing everything on to her relations with him, which she had hitherto avoided thinking about. "What was it he sought in me? Not love so much as the satisfaction of vanity." She remembered his words, the expression of his face, that recalled an abject setter-dog, in the early days of their connection. And everything now confirmed this. "Yes, there was the triumph of success in him. Of course there was love too, but the chief element was the pride of success. He boasted of me. Now that's over. There's nothing to be proud of. Not to be proud of, but to be ashamed of. He has taken from me all he could, and now I am no use to him. He is weary of me and is trying not to be dishonorable in his behavior to me. He let that out yesterday—he wants divorce and marriage so as to burn his ships. He loves me, but how? The zest is gone, as the English say. That fellow wants every one to admire him and is very much pleased with himself," she thought, looking at a red-faced clerk, riding on a riding-school horse. "Yes, there's not the same flavor about me for him now. If I go away from him, at the bottom of his heart he will be glad."

This was not mere supposition, she saw it distinctly in the piercing light, which revealed to her now the meaning of life and human relations.

"My love keeps growing more passionate and egoistic, while his is waning and waning, and that's why we're drifting apart." She went on musing. "And there's no help for it. He is everything for me, and I want him more and more to give himself up to me entirely. And he wants more and more to get away from me. We walked to meet each other up to the time of our love, and then we have been irresistibly drifting in different directions. And there's no altering that. He tells me I'm insanely jealous, and I have told myself that I am insanely jealous; but it's not true. I'm not jealous, but I'm unsatisfied. But ..." she opened her lips, and shifted her place in the carriage in the excitement, aroused by the thought that suddenly struck her. "If I could be anything but a mistress, passionately caring for nothing but his caresses; but I can't and I don't care to be anything else. And by that desire I rouse aversion in him, and he rouses fury in me, and it cannot be different. Don't I know that he wouldn't deceive me, that he has no schemes about Princess Sorokina, that he's not in love with Kitty, that he won't desert me! I know all that, but it makes it no better for me.

If without loving me, from *duty* he'll be good and kind to me, without what I want, that's a thousand times worse than unkindness! That's—hell! And that's just how it is. For a long while now he hasn't loved me. And where love ends, hate begins. I don't know these streets at all. Hills it seems, and still houses, and houses ... And in the houses always people and people ... How many of them, no end, and all hating each other! Come, let me try and think what I want, to make me happy. Well? Suppose I am divorced, and Alexey Alexandrovitch lets me have Seryozha, and I marry Vronsky." Thinking of Alexey Alexandrovitch, she at once pictured him with extraordinary vividness as though he were alive before her, with his mild, lifeless, dull eyes, the blue veins in his white hands, his intonations and the cracking of his fingers, and remembering the feeling which had existed between them, and which was also called love, she shuddered with loathing. "Well, I'm divorced, and become Vronsky's wife. Well, will Kitty cease looking at me as she looked at me to-day? No. And will Seryozha leave off asking and wondering about my two husbands? And is there any new feeling I can awaken between Vronsky and me? Is there possible, if not happiness, some sort of ease from misery? No, no!" she answered now without the slightest hesitation. "Impossible! We are drawn apart by life, and I make his unhappiness, and he mine, and there's no altering him or me. Every attempt has been made, the screw has come unscrewed. Oh, a beggar-woman with a baby. She thinks I'm sorry for her. Aren't we all flung into the world only to hate each other, and so to torture ourselves and each other? Schoolboys coming—laughing—Seryozha?" she thought. "I thought, too, that I loved him, and used to be touched by my own tenderness. But I have lived without him, I gave him up for another love, and did not regret the exchange till that love was satisfied." And with loathing she thought of what she meant by that love. And the clearness with which she saw life now, her own and all men's, was a pleasure to her. "It's so with me and Pyotr, and the coachman, Fyodor, and that merchant, and all the people living along the Volga, where those placards invite one to go, and everywhere and always," she thought when she had driven under the low-pitched roof of the Nizhigorod station, and the porters ran to meet her.

"A ticket to Obiralovka?" said Pyotr.

She had utterly forgotten where and why she was going, and only by a great effort she understood the question.

"Yes," she said, handing him her purse, and taking a little red bag in her hand, she got out of the carriage.

Making her way through the crowd to the first-class waiting-room, she gradually recollected all the details of her position, and the plans between which she was hesitating. And again at the old sore places, hope and then despair poisoned the wounds of her tortured, fearfully throbbing heart. As she sat on the star-shaped sofa waiting for the train, she gazed with aversion at the people coming and going (they were all hateful to her), and thought how she would arrive at the station, would write him a note, and what she would write to him, and how he was at this moment complaining to his mother of his position, not understanding her sufferings, and how she would go into the room, and what she would say to him. Then she thought that life might still be happy, and how miserably she loved and hated him, and how fearfully her heart was beating.

CHAPTER XXXI

A BELL RANG, SOME YOUNG MEN, UGLY AND IMPUDENT, AND AT THE SAME time careful of the impression they were making, hurried by. Pyotr, too, crossed the room in his livery and top-boots, with his dull, animal face, and came up to her to take her to the train. Some noisy men were quiet as she passed them on the platform, and one whispered something about her to another—something vile, no doubt. She stepped up on the high step, and sat down in a carriage by herself on a dirty seat that had been white. Her bag lay beside her, shaken up and down by the springiness of the seat. With a foolish smile Pyotr raised his hat, with its colored band, at the window, in token of farewell; an impudent conductor slammed the door and the latch. A grotesque-looking lady wearing a bustle (Anna mentally undressed the woman, and was appalled at her hideousness), and a little girl laughing affectedly ran down the platform.

"Katerina Andreevna, she's got them all, *ma tante!*" cried the girl.

"Even the child's hideous and affected," thought Anna. To avoid seeing any one, she got up quickly and seated herself at the opposite window of the empty carriage. A misshapen-looking peasant covered with dirt, in a cap from which his tangled hair stuck out all round, passed by that window, stooping down to the carriage wheels. "There's something familiar about that hideous peasant," thought Anna. And remembering her dream, she moved away to the opposite door, shaking with terror. The conductor opened the door and let in a man and his wife.

"Do you wish to get out?"

Anna made no answer. The conductor and her two fellow-passengers did not notice under her veil her panic-stricken face. She went back to her corner and sat down. The couple seated themselves on the opposite side, and intently but surreptitiously scrutinized her clothes. Both husband and wife seemed repulsive to Anna. The husband asked, would she allow him to smoke, obviously not with a view to smoking but to getting into conversation with her. Receiving her assent, he said to his wife in French something about caring less to smoke than to talk. They made inane and affected remarks to one another, entirely for her benefit. Anna saw clearly that they were sick of each other, and hated each other. And no one could have helped hating such miserable monstrosities.

A second bell sounded, and was followed by moving of luggage, noise, shouting and laughter. It was so clear to Anna that there was nothing for any one to be glad of, that this laughter irritated her agonizingly, and she would have liked to stop up her ears not to hear it. At last the third bell rang, there was a whistle and a hiss of steam, and a clank of chains, and the man in her carriage crossed himself. "It would be interesting to ask him what meaning he attaches to that," thought Anna, looking angrily at him. She looked past the lady out of the window at the people who seemed whirling by as they ran beside the train or stood on the platform. The train, jerking at regular intervals at the junctions of the rails, rolled by the platform, past a stone wall, a signal-box, past other trains; the wheels, moving more smoothly and evenly, resounded with a slight clang on the rails. The window was lighted up by the bright evening sun, and a slight breeze fluttered the curtain. Anna forgot her fellow-passengers, and to the light swaying of the train she fell to thinking again, as she breathed the fresh air.

"Yes, what did I stop at? That I couldn't conceive a position in which life would not be a misery, that we are all created to be miserable, and that we all know it, and all invent means of deceiving each other. And when one sees the truth, what is one to do?"

"That's what reason is given man for, to escape from what worries him," said the lady in French, lisping affectedly, and obviously pleased with her phrase.

The words seemed an answer to Anna's thoughts.

"To escape from what worries him," repeated Anna. And glancing at the red-cheeked husband and the thin wife, she saw that the sickly wife considered herself misunderstood, and the husband deceived her and encouraged her in that idea of herself. Anna seemed to see all their history and all the crannies of their souls, as it were turning a light upon them. But there was nothing interesting in them, and she pursued her thought.

"Yes, I'm very much worried, and that's what reason was given me for, to escape; so then one must escape: why not put out the light when there's nothing more to look at, when it's sickening to look at it all? But how? Why did the conductor run along the footboard, why are they shrieking, those young men in that train? why are they talking, why are they laughing? It's all falsehood, all lying, all humbug, all cruelty! ..."

When the train came into the station, Anna got out into the crowd of passengers, and moving apart from them as if they were lepers, she stood on the platform, trying to think what she had come here for, and what she meant to do. Everything that had seemed to her possible before was now so difficult to consider, especially in this noisy crowd of hideous people who would not leave her alone. One moment porters ran up to her proffering their services, then young men, clacking their heels on the planks of the platform and talking loudly, stared at her; people meeting her dodged past on the wrong side. Remembering that she had meant to go on further if there was no answer, she stopped a porter and asked if her coachman were not here with a note from Count Vronsky.

"Count Vronsky? They sent up here from the Vronskys just this minute, to meet Princess Sorokina and her daughter. And what is the coachman like?"

Just as she was talking to the porter, the coachman Mihail, red and cheerful in his smart blue coat and chain, evidently proud of having so successfully performed his commission, came up to her and gave her a letter. She broke it open, and her heart ached before she had read it.

"I am very sorry your note did not reach me. I will be home at ten," Vronsky had written carelessly....

"Yes, that's what I expected!" she said to herself with an evil smile.

"Very good, you can go home then," she said softly, addressing Mihail. She spoke softly because the rapidity of her heart's beating hindered her breathing. "No, I won't let you make me miserable," she thought menacingly, addressing not him, not herself, but the power that made her suffer, and she walked along the platform.

Two maid-servants walking along the platform turned their heads, staring at her and making some remarks about her dress. "Real," they said of the lace she was wearing. The young men would not leave her in peace. Again they passed by, peering into her face, and with a laugh shouting something in an unnatural voice. The station-master coming up asked her whether she was going by train. A boy selling kvas never took his eyes off her. "My God! where am I to go?" she thought, going farther and farther along the platform. At the end she stopped. Some ladies and children, who had come to meet a gentleman in spectacles, paused in their loud laughter and talking, and stared at her as she reached them. She quickened her pace and walked away from them to the edge of the platform. A luggage train was coming in. The platform began to sway, and she fancied she was in the train again.

And all at once she thought of the man crushed by the train the day she had first met Vronsky, and she knew what she had to do. With a rapid, light step she went down the steps that led from the tank to the rails and stopped quite near the approaching train.

She looked at the lower part of the carriages, at the screws and chains and the tall cast-iron wheel of the first carriage slowly moving up, and trying to measure the middle between the front and back wheels, and the very minute when that middle point would be opposite her.

"There," she said to herself, looking into the shadow of the carriage, at the sand and coal-dust which covered the sleepers— "there, in the very middle, and I will punish him and escape from every one and from myself."

She tried to fling herself below the wheels of the first carriage as it reached her; but the red bag which she tried to drop out of her hand delayed her, and she was too late; she missed the moment. She had to wait for the next carriage. A feeling such as she had known when about to take the first plunge in bathing came upon her, and she crossed herself. That familiar gesture brought back into her soul a whole series of girlish and childish memories, and suddenly the darkness that had covered everything for her was torn apart, and life rose up before her for an instant with all its bright past joys. But she did not take her eyes from the wheels of the second carriage. And exactly at the moment when the space between the wheels came opposite her, she dropped the red bag, and drawing her head back into her shoulders, fell on her hands under the carriage, and lightly, as though she would rise again at once, dropped on to her knees. And at the same instant she was terror-stricken at what she was doing. "Where am I? What am I doing? What for?" She tried to get up, to drop backwards; but something huge and merciless struck her on the head and rolled her on her back. "Lord, forgive me all!" she said, feeling it impossible to struggle. A peasant muttering something was working at the iron above her. And the light by which she had read the book filled with troubles, falsehoods, sorrow, and evil, flared up more brightly than ever before, lighted up for her all that had been in darkness, flickered, began to grow dim, and was quenched forever.

PART EIGHT

——————

CHAPTER I

A LMOST TWO MONTHS HAD PASSED. THE HOT SUMMER WAS HALF OVER, BUT Sergey Ivanovitch was only just preparing to leave Moscow.

Sergey Ivanovitch's life had not been uneventful during this time. A year ago he had finished his book, the fruit of six years' labor, "Sketch of a Survey of the Principles and Forms of Government in Europe and Russia." Several sections of this book and its introduction had appeared in periodical publications, and other parts had been read by Sergey Ivanovitch to persons of his circle, so that the leading ideas of the work could not be completely novel to the public. But still Sergey Ivanovitch had expected that on its appearance his book would be sure to make a serious impression on society, and if it did not cause a revolution in social science it would, at any rate, make a great stir in the scientific world.

After the most conscientious revision the book had last year been published, and had been distributed among the booksellers.

Though he asked no one about it, reluctantly and with feigned indifference answered his friends' inquiries as to how the book was going, and did not even inquire of the booksellers how the book was selling, Sergey Ivanovitch was all on the alert, with strained attention, watching for the first impression his book would make in the world and in literature.

But a week passed, a second, a third, and in society no impression whatever could be detected. His friends who were specialists and savants, occasionally— unmistakably from politeness—alluded to it. The rest of his acquaintances, not interested in a book on a learned subject, did not talk of it at all. And society generally—just now especially absorbed in other things—was absolutely indifferent. In the press, too, for a whole month there was not a word about his book.

Sergey Ivanovitch had calculated to a nicety the time necessary for writing a review, but a month passed, and a second, and still there was silence.

Only in the *Northern Beetle*, in a comic article on the singer Drabanti, who had lost his voice, there was a contemptuous allusion to Koznishev's book, suggesting that the book had been long ago seen through by every one, and was a subject of general ridicule.

At last in the third month a critical article appeared in a serious review. Sergey Ivanovitch knew the author of the article. He had met him once at Golubtsov's.

The author of the article was a young man, an invalid, very bold as a writer, but extremely deficient in breeding and shy in personal relations.

In spite of his absolute contempt for the author, it was with complete respect that Sergey Ivanovitch set about reading the article. The article was awful.

The critic had undoubtedly put an interpretation upon the book which could not possibly be put on it. But he had selected quotations so adroitly that for people who had not read the book (and obviously scarcely any one had read it) it seemed absolutely clear that the whole book was nothing but a medley of high-flown phrases, not even—as suggested by marks of interrogation—used appropriately, and that the author of the book was a person absolutely without knowledge of the subject. And all this was so wittingly done that Sergey Ivanovitch would not have disowned such wit himself. But that was just what was so awful.

In spite of the scrupulous conscientiousness with which Sergey Ivanovitch verified the correctness of the critic's arguments, he did not for a minute stop to ponder over the faults and mistakes which were ridiculed; but unconsciously he began immediately trying to recall every detail of his meeting and conversation with the author of the article.

"Didn't I offend him in some way?" Sergey Ivanovitch wondered.

And remembering that when they met he had corrected the young man about something he had said that betrayed ignorance, Sergey Ivanovitch found the clue to explain the article.

This article was followed by a deadly silence about the book both in the press and in conversation, and Sergey Ivanovitch saw that his six years' task, toiled at with such love and labor, had gone, leaving no trace.

Sergey Ivanovitch's position was still more difficult from the fact that, since he had finished his book, he had had no more literary work to do, such as had hitherto occupied the greater part of his time.

Sergey Ivanovitch was clever, cultivated, healthy, and energetic, and he did not know what use to make of his energy. Conversations in drawing-rooms, in meetings, assemblies, and committees—everywhere where talk was possible— took up part of his time. But being used for years to town life, he did not waste all his energies in talk, as his less experienced younger brother did, when he was in Moscow. He had a great deal of leisure and intellectual energy still to dispose of.

Fortunately for him, at this period so difficult for him from the failure of his book, the various public questions of the dissenting sects, of the American alliance, of the Samara famine, of exhibitions, and of spiritualism, were definitely replaced in public interest by the Slavonic question, which had hitherto rather languidly interested society, and Sergey Ivanovitch, who had been one of the first to raise this subject, threw himself into it heart and soul.

In the circle to which Sergey Ivanovitch belonged, nothing was talked of or written about just now but the Servian War. Everything that the idle crowd usually does to kill time was done now for the benefit of the Slavonic States. Balls, concerts, dinners, matchboxes, ladies' dresses, beer, restaurants—everything testified to sympathy with the Slavonic peoples.

From much of what was spoken and written on the subject, Sergey Ivanovitch differed on various points. He saw that the Slavonic question had become one of those fashionable distractions which succeed one another in providing society with an object and an occupation. He saw, too, that a great many people were taking up the subject from motives of self-interest and self-advertisement. He recognized that the newspapers published a great deal that was superfluous and exaggerated, with the sole aim of attracting attention and outbidding one another. He saw that in this general movement those who thrust themselves most forward and shouted the loudest were men who had failed and were smarting under a sense of injury—generals without armies, ministers not in the ministry, journalists not on any paper, party leaders without followers. He saw that there was a great deal in it that was frivolous and absurd. But he saw and recognized an unmistakable growing enthusiasm, uniting all classes, with which it was impossible not to sympathize. The massacre of men who were fellow-Christians, and of the same Slavonic race, excited sympathy for the sufferers and indignation against the oppressors. And the heroism of the Servians and Montenegrins struggling for a great cause begot in the whole people a longing to help their brothers not in word but in deed.

But in this there was another aspect that rejoiced Sergey Ivanovitch. That was the manifestation of public opinion. The public had definitely expressed its desire. The soul of the people had, as Sergey Ivanovitch said, found expression. And the more he worked in this cause, the more incontestable it seemed to him that it was a cause destined to assume vast dimensions, to create an epoch.

He threw himself heart and soul into the service of this great cause, and forgot to think about his book. His whole time now was engrossed by it, so that

"It's a pity you're going away," said Stepan Arkadyevitch. "To-morrow we're giving a dinner to two who're setting off—Dimer-Bartnyansky from Petersburg and our Veslovsky, Grisha. They're both going. Veslovsky's only lately married. There's a fine fellow for you! Eh, princess?" he turned to the lady.

The princess looked at Koznishev without replying. But the fact that Sergey Ivanovitch and the princess seemed anxious to get rid of him did not in the least disconcert Stepan Arkadyevitch. Smiling, he stared at the feather in the princess's hat, and then about him as though he were going to pick something up. Seeing a lady approaching with a collecting-box, he beckoned her up and put in a five-rouble note.

"I can never see these collecting-boxes unmoved while I've money in my pocket," he said. "And how about to-day's telegram? Fine chaps those Montenegrins!"

"You don't say so!" he cried, when the princess told him that Vronsky was going by this train. For an instant Stepan Arkadyevitch's face looked sad, but a minute later, when, stroking his mustaches and swinging as he walked, he went into the hall where Vronsky was, he had completely forgotten his own despairing sobs over his sister's corpse, and he saw in Vronsky only a hero and an old friend.

"With all his faults one can't refuse to do him justice," said the princess to Sergey Ivanovitch as soon as Stepan Arkadyevitch had left them. "What a typically Russian, Slav nature! Only, I'm afraid it won't be pleasant for Vronsky to see him. Say what you will, I'm touched by that man's fate. Do talk to him a little on the way," said the princess.

"Yes, perhaps, if it happens so."

"I never liked him. But this atones for a great deal. He's not merely going himself, he's taking a squadron at his own expense."

"Yes, so I heard."

A bell sounded. Every one crowded to the doors. "Here he is!" said the princess, indicating Vronsky, who with his mother on his arm walked by, wearing a long overcoat and wide-brimmed black hat. Oblonsky was walking beside him, talking eagerly of something.

Vronsky was frowning and looking straight before him, as though he did not hear what Stepan Arkadyevitch was saying.

Probably on Oblonsky's pointing them out, he looked round in the direction where the princess and Sergey Ivanovitch were standing, and without speaking lifted his hat. His face, aged and worn by suffering, looked stony.

Going onto the platform, Vronsky left his mother and disappeared into a compartment.

On the platform there rang out "God save the Tsar," then shouts of "hurrah!" and *"jivio!"* One of the volunteers, a tall, very young man with a hollow chest, was particularly conspicuous, bowing and waving his felt hat and a nosegay over his head. Then two officers emerged, bowing too, and a stout man with a big beard, wearing a greasy forage-cap.

CHAPTER III

SAYING GOOD-BYE TO THE PRINCESS, SERGEY IVANOVITCH WAS JOINED BY Katavasov; together they got into a carriage full to overflowing, and the train started.

At Tsaritsino station the train was met by a chorus of young men singing "Hail to Thee!" Again the volunteers bowed and poked their heads out, but Sergey Ivanovitch paid no attention to them. He had had so much to do with the volunteers that the type was familiar to him and did not interest him. Katavasov, whose scientific work had prevented his having a chance of observing them hitherto, was very much interested in them and questioned Sergey Ivanovitch.

Sergey Ivanovitch advised him to go into the second-class and talk to them himself. At the next station Katavasov acted on this suggestion.

At the first stop he moved into the second-class and made the acquaintance of the volunteers. They were sitting in a corner of the carriage, talking loudly and obviously aware that the attention of the passengers and Katavasov as he got in was concentrated upon them. More loudly than all talked the tall, hollow-chested young man. He was unmistakably tipsy, and was relating some story that had occurred at his school. Facing him sat a middle-aged officer in the Austrian military jacket of the Guards uniform. He was listening with a smile to the hollow-chested youth, and occasionally pulling him up. The third, in an artillery uniform, was sitting on a box beside them. A fourth was asleep.

Entering into conversation with the youth, Katavasov learned that he was a wealthy Moscow merchant who had run through a large fortune before he was two-and-twenty. Katavasov did not like him, because he was unmanly and effeminate and sickly. He was obviously convinced, especially now after

We lived on the ground-floor, but there was no reckoning on anything. You know, of course, that he had shot himself once already on her account," she said, and the old lady's eyelashes twitched at the recollection. "Yes, hers was the fitting end for such a woman. Even the death she chose was low and vulgar."

"It's not for us to judge, countess," said Sergey Ivanovitch; "but I can understand that it has been very hard for you."

"Ah, don't speak of it! I was staying on my estate, and he was with me. A note was brought him. He wrote an answer and sent it off. We hadn't an idea that she was close by at the station. In the evening I had only just gone to my room, when my Mary told me a lady had thrown herself under the train. Something seemed to strike me at once. I knew it was she. The first thing I said was, he was not to be told. But they'd told him already. His coachman was there and saw it all. When I ran into his room, he was beside himself—it was fearful to see him. He didn't say a word, but galloped off there. I don't know to this day what happened there, but he was brought back at death's door. I shouldn't have known him. *Prostration complète,* the doctor said. And that was followed almost by madness. Oh, why talk of it!" said the countess with a wave of her hand. "It was an awful time! No, say what you will, she was a bad woman. Why, what is the meaning of such desperate passions? It was all to show herself something out of the way. Well, and that she did do. She brought herself to ruin and two good men—her husband and my unhappy son."

"And what did her husband do?" asked Sergey Ivanovitch.

"He has taken her daughter. Alexey was ready to agree to anything at first. Now it worries him terribly that he should have given his own child away to another man. But he can't take back his word. Karenin came to the funeral. But we tried to prevent his meeting Alexey. For him, for her husband, it was easier, anyway. She had set him free. But my poor son was utterly given up to her. He had thrown up everything, his career, me, and even then she had no mercy on him, but of set purpose she made his ruin complete. No, say what you will, her very death was the death of a vile woman, of no religious feeling. God forgive me, but I can't help hating the memory of her, when I look at my son's misery!"

"But how is he now?"

"It was a blessing from Providence for us—this Servian war. I'm old, and I don't understand the rights and wrongs of it, but it's come as a providential blessing to him. Of course for me, as his mother, it's terrible; and what's worse, they say, *ce n'est pas très bien vu à Pétersbourg.* But it can't be helped! It was the one thing that could rouse him. Yashvin—a friend of his—he had lost all he had at cards and he was going to Servia. He came to see him and persuaded him to go. Now it's an interest for him. Do please talk to him a little. I want to distract his mind. He's so low-spirited. And as bad luck would have it, he has toothache too. But he'll be delighted to see you. Please do talk to him; he's walking up and down on that side."

Sergey Ivanovitch said he would be very glad to, and crossed over to the other side of the station.

CHAPTER V

IN THE SLANTING EVENING SHADOWS CAST BY THE BAGGAGE PILED UP ON THE platform, Vronsky in his long overcoat and slouch hat, with his hands in his pockets, strode up and down, like a wild beast in a cage, turning sharply after twenty paces. Sergey Ivanovitch fancied, as he approached him, that Vronsky saw him but was pretending not to see. This did not affect Sergey Ivanovitch in the slightest. He was above all personal considerations with Vronsky.

At that moment Sergey Ivanovitch looked upon Vronsky as a man taking an important part in a great cause, and Koznishev thought it his duty to encourage him and express his approval. He went up to him.

Vronsky stood still, looked intently at him, recognized him, and going a few steps forward to meet him, shook hands with him very warmly.

"Possibly you didn't wish to see me," said Sergey Ivanovitch, "but couldn't I be of use to you?"

"There's no one I should less dislike seeing than you," said Vronsky. "Excuse me; and there's nothing in life for me to like."

"I quite understand, and I merely meant to offer you my services," said Sergey Ivanovitch, scanning Vronsky's face, full of unmistakable suffering. "Wouldn't it be of use to you to have a letter to Ristitch—to Milan?"

"Oh, no!" Vronsky said, seeming to understand him with difficulty. "If you don't mind, let's walk on. It's so stuffy among the carriages. A letter? No, thank you; to meet death one needs no letters of introduction. Nor for the Turks ..." he said, with a smile that was merely of the lips. His eyes still kept their look of angry suffering.

"Yes; but you might find it easier to get into relations, which are after all essential, with anyone prepared to see you. But that's as you like. I was very

for their luncheon, Kitty ran out onto the balcony, enjoying the freedom, and rapidity of movement, of which she had been deprived during the months of her pregnancy.

"It's Sergey Ivanovitch and Katavasov, a professor," she said.

"Oh, that's a bore in this heat," said the prince.

"No, papa, he's very nice, and Kostya's very fond of him," Kitty said, with a deprecating smile, noticing the irony on her father's face.

"Oh, I didn't say anything."

"You go to them, darling," said Kitty to her sister, "and entertain them. They saw Stiva at the station; he was quite well. And I must run to Mitya. As ill-luck would have it, I haven't fed him since tea. He's awake now, and sure to be screaming." And feeling a rush of milk, she hurried to the nursery.

This was not a mere guess; her connection with the child was still so close, that she could gauge by the flow of her milk his need of food, and knew for certain he was hungry.

She knew he was crying before she reached the nursery. And he was indeed crying. She heard him and hastened. But the faster she went, the louder he screamed. It was a fine healthy scream, hungry and impatient.

"Has he been screaming long, nurse, very long?" said Kitty hurriedly, seating herself on a chair, and preparing to give the baby the breast. "But give me him quickly. Oh, nurse, how tiresome you are! There, tie the cap afterwards, do!"

The baby's greedy scream was passing into sobs.

"But you can't manage so, ma'am," said Agafea Mihalovna, who was almost always to be found in the nursery. "He must be put straight. A-oo! a-oo!" she chanted over him, paying no attention to the mother.

The nurse brought the baby to his mother. Agafea Mihalovna followed him with a face dissolving with tenderness.

"He knows me, he knows me. In God's faith, Katerina Alexandrovna, ma'am, he knew me!" Agafea Mihalovna cried above the baby's screams.

But Kitty did not hear her words. Her impatience kept growing, like the baby's.

Their impatience hindered things for a while. The baby could not get hold of the breast right, and was furious.

At last, after despairing, breathless screaming, and vain sucking, things went right, and mother and child felt simultaneously soothed, and both subsided into calm.

"But poor darling, he's all in perspiration!" said Kitty in a whisper, touching the baby.

"What makes you think he knows you?" she added, with a sidelong glance at the baby's eyes, that peered roguishly, as she fancied, from under his cap, at his rhythmically puffing cheeks, and the little red-palmed hand he was waving.

"Impossible! If he knew any one, he would have known me," said Kitty, in response to Agafea Mihalovna's statement, and she smiled.

She smiled because, though she said he could not know her, in her heart she was sure that he knew not merely Agafea Mihalovna, but that he knew and understood everything, and knew and understood a great deal too that no one else knew, and that she, his mother, had learned and come to understand only through him. To Agafea Mihalovna, to the nurse, to his grandfather, to his father even, Mitya was a living being, requiring only material care, but for his mother he had long been a mortal being, with whom there had been a whole series of spiritual relations already.

"When he wakes up, please God, you shall see for yourself. Then when I do like this, he simply beams on me, the darling! Simply beams like a sunny day!" said Agafea Mihalovna.

"Well, well; then we shall see," whispered Kitty. "But now go away, he's going to sleep."

CHAPTER VII

A GAFEA MIHALOVNA WENT OUT ON TIPTOE; THE NURSE LET DOWN THE blind, chased a fly out from under the muslin canopy of the crib, and a bumblebee struggling on the window-frame, and sat down waving a faded branch of birch over the mother and the baby.

"How hot it is! if God would send a drop of rain," she said.

"Yes, yes, sh—sh—sh—" was all Kitty answered, rocking a little, and tenderly squeezing the plump little arm, with rolls of fat at the wrist, which Mitya still waved feebly as he opened and shut his eyes. That hand worried Kitty; she longed to kiss the little hand, but was afraid to for fear of waking the baby. At last the little hand ceased waving, and the eyes closed. Only from time to time, as he went on sucking, the baby raised his long, curly eyelashes and peeped at his mother with wet eyes, that looked black in the twilight. The nurse had left off fanning, and was dozing. From above came the peals of the old prince's voice, and the chuckle of Katavasov.

At first, marriage, with the new joys and duties bound up with it, had completely crowded out these thoughts. But of late, while he was staying in Moscow after his wife's confinement, with nothing to do, the question that clamored for solution had more and more often, more and more insistently, haunted Levin's mind.

The question was summed up for him thus: "If I do not accept the answers Christianity gives to the problems of my life, what answers do I accept?" And in the whole arsenal of his convictions, so far from finding any satisfactory answers, he was utterly unable to find anything at all like an answer.

He was in the position of a man seeking food in toy-shops and tool-shops.

Instinctively, unconsciously, with every book, with every conversation, with every man he met, he was on the lookout for light on these questions and their solution.

What puzzled and distracted him above everything was that the majority of men of his age and circle had, like him, exchanged their old beliefs for the same new convictions, and yet saw nothing to lament in this, and were perfectly satisfied and serene. So that, apart from the principal question, Levin was tortured by other questions too. Were these people sincere? he asked himself, or were they playing a part? or was it that they understood the answers science gave to these problems in some different, clearer sense than he did? And he assiduously studied both these men's opinions and the books which treated of these scientific explanations.

One fact he had found out since these questions had engrossed his mind, was that he had been quite wrong in supposing from the recollections of the circle of his young days at college, that religion had outlived its day, and that it was now practically non-existent. All the people nearest to him who were good in their lives were believers. The old prince, and Lvov, whom he liked so much, and Sergey Ivanovitch, and all the women believed, and his wife believed as simply as he had believed in his earliest childhood, and ninety-nine hundredths of the Russian people, all the working people for whose life he felt the deepest respect, believed.

Another fact of which he became convinced, after reading many scientific books, was that the men who shared his views had no other construction to put on them, and that they gave no explanation of the questions which he felt he could not live without answering, but simply ignored their existence and attempted to explain other questions of no possible interest to him, such as the evolution of organisms, the materialistic theory of consciousness, etc.

Moreover, during his wife's confinement, something had happened that seemed extraordinary to him. He, an unbeliever, had fallen into praying, and at the moment he prayed, he believed. But that moment had passed, and he could not make his state of mind at that moment fit into the rest of his life.

He could not admit that at that moment he knew the truth, and that now he was wrong; for as soon as he began thinking calmly about it, it all fell to pieces. He could not admit that he was mistaken then, for his spiritual condition then was precious to him, and to admit that it was a proof of weakness would have been to desecrate those moments. He was miserably divided against himself, and strained all his spiritual forces to the utmost to escape from this condition.

CHAPTER IX

THESE DOUBTS FRETTED AND HARASSED HIM, GROWING WEAKER OR STRONger from time to time, but never leaving him. He read and thought, and the more he read and the more he thought, the further he felt from the aim he was pursuing.

Of late in Moscow and in the country, since he had become convinced that he would find no solution in the materialists, he had read and reread thoroughly Plato, Spinoza, Kant, Schelling, Hegel, and Schopenhauer, the philosophers who gave a non-materialistic explanation of life.

Their ideas seemed to him fruitful when he was reading or was himself seeking arguments to refute other theories, especially those of the materialists; but as soon as he began to read or sought for himself a solution of problems, the same thing always happened. As long as he followed the fixed definition of obscure words such as *spirit, will, freedom, essence,* purposely letting himself go into the snare of words the philosophers set for him, he seemed to comprehend something. But he had only to forget the artificial train of reasoning, and to turn from life itself to what had satisfied him while thinking in accordance with the fixed definitions, and all this artificial edifice fell to pieces at once like a house of cards, and it became clear that the edifice had been built up out of those transposed words, apart from anything in life more important than reason.

At one time, reading Schopenhauer, he put in place of his *will* the word *love,* and for a couple of days this new philosophy charmed him, till he removed a little away from it. But then, when he turned from life itself to glance at it again, it fell away too, and proved to be the same muslin garment with no warmth in it.

of agriculture at Pokrovskoe going so as to yield an income. Just as incontestably as it was necessary to repay a debt was it necessary to keep the property in such a condition that his son, when he received it as a heritage, would say "thank you" to his father as Levin had said "thank you" to his grandfather for all he built and planted. And to do this it was necessary to look after the land himself, not to let it, and to breed cattle, manure the fields, and plant timber.

It was impossible not to look after the affairs of Sergey Ivanovitch, of his sister, of the peasants who came to him for advice and were accustomed to do so—as impossible as to fling down a child one is carrying in one's arms. It was necessary to look after the comfort of his sister-in-law and her children, and of his wife and baby, and it was impossible not to spend with them at least a short time each day.

And all this, together with shooting and his new bee-keeping, filled up the whole of Levin's life, which had no meaning at all for him, when he began to think.

But besides knowing thoroughly what he had to do, Levin knew in just the same way *how* he had to do it all, and what was more important than the rest.

He knew he must hire laborers as cheaply as possible; but to hire men under bond, paying them in advance at less than the current rate of wages, was what he must not do, even though it was very profitable. Selling straw to the peasants in times of scarcity of provender was what he might do, even though he felt sorry for them; but the tavern and the pot-house must be put down, though they were a source of income. Felling timber must be punished as severely as possible, but he could not exact forfeits for cattle being driven onto his fields; and though it annoyed the keeper and made the peasants not afraid to graze their cattle on his land, he could not keep their cattle as a punishment.

To Pyotr, who was paying a money-lender ten per cent a month, he must lend a sum of money to set him free. But he could not let off peasants who did not pay their rent, nor let them fall into arrears. It was impossible to overlook the bailiff's not having mown the meadows and letting the hay spoil; and it was equally impossible to mow those acres where a young copse had been planted. It was impossible to excuse a laborer who had gone home in the busy season because his father was dying, however sorry he might feel for him, and he must subtract from his pay those costly months of idleness. But it was impossible not to allow monthly rations to the old servants who were of no use for anything.

Levin knew that when he got home he must first of all go to his wife, who was unwell, and that the peasants who had been waiting for three hours to see him could wait a little longer. He knew too that, regardless of all the pleasure he felt in taking a swarm, he must forego that pleasure, and leave the old man to see to the bees alone, while he talked to the peasants who had come after him to the bee-house.

Whether he were acting rightly or wrongly he did not know, and far from trying to prove that he was, nowadays he avoided all thought or talk about it.

Reasoning had brought him to doubt, and prevented him from seeing what he ought to do and what he ought not. When he did not think, but simply lived, he was continually aware of the presence of an infallible judge in his soul, determining which of two possible courses of action was the better and which was the worse, and as soon as he did not act rightly, he was at once aware of it.

So he lived, not knowing and not seeing any chance of knowing what he was and what he was living for, and harassed at this lack of knowledge to such a point that he was afraid of suicide, and yet firmly laying down his own individual definite path in life.

CHAPTER XI

THE DAY ON WHICH SERGEY IVANOVITCH CAME TO POKROVSKOE WAS one of Levin's most painful days. It was the very busiest working-time, when all the peasantry show an extraordinary intensity of self-sacrifice in labor, such as is never shown in any other conditions of life, and would be highly esteemed if the men who showed these qualities themselves thought highly of them, and if it were not repeated every year, and if the results of this intense labor were not so simple.

To reap and bind the rye and oats and to carry it, to mow the meadows, turn over the fallows, thrash the seed and sow the winter corn—all this seems so simple and ordinary; but to succeed in getting through it all every one in the village, from the old man to the young child, must toil incessantly for three or four weeks, three times as hard as usual, living on rye-beer, onions, and black bread, thrashing and carrying the sheaves at night, and not giving more than two or three hours in the twenty-four to sleep. And every year this is done all over Russia.

CHAPTER XII

L EVIN STRODE ALONG THE HIGHROAD, ABSORBED NOT SO MUCH IN HIS THOUGHTS (he could not yet disentangle them) as in his spiritual condition, unlike anything he had experienced before.

The words uttered by the peasant had acted on his soul like an electric shock, suddenly transforming and combining into a single whole the whole swarm of disjointed, impotent, separate thoughts that incessantly occupied his mind. These thoughts had unconsciously been in his mind even when he was talking about the land.

He was aware of something new in his soul, and joyfully tested this new thing, not yet knowing what it was.

"Not living for his own wants, but for God? For what God? And could one say anything more senseless than what he said? He said that one must not live for one's own wants, that is, that one must not live for what we understand, what we are attracted by, what we desire, but must live for something incomprehensible, for God, whom no one can understand nor even define. What of it? Didn't I understand those senseless words of Fyodor's? And understanding them, did I doubt of their truth? Did I think them stupid, obscure, inexact? No, I understood him, and exactly as he understands the words. I understood them more fully and clearly than I understand anything in life, and never in my life have I doubted nor can I doubt about it. And not only I, but every one, the whole world understands nothing fully but this, and about this only they have no doubt and are always agreed.

"And I looked out for miracles, complained that I did not see a miracle which would convince me. A material miracle would have persuaded me. And here is a miracle, the sole miracle possible, continually existing, surrounding me on all sides, and I never noticed it!

"Fyodor says that Kirillov lives for his belly. That's comprehensible and rational. All of us as rational beings can't do anything else but live for our belly. And all of a sudden the same Fyodor says that one mustn't live for one's belly, but must live for truth, for God, and at a hint I understand him! And I and millions of men, men who lived ages ago and men living now—peasants, the poor in spirit and the learned, who have thought and written about it, in their obscure words saying the same thing—we are all agreed about this one thing: what we must live for and what is good. I and all men have only one firm, incontestable, clear knowledge, and that knowledge cannot be explained by the reason—it is outside it, and has no causes and can have no effects.

"If goodness has causes, it is not goodness; if it has effects, a reward, it is not goodness either. So goodness is outside the chain of cause and effect.

"And yet I know it, and we all know it.

"What could be a greater miracle than that?

"Can I have found the solution of it all? can my sufferings be over?" thought Levin, striding along the dusty road, not noticing the heat nor his weariness, and experiencing a sense of relief from prolonged suffering. This feeling was so delicious that it seemed to him incredible. He was breathless with emotion and incapable of going farther; he turned off the road into the forest and lay down in the shade of an aspen on the uncut grass. He took his hat off his hot head and lay propped on his elbow in the lush, feathery, woodland grass.

"Yes, I must make it clear to myself and understand," he thought, looking intently at the untrampled grass before him, and following the movements of a green beetle, advancing along a blade of couch-grass and lifting up in its progress a leaf of goat-weed. "What have I discovered?" he asked himself, bending aside the leaf of goat-weed out of the beetle's way and twisting another blade of grass above for the beetle to cross over onto it. "What is it makes me glad? What have I discovered?

"I have discovered nothing. I have only found out what I knew. I understand the force that in the past gave me life, and now too gives me life. I have been set free from falsity, I have found the Master.

"Of old I used to say that in my body, that in the body of this grass and of this beetle (there, she didn't care for the grass, she's opened her wings and flown away), there was going on a transformation of matter in accordance with physical, chemical, and physiological laws. And in all of us, as well as in the aspens and the clouds and the misty patches, there was a process of evolution. Evolution from what? into what?—Eternal evolution and struggle…. As though there could be any sort of tendency and struggle in the eternal! And I was astonished that in spite of the utmost effort of thought along that road I could not discover the meaning of life, the meaning of my impulses and yearnings. Now I say that I know the meaning of my life: 'To live for God, for my soul.' And this meaning, in spite of its clearness, is mysterious and marvelous. Such, indeed, is the meaning of everything existing. Yes, pride," he said to himself, turning over on his stomach and beginning to tie a noose of blades of grass, trying not to break them.

"And not merely pride of intellect, but dulness of intellect. And most of all, the deceitfulness; yes, the deceitfulness of intellect. The cheating knavishness of intellect, that's it," he said to himself.

then? Why, they'd die of hunger! Well, then, leave us with our passions and thoughts, without any idea of the one God, of the Creator, or without any idea of what is right, without any idea of moral evil.

"Just try and build up anything without those ideas!

"We only try and destroy them, because we're spiritually provided for. Exactly like the children!

"Whence have I that joyful knowledge, shared with the peasant, that alone gives peace to my soul? Whence did I get it?

"Brought up with an idea of God, a Christian, my whole life filled with the spiritual blessings Christianity has given me, full of them, and living on those blessings, like the children I did not understand them, and destroy, that is try to destroy, what I live by. And as soon as an important moment of life comes, like the children when they are cold and hungry, I turn to Him, and even less than the children when their mother scolds them for their childish mischief, do I feel that my childish efforts at wanton madness are reckoned against me.

"Yes, what I know, I know not by reason, but it has been given to me, revealed to me, and I know it with my heart, by faith in the chief thing taught by the church.

"The church! the church!" Levin repeated to himself. He turned over on the other side, and leaning on his elbow, fell to gazing into the distance at a herd of cattle crossing over to the river.

"But can I believe in all the church teaches?" he thought, trying himself, and thinking of everything that could destroy his present peace of mind. Intentionally he recalled all those doctrines of the church which had always seemed most strange and had always been a stumbling-block to him.

"The Creation? But how did I explain existence? By existence? By nothing? The devil and sin. But how do I explain evil? ... The atonement? ...

"But I know nothing, nothing, and I can know nothing but what has been told to me and all men."

And it seemed to him that there was not a single article of faith of the church which could destroy the chief thing—faith in God, in goodness, as the one goal of man's destiny.

Under every article of faith of the church could be put the faith in the service of truth instead of one's desires. And each doctrine did not simply leave that faith unshaken, each doctrine seemed essential to complete that great miracle, continually manifest upon earth, that made it possible for each man and millions of different sorts of men, wise men and imbeciles, old men and children—all men, peasants, Lvov, Kitty, beggars and kings to understand perfectly the same one thing, and to build up thereby that life of the soul which alone is worth living, and which alone is precious to us.

Lying on his back, he gazed up now into the high, cloudless sky. "Do I not know that that is infinite space, and that it is not a round arch? But, however I screw up my eyes and strain my sight, I cannot see it not round and not bounded, and in spite of my knowing about infinite space, I am incontestably right when I see a solid blue dome, and more right than when I strain my eyes to see beyond it."

Levin ceased thinking, and only, as it were, listened to mysterious voices that seemed talking joyfully and earnestly within him.

"Can this be faith?" he thought, afraid to believe in his happiness. "My God, I thank Thee!" he said, gulping down his sobs, and with both hands brushing away the tears that filled his eyes.

CHAPTER XIV

L EVIN LOOKED BEFORE HIM AND SAW A HERD OF CATTLE, THEN HE CAUGHT sight of his trap with Raven in the shafts, and the coachman, who, driving up to the herd, said something to the herdsman. Then he heard the rattle of the wheels and the snort of the sleek horse close by him. But he was so buried in his thoughts that he did not even wonder why the coachman had come for him.

He only thought of that when the coachman had driven quite up to him and shouted to him. "The mistress sent me. Your brother has come, and some gentleman with him."

Levin got into the trap and took the reins. As though just roused out of sleep, for a long while Levin could not collect his faculties. He stared at the sleek horse flecked with lather between his haunches and on his neck, where the harness rubbed, stared at Ivan the coachman sitting beside him, and remembered that he was expecting his brother, thought that his wife was most likely uneasy at his long absence, and tried to guess who was the visitor who had come with his brother. And his brother and his wife and the unknown guest seemed to him now quite different from before. He fancied that now his relations with all men would be different.

"I mean that I'm fully convinced that the solution of the problems that interest me I shall never find in him and his like. Now..."

But Katavasov's serene and good-humored expression suddenly struck him, and he felt such tenderness for his own happy mood, which he was unmistakably disturbing by this conversation, that he remembered his resolution and stopped short.

"But we'll talk later on," he added. "If we're going to the bee-house, it's this way, along this little path," he said, addressing them all.

Going along the narrow path to a little uncut meadow covered on one side with thick clumps of brilliant heart's-ease among which stood up here and there tall, dark green tufts of hellebore, Levin settled his guests in the dense, cool shade of the young aspens on a bench and some stumps purposely put there for visitors to the bee-house who might be afraid of the bees, and he went off himself to the hut to get bread, cucumbers, and fresh honey, to regale them with.

Trying to make his movements as deliberate as possible, and listening to the bees that buzzed more and more frequently past him, he walked along the little path to the hut. In the very entry one bee hummed angrily, caught in his beard, but he carefully extricated it. Going into the shady outer room, he took down from the wall his veil, that hung on a peg, and putting it on, and thrusting his hands into his pockets, he went into the fenced-in bee-garden, where there stood in the midst of a closely mown space in regular rows, fastened with bast on posts, all the hives he knew so well, the old stocks, each with its own history, and along the fences the younger swarms hived that year. In front of the openings of the hives, it made his eyes giddy to watch the bees and drones whirling round and round about the same spot, while among them the working bees flew in and out with spoils or in search of them, always in the same direction into the wood to the flowering lime-trees and back to the hives.

His ears were filled with the incessant hum in various notes, now the busy hum of the working bee flying quickly off, then the blaring of the lazy drone, and the excited buzz of the bees on guard protecting their property from the enemy and preparing to sting. On the farther side of the fence the old bee-keeper was shaving a hoop for a tub, and he did not see Levin. Levin stood still in the midst of the beehives and did not call him.

He was glad of a chance to be alone to recover from the influence of ordinary actual life, which had already depressed his happy mood. He thought that he had already had time to lose his temper with Ivan, to show coolness to his brother, and to talk flippantly with Katavasov.

"Can it have been only a momentary mood, and will it pass and leave no trace?" he thought. But the same instant, going back to his mood, he felt with delight that something new and important had happened to him. Real life had only for a time overcast the spiritual peace he had found, but it was still untouched within him.

Just as the bees, whirling round him, now menacing him and distracting his attention, prevented him from enjoying complete physical peace, forced him to restrain his movements to avoid them, so had the petty cares that had swarmed about him from the moment he got into the trap, restricted his spiritual freedom; but that lasted only so long as he was among them. Just as his bodily strength was still unaffected, in spite of the bees, so too was the spiritual strength that he had just become aware of.

CHAPTER XV

DO YOU KNOW, KOSTYA, WITH WHOM SERGEY IVANOVITCH TRAVELED ON his way here?" said Dolly, doling out cucumbers and honey to the children; "with Vronsky! He's going to Servia."

"And not alone; he's taking a squadron out with him at his own expense," said Katavasov.

"That's the right thing for him," said Levin. "Are volunteers still going out then?" he added, glancing at Sergey Ivanovitch.

Sergey Ivanovitch did not answer. He was carefully with a blunt knife getting a live bee covered with sticky honey out of a cup full of white honeycomb.

"I should think so! You should have seen what was going on at the station yesterday!" said Katavasov, biting with a juicy sound into a cucumber.

"Well, what is one to make of it? For mercy's sake, do explain to me, Sergey Ivanovitch, where are all those volunteers going, whom are they fighting with?" asked the old prince, unmistakably taking up a conversation that had sprung up in Levin's absence.

"With the Turks," Sergey Ivanovitch answered, smiling serenely, as he extricated the bee, dark with honey and helplessly kicking, and put it with the knife on a stout aspen leaf.

"But who has declared war on the Turks?—Ivan Ivanovitch Ragozov and Countess Lidia Ivanovna, assisted by Madame Stahl?"

"Here, then, ask him. He knows nothing about it and thinks nothing," said Levin. "Have you heard about the war, Mihalitch?" he said, turning to him. "What they read in the church? What do you think about it? Ought we to fight for the Christians?"

"What should we think? Alexander Nikolaevitch our Emperor has thought for us; he thinks for us indeed in all things. It's clearer for him to see. Shall I bring a bit more bread? Give the little lad some more?" he said addressing Darya Alexandrovna and pointing to Grisha, who had finished his crust.

"I don't need to ask," said Sergey Ivanovitch, "we have seen and are seeing hundreds and hundreds of people who give up everything to serve a just cause, come from every part of Russia, and directly and clearly express their thought and aim. They bring their halfpence or go themselves and say directly what for. What does it mean?"

"It means, to my thinking," said Levin, who was beginning to get warm, "that among eighty millions of people there can always be found not hundreds, as now, but tens of thousands of people who have lost caste, ne'er-do-wells, who are always ready to go anywhere—to Pogatchev's bands, to Khiva, to Servia ..."

"I tell you that it's not a case of hundreds or of ne'er-do-wells, but the best representatives of the people!" said Sergey Ivanovitch, with as much irritation as if he were defending the last penny of his fortune. "And what of the subscriptions? In this case it is a whole people directly expressing their will."

"That word 'people' is so vague," said Levin. "Parish clerks, teachers, and one in a thousand of the peasants, maybe, know what it's all about. The rest of the eighty millions, like Mihalitch, far from expressing their will, haven't the faintest idea what there is for them to express their will about. What right have we to say that this is the people's will?"

CHAPTER XVI

SERGEY IVANOVITCH, BEING PRACTICED IN ARGUMENT, DID NOT REPLY, BUT AT once turned the conversation to another aspect of the subject.

"Oh, if you want to learn the spirit of the people by arithmetical computation, of course it's very difficult to arrive at it. And voting has not been introduced among us and cannot be introduced, for it does not express the will of the people; but there are other ways of reaching that. It is felt in the air, it is felt by the heart. I won't speak of those deep currents which are astir in the still ocean of the people, and which are evident to every unprejudiced man; let us look at society in the narrow sense. All the most diverse sections of the educated public, hostile before, are merged in one. Every division is at an end, all the public organs say the same thing over and over again, all feel the mighty torrent that has overtaken them and is carrying them in one direction."

"Yes, all the newspapers do say the same thing," said the prince. "That's true. But so it is the same thing that all the frogs croak before a storm. One can hear nothing for them."

"Frogs or no frogs, I'm not the editor of a paper and I don't want to defend them; but I am speaking of the unanimity in the intellectual world," said Sergey Ivanovitch, addressing his brother. Levin would have answered, but the old prince interrupted him.

"Well, about that unanimity, that's another thing, one may say," said the prince. "There's my son-in-law, Stepan Arkadyevitch, you know him. He's got a place now on the committee of a commission and something or other, I don't remember. Only there's nothing to do in it—why, Dolly, it's no secret!—and a salary of eight thousand. You try asking him whether his post is of use, he'll prove to you that it's most necessary. And he's a truthful man too, but there's no refusing to believe in the utility of eight thousand roubles."

"Yes, he asked me to give a message to Darya Alexandrovna about the post," said Sergey Ivanovitch reluctantly, feeling the prince's remark to be ill-timed.

"So it is with the unanimity of the press. That's been explained to me: as soon as there's war their incomes are doubled. How can they help believing in the destinies of the people and the Slavonic races … and all that?"

"I don't care for many of the papers, but that's unjust," said Sergey Ivanovitch.

"I would only make one condition," pursued the old prince. "Alphonse Karr said a capital thing before the war with Prussia: 'You consider war to be inevitable? Very good. Let every one who advocates war be enrolled in a special regiment of advance-guards, for the front of every storm, of every attack, to lead them all!'"

"A nice lot the editors would make!" said Katavasov, with a loud roar, as he pictured the editors he knew in this picked legion.

"But they'd run," said Dolly, "they'd only be in the way."

"Oh, if they ran away, then we'd have grape-shot or Cossacks with whips behind them," said the prince.

holding their hats on, strode with long steps beside her. They were just at the steps when a big drop fell splashing on the edge of the iron guttering. The children and their elders after them ran into the shelter of the house, talking merrily.

"Katerina Alexandrovna?" Levin asked of Agafea Mihalovna, who met them with kerchiefs and rugs in the hall.

"We thought she was with you," she said.

"And Mitya?"

"In the copse, he must be, and the nurse with him."

Levin snatched up the rugs and ran towards the copse.

In that brief interval of time the storm-clouds had moved on, covering the sun so completely that it was dark as an eclipse. Stubbornly, as though insisting on its rights, the wind stopped Levin, and tearing the leaves and flowers off the lime-trees and stripping the white birch branches into strange unseemly nakedness, it twisted everything on one side—acacias, flowers, burdocks, long grass, and tall tree-tops. The peasant girls working in the garden ran shrieking into shelter in the servants' quarters. The streaming rain had already flung its white veil over all the distant forest and half the fields close by, and was rapidly swooping down upon the copse. The wet of the rain spurting up in tiny drops could be smelt in the air.

Holding his head bent down before him, and struggling with the wind that strove to tear the wraps away from him, Levin was moving up to the copse and had just caught sight of something white behind the oak-tree, when there was a sudden flash, the whole earth seemed on fire, and the vault of heaven seemed crashing overhead. Opening his blinded eyes, Levin gazed through the thick veil of rain that separated him now from the copse, and to his horror the first thing he saw was the green crest of the familiar oak-tree in the middle of the copse uncannily changing its position. "Can it have been struck?" Levin hardly had time to think when, moving more and more rapidly, the oak-tree vanished behind the other trees, and he heard the crash of the great tree falling upon the others.

The flash of lightning, the crash of thunder, and the instantaneous chill that ran through him were all merged for Levin in one sense of terror.

"My God! my God! not on them!" he said.

And though he thought at once how senseless was his prayer that they should not have been killed by the oak which had fallen now, he repeated it, knowing that he could do nothing better than utter this senseless prayer.

Running up to the place where they usually went, he did not find them there. They were at the other end of the copse under an old lime-tree; they were calling him. Two figures in dark dresses (they had been light summer dresses when they started out) were standing bending over something. It was Kitty with the nurse. The rain was already ceasing, and it was beginning to get light when Levin reached them. The nurse was not wet on the lower part of her dress, but Kitty was drenched through, and her soaked clothes clung to her. Though the rain was over, they still stood in the same position in which they had been standing when the storm broke. Both stood bending over a perambulator with a green umbrella.

"Alive? Unhurt? Thank God!" he said, splashing with his soaked boots through the standing water and running up to them.

Kitty's rosy wet face was turned towards him, and she smiled timidly under her shapeless sopped hat.

"Aren't you ashamed of yourself? I can't think how you can be so reckless!" he said angrily to his wife.

"It wasn't my fault, really. We were just meaning to go, when he made such a to-do that we had to change him. We were just ..." Kitty began defending herself.

Mitya was unharmed, dry, and still fast asleep.

"Well, thank God! I don't know what I'm saying!"

They gathered up the baby's wet belongings; the nurse picked up the baby and carried it. Levin walked beside his wife, and, penitent for having been angry, he squeezed her hand when the nurse was not looking.

CHAPTER XVIII

DURING THE WHOLE OF THAT DAY, IN THE EXTREMELY DIFFERENT conversations in which he took part, only as it were with the top layer of his mind, in spite of the disappointment of not finding the change he expected in himself, Levin had been all the while joyfully conscious of the fulness of his heart.

After the rain it was too wet to go for a walk; besides, the storm-clouds still hung about the horizon, and gathered here and there, black and thundery, on the rim of the sky. The whole party spent the rest of the day in the house.

No more discussions sprang up; on the contrary, after dinner every one was in the most amiable frame of mind.

And what a happy day we've had altogether. And you're so nice with Sergey Ivanovitch, when you care to be.... Well, go back to them. It's always so hot and steamy here after the bath."

CHAPTER XIX

GOING OUT OF THE NURSERY AND BEING AGAIN ALONE, LEVIN WENT BACK at once to the thought, in which there was something not clear.

Instead of going into the drawing-room, where he heard voices, he stopped on the terrace, and leaning his elbows on the parapet, he gazed up at the sky.

It was quite dark now, and in the south, where he was looking, there were no clouds. The storm had drifted on to the opposite side of the sky, and there were flashes of lightning and distant thunder from that quarter. Levin listened to the monotonous drip from the lime-trees in the garden, and looked at the triangle of stars he knew so well, and the Milky Way with its branches that ran through its midst. At each flash of lightning the Milky Way, and even the bright stars, vanished, but as soon as the lightning died away, they reappeared in their places as though some hand had flung them back with careful aim.

"Well, what is it perplexes me?" Levin said to himself, feeling beforehand that the solution of his difficulties was ready in his soul, though he did not know it yet. "Yes, the one unmistakable, incontestable manifestation of the Divinity is the law of right and wrong, which has come into the world by revelation, and which I feel in myself, and in the recognition of which—I don't make myself, but whether I will or not—I am made one with other men in one body of believers, which is called the church. Well, but the Jews, the Mohammedans, the Confucians, the Buddhists—what of them?" he put to himself the question he had feared to face. "Can these hundreds of millions of men be deprived of that highest blessing without which life has no meaning?" He pondered a moment, but immediately corrected himself. "But what am I questioning?" he said to himself. "I am questioning the relation to Divinity of all the different religions of all mankind. I am questioning the universal manifestation of God to all the world with all those misty blurs. What am I about? To me individually, to my heart has been revealed a knowledge beyond all doubt, and unattainable by reason, and here I am obstinately trying to express that knowledge in reason and words.

"Don't I know that the stars don't move?" he asked himself, gazing at the bright planet which had shifted its position up to the topmost twig of the birch-tree. "But looking at the movements of the stars, I can't picture to myself the rotation of the earth, and I'm right in saying that the stars move.

"And could the astronomers have understood and calculated anything, if they had taken into account all the complicated and varied motions of the earth? All the marvelous conclusions they have reached about the distances, weights, movements, and deflections of the heavenly bodies are only founded on the apparent motions of the heavenly bodies about a stationary earth, on that very motion I see before me now, which has been so for millions of men during long ages, and was and will be always alike, and can always be trusted. And just as the conclusions of the astronomers would have been vain and uncertain if not founded on observations of the seen heavens, in relation to a single meridian and a single horizon, so would my conclusions be vain and uncertain if not founded on that conception of right, which has been and will be always alike for all men, which has been revealed to me as a Christian, and which can always be trusted in my soul. The question of other religions and their relations to Divinity I have no right to decide, and no possibility of deciding."

"Oh, you haven't gone in then?" he heard Kitty's voice all at once, as she came by the same way to the drawing-room.

"What is it? you're not worried about anything?" she said, looking intently at his face in the starlight.

But she could not have seen his face if a flash of lightning had not hidden the stars and revealed it. In that flash she saw his face distinctly, and seeing him calm and happy, she smiled at him.

"She understands," he thought; "she knows what I'm thinking about. Shall I tell her or not? Yes, I'll tell her." But at the moment he was about to speak, she began speaking.

"Kostya! do something for me," she said; "go into the corner room and see if they've made it all right for Sergey Ivanovitch. I can't very well. See if they've put the new wash-stand in it."

"Very well, I'll go directly," said Levin, standing up and kissing her.

"No, I'd better not speak of it," he thought, when she had gone in before him. "It is a secret for me alone, of vital importance for me, and not to be put into words.

"This new feeling has not changed me, has not made me happy and enlightened all of a sudden, as I had dreamed, just like the feeling for my child. There was no surprise in this either. Faith—or not faith—I don't know what it is—but this feeling has come just as imperceptibly through suffering, and has taken firm root in my soul.

"I shall go on in the same way, losing my temper with Ivan the coachman, falling into angry discussions, expressing my opinions tactlessly; there will be still the same wall between the holy of holies of my soul and other people, even my wife; I shall still go on scolding her for my own terror, and being remorseful for it; I shall still be as unable to understand with my reason why I pray, and I shall still go on praying; but my life now, my whole life apart from anything that can happen to me, every minute of it is no more meaningless, as it was before, but it has the positive meaning of goodness, which I have the power to put into it."